One Hundred Years at Hillsborough

2nd September 1899–1999

Jason Dickinson

Published by
The Hallamshire Press

in association with
Sheffield Wednesday Football Club Limited

1999

©1999 Sheffield Wednesday Football Club Limited

Published by The Hallamshire Press Limited
in association with Sheffield Wednesday Football Club Limited

Typeset by The Hallamshire Press Limited
Broom Hall
Sheffield S10 2DR
England

Printed in Singapore

British Library Cataloguing in Publication Data:
  A catalogue record for this book is available from the British Library.

ISBN 1 874718 29 6

Contents

Acknowledgements

When the idea of writing *100 Years at Hillsborough* was first suggested to me in late January the task seemed a daunting one, especially considering the time constraints imposed. I accepted the challenge and, by burning the candle at both ends I managed to complete the book by the deadline, however, it would be remiss of me not to acknowledge the help of several people along the way.

My biggest thanks go to fellow Wednesday historian, John Brodie, who not only loaned me a multitude of photographs and memorabilia but was always willing to aid my research. Also a big thank you to my mother, Doreen, who diligently read through all my work.

I much appreciate the assistance of Andrea Brooks, Sharon Lane and Andy Berry of *Sheffield Wednesday* along with the help I received from Pauline Climpson, Andrew Fyfe and Jenny Sayles of *The Hallamshire Press*. I also extend many thanks to the staff at the Local Studies Department at Sheffield City Library, where, over several years, I have researched the history of the Club and its players. Also to *Sheffield Newspapers* for permission to use pictures from the 1950s and 60s and, of course, special thanks to Steve Ellis the official Wednesday photographer, for permission to use his photographs from the last 25 years.

Finally, I am grateful to friends Mick Grayson and Steve Clarke for their help when writing the chapter relating to the history of the ground

Chapter 1

Pre-Hillsborough and the move from Olive Grove
1867–1899

It would be remiss to cover the last hundred years of Sheffield Wednesday's history without looking briefly at the club's origins and their subsequent fortunes before they secured Owlerton as their home. To find the seeds of today's multi-million pound Premiership club you have to go all the way back to 1820, when 'The Wednesday Cricket Club' was formed by a group of local businessmen whose half-day happened to fall on a Wednesday; and they quickly became a force on the local cricket scene. Following the formation of Sheffield FC in 1857, and Hallam FC in 1860—and, as Association Football rapidly started to gain in popularity—a group of Victorian gentlemen-members of the cricket club decided that, in order to keep the cricketers together during the period from September to April, the time was ripe to form a football section. On 4th September 1867 an historic meeting took place at the Adelphi Hotel where the Crucible theatre now stands. During this, a brewery traveller, John Pashley, rose to his feet to propose 'that a football club be formed in connection with the cricket club, and that no body of persons shall be empowered to sever the two clubs without the unanimous consent of a general meeting, six days notice to be given to every member of the two clubs'. The motion was duly seconded by William Littlehales, and a football club was born; with financial agent, Ben Chatterton elected first President, and John Marsh as first secretary and playing captain. The colours of blue and white were adopted and plans were then formulated for the new club's first season.

It was once thought that it was not until New Year's Eve, 1867 that 'The Wednesday Football Club' played their first ever match against a Dronfield team. Recent research, however, has revealed that the club played at least eleven matches before that date. Indeed, on 12th October 1867, just over a month after their formation, Wednesday's members played a practice game at their first home ground of Highfield; and a week later played the first game in their history when they beat the Mechanics club at Norfolk Park by three goals and four rouges to nil. It should be noted that at the time, goal posts were only four yards apart, with the crossbar nine feet from the ground. Four yards from each goal post was a further 'rouge' post, and if the ball passed between the inner post and outer post, then a rouge was scored. Those points were, however, only used if a game was tied, and within a year the rule was abolished. Before the turn of the year two defeats against the Garrick Club were recorded for posterity in the local press, and it wasn't long before Wednesday played their first ever 'competitive' series of games, when, in early February they entered the new Cromwell Cup. The trophy's benefactor, Oliver Cromwell, was then a member of the Garrick

and Manager of the Theatre Royal. Four teams entered for a competition, which was for clubs two years old or under. Wednesday beat the Mackenzie Club 4–0 in the first game, to set up a Bramall Lane final with the Garrick, who at the time were considered to be the best side in Sheffield. The final, played before 600 fans, was goalless at the final whistle; and it was decided to play on until one of the teams scored. Ten minutes into the extra time Wednesday scored, and John Marsh was carried from the ground by jubilant spectators after winning the trophy, thanks to a 'golden goal' scored some 129 years before FIFA decided to introduce the rule! The club finished their first season with a friendly against the Wellington club, and then by holding a sports day at Bramall Lane as their first ever fund raising event.

In 1868, Wednesday welcomed John Holmes onto their committee. He would go on to play a prominent role in their early development, first taking on the job of treasurer and then becoming Club President in 1887. The club's second season was limited to friendly games against the likes of Heeley, Mechanics, Pitsmoor and Broomhall, and in 1870 the club made Myrtle Road their second home. Henry Hawksley became the Club President and the famous brothers, William and Charles Clegg, joined the Wednesday club. Two years later the latter would play for England in their first ever International match, and both appeared in October 1870, in the first ever published line-up for a Wednesday game; which resulted in a 1–1 home draw with Mackenzie. For posterity the following twelve men (it was many years before the game of football settled into an eleven-a-side format) represented Wednesday at Myrtle Road, with Sampson netting the home goal:

J. Marsh, C. Mills, W. Clegg, J. Clegg, J. Hollingsworth, G. Sampson, F. Butler, T. Cawthorn, W. Ward, C. Stokes, H. Parker.

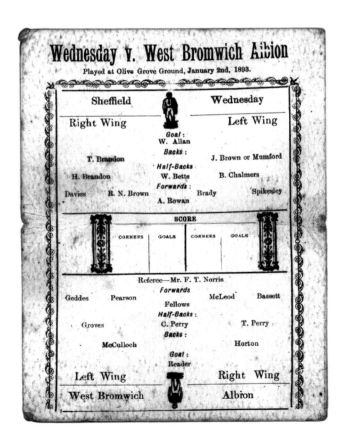

The same season saw Wednesday lose at Fir Vale after playing with only seven men, and in October 1871 a home game with Mackenzie was abandoned after 20 minutes when the ball burst and another could not be found! As the 1870s progressed, so did Wednesday; and in the 1872–73 season the club organised home and away games with the Derby County Association, winning a fourteen-a-side encounter at Bramall Lane in November, and triumphing in Derbyshire in early February. The following campaign saw Wednesday play a total of 25 times at first, second and third team levels, and saw the first appearance of an early goal-scoring hero, Bob Gregory. However, the club lost an outstanding player and founder member, John Marsh, with William Littlehales stepping into his secretarial shoes and William Stacey becoming the new captain.

One of the greatest players in Wednesday's early history was the outstanding left-winger, Billy Mosforth, who made his first appearance in a blue and white shirt in October 1875, at Thurlstone, against a team called Crystal Palace. The diminutive Mosforth, who in his playing days was the idol of the Wednesday followers and was affectionately known to them as 'The Little Wonder', won the first of his nine England caps aged just nineteen. At a time when team-play was a concept yet to be embraced, the individual talents of Mosforth made him stand out from the norm, and he continued to delight Wednesday supporters until late in 1889, when he moved to the newly formed Sheffield United club.

The 1875–76 season also saw Wednesday travel outside England for the first time, when, in April 1876, they lost 2–0 to Clydesdale in Glasgow. Again in 1876, a young Arthur Dickinson joined the committee to start a 44-year association with the club. Four years earlier, in 1872, the Football Association had introduced its Challenge Cup competition. Such was its success that the Sheffield Association followed their lead, and in the 1876–77 season the Sheffield equivalent was staged for the first time, to enormous local interest (the competition survives today under the guise of the Senior Cup). Football was now becoming hugely popular and Wednesday, one of 25 teams who entered the new tournament, had the pleasure of playing in the first ever game on 21st October 1876, when they beat Parkwood Springs in front of 1,000 fans at Myrtle Road. Further victories over Kimberworth, Attercliffe and Exchange followed, and led to a Bramall Lane meeting with Heeley in the Final. A tremendous tussle was played out in front of an unprecedented crowd of 8,000, with Heeley leading 3–0 at the interval. However, Wednesday stormed back to equalise and force the game into extra time, with Skinner hitting a sensational winner. Wednesday were therefore the first holders of the new £50 trophy, and would engrave their name on the Cup a total of five times in its first eleven seasons, before the arrival of league football diminished its appeal. Incidentally, J.J. Lang was in that Cup winning side, he is widely recognised as being the first professional player to play in English football. At that time, professionalism was seen as a great evil, and although Lang was employed by a member of the club's committee, he actually spent most of his time reading the paper and later admitted receiving payment for playing. A year later his fellow Scots from Glasgow Rangers made their first ever visit to Sheffield, to play Wednesday in a

Bramall Lane friendly. As the decade drew to a close, the club was now firmly established as the top dogs in Sheffield—a position which was strengthened in March 1879 when Wednesday won 3–2 at Bramall Lane, to became the first winners of the new Wharncliffe Charity Cup, with a Woodcock hat-trick being enough to beat their old rivals, Heeley.

The 1880s were, without doubt, the decade that shaped the club we know today. Wednesday entered the FA Cup for the

Extracts from an early 'minute book'— note the wrong date of formation.

first time, then adopted professionalism, finally secured their own ground, and played in their first league competition. The first feat was achieved when Wednesday travelled to Blackburn in December 1880 for a second round tie, after receiving a first round bye following the withdrawal from the competition of scheduled opponents, Queen's Park. Wednesday started their Cup history in fine style with a 4–0 win, with Bob Gregory helping himself to a hat-trick. However, the team eventually lost in the quarter finals at Darwen. In the following season, Wednesday proved their debut run in the FA Cup had not been a fluke as they went all the way to the last four, where they again encountered Blackburn Rovers at the Huddersfield rugby club. The match ended in a goalless draw, with Rovers progressing in the replay by winning 5–1. By this time Wednesday had established a reputation of being Cup fighters and became the team to fear in the competition. Another change of home venue preceded the 1882–83 campaign, with Roberts' Farm (situated off Hunter's Bar) used for the first time in November 1882, in a friendly with Thurlstone which Wednesday won 5–0. Two weeks earlier Wednesday had crushed Spilsby 12–2 at Bramall Lane in the FA Cup, with Gregory scoring five times. For the third consecutive season they then went all the way to the quarter finals, this time with Notts County stopping their progress by winning 4–1 at Bramall Lane. However, victory in the Sheffield Cup and in the Wharncliffe Cup was more than ample consolation for a side containing the talents of Mosforth, Tom Cawley and Jack Hunter.

Billy Mosforth

Tom Cawley

Harry Winterbottom

1885–86 Member's Card

The year 1883 proved to be significant, as The Wednesday Football Club officially split from the Cricket club following claims by the footballers that their exploits were making all the money, but the cricketers were spending it! The season of 1883–84 saw Wednesday's early Cup record dented when Staveley knocked them out at the first hurdle; and this saw the start of several difficult seasons for the club, with problems occurring both on and off the pitch. During this time, Wednesday's playing reputation was badly hit, and they fell to some shocking defeats, including a 12–0 reverse at Blackburn Olympic, as well as home defeats of 7–0 to Nottingham Forest and 8–2 to Derby County. Moreover, Wednesday won only one FA Cup tie in the three seasons that followed, and were embarrassed when they failed to appear at all in the 1886–87 competition, after secretary, Jack Hudson submitted a late application. This followed persistent administration problems as the club tried without much success to replace the departed secretary, William Littlehales. However, the real problem for Wednesday was clearly on the pitch, for the adoption of professionalism—especially over the Pennines in Lancashire—threatened their very future.

It was obvious that a crisis was looming, with Hunter's error regarding the late application for the FA Cup proving to be the catalyst for wholesale change. A local works club, Lockwood Brothers, had their application to enter the Cup accepted, and several of Wednesday's top players agreed to turn out for them—including Tom Cawley, Harry Winterbottom and Billy Mosforth. The Sheffield works side promptly stunned the football world by reaching the quarter finals, with the consequences being dramatically brought home to Wednesday officials when they could only raise ten players for the trip to Halliwell; and where they consequently suffered a 16–0 drubbing. The situation came to a head in April 1887 when, with Wednesday standing steadfastly against professionalism, several prominent Wednesday players combined with other local sportsmen to form a new club to be called Sheffield Rovers. After agreeing to adopt professionalism, the team then played the two games required to enter the following season's FA Cup, and were duly accepted. Two meetings then took place which would change Wednesday's history. Firstly, at a Sheffield Rovers meeting, the blue and white die-hard, Tom Cawley said he thought Wednesday should be allowed one final opportunity to say 'yes' to the payment of players. His suggestion was adopted and, at a special meeting of the Wednesday club, the players simply stated that either Wednesday gave in to their payment demands or they would switch their allegiance to Sheffield Rovers; thus signalling the death knell for Wednesday as a major force. Wednesday had no choice, they agreed to pay the

players five shillings for home games, and seven shillings and sixpence for away games—a new era had begun.

The year of 1887 was without doubt a pivotal time in Wednesday's early history. After the momentous decision to turn professional, they then secured the exclusive use of a home ground. Several different home venues had been used in the twenty years since their formation, and the need for their own ground was becoming increasingly urgent—if only from a financial point of view because of the new professional status. The main problem was that once the visitors and the venue had taken their share, at times Wednesday would be lucky if they received a sixth of the gate receipts from a big game at Bramall Lane. In the summer of 1887, the club committee therefore signed a seven year lease with the Duke of Norfolk for a piece of somewhat swampy land off Queen's Road. After spending over £5,000 bringing the enclosure up to scratch, and having christened the ground, 'Olive Grove', the mighty Blackburn Rovers came to Sheffield to officially open the new ground in September 1887; with Wednesday fighting back from 4–1 behind to share eight goals after Billy Mosforth had scored the first goal on the new ground. Wednesday played 25 times in their first season at Olive

Olive Grove

Grove, with over 9,000 cramming into the enclosure for a smallpox-delayed FA Cup defeat to Preston, and to witness ten goals put past Eckington Works in a Sheffield Cup tie. The following summer saw the Football League formed, but Wednesday were initially refused entry to the new competition. The club had to content themselves with a diet of friendlies and minor cup ties, with the likes of Hearts and Clyde Glasgow providing a cross-border challenge. However, the public enthusiasm for such games was waning, and Wednesday became leading players in the formation of the Football Alliance League in the summer of 1889, with club official, John Holmes, appointed as the first President. The founding members of the new league included Manchester United and Nottingham Forest, though Wednesday swept all before them in their debut season, lifting the Championship after getting off to a winning start by beating Bootle at Olive Grove in their first ever Alliance League fixture. Leading Wednesday to the title were the likes of Teddy Brayshaw, goalie Jim Smith, captain Tom Cawley, and Harry 'Toddles' Woolhouse. The latter was one of the real characters of the club's non-league years, and once wrote a letter to the Wednesday's secretary which simply read:

Dear Mr. Dickinson

I AM ILL.
I believe you are having oxtail soup at the ground today; if so I should like some.

Toddles

It was without doubt a glorious season for Wednesday. Not only did they win the Alliance League but went all the way to the final of the FA Cup for the first time, having overcome Bolton Wanderers in the semi-final at Perry Bar, then the home of Aston Villa. The Final saw the club pitted against the Football League side, Blackburn Rovers, at the Kennington Oval. The Lancastrians proved to be far too strong, however, with a Mickey Bennett second-half goal being a mere consolation in a 6–1 beating.

The increasing popularity of football was emphasised the following season when, despite a dreadful season as the club went from 'prince to pauper' and finished bottom of the table, Wednesday's average attendance in the Alliance League rose by almost 40 per cent, to over 5,000. Two games, however, did stand out. The first was played in December 1890 against Sheffield United, who were then boasting the nickname of 'The Cutlers'. United lost 2–1 at Olive Grove in the first ever meeting of the City's professional clubs. Wednesday's nickname until just before the First World War was 'The Blades', and they won the game against 'The Cutlers' thanks to goals from Harry Winterbottom and 'Toddles' Woolhouse; with the great Harry Brandon making his first appearance in a blue and white shirt under the pseudonym of Todd. The second memorable encounter came in mid-January, in the FA Cup, when Woolhouse hit five goals as Wednesday put twelve past Halliwell without reply—and set a club record victory which, in all probability, will never be bettered. Four different sides from Glasgow visited Olive Grove in the same season, and in September 1891 Wednesday played foreign opposition for the first time when a Canadian touring side were beaten in front of a bumper crowd of 6,000. The club played an astonishing 60 games in 1891–92, including an 8–1 friendly win at Woolwich Arsenal, and a nine goal romp at home to St Mirren, before finishing fourth in the Alliance League. However, a stormy home game with Derby County which finished goalless after Archie Goodall and Wednesday's Jack Brandon were sent off, was, perhaps, of the greatest significance, for it proved to be Wednesday's last as a non-league team. In the following summer, the Football League was extended and Wednesday were elected straight into the First Division.

In preparation for the move to the big-time, Wednesday spent around £2,000 upgrading Olive Grove, including the building of a 1,000-seater stand. To herald the dawn of a new era, Secretary, Arthur Dickinson, was instrumental in bringing in the talents of Fred Spiksley, Harry Davis and Alec Brady to Sheffield. Dubbed the 'Olive Grove Flyer', Spiksley became a living legend at Olive Grove, and in Wednesday's debut season in the Football League, he was the top scorer with sixteen goals. The club's league campaign started with a 1–0 win at Notts County; Tom Brandon entering the history book as Wednesday's first goal scorer in the competition. Accrington Stanley were then beaten 5–2 in Wednesday's first home game. The team rode high in the table until the new year, however, following a slump, it was only with a final day victory that the club ensured they did not have to compete in the end of season test matches—a forerunner of today's play-offs which then involved clubs from both divisions. In the FA Cup, Wednesday reached the last eight, but not before Derby County were controversially overcome after a series of protests and counter protests in the first round. After losing a Cup tie in those days, it was the vogue to lodge some kind of protest about the ineligibility of an opposing player, or to complain about the ground conditions, in order to force a replay. This farcical situation was eventually stamped out by the FA, when they took the blindingly obvious step of insisting that such protests must be made before the match.

Wednesday won 3–2 at home in this campaign, only for a Derby protest to force a replay which the opposition won 1–0. It was then Wednesday's turn to protest, of course, and they succeeded in forcing a third match; with the tie finally being

settled back at Olive Grove, when Wednesday won 4–2. In the summer of 1893 the club became a limited company, issuing fifty, £5 shares. In the season that followed, in the home match with Derby County, Alec Brady became the first player to score a league hat-trick for the club. That campaign saw an amazing three league games abandoned for three different reasons: snow claimed the Olive Grove game with Stoke, rain denied an

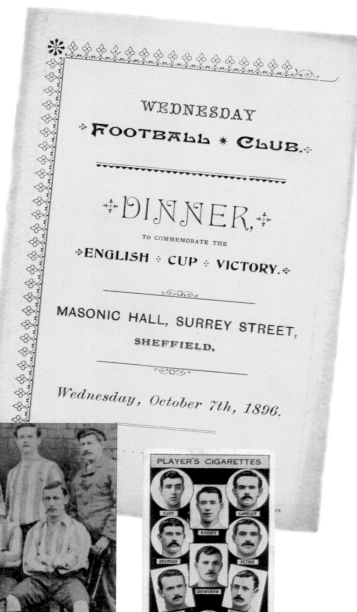

April, 1896
(Left to right) back: H. Brandon, Massey, Earp, Jamieson, Langley; middle: T. Crawshaw, Brash, Brady, Petrie, Davis, Spiksley; front: Bell

away match with Darwen, and fog prevented the home game with the same team! With newcomers Ambrose Langley and Jack Earp in their side, Wednesday finished twelfth in the league but won through to the semi-final of the Cup. There, Bolton Wanderers gained revenge for their defeat four years earlier by winning 2–1 at Fallowfield in Manchester. An upwards move in the league to eighth place was followed by yet another semi-final appearance. This again ended in disappointment when West Bromwich Albion won 2–0 to dash dreams of a Final appearance. However, it was a home game with Stoke in early April 1895 that grabbed all the headlines when the Blackburn referee, Mr Lewis, who had performed poorly at Olive Grove a fortnight earlier, was hooted and jeered by the unforgiving home crowd. After a number of increasingly erratic second-half decisions, Lewis felt he could no longer take the abuse, and, with fifteen minutes remaining, he halted the game. At this juncture a fan in the Heeley end of the ground threw a grass sod at the official, which just missed him, then the referee left the field and abandoned the match. Fears of a ground closure proved to be unfounded, though, five days later at a Football League meeting, Wednesday were 'severely censured' as to the conduct of their fans and were effectively put on probation.

Following many near misses, the club's ninth season at Olive Grove proved to be Wednesday's best of the 19th century, as an eighth place league finish was overshadowed by a first victory in the FA Cup final in the club's history. With Tommy Crawshaw firmly established and Spiksley still in imperious form, Wednesday overcame the challenge of Southampton St Mary's, Sunderland, Everton, and Bolton Wanderers to set up a Final against Wolves at the Sydenham ground, Crystal Palace. A crowd of almost 50,000 watched the game, with the

fans who sported the blue and white favours celebrating within a minute of the 4 o'clock kick off, as Fred Spiksley netted. Wolves levelled through Black after ten minutes, but within a further ten minutes Spiksley scored again. This proved enough to ensure that, at the final whistle, the President of the FA, Lord Kinnaird, would hand the trophy to the Wednesday captain, Jack Earp, after a thoroughly deserved victory. Two days later Wednesday brought the Cup home to Sheffield, parading through the streets of the city to an enthusiastic reception from the massed ranks of Wednesday supporters, before bringing their celebrations to an end at a sold-out Empire Theatre. The club wound up the season with friendly games in Scotland at Third Lanark, Hearts and St Mirren; and a Gala Dinner was held to commemorate the great triumph of 18th April 1896. The following eleven players represented the club on that historic day:
Massey, Earp, Langley, H. Brandon, T. Crawshaw, Petrie, Ferrier, Brady, Bell, Davis, and Spiksley.

The Cup celebrations had only just died down, when, in July 1896, the first rumours surfaced of a possible ground move. These fears were calmed, but after finishing sixth and fifth respectively in the next two seasons it was announced that the lease on Olive Grove, due for renewal in September 1898, would not be available as the Railway Company who co-owned the land with the Sheffield Corporation needed to extend the Northern Line. The club were given permission to play the 1898–99 season at Olive Grove, but a new ground would be needed if league football was to continue. In the summer of 1898 it was reported that the club were on the brink of signing a 20-year lease on the Sheaf House ground, a short distance from Olive Grove, with a nominal rent agreed with the landlords, Mappins Brewery. Permission was

WEDNESDAY'S FUTURE HOME

THE RESULT OF THE POLLING

We are informed that the voting at Olive Grove on Saturday last as to the future home of the Wednesday club resulted in over 10,000 cards being returned. Of these several hundred were spoiled from one cause or another, the actual result being:—

For Carbrook	4,767
For Owlerton	4,115
Neutral	124
For Sheaf House (written across the card)	16

required for this from the magistrates at the forthcoming 'Brewster sessions', and when Wednesday made no application, it emerged the brewery had suddenly hiked their rent demand. Wednesday, it seemed, believed their increasing desperation was being taken advantage of, and so the deal had fallen through. The club was therefore back to square one, with their final season at Olive Grove already under way and no new home on the horizon.

Attention then switched to alternative venues at Carbrook and Owlerton, with the former becoming the definite favourite. At the time there was little other than green fields beyond the Hillsborough Barracks, and it was felt to be much easier for that core of Wednesday support residing in the Heeley area to travel to nearby Carbrook. However, in November 1898, Wednesday decided to test public opinion, with voting slips being handed out at the home game with Aston Villa. Over 10,000 were returned, Carbrook polling 4,767 votes to Owlerton's 4,115. Incidentally, that game with Villa became memorable for unique reasons. The match was abandoned after 79 minutes because of fading light, with Wednesday 3–1 ahead and, instead of the whole game being replayed as would seem necessary, it was inexplicably decided to play out only the remaining 10 minutes. This duly occurred in March 1899, with Richards adding a fourth goal for the home side before the teams went on to play a full ninety minutes in a benefit match for Harry Davis. The victory against Aston Villa was more than welcome, for Wednesday were struggling desperately against relegation, with the future of the whole

club hanging in the balance. In early April 1899 a special general meeting of the club was held at the Maunche Hotel, at which plans were announced for a share issue which, it was hoped, would raise £5,000. It was President, John Holmes, who announced the good news the fans had been long been waiting for, that the money was required as Wednesday were poised to acquire a plot of land at Owlerton. The committee had considered other sites but were in unanimous agreement that Owlerton was the best they could secure for the building of their new home.

There was a degree of sadness all round among the 4,000 in attendance, nine days later, when Newcastle United visited for Olive Grove's final bow. Not only had relegation been confirmed a few days previous, but the fans also mourned the loss of a popular home which had played a major part in Wednesday's development. Unfortunately there was no fairy tale ending for the old ground, as the Geordies won 3–1, with Hutton scoring the final goal by a Wednesday player at Olive Grove. Today the Olive Grove Council depot stands on the site of the old ground, where a plaque has been erected to mark the significance of the venue. Yet, for Wednesday, the move away from the centre of Sheffield would prove to be a masterstroke, and one which would lead the club to greater honours.

The club was represented at the final game by: Massey, Earp, Langley, Ferrier, T. Crawshaw, Ruddlesdin, Bosworth, Pryce, Hutton, Wright, Spiksley.

March, 1890
(Left to right) back: Holmes, Smith, Nixon, Waller, Woolhouse, Pearson, Mumford, Muscroft; middle: Cawley, Brayshaw, Winterbottom, Bennett, Betts; front: Dungworth, Ingram, Morley

Chapter 2

The Early Years
1899–1919

1899–1900
OWLS MAKE PERFECT START TO LIFE AT OWLERTON

Without doubt the story that dominated the summer of 1899 was Wednesday's search for a new ground to replace Olive Grove. However, an equally important event occurred in June when 'The Wednesday F. C. (Limited)' was registered to take over the incorporated Wednesday Football Club. The change to a limited company was overseen by the secretary, Arthur Dickinson, with the aim of the new club stated as being: 'to acquire freehold estate in the parish of Ecclesfield and to promote the practise and play of football, cricket, tennis, cycling and other sports'. A total of twenty two directors were appointed, including the Clegg brothers, John Holmes, and Dickinson himself; it would be these gentlemen who would oversee the subsequent move to Owlerton. Meanwhile, after suffering relegation from the top flight in April 1899, the committee decided to make changes to the playing personnel. This resulted in Archie Brash arriving from Crewe Alexandra, Harry Millar from Reading, William Simmons and E. Rand from Parkgate United, and T. Fish from Birtley. The only player to depart was William Gooing, who went to neighbours Chesterfield, though trainer Johnson also left, with the vacancy filled with the appointment of Paul Frith. When the players reported back after their summer break, they started pre-season training at the old Sheaf House ground. And, as Owlerton was still in the throws of construction, they were forced to use the Niagara Grounds at Wadsley Bridge for a series of three public practice matches. Finally, if you wanted to guarantee a seat in the new enclosure, season tickets could be obtained from Wednesday's registered offices at Barkers Pool in the centre of Sheffield. These cost ten shillings and sixpence, the equivalent of about 52 new pence one hundred years later.

The fixture list ensured Wednesday's first ever game in the Second Division would take place at their new ground, with the tenants making a perfect start by putting five goals past their Derbyshire visitors, Chesterfield. This was followed by a win at Gainsborough Trinity, before the club had their fingers burnt in the transfer market; for, after selling William Hemingfield to Grimsby Town for £75, the Football League committee promptly intervened and lowered the fee to just £25! Another excellent crowd of around 12,000 then witnessed a second home win before Wednesday dropped their first points in a surprise goalless away draw with the bottom club, Loughbrough. Wednesday had settled into their new surroundings in fine style, however, and won all six games played at Owlerton in the first half of the season. The highlight of the half-dozen was a 6–0 romp against Luton Town, when the legendary Fred Spiksley helped himself to a hat-trick. Wednesday were no less impressive away from home; and it wasn't until the return game with Chesterfield in late December that they suffered their first defeat. Their position at the top of the division was maintained despite this, and the disappointment of the club supporters was eased somewhat by the Boxing Day result; for their side had won at Bramall Lane in a fiercely contested friendly against League Champions, Sheffield United.

Despite victories in their first two home games of the New Year, Wednesday slipped off the top of the table as Bolton Wanderers sneaked ahead. However, it was then FA Cup time, with the self-same Bolton beaten by Wednesday, to set up a memorable three game tussle with Sheffield United. Before the first tie at Bramall Lane, Wednesday re-entered the transfer

---

THIS DAY
WEDNESDAY GROUND, OWLERTON, SHEFFIELD
LEAGUE CHAMPIONSHIP

OPENING NEW GROUND

WEDNESDAY
v.
CHESTERFIELD

THE LORD MAYOR OF SHEFFIELD WILL KICK-OFF
AT 3 O'CLOCK
ADMISSION 6d, Boys 3d
Stand 6d extra.

market, signing Harry Davis from Barnsley—with William Simmons moving on loan for the remainder of the season in the opposite direction. The new signing did not appear in any of the Cup ties, and was probably quite pleased about this, for after two games at Bramall Lane, the final game of the trilogy saw passions boil over. The initial tie had been lost to snow early in the second half, with the teams locked in a goalless stalemate. After two further postponements, a 1–1 draw was fought out in a game in which the Owls' goalkeeper, Massey, was forced to leave the field for several minutes after being kicked by United's, Beer. The two sides, however, seemed to have only been warming up for the third clash at Owlerton, a match which has gone down in history as the perhaps the fiercest ever derby clash. The referee had actually warned both sides about their conduct before the game, but no prisoners were taken in the first half, which ended with Wednesday down to ten men after George Lee broke his leg in an accidental collision with Thickett. Soon after the interval Langley conceded a penalty which Needham converted to put the 'Cutlers' ahead. Wednesday were then reduced to nine men as Pryce went 'over the top' on Hedley and was ordered off. Near the end Hedley himself was carried off, having been hacked down by Langley, who became the second man to be dismissed. The home side were now down to eight men and a late goal wrapped up the game for United in a match that would be talked about in Sheffield for decades.

With Wednesday out of the Cup they redoubled their efforts in the league and quickly regained the top spot from the Wanderers. With the club seemingly heading towards promotion they then had to face the consequences of that Cup

battle with United, for the FA launched an inquiry into the events. The outcome was that Ambrose Langley was suspended for one month, and John Pryce for two weeks: though the latter was probably not too distressed, for Wednesday did not play for almost two weeks, by which time his ban was almost over! On the field of play, a home win over Port Vale secured promotion back to the top flight at the first attempt; and by beating Middlesbrough on the last day of the season, Wednesday not only clinched the Championship, but became one of only seven teams in the history of English soccer to complete a home league programme without dropping a point. The season therefore finished on a high note, a great contrast to the events of twelve months earlier, when the future of the club was in doubt after they had lost Olive Grove, and Wednesday had suffered relegation for the first time in their history. It had indeed been a glorious debut season for the new ground.

Tom Crawshaw

The Directors of
The Wednesday Football Club, Limited,
request the honour of the Company of

_____ and lady

To the Opening of the New Ground at Owlerton,
on Saturday next, September 2nd, 1899,
The Lord Mayor of Sheffield, Ald. W. E. Clegg,
will kick-off at 3.0 p.m. prompt.

1900–01
WEDNESDAY CONSOLIDATE BACK IN THE TOP FLIGHT

Almost immediately after reclaiming their First Division place, Wednesday took steps to strengthen the side; and inside a twelve-day period a total of five new players were engaged for the following season. The first to arrive, from Scottish club Third Lanark, was W. McWhinnie. He was joined soon after by Jack Malloch from Dundee, and goalkeeper, Frank Stubbs, from Loughborough. In those days Scotland was awash with English scouts looking for talent; though doubts were expressed at the expense when Wednesday broke their transfer record by splashing out £200 on the Glasgow Clyde centre-forward, Andrew Wilson. However, the fact that 'Andra' went on to become the club's all-time record goal scorer probably justified the original outlay! The last of the quintet, Matt Moralee, was signed from North East club, Hebburn Argyle. In mid-June the club released their first ever annual report and financial statement, the accounts showing a recorded deficit of just over £500. However, considering the enormous costs incurred in moving grounds, the directors believed the loss 'to be not very large', and commented that the club should soon be in profit. The summer period saw two players leave Owlerton; after seven seasons with Wednesday, Jack Earp joined Stockport County in a player-coach capacity, and Archie Brash was sold to Leicester Fosse for a £60 fee.

The First Division campaign kicked off with an entertaining draw at Hyde Road against Manchester City. Then, at Owlerton, it was 'as-you-were', as Wednesday won their first two home fixtures to settle comfortably into a top ten position. In the process they also launched their first, proper, match day programme. Around the same time, Wednesday drew 1–1 with Barnsley in a friendly arranged to officially open the Tykes new Oakwell enclosure. Wednesday fans were then shocked as Preston won at Owlerton to end the one hundred per cent record of league victories at the new ground, which stretched back some twenty games. Incredible as it may seem to modern eyes, the club's next home fixture was then postponed because their opponents, Wolves, had arranged to play the famous amateur side, The Corinthians, on the same afternoon—with the full backing of the Football League! When they returned to league action, Wednesday quickly got back to winning ways at home; and this excellent Owlerton record kept them out of trouble—for, by the turn of the year, the 'Blades' had failed to record a win on foreign soil. One of these away reverses came down the road at Bramall Lane when, before the game began, a glimpse was afforded of 'training' in the early part of the 1900s. This started with the Wednesday players taking a brisk walk in the bracing air of Ecclesfield, before taking dinner, having a good rest, and then walking back to Owlerton to arrive in the late afternoon. What these early professionals would have made of today's high-tempo training techniques in anyone's guess.

As the local press hailed the beginning of the 20th century, a huge crowd of 25,000 flocked to Owlerton to see a victory over Wolves. However, an equally large gathering was to be bitterly disappointed a few weeks later, as Bury followed up a league victory at Owlerton by knocking Wednesday out of the Cup at the first round stage. The former game made the headlines for all the wrong reasons for, after the referee had made some unpopular decisions in favour of Bury, an angry mob ambushed the visiting team on Penistone Road as they headed towards the station. Pelted with mud and stones by the angry fans, many of the visitors received cut heads before they could push through the mob. The Bury officials seemed set to

Herrod Ruddlesdin

report the matter to the FA, but a somewhat remorseful telegram from Wednesday ensured the matter was eventually dropped—much to the relief of those in Owlerton. Incidentally, on the Saturday before the aforementioned Cup tie, all sports events had been cancelled as the country was in deep mourning following the death of Queen Victoria. The month of February finished on a brighter note for Wednesday, however, as they secured the signatures of Jack Lyall and William Gosling from the happy-hunting-ground of North Eastern, non-league football. Following a narrow win in Kensington against The Corinthians, Wednesday returned home to crash four goals past Stoke and move back towards mid-table safety after a disappointing run of results from the turn of the year. By the time the 'Cutlers' from Bramall Lane visited Owlerton for the final game of the season, Wednesday were already safe in mid-table; and a goal from Andrew Wilson early in the second half ensured sweet revenge for the Wednesdayites.

At the season's end Wednesday had failed to win a single game away from home. Thankfully, though, they had earned win-bonuses in all but four of their home fixtures; and this ensured the return to top flight football had been satisfactory. Moreover, the addition of quality players such as Jack Lyall and Andrew Wilson would prove to be the building blocks for future success.

1901–02
WEDNESDAY EXPERIENCE SEASON OF DISAPPOINTMENT

Wednesday fans had hoped, that, after consolidating their place back in the top flight, the side would produce the kind of football that would match the opulent Owlerton ground—which had become one of the best enclosures in the Country. However, local opinion had it that Wednesday, although having no fears of being involved in a relegation scrap, did not really possess the playing staff to make a realistic challenge for the Championship. The summer had seen the club retain the majority of their best players (the concept of long-term contracts was still many decades away, with players signing on a seasonal basis, and simply not being retained come April if their services were no longer required); though there was no big name signing. The fans therefore had to be content with the recruitment of a number of promising local players. Amongst the youngsters signed, was Herrod Ruddlesdin's brother, from Birdwell; Hutton, who returned after a season at Worksop Town; and centre-forward, Joe Ryalls, from Montrose Works. None of the trio went on to make any long term impact on the first team; and only the return of William Dryburgh, after two years with Millwall, could be deemed a success. The other summer signing, the outstanding amateur player, Vivian Simpson, would not agree professional terms with Sheffield FC, but signed league forms for Wednesday. Off the pitch, the club supported West Bromwich Albion's proposal to extend the football league to forty clubs, but were voted down at the League's AGM; though Wednesday's application to enter their reserve team into the Midland League was accepted.

Five days before the first team kicked off their Division One campaign at home to Grimsby Town, the club's reserves played their first ever Midland League game. This must have been an enjoyable introduction to the new league, for the Derby County reserve team were thrashed 13–1 at Owlerton, with Jack Beech grabbing five of the goals. The first Saturday in September saw 'The Fishermen' from Grimsby visit Owlerton; and though they lost McConnell through injury after just twenty minutes, it needed a late surge from Wednesday to get their season off to an opening day 3–1 success. Wednesday's first away game took them to Notts County, with the main talking point after the match relating to the Blades' keeper, Frank Stubbs. He, it was felt, had given an inexplicably poor second-half display which contributed greatly to the home side's 6–1 victory. It later emerged that Stubbs had been concussed in the first half, and literally did not know what he was doing! In the match with County, Wednesday were missing both Davis and Dryburgh because of an early season injury crisis, this prompted the club to re-engage Topham, who had played briefly in the club's first season at Owlerton. Meanwhile, although it seems unbelievable now, Wednesday

then had to apply to the Football Association for permission to pay half wages to their inside-forward, Jock Wright while he was suspended—as he had a wife and two children to support!.

Back in the early part of the century the game of association football was still in its infancy in many parts of the country, and Wednesday did their best to encourage the growth in the sport by occasionally playing exhibition games. One such match took place in September of this 1901–02 season, when a huge crowd of around 5,000 packed into the tiny ground at Barrow and saw Wednesday win 5–2. Back in the bread and butter of the league, the Blades were ensconced in mid-table, with their only away win to date having somewhat ironically been achieved at the home of the reigning Champions, Liverpool. The Anfield victory was long overdue, for it was Wednesday's first away win in top flight football since one secured at West Bromwich Albion in March 1898—some 39 games earlier. By the turn of the year, the club's only realistic hope of success came in the shape of the FA Cup. However, these fancies were quickly dashed at Owlerton, when a record crowd of over 30,000 saw Wednesday bow out at the first hurdle, losing to Sunderland in one of the outstanding last

sixteen ties. Sandwiched by a victory against The Corinthian amateurs in London, Wednesday then lost their next two league games to slip down to 14th place in the eighteen-strong First Division.

Problems also occurred off the field, with Wednesday forced to suspend William Gosling for a month after he had been convicted of being drunk and disorderly on a public highway. This was subsequently cut by one week after Gosling was said to have behaved himself; though the same player was back in hot water near the end of the season. Suspended after failing to turn up for a reserve game against Worksop by a committee who were growing tired of his antics, Gosling was eventually given a free transfer at the end of the campaign. Meanwhile, there was discontent amongst the club's shareholders, and they decided to call a special meeting to discuss their dissatisfaction at how the club was being run. Unfortunately for the organisers, in the period between the meeting being arranged and it actually taking place, Wednesday suddenly started to string together some impressive results; including a best ever First Division run of three consecutive away wins. These successes diluted the shareholders complaints somewhat, though the Chairman was still able to make several

relevant points which 'they hoped the Wednesday directors present would take on board'. A major gripe of the shareholders was that the club had underachieved since entering the league nine years previously. They also believed, it was said, that the club should not only appoint a paid assistant to honorary secretary, Arthur Dickinson, but take on an experienced trainer-manager to mould the club's playing squad into a title-winning side. Both recommendations were eventually adopted, though it would take seventeen years for the second to occur! Before the end of the season the club entered the transfer market to sign William Bartlett from Gateshead NER for £25; while, on the field of play, Wednesday finished where they had started—in mid-table—after a fairly uneventful campaign. However, a somewhat better season loomed on the horizon.

F. Spiksley

1902–03
CHAMPIONS FOR THE FIRST TIME

After the problems encountered in the previous season Wednesday hoped for a more tranquil campaign in 1902–03. As was the case in those days, the club did most of their transfer business immediately after the end of the season, and in sharp contrast to twelve months earlier, the three senior players who were now brought to the club all proved to be of long term benefit. The first capture saw the Blades make a quick return visit to Gateshead NER, Bartlett's old side, and sign the 20-year-old inside-forward, James Stewart. After taking a season to break into the side this young man would go on to score 59 times in a six year stay. Stewart was followed into Owlerton by two more players who would become fixtures in the side after a settling-in period. Firstly, left-back, Harry Burton signed from Attercliffe, and then left-winger, George Simpson, arrived from Jarrow, the North-East non-league outfit. Fringe players, James Melia and William Simmons, left Owlerton and joined Preston North End and Doncaster Rovers respectively, and one more important signing was made as William Tolly of Chapeltown was appointed the club's first groundsman. The summer also saw the famous Olive Grove programme seller, Billy Whitham, again given the rights to sell the clubs programmes and books, for which pleasure he was charged a £21 fee.

The new fixture list caused great excitement in the City, for it paired United and Wednesday together at Bramall Lane on the opening day. Over 20,000 filled the ground and witnessed a great start for the visitors, as goals from Fred Spiksley, Andrew Wilson and Harry Davis helped Wednesday to a tremendous 3–2 victory. The club then won their next two games to hold joint leadership of the division as the league tables started to take shape. A defeat at Newcastle United followed, but a visit to Notts County on 'Goose Fair' Friday saw the Sheffield FC amateur player, Hounsfield, brought into the side, as Wednesday won for the third time on their travels, and became outright league leaders for the first time in their history. However, consecutive defeats then saw the team slip from the top spot; but, as winter dawned, the club consolidated a top six position, thanks, in the main, to a remarkable away record which brought six wins in eleven games. During the excellent opening first half to the season, the Wednesday committee sold Jock Wright to Hamilton Academicals, after he'd played 110 games for the club. Also, they decided not to entertain a compensation claim from Swift, the Walsall Town, Midland League club goalie, who had written complaining that his false teeth had been broken during a game at Owlerton! The only other behind-the-scenes event of note saw Wednesday launch court proceedings against a gateman who had defrauded the club of a significant amount of gate money.

A run of five consecutive home wins over the Christmas and New Year period pushed Wednesday into second place behind leaders, West Bromwich, with Andrew Wilson and Harry Davis both grabbing hat-tricks in the process. The FA Cup run then lasted only two games with a replay defeat being suffered at Blackburn Rovers. However, following a friendly win on the South coast at Portsmouth, Wednesday regained top spot on goal average—thanks to Ambose Langley's first-half penalty kick against Nottingham Forest. The club then played another 'missionary' game, when, somewhat embarrassingly, they were held to a 2–2 draw by a select side from the West Yorkshire based Heavy Woollen District League. Despite this hiccup, Wednesday travelled to third-placed Sunderland a fortnight later, where, thanks to an Andrew Wilson goal, they recorded a critical 1–0 win against a side considered their main challengers; and one which had been unbeaten since losing at Owlerton back in November. All the headlines came

.. The ..
Wednesday

Football
.. Club, .

LIMITED.

§   §

BANQUET,

. . . AT THE . . .

MASONIC HALL,

On MONDAY, AUGUST 24th. 1903.

TO COMMEMORATE THE WINNING OF THE

LEAGUE CHAMPIONSHIP,

AND THE

MIDLAND LEAGUE CHAMPIONSHIP.

SHEFFIELD CHALLENGE.

AND WHARNCLIFFE CHARITY CUPS.

Chairman ... ... Ald. GEO. SENIOR, J.P.

T. WOODCOCK, SHEFFIELD.

from events off the pitch, however, for during the game the visiting players and the referee were constantly pelted with oranges; and, after the match, an angry mob of Sunderland hooligans waited outside the ground for the poor old referee, who was somehow smuggled out of the ground. It was then Wednesday's turn to face the music, and they were assailed with stones and various missiles. It was fortunate there were no serious injuries, for as the players and officials pulled away in their horse-drawn waggonette, the mob chased them down the road, throwing anything they could get their hands on. Wednesday later reported the incident to the Football Association and the Sunderland ground was closed for two weeks, a disruption which certainly could not have helped their challenge for the Championship. Following that victory at Roker Park, the Blades remained top of the table until the last game of the season, when West Bromwich were beaten at Owlerton. However, they could still not be crowned Champions, for Sunderland had one game still to play—and if they were to beat their great rivals, Newcastle, at St James' Park, then the title would go to Wearside. A week later Wednesday found themselves in Devon, where a remarkable crowd of 16,000 turned out in this rugby dominated area to see Notts County and Wednesday contest the 25 guinea, Plymouth Bowl. The Wednesday captain, Ambrose Langley

duly lifted the trophy after a 2–0 win, and received a lavish gold winners-medal. However, events hundreds of miles to the north dominated the proceedings, and when news came through that Sunderland had lost 1–0 to Newcastle, the celebrations began in earnest.

Incidentally, the Wednesday reserves were in action at Owlerton on that same day, and when Billy Whitham put the Sunderland result on the scoreboard, the game was held up for several minutes because of the celebrations. Before returning home, the new Champions shared four goals with Bristol City, and put six past the Welsh side, Aberaman. On their return from Cardiff, the team was met at the Midland Station by the Sheffield Recreation Band, who played at Owlerton on match days. The players were then driven through the streets of Sheffield to the acclaim of their fans, before completing a glorious day by dining at the Carlton restaurant and watching a variety show at The Empire Theatre. Without doubt, this had been the best season in the Club's history; for in addition to the two trophies captured by the first team, the reserves recorded the treble of the Wharncliffe Charity Cup, the Sheffield Challenge Cup and the Midland League Championship. The Chairman of the Shareholders group had probably resigned by now!

The Plymouth Bowl

1903–04
WEDNESDAY RETAIN THE CHAMPIONSHIP

After sweeping all before them in the previous season, Wednesday fans approached the 1903–04 season with their confidence sky high, for the Championship winning team was retained and a handful of useful new recruits were added. The major newcomer was Grimsby Town half-back, William Hemingfield, arriving for a second spell. He had previously appeared in the club's first season at Owlerton, and returned now for a £75 fee. Others who signed in were the youngsters W. Eaton, F. Levick and Oliver Tummon, the latter eventually establishing himself in the first eleven after signing from the Sunday School club, South Street; with the only departures being Hutton and Fish. Meanwhile, those Wednesday fans who wished to reflect on the club's recent glories could visit the Sheffield Telegraph offices where the quintet of trophies were put on display. Other events in the off-season saw Wednesday apply to have a telegraph wire extension installed from Hillsborough Park to Owlerton; a celebration dinner held at the Masonic Hall on Surrey Street; and League Championship medals ordered for the players, at £3 apiece. Permission was also granted for a summer gala to be held at Owlerton—with a proviso for the organisers that elephants were to be kept on the pitch!

The new season kicked off with a visit to the Hawthorns, where a second-half strike from Harry Chapman gave Wednesday the perfect start against home side, West Bromwich Albion. This early form was maintained and victory over Nottingham Forest in the club's sixth game of the season put them back on top of the table. And, though Wednesday were quickly displaced after a setback at Wolves, the Blades were again a major league force, remaining in the top three for the rest of the year. Dominant at home, Wednesday would not taste defeat at Owlerton during the whole campaign; and an occasional away success kept them in touch with the league leaders, Sheffield United. When the two City sides met in mid-December, United were top of the league and Wednesday were second; the first and only time this has occurred. There was, of course, huge interest in the game, with hundreds locked out as over 30,000 packed into Bramall Lane. Not surprisingly the game ended all square, with 'The Cutlers' remaining at the summit for the time being; though they would eventually fade to finish down in seventh place. Wednesday then entered the transfer market engaging the Whitwick White Cross goalkeeper, Richard Jarvis; centre-forward Fred Robson, from the little-known Scotswood-on-Tyne FC; while reserve team player, Albert Kaye, was transferred to Stockport County. The Christmas period saw a fully deserved benefit match held for long-serving full-back, Billy Layton. He had spent nine seasons at the club and was a vital member of the Wednesday's legendary 'L' back line of Jack Lyall, Layton and Ambrose Langley.

The New Year started with a splendid 4–0 home win over Wolves, with the renowned amateur, Vivian Simpson, scoring twice; and by the time Wednesday made the long trek to Plymouth Argyle in the First Round of the FA Cup, they had re-taken top spot from their City rivals. Wednesday, of course, had fond memories of Home Park, having heard of their League Championship success there as they won the Plymouth Bowl some nine months earlier. This time, however, they met a newly formed home side who were in their first season in the Southern League. An 'Andra' Wilson brace looked to be sending the Champions through, though the non-leaguers gave Wednesday a fierce contest, with Peddie heading home a last minute equaliser. Wednesday comfortably progressed in the replay, however, to set up a meeting with Manchester United. This, without doubt, was inside-forward, Vivian Simpson's day, for after scoring a first minute goal he received rough treatment from the Mancunian defenders, yet

shook off their unwelcome attentions to grab a hat-trick as United were thrashed 6–0, and Wednesday reached the last eight of the competition. It then needed a replay to overcome the challenge of non-league giants, Tottenham Hotspur, to secure a Goodison Park semi-final clash with Manchester City, which attracted over 45,000 fans to the Merseyside enclosure. The fact that Wednesday were playing a Lancashire team on a Lancashire ground, with a Lancashire referee and linesman officiating, somewhat rankled the 4,000 Wednesday supporters who had crossed the Pennines! As it was, even the pre-match marching band turned out to be the one that played at City's home games. For Manchester City, who sat in second place behind Wednesday in the league table, the semi-final was therefore as close to a home-tie as it could possibly be. Even these factors, however, were no real excuse for the poor Wednesday performance; as the travelling support saw their side fail, and the chance of a momentous double disappear in a 3–0 reverse.

There was still the small matter of the league to concentrate on, however, and, somewhat ironically, seven days later the Blades gained swift revenge when City were beaten at Owlerton, thus extending Wednesday's lead at the top of the table. Consecutive away defeats, with a tremendous 3–0 home win over United at Owlerton sandwiched in between, then kept the Championship pot boiling, and, following a win over Aston Villa in the final home game, Wednesday held a one point lead over Manchester City, with one game to play. The top two both had away engagements on the final day, with City making a return visit to Goodison Park to face Everton, and Wednesday making the short journey south to oppose Derby County. Wednesday, of course, knew that what happened on Merseyside would be irrelevant if only they could secure a victory at the Baseball Ground. They could hardly have had a better start when, after just three minutes, Harry Davis set up Harry Chapman to send a fierce low drive clean past Maskery in the home goal. Wednesday continued to attack and though they experienced a few scares in the second half, they were always in control. When Harry Davis netted a second with just ten minutes remaining he thus ensured the Championship would remain in Sheffield, with Wednesday becoming only the third club to retain the title. Although Wednesday scored only 48 goals in the whole season, with Harry Chapman being the top scorer with 16, the defence conceded only 28 times, and this was a major factor in another glorious season for the Wednesday fans.

THE WEDNESDAY
FOOTBALL CLUB.
LIMITED.

Banquet
* * AT THE * *
MASONIC HALL,

· ON ·

Friday, May 20th 1904.

To Commemorate the winning of the
Football League Championship
for the second year in succession.

Chairman:
Ald. GEO. SENIOR, J.P.

Wednesday Football Club Limited,

DINNER,

At the Masonic Hall, Surrey Street, Sheffield,
FRIDAY, MAY 20TH. 1904.

To Commemorate the winning of the Football League Championship
for the second year in succession.

DINNER 7-30 P.M.
MORNING DRESS.

A. J. DICKINSON,
Hon. Sec.

1904–05
INCREDIBLE START BUT THE CROWN SLIPS

The task for the new season was simply to become the first team ever to win the Football League Championship in three consecutive seasons. The Wednesday committee again decided not to make many changes to the club's playing personnel, with only a handful of players moving. There were four departures, including Fred Thackeray, Matt Moralee and Jack Beech, who went to Gainsborough Trinity, Doncaster Rovers and Barnsley, respectively. However, it was also the end of an historic era; for 'The Olive Grove Flyer', Fred Spiksley—the last of those who played in Wednesday's first ever league game back in 1892—was given a free transfer after making over 300 hundred appearances in the blue and white shirt. The diminutive Spiksley had been the darling of the Olive Grove crowd and had won numerous club and International honours in his fourteen seasons at Wednesday. The only newcomer to make an impact proved to be the 21-year-old full-back, Hugh Slavin, who signed from Birkenhead. Following two seasons of uninterrupted success, the club were now described as being in the healthiest financial position in their history, with a huge profit of almost £2,000 reported for the year to May 1904.

Even the most optimistic of fans could hardly have predicted the start that Wednesday would make to the new season, for they proceeded to win their first seven games stunning the English football world. The unbelievable opening salvo included a 3–1 win at Middlesbrough on the opening day, a 4–1 victory at Bury, and comprehensive home successes over Wolves and Stoke. However, in just as dramatic a style, the proverbial wheels then fell off, with three consecutive defeats kicking off at the old foes, Sunderland. Woolwich Arsenal then became the first side to win at Owlerton since December 1902, some 31 matches earlier. Following this, one of the greatest games ever seen at Hillsborough took place, when ten goals were shared with Everton. However, the defensive frailties revealed in that game must have worried the club officials, and by Christmas they had seen their charges slide away to eleventh place, following a six-goal mauling at St James' Park and a Boxing Day defeat at Nottingham Forest. The old year, though, was seen out in style, as Middlesbrough were hit for five on New Year's Eve, restoring hopes that a revival might see the Blades move back into title contention.

The first game of 1905 resulted in a splendid home win over Preston. After a defeat at Molineaux, however, the committee decided to act, and two days later duly broke the club transfer record by splashing out £300 on Stockport County's 'clever' inside-forward Tom Brittleton. The new man made a winning debut, as a Jimmy Stewart treble helped to beat Bury 4–0. Brittleton would prove to be one of Wednesday's best ever

captures, remaining a first team regular for an astonishing fifteen seasons. As far as the league was concerned, though, Wednesday had fallen too far and too quickly to come back into Championship contention, and so interest turned to the Cup, where, after Blackburn Rovers were beaten at Ewood Park and Portsmouth overcome at Owlerton, Wednesday were drawn at Preston in the last eight. A huge hike in prices by the home club meant less than 12,000 attended the tie, and those that did saw the home side move ahead after only three minutes. An equaliser from Andrew Wilson forced an Owlerton replay on the following Thursday afternoon, and the replay resulted in a comprehensive 3–0 victory for Wednesday. For the second season running the team entered the semi-final stage but this time with Newcastle waiting at Hyde Road, the home of Manchester City. Before the game the streets of Manchester were a colourful sight as thousands of Wednesday fans outnumbered their Geordie counterparts and made a great noise with their rattles and horns. The Wednesday squad had been training at Buxton and when they finally arrived at the ground, just past three o'clock, the newsmen were able to glean the information that Hugh Slavin was to replace stalwart, Billy Layton in defence. Wednesday

Harry Chapman

started the better of the two sides, but after 18 minutes a mistake from Stewart presented the ball to the United left wing. They eventually supplied Jimmy Howie who fired past Jack Lyall into the Wednesday net. From that point on the game was played at a frantic pace, with Wednesday counting themselves unlucky to still be in arrears at the break. The second period was played out in the same vein, with the Geordies lucky not to concede a penalty kick when McCombie clearly handled near the goal line, an incident the referee somehow missed. Despite their best efforts, however, Wednesday could not grab the vital equaliser and the North

East fans were celebrating at the end of ninety minutes, with the Blades again falling agonisingly at the penultimate stage. It was then back to the league for the beaten semi-finalists, and after taking two points off Notts County on the following Saturday, Wednesday then failed to register a win in their last five games. These included a disappointing 4–2 defeat to United at Bramall Lane. To sum up a poor finish to the season the club then played a 'thank-you' match at Buxton, for they had provided their Silverlands ground for training before the Cup semi-final. Even here, a full strength Wednesday team somehow managed to lose 4–3 to the minnows.

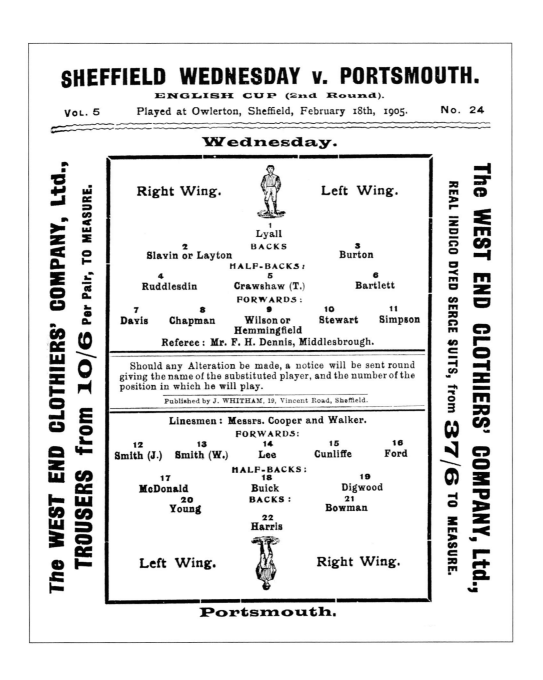

1905–06
FA CLOSE OWLERTON AFTER PRESTON FRACAS

Following the relative failure of a ninth place in the league, and a Cup semi-final defeat, the supporters of the Wednesday club were impatient for the club to return to their former glories. Injury and illness to key players were highlighted as being the main reasons behind the disappointments of the previous campaign, but the club may also have believed that other matters were to blame, for they brought several new faces to Owlerton during the summer months. The first newcomer was Joseph Jameson who arrived from that regular source, Wallsend Park Villa. The somewhat unfortunately named Christopher Crapper was the next to sign from South Kirkby Colliery. Walter Holbem, who'd built a big reputation in local football with Heeley Friends, also arrived; along with Frank Rollinson, who was also a member of the Heeley club. The biggest capture of the period was the purchase of Grimsby Town's highly rated forward, John Reynolds, for £275; though he would be a big disappointment, as he only played twice for Wednesday in two seasons. Wednesday went into the new season with a total of 21 professionals on their books, plus the likes of amateurs, Vivian Simpson and George Hoyland. One name was missing, however—that of Ambrose Langley—for after being awarded a free transfer by the club, he ended his 12 year, 318 game association by signing for Hull City. Also heading for the exit door was W. McWhinnie, who returned north of the Border to sign for Hibs. There was sadness, too, when the director, John Mastin died. His construction company had been instrumental in building both Olive Grove and Owlerton.

For the second consecutive season Wednesday made an excellent start to their league campaign; and though not as spectacular as the one twelve months earlier, it was equally effective. One defeat in their first eleven outings put Wednesday at the top of the First Division rankings, where they remained until late November. This splendid opening included a great derby win at Bramall Lane, with Chapman and Stewart netting in a 2–0 scoreline. It also saw the first ever top flight win at Woolwich Arsenal; and this, as todays fans know, is never an easy task for Wednesday! A mini slump before the festive celebrations then resulted in the Blades falling to fifth, but this time Wednesday quickly revived and remained in the top six placings for the rest of the season. As 1905 drew to a close, the club said good-bye to Tommy Crawshaw's brother, Percy, who had given six years loyal service to the club, making the occasional first team appearance. Crawshaw's contract was cancelled by mutual consent in order that he could take over the running of a public house in the city centre—at that time it was strictly taboo to work as a publican and play professional football. Also departing the club was outside-right, Joe Ryalls, who made the short trip to sign for neighbours, Barnsley.

Before the New Year was seen in, Jimmy Stewart became the first Wednesday player to score four times in a league game, when Wolves were vanquished at Owlerton on Boxing Day. At the summit, the league was then so congested, that only one point separated the top three clubs, and a home draw with Bury in the opening game of 1906 was enough to send Wednesday into second place. Liverpool suddenly started to open up a lead at the top, however, and this would eventually see them crowned Champions by an impressive six point margin. Before Wednesday started on the Cup trail that year they secured the services of half-back, Pattison Proud, from the famous North East club, Bishop Auckland; and a victory over Bristol Rovers opened their Cup campaign before the fellow Southern League outfit, Millwall, earned a draw at Owlerton. Thankfully, Wednesday played more like a club of their standing in the North Greenwich replay, and, after a 3–0 win, progressed to a home meeting with Nottingham Forest. Over 36,000 packed Owlerton, just fifty spectators short of the ground record set a year earlier, with the majority delighted as Wednesday cruised through to yet another quarter final—their third in a row. However, a trio of consecutive semi-final appearances was not to be, as, this time, in a thrilling tie at Everton, the 'Blades' came back from a 4–1 half time deficit to exit by the odd goal in seven—Harry Davis having missed from the penalty spot.

Incidentally, the home Cup tie with Forest caused post-match problems for Wednesday, after two spectators wrote to the club complaining of their day out at Owlerton. A Mr Bird of Attercliffe wrote saying that his coat had been ripped by a rusty nail as he was coming through the turnstile, and asked for compensation. And, somewhat bizarrely, a Mr Wagstaff wrote saying he had left his coat on a nail at the Penistone Road end of the ground; he had the cheek to ask for compensation for his memory lapse! If the fans and their coat escapades had been the only problems they faced, then the club's committee would have been content. Unfortunately this was not the case, for they then had to deal with the fall-out which accrued from a bad-tempered home league game with Preston. The actual match was poorly refereed, and both sets of players did not shirk in tackle. This produced a truly fierce encounter which only needed a spark to ignite an explosion. The game, somewhat surprisingly, finished with 22 players still on the pitch. At its conclusion, the Preston director, T. Houghton did not help matters, when he abused the home fans as he walked past them to the dressing rooms. The visiting players then conducted themselves in a 'vulgar' manner from the dressing room windows at the end of the game, which in turn resulted in a mob of Wednesday fans throwing stones and other missiles and attacking the Preston players as they travelled from the ground to their hotel. The

William Layton

disturbances were reported by the Preston director, though his protest rebounded somewhat, when, at an FA Commission in London, he was banned for a month for his behaviour, and the Preston players were each fined £1. Despite being absolved of blame for the incidents, Wednesday did not escape censure, and the commission ordered Owlerton to be closed for fourteen days from 26th February 1906. Ironically, the club had played Nottingham Forest just two days earlier at the ground and their next scheduled home game was on March 24th against Woolwich Arsenal, so the closure had little, if any, effect. Posters warning spectators about their conduct were pinned up at the Arsenal game—which doubled as a benefit match for both Herrod Ruddlesdin and Harry Chapman—with the subsequent 4–2 victory completing an always satisfying double over the Gunners. The win lifted the club into fourth place, and with only one defeat in their last seven games, the season finished on a high note; with star-forward, Jimmy Stewart, becoming the first Wednesday player to score twenty league goals in a First Division season for the club.

Harry Chapman

1906–07
CUP GLORY AT CRYSTAL PALACE

With the experience of league and cup success in four consecutive seasons, Wednesday had established themselves as one of the major forces in the English game; and so a title challenge was almost expected at the start of each season. Moreover, considering the quality of players available to Wednesday in the early years of this century, it is not churlish to suggest that a challenge for the major honours would have been expected by the supporters, having seen several of the old guard replaced with players of equal talent, such as Brittleton, Burton and Bartlett. The Wednesday club thus decided against entering the market for big name signings in the summer of 1906, relying instead on last season's retainees, together with several promising youngsters spotted by a certain Bob Brown, who was deservedly retained as Wednesday's scout in the North East. The goalie, William Crinson from the Sunderland club, Southwick, was among the recruits, with Daniel Napier from Wallsend Park Villa, and inside-forward Billy Lloyd, completing the trio of captures from non-league soccer when the latter signed from Jarrow. The summer again saw trainer Paul Frith take pre-season training to ensure the players would be amongst the fittest in the league for the new campaign.

The season kicked off with a somewhat dour and goalless draw at Bury. Then, as per usual, Wednesday were quickly out of the blocks and a five game unbeaten spell ensured another top three position was secured in the early league tables. A stunning 5–1 defeat at Newcastle United ended the run, but confidence was restored with a comfortable win over Sheffield United in a charity game. As Christmas approached, Wednesday might well have harboured genuine hopes of a third title in five years, for they sat just a single point behind the leaders, Everton. However, over the festive period their form was patchy, and Wednesday's chances of an FA Cup success were looking bleak when, a minute into the second half of the first round tie at Owlerton, the Wolves centre-forward, Wooldridge, put his side two goals ahead. Helped on by a vociferous home crowd, Wednesday then stormed back, and George Simpson capped a tremendous recovery by scoring the winning goal to put his side on the road that would lead all the way to the final. From that moment the Cup took over, with Wednesday's league form suffering to the extent that by the season's end they had slipped into the bottom half of the table. Probably, this was of little consequence to the Wednesdayites, for 300 of them travelled to the Dell to see a 1–1 draw, before Wednesday progressed in the replay. The draw for the third round brought Sunderland and Wednesday together for the fourth time in the competition, with the 'Mackems' the favourites to go through after forcing a goalless draw at Owlerton. In front of a new record Roker Park crowd, the Blades pulled the tie out of the proverbial fire and went through to the next round thanks to

George Simpson's first-half goal. This was despite playing the last twenty minutes without Harry Davis, who had the misfortune to fracture his right leg. Ten days later Wednesday's own ground record was broken when over 37,000 packed Owlerton to see the quarter-final meeting with Liverpool. As the final whistle blew, those wearing blue and white favours were celebrating, Wednesday had reached yet another semi-final. Before the meeting with Woolwich Arsenal for a place in the final, the club committee decided it was again time to enter the transfer market. A new club record fee of £500 brought James Maxwell to Sheffield from Kilmarnock.

On a perfect day for football, the semi-final tie took place at St Andrew's; with hordes of Wednesday fans making the train journey to Birmingham in the hope that this would be third time lucky, following two previous losses at the same stage. After just nine minutes those hopes were hit when Garbutt put the Gunners ahead. However, Andrew Wilson equalised ten minutes later, then eight minutes into the second half 'Andra' was on hand to put the blue and whites ahead, after Jimmy Stewart's fierce shot had come back off the crossbar. Wednesday dominated the second period, though the Londoners were still capable of grabbing an equaliser—a situation which had the game on a knife edge. The tension

evaporated in the final minute for the Wednesdayites when man of the match, Andrew Wilson, set up Jimmy Stewart. He duly fired past Sharp sealing Wednesday's place in the showpiece of English football. As is often the case, Wednesday's first league opponents after the semi-final were their Cup victims, and at the Manor Ground—the Gunners home until 1913—Arsenal were avenged, scoring the only goal of the game. A week later a bumper Owlerton crowd saw Stoke earn a surprise 1–0 win, secured despite having their centre-forward sent off in a strange second-half incident. With the visitors having taken the lead, Wednesday had poured forward and won a penalty after Wilson was pulled down in the area. However, the Stoke forward, Fielding, was not best pleased with the decision, and as the referee motioned to place the ball on the spot, Fielding knocked it from the official's hands and was subsequently sent from the field for petulance. The delay certainly did not help Wednesday winger, Jack Reynolds, for he promptly fired the spot-kick straight at Rathbone, the Stoke custodian. Three days later, Frank Foxall was signed from Football League club, Gainsborough Trinity. Many fans must have been saving for the trip to Crystal Palace, because, on what admittedly was a foul and rain lashed day, only 3,000 attended Owlerton in the team's final game before the Cup Final meeting with Everton.

It was now almost a tradition for the 'Northern hordes'—a tiresome description used by the London press—to incorporate a tour of the City on Cup Final Day. Wednesday fans were no different, and hundreds filled open-topped buses to 'do' the grand tour—if only to fill the gap between breakfast time and the game. At the kick-off over 84,000 filled the large but somewhat basic ground at Sydenham; and with the pre-match preliminaries over, Wednesday faced a sharp breeze as Tom Crawshaw lost the toss. The game was an open affair with first blood going to Wednesday after 20 minutes. A low shot from Harry Chapman was fumbled by Scott in the Everton goal, and, as the Sheffielders appealed for a goal, Jimmy Stewart crashed home the loose ball to dispel any doubts (after the match the referee stated the goal was Chapman's, though history has credited the goal to Stewart). Five minutes before the interval Sharp levelled for the Toffeemen, with the game looking set for extra time as an even second half entered its final minutes. However, with 86 minutes on the clock, Andrew Wilson received the ball on the right and, from near the touch-line, whipped in a perfect cross for George Simpson to send a glancing header past Scott and win the Cup for Wednesday. Captain, Tommy Crawshaw, lifted the trophy and on their return to Sheffield the Wednesday team rode through the packed streets of Sheffield to take the acclaim of the delirious fans. The parade snaked to the Town Hall, with the Corporation band playing 'See the Conquering Hero Comes' and 'Play Up Wednesday Boys'. Following the various speeches, the team stepped out onto the balcony, where Crawshaw raised the Cup to the tumultuous cheers of an estimated crowd of 50,000. The club still had three league games to play, accruing a couple of draws in the process. A memorable season ended at Buxton, where the locals had a rare opportunity to see the famous FA Cup before their side were beaten 5–1 in another 'thank you' match for the use of the Derbyshire club's facilities throughout the campaign.

1907-08
CUP SHOCKER FOR HOLDERS

With the FA Cup safely in their possession, the summer of 1907 could hardly pass quickly enough for the club's support, for hopes were again high that a mix of newly arrived young blood and the best of last season's team might well combine to produce yet another tilt at the League Championship. The Cup winning team were all re-signed, although, initially, Jimmy Stewart stalled on a new deal. Meanwhile, the strong non-league scene in the North East was again raided to bring several newcomers to Owlerton. These included the outside-left, Thomas Bolland, from Washington United; Walter Miller and James Taylor, both from that annual source, Wallsend Park Villa; and Armstrong from the Sunderland club, Southwick. Closer to home, Kilnhurst's 'fearless' full-back, Harry Caterer was added to the ranks, with the £30 fee seeming almost to be mere loose change to Wednesday after they received £2,600 from the Football Association as their share from the Cup run. Among the departures from Owlerton were John Reynolds, Pattison Proud, and reserve team top scorer, Adam Stewart. Meanwhile, the undoubted highlight of the close season was the lavish banquet held at the Masonic Hall to celebrate their Cup success.

Wednesday made a highly promising start to the new campaign, as per usual, and a five game unbeaten run, including four straight wins, put them top of the league tables. During this spell, and as part of the transfer deal of Frank Foxall from Gainsborough Trinity, the Blades visited Northolme to play a friendly match. It was a home game against First Division 'new boys', Bristol City, which took Wednesday to the summit, though they had a real scare when, mid-way through the second half, their 4–0 lead was reduced as City scored three times in seven minutes before a late 'Andra' Wilson goal calmed the home nerves. Wednesday lost the top spot after coming unstuck at Manchester City, but, despite showing some inconsistent form, the club maintained their challenge throughout the winter months. During that time they secured an excellent 3–1 derby win at Bramall Lane, with the highlight of the period arriving in late November when the league leaders, Manchester United, travelled to second placed Wednesday. An eagerly anticipated game set a new record crowd for Owlerton and the for City of Sheffield, as 38,397 packed the ground to see a home victory after a tremendous tussle in fog-bound conditions. Ironically, a fortnight later, a serious breakdown on the Hillsborough tramway line meant a record low crowd of only 2,500 fans attended the 5–2 home win over Bolton Wanderers! The period also saw a Frank Bradshaw hat-trick help the Blades thrash Woolwich Arsenal 6–0 on New Year's Eve; and Christopher Crapper sold off to Grimsby Town. Meanwhile, the club committee must have had a premonition of what was in store, for when the FA Cup draw was made and Wednesday were set to travel to play Southern

League, Norwich City, the committee tried unsuccessfully to persuade the Canaries to switch the tie to Owlerton for a £300 guarantee.

Wednesday sat in second place as the New Year dawned, and though they were eight points behind the runaway leaders, Manchester United, it was the Cup and their defence of their trophy that was the main priority. As holders, the Blades were easily expected to see-off the challenge of non-league, Norwich City. However, when the 500 travelling Wednesday fans arrived at Newmarket Road, they found the game was to be played on an ice-bound pitch. On several occasions the match had to be halted, to allow the players to recover from their tumbles on the rock hard surface. Suffice to say, the pitch was such that the match would not have been played today; however, attitudes were very different back in 1908, and a fanatical home crowd saw their home side adapt to the conditions to send the holders crashing out of the competition by two goals to nil. A week later only a handful of disappointed Wednesday fans made the trip to Notts County, when a 2–1 victory cheered the loyal supporters somewhat; however, they then saw the team put five goals past Manchester City, dispelling fears of a Cup hangover. Shortly after this, the Blades paid a first ever visit to Park Avenue, to play the Bradford club in a friendly; and the double was then completed over Sheffield United. With no real chance of being able to catch the league leaders, Manchester United, the not inconsiderable prize of being runners up was still to be played for, and with ten games remaining Wednesday were the club then in possession of the place. The season was, however, to end in disappointing fashion. Wednesday only won two further games, and conceded four goals at Bank Street (the home of Manchester United—which, incidentally, was slated as being unfit for top flight football in that season) and six goals at Middlesbrough. One of the two victories came in the home game with Nottingham Forest—which doubled as a

benefit match for Jack Lyall and Gavin Malloch. The other came at Roker Park, where Wednesday's Indian sign over Sunderland continued. The gloom surrounding the club deepened in April that year, when John Holmes (who had joined the club back in 1868 and had played a prominent role in its subsequent development) passed away, leaving only Arthur Dickinson from the old guard. In retrospect, the same month saw two significant high spots occur, for two players were signed for peanuts, and they would go on to give tremendous service to the club over the ensuing years. The unmistakable hand of that expert North East scout, Bob Brown was again behind the moves, which saw £10 purchase Jimmy Spoors from Jarrow FC, and the signing of John 'Teddy' Davison from Gateshead St Chad's; the latter going on to become one of the best goalkeepers in the long history of the club. Despite suffering a late slump in the league, Wednesday still finished in fifth place, and a goal tally of 73 set a new club record in top flight football. Andrew Wilson netted 19 of these to finish top scorer in another eventful season.

Crawshaw in his element.

A Glorious Goal

1908–09
MORE CUP MISERY IN A SEASON OF CHANGES

The 1908–09 close-season ranks as one of the busiest in the club's early history, with wholesale changes taking place both on and off the pitch. On the playing side there were several notable departures, with the transfer of the unsettled Jimmy Stewart perhaps creating the biggest story. Wednesday had offered the brilliant inside-forward the maximum wage possible, but Stewart was believed to be hankering for a move back to his North East roots, and for the second season running he refused to sign. After his transfer request was refused he applied direct to the FA and negotiations opened with Newcastle United soon after this. Wednesday rejected an initial offer of £500, and eventually succeeding in talking the Geordies up to a fee of £1,000—the biggest sale in the club's history by a large margin. Stewart was not the major departure, however, for the captain, Tommy Crawshaw, who had taken over a public house as a prelude to his retirement, was given a free transfer and signed for neighbouring Chesterfield. Without doubt Crawshaw was one of Wednesday's best ever players, playing over 450 games for the club, winning ten England caps, two League Championship medals and two FA Cup winners medals, as well as providing expert leadership both on and off the pitch.

Crawshaw, the second capped player to depart, was followed soon after this by yet another, as Herrod Ruddlesdin signed for Northampton Town. The disappointing big-money capture, James Maxwell, then moved onto Woolwich Arsenal, and William Crinson and Walter Hemmingfield also headed for the exit door. After becoming the licensee of a public house at Wadsley Bridge, Harry Davis hung up his boots after 235 games for the club, and then accepted a coaching position with Wednesday. Meanwhile, to replace the stalwart, Crawshaw, the club bought English McConnell from Sunderland in what proved to be the only senior capture of the close season. Several youngsters, who subsequently failed to make the grade, were signed, and, off-the-pitch, the long-time trainer, Paul Frith, was not retained, in due course he moved on to Bradford Park Avenue. After advertising the position, the club ultimately appointed Charlie Parramore as his replacement. Bob Brown, who had given years of outstanding talent spotting service, was then appointed as assistant to secretary, Arthur Dickinson at the princely sum of £3 per week. Meanwhile, in an incident packed summer, the Owlerton pitch was completely dug up and re-laid in an attempt to solve a dandelion problem! Finally, Andrew Wilson was elected as captain to replace the sadly departed Crawshaw.

Despite these wholesale changes, optimism was again high for the new campaign, hopes being boosted by yet another good start which began with an opening day draw at Leicester Fosse. After Sunderland brought Wednesday's unbeaten start to the season to an end, a home win over Bristol City saw Teddy Davison make his debut for the injured Jack Lyall. A week later almost 40,000 were at Stamford Bridge to watch the

northerners go 2–0 ahead after just ten minutes, only for the Pensioners to fight back and earn a point. Wednesday also had to be content with a point at Blackburn after throwing away a two goal advantage, while the pre-Christmas home game with Bury fluctuated wildly, as Wednesday took a two goal lead, fell 3–2 behind, drew level, and then clinched a last minute win when 'Andra' Wilson netted in a goal mouth scramble. December saw the club enter the transfer market again, as Frank Stringfellow was signed from Ilkeston United and Henry Hamilton came in from Craghead United. Early in the new year, Gavin Malloch joined Barnsley on trial, and keeper Henry Kinghorn was secured from the Scottish junior club, Keith Athletic. A Christmas double header with Sheffield United saw a home win apiece, then, for the second season running, not only were Woolwich Arsenal the last opponents of the old year, but they again conceded six goals, with 'Andra' Wilson this time being the hat-trick hero. The victory over Arsenal left Wednesday in fourth place, five points behind the leaders, Everton. Early in the New Year, they started to close in on the Merseysiders, but then the FA Cup proved a distraction.

The Cup trail started with a comfortable home win over a Stoke side who had just resigned from the Football League because of financial problems. Wednesday then found themselves two goals

in arrears early in the second half in the next round at Portsmouth, though the young winger, Oliver Tummon saved the day with a late brace—including a last minute equaliser—and the Blades went through in the replay. The next round brought the Second Division minnows, Glossop North End (previous publications have relegated them to non-league status) to Owlerton. The fans were treated to the strange pre-match sight of the Wednesday monkey mascot (sent to English McConnell by a friend in Southampton) being led out onto the field dressed in blue and white garb! Wednesday were expected to brush aside the challenge of The Peakites but allowed complacency to creep into their play and, as a result, the visitors were ahead by a penalty kick at the break. Early in the second half the huge crowd sighed with relief when Wednesday were themselves awarded a penalty. However, Tom Brittleton's effort was saved by Butler, in the North End goal. Wednesday then redoubled their efforts, and, with time running out, they won another penalty, only for Harry Burton to fire this one against the crossbar. Disastrously, the side had duly crashed out on another calamitous Cup afternoon. A trio of league defeats followed, effectively ending any hopes of a league success. Meanwhile, Belfast Celtic's Archie Hunter became the latest signing, and a shock deal saw Harry Burton and fellow stalwart, George Simpson join West Bromwich Albion for a joint fee of £850. Following their departure, Wednesday lost five of their last eight games, slipping out of the top three places. The defeats included a 5–2 home setback to Sunderland, the heaviest home defeat since the move to Owlerton. In many ways, however, it had been a transitional season for the club and a final position of fifth in the league seemed a more than satisfactory return.

THE OWL'S VICTIM

The Chelsea Pensioner: "You young varmint—to treat an old fellah like this!"
(Wednesday easily defeated Chelsea at Owlerton.)

Wednesday 3, Portsmouth 0
FA Cup tie as seen by an artist of the day

1909–10
TERRIBLE START ENDS IN MID TABLE

Before a ball was kicked, the Wednesday secretary, Arthur Dickinson, commented: 'We are always there or thereabouts'. The club's consistent performances in the league since moving to Owlerton suggested that his prediction might again be proved to be correct in the new season. The summer lay-off again saw another large turnover in playing personnel, with Gavin Malloch, James Jameson, Armstrong, Harry Caterer and Thomas Bolland all leaving for pastures new. There were several newcomers with Warren arriving from Belfast Celtic, Harry Bentley from Heeley Friends, Finlay Weir from the Scottish junior side, Maryhill, and Teddy Worrall from the old friends at Buxton. Sam Kirkman was then engaged for £40 from Carlisle United, and the club signed the Scottish Junior International, James Miller, and another ex-Belfast Celtic player, Patrick 'Paddy' O'Connell. Meanwhile, the club reached an impasse with Jack Lyall and English McConnell, both of whom refused to re-sign despite being offered the maximum terms possible under the FA rules. The former never returned to training and was subsequently sold to Manchester City after the start of the new season, while McConnell returned to the side in early October—though his days were numbered.

The Wednesday supporters must hardly have known how to react at the beginning of the league campaign for, in stark contrast to the norm, they watched as their team earned only two draws in the opening six games, and slumped to the foot of the table. Fortress Owlerton was witness to three successive home defeats, including a 5–1 reverse to Middlesbrough in the first home game of the season, and it wasn't until a Rollinson brace helped to secure a 4–1 win over Preston that the rot was stopped. The Wednesday inside-left then grabbed a hat-trick as Newcastle were put to the sword; as, thankfully, the Blades pulled away from the lower reaches to achieve a mid-table spot by Christmas. A quickfire festive double over Manchester United helped further the cause and put Wednesday in good heart for their FA Cup First Round trip to Southern League Champions, Northampton Town. It seemed Wednesday had learnt the lesson from their previous matches against such minnows, fighting tooth and nail to bring the Cobblers back to Owlerton with a goalless draw. However, the Cup gods were obviously still not fully recompensed for the Blades victory three years earlier, and they thus decreed that a 69th minute goal from Walker would embarrass Wednesday yet again, as the non-leaguers triumphed in Sheffield.

The Cup exit triggered another foray into the transfer market, first bringing full-back, Robert McSkimming from Albion Rovers, to be followed by Robert Hunter from Birtley, County Durham. By this time Andrew Wilson had started a secondary career as a fruit merchant; and the home game against Liverpool was designated as a benefit game for both Frank Bradshaw and Billy Layton—the latter receiving the honour

for the second time since joining in 1894. A 5–0 defeat at Aston Villa was notable not only for the home side's five second-half goals, but also because of the inexplicable behaviour of Wednesday's Irish International, English McConnell. The likes of what occurred on the pitch had never been seen before, for after Villa netted their second goal, McConnell ceased to take any further part in the game, strolling around the field and making no attempt to get near the ball. When Villa scored again McConnell was standing away on the touch line, opposite the centre circle. At one point he was seen to simply stop playing and fold his arms, letting the home players surge past him. Not surprisingly, within weeks McConnell was shipped out to Chelsea, with no explanation ever forthcoming for his bizarre behaviour at Villa Park. A week later, in the Sheffield derby, Wednesday lost at home to United and were reduced to ten men near the end when Walter Holbem was sent off after he had cynically scythed down Robbins, the Cutlers' winger. The home game with Bristol City was also peculiar, disproving the myth that it is only in recent times that top flight clubs have been crammed with non-English players. This particular game saw fourteen Scotsmen and two Irishmen take the field, even the referee was a Scot. The Owls goals in a 2–1 win were netted by debut makers, James Robertson and George Murray, both of whom made perfect starts after joining from Motherwell. Both newcomers were full Internationals, Murray for Ireland and Robertson for Scotland. The Scotsman's main reason for moving to Wednesday was unique, in that he was of a scholastic nature and came to Sheffield in order to study at the City University. Before the curtain came down on another season of restructuring, and one which eventually resulted in a mid-table finish for the club, both Hamilton and Bartlett were transferred to Midland League, Huddersfield Town. This would not be the end of the transfer activity, as the club committee attempted to rebuild the side following a decade of success.

Andrew Wilson

1910–11
FIRST FOREIGN TOUR

As the disappointing 1909–10 season drew to a close, Wednesday took steps to rectify matters. The list of professionals who started the following season was thus greatly changed. For the most part, the changes were a result of departures from Owlerton, with several experienced players leaving for pastures new. Top of that particular list was the veteran, Billy Layton, who became the last to leave of the famous back line of Layton, Jack Lyall and Ambrose Langley—the affectionately named 'three L's'. The full-back signed for non-leaguers, Whitwell, on a free transfer after 361 games for Wednesday. One surprise departure was forward, Frank Bradshaw, who, only twelve months after he had finished as Wednesday's top league goal scorer, was sold to Southern League Northampton Town, along with his team mate, Napier. Also departing were Fred Foxall, Oliver Tummon and Archie Hunter, to Birmingham, Gainsborough Trinity and Glentoran respectively; and the experienced Hugh Slavin was not retained. There was a total of five newcomers, with Teddy Glennon proving to be the crucial capture from Denaby United, with Martin Bradley signing in from the same Doncaster club. Lawrie Burkinshaw arrived from Mexborough Town, P. Wright from Heanor Town, and Michael Dowling from St Mirren. Meanwhile, the club's accounts made poor reading for the shareholders, as a considerable loss of over £2,000 was reported. This, it was felt, was caused by a poor league showing and yet another disastrous Cup campaign, which had resulted in very little revenue from the lucrative competition. Not surprisingly the gates were also down, though this was linked to events at the start of the previous season when the league players had almost gone on strike as they unsuccessfully battled to form a union. Whatever the reasons, it was a sharp reminder that success on the field was vital if the club hoped to maintain its well paid playing staff.

With Tom Brittleton appointed the new captain, Wednesday kicked off their league campaign at White Hart Lane, where, despite an early goal from Harry Chapman, Tottenham came back to win 3–1. The club's first two-point haul came at Notts County in the fourth game of the season. However, the lack of an out-and-out goal scorer meant that mid-table was Wednesday's wont in the first half of the season. To meet the problem the club tried out Murray, Brittleton, Dowling, O'Connell and even Wilson at centre-forward, but it wasn't until the new year that the arrival of one man solved this particular problem. A quickfire double from Chapman had beaten rivals United in the derby at Owlerton, and following a 6–1 setback at Blackburn Rovers, Wednesday returned home to take their frustrations out on Nottingham Forest who conceded five goals—with four of Wednesday's front line finding the net. Christmas was certainly not a happy one for fans of the blue and white persuasion, for their side left mid-table behind and slipped into the relegation zone following

another home defeat, this time to Newcastle United. Thankfully, only four days of the season were spent in the bottom two as Wednesday recorded their now traditional New Year's Eve home win over a London side, in this instance Tottenham Hotspur, to move out of the danger zone.

As usual the New Year brought new hope in the shape of the FA Cup. However, the fans must have groaned when their side again drew non-league opposition, this time in the shape of Southern League, Coventry City. To many people today the term 'non-league' suggests a side consisting of bricklayers, postmen and the like; however, before the Great War the Football League consisted of only two divisions. The fully professional Southern League effectively acted as an unofficial Third Division (in 1920 the Football League was extended, with Division One of the Southern League being voted *en masse* into the competition). Looked at from this perspective, it is perhaps not surprising that Southern League teams regularly knocked Football League sides out the FA Cup (one of their members, Tottenham, actually lifted the trophy back in 1901). Wednesday should have realised by now that, as with Norwich City and Northampton Town before them, Coventry would be no pushovers. However, despite the Owlerton club having home advantage, yet another disastrous Cup afternoon saw the Midlands club score the winning goal with twelve minutes remaining, leaving the Wednesday's fans, the officials and the bank manager in sombre mood.

The club were now left to concentrate on their worrying league position, though one week's transfer activity would solve this problem as Wednesday added three more Scotsmen to their ranks. Non-league club, Leith, was the source for both half-back James Campbell and forward Marr Paterson, while the club record £1,000 capture of centre-forward, David McLean, proved to be the catalyst that would turn the club's fortunes

J.T. Brittleton

around. If any man disproved the old adage 'one man doesn't make a team', then it was surely the outstanding McLean. When he joined Wednesday they sat in sixteenth place with only eight wins to their credit. However, after his arrival Wednesday proceeded to win nine times in their final thirteen games and soared up the league table to a final placing of fifth. Although McLean only scored twice, his overall play was excellent and with him at his side, Andrew Wilson more than doubled his seasonal goal tally. Saying that, the contribution of Campbell could not be overlooked either, for in the Scots defender Wednesday had finally found a replacement for the long since departed, William Bartlett, in the problem area of full-back.

The club's tremendous finish to the season reached a peak in their final away game when doubles from both Wilson and Robertson helped beat host club Nottingham Forest 6–0, and post a record league away win that has only once been equalled in the ensuing 89 years. The highly satisfying end to the season was a prelude to Wednesday's first ever foreign tour, in which they played games in Sweden and Denmark. It took the Wednesday party of fourteen players, four directors and two trainers an astonishing 49 hours to reach Gothenburg after leaving Sheffield, with a few meals deposited in the North Sea after several bouts of *mal de mer* struck the travellers! On arriving at their destination, the party watched the English Cup holders, Bradford City, lose to a Swedish select side. This was followed by a sightseeing tour, before a Gothenburg side were beaten 5–0 in Wednesday's first ever Sunday game. After the match, the old hero, Fred Spiksley, who had accepted an invitation to coach in Sweden, joined the party and ran the line as a Swedish select team were beaten 2–0 in the next friendly. Wednesday then journeyed to Denmark, where, in front of the Crown Prince of Denmark they officially opened the country's new stadium by overcoming the Danish national team by three goals to two. The club also won their two other games in the country by the same score, and, after five games in seven days, they returned home a little tired but delighted after a successful first foray onto foreign soil.

O'CONNELL
SHEFFIELD WEDNESDAY

1911–12
WEDNESDAY HOST THEIR FIRST CUP SEMI-FINAL

Following the remarkable finish to the previous season, the club's players, officials and supporters all exuded optimism for the new term, with most firmly believing that Wednesday had finally found the formula that would bring the glory days back to Owlerton. The club's successful foreign tour had also manifested an improved team spirit and the local scribes could see nothing but a successful season on the horizon. The club was obviously happy with their playing staff, as the close season produced no major signings, with only a handful of untried local players secured—including two goalies, Clarke and Hustler, half-back Dexter, and forwards Hemstock, Moore and Beech. Among the players to depart were Kinghorn, Murray, Rollinson, Stringfellow and Bradley; while Wednesday looked somewhat dimly on Walter Holbem's 'outrageous' demand that before re-signing he be guaranteed a benefit match before Christmas. He was immediately transfer listed and three days before the opening game of the new season was sold to Everton as Wednesday quickly dispensed of their 'rebellious' left-back. The summer also saw major changes behind the scenes, with Wednesday disappointed to lose the services of team 'manager' Bob Brown, who moved to the south coast to become secretary-manager at Southern League, Portsmouth. As Arthur Dickinson was then the only honorary secretary in the league (i.e. receiving no payment for his tireless work), Brown had been of great assistance to him since joining the club on a full-time basis. It is also interesting to note that once Brown relinquished his position as the club's scout in the North East on moving to Sheffield, the pool of outstanding talent that had supplied the club with the likes of Jack Lyall, Teddy Davison and Jimmy Stewart had almost totally dried up—a tribute to the scouting skills of Brown who, early in 1920, would make a triumphant return to lead Wednesday to the best period in their history. Also leaving was trainer Charlie Parramore, with Ted Kinnear appointed to the position.

All the hopes for the new season evaporated within a few short weeks, however, as Wednesday lost four of their five opening games to slump to the foot of the league table. A terrific 4–0 home win over Spurs got Wednesday off the mark, but there was to be no sudden revival, for they remained in the bottom two until late October. After fighting back from a two goal deficit at home to Liverpool to earn a point, some confidence was restored a week later with the first away win of the season at Aston Villa. Even with McLean scoring on a regular basis on his way to equalling the club's seasonal goal scoring record, it was Wednesday's poor finishing that was their downfall. It was very much a case of 'if McLean does not find the net, then victory would be unlikely'. After conceding an injury-time equaliser to Sheffield United, a win over Oldham resulted in a move out of the bottom three, and slowly, as the weeks passed, Wednesday moved up to a more respectable mid-table position. In fact, in a run of games from early November to early March, Wednesday lost only once, during which time Sunderland visited Owlerton and were humiliated by eight goals to nil, as a new club record league win was established.

By the time Wednesday visited Middlesbrough for a first round FA Cup tie they had soared to sixth place and, despite having Weir sent off, were confident of progressing in the Cup after earning a goalless draw on a mud bath of a pitch. Over 30,000 attended the Owlerton replay, though the majority were to be disappointed as the jinx struck again, sending Wednesday tumbling out at the first hurdle for the fourth time in the five seasons since Tommy Crawshaw had lifted the trophy at Crystal Palace. Once again the Blades were idle on the day of the second round, but, at least, their league revival meant the Championship was still not an unattainable dream; and, after drawing at home to City rivals United, Wednesday moved into second place, three points behind leaders Blackburn Rovers. Despite their form then stuttering somewhat, Wednesday were still in second place with only six games to play. However, a loss at Bolton hit their hopes, before a shocking 5–1 defeat at Yorkshire rivals, Bradford City, completely obliterated them. The runners up spot was still a prize to play for, but further disappointments away from home ensured Wednesday would slip down to fifth place, eight points behind the Champions from Ewood Park. Late in the season the club received what was thought to be a long overdue honour for their modern enclosure, when the Cup semi-final replay between West Bromwich Albion and Blackburn Rovers became the first to be held on a Wednesday ground. A crowd of just over 20,000 attended the mid-week game and saw a goal from Albion's Pailor send his side through to a final meeting with Barnsley, and deny Rovers the chance to complete a league and cup double. Meanwhile, before the end of the season, Wednesday again raided local football to sign Charles 'Chas' Brelsford from Kilnhurst Town, J. W. Lamb from Bolsover Colliery, and Horace Nicholson from Highthorn Mission. If Wednesday's start to the season had been better there is little doubt that the Championship flag could well have been flying over Owlerton. However, the outstanding goal scoring of David McLean, whose 25 league goals were the highest tally recorded in the top flight by a Wednesday player, and the record win over Sunderland, ensured the season was another memorable one.

1912–13
TITLE SLIPS AWAY DESPITE McLEAN'S RECORD HAUL

As was the case in the previous summer, Wednesday did not see any reason to enter the transfer market for senior players in this off-season period. With hindsight, however, this lack of major investment was probably the main reason that the League Championship did not find its way to Owlerton—for Wednesday were, arguably, only one, or at worst two, top class players short of again becoming a major force in the game. All the newcomers were untried youngsters, who the club hoped would turn from 'ducklings into swans'; and none of the departures could be considered first team regulars. The first to leave was veteran Harry Chapman, leaving Andrew Wilson as the only survivor of the Championship teams. Chapman signed for Hull City after having scored over a hundred times in nearly 300 games since joining Wednesday at the start of the century. He was later joined at Hull by Patrick O'Connell, while Paterson returned to Scotland, Dexter joined Bob Brown at Fratton Park, and Warren sailed back to his native Ireland to sign for the Dublin side, Shelbourne. This summer also witnessed one highly significant event, when the Wednesday player, George Robertson, presented the club with a mascot in the shape of an Owl. The monkey introduced by English McConnell some years earlier had not brought much luck, though Wednesday now stressed that they hoped the gift of this mascot would not lead to them being known as the Owls instead of their real *nom de plume* of 'The Blades'! Somehow the club failed to get their wish, and a nickname was born; especially when the Owl was placed under the roof of the North stand in October, and Wednesday promptly won their next four games without conceding a goal!

Wednesday opened the new season with a visit from League Champions Blackburn Rovers, and the fans were in high spirits when a McLean double secured the downfall of the Lancastrians. Three more wins followed, leaving Wednesday in the top three before the visit to Aston Villa, where the Owls' unbeaten start came to an end in quite extraordinary circumstances. The record 10–0 defeat the club suffered that afternoon was simply a mystery, for the Owls had an equal share of the play. Yet every time Villa attacked, the ball seemed to find its way into Davison's goal. Such was the astonishment at the score that a rumour circulated in Sheffield that Wednesday's keeper had played with a broken leg. The Owls had started and finished with eleven fit men, however, and were at a loss to explain how one of the best teams in the league could possibly lose a game by ten clear goals. Rumours of the club's death at Villa Park were greatly exaggerated, however, and a week later a Wright goal put the Owls back on track with a home success over Liverpool. Wednesday then embarked on a spell of five consecutive clean sheets which brought four wins and took the Owls up into second position. Meanwhile, after spending a one month trial period at White Hart Lane, Finlay Weir was signed on a permanent basis by Tottenham; and James Yates was engaged as the Owls' new scout in the North East. Fans then flocked to Owlerton to witness a titanic struggle on Christmas morning, when George Robertson put Wednesday one up after only 30 seconds against the league leaders, Sunderland. The 'Mackems' fought back though, and netted a crucial 86th minute winner. Within twenty-four hours, the Owls were avenged, winning away at Roker Park; and, following a thrilling New Year's Day draw with Derby County which attracted a new record crowd to Owlerton, Wednesday went to the top of the division for the first time in the season.

With Wednesday leading the Championship race, they were installed as one of the favourites for the FA Cup. This faith was rewarded when star forward, David McLean scored four at home to Grimsby Town, and a treble in a tremendous 6–0 replay win over Chelsea, to send his side into a third round derby clash at Second Division, Bradford Park Avenue. Over 8,000 Owls fans travelled into deepest Yorkshire fully expecting the hot favourites, Wednesday, to progress. They should have known better, for the home side pulled off one of the greatest results in their history to win 2–1 in the day's shock result. It was a bad few days for the club, as a week earlier a 2–1 defeat at Liverpool had seen them knocked off the top of the league. Wednesday, however, bounced back, and goals from Robertson and McLean secured a 2–0 derby win at Bramall Lane to leave them in pole position with ten

AT HILLSBOROUGH.

The owl of Hillsborough : "Look 'ere, you're asking for it, y'know"
(Derby County were at Hillsborough today.)

games to play. The Championship had now become a three horse race, with Sunderland and Villa the main rivals. The top spot was traded several times, with a superb 5–2 win at Woolwich Arsenal putting Wednesday back on top. The North East side then took over top spot when the Owls could only draw at Manchester City, after being two goals in arrears with twenty minutes remaining. However, it was the home game with Newcastle United that produced the hammer blow, when Sunderland's great local rivals won 2–1 at Owlerton. The club now had to rely on the failings of others, but despite beating West Brom in Andrew Wilson's second benefit game (which was badly hit by heavy rain), the Championship went to Wearside. A last-day defeat at Everton meant Wednesday finally slipped down to third place, a disappointing end to a season of what-might-have-beens.

Despite finishing with no silverware, it had been a tremendous season, with David McLean at the forefront. His 38 League and Cup goals not only set a new seasonal goal scoring record for his club, but meant he topped the First Division scoring charts as well. The Owls' centre-forward missed only two games and, incredibly, in the whole season, Wednesday used only sixteen players; with the same eleven playing the majority of the fixtures, and ten players missing two games or less, usually caused by International call ups. This

almost ever-present line up was a crucial factor in the Championship challenge, and barring unforeseen circumstances it was sincerely hoped the same combination of relatively young players would serve Wednesday for many years and bring them close to honours again in 1913–14.

"THE MARCH OF THE OWLERTON MEN"

The Owl of Owlerton : I'll Scotch 'em!"

(Bradford and the Owls (who meet in the Cup tie next Saturday), have seven and five Scotsmen respectivey in their teams.)

"THAT'S DONE IT."

Miss Championship : "All is over between us."
The Owl : "Ah! hic! You love another! hic!!"

(Wednesday by losing to Newcastle last Monday spoilt their chance of winning the Championship.)

1913–14
McLEAN STAND OFF TRIGGERS RELEGATION SCRAP

The summer of 1913 saw work start on the club's new ultra modern South Stand. But for Wednesday fans the real story of the close season involved the prolific centre-forward, David McLean, who refused to re-sign after his unprecedented demand for a three year contract had been turned down by the club. Wednesday had offered McLean the maximum wage of almost £5 a week, and promised him a benefit game with £350 guaranteed. After he turned down that offer the Owls reached a compromise and agreed to give him a two year deal; but McLean, then asked for a £400 benefit game, and when this was refused he returned to Scotland, and into footballing obscurity with non-league, Forfar. The loss of the league's top scorer was, of course, an immeasurable blow to Wednesday, and was the main topic of conversation amongst the fans, who, not surprisingly, wondered if the team could cope with the loss of such a vital member. As a direct replacement Wednesday brought the Swindon centre-forward, Jack Burkinshaw to Owlerton, where he joined his brother Lawrie. Other newcomers included the Mansfield Mechanics goalie, George Streets; the promising local youngster, Jimmy Gill; and Silverwood Colliery forward, Henry Platts. The summer also saw the club announce a record profit of over £5,000, while ex-player Ambrose Langley returned from Hull City to become Arthur Dickinson's assistant, almost a year after Bob Brown had vacated the role.

With Teddy Davison injured in the pre-season practice game, the new goalie, Streets was between the sticks when Wednesday made a winning start to the season at Bolton Wanderers. Five days later, Manchester United were Wednesday's first home opponents, and, with the new stand in partial use, many spectators arrived early to view the impressive structure. Incidentally, that game was also the first to be officially played at Hillsborough, as early in September 1913 the directors altered the name of the enclosure, announcing that from that day forth the ground would be called 'Hillsborough'. Within a year the club had therefore renamed their home venue and collected a new nickname. The changes were only cosmetic, however, for back on the field Manchester United won 3–1, and, in a desperately disappointing start, the Owls would go on to lose five times at Hillsborough before the end of the year. Highlights were rare as the club toiled in the bottom half of the table, with a Teddy Glennon winner at Bramall Lane being a definite high. A mini revival then lifted Wednesday into the top ten, at which point, following a tip-off from McSkimming, they entered the transfer market to sign James McGregor from Albion Rovers, and youngster Oscar Bretnall from Midland Athletic. However, only two wins accrued in the thirteen league encounters that followed, and by late January Wednesday had slipped to second bottom, and were facing a battle to retain their top flight status. During that spell, the long serving Andrew Wilson was made captain for the day when the visit of Bradford City was designated as his

third benefit match—his second having been ruined by terrible weather. It looked as if he was to be unlucky again, for heavy showers fell all morning; however, the weather cleared and 'Andra' purchased cigars and champagne for his team-mates before receiving the healthy gate receipts of almost £450.

The New Year could not have started any worse for Wednesday, as Burnley recorded a 6–2 Hillsborough win, a scoreline that would remain the Owls heaviest home defeat for over 78 years. Brighter news was on the horizon, however, as David McLean had a sudden change of heart, and, after Wednesday had paid Forfar £250 to get him back, he returned to first team duty. His comeback game resulted in a five goal mauling at Preston, a week after Wednesday had progressed in the FA Cup, following a controversial home win over Notts County. The teams were tied at 2–2 when, early in the second half, the County keeper, Iremonger pounced on the ball at his near post. In the ensuing scramble, several Wednesday players dived on top of him to try and force the ball over the line. When the referee finally called a halt to the melee he was pointing towards the half way line, having, to everyone's amazement, awarded the home side with what proved to be the winning goal. The goalie, who was then

Jimmy Gill

Teddy Glennon

stood in his goal supported by two County players, collapsed before the game was re-started and was carried off suffering concussion—after an incident which the referee deemed did not to contain any dangerous play by the Wednesday players! The County players were furious, and though general opinion held that the goal should not have been allowed, they were forced to play out the remaining forty minutes with only ten men, and subsequently exited the Cup. This was not the end of the story, however, County appealed to the FA, and, at a meeting in Sheffield, their protest was dismissed.

Once the dust had settled on this Cup tie, Wednesday could look forward to the second-round clash at Wolves. This ended in a draw, forcing a Hillsborough replay which saw a Kirkman goal put the Owls through. The game, however, unfortunately entered the history books for all the wrong reasons, following an incident which occurred with twelve minutes remaining. With Wednesday attacking the Leppings Lane end of the ground and McLean about to shoot, there was a surge of supporters on the packed Penistone Road embankment, which resulted in a newly-built retaining wall collapsing, suddenly sending fans and debris cascading onto the spectators below. It was a moment or two before everyone realised the enormity of the situation; but once the game had been stopped, literally thousands of spectators rushed across the pitch to the scene of the accident. Thankfully, confusion did not reign and the injured were carried to the dressing rooms which acted as a makeshift casualty ward. Incredibly, there were no fatalities, though 75 people were admitted to hospital with various broken bones and the like, with the majority being allowed to go home once they had been treated. After considerable delay the officials decided to re-start the match, though Wolves were reluctant, and their keeper, Peers, did not re-appear, having

fainted at the sight of the injured. The game was played to a conclusion but at the finish Wolves protested to the FA, stating that the referee had played five minutes under time, and that the game should have been abandoned. The FA were not impressed, however, and Wednesday were allowed to progress to a home clash with Southern League, Brighton. Incidentally, after the game, Wednesday announced that they would compensate any injured persons who made a reasonable claim, and, in the end, over £500 was paid to claimants.

The game with Brighton not only brought an end to the terrible run of defeats against non-league sides, but led directly to the £1,000 transfer to Hillsborough of the Brighton half-back, David Parkes, who, within the week, was a Wednesday player. He came in for the injured McSkimming, but was cup-tied for the quarter final clash with Aston Villa. This broke all attendance records for the City, as over 57,000 crammed into Hillsborough. However the majority were to be disappointed, as a goal two minutes from the break by Villa's Edgley took the Birmingham club into the semi-finals and left the home side to concentrate on their precarious league position. That position was then eighteenth, following a splendid home win over Sheffield United; and, with McLean scoring nine times in fifteen league starts, Wednesday slowly climbed out of trouble—with league leaders, Blackburn Rovers, beaten at Hillsborough along the way. A win at the Champions, Sunderland followed, before Wednesday started to build early for the new season by signing Alf Capper from Witton Albion, Edwin Hughes from Chester, and selling Wright to West Ham United in the process. A point in their penultimate home game was enough to guarantee another season of First Division football for Wednesday, producing a happy end to a season which had been fraught with problems both on and off the field.

Sheffield Wednesday 1913–14
Back row: L. Burkinshaw, Worrall, Davison, Spoors, McSkimming, Brittleton; Front row: J. Burkinshaw, Kirkman, Campbell, McLean, Wilson, Robertson, Wright.

1914–15
TRANSFER RECORD SMASHED AS WAR BREAKS OUT

The summer of 1914 was dominated by non-football events, for the Balkans crisis meant the world was about to be plunged into a bloody conflict that would last four years. As the situation worsened football started to become affected. Wednesday lost three players to the draft, including key defender Jimmy Campbell, and their new signing, Doig. Circumstances thus dictated that very little transfer activity took place in the off-season, due largely to the fundamental uncertainty caused by the imminent outbreak of war. However, the one major signing by Wednesday stunned their followers, when they almost doubled their previous record deal by splashing out £1,975 on Clyde left-back, Jimmy Blair. Unfortunately, Wednesday fans had a wait to see their record signing in action, for a week before the club's practice game Blair crashed his motorcycle and promptly missed the opening five games of the new season. In a prime example of 'closing the stable door once the horse had bolted', Wednesday's committee then banned all players from riding cycles and motor cycles, warning their wages would not be paid if they were injured as a result of an accident. Incidentally, Blair's first season at Hillsborough did not get any better, as he started only twenty games due to a serious bout of influenza and, somewhat unbelievably, another motor accident! Although only a handful of players arrived at the club, several departed, with James Miller signing for Airdrie, Lawrie Burkinshaw for Rotherham Town, Beech going to Brighton, and both Clarke and Monaghan joining Midland League, Scunthorpe United. The month of July also saw a unique event held at the ground, when a Boy Scout rally was attended by the founder of the movement, Lord Baden Powell. Meanwhile, the clouds of war manifested themselves amongst the Hillsborough playing staff, when Wednesday arranged for them to take drill instruction.

When Britain finally entered the War the season had already begun. After consultation, the football authorities decided to complete the season, much against the public opinion of the time. Several measures were introduced to forestall this, including the paying of a percentage of gate receipts into a general war fund, and the agreement of top flight players to take a pay cut—which would be paid into a relief fund to be used to fund the payroll of those smaller clubs who faced financial hardship. In an unselfish gesture all Wednesday's players and staff agreed to the latter measure, and captain Tom Brittleton, who spoke on behalf of the playing personnel, commented that they had agreed wholeheartedly and unanimously to the deduction. Against this backdrop, Wednesday had in fact started the season well and were the early leaders, with McLean grabbing the headlines again after scoring a hat-trick in consecutive home games; including a five minute treble against Bradford Park Avenue. The realities

of war were then shown in the home game with Manchester City, when several wounded Belgian soldiers were in attendance as Wednesday won 2–1 to remain in the Championship race.

As 1915 dawned, the Owls were still holding a top three position, and hopes were high of finally lifting some silverware, as progress had also been made through to the last sixteen of the FA Cup. The third round of that competition brought old rivals, Newcastle United, to Hillsborough, which, after having a blatant last minute penalty refused by the referee, the Owls lost 2–1, in what proved to be their last Cup tie for five years. Back in the bread and butter of the league, the Owls hit top spot following an astonishing seven goal showing against Bolton Wanderers.

Lord Baden Powell, founder of the Boy Scouts, addresses a rally at Hillsborough

To the bitter disappointment of their long suffering fans, Wednesday then won only twice more in their final ten games, thus ruining any chance of bringing the Championship trophy to Hillsborough. One of the crucial matches in the run in came at title rivals, Manchester City, where, on a disastrous afternoon at Hyde Road the Owls conceded four goals to tumble out of the top three. A victory at home to Cup finalists Chelsea boosted spirits, but by this time the league was out of reach and Wednesday's last 'peacetime' game for four seasons resulted in a tame, goalless home draw with Burnley. In the end, it had been a frustrating finish to a highly promising season, as the race for the Championship was one of the tightest for many years and, despite Wednesday's late slump, they only finished an agonising three points behind the eventual Champions, Everton.

"AT THE FRONT" (of the League Table).

General Owlerton : "It's no good! I can't advance while the enemy hold the first trench."
(Wednesday, who are next to Manchester City at the top of the table, entertain the leaders at Hillsborough next Saturday.)

Wednesday Football Club Limited.

The Directors, being desirous of giving the Shareholders an opportunity of seeing over the New Stand, &c., request the pleasure of the company of

———————— and Lady

at the Wednesday Ground, on the afternoon of Saturday, the 20th of June, 1914, from 3.30 to 5.30.

AFTERNOON TEA.

A. J. Dickinson,
HON. SECRETARY.

1915–19
WEDNESDAY IN THE GREAT WAR

Though football had retained its status quo in 1914–15, the following season saw wholesale changes as the Football League was divided into various regional sections. For the southern clubs the London Combination was created, while Lancashire and Midland sections were formed to accommodate the remainder. The Owls were placed in the Midland section, but the squad that started the 1915–16 campaign was missing several well known faces. The draft and war work denied Wednesday the services of Jimmy Blair, Bob McSkimming, George Robertson and David McLean, all of whom returned to their native Scotland; none would return until the end of hostilities. Wednesday were also forced to play on without the talents of Teddy Davison, Sam Kirkman and David Parkes, to name just three. The Owls decided to withdraw their reserve team from the Midland League and even agreed not to issue a fixture list, instead, posters were pasted around the ground advertising any forthcoming games. However, the biggest change occurred when the FA announced that, until further notice, no players should receive payment and that anyone could play where it was convenient for them. The introduction of the Registration Act in 1915 also put more pressure on the football clubs, for it was decided that games could only be played on Saturdays and Bank Holidays, in order not to interfere with the making of munitions, etc. The Owls actually voted against football continuing, but when they were voted down they started to prepare for their first ever season of wartime soccer by signing several players who had been posted in Sheffield. These included the Exeter City centre-forward, Goodwin; Tasker and Womack from Birmingham; and Harrop of Aston Villa.

Wednesday made a wretched start to the new campaign by losing their first five games, conceding seventeen goals in the process. Two wins in late October, however, dragged them off the bottom of the fourteen strong league. As the likes of Stapleton and Tom Brelsford were drafted into the side, the Owls defence tightened considerably, and from October 23rd to February 19th, Wednesday lost only three times—two of the three to Champions, Nottingham Forest—to make rapid strides up the league table. Meanwhile, Arthur Dickinson was having to use all his skills to keep the club going, for the loss of so many players meant that on many occasions he was not sure he could raise a side; and had Wednesday not decided to run a reserve team, the situation would almost certainly have reached crisis point. On the financial front, matters were better than Wednesday had anticipated, despite crowds having dwindled; and by November it looked as if costs would not only be covered but that a profit might even accrue. Amongst the newcomers was Tom Cawley Jnr., following in the footsteps of a famous father who had played for Wednesday in their non-league days; as well as winger, Hatton. Khaki

Womack

uniformed soldiers were now a regular sight at Hillsborough, with over 800 taking advantage of free admission to attend the home game against Lincoln City. The Christmas morning home game with Nottingham Forest attracted the best gate of the season, but was fraught with problems. Forest were 40 minutes late arriving and the non-appearance of ten gatemen ensured that the kick-off was delayed as thousands were stranded outside the ground. This was indicative of wartime football in Sheffield, and, like many clubs, Wednesday were glad when the season was over, for it had been a constant struggle to put a representative side onto the field of play. Of the side that almost brought the title to Hillsborough in the previous season only Tom Brittleton, Teddy Glennon and Andrew Wilson (top scorer with 16) appeared on a regular basis. The majority of the others never figured at all, as the club were forced to use a total of 46 players, many being untried youngsters. Problems continued right until the end of the season, when fifteen minutes from the beginning of the home game with leaders Grimsby Town, the Owls had only seven players in their dressing room. By kick-off they had reached the requisite eleven and proceeded to beat the Mariners to record their first win in the subsidiary competition. However, despite the problems, the season had been a learning curve for the club and a mid-table position was seen as a satisfactory outcome.

The club accounts showed that income exceeded expenditure in the year ending 30th April 1916, and that over 15,000

C. Brelsford   *Hatton*   *T.E. Crawshaw*

soldiers, including a considerable number who had been wounded at the front, had been admitted free to games at Hillsborough in the past season. The profit was mainly attributed to the fact that the players now gave their services free of charge, but other expenses had been reduced to ensure Wednesday would continue to provide football for the Sheffield public. The summer of 1916 also saw news breaking about several of the players who had graced Hillsborough before the outbreak of the war, with Sam Kirkman, Harry Bentley and Jimmy Campbell all on the front in France. There was bad news about the outstanding half-back, David Parkes, who had broken his leg playing for non-league, Cradley Heath. The fracture, it seemed, had not been set properly and it was believed that Parkes might never play again.

After the pessimism shown by the club towards the first season of wartime football, the situation twelve months later was markedly different, for it had been demonstrated that the public wanted football; and so the Wednesday management decided to approach the new season with added enthusiasm. They therefore attempted to gather a side that could challenge for honours, and pulled off a coup by securing the services of Newcastle United Internationals, Wilfred Low and Billy Hibbert, both of whom would be stationed in Sheffield. Strangely enough, Hibbert never appeared for the club, and Low played only twice. The one man who would play on a regular basis was Ayr United goalkeeper, Jack Lyall, who returned to Hillsborough eight years after leaving for

Manchester City. Also helping Wednesday would be Huddersfield's Islip, and Harrop from Aston Villa, while Womack returned to Birmingham after they resumed operations. Meanwhile, after being released at the end of the previous season Ambrose Langley was re-engaged, but this time as trainer. The Midland Section had now expanded to sixteen clubs and the Owls opened with a draw at Chesterfield before losing their first home game in somewhat bizarre circumstances to Bradford City. The visitors won 3–1, though two of their goals actually came from Wednesday player, Tom Cawley who was included in the Bradford forward line because they had arrived a man short after one of their enlisted players failed to put in an appearance. To make matters worse for the above-average crowd of 6,000, Burkinshaw missed a second-half penalty in a game in which Wednesday players netted three of the game's four goals but still managed to lose! Other than in the self-inflicted Bradford defeat, the Owls were strong at home in the first half of the season. However, any chance of league honours was ruined by an appalling record on their travels, producing only three points before the end of the year and leaving Wednesday just four places off the foot of the table. There was sadness, too, when the pre-war reserve team player, James Monaghan was reported to have been killed in action. The biggest South Yorkshire gate of the season at Hillsborough, witnessed a Sheffield derby which ended all square. The New Year also saw honorary trainer, John Davis, pass away, before Wednesday played Bradford City in a stormy Hillsborough game. With the Owls leading by a single goal, the game was only three minutes from its conclusion when Tom Brelsford and the Bradford City player, Torrance, collided in the centre circle, with Brelsford falling to the ground. Instantly the two players started to fight, but despite being separated by the referee they got away and started to scrap again. At this point three spectators, two of them sailors, jumped over the railings on the far side of the ground and sprinted across the pitch, ploughing into the mass of players with fists flailing. As soon as it was seen that the invaders were not being dealt with, hundreds of spectators flooded onto the pitch and the referee had no choice but to abandon the game. Along with the players, he then had to try to fight his way to the dressing rooms. It later transpired the referee had sent Torrance off, and his refusal to walk then triggered the whole sorry scene. Wednesday could consider themselves lucky that these events did not happen in peacetime football, for they would probably have had the proverbial book thrown at them. The playing season ended on a high, with three wins recorded over Sheffield United, including a thrilling 4–3 win at Bramall Lane in the subsidiary competition. In the final league game of the campaign, the Owls recorded their biggest victory of the war period when a hat-trick from Jack Burkinshaw helped his side to a resounding 7–1 win. However, the second season of wartime football had proved an overall disappointment for the club, with a second place in the four team subsidiary competition being no consolation for a poor league performance which left Wednesday just three places off the bottom.

Wednesday entered the 1917–18 season unsure of the size or quality of the squad they would have at their disposal. Several talented youngsters who had made a big impact at the back end of the previous campaign were retained, while those old hands such as Andrew Wilson (who was employed in Sheffield), Teddy Glennon and Jack Burkinshaw would be able to offer their services. Tom Brelsford also hoped to turn out, despite having joined the Army, though Jack Lyall certainly would not, for he was now in India. In a letter to secretary, Arthur Dickinson, Lyall described how he had to undertake a 2,000 mile journey to play in a cup-tie for his regimental side. The Owls could not have made a worse start to the new season, for only two goals were scored in a run of five consecutive defeats. These ended eventually, when goals from Wilson and Burkinshaw earned victory at Leicester City. However, six wins in their next seven home games, including a derby win over United on Boxing Day, soon lifted Wednesday into a mid-table position. The run of home successes included a 7–2 win over Lincoln City, in which seven different Wednesday players put their names onto the score sheet, but then ten defeats in their fourteen away games

ensured another disappointing finish. Once the league season had come to a close, a series of games were played in aid of the National Footballers War Fund, and, after drawing at Anfield, the Owls overcame Liverpool at Hillsborough to at least send their loyal supporters into the summer break with a victory to cheer.

With the Great War starting to turn in the Allies direction, the 1918–19 season was approached in optimistic fashion, and Wednesday played their part by actually winning one of their opening five league games! The home game with Coventry was certainly eventful, as an excellent crowd of 10,000 saw the return after four years, of the outstanding centre-half, Jimmy Campbell. They then watched a match which was more reminiscent of pre-war Cup tie football, with Wednesday's William Stapleton being sent off for striking an opponent, as the Owls chalked up a 3–0 success. A quickfire double over neighbours Barnsley lifted Wednesday to the dizzy heights of eighth place, before five consecutive losses, including a seven goal mauling at Leicester City, plunged them back into the lower reaches. On 11th November 1918, two days after that defeat at Filbert Street, an armistice was signed with Germany, the horror of the trenches finally ended, and the First World War was consigned to history. A splendid 4–0 Yuletide morning home win over United ensured the Christmas celebrations could continue in the city's blue and white households, although 35,000 then watched as Sheffield United, now 'The Blades', were avenged at Bramall Lane on the following day. The New Year saw the club's form fluctuate, as playing personnel was continuously altered. Once again Wednesday eventually had to be content with a lowly position as Nottingham Forest won their second Championship of the War. The season was extended into late May, and after losing 4–1 at home to Lancashire Champions, Everton, in a Hillsborough friendly, Wednesday then travelled to Goodison Park a week later to record a surprise 2–1 victory and bring the curtain down on four seasons of wartime soccer, with fans now able to look forward to a return to normality on the football field.

Memory Match

Sheffield Wednesday Football Club.

Day and Date _Sat September 2nd 1899_

Time left Home _____ Time Returned _____

Description of Match _League_

Name of Opposing Club _Chesterfield_

Where Played _Owlerton_

Time of Kick-off _3 pm_

Goal Keeper _Massey_

R. Back _Earp_

L. Back _Langley_

R. H. Back _Ferrier_

C. H. Back _T Crawshaw_

L. H. Back _Ruddlesdin_

R. O. Forward _Brash_

R. I. do. _Pryce_

Centre do. _Millar_

L. I. do. _Wright_

L. O. do. _Spiksesley_

Reserve _____

Linesmen _Messrs Wallis + Cropper_

Referee _Mr. G. W. Horrocks_

Result _Wednesday 5 Chesterfield 1_

Remarks _____

Sheffield Wednesday 5
Chesterfield 1

After losing their home at Olive Grove and suffering relegation from the First Division in April 1899, the immediate future looked bleak for Wednesday. But the picture changed completely within five months, as the club prepared to open their new ground at Owlerton. One major worry for the club was the distance of Owlerton from the City centre. However, those fears calmed when an excellent crowd of around 12,000 attended the first game on the new enclosure, which was still under construction, with only the old Olive Grove stand offering any cover. The visitors for Wednesday's first ever Second Division game were the newly elected league members, Chesterfield, and various dignitaries honoured the club with their presence, including the Lord Mayor of Sheffield, and the ex-Wednesday player, William Clegg. The appearance of both sides was greeted warmly by the enthusiastic crowd, with new signings Archie Brash and Harry Miller appearing for the first time in blue and white.

After the Wednesday captain, Jack Earp, had won the toss for ends, it was the Lord Mayor who had the honour of kicking off the first ever game at Owlerton. His long punt was quickly returned by Ambrose Langley and within the first minute, Harry Millar almost wrote his name into the history books when he watched his shot strike an upright. The men from Derbyshire could not get past the half-way line in the very early stages, however, after ten minutes and totally against the run of play, they broke away to snatch the lead. A strong run from Geary took him near the by-line, and from his centre, Herbert Munday not only had the distinction of becoming the first man to score on Wednesday's new ground, but was also the scorer of Chesterfield's first ever goal in league soccer—much to the delight of the contingent of visiting supporters who had made the short journey. The Spireites were now playing with 'pluck and dash' and Munday was denied a second when his goal was ruled offside. Wednesday were determined their big day was not going to be ruined, however, and after 33 minutes Brash centred for the hero of Olive Grove, Fred Spiksley, to net the equaliser. Within five minutes Bob Ferrier had put the Blades ahead, as in an end-to-end game, Geary almost grabbed a leveller before an entertaining first period ended as half-time was called.

Early in the second half Spiksley had a goal chalked off for offside, and, after scares at both ends, Wednesday extended their lead after 64 minutes, as Millar's long shot struck the underside of the bar and bounced down back into play. The Blades appealed that the ball had crossed the line, and, after consulting his linesmen, the referee allowed the rather doubtful goal to stand. The visitors sense of injustice was heightened a few minutes later when, at the precise moment Munday dashed the ball into the net, the official blew for a foul by Wednesday's Earp, thereby disallowing the Chesterfield goal. The home side then went back on the offensive and Brash, the promising new forward, supplied Millar who fired in his side's fourth goal. Wednesday's superior fitness, which was probably due to their new trainer, Paul Frith, had by now started to show through and with nine minutes left on the watch, and as Chesterfield tired, Wednesday completed a memorable afternoon as Spiksley set up a deserved goal for Archie Brash. The game had been played at a fast pace, with the standard of football on show being better than many of the First Division games on show at Olive Grove in the previous season. Moreover, the loyal fans who had followed Wednesday out to the 'wilds' of Owlerton were now seeing only the beginning of a glorious first season at their new enclosure.

Wednesday: Massey, Earp, Langley, Ferrier, T. Crawshaw, Ruddlesdin, Brash, Pryce, Millar, Wright, Spiksley

Chesterfield: Hancock, Pilgrim, Fletcher, Ballantyne, Bell, Downie, Morley, Thacker, Gooing, Munday, Geary

Referee: Mr J. Horrocks (Bury)

Memory Match

With Wednesday heading for a second consecutive League Championship, hopes were understandably high that the FA Cup might also be captured; especially when the second round draw handed Wednesday a home tie with Second Division side, Manchester United. A damp and drizzly day did not stop 22,051 fans paying receipts of just over £740 after making their way to Owlerton, where they discovered that Jimmy Stewart and Jock Malloch were missing from a Wednesday side which had been held at home by Sunderland a week earlier. In their places George and Vivian Simpson were substituted, the latter being an outstanding inside-forward who remained strictly amateur throughout his career. Of course, in those early days of the century, there was always fine line between the standards of the amateur and professional game, with many players deciding to play for love of the game while pursuing other careers. With the rewards on offer to professional players being nothing like today's inflated returns, the financial inducements on offer then were easy for many 'gentlemen' to resist. Also, in many quarters, the professional player was still frowned upon, despite the payment of players having occurred for almost twenty years. The England side, for example, still lined up with amateurs from the likes of The Corinthians, and for many years Wednesday would have one or two players on their books who played on a strictly amateur basis.

The presence of Vivian Simpson would be the major talking point of a Cup-tie which opened in sensational style. Inside the first minute Beech won a corner from which Ferrier's shot was fumbled by Sutcliffe, allowing 'V.S.' to drive home the opening goal. Legend states that before he scored, Vivian had already been almost knocked unconscious by the uncompromising United defenders; however, he showed no ill-effects in giving his side the perfect start. In the early stages, the visitors conceded a flurry of free-kicks, allowing Wednesday to keep the pressure on; so that both Jack Beech and the affectionately named 'V.S.' (the vogue in the early years was to differentiate between amateurs and professionals by prefixing the former with the initials of their christian names) went close to scoring a second goal. United could not keep the blue and white tide at bay, and after 17 minutes Harry Davis sent in a low shot which was not properly dealt with, and Sutcliffe let the ball pass into the net. After Wednesday's second, the Mancunians finally started to 'play up' and Lyall, in the home goal, was called into action. However, it was the trickery of V.S. that lightened the game, and twice he was heavily fouled on the edge of the box when shaping to shoot.

The visitors started the second half with only ten men after Downie received what was described as a 'slight concussion of the brain' though within seven minutes he had returned to the fray. The Blades then lost Beech for several minutes when he had to be carried off. During his absence, Harry Davis ran onto a Ruddlesdin free-kick to fire a third goal past the Manchester custodian. Beech then returned to a tremendous ovation, and, after Lyall had pulled off a brilliant save from Morrison, Wednesday went on to dominate the remainder of the game, with wing men Davis and George Simpson causing havoc in the visiting back line. The home side promptly netted three more in the final fifteen minutes, with V.S. scoring number four and his namesake, George, heading in the fifth. The best goal of the game was still to come, however, as, in the final minute, V.S. raced onto a pass from Davis before beating several opponents to flash the ball pass Sutcliffe for an outstanding hat-trick. It had been a comprehensive victory for Wednesday in which Vivian Simpson played the game of his life. The Sheffield born player ended his seven year association with the club in 1907, having scored eleven times in 38 games. His story has a tragic end, however, for he was killed fighting for his country on the Western Front in April 1918, at the age of just thirty-three.

Wednesday: Lyall, Layton, Burton, Ferrier, T. Crawshaw, Ruddlesdin, Davis, Chapman, Beech, V.S. Simpson, G. Simpson

Manchester United: Sutcliffe, Bonthron, Hayes, Downie, Griffiths, Cartwright, Schofield, Morrison, Pegg, Arksden, Robertson

Sheffield Wednesday

Manchester United

Memory Match

Sheffield Wednesday 5

Everton 5

The meeting of third placed Wednesday—who were chasing a hat-trick of titles—and fourth placed Everton attracted just over 12,000 fans to Owlerton. Few, however, could have predicted the extraordinary ninety minutes that would follow. A week earlier, a defeat at Derby had knocked Wednesday off the top of the table and, when the sides ran out, the supporters were no doubt dismayed to find that Jock Malloch and their outstanding keeper, Jack Lyall, were both missing. The latter had been kept out by a bad foot injury, with the inconsistent Richard Jarvis taking his place, and amateur Vivian Simpson was recalled to the side to replace Malloch.

On a crisp winter afternoon Wednesday won the toss and elected to defend the Leppings Lane goal. Before they could settle, however, they were a goal in arrears. After only two minutes, Layton allowed Young to run on to fire past Jarvis, who really should have done more to deny the Toffeemen's centre-forward. It was a lively opening, and after Jarvis had denied Young's second attempt, the Blades equalised when a George Simpson cross was knocked down by Stewart for Harry Davis to score with a crisp low shot. The home fans then watched in stunned silence as their high-riding side was totally outplayed by the visiting eleven for the remainder of the half; with the visitors galloping into a 5–1 lead before the half-time whistle sounded. A superb burst of football had resulted in Everton netting twice inside two minutes through Settle, with his second being the result of bad handling by Jarvis rather than anything else. Hardman then crashed a fourth into the Wednesday net, and, on the stroke of half-time, Abbott completed his side's nap hand following a corner, leaving Wednesday with an almost impossible task in the second period.

Whatever the trainer, Paul Frith, said in the dressing room at the interval certainly worked, as from the whistle Wednesday went on the attack, with Davis—although in an offside position—firing against a post. Wednesday's early dash was repelled, however, and the game became a more even affair; and though the Merseysiders were not performing as they had in the first period, they were still playing well enough to keep the home side at bay. Then, with eighteen minutes gone, the Blades attacked down the left, and as George Simpson ran into the box he was pulled down by Balmer to give Wednesday a penalty. The spot-kick was entrusted to Jimmy Stewart who netted at the second attempt after his initial shot had been parried by Scott, and this at least gave Wednesday some hope. The visiting keeper had been hurt during the penalty scramble but played on and was put under severe pressure as Wednesday camped in the Everton half. Mid-way through the half, the goalie raced out to intercept a ball but misjudged the situation, leaving George Simpson to poke the ball past him and watch as it rolled slowly into the empty net from the narrowest of angles. Roaring their side on, the home fans were boosted further when Scott was forced to retire. Half-back Abbott took his place between the sticks; and with Vivian Simpson in irresistible form the Blades now poured forward. Stewart then shot against a post and, with ten minutes remaining, Wednesday won a corner. From the ensuing scramble Vivian Simpson netted to make the score 5–4. Excitement in the ground had now reached fever pitch and further drama followed, when, after Jarvis had saved superbly, Harry Davis lost his head and was sent off for striking Hardman in the face. Both sides were now down to ten men, but this astonishing game had one final twist in its tail, as, in the final thirty seconds, Wednesday made one last desperate effort and, from a free kick taken by Bob Ferrier, the ball was 'rushed through' to thunderous applause from the exhausted crowd who had witnessed one of the most remarkable league games ever played.

Wednesday: Jarvis, Layton, Burton, Ferrier, T. Crawshaw, Ruddlesdin, Davis, Stewart, Wilson, V.S. Simpson, G. Simpson

Everton: Scott, Balmer, Crelley, Ashworth, Taylor, Abbott, Sharp, McDermott, Young, Settle, Hardman

Referee; Mr F. Heath (Birmingham)

Memory Match

All the indications were that the Boxing Day meeting with Sunderland at Owlerton would be a close affair. Both sides had drawn at Blackburn in their last away forays, and this pointed to an even contest. Indeed, the teams were so close that, before the game, their goals records were identical, with 31 goals for and 27 against. The public evidently anticipated a good game, for there was an attendance of around 33,000, of whom 29,995 paid just over £912 at the gate. Wednesday were unchanged from the aforementioned draw at Ewood Park on Christmas Day, with Sunderland showing just one change from the team that had won 2–0 at Bury on the previous day; Forster moving to right-back to replace Troughear, and Tait coming into the side to fill the vacancy created by Forster's positional change.

From the start it became obvious that Wednesday's forwards were in fine fettle, and inside the first thirty seconds an Andrew Wilson effort was well saved by Scott in the Sunderland goal. The visitors then made a tentative attack, but Wednesday countered to take the lead after 4 minutes, as George Robertson pulled the ball back from the by line for Sam Kirkman to deliberately shoot into the far corner of the net. Soon after, the Sunderland captain, Thomson, was injured and left the field for ten minutes. During this time Wednesday attacked constantly without scoring, though Kirkman did get the ball in the net, but after the whistle had already gone because of an injury to Scott. Ironically, with visitors back to eleven men, Wednesday played even better, and the inevitable second goal arrived after 25 minutes when Kirkman fired home a great shot. Thomson again left the field with what was later discovered to be a ruptured thigh muscle. The Sunderland defence, which was already struggling to cope with the tremendous speed and footwork of the Wednesday attack, now fell apart completely, parting like the Red Sea as Wednesday crashed in an astonishing five goals in a thirteen minute period. The goal glut started on the half-hour, when a great passing move ended with David McLean scoring with a terrific low drive. Five minutes later, Robertson, although fouled, managed to keep his feet to cross for Teddy Glennon to rush the ball into the net. Two minutes later Robertson was again the supplier as he crossed for McLean to make no mistake; with Wilson setting up a sixth which was converted by Teddy Glennon. To end the most remarkable period of scoring seen at Owlerton, David McLean then completed his first hat-trick for the club when he ran straight through the middle of a demoralised defence to fire home goal number seven.

It would be fair to say the Wednesdayites probably enjoyed their half-time refreshments, and might well have spent the interval dreaming of seeing their side net double figures for the first time in league football. Their wish certainly looked to be coming true, for the second half was only ten minutes old, when, with Forster in hot pursuit, McLean ran almost from the half-way line to fire his fourth goal past Scott, as the keeper advanced from his line. Perhaps not surprisingly, Wednesday then eased up somewhat, and the McLean strike proved to be the last of the afternoon as Wednesday recorded a new club record league win. The drama was not over yet, however, for the slippery surface was such that when Robertson fired a shot at Scott with ten minutes remaining, his momentum caused him to accidentally collide with the Sunderland custodian, catching the poor keeper in the jaw with his knee. Scott was carried off with concussion and was eventually taken to the Royal Hospital with a broken jaw. The visiting keeper certainly did not experience much in the way of luck on his visits to Owlerton. Several years earlier, in 1904, he had been the man between the sticks for Everton in the famous 5–5 draw; a match in which he was also carried off injured! After Scott's departure, Holley went in goal. However, despite creating several opportunities Wednesday, it seemed, decided not to profit from their nine-man opponents misfortune, and made no real attempt to place the ball in the net in a somewhat low-key ending to a dramatic game

Wednesday: Davison, Worrall, Spoors, Brittleton, Weir, Campbell, Kirkman, Glennon, McLean, Wilson, Robertson

Sunderland: Scott, Forster, Milton, Cuggy, Thomson, Tait, Mordue, Buchan, Young, Holley, Bridgett

Referee: Mr F. Kirkham (Ben Rhydding)

'Teddy' Davison

Sheffield Wednesday
8
Sunderland
0

Memory Match

Football League Division One
Wednesday 1st January 1913

David McLean

Sheffield Wednesday
3
Derby County
3

With David McLean and Wednesday firing on all cylinders, there was a real possibility of the Championship coming to Owlerton. So when title rivals, Derby County, visited Sheffield on New Year's Day 1913, the interest was such that a bumper holiday crowd of over 40,000 flocked to the ground. Wednesday sat second in the table before the kick-off, after a 2–1 win over Spurs three days earlier. The team sheet showed one change, with Sam Kirkman replacing Jack Burkinshaw; while the Derbyshire visitors included goal scoring legend, Steve Bloomer in their ranks, who in his County career amassed a staggering 332 goals.

The soft Owlerton pitch ensured the game was played at a fast pace, with chances coming at both ends in an even first half. However, despite this, Wednesday found themselves two goals in arrears at the break, as Derby converted the few opportunities that came their way. A picture book goal put the visitors ahead after nine minutes, when Sharpe's right-wing cross was superbly headed into the net by Horace Barnes. It was 2–0 mid-way through the period, as centre-forward, Henry Leonard ran through a gaping hole in the Wednesday back line to fire past an exposed Teddy Davison. Wednesday had the proverbial mountain to climb at the half-time break and this turned into a Mount Everest, when, twenty minutes into the second half, Leonard—looking to be obviously offside—again outpaced the disorganised home defence to send a fierce low drive past the helpless keeper. Within a minute it was apparently 4–0, as Barnes netted following a corner. Thankfully, for the home fans, the Staffordshire official saw reason to disallow the goal for offside and Wednesday remained three goals in arrears.

Despite being in a seemingly impossible position Wednesday continued to push forward, and with fifteen minutes remaining they scored what appeared to be a consolation goal. James Campbell and Robertson combined to supply Andrew Wilson, who in turn sprayed a neat pass to David McLean to fire into the net. Driven on by their inspirational captain, Tom Brittleton, Wednesday again came at the Derby back line, and, as the Rams counter-attacked, the last ten minutes became a thrilling spectacle for the crowd. With six minutes remaining, Wednesday reduced the deficit further when McLean took a pass from Campbell to sprint clear and fire past Lawrence. Within a minute the ground exploded again, as unbelievably, the scores were tied when a brilliant centre from George Robertson was deftly turned into the net by Kirkman. The last five minutes were fast and furious, but futile; and this memorable game eventually ended all square. Wednesday's point was enough to send them back to the top of the First Division table following West Brom's defeat at Middlesbrough.

Wednesday: Davison, Worrall, Spoors, Brittleton, McSkimming, Campbell, Kirkman, Glennon, McLean, Wilson, Robertson

Derby: Lawrence, Atkin, Betts, Barbour, Buckley, Richards, Sharpe, Bloomer, Leonard, Barnes, Neve

Referee: Mr T. Kirkham (Burslem)

Memory Match

When a postponed league game with struggling Bolton Wanderers was re-arranged for a Monday evening in early March, it gave Wednesday the perfect opportunity to step up their Championship challenge by earning the two points required to leap above the current league leaders, Oldham Athletic. Two days previous, the Owls had earned a hard fought draw away to title rivals, Blackburn Rovers, and were now fully expected to overcome the Lancashire challenge. The Burnden Park club were only one point off the bottom of the table and would remain in trouble to the end, eventually avoiding relegation by a mere point. Wednesday retained the same eleven who had turned out at Ewood Park, with a new right-wing combination of Alf Capper and Jimmy Gill keeping their places. Despite the afternoon kick-off, there was good attendance of around 7,000.

From the first whistle Wednesday swarmed around the visitors penalty area, with the Bolton keeper, Edmondson, a busy man, saving from Brittleton, Robertson, Parkes and Wilson inside the opening fifteen minutes. Wanderers were then unfortunate to lose their left-back, Feebury, with a knee strain. He returned after twelve minutes but was little more than a passenger, until, twenty minutes into the second half—and with his team five goals in arrears—he gave up the ghost and hobbled off the field. Though, had he been fit for the whole ninety minutes, it is debatable whether the scoreline would have changed much, such was the one-sided nature of the match; for it was only a matter of time before the opening goal came Wednesday's way. This occurred after 15 minutes and came from the unusual source of half-back, David Parkes, who netted his first goal for the club in a goal mouth melee that followed on from a corner. The Owls continued to push forward and by half-time had scored twice more, first through a Teddy Glennon header, and then with a close range effort from Jimmy Gill, after tremendous work from Glennon. Such was the home side's overwhelming dominance, that when Parkes was forced to pass the ball back to Davison after the third goal was scored, this gave the Wednesday custodian his first touch!

The Bolton defence was no doubt glad to hear the half-time whistle, but had another half to play in which their priority was no doubt simply to keep the score to a respectable level. This they managed in the early stages of the second period, but were lucky not to be reduced to ten men when Thomas and Spoors collided in an off-the-ball incident, which was not properly seen by the referee. After tumbling to the floor, Bolton's Thomas was seen to kick the Wednesday right-back full in the mouth. Spoors retaliated and the duo 'sparred' on, with the visiting player getting the points decision before the referee separated them, severely censuring both for their ungentlemanly conduct. The Bolton defender seemed to have escaped lightly; however, this was not the case for his side, as Wednesday added a fourth through George Roberton's low drive, and a fifth from the foot of veteran Andrew Wilson. When Alf Capper scored Wednesday's sixth after 73 minutes it meant all five forwards had found the net. Then, with ten minutes remaining, Harry Bentley scored only his second goal in a blue and white shirt, becoming the seventh different scorer, and setting a club record which has never been matched. The visitors were a sorry outfit by the end, with only Edmondson, the overworked keeper, emerging with any credit, as Wednesday went a point clear at the summit and prompted humorist newsboys on the following day to shout: 'Extra special—latest cricket scores'.

Wednesday: Davison, Spoors, McSkimming, Brittleton, Parkes, Bentley, Capper, Gill, Glennon, Wilson, Robertson

Bolton Wanderers: Edmondson, Wilson, Feebury, Fay, Rowley, Thomas, Donaldson, Jones, Lillycrop, Smith, Viszard

Referee: Mr A. Warner (Nottingham)

MUNITIONS AND FOOTBALL

Alf Capper

Sheffield Wednesday 7
Bolton Wanderers 0

Between the Wars
1919–1939

1919–20
FROM BAD TO WORSE

The end of the Great War saw football return to its pre-war status quo. This meant the Owls would be back in top flight football after an enforced break of four seasons. However, before the season kicked off, the Owls had a taste of the problems that lay ahead, as star players David McLean and Jimmy Blair refused to accept the terms offered by Wednesday. The former eventually signed, but an impasse was reached with Scottish International, Blair, who flatly refused to return for the start of the campaign. The Owls record signing asked that the war period be counted towards his benefit. As he had not played the requisite number of games, however, Wednesday were not allowed by the rules to meet his demands. Moreover, he also wrongly believed the club would not allow him to secure employment to supplement his maximum wage of £8 a week. The club stood their ground and refused to release him, and so Blair signed for non-league outfit, Alloa Athletic. Though their captain remained in Scotland, the Owls decided to keep faith with the majority of their pre war squad, with a few additions such as Oliver Levick and Percy Reed. They also appointed a new trainer in Scot, William Barr.

Once the season began it quickly became apparent that Wednesday were set for a campaign of struggle, when they failed to find the net in their first three games, and slumped to the lower reaches of the league. Wednesday needed seven attempts before securing their first success; though this proved sweet when United were vanquished 2–1 at Hillsborough in a fierce derby clash. Unfortunately, the Blades won 3–0 in the return game a week later, and by the start of November Wednesday were bottom, having scored only six times in a dozen games. Off the field, Jimmy Blair finally returned after a two month absence, but the prolific pre-war marksman, McLean, was still unhappy and it was no surprise when he was sold to Bradford Park Avenue after scoring one hundred goals for the Owls. Meanwhile, on his demobilisation from the Army, William Harvey joined Wednesday, along with centre-half, Harry O'Neill, from Wallsend. The Owls then signed Joe Edmondson and Arthur Price in the mass sale from Leeds City, which occurred after the club had been disgraced and expelled from the Football League.

Consecutive wins against Derby and West Bromwich failed to lift Wednesday off the foot of the table, and, to compound their problems, forward Sam Kirkman contracted malaria; while new signing Gilmour was injured on his debut for the reserves and was to be out of action for six months. The Directors were now beginning to come under fire for chopping and changing the team and for not purchasing star players. In an attempt to stop the rot they raided Scottish

Jimmy Blair

George Wilson

clubs on three occasions inside a fortnight, purchasing centre-forwards Colin McKay and Fletcher Welsh, plus half-back Robert Eggo. Unfortunately, none of the new players made a lasting impression and the Owls remained in deep trouble. The gloom surrounding the club was then increased, when, in front of a bumper mid-week crowd, Wednesday crashed embarrassingly out of the FA Cup to non league Darlington, after having drawn 0–0 in the North East. Incidentally, the Hillsborough Cup tie was played in a blizzard. This prompted Wednesday's amateur winger, William Harvey, to buy himself a pair of Corinthian 'knickers' so that he would be able to put his hands in the pockets during the game to prevent himself from catching a cold!

George Shelton was another new arrival, from the local club Star Inn. However, players such as this, signed from the Attercliffe Alliance League, were not going to turn the season round; and as deadline day dawned, the Owls were already looking doomed. Wednesday then shocked their fans by breaking the club's transfer record to sign Blackpool's star centre-back, George Wilson, before capturing Fulham inside-forward, John McIntyre. The duo appeared for the first time in a promising draw at Chelsea, but it was asking a great deal from the pair that they settle in straight away. Such was the Owls plight, that within five games they were relegated from the top flight after a home defeat to the Stamford Bridge side. In fact, with only seven wins recorded all season, Wednesday were destined to go down with five games still remaining; and in the process, they used what is still a club record of 41 players. In retrospect, an over-reliance on pre-war players and the lack of a regular marksman seemed to be the main reason for one of the club's worst seasons in their history. And, as is often the case with a struggling side, Lady Luck deserted them as several key players picked up lengthy injuries.

THE

FOOTBALL BOOT

OF THE SEASON.

Wear our famous " K.O." BOOT,
(KNOCKOUT),

MADE THROUGHOUT BY HAND.

1920–21
A SEASON OF CONSOLIDATION

Preparation for the first Wednesday season in the Second Division for over twenty years was far from ideal, as the fallout from the disastrous 1919–20 campaign saw several changes on and off the pitch. On the field of play, Wednesday cut a swathe through their playing staff, and in May 1920 an astonishing total of twenty one players were transferred or released. Among the departures was long serving wing-half, Tom Brittleton, who signed for Stoke City after fifteen years service and 372 games. Several young players were signed for the forthcoming season, with Fred Kean proving to be the real success of the group. Arguably the greatest loss to the club came in June 1920, when, at a stormy Annual General Meeting, long-serving secretary-manager, Arthur Dickinson, announced he was resigning the post he'd held for 29 years. To replace the vastly experienced administrator, the Owls appointed Mr Robert Brown to the post. For ten years prior to the Great War, he had acted as assistant to the departing Dickinson. Trainer, William Barr, was another departure, leaving to join Huddersfield Town (Jerry Jackson would be his replacement); and to complete an eventful summer, the Owls learned that winger William Harvey had contracted pneumonia during a tour with the FA in South Africa, and had now been hospitalised.

An unremarkable start to the new season saw Wednesday record three consecutive goalless draws, two of which came against neighbours Barnsley. The goal famine ended with a Johnny McIntyre strike in the 3–1 home defeat to Stoke. McIntyre then went on to hit nine in the next five games, including his first hat-trick for the club, as the Owls moved to mid table. However, six games without a win (in which McIntyre was sent off in the home game with Birmingham) saw a drop to the fringes of the relegation zone and prompted several moves into the transfer market. Jack Bellas the Shildon winger, together with George Prior and Sid Binks from Blyth and Bishop Auckland arrived at the club. There was also one significant departure, with arguably the best player on the club's books, Scottish International Jimmy Blair, going for a record fee to Cardiff City. The Scot's final appearance was at West Ham, where Sid Puddefoot hit all four for the home side. Wednesday then failed to score in nine out of eleven games between the end of October until the turn of the year, leaving them in serious relegation danger and lying third from bottom.

In early January the signing of Huddersfield centre-forward, Sam Taylor, would prove to be the season's catalyst. However, his influence was not immediately apparent, as the Owls went out of the Cup (after having set a new record attendance in the replay with Everton). They were then involved in a strange incident at Port Vale, where, at the end of the first half, the

Teddy Davison

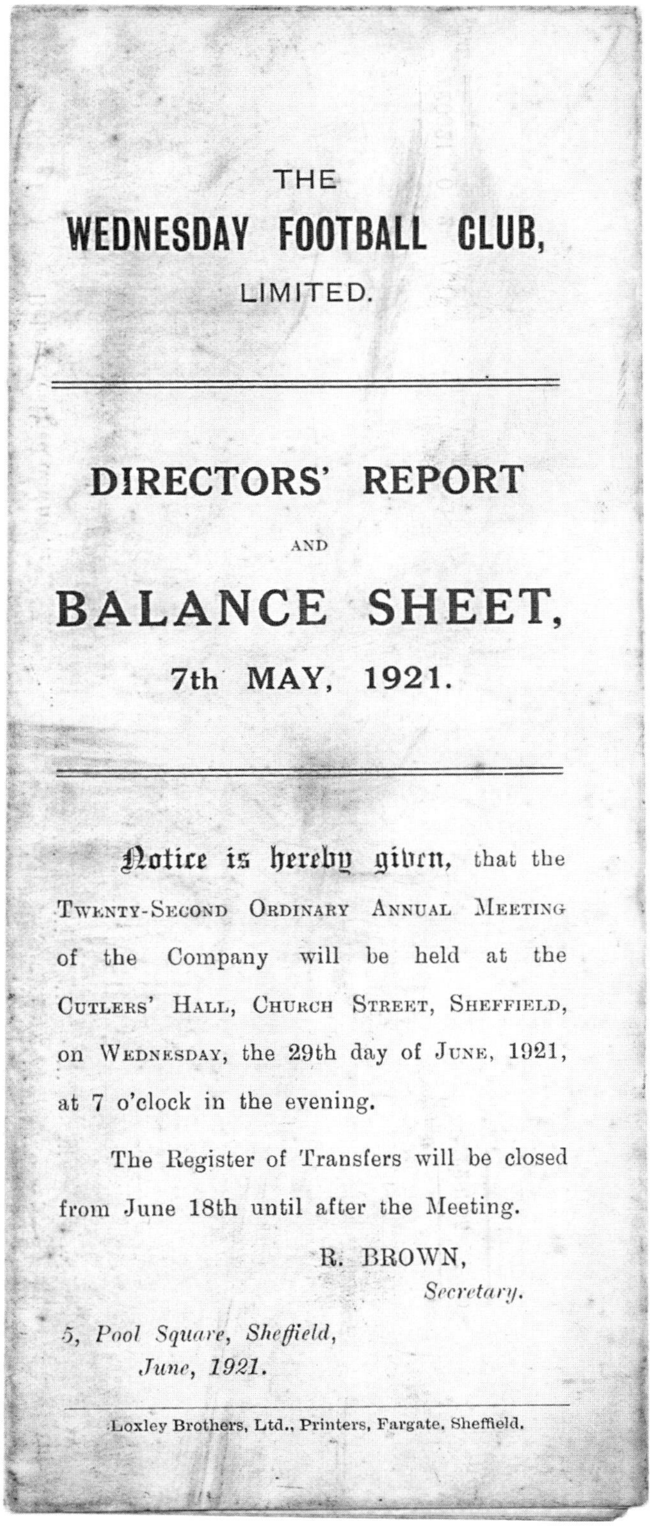

THE

WEDNESDAY FOOTBALL CLUB,

LIMITED.

DIRECTORS' REPORT

AND

BALANCE SHEET,

7th MAY, 1921.

Notice is hereby given, that the TWENTY-SECOND ORDINARY ANNUAL MEETING of the Company will be held at the CUTLERS' HALL, CHURCH STREET, SHEFFIELD, on WEDNESDAY, the 29th day of JUNE, 1921, at 7 o'clock in the evening.

The Register of Transfers will be closed from June 18th until after the Meeting.

R. BROWN,
Secretary.

5, Pool Square, Sheffield,
June, 1921.

Loxley Brothers, Ltd., Printers, Fargate, Sheffield.

referee discovered he had played three minutes short and promptly had to clear the pitch of the oncoming band in order to play out the remaining time!

After their Cup exit, Wednesday started to shown signs of revival in the league, and a tremendous unbeaten run of ten games, including five straight wins, quickly banished relegation fears; with the run culminating in an astonishing 6–0 victory over Cup Finalists, Wolves. In the following home game against Bury, the kick-off was delayed due to the non-arrival of a linesman. However, this was easily rectified, when, with the blessing of the opposition, Owls reserve keeper, Arnold Birch, took his place.

Wednesday eventually finished in a praiseworthy tenth position, with free scoring Johnny McIntyre proving to be their saviour, netting a tremendous 27 times—more than the rest of the team put together. At the end of the season the Owls had a chance to add silverware to their trophy room. These hopes were dashed, however, when neighbours, United won at Hillsborough in the first-ever final of the new Sheffield County Cup competition.

1921–22
A LATE SURGE TO MID TABLE

After securing a top ten finish in the previous campaign, hopes for a promotion push in '21–'22 were high amongst the Hillsborough faithful. In an attempt to reclaim their top flight place, the Owls brought several new players into the club during the summer months. First to arrive was the Portsmouth duo of James Armstrong and Emil Thompson, while centre-forward, Archie Ratcliffe, arrived to hopefully link up with the prolific Jimmy McIntyre. Also arriving at Hillsborough were George Holmes and Fred Lunn. Among the departures were Bert Eggo, Percy Reed, Alf Capper and Billy Harvey—the latter joining Birmingham after having returned from the Southern Hemisphere after his bout of pneumonia. Wednesday were also boosted by the annual report. This showed the club to be in its healthiest position for many a year, with a profit of over £8,000 announced, thanks to a 35% rise in match receipts to nearly £34,000.

The Owls kicked off the new season with a derby encounter against neighbours Barnsley; however, the visitors went away with the points, dashing Wednesday's hopes of a good start. Forty eight hours later a Sam Taylor goal at the Baseball Ground earned the first two point haul of the season, before the Tykes completed a quickfire double with a 2–0 success at Oakwell. It was generally a disappointing start, for Wednesday won only one of their opening seven league games, and found themselves struggling in the lower echelons of the Second Division table. Thankfully, a revival did take place in October, when three wins in four games lifted the Owls to mid table. That month also saw the arrival of key man, Frank Froggatt, from Denaby United; who, for his £300 fee, would prove to be one of the club's best ever purchases.

Wednesday remained inconsistent as autumn dawned, however, although a brace from Jimmy Lofthouse helped the Owls to their biggest win of the season against Blackpool at Hillsborough in late November. There then was more movement on the transfer front as Norwich full-back, George Gray arrived. This was twenty four hours before Armstrong ended an unhappy six month stay by joining the Canaries. Tom Ramsbottom then joined the Owls from Welsh side, Pontypridd; yet Wednesday simply could not get out of their mid-table rut.

As Christmas approached, the club were again rocked, when, for the second season running, they encountered severe difficulties with one of their star players. This time it was the previous season's top scorer, Johnny McIntyre, who was placed on the transfer list. This occurred after mystery problems between McIntyre and the club had come to a head, prompting Wednesday to take a firm line with the Scot by making the popular forward available for transfer. It was the beginning of the end for McIntyre, and to the general dismay of Owls fans their eight-goal top scorer was sold for a large fee to Division One side, Blackburn Rovers.

The club was hit by tragedy early in the New Year, when 'A' team player, George Pennington, died of pneumonia just before the Owls crashed out of the Cup at Park Avenue. Stoke then won at Hillsborough amidst a snowstorm, while a shocking home loss to Forest set alarm bells ringing, as Wednesday dropped into the bottom eight. The slide prompted Bob Brown to re-enter the transfer market, and inside a fortnight a treble swoop brought 'Darkie' Lowdell and Charlie Petrie to the club (from Ton Pentre and Stalybridge Celtic respectively). He also captured the signature of Bury centre-forward, Jimmy Trotter; who would go on to become one of the greatest goalscorers in the club's history. It took a while for the new players to gel, however, and defeats continued—though a surprise treble from Charlie Binney helped the Owls to a win over Coventry City. Off the field, Wednesday applied to join the Central League, while another arrival at Hillsborough was Welsh Amateur International T. Wolfe from Swansea Town.

Fears of a drop into regional Third Division football were thankfully allayed in the final eight games of the season, during which time the Owls remained unbeaten, recording five wins in the period. Consecutive home wins over Port Vale and West Ham started the revival, and only a missed penalty from Tom Brelsford denied them two points in the Hillsborough game with Hull City. A terrific second half display saw off Bury, while a victory over Leicester on the season's final day ensured the Owls would finish exactly where they had twelve months earlier—in tenth position. In what proved to be another re-run of the previous campaign, Wednesday's last game of the season came in the final of the new Sheffield County Cup at Oakwell. There it needed an injury time winner from Barnsley's Ernie Hine to again dash Wednesday's hopes of silverware. The final acts of the season saw Wednesday sign Sid Binks on pro forms, while the club's retained list revealed that a total of ten players with first team appearances to their name would not be re-engaged.

Fred Kean

1922–23
NEW RECORD ATTENDANCE SET

As Wednesday prepared for a third consecutive season in Division Two football, many fans hoped Bob Brown's 1920 prophecy would come to pass. On his return as Secretary-Manager, he'd expressed the opinion it would take Wednesday three seasons to fight their way back to the top flight of English soccer.

In an attempt to achieve that goal, Brown now brought several new players to Hillsborough, starting with the capture of Sheffield-born full-back, Walter Dickinson from Bradford Park Avenue. Soon after this, veteran left-winger, Horace Henshall arrived from Notts County to fulfil the role of player and reserve team coach. The big summer signing, however, was Welsh International right-winger, Rees Williams, who was signed from the then league side, Merthyr Town. Basil Wood was signed from Leeds, and Fletcher, the Darnall Old Boys goalkeeper also arrived. Fletcher, intriguingly, was said to have played league football during a spell at Bury under the name of Younger! There were several departures, with former Wednesday record scorer, Andrew Wilson, signing both O'Neill and Lunn in his capacity as Bristol Rovers manager; and Billy Taylor joining Midland League, Doncaster Rovers. Off the field, the club's reserve team again had to be satisfied with Midland League soccer, for their application to join the Central League was rejected at the AGM. Meanwhile, the club released their accounts showing a loss of almost £6,000. This was attributed to poor attendances suffered because of terrible weather experienced at all but one of Wednesday's home games since the Christmas period.

Debut boy, Sid Binks, ensured Wednesday experienced a winning start to the new season, as he hit the opening day clincher at Rotherham County. The centre-forward was again on target two days later when Manchester United were beaten; and, after three games, the Owls found themselves sitting in second position—their best start to a season for over eight years. They soon came back down to earth, however, when a run of five games without a win saw them drop to mid table. The month of September also saw Wednesday embark on a mini tour of South Wales, with games at Swansea Town and non leaguers, Ton Pentre; the latter arranged as part of the deal which brought 'Darkie' Lowdell to Sheffield some six months earlier. Back in the league the rot was stopped with two points at home to Fulham. However, Wednesday were struggling to find the net, and so Bob Brown went back in the transfer market to capture the Newcastle United inside-forward, Andrew Smailes. The new man made a goal scoring debut in a draw at Clapton Orient, before a hat trick from Sam Taylor ensured a comfortable victory in the return fixture.

As Christmas approached, the Owls moved back into the top six after a tremendous 4–2 win at Oakwell, having trailed 2–0 at the break. This, however, was a prelude to a terrible run of results which brought only three points out of a possible twelve. The Cup proved to be a welcome distraction, with the Owls winning through to the last sixteen after beating Barnsley in front of the biggest crowd ever seen in Sheffield (66,103). In retrospect, the January results would take a back seat, as the future success of the club was effectively secured with the signings of a trio of players who would be instrumental in helping Wednesday back to the promised land. First to arrive was full-back, Billy Felton from Grimsby Town; followed soon after by classy half-back, Ernest Blenkinsop, signed for over £1,000 from Hull City. The final capture was Worksop Town keeper, Jack Brown, who was regarded as the best custodian in the Midland League, and who would appear in over five hundred games for Wednesday across the ensuing fifteen seasons.

Fellow Second Division side, Derby County, ended the cup run, while back in the league the Owls excellent home form ensured they remained on the fringes of the top six. However, poor form on their travels, characterised by an embarrassing 2–0 defeat in a friendly at Bishop Auckland, meant Wednesday would have to wait at least another twelve months for a promotion push.

Attempts by the Owls to win the County Cup again hit the rocks with a defeat at Rotherham County, though consolation came with a victory at Bramall Lane in a benefit game. The final signing of the season saw Joseph Harron arrive from York City, while a league defeat in their last home game saw the Owls drop to a final eighth position. It seems that the stress created by the Owls unpredictability was not confined to the supporters, for at the end of the season it was reported that winger, Charlie Binney was seriously ill with a nervous breakdown! Wednesday finally did win a trophy, when the second team—with Jimmy Trotter top scoring with twenty goals—lifted the Midland League Championship in what proved to be their final season in the competition.

Sid Binks

1923–24
WEDNESDAY'S OLDEST PLAYER

For the third consecutive season Wednesday fans hoped this would be the campaign in which the Owls finally regained their rightful place in the top flight of English football. The close season was extremely quiet, with Durham City winger, Joe Wilson being the only one senior player to arrive. Among the departures was Walter Dickinson, who was bluntly described in the local press as being 'a clever player but slow'. Wednesday were then frustrated when Jack Bellas moved to Midland League Mansfield Town for a £500 fee, because the Stags were not then a league side, and the ruling of the day meant they were not required to pay a fee for his services.

The summer months saw Wednesday elected to the Central League; and, in June, the football world was shocked to learn of the arrest of ex Owls trainer, William Barr, at the end of an FA enquiry into a payments scandal at his Port Vale club. Barr had originally blown the lid on the scandal, but after being accused by the Vale Chairman of obtaining £15 from him by false pretences, he was hauled into court pleading his innocence. Quickly acquitted on all charges, he was allowed to return to the profession which had seen him spend a year at Hillsborough in the nightmare season of 1919–20.

Hopes for a positive start were quickly dashed when the Owls picked up only one solitary point from their first three games. The second of those fixtures saw a 2–0 defeat at Port Vale, but the result was only half the story; for when Wednesday departed on the 1.48 p.m. train out of Sheffield, Billy Felton and Rees Williams were missing, having managed to miss the proverbial boat! The two players failed to make it to the Potteries under their own steam, and to make up the numbers Wednesday drafted in travelling reserve, Charlie Petrie. To everyone's amazement they also included their 46-year-old trainer, Jerry Jackson, who'd never played league football before. Starting the game out on the right wing, Jackson entered the record books as the club's oldest player; and performed pluckily before the pace forced him to retire with ten minutes of the first half remaining. Incidentally, after the game the two absent players were fined the princely sum of £5 apiece by the League management committee.

The Owls' first win of the season came in the return game with Vale, yet at the end of September Wednesday were near the foot of the table after a heavy loss at Fulham. A move into the transfer market was then made to bring both Thomas Harvey and Joe Gill to the club, before Andy Smailes moved to Bristol City in a swap that brought William Walker in the opposite direction. The latter's home debut proved to be a turning point in Wednesday's season, when his brace in a big win over Nelson sparked the Owls on a seven game unbeaten run which lifted them into the top ten.

Sam Taylor

Jerry Jackson

THE HIPPODROME

SHEFFIELD.

TWICE NIGHTLY :-: 6.30 and 8.40.
MATINEES—AS ANNOUNCED.
— ALWAYS BRIGHT AND SELECT. —

The Wednesday v. Crystal Palace.

Played at Hillsboro', Sheffield, December 22nd, 1923.

T H E H I P P O D R O M E

Wednesday.

Right Wing.   Left Wing.

Goal.
1
Davison

2   3
Felton   Blenkinsopp

Half-Backs.
4   5   6
Kean   Wilson   Brelsford

Forwards.
7   8   9   10   11
Williams Walker Binks   Petrie Harron

Referee : Mr. F. A. Freemantle.

Should any alteration be made, a notice will be sent round giving the name
of the substituted player, with the number of the position in which he will play.

Linesmen : Messrs. W. F. Parr & N. Shuker.

Forwards.
12   13   14   15   16
Harry   Morgan Hoddinott   Whitworth   G. Nicholson

Half-Backs.
17   18   19
Feebery   Cracknell   M'Cracken

20   Backs.   21
Cross   Little

Goal.
22
Alderson

Left Wing.   Right Wing.

6.30   **Crystal Palace.**   **8.40**

T H E H I P P O D R O M E

Just before Christmas, Crystal Palace were crushed at Hillsborough; and victory over Coventry on Boxing Day was secured on a snow bound pitch, with the goal posts painted blue. The festive period was marred by tragedy, however, when, on Christmas Day in a Wharncliffe Charity Cup tie, reserve player, Tom Armitage was seriously injured and rushed to the Royal Infirmary. An emergency operation was seemingly successful, but Armitage suffered a relapse soon after and sadly died at the tender age of 24, four days after the fateful game. As the New Year dawned, Wednesday cruised past Leicester in the Cup, despite Sid Binks managing to miss two penalties; while an improved league performance saw a climb to seventh place. Defeat at Elland Road (after a 'good journey' which took only two hours) was followed by a disappointing replay loss at Bristol City in the Cup. However, hopes were still high for a top-six finish.

Sixth place was duly reached with a comfortable home win over Stockport County. But then the rot set in, as three straight defeats were recorded to see Wednesday tumble back down into mid-table. With promotion now an impossible dream the Owls decided not to sign any big 'name' players, but took on several young players—none of whom would go on to play first team football. Spirits were raised after a Sam Taylor treble saw off South Shields, but a week later it was Wednesday who conceded five in a heavy defeat at Bury, before Sid Binks became the third Owls player in the campaign to grab a Cup hat-trick in the revenge win at Ashton Gate. Defender, Fred Kean then followed the trend by hitting all three in a friendly win at Bishop Auckland, before the Owls rounded off their season with a home win over Manchester United (new signing, George Ayres from Charlton, scoring on his debut) to leave Wednesday back in eighth place, seven points off the promotion places.

1924–25
A SEASON OF DISAPPOINTMENT

In what looked to be the most competitive Second Division since the end of the War, manager Bob Brown realised his Wednesday side would need to be strengthened if the long awaited promotion push was to become a reality. Optimism was again high amongst the Hillsborough faithful, and this was strengthened by a series of forays into the transfer market which resulted in the arrival of six new players.

First to sign was Port Vale winger, Arthur Prince. Wednesday then secured one of their best transfers of the whole decade, when inside-forward Billy Marsden, the understudy to the famous Charlie Buchan of Sunderland, arrived in Sheffield. On the day Marsden arrived, two new faces appeared at the club, as Brown restructured his backroom staff to bring both George Utley and Chris Craig onto the coaching staff. A double swoop then brought William Collier and William Inglis from Scottish club, Raith Rovers, while further signings included reserve keeper Tony Carr from Newport County, and half-back George Toone from Watford. The Toone transfer saw George Prior move in the opposite direction and other departures included Joe Sykes, Tom Brelsford and William Walker (who joined Weymouth as player-manager).

Wednesday's opening match of the new season was a momentous day for their hosts, Crystal Palace, as this was the first game to be played at their new Selhurst Park ground. Because of industrial action, the single stand was incomplete, and the majority of a bumper crowd went away unhappy as debut boy, Billy Marsden, grabbed the only goal of the game after just four minutes. Unfortunately, the Owls couldn't build on this flying start, losing at home forty eight hours later; and, after the early skirmishes, they found themselves lodged firmly in mid table.

Away from football there was sadness when an important part of club history died, with the original Wednesday Cricket Club (formed in 1820) wound up, largely because they lacked a home to call their own.

A treble from Ayres pushed Wednesday to the fringes of the top six, but this was as close as they would get all season, for three straight defeats then pushed them back down the league ladder. Another move into the transfer market occurred, when, at a record fee for his club, inside-right Harold Hill moved to Hillsborough from Notts County. The new signing netted on his debut, and with the emerging Jimmy Trotter starting to find the net it began to look as if Wednesday might well have the forward line to move them upwards. Indeed, over the next few weeks Trotter hit a rich seam of form, netting ten times in nine starts. This culminated in an astonishing home game with Portsmouth,

A. Prince

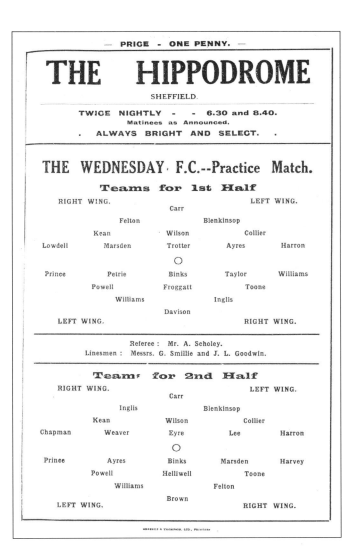

THE HIPPODROME

SHEFFIELD.

TWICE NIGHTLY - - 6.30 and 8.40.
Matinees as Announced.
. ALWAYS BRIGHT AND SELECT. .

THE WEDNESDAY F.C.--Practice Match.

Teams for 1st Half

RIGHT WING.   LEFT WING.

Carr

Felton   Blenkinsop

Kean   Wilson   Collier

Lowdell   Marsden   Trotter   Ayres   Harron

○

Prince   Petrie   Binks   Taylor   Williams

Powell   Froggatt   Toone

Williams   Inglis

Davison

LEFT WING.   RIGHT WING.

Referee : Mr. A. Scholey.
Linesmen : Messrs. G. Smillie and J. L. Goodwin.

Teams for 2nd Half

RIGHT WING.   LEFT WING.

Carr

Inglis   Blenkinsop

Kean   Wilson   Collier

Chapman   Weaver   Eyre   Lee   Harron

○

Prince   Ayres   Binks   Marsden   Harvey

Powell   Helliwell   Toone

Williams   Felton

Brown

LEFT WING.   RIGHT WING.

GREENUP & THOMPSON, LTD., PRINTERS.

Billy Felton

where he scored all five Wednesday goals. Meanwhile, off the field, the Owls trio of Inglis, Collier and Sam Taylor all refused offers to play in the US for a tempting £14 a week; while Sid Binks left for Huddersfield with winger Eddie Richardson arriving as part of the deal.

The Christmas period was certainly not a merry one for the Owls. In a disastrous home game with Blackpool, Wednesday crashed to their biggest ever home defeat (6–2)—it would be almost 67 years before they suffered a heavier home loss. Thankfully, the reaction to the humiliation was positive, and, as the New Year dawned, the distraction of the Cup brought a welcome home win over Manchester United (whose one-legged mascot hopped bizarrely round the pitch before the game). The draw for the next round put the City into a frenzy of anticipation, for Wednesday were sent to Bramall Lane. There, on a mud bath of a pitch, a brace from Trotter inside the first ten minutes put the Owls in command. However, their First Division rivals stormed back to level the scores before twenty minutes had been played, then grabbed a second-half winner—in a season which would see them go on to win the trophy. The hangover following the defeat dealt the Owls a 6–1 thrashing at Filbert Street a week later; and, most worryingly, Wednesday were now slipping into the lower echelons of the division.

A string of defeats followed, pushing Wednesday down to fourth from bottom, and this prompted yet another move into the transfer market. The intention this time was simply to attempt to stop the alarming slide, and Sam Powell from Leeds United, and Blackpool captain Matt Barress—who'd netted a hat-trick in the aforementioned Christmas Day debacle at Hillsborough—arrived at the club. The former made an immediate impact, scoring the only goal against Barnsley on his home debut; and went to hit a treble against Fulham to ease fears of a drop into regional football. However, it needed a terrific win over Hull in the penultimate home fixture to finally banish those fears, and in the end a final position of fourteenth was secured. Overall, there was general disappointment among the Wednesday fans at the season's conclusion, for the Owls had failed to even challenge for promotion with what, on paper, had seemed to be their strongest side for many a year. The mood was certainly not helped by the Blades Cup success; but still, hope was expressed in the local press that next season would belong to Wednesday.

1925–26
PROMOTION AT LAST!

Despite the disappointment of the previous campaign, manager Brown was convinced that the nucleus of his squad would be good enough to finally take Wednesday back to where they belonged. This was the main reason that only three new players arrived in the summer; the first being the prolific Crystal Palace centre-forward, George Whitworth, who joined after netting fifty times in 118 games for the Selhurst Park club. The second newcomer was Wolves inside-forward, Fred Marson; while just before kick off, Wednesday signed pacey winger, Lewis Bedford from Walsall.

Exiting Hillsborough were several players who had failed to make a lasting impression during their time in Sheffield. These included the likes of Collier and Inglis, who'd only joined twelve months earlier; plus Charlie Petrie and Sam Taylor. However, one undesirable departure from the club was of ex England International defender, George Wilson, who, after refusing to re-sign, inexplicably dropped into Division Three (North) soccer to become Nelson's record signing at £2,500. As part of the deal, Wilson became landlord of the Prince of Wales Hotel in Nelson; and this was believed to be the reason why he effectively sacrificed any hope of reclaiming his International place. Behind the scenes the coaching staff again altered, as Utley departed and was replaced by Rotherham Town trainer, William Hodgkiss, who became assistant to Chris Craig (who was himself promoted from reserve trainer). Finally, season ticket prices were issued which allowed women to gain admission for roughly a third of the price of the club's male supporters!

For once Wednesday were quick out of the blocks when the season got underway, and a five game unbeaten start saw them lying comfortably in third place. The last of those fixtures, against Preston, saw Trotter give the fans a taste of things to come, when he scored four times. Two weeks later the now familiar chant of 'Trott, Trott, Trott, Trott, Trotter, score a little goal for me' rang out around Hillsborough, as the unstoppable forward grabbed five (his first four coming in a crazy five minute period) in the demolition of poor Stockport. With their forward line firing on all cylinders the Owls settled into second place, with enthusiasm high that a promotion challenge could finally become reality after several false dawns. A chance of moving into top place was lost when promotion rivals, Derby inflicted the first home defeat of the season. However, a comfortable home win over neighbours Barnsley kept the Owls in touch at the summit. On the transfer front, Wednesday captured Wath Athletic's diminutive and much sought after 17-year-old winger, Jack Wilkinson; while a double swoop saw Welsh Internationals Beadles and McIlvenny sign from Cardiff City.

Goalkeeper Jack Brown

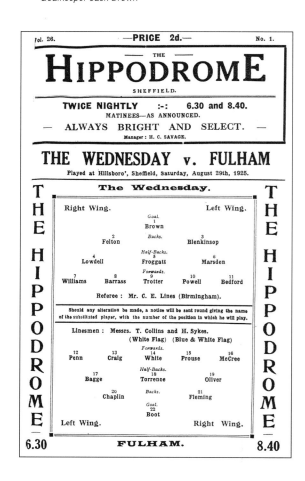

ABOUT OUR PLAYERS.

P	Stands for Players, who have made a name 'tis true— The first one is Jack Brown and a clever goalkeeper too.
L	Stands for Leading light and all good judges say— The Welsh boy, Rees Williams, he's a leading light to-day.
A	Stands for Active, and for able, and for art— Trotter, he's an artist, and he ably plays his part.
Y	Stands for Youth and there's a youth with brains, and wise— The winger, Wilkinson, he's always on the job and tries.
U	Stands for Useful, and I'm sure you're well aware— That Froggatt as our captain, always does his share.
P	Stands for Peerless, and the fact it still remains— That Blenkinsop, he's a masterpiece with grit, and pluck and brains
W	Stands for Workmanlike, meaning action, sharp and clean— And don't forget this is our half-back, Freddie Kean.
E	Stands for Eager, ever-ready and always in the fray, This is our forward Powell, a real strong player on his day.
D	Stands for Daring and deliberate, this I'm sure you'll all admit— That Walker, our Scotch full back will always do his bit.
N	Stands for Nippy, and it also stands for neat,— And Marsden he is nippy, his shots at goal are quite a treat.
E	Stands for Energy, and this combined with pluck and skill,— Well, we have a forward, you'll guess his name is Hill.
S	Stands for Safe and sound, that's what a full back should always be, Now there's Billy Felton, who plays a game of high degree.
D	Stands for Deeds, now these are full of skill and craft— Our clever forward, Barrass, he's the schemer fore and aft.
A	Stands for Ability, so willing and so able— So when they speak of Lowdell's skill—believe it—it's no fable.
Y	Stands for Yeoman, these are services so well rendered— Now from A. Prince they must be well intended.

S O when you're watching Wednesday and sharing in their joys—
Well don't forget Chris. Craig, he's the trainer of the boys—
The Blues they are a brilliant team and honor they deserve,—
Perhaps even the Officials, and the lads who've been reserve.

H.H.

Harold Hill

Harold Hill's reintroduction into the side at about this time seemed to be an inspired move, for his arrival coincided with a rise to the top of the table, after Chelsea were vanquished at Hillsborough. A free scoring Owls side remained in the top two in the run up to Christmas, and before the New Year was toasted they hit the fifty goal mark in league football, thanks to a nine goal Xmas bonanza in two meetings with Bradford City. The new year started poorly, however, as a heavy defeat at Fulham was followed by a surprise FA Cup exit at Division Three (North) club, New Brighton. Thankfully, this proved to be only a minor blip, as Wednesday proceeded to record five consecutive wins to move clear at the top of the table, with Derby in their slipstream.

Brough Fletcher, a new arrival at Hillsborough from Barnsley, was signed to act as captain to the reserve team, as well as to coach the club's younger players. Another new face was Bradford City right-back, Tom Walker, who was not in the side which travelled in late February to the Baseball Ground for the crunch meeting with the Rams. Unfortunately, the home side repeated their 4–1 win at Hillsborough earlier in the season, to close the gap at the top. In the next away game, the Owls could only draw at Swansea and in the process had Sam Powell sent off. A record league crowd for Oakwell then saw a 1–1 draw, before a wobbling Wednesday succumbed to their second home defeat of the campaign. However, despite this attack of the jitters, the Owls were still top and remained so for the remainder of the season, after winning six of their final seven games. This unbeaten run was preceded by a heavy defeat at Darlington, who were inspired by a certain Mark Hooper. Three straight wins, however, then set up a crucial clash at third placed, Chelsea. At Stamford Bridge a huge crowd of over 41,000 saw Wednesday battle to what looked like a well earned point, before disaster struck two minutes from time when Marsden handled in the box to concede a penalty. Keeper Jack Brown proved to be the hero, however, brilliantly saving the spot kick to leave Wednesday three points off promotion. Aptly, it was a Jimmy Trotter double at Southampton which finally secured promotion, before a home win over Blackpool meant the champagne could be opened to celebrate the capture of the Second Division Championship.

It had proved to be a truly momentous season in the club's history, as their 88 goals in league football was a club record. Jimmy Trotter, in topping the Division Two scorers chart with 37 league goals, set an individual seasonal league record, beating David McLean's 30 goals back in 1912–13. However, the true secret of their success seemed to lie in the fact that seven players had played in at least forty league games, with inspirational captain, Frank Froggatt an ever present, as he led Wednesday back to the promised land from whence they'd come six years earlier.

1926–27
TROTTER TO THE RESCUE!

As they prepared for their first season in the top flight in seven years, Wednesday decided against wholesale change, relying instead on the Division Two Championship squad with a few choice additions. Two major arrivals during the close season were half-back, Herbert Burridge from Darlington, and Rochdale's prolific inside-forward, Harry Anstiss, who in two seasons at Spotland had scored 42 times in only 70 games. Alex Cruickshank was also signed from Merthyr Town. An all-round sportsman, in the previous summer Cruikshank had scored over 600 runs for the Scotland cricket team.

There were several departures, including George Ayres, Matt Barrass and Welsh International, Harry Beadles; with the last named leaving after failing to make a single appearance. However, the most significant departure was that of legendary goalie, 'Teddy' Davison, who, after 18 years and 424 games for the Owls, signed for non-league Mansfield Town. Off the pitch there was debate at the club's AGM concerning the actual name of the club ('The Wednesday' as opposed to 'Sheffield Wednesday'); and in August, Wednesday held a banquet to celebrate their promotion success, at which, with impeccable timing, Richard Sparling launched his seminal book on the Owls, entitled *The Romance of The Wednesday*.

Handed a home tie with the Blades, Wednesday couldn't have asked for a more high profile fixture to welcome them back into the big time. The biggest crowd of the season packed into Hillsborough, though the majority would go home disappointed—despite a brace from Jimmy Trotter, United scored twice in the last seven minutes to take the points. It would be fair to say that the Owls defence struggled to cope with the First Division forward lines in the early weeks, for they conceded seven at Spurs, followed by five at Filbert Street, before the first points and a clean sheet came in a home win over West Ham. Even early in the season it became obvious that Wednesday's survival would depend on their home record, with the final analysis revealing the Owls failure to record a win on their travels all season. A first hat-trick of the season for Trotter helped vanquish Everton, during a run of games at Hillsborough that brought nine wins out of ten and kept Wednesday comfortably in the top half of the table. Among these was a first ever league meeting with Huddersfield Town, while a victory over Newcastle lifted the Owls to the dizzy heights of sixth place. Away from the action, Lewis Bedford returned to Walsall, while Glasgow Rangers inside-forward, Daniel Kirkwood arrived in Sheffield.

The New Year brought mixed fortunes, with Bury becoming the first team to win at Hillsborough since the season's

J. TROTTER

400 SHEFFIELD WED.

SHEFFIELD WEDNESDAY
FOOTBALL CLUB.

DINNER

To celebrate the winning of the 2nd Division League Championship, Season 1925-26, and of the 60th Anniversary of the founding of the Club.

HELD AT THE
ROYAL VICTORIA STATION HOTEL,
SHEFFIELD.

Friday, 6th August, 1926.

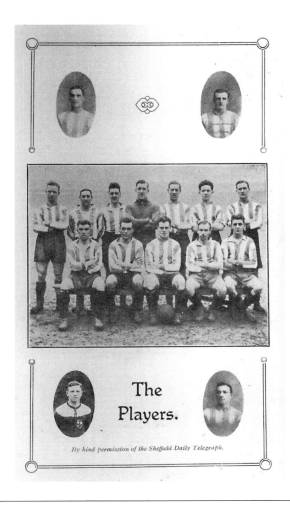

The
Players.

By kind permission of the Sheffield Daily Telegraph.

opening day. Progress in the Cup came against Division Three (South) club, New Brighton. Sheffield United then completed the double in front of their biggest ever league crowd (just over sixty thousand). This was followed by the Owls FA Cup exit in a replay at South Shields; however, in retrospect, these results took a back seat to a trio of transfer deals which would play a major part in the success which would follow before the decade was out. First to arrive was the 5ft 4in Darlington winger, Mark Hooper, followed soon after by Port Vale inside-forward, Alf Strange (Anstiss going to Burslem as part of the deal). The third Bob Brown capture was Brentford forward, Jack Allen, who would eventually replace Jimmy Trotter as the Owls number one marksman. Of the three new men, only Allen appeared on a regular basis, netting his first goal in the comprehensive home win over Sunderland.

A run of five consecutive away defeats pushed the Owls down to fifteenth by the end of February. The nadir of this shocking away form was reached soon after, when future Owl, Jackie Whitehouse scored four as Derby romped to an 8–0 home victory. Seven days later the Owls bounced back from the Baseball Ground debacle with a home win over Manchester United, in a game in which Billy Fenton, the Wednesday reserve full-back, ran the line after one of the appointed linesmen failed to put in an appearance. Thankfully for Wednesday, fears of dropping into the relegation zone were unfounded, for in Jimmy Trotter they possessed one of the country's most prolific strikers; and one who seemed to score almost every time the Owls appeared at home (he failed to find the net only six times in twenty-three home games). Trotter ended the season with 39 league and cup goals to his name, finishing with the accolade of Division One top scorer, having netted half of the Owls 75 league goals. In the end, Wednesday finished in a comfortable fifteenth place; and it was perhaps fitting that the final goal of the season went to Jimmy Trotter, who more than anyone had ensured the Owls could build on their newly won First Division status.

1927–28
THE GREAT ESCAPE

The summer of 1927 was one of the quietest in the club's history, with only minor changes made to a squad which had kept the Owls comfortably in Division One in their first season back in the top flight. There were several low key arrivals, with Norman Smith joining from Wombwell, along with the Jarrow FC duo of MacDougall and William Smith. Behind the scenes, W. Hopkins was appointed as assistant trainer to Chris Craig, while reserve player, William Powell dropped into non-league football. In retrospect, the most crucial signing came early in August when Tottenham's classy ex-England International inside-forward, Jimmy Seed, joined Wednesday. Somewhat surprisingly he had been deemed surplus to requirements at White Hart Lane, arriving at Hillsborough in a straight swap deal for 'Darkie' Lowdell— a decision which would rebound spectacularly on the North Londoners come May.

The season started in disastrous fashion for Wednesday when they suffered a 4–0 drubbing at Goodison Park. This was followed by a home defeat to Manchester United, for whom Partridge netted after just 25 seconds. It became apparent that all was not well on the field of play, and that unless Bob Brown could turn the situation round quickly, the Owls would be set for a season of struggle. The first victory finally came in game six; and a week later a hard fought draw at Bramall Lane lifted hopes that a revival was around the corner. However, this proved to a be false dawn, and after losing a 3–1 lead in a seven goal thriller at Newcastle, the Owls slumped to the foot of the table. Despite a succession of defeats, Wednesday were still finding the net on a regular basis (unfortunately, so were their opponents—with more success!) and occasionally the side clicked, witnessed by a four goal win over Bury which temporarily took the Owls off the bottom. Meanwhile, off the field, winger Rees Williams was sold to Manchester United after losing his place to Mark Hooper; while full-back, Ernest Hatfield, arrived from nursery club, Wombwell. Frank Froggatt, the Sheffield born centre-back who'd captained Wednesday to the Second Division title less than eighteen months earlier, then departed the club. However, the major transfer news of the period concerned Blackburn Rovers and England centre-forward, Ted Harper, who the Owls secured for a reputed club record fee of over £4,000.

Harper's debut came in an astonishing game at Derby County, with the new signing grabbing a hat-trick to make a sensational start to his Wednesday career as the Owls won 6–4 after trailing 3–1 at the interval. Just before the Christmas fixtures the Huddersfield Town full-back, Norman Smith, became the latest signing. He was probably wishing he hadn't moved, however, as Wednesday earned only two draws in their next six games, including a shocking home

defeat to his old club, and the Owls again dropped to the foot of the table. The FA Cup proved a welcome distraction from Wednesday's league worries, as they progressed to the last sixteen following a home success over Bournemouth and Boscombe and a victory at Swindon Town. This earned a tie with neighbouring United, where a combined attendance of over 116,000 watched a draw at Hillsborough before a Harry Johnson hat-trick helped the Blades to a 4–1 replay win. This further deepened the gloom amongst the blue and white half of the City. Three days after the Cup exit, a new left-winger, Ellis Rimmer, made his debut after completing a big money move from Tranmere Rovers. However, he was unable to reverse Wednesday's fortunes, which had seen them play thirty games with a paltry five wins to their credit.

The situation seemed hopeless, with the inquest in the local press seemingly already underway as to what had gone wrong in a season that promised so much. Morale lifted momentarily after a nap hand win over Burnley; though a defeat at Bury put Wednesday a massive seven points adrift at

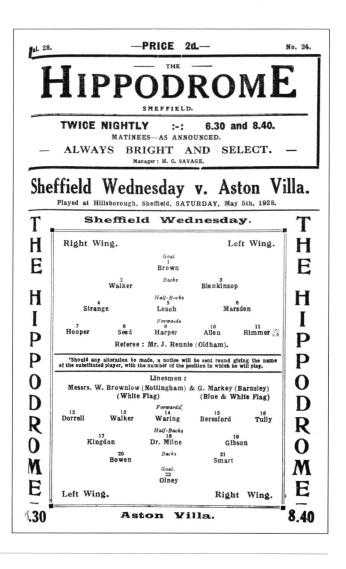

the foot of the table. A minor miracle was obviously needed to avoid the drop back into Division Two, though another big home win followed. After earning a point at Leicester, the Owls went into the Easter programme with their deficit at the bottom cut to four points. Two meetings over the holiday period with Tottenham would, in the final analysis, prove vital for both clubs, with Jimmy Seed inspiring Wednesday to record a superb double, thanks to five goals from top scorer, Mark Hooper. An Easter Tuesday home win over Spurs put the Owls just three points from safety (two were relegated in those days) and Wednesday fans were starting to believe that perhaps the cause was not yet lost. This feeling grew after a great win at West Ham. However, despite a stunning victory at Sunderland in their penultimate away game, Wednesday still lay in bottom place, though four clubs were now only one point better off. An amazing unbeaten run of six wins and two draws meant that if the Owls could earn anything from their 'game in hand' at Highbury, they'd be out of the bottom two. Unfortunately a goal by Brain looked to have won the game for the Gunners, when, in a sensational finish, up popped

Jimmy Seed to head home a last minute equaliser. This moved Wednesday into 19th place, ahead on goal average of the three clubs immediately below them. Everything was now set for one of the most incredible relegation dog fights of all time, as, on the final day, only two points separated twelfth place Liverpool from bottom club Manchester United. At home, at Hillsborough, Wednesday were masters of their own destiny and didn't disappoint as a 2–0 win saw hero, Jimmy Seed carried from the field by joyous home fans who had seen the culmination of one of the greatest escapes from relegation in the history of the English game. When the results filtered through that day, it was revealed that Middlesbrough were down and, ironically for Wednesday's veteran captain, they were joined by Spurs, who'd finished their fixtures early and were on their way to a friendly in Amsterdam, never for one moment thinking relegation would befall them. This truly incredible finish by Wednesday would prove to be only the beginning of a change in fortune.

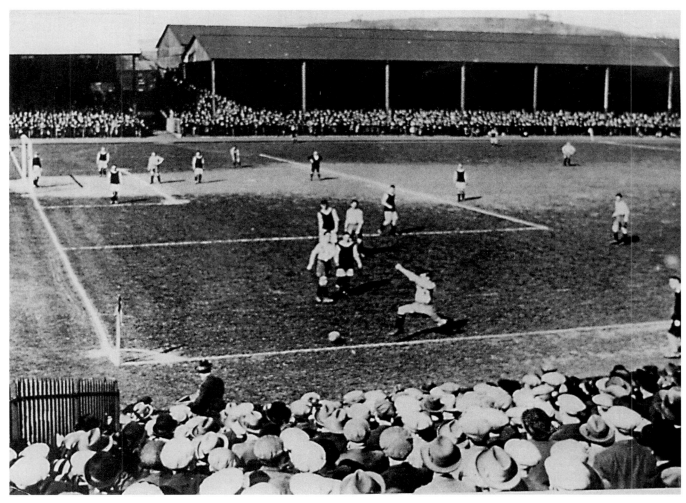

Wednesday v. Aston Villa—'The Great Escape' is completed

1928–29
CHAMPIONSHIP COMES TO HILLSBOROUGH

After the momentous finish to the previous season, confidence was high that Wednesday would be able to carry their form over into the new campaign. During the close season Wednesday were actually criticised by many supporters for not having added any 'big name' players to their rosta. This, however, seemed harsh, for earlier in the year the Owls had spent heavily. For instance, a £12,000 outlay on transfer fees, in order to avoid the drop and build for the future, had created a recorded loss in the annual accounts. Indeed, such was Bob Brown's confidence in his side, that he only entered the transfer market on one occasion, bringing inside-forward, Harry Gregg, from Darlington. Exiting Hillsborough were Fred Marson, Arthur Prince and Dan Kirkwood; while plans for a shelter/refreshment area at the Leppings Lane end were announced. Meanwhile, at the pre-season practise game, the crowd were met with the rare sight of three sets of brothers appearing for Wednesday, with the Felton, Rimmer and Wilson families all represented.

It would be fair to say the fixture list was not kind to Wednesday, for in the first ten days of the season they were twice required to meet the League Champions, as well as the Cup holders. The Owls made a great start, however, as Arsenal were beaten at Hillsborough in a game in which the visitors came out wearing numbers on the back of their shirts—the first time the idea had been used in league football. Wednesday then earned a superb draw at champions, Everton, before posting their intentions for the season by registering a single goal victory in the return game. The Owls home record would be vital to their season, and, after a 6–0 debacle at bogey club Derby, Wednesday returned to Hillsborough for a derby clash with United. Almost 45,000 packed into the ground, with the majority in celebratory mood at the finish, as Wednesday recorded their biggest ever league victory over the Blades in peacetime league soccer. A game at Portsmouth in early October saw another away defeat for Wednesday, with the match holding great significance as a positional change saw inside-forward, Jack Allen, move to centre-forward in place of Ted Harper. Allen netted in that defeat and never looked back, scoring three at home to Birmingham seven days later, and all four as Wednesday earned their first away win of the season at Bury. Off the pitch, Fred Kean left for Bolton, with the Owls receiving a club record fee for his services.

A second away win at Yorkshire rivals, Leeds, lifted Wednesday into second place, and victory over Liverpool in late November lifted the Owls to the top of the First Division for the first time since March 1915. The Yuletide period proved vital, for after Manchester City were vanquished the Owls faced two top-of-the-table Hillsborough clashes against

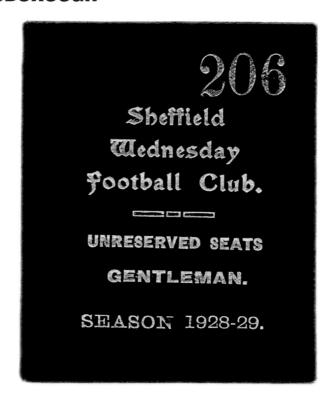

206

Sheffield Wednesday Football Club.

UNRESERVED SEATS

GENTLEMAN.

SEASON 1928-29.

THE STORM BEFORE THE SUNSHINE.

THE

FOOTBALL ASSOCIATION

Patron: His Majesty The King
President: Sir Charles Clegg, J.P.

□

International Trial Match

ENGLAND

versus

THE REST

□

PLAYED ON THE GROUND OF THE

SHEFFIELD WEDNESDAY F.C.

ON

MONDAY, FEB. 4TH, 1929

Kick-off 3 p.m.

Huddersfield and Blackburn. The first saw a new record attendance for a league game at the ground, as Wednesday reached the fifty goal mark, thanks to a late equaliser from Gregg (Hooper having missed a penalty). The meeting with second place Rovers was even more crucial, and on a snow covered pitch Jack Allen's shot through a crowded goal mouth put Wednesday five points clear at the top of the league.

The FA Cup run lasted only two games, for after victory at league side, Wigan Borough, the Owls crashed out at Second Division, Reading. As is often the case at such a moment, Wednesday could then declare they were now concentrating on the league; and a hard fought point at Bramall Lane kept them with a four point advantage at the top. Incredibly, from mid December until the end of the season, Wednesday then failed to win away from home. However, their tremendous home record meant that the chasing pack struggled to keep pace, and by late March the dream was becoming a reality, with the Owls holding a substantial five point lead over second placed Sunderland. Away from the action, Bob Brown boosted the Championship challenge by capturing the signature of Derby inside-forward, Jack Whitehouse. This was followed soon after by the arrival of Len Hargreaves from Sunderland; with Billy Felton going in the opposite direction. Highly rated full-back, George Beeson, then signed from Chesterfield, as the prolific scoring of Jack Allen led directly to the departure of Ted Harper to Tottenham.

The mid-week thrashing of West Ham set a new First Division points record for the Owls and meant that the home game with Burnley could decide the title. Wednesday went into the game holding a three point lead, with the chasing pack having only two games left. A win would therefore be sufficient, though the visitors obviously hadn't read the script, for they stunned the home fans by taking the lead with only twenty minutes remaining. However, Wednesday stormed back to equalise through—who else, but—Jack Allen (who finished the season with 35 goals to his name), and they then poured forward in the last nine minutes in an attempt to grab the winner. Although they failed, in the end this did not matter, for news had filtered through that their main rivals, Leicester, had drawn. Wednesday were thus crowned Champions for the first time for 25 years. The inspirational captaincy of Jimmy Seed and the goal-scoring talents of Allen were key factors in the success, though a terrific team spirit in the side was the main reason why the Owls could progress from bottom to top inside a six month period, and stay at the summit for three quarters of the season. To complete a glorious campaign, the club's reserve side won the Central League for the first time. At the season's end, the title-winning squad earned a well deserved busman's holiday, as Wednesday embarked on a three week, six-game tour of Switzerland.

1929–30
SO CLOSE TO THE DOUBLE

After winning the Championship, Wednesday were now faced with the not inconsiderable task of retaining the title. As was the case twelve months earlier, the club decided to keep faith with last season's squad; the only arrival of note being Stockport County's highly-rated 18-year-old inside-forward, Harry Burgess. Another arrival of interest was that of Mark Hooper's brother, Chris, from Darlington; while Chesterfield's Tom Neale completed a trio of summer signings, and Harold Hill was among the departures. At the club's Annual General Meeting, it was proposed to officially change the name of the club from The Wednesday FC Ltd. Debate on the subject had raged across several years and three years earlier it had been agreed that for all general purposes the club should now be known as Sheffield Wednesday. The motion was seconded on this occasion, however, and from June 1929 the club title changed to Sheffield Wednesday Football Club Limited.

The season got off to an amazing start, when, in the traditional Whites v. Stripes curtain raiser, the Stripes netted ten times—Jack Allen getting into an early scoring groove with a treble. A tremendous four goal win at Portsmouth was then recorded on day one, and it looked to be business-as-usual when a home win put the Owls on top as the first league tables were published. However, there was a shock in store for the Hillsborough faithful, when, over the next fortnight, not only did Arsenal become the first team to win in Sheffield since February 1928, but Leeds duly repeated the trick in the following home fixture. In total contrast, Wednesday's away form was so good, that by early October they already had four victories to their name, surpassing their tally from the whole of the Championship season. As winter started to close in, the Owls had settled into second place. It seemed as if their famous forward line of Hooper, Seed, Allen, Burgess and Rimmer simply could not stop scoring, for they netted four goals at home to Leicester and Blackburn, four at Goodison Park, and a magnificent seven at home to Manchester United. Ironically, it was a home draw against Pompey that took Wednesday back to the top, on a pitch that was so muddy that three tosses of the pre-match coin were required before it would fall flat! Meanwhile, Tom Mackey arrived from non-leaguers West Hartlepool; and the Sheffield Wednesday Supporters Club held their first ever meeting.

The new year opened with a top of the table clash at Maine Road, where, in an astonishing game, almost 60,000 saw the home side come back from being three down to earn a point in what was described as the game of the season. With seven wins in their next eight games, and scoring 26 times in the process, Wednesday stretched their lead at the top, and progressed to the last eight of the Cup. There, after earning a draw at Forest, they won the replay to set up a semi-final

Supporters Club members' card

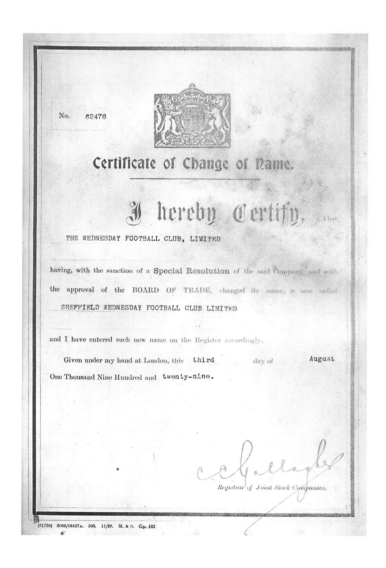

CHAMPIONSHIP STAYS AT HILLSBOROUGH.

ON MONDAY THE CHAMPS GOT A RATHER NASTY TUPPING WHEN THEY BEARDED THE RAMS IN THEIR OWN FIELD.

BUT. YESTERDAY THOSE RAMS CAME TO THE SLAUGHTER AND WEDNESDAY TO JOURNEYS END

LEAGUE CHAMPIONSHIP.

SHEFFIELD WEDNESDAY FOOTBALL CLUB.

✠

Admit Bearer

TO THE

Lord Mayor's Reception

TO BE HELD AT THE

Town Hall, Sheffield,

On Tuesday, 6th May, 1930

at 5.0 p.m.

AFTERNOON TEA.   R. BROWN, SECRETARY.

meeting with Huddersfield Town. The possibility of Wednesday becoming the first team to complete the double this century was now the topic of conversation among Wednesday fans, however, to bring the dream closer to reality and reach Wembley, they first had to overcome the Terriers at Old Trafford. Unfortunately, it was Birmingham referee, Mr Lines, who stole the headlines. Two astonishing decisions turned the game away from a Wednesday side who were left with only a feeling of injustice to take back to Sheffield. The Owls were the first to score through Hooper. Then, just before half-time, Lewis blatantly knocked the ball onto Jackson with his hand. The Town attacker hesitated as though waiting for a whistle, and when none came he ran on to fire home. To the amazement of the crowd and despite Wednesday protests, the goal was allowed to stand. With seventeen minutes remaining Jackson netted a second. In the final minute as the Owls poured forward, a Seed pass saw Jack Allen seemingly fire home a deserved equaliser. As the ball was passing over the goal line the referee blew his whistle for full-time and promptly disallowed the goal, thus denying Wednesday a replay. The Owls bounced back from the disappointment to beat West Ham, and followed this with a superb win at Anfield. There, despite lacking Strange, Blenkinsop, Marsden and Hooper (all of whom were on International duty) they won 3–1, helped by new signing, Walter Millership, who had arrived from Bradford Park Avenue.

A defeat at Leeds kept the Championship pot boiling, and when their main rivals, Derby, won 4–1 at the Baseball Ground, the Owls lead was cut to three points. Twenty four hours later the crunch return fixture took place and Wednesday duly stormed to a resounding 6–3 win to retain the Championship, with four games still to play. The Owls continued to amass points and goals once the title had been secured, and by the end of the season had not only equalled the 60 points record league tally, but finished with a club record 105 goals to their name. In the end the Owls finished a massive ten points clear (another record) and were now firmly established as the outstanding team in English football. This was thanks to a solid defence and an outstanding attack which had netted 122 times in League and Cup football (the reserves also crashed home 114 goals!)— Jack Allen again leading the way with 39 goals to his credit.

1930–31
RECORD LEAGUE VICTORY

In an attempt to secure a hat-trick of League Championships, manager Bob Brown made several forays into the transfer market in the summer of 1930. The end of the previous campaign had seen Wednesday make a total of nine senior professionals available for transfer. However, the first departure was not on the list, as Jack Wilkinson signed for Newcastle United after failing to displace Ellis Rimmer. It was also the end of an era when prolific scorer, Jimmy Trotter—who'd not been used at all in the first team in the previous season—left for Torquay United after netting 113 goals for the Owls. Other departures included Bert Burridge to Oldham Athletic, William Hodgkiss to Reading, and Norman Smith, who joined Queen's' Park Rangers. New arrivals included the Manchester United centre-forward, Jack Ball, plus the defensive duo George Nevin and Joe Peacock signed from Newcastle United. The former arrived on a free transfer after appealing to the Football League to have his £1,000 transfer fee removed. Meanwhile, one player who missed the start of the new season was the outstanding half-back, Billy Marsden who, in May that year, was seriously injured playing for England in Germany; an injury which would eventually force a premature end to his career.

The Owls assault on the treble started with a last minute own goal winner, at home to Newcastle United; before a defeat at Villa Park somewhat dampened the enthusiasm of the Wednesday faithful. A draw at Bramall Lane, after Harry Burgess had put the Owls ahead after just thirty seconds, was the prelude to a win at Grimsby, where new attacker, Jack Ball found the net for the first time in a blue and white shirt. By mid October Wednesday had climbed into the top six, and therefore travelled in good heart to Stamford Bridge to face Arsenal in the FA Charity Shield. However, it was 2–0 to the Gunners at the break, and despite Burgess pulling a goal back in the second period, the Owls first chance of silverware slipped away. Off the pitch, a trio of new arrivals checked in, with Rotherham United inside-forward, Victor Wright, followed by Everton half-back, Tom Robson. Ted Catlin then signed amateur forms from Northern League club South Bank.

November proved a pivotal month in Wednesday's season, for they found their scoring touch in a dramatic fashion, with three players recording hat-tricks in the process; though they lost a crucial top-of-the-table clash with leaders, Arsenal, which seriously dented their title hopes. It was Jack Ball who grabbed two of the trebles, while Mark Hooper added the third, and even Ellis Rimmer caught the bug, netting three in a 6–0 friendly win at Millmoor in a fund raising match for the impoverished home side. The crunch game with Arsenal was the one that simply had to be won, and the Sheffield fans

Mark Hooper

..The tragically sudden death of Mr. A. J. Dickinson came as a great shock to his colleagues on the board of directors, and to all supporters of the Wednesday club.

Mr. Dickinson had an intimate association with the management of the Wednesday club for half a century, and was universally esteemed in football circles, not only for his work for his own particular club, but for his valuable services on the Football Association Council, the League Management Committee, and the Sheffield and Hallamshire County Football Association.

We ask that our spectators will observe one minute's silence before the kick-off to-day, as a tribute of respect to one of the great figures of the game, who will be sadly missed but affectionately remembered.

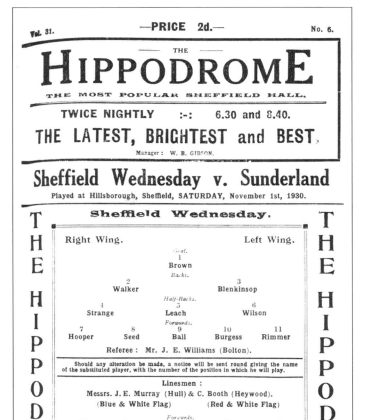

Vol. 31.　　　—PRICE 2d.—　　　No. 6.

THE
HIPPODROME
THE MOST POPULAR SHEFFIELD HALL.

TWICE NIGHTLY　:-:　6.30 and 8.40.
THE LATEST, BRIGHTEST and BEST.
Manager : W. B. GIBSON.

Sheffield Wednesday v. Sunderland
Played at Hillsborough, Sheffield, SATURDAY, November 1st, 1930.

Sheffield Wednesday.

Right Wing.　　　　　　　Left Wing.

Goal.
1
Brown

Backs.
2　　　　　　　　　　3
Walker　　　　　　Blenkinsop

Half-Backs.
4　　　　5　　　　6
Strange　　Leach　　Wilson

Forwards.
7　　8　　9　　10　　11
Hooper　Seed　Ball　Burgess　Rimmer

Referee : Mr. J. E. Williams (Bolton).

Should any alteration be made, a notice will be sent round giving the name of the substituted player, with the number of the position in which he will play.

Linesmen :
Messrs. J. E. Murray (Hull) & C. Booth (Heywood).
(Blue & White Flag)　　(Red & White Flag)

Forwards.
16　　15　　14　　13　　12
Connor　Leonard　Gurney　Urwin　Robinson, G.

Half-Backs.
19　　18　　17
Andrews　McDougall　Clunas

Backs.
21　　　　　　20
Shaw　　　　　Murray

Goal.
22
Robinson, R.

Left Wing.　　　　　　　Right Wing.

6.30　　　　Sunderland.　　　　8.40

Harry Burgess

turned out in force to give Wednesday their biggest crowd of the season. The build up to the game was marred, however, by the death of director, Arthur Dickinson, one of the clubs greatest administrators. He had served the Owls for almost forty years, the majority of which saw him hold the post of secretary-manager. During this time, Wednesday attained league status, moved from Olive Grove to Hillsborough, and had won several major honours. A minute's silence was observed before the game, with the week looking set for a happy ending, as Ball put the Owls ahead early in the first half. Unfortunately, it wasn't to be, for Lambert struck twice, with the winner coming just five minutes from time. This pushed Wednesday down to third place and extended Arsenal's lead at the top of the table. Consecutive wins then saw the Owls hit the front after an astonishing scoring burst which brought them 24 goals in only four games! It seems fitting that Wednesday took over the top spot after the final game of the quartet, at home to Birmingham, when, despite having missed a penalty, the Owls recorded their biggest ever league win in the club's long history.

After a spell in second place, the Owls moved back to the summit in mid January, a week after hitting six in a runaway FA Cup victory at Gateshead. Over a period of several weeks they continued to trade positions in the race for the championship with Arsenal; while, away from the league, Wednesday's chances of Cup glory ended at Oakwell. On the transfer front, custodian Jack Breedon arrived from their cup victors, with George Stephenson and Tom Davison signing from Derby County. Bob Gregg, a regular in the club's '28–'29 title winning team, left Hillsborough, and that recent darling of the faithful, Jack Allen, was placed on the transfer list after failing to win his place back from Jack Ball. Unfortunately, the title run-in proved to be an anti-climax for Wednesday fans, for three straight defeats saw them slip behind the top two. They never recovered, winning only five of their final thirteen games, finishing a massive fourteen points behind the eventual champions, Arsenal. The loss of key-man, Jimmy Seed, for several of those games was a contributory factor in this poor finish. However, the task of winning three titles in a row was always going to be a difficult feat, and Owls fans surely couldn't have been too disappointed with 102 league goals and a final position of third.

1931–32
THIRD AGAIN DESPITE KEY DEPARTURES

Despite finishing in third place in 1930–31, the immediate close season was an unhappy time for Wednesday. Three players who had played vital roles in the two recent championship successes became unavailable in contrasting circumstances. Without doubt the biggest blow came, when, in a shock move, inspirational captain, Jimmy Seed announced he was leaving to take up the vacant manager's position at Clapton Orient, at the tender age of thirty. The inside-forward would prove to be almost irreplaceable; and to compound matters, a few days later it was announced that International half-back, Billy Marsden had been forced to hang up his boots after failing to recover from an injury he'd received playing for his Country. The FA agreed to pay Marsden £700 compensation, with Wednesday receiving £2,000—woefully inadequate sums considering the loss. To complete a trio of departures, prolific scorer Jack Allen left for Newcastle in a move which would seem almost incomprehensible to modern eyes; as he'd netted 90 times for the Owls in just 109 games. Jack Ball, however, was now in possession of the number nine shirt, and the club allowed Allen to move to pastures new. Reserve goalie, Dick Mellors also left, with the one signing of note being Horace Burrows, arriving from Mansfield Town. Meanwhile, a backroom change saw Joe McClelland appointed as assistant manager to Bob Brown.

The loss of so many top class performers looked to have made little difference to the Owls when the season kicked off, as they made one of the most sensational starts ever seen in league football. They began with a 6–1 romp at Blackburn, with George Stephenson netting four. Eleven goals then went into the opposition net in two Hillsborough games. A brilliant 3–2 win followed at Chelsea, after Wednesday had found themselves two behind after just fourteen minutes. This saw the Owls comfortably settled in first place, with an astonishing twenty goals to their tally. The bubble then burst with a four goal mauling at Middlesbrough. This was followed by four consecutive away losses, culminating in an afternoon of disaster at Goodison Park where the legendary centre-forward, Dixie Dean plundered five goals, as Everton won 9–3. This debacle in Liverpool pushed Wednesday to seventh place, though, within five games, they were back in second spot after having overcome the Blades in a thrilling derby clash.

Just before the festive fixtures, Bob Brown entered the transfer market to compete the signing of three new players. The first to arrive was Wilf Aspinall, followed soon after by Derby County's Gavin Malloch and Hull City's William Gowdy—the latter signing on Christmas Eve. By this time Arsenal had become the first team to win at Hillsborough,

The Football Association.

Patron - His Majesty the King.
President - Sir Charles Clegg, J.P.

Marsden Trust Fund Match.

F.A. XI.
(Canadian Tour Players)
v.
A Combined XI. of
SHEFFIELD
(Wednesday & United F.C's.)

To be played on the Ground of the
SHEFFIELD WEDNESDAY F.C.,
Hillsborough, Sheffield,
On MONDAY. 28th SEPT., 1931.

Kick-off 5.30 o'clock.

Gavin Malloch

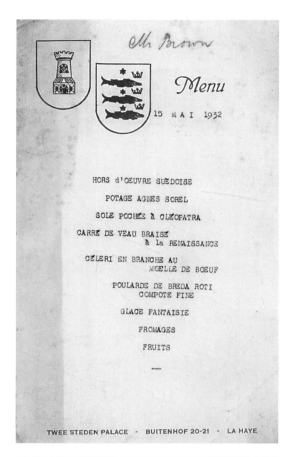

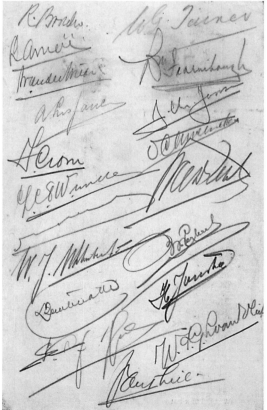

Signed dinner menu from the tour of Holland

while a farcical home game with Manchester City went ahead despite the pitch being frozen solid and covered with more sand than there is on Blackpool beach, as well as being shrouded in dense fog (it took a lot to get a game called off in those days). City caused a minor sensation by wearing boots with rubber soles and studs, and the major aim—to avoid breaking bones—was thankfully achieved by both teams, with the honours even. The New Year saw Harry Millership switched to centre-forward for the first time, to which he responded with a hat-trick in the next home game with Blackburn. The Cup trail began with a tricky tie at White Hart Lane, with a second half equaliser from Rimmer bringing the Londoners back to Hillsborough. There the Owls finished the job. The next round saw a little bit of history made as, for the first time in the club's history, two players netted hat-tricks in a competitive game. However, the Cup run ended in a replay with those perennial foes, Chelsea, with over 60,000 watching Wednesday exit at the last sixteen stage.

Back in the league another mini revival was needed to boost Wednesday after they had slumped to tenth position. However, a shocking home loss to West Brom effectively ruled out any hope of a title challenge. Somewhat typically for Wednesday, they then hit top form when the cause seemed lost; and a quartet of wins pushed them to third, after five second half strikes at home to West Ham saw them pass the fifty goal mark at home in league football. Meanwhile, away from the action, reserve utility player, Charlie Wilson was sold to the Division One basement club, Grimsby Town. The Owls remained in the top three for the rest of the season and, in the final analysis, they finished only six points behind the champions, Everton, who, significantly, had completed the double over Wednesday.

The Owls did manage to finish the season with some silverware, however, for in the final of the County Cup, Barnsley were beaten 3–0 at Bramall Lane. This was a game which saw Mark Hooper pick up an injury which would see him miss the trip to Maine Road five days later. Normally this would not have been of any real significance; however, in Hooper's case it meant he missed his first game in Wednesday colours since 31st March 1928—a remarkable run of 189 consecutive appearances. Finally, at the season's end, the Owls embarked on their first ever tour of Holland, where a Hague select eleven were vanquished 8–1, before a game with Austrian side, Nicholson, ended 2–2 to complete another high scoring season.

1932–33
TITLE CHANCE SLIPS AWAY

For the first time in several years the pre-season mood was one of apprehension amongst the Hillsborough faithful, with concern expressed as to how an ageing team could maintain the club's position as one of the powers in English football. Bob Brown was confident about his team's chances, however, and promised not to his alter his tactics of 'pursuing a forward policy'. Despite the concerns, Wednesday retained all but one of the previous season's professionals, adding only two senior players during the summer months. Centre-forward, Alex Law arrived from Scottish junior club, Fauldhouse; but the crucial signing proved to be that of inside-forward, Ronnie Starling, who was brought from Newcastle United and became a capable successor to the much-missed Jimmy Seed. Only one departure of note took place, with Tom Davison signing for Coventry City; though there was sadness in August '32 when Wednesday director, Sir William Clegg passed away. Along with his brother, Charles, he had played for the club in the 1870s, and, after being elected in 1899, he'd served on the Wednesday board for 33 years.

Wednesday experienced a mixed start to the new season, and, with half a dozen games played, found themselves in mid-table after failing to earn a single point away from home. The Hillsborough game with United proved to be one of the best ever derby meetings, with fortunes fluctuating rapidly before the spoils were shared in a six goal thriller. Then, after losing a fourth consecutive away game, the side suddenly started to click, coinciding with a return to form of Harry Burgess. A terrific run of nine unbeaten games saw the Owls soar to second position, which, in this purple patch, included five and six goal salvos at Wolves and Aston Villa respectively. This change of fortune, combined with a still unbeaten home record, meant that a Championship challenge was certainly on the cards. The Christmas period brought five points out of six, with the Boxing Day game at Maine Road seeing Wednesday amazingly awarded their tenth penalty of the season—Jack Ball having successfully converted seven of the spot kicks. The first game of the New Year captured the imagination of the Sheffield public, as reigning champions and league leaders, Arsenal visited Hillsborough for a 'must win' game for Wednesday. Such was the enormous interest, that a new record league crowd packed into the ground and were rewarded when a titanic struggle ended in the Owls' favour, cutting the Gunners' lead at the top to only three points.

Wednesday then came back down to earth with a bump, when, in a Saltergate replay, their second division neighbours, Chesterfield, netted four times in the first twenty five minutes to knock the Owls out of the Cup. To fill the gap caused by the Cup exit, the Owls welcomed the famous

Wednesday v. United

amateur outfit, The Corinthians, to Hillsborough. However, a desperately low crowd showed the enthusiasm for these fixtures was no longer there, and this proved to be the southerners last visit to Sheffield. Meanwhile, in the First Division, Wednesday fans were the top dogs in the City of Sheffield, as their team won at Bramall Lane for the first time since the Great War, to maintain their title challenge. Changes then took place in the Owls' backroom staff, as George Irwin took over from Sam Powell as assistant trainer. On the playing side, Vic Wright went to Rotherham United along with a fee, as George Bratley arrived in exchange. Victory over Wolves in early March took the Owls to within two points of Arsenal, with a game in hand, but the win was costly, for influential wing-half Tony Leach was sent off after clashing with Hartill, and was subsequently banned for 28 days by the Football Association. The Owls were thus forced to rearrange their back line, with the out-of-favour attacker, Harry Millership, tried out at half-back. Bratley was given his debut game, and even Billy Smith was brought in from the cold for his first game in almost eighteen months. The disruption seemed to have an effect on Wednesday and, much to their fans acute disappointment, the last nine games of the campaign yielded only six points out of a possible eighteen, with one solitary victory and three draws.

Any chance of the title was lost in April. Wednesday were beaten 4–2 by Arsenal in a crunch Good Friday meeting at Highbury, before Aston Villa became the only club to win at Hillsborough during the campaign. With the chance of the championship gone, Wednesday picked up some consolation silverware by winning the next best thing—the Scunthorpe Hospital Cup! After triumphing 2–1 on the East Coast, the Owls then embarked on a whistle-stop mid-week tour of Ireland, where 15,000 gathered in Belfast to see Linfield beaten 2–0. Forty eight hours later, the Dublin club, Shelbourne were defeated 4–1 before a similar sized crowd, all of whom were delighted by the 'clever play' of their English visitors. The Owls then rushed back to Blighty to complete their season at Liverpool. A feeling of frustration must surely have been prevalent, for Wednesday finished only seven points behind champions, Arsenal, despite an awful finish to a season in which the Owls' destiny had been in their own hands but had slipped agonisingly from their grasp.

Ellis Rimmer, Jack Brown, Leach, Mark Hooper

1933–34
RECORD CROWD FOR HILLSBOROUGH
BUT THE BOB BROWN ERA COMES TO A CLOSE

After coming so close to a third league title in five years, manager Bob Brown made only minor alterations to his squad. Thomas Brolly from the Irish side, Glenavon, was the only senior player arriving at Hillsborough during the close season, with departures including George Stephenson and William Gowdy. As the economic depression of the times hit football hard, the club's annual accounts showed a worrying drop of twenty percent in gate receipts. The most significant event of the summer, however, came in July, when Bob Brown was devastated by the sudden death of his wife as they holidayed in Blackpool. This was to have a far reaching effect on the history of the club.

The Owls kicked off the season with a fine win at Manchester City, before consecutive home defeats were followed by a single goal loss at Villa. This put Wednesday in eighteenth place in the early tables. The ship was steadied somewhat with a tremendous win over the Cup holders at Everton; however, soon after this the club was rocked when manager, Bob Brown announced he was resigning his post due to ill health—with assistant manager Joe McClelland taking temporary charge. The meticulous Brown originally joined Wednesday around the turn of the century, scouting in his native North East and then later working in the club's offices. His career had taken off after joining Southern League, Portsmouth as secretary-manager. After winning two titles he eventually returned to Hillsborough in the 1920 close season following a short spell at Gillingham. Brown's legacy as arguably the club's greatest professional manager, was three Championship successes and the signing of several of the best players ever to play for Wednesday, such as Ernest Blenkinsop, Jimmy Trotter and Jimmy Seed. However, after the tragic loss of his wife, Brown was never the same, and after falling ill early in the season he decided his only course of action was to give up his post and end one of the most successful eras in the club's history. Sadly, Brown would live for only a further eighteen months, as in March 1935 he collapsed while on a scouting mission for Chelsea and died in hospital. After accepting his resignation, the Owls immediately tried to persuade Charlton boss, Seed, to return to Sheffield. He refused, however, and it would be almost three months before a new man was appointed to the post.

Back in the league, Wednesday were struggling to get out of the bottom six. A home defeat to United didn't help the mood of the blue and white side of the City, though a 6–1 County Cup win at Barnsley was a welcome confidence boost. Only five wins in their opening seventeen games, however, meant that Wednesday were in deep trouble at the foot of the table, with relegation clouds forming. The Owls were a rudderless

Training at Cleveleys

ship and matters were not helped in November when the club announced that St Johnstone secretary-manager, Thomas Muirhead, was to be the new Sheffield Wednesday boss. Unfortunately, the Owls hadn't actually received the all-clear from the Scottish club, and nineteen days after his 'appointment' an emergency meeting in Perth finally saw the move fall through. A fortnight later Wednesday did finally get their man, when the Aston Villa player, Billy Walker was appointed manager—a month after he'd brought his Villa Park playing career to a close. To say that Walker made a favourable impact would be a gross understatement, as Wednesday immediately won four consecutive games to begin an unbeaten run which stretched to an amazing sixteen league and cup matches. The new boss started with a splendid win at Anfield, and, by the Christmas period, Wednesday had moved up to mid-table. Walker then entered the transfer market, bringing Manchester United centre-forward, Neil Dewar to Hillsborough in exchange for Jack Ball, who returned from whence he came. Dewar certainly made an impression, for 24 hours after signing for Wednesday he created a minor sensation by eloping and marrying the daughter of a Manchester United director!

With league worries behind them, Wednesday turned to the Cup, where a win at Millmoor and a replay success over Oldham set up a last sixteen clash with Manchester City. The interest in the tie was quite phenomenal and resulted in an all-time Hillsborough record crowd of 72,841, with many thousands locked out. The Owls, however, could only draw the home game, and would have to wait another season for Cup glory after losing 2–0 in the subsequent replay. Off the field, the Hillsborough faithful were shocked by the sensational move of Ernest Blenkinsop. Dubbed the 'Prince of half backs', Blenkinsop was sold for a large fee to Division One rivals, Liverpool, after playing in over 400 hundred games for Wednesday, and gaining sixteen England caps. After exiting the Cup, the Owls' league form suffered, with a 5–1 debacle at Bramall Lane as the nadir. Victory at Chelsea, however, saw a rise to the dizzy heights of fifth place, before a poor run up to the end of the season saw the Owls finish outside of the top ten for the first time in six years. Other events of note saw George Nevin transferred back from Manchester United, and Wednesday again stricken by tragedy when trainer Chris Craig (who had been at Hillsborough ten years) passed away after a short illness. After retaining the Scunthorpe Hospital Cup, then winning the Scarborough version and finally lifting the County Cup, Wednesday wrapped up their season in Scandinavia. In completing a whistle-stop twelve day tour, the Owls won all but one of their four games in Sweden, netting 22 goals in the process, before Copenhagen were beaten 7–0 and the Danish national side hit for six.

Manager Billy Walker

SHEFFIELD WEDNESDAY FOOTBALL CLUB

Official Souvenir Handbook
For Season 1933-34

RECORD OF ACHIEVEMENTS
PLAYERS :: FIXTURES
LEAGUE TABLES
&c.

Compiled by the

SHEFFIELD WEDNESDAY SUPPORTERS CLUB

1934–35
CUP GLORY

After the relative disappointment of the previous campaign, boss Billy Walker resisted the temptation to make wholesale changes to the playing personnel, and only a handful of transfer moves were undertaken in the close season. The first to arrive was the St Johnstone winger, Joe Brown. Soon after this another of the key players from the Owls Championship seasons left, with Tony Leach departing to Newcastle after 260 appearances for Wednesday. Also on his way out was Tommy Jones, who finally admitting defeat in trying to displace stalwart, Mark Hooper from the left wing. On the verge of the season, Wednesday then managed to pull the proverbial rabbit out of the hat, when, in a sensational move, they signed Aston Villa's Scottish International full-back, Joe Nibloe—with George Beeson moving to Villa Park as part of the deal. The only other transfers of note saw Wilf Sharp arrive from Airdrie, with Harry Nicholls coming in from non-league Hednesford Town. There was also good news on the financial front, as the annual accounts showed a healthy profit. From a present day point of view, they also interestingly revealed that only one half of Wednesday's net income of £27,000 was needed to pay the wage bill.

The opening game of the season, at home to Stoke, saw the Owls launch a new large-style match programme. While on the field, Wednesday made a fine start by netting four goals. Victory at Chelsea four days later put Wednesday top of the first tables published, but then a run of five defeats in the next six away trips ensured the Owls would not maintain their lofty position. In addition to league commitments Wednesday made a first-ever visit to Halifax for a benefit game, and then crashed to a shock County Cup loss at Millmoor. Back in the league, Wednesday found themselves stranded in mid table. For despite boasting an unbeaten home record their aforementioned away form failed to improve, with consecutive 4–0 away defeats at Huddersfield and at Villa no doubt leaving manager Walker to scratch his head. Off the pitch, assistant manager Joe McClelland tendered his resignation; while centre-forward, Jack Palethorpe, arrived from Preston North End, and youngster, Jack Surtees was signed after a successful trial period.

In early December Wednesday welcomed an Austrian touring team to Hillsborough, with three second-half goals ensuring that the Owls were the first side to beat the visitors on their English tour. Meanwhile, a good Christmas period, which saw Wednesday rise to fifth place, included a splendid Palethorpe treble in a 4–0 win at Birmingham. A single goal win over Manchester City then moved the Owls up another place, to generate talk of a possible title challenge in and around Sheffield 6. While progress was being made in the league, the Owls were also progressing through to the last sixteen of the Cup, where a trip to Norwich City led directly to one of the strangest games ever to be staged at Hillsborough. Home for the Canaries at this time was 'The Nest', a small and rather cramped enclosure which would have certainly come as something of a culture shock to the Owls players. In an attempt to overcome their unfamiliarity, Wednesday arranged a special practice match on the Tuesday afternoon before the Cup tie. The unemployed were invited to attend and to line up, three and four deep, on all sides of a shorter and narrower pitch. Surrounded by this human wall, the Wednesday players certainly felt cramped, with the forwards tending to get in each others way, so that most goal efforts soared well over the bar. However, with manager, Billy Walker sitting in the scorebox barking instructions through a microphone, the players slowly grew accustomed to their surroundings, and at the end of the trial he was able to declare that the game had exactly answered his purpose. This somewhat bizarre dress rehearsal must have helped, however, for in difficult conditions Wednesday beat City 1–0, thanks to a late goal from Rimmer. Incidentally, just before the Norwich game the local press reported that the Owls were talking to the protégé, 15-year-old forward, Thomas Lawton, and that he looked set to sign once he was old enough (obviously he didn't sign, for thankfully—as we all know now—Tommy Lawton never really made the grade, did he?)

Match programme v. Grimbsy Town

Wednesday v. Manchester City

Wolves v. Wednesday, FA Cup—Palethorpe heads for goal

As Cup fever grew, the Owls maintained a lofty league position, so that the double still looked to be a possibility, especially after Arsenal were beaten at Hillsborough to see Wednesday through to the semi-final. One transfer which did go through then was of Harry Burgess to Chelsea, while there was sadness at the news of the death of ex-manager, Bob Brown. The Cup semi-final against Burnley took place at Villa Park. A superb display from Wednesday saw a comfortable 3–0 win recorded, with two goals from Rimmer and one from Palethorpe securing a first-ever visit to Wembley Stadium. Back in the league, Arsenal were pulling clear at the summit, with third position certainly on for Wednesday. This proved to be their final placing as they completed the season unbeaten at home.

Cup Final preparations dominated everyone's thoughts, however, and this led to an event which could never occur in modern times. With well over 10,000 applications received for Final tickets, Billy Walker's scheme to resolve the problem of a fair distribution required that all the requests be placed in three large tubs in the boardroom. To ensure absolute impartiality, two men from the Sheffield Institute for the Blind were then asked to make the draw! Five days before the Cup Final, Wednesday and West Brom played out a dress rehearsal at The Hawthorns, where youngster, Jackie Robinson made his debut for the Owls in a 1–1 draw. The final was a close encounter, with goals from Palethorpe and Hooper ensuring that with only three minutes remaining the teams were deadlocked at two goals apiece. Ellis Rimmer then dramatically struck twice in the final moments to bring the Cup to Sheffield for the first time in 28 years, triggering wild celebrations back in the city. After the Final, the Owls still had two league games to play and at the last home fixture the Cup was paraded to the delight of the assembled spectators. Two days later, Wednesday lost a Charity match at Grimsby, and then embarked on a two week tour of Denmark which resulted in several large victories and some remarkable attendances (a record 30,000 crowd at a game in Copenhagen). On the way home, Wednesday stopped off in Paris to beat Racing Club 4–0, and brought to an end a long and ultimately successful season.

Sheffield Wednesday – Cup Winners 1935

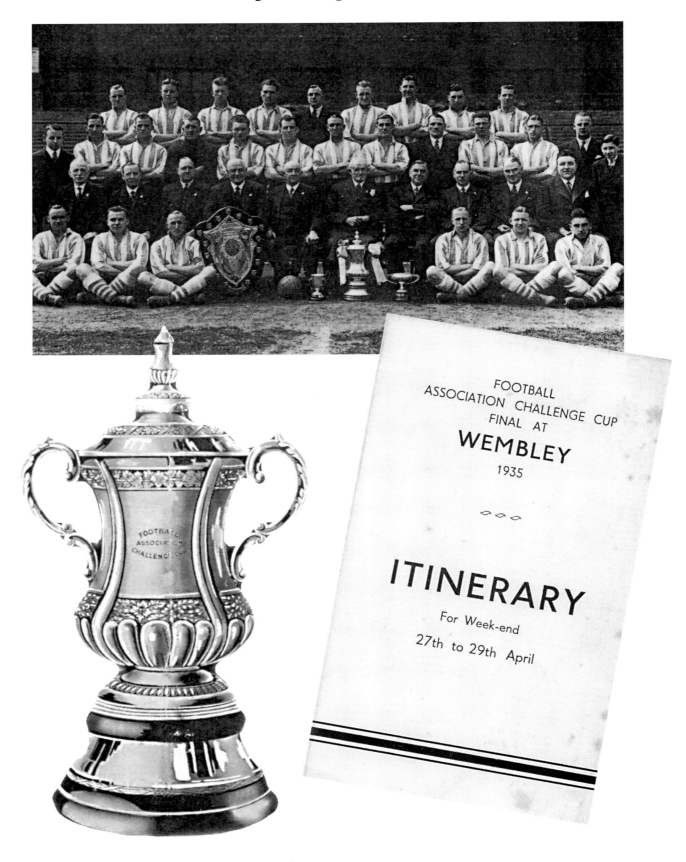

FOOTBALL
ASSOCIATION CHALLENGE CUP
FINAL AT
WEMBLEY
1935

⬦ ⬦ ⬦

ITINERARY
For Week-end
27th to 29th April

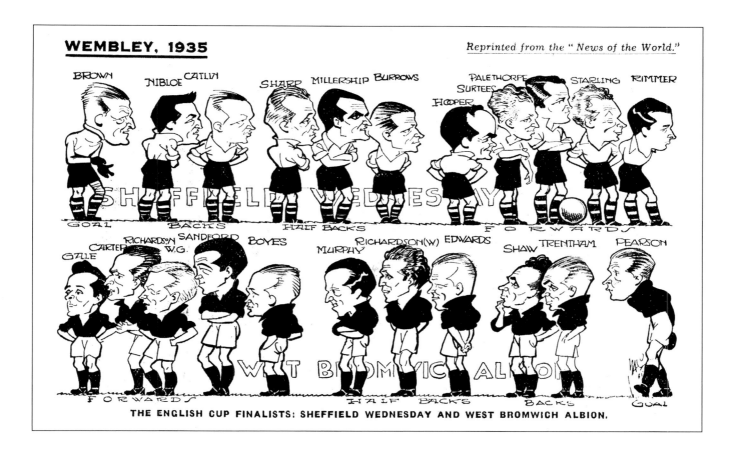

WEMBLEY, 1935

Reprinted from the " News of the World."

BROWN — NIBLOE — CATLIN — SHARP — MILLERSHIP — BURROWS — HOOPER — PALETHORPE — SURTEES — STARLING — RIMMER

GOAL — BACKS — HALF BACKS — FORWARDS

GALE — CARTER — RICHARDSON W.G. — SANDFORD — BOYES — MURPHY — RICHARDSON (W) — EDWARDS — SHAW — TRENTHAM — PEARSON

FORWARDS — HALF BACKS — BACKS — GOAL

THE ENGLISH CUP FINALISTS: SHEFFIELD WEDNESDAY AND WEST BROMWICH ALBION.

'By Jove old boy—it's the FA Cup!'

1935–36
AFTER THE LORD MAYOR'S SHOW

With the FA Cup safely in the trophy room, Wednesday seemed content with their playing staff. As a result there was minimal transfer activity in the close season, with players mostly departing from Hillsborough. However, the first move of the summer saw Wednesday finally capture the signature of Preston North End inside-forward, George Bargh, a player they'd unsuccessfully tried to sign during the previous season. The only other arrival must surely have puzzled the Wednesday support, for the Manchester City reserve winger, Percival was signed even though he had been unable to break into City's team because of the form of Ernie Toseland (who, somewhat ironically, would be signed by the Owls in 1939). Meanwhile, another link with the Wednesday championship sides of the late '20s was severed when Alf Strange was allowed to leave for Bradford Park Avenue on a free transfer. Alex Law, Jack Breedon and Thomas Brolly also left the club, and, in August, the club announced plans for a proposed share issue of 700 £10 shares, the proceeds of which would be used to pay off a £3,300 mortgage and £3,700 debentures.

When the eagerly awaited season finally kicked off, the Owls made a perfect start with a superb victory at Villa Park. This was followed by a point gained at Bolton. However, instead of then returning to play their first home league game, Wednesday hosted a double-header, cross-border clash with Glasgow Rangers. This saw the Scottish giants hold the Owls

at Hillsborough, before winning 2–0 at Ibrox Park two weeks later. The Owls first two home games were then drawn, before Huddersfield became the first team to win at Hillsborough since April 1934. This left Wednesday in a disappointing mid-table position. Off the pitch, Wednesday transferred Bernard Oxley to Plymouth for a large fee, while Mansfield Town full-back, Jack Ashley, and Wolves defender, Richard Rhodes, arrived in Sheffield. Defeat at Portsmouth came after a 2–0 lead was lost; but then a hat-trick of home wins lifted the Owls to sixth place before they travelled to Highbury to face the home side in the Charity Shield. There, in front of a poor crowd of only 13,000, a strike from Neil Dewar was enough to secure the trophy for the first and only time in Wednesday's history.

Winning the Charity Shield seemed to have an unfortunate and adverse effect on Wednesday's form, for in the following three games they managed to concede seventeen goals and slumped into the lower reaches of the First Division. It was quickly becoming apparent that action was needed if Wednesday were to challenge for honours, and therefore it came as something of a surprise when Jack Palethorpe— who had scored in the Cup Final just seven months earlier— was sold to Villa. This left Dewar as the club's only recognised No. 9. The Owls then undertook a rather ill-advised trip to northern France for a Sunday afternoon

Manager, Billy Walker, and Chairman, W. Turner, address the Supporters' Club

friendly with a Ligue du Nord representative team. This required Wednesday to leave immediately after a stormy home game with Chelsea, and then travel non-stop in order to fulfil the Continental engagement less that 24 hours later. The subsequent 3–2 defeat in Lille probably showed that Wednesday had, in fact, bitten off more than they could chew in arranging such a bizarre fixture. By the end of the year alarm bells were starting to ring, with Wednesday only two places off the foot of the table—despite a comprehensive Christmas holiday win over Villa. League worries were put aside, however, as Wednesday started their defence of the Cup; though it needed extra time in a replay to see off lowly Crewe, before Newcastle forced a draw at Hillsborough. The mid-week St James' Park return match was played on a mud bath of a pitch, with the Owls unable to voice any real complaints about a 3–1 defeat. This left them with only Division One safety to aim for, in an increasingly poor campaign.

In an attempt to boost their fortunes, the club secured the transfer of West Brom's International inside-right, Joe Carter. Within days, however, the deal hit a snag when it seemed Carter was unfit to play after injuring his knee in an accident at home. The transfer was officially cancelled six days after

his 'signing', when his old club admitted that Carter had actually been injured before leaving for Sheffield and would need a cartilage operation to remedy the problem. The Owls then switched to 'Plan B', signing Thomas Grosvenor from Birmingham City, Charles Luke from Huddersfield Town, and the Swansea Town captain, Harry Hanford. After a brilliant fightback from three goals down earned the Owls a point at home to Brentford, they travelled to St Andrews where heavy snow caused the match to be abandoned in the first half; with the only real entertainment occurring as spectators ran onto the pitch to start an impromptu snowball fight which then spread into the stands!

Before Easter a mini revival had seemingly lifted Wednesday out of immediate danger, but the table was so congested that a 5–0 defeat at Ayresome Park on Easter Monday saw the Owls drop into one of the two relegation places for the first time, with just five games left to play. Thankfully, a tremendous 3–0 win at Stoke followed, while a point secured in the final home game was enough to ensure safety; though this was not enough to stop the post-mortem that followed a bitterly disappointing campaign. At the season's end, Wednesday embarked on their now traditional tour of Denmark, and duly maintained their unbeaten record in Scandinavia.

Ted Catlin

1936–37
NO ESCAPE THIS TIME

After their brush with relegation in the previous campaign, manager Billy Walker promised the Owls fans that they would see a new 'all-up' attack in the forthcoming season which would bear comparison with the tactics used in both championship winning seasons of the late 1920s. To turn the club's fortunes round, Walker made several forays into the transfer market in an attempt to find the elusive winning formula. The first arrival, however, was not a player but ex-United star, Tom Sampy, who joined as player-coach to the 'A' team—with Wednesday full-back, Tom Walker acting as trainer. With veteran Jack Brown coming to the end of a glittering career, the Owls signed not one but two new goalies, with teenager Roy Smith arriving from Selby Town, and Derek Goodfellow coming in from Gateshead. Other newcomers included Irish International, James McCambridge and 17-year-old Mansfield Town forward, Allenby Driver; while Sharp, Bruce and Bargh all left Hillsborough for pastures new.

Wednesday's new attacking formation bore fruit in the opening game of the new season, as Sunderland were put to the sword at Hillsborough. However, defensive frailties were soon exposed, as fourteen goals were conceded in the next four outings; including four in an astonishing ten goal home game with Everton in which both defences seemed to have a short holiday for ninety minutes. The Owls then embarked on a nine-game spell without a win, and saw them drop into the bottom four. This triggered further transfer activity, with the surprise move of Jack Surtees to Forest. Meanwhile, there was trouble afoot behind the scenes, as Grosvenor, McCambridge and Rhodes were all put on the transfer list and dropped out of the first team picture to further deplete a struggling squad. After losing a County Cup tie at Barnsley, the Owls were boosted by a home win over Middlesbrough; but despite a splendid pre-Christmas goal bonanza against Manchester City, Wednesday started the New Year third from bottom of the First Division table.

Without doubt, a major problem lay in the crucial position of centre-forward. The likes of Jack Ball and Jack Palethorpe had not been adequately replaced, and when new signing, Albert Shelley, was given his debut early in January he became the sixth man to lead the Owls attack. Manager Walker was said to be actively seeking a new No. 9, but there was a major shock in store for Wednesday fans when, 24 hours after rejecting a huge bid from Arsenal for brilliant inside-forward Jackie Robinson, the Owls captain Ronnie Starling—who had led the club FA Cup success just eighteen months earlier—was sensationally sold to Aston Villa for a record club fee of £8,000. James McCambridge then departed to Hartlepool, and as the club tried to deflect criticism, Walker took an unusual step for the 1930s, of

Mark Hooper's contract with Sheffield Wednesday

arranging for a sports psychologist to lecture the players in an attempt to improve their mental toughness for the relegation scrap ahead. And although the gentleman in question was actually chaplain to two big London mental hospitals, there was no miracle cure for the Owls' ills; for after they had exited from the Cup at Goodison Park, Wednesday continued to just about keep their head above the waterline in the relegation zone.

A tremendous win over league leaders, Charlton, revived hopes of a move up the table. But a shocking five goal reverse at Grimsby, seven days later, quickly burst the bubble.

John Roy from Mansfield, and Crook Town winger, Tommy Ward, joined the club, but as deadline-day passed there was still no new centre-forward—despite the best efforts of Billy Walker, who had twice undertaken scouting trips north of the border. Back on the field, a crucial relegation clash with Bolton went the Owls' way, but a hat-trick of defeats followed; and, with only four games left to play, Wednesday disastrously dropped into the bottom two for the first time. The game at Stoke saw Webster become the ninth centre-forward to be tried out—but, on this issue, the horse had definitely bolted; and Wednesday's problem became glaringly apparent at the season's end when Neil Dewar finished top scorer with only ten goals to his name. A desperate home defeat to West Brom looked to have sealed their fate; but then four days later a first away win of the season in the return game kept hopes alive and set up the team for a trip to Maine Road. Unfortunately for Wednesday, Manchester City needed a win to secure the Championship, and in front of a 55,000 crowd it was obvious the Owls simply couldn't cope with the rampant home side as they crashed to a 5–1 defeat to confirm their relegation from the top flight after an eleven year tenure. The Owls wrapped up the season with a defeat at Huddersfield to finish four points from safety. To bring the curtain down on a truly miserable season, Wednesday then travelled to non-league Scunthorpe to defend the Hospital Cup—and promptly lost 3–0. Roll on the summer!

A Wednesday training session

ALMOST RELEGATED AGAIN AS WALKER DEPARTS

Manager, Billy Walker was a busy man in the transfer market as the Owls first season back in Division Two beckoned, with Newcastle United forward, Harry Ware, being the first player to sign on the dotted line. A week later, Grosvenor departed for Bolton Wanderers; and soon after this Sid Chedgzoy (whose father, Sam, played 300 times for Everton) arrived from Cheshire League champions, Runcorn. The other major transfer saw Neil Dewar sold back to Third Lanark (for a record fee for the Scottish League club). Off the field, trainer George Irwin left for Crystal Palace after four years service, with ex-player, Sam Powell, promoted to fill the vacancy. Meanwhile, the release of the annual accounts showed that despite relegation a large profit had been realised on the previous season (as opposed to a massive loss in '35–'36). Unfortunately, from the fans point of view, the main reason for the increase was that net transfer payments had dropped significantly as Wednesday sold high and bought low.

Hopes of a good start in their new surroundings were quickly dashed, when, after losing an opening day derby clash at Chesterfield, the Owls won only one of their first eight games and slumped to third from bottom in the Division Two table. During this period Wednesday signed centre-forward, Ernest Matthews, from Bury—a move probably triggered by the fact that Ware, the new forward, had failed to make an impression, and had proved to be a better half-back than goal scorer! Fred Walker arrived at Hillsborough after a trial period, while legendary keeper, Jack Brown, ended a mammoth fourteen season, 507-game association with the club when he joined Hartlepool United. On the same day, Wednesday sent a letter to the FA. This alleged Harry Ware had been punched off the ball by a Norwich City player in a home game played three days previously, and this had resulted in a broken jaw for the Owls' player. The month of September was certainly busy, for in addition to the above activity, the club was also fined two guineas by the FA for fielding the unregistered Curry at Aston Villa on the eighteenth of the month.

A goal from veteran Ellis Rimmer was enough to beat West Ham and set the fans up for the home derby with the Blades. Over 50,000, including the crew of HMS Sheffield, attended a game which was broadcast live across the 'Empire'. Unfortunately for those supporters wearing the blue and white favours it was another black day, as a solitary second-half goal condemned Wednesday to a painful home defeat. Three new players then joined the Owls, with Bill Pickering, Fred Lester and Cyril Walker all arriving at Hillsborough to bring aid to a side which had slipped to the bottom of the table after a 4–1 derby defeat at Oakwell in early November. However, a remarkable home win over Luton quickly hauled them off the bottom rung, though this was achieved without

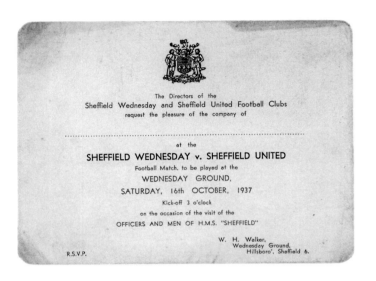

Horace Burrows

manager, Billy Walker, who days earlier had stunned the club by tendering his resignation, which had been accepted by the board. A managerless Owls then earned their first away win of the season at Coventry, and by the end of the year, Wednesday were just outside the bottom two, with a second successive relegation scrap on their hands. Off the field, Ware was sold to Norwich city—a somewhat surprising event given the fall-out from the Hillsboro' meeting earlier in the season; while Len Massarella joined from Denaby United.

In the final days of 1937 the Owls announced that after a six week search they had offered the post of manager to Notts County boss, Jimmy McMullan. He had accepted the position, and, after County had agreed to the move, he took up his new post early in the New Year—just in time to oversee the Cup tie with Burnley, which saw the Owls concede a last minute equaliser. They exited the competition in the replay, though in the league a mini revival was underway. This saw the Owls move into the safety of mid-table. However, four consecutive defeats, including the return game at Bramall Lane, pushed Wednesday back down into the bottom three, despite the arrival of Douglas Hunt from Barnsley. The first foray into the transfer market by McMullan had seen Luke sold to Blackburn. His next sale brought a wave of criticism to the club from the fans, for the

outstanding young inside-forward, George Drury, left for Arsenal. The move was a shock for the Wednesday faithful, whose side were fighting the drop. It also came as a surprise to the player, for he was unaware of a possible move until the day of the transfer. The club's shareholders threatened to arrange a protest meeting, and in order to placate the supporters, Wednesday immediately entered the market, signing Scottish International, Charlie Napier from Derby, and Bill Fallon from Notts County. The young goalie, Albert Morton, was also brought in, but it was the more senior signings who played a prominent role in the run in to the end of the season. Hunt hit the winner at Forest, and the same player grabbed a vital brace in Wednesday's final home game to lift them out of the bottom three; and the Owls went into the final game at Tottenham lying just one point outside the relegation places. An early goal from Fallon, however, settled the nerves, before Hunt struck early in the second half to put Wednesday two up. The home side quickly pulled a goal back, though the Owls hung on for a crunch victory which ensured they would not drop into regional football just twelve months after falling from the top flight. In the end Wednesday finished two points from the drop zone, and most supporters were more than happy to see the back of a season so full of drama and disappointment.

1938–39
A POINT AWAY FROM PROMOTION!

After the acute disappointment of the previous campaign, when the Owls finished in their lowest ever position in their history, the fans were generally not too optimistic about the chances of launching a promotion challenge in the forthcoming season. During the summer months three new players were secured by Jimmy McMullen, with Manchester North End inside-forward, Francis Dillon, being the first to sign. Arguably the best capture, however, was that of half-back, David Russell, who was snapped up from Scottish Cup winners, East Fife during a scouting trip north of the Border. The trio of signings was completed by Idris Lewis, who arrived from Swansea Town in exchange for Richard Rhodes. The only other departure of note involved Cyril Walker, who was signed by his old boss Billy Walker for the ambitious non-league club Chelmsford City.

A pre-season win over the Blades—one of many derby games arranged around the Country to celebrate fifty years of the Football League—put Owls fans in good heart. This was maintained as Wednesday shot to the top of the early tables after a five game unbeaten start to the season. The first defeat came in a local derby at Saltergate, and a run of three successive away losses then saw Wednesday drop out of the top six by mid October. During that month, Thurnscoe Victoria forward, Walter Aveyard, signed pro forms; while in the derby clash at Bramall Lane the two professional city sides served up a dismal 0–0 draw in front of over 45,000 fans. A home loss, soon after, to Newcastle saw Wednesday slip to mid table; but then, in a spell of twelve days, Douglas

Hunt took centre stage as he crashed home ten goals in two games. After having drawn at Millmoor in the County Cup, Hunt netted all four in the Hillsborough replay, before—in the home game with Norwich City—the centre-forward became the only Wednesday player ever to net a double hat trick in league soccer, when he grabbed six goals in a 7–0 romp against the Canaries.

After hitting Norwich for seven, the Owls netted another five at Newcastle. Goal scoring was now seemingly not a problem as Wednesday settled into a position just outside the promotion places. However, off the field, there were problems galore. Firstly, Len Massarella had to attend a Doncaster inquest after he knocked over and killed a cyclist. Thankfully for the Wednesday player, he was cleared of any blame after evidence was given that the cyclist had swerved into his path. The motor car was also prominent in a second unfortunate incident just before Christmas, when a vehicle containing the Wednesday duo, Ted Catlin and Bill Fallon, skidded in the heavy snow on Penistone Road near Wadsley Bridge, and crashed into a telegraph pole. Both players were rushed to hospital, and it was several weeks before the pair could return to first team action after recovering from their injuries. The New Year brought the FA Cup and a home tie with Southern League giants, Yeovil Town. They held the Owls to a draw at Hillsborough, before Wednesday saved their blushes by winning 2–0 in the West Country replay. The reward was another home draw against Chester, but once again Wednesday couldn't make the ground advantage count and

SHEFFIELD WEDNESDAY F.C. 1938-39

Back Row (left to right)—H. Hanford, D. A. Hunt, J. A. Ashley, D. O. Goodfellow, W. Millership, C. E. Napier, H. Burrows and S. Powell (trainer).
Front Row—D. Russell, F. Walker, I. Lewis, L. Massarella, A. E. Catlin, J. Robinson and W. J. Fallon.

Charlie Napier

another jackpot draw ensued. The second meeting also ended all-square. This led to a second replay at Maine Road, where goals from Robinson and Hunt secured a place in the last sixteen of the Cup. So far it had taken Wednesday five games to progress two rounds; and, amazingly, their fifth round clash with Chelsea also took three games to settle—in front of a combined attendance of over 160,000. After earning a goalless draw at Stamford Bridge, the home replay then ended all-square to set up a game at the neutral (!) venue of Highbury. There the Owls' lengthy cup exploits ended in a 3–1 defeat.

Back in the league, history was made in the home game with Bradford Park Avenue. For the first time in a game played in Sheffield, two players were sent off in a league fixture, as Avenue's Stabb and Hallard were dismissed within a minute of each other. Not surprisingly the Owls won that fixture, and at the beginning of March had climbed to third place, four points behind second placed Sheffield United. The meeting with the Blades was therefore of vital importance, and it was Wednesday who took the spoils at Hillsborough, thanks to a solitary goal from Fallon. After boosting their promotion credentials by signing Manchester City winger, Ernie Toseland, Wednesday would go on to lose only one of their final twelve games, and to inflict tremendous pressure on the top two. This reached a climax on the final day of the season, when victory over Spurs lifted Wednesday into second place, one point clear of the Blades. Unfortunately for Wednesday, their City rivals still had to complete their fixtures, and a week later there was a fair sprinkling of Wednesday fans at Bramall Lane to cheer on the visiting Tottenham side. There was not much to cheer for the Wednesday contingent, however, for United proceeded to crush their visitors 6–1, and to agonisingly snatch promotion from the Owls grasp at the last moment. Forty eight hours later, the Owls had a chance for revenge when they visited Bramall Lane in the final of the County Cup. The tie, however, ended 0–0, with the two sides eventually agreeing to keep the trophy for six months apiece. Yet Wednesday did finish the season with some silverware, as the Scunthorpe Hospital Cup was won once again. However, this was scant consolation in a season in which the Owls came within a whisper of regaining their top flight status.

Memory Match

It was more like a damp November day than a Spring afternoon when the old enemies met in the first ever full international fixture to be played at Hillsborough. As the rain lashed down, the murky Sheffield streets were brightened only by the appearance of those pockets of Scotsmen who had made the overnight trip from their homeland. Many sported the national headdress, the colourful Tam O'Shanter adorned with a pheasant's feather. Some had brought their national instrument of torture, otherwise known as the bagpipe. All roads led to Owlerton, and the tram company laid on no fewer than 107 special cars to ferry the supporters from the City Centre to a sodden Hillsborough ground. Pre-match predictions had pointed to a record crowd of over 60,000, but the rain drove the actual crowd down to a disappointing figure of 25,563.

England lined up as selected, captained by West Brom veteran, Jesse Pennington; while Wednesday were represented in the Scottish line-up by left-back, Jimmy Blair, winning the second of the two caps he earned during the time he was on the Owls' books. Not surprisingly the pitch looked as soft as a 'Yorkshire Pudding'. Indeed the rain ensured a slippery surface, and this was to become a factor in the astonishing game that was about to unfold. After the pre-match photographs had been taken, Pennington won the toss for England and elected to defend the Penistone Road end.

England were the quickest off the blocks and went ahead after just nine minutes when centre-forward, Jack Cock, netted from close range from a centre from Wallace. The home side hardly had time to celebrate their success, however, when, two minutes later, the Scots were level as Pennington failed to control the greasy ball, allowing Miller to drive home an equaliser. The crowd were buzzing as the amazing start to the game continued at a pace; for two minutes later, England surged back into the lead. This time it was Quantrill who netted, after Wallace had seen his fierce shot parried by Campbell in the Scotland goal. Incredibly a fourth goal soon followed, and this went to the visitors as the luckless Pennington again failed to control a cross, and allowed Wilson to easily net a second equaliser for the Jocks. After Campbell had saved bravely from Cock, it was Scotland who surged ahead for the first time as the half hour elapsed. The home side's creaky defence was again exposed as good interpassing inside the area led to Donaldson scoring with a cross shot. With five minutes of the half remaining, and to complete a miserable first half for the pre-game favourites, Scotland then scored yet again through Miller; leaving those Englishmen in the crowd stunned by the events of a sensational six goal period.

England turned out in fresh kit at the start of the second half, while the Scots brought their mud back out with them. However, it appeared it would need more than clean shirts to turn the game around for the homesters. England attacked with gusto from the whistle, but fine Scottish defending denied an early breakthrough—though hopes were raised of a comeback, when, after 58 minutes, Kelly shook off the attentions of Blair before crashing home a magnificent shot. England now threw everything at the 'Caledonians', and after 68 minutes it was four apiece as Morris's low drive just evaded Campbell's dive. The crowd then held its collective breath as a Kelly shot flew past Campbell, struck the inside of the post but then rebounded back into play. With seventeen minutes remaining, the prospect of what had seemed an unlikely recovery was completed, when superb wing play from Quantrill saw him centre for Bob Kelly to joyously drive a fifth England goal past the despairing Campbell. To rub salt into the wounds, Scotland were immediately reduced to ten men, when their custodian was forced to leave the field after having been injured attempting to stop the goal (Gordon taking his place before Campbell returned a few minutes later). The sound of bagpipes urged the Scots forward in the final minutes, and at the last gasp Hardy had to brilliantly save a superb Patterson effort in order to maintain the English advantage. This proved to be the final act of the game, and when the referee brought the curtain down there was tremendous cheering around the ground after one of the most sensational International games ever played on these shores.

England: Hardy (A. Villa), Longworth (Liverpool), Pennington (West Brom), Ducat (A. Villa), McCall (Preston), Grimsdell (Tottenham), Wallace (A. Villa), Kelly (Burnley), Cock (Chelsea), Morris (West Brom), Quantrill (Derby).

Scotland: Campbell (Partick), McNair (Celtic), Blair (The Wednesday), Bowie (Rangers), Low (Newcastle), Gordon (Rangers), Donaldson (Bolton), T. Miller (Liverpool), Wilson (Dunfermline), Patterson (Leicester), Troup (Dundee).

Twopence.

Souvenir Programme

OF THE

FORTY-FOURTH MATCH

BETWEEN

ENGLAND

AND

SCOTLAND

On the Ground of

THE WEDNESDAY CLUB,
HILLSBOROUGH, SHEFFIELD,

SATURDAY, APRIL 10th, 1920.

KICK OFF 3-30.

SHEFFIELD INDEPENDENT PRESS, LTD.

England
5
Scotland
4

Memory Match

FA Cup Semi-Final
Saturday 19th March 1921

J. Seed

Tottenham Hotspur 2
Preston North End 1

In the second FA Cup Semi-Final to be played on the Hillsborough ground, the Sheffield public were treated to a classic North versus South encounter, with the winners widely expected to go on to lift the trophy. The Southerners were favourites and, if the luck of the toss—taken an hour before the kick off—had decided the game, then Preston might well have gone straight back across the Pennines. For the Spurs captain, Grimsdell, won three times—for choice of shirts, choice of dressing rooms and choice of ends. Incidentally, the local press reporter wasn't too keen on the red shirts picked by Tottenham, for he thought 'they had evidently seen the wash tub too often'. Spurs were at full strength, while Preston—decked out in blue—had to bring novice winger, Knight into their side to replace the unfit Woodhouse.

Fifteen minutes before the kick-off a Preston supporter who had walked all the way from Deepdale appeared in front of the South Stand dressed in a natty white waistcoat, with a huge horse shoe slung around his neck. He began chatting to the fans but was suddenly pelted with oranges and coppers. For a full five minutes he became the victim of 'merry makers' before the local constabulary moved him to quieter quarters. It was estimated that a crowd of 55,000 were in the ground as kick-off approached (the official attendance was actually 44,668); and, after the Lord Major of Sheffield had taken his seat, the teams came onto the field of play.

A scrappy opening period saw Preston create the best chance, with a fierce, low shot from Roberts well saved by Hunter. The offside flag then denied Spurs on two occasions, as first, Banks and then Bliss found the rigging. As the second of these goals was being chalked off, an aggressive undercurrent to the game suddenly boiled to the surface, after the Preston full-back, Speaks, had punched Banks in the face and the teams began scuffling behind the ref's back. Soon after this, Dimmock fired against the bar. From the rebound the future Wednesday hero, Jimmy Seed, saw his effort also strike the bar and then rebound to safety. There was no doubt Spurs were dominating, and the Lancastrians were more than happy to hear the half-time whistle.

Tottenham didn't have to wait long for the breakthrough, however, for six minutes into the second half a superb three-man move ended with Bert Bliss driving the ball home. Just after this Spurs were denied a blatant penalty when Doolan knocked the ball down with his hand. Then, five minutes after his first strike, Bliss added a splendid second as he beat two men before crashing a rasping drive into the top corner of the net. Their opponents were now looking a well beaten side; yet, almost out of the blue, Preston pulled a goal back after 58 minutes through a Jeffries effort. This short-lived goal glut was then followed by a quiet passage of play, as Spurs reasserted their authority on the game, with North End striving in vain for a leveller. In the end Tottenham held on comfortably, and in Bliss and Dimmock had the best two players on the pitch. The pair would go on to grace the Stamford Bridge Final versus Wolves, which the Londoners would win 1–0, thanks to a strike from the aforementioned Dimmock.

Tottenham: Hunter, Clay, MacDonald, Smith, Walters, Grimsdell, Banks, Seed, Cantrell, Bliss, Dimmock

Preston North End: Causer, Doolan, Speak, Waddell, McCall, Mercer, Rawlings, Jeffries, Roberts, Quinn, Knight

Referee: Mr Forshaw

Memory Match

As soon as the FA Cup draw paired Wednesday and Barnsley, the build-up to the game began, with tremendous interest sparked in both camps. The Tykes had overcome Swindon to reach the second round (which in those days was equivalent to today's fourth round); while Wednesday had cruised past New Brighton to set up the Derby clash. When the big day arrived and the two sets of supporters made their way to Hillsborough, the conditions couldn't have been better, for the sun was shining brightly. At the ground a huge throng of supporters packed the enclosure, the massive interest in the game was such that thousands were locked out, as, with fifteen minutes still to go to the kick-off, the gates had to be closed. At the Leppings Lane end of the ground hundreds of spectators climbed onto the roof of the stands and advertisement hoardings, with many others attempting to get a glimpse of the game from the adjoining houses, and, just before the start, a hundred or so fans sprinted across the pitch to take up a position in front of the stand. As the kick-off approached there was an ominous swaying on the tightly packed Spion Kop, and it wasn't long before people on the verge of fainting were being passed down from the back to the front, to be dealt with by the Ambulance men.

These were the incredible scenes that greeted the players as they came out in front of what proved to be a new Sheffield record crowd of 66,103. Both sides wore black armbands as a show of respect to the recently deceased FA President, Lord Kinnaird. Fletcher, the Barnsley captain, won the toss. This meant Wednesday had to defend the Penistone Road end in the first half, with the sun and wind against them. The Owls had suffered a pre-match double blow, when Sam Taylor and Tom Brelsford both failed fitness tests; Barnsley remained unchanged. The home side started the better of the two teams, though early pressure brought little in the way of clear cut chances—and it was actually the Wednesday keeper, Teddy Davison, who had to make the first save, receiving a whitewash mark on his jersey after being trapped against a post by a visiting attacker. From the ensuing corner the ball went straight into the net. Fortunately for Wednesday, in those days a goal could not be scored direct from a corner and so the tie remained goalless. Tackles were flying in all over the field in a rousing encounter; however, when the first goal was scored, with three minutes of the half remaining, it went the way of the visitors, as Wednesday full-back, Jack Bellas, conceded a corner. Curran's flag kick was cleverly headed home by Baines, who promptly showed his joy by dashing down the field 'madly waving his arms about'. Wednesday then encamped in the Tykes half for the remaining minutes of the period, but at the interval it was still 1–0 to the men from Barnsley.

With the wind in their favour the Owls went straight on the attack in search of an equaliser, and within five minutes of the restart it duly arrived from the boot of Andy Smailes. A cross from 'Darkie' Lowdell was mis-kicked high into the air by the Barnsley back, Beaumont, and when the ball came down there was an almighty scramble near the post before it was despatched into the net. The identity of the scorer became known only when Wednesday's inside-forward was congratulated by his ecstatic team mates. The goal spurred both sides on to greater effort and the game became an end-to-end encounter, with the Reds giving as good as they got. Ten minutes into the half, the crowd erupted when the Owls grabbed a second goal, as Lowdell again got away down the right before centring. Barnsley keeper Gale ran out to collect the bouncing ball, but Lowdell was following up and promptly charged the custodian who subsequently dropped the ball. With Lowdell and Gale in a heap on the floor, Sid Binks scented an opportunity and dashed in; and before the Barnsley defenders realised what had happened, he'd driven the ball into an empty net from around twelve yards distance. Play then became somewhat stormy, with the Owls captain, George Wilson, carrying on a running battle with Halliwell, the Tykes forward. This only calmed down when the latter was severely reprimanded by the referee. As the game entered its final five minutes the visitors piled on the pressure, winning several corners in the process, one of which saw Davison having to save brilliantly from Halliwell. However, the Owls managed to hold on, and as the final whistle was blown hundreds of spectators invaded the pitch from all sides to pat the Wednesday men on the back for their tremendous efforts in securing a place in the last sixteen of the Cup.

Wednesday: Davison, Bellas, Blenkinsop, Kean, Wilson, Sykes, Williams, Lowdell, Binks, Smailes, Henshall

Barnsley: Gale, Gittins, Armstrong, Fletcher, Beaumont, Barnes, Curran, Hine, Wainscoat, Halliwell, Newton

Referee: Mr E. Shutt (Burnley)

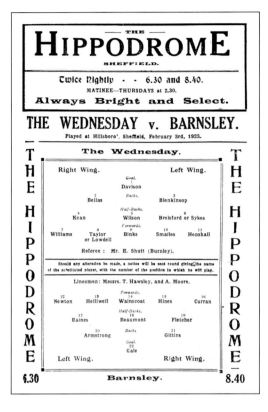

Sheffield
Wednesday
2
Barnsley
1

Memory Match

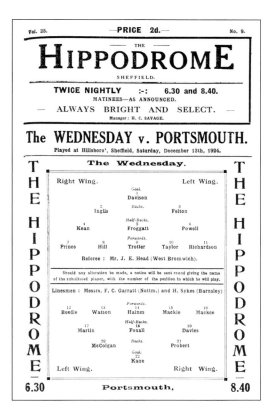

Sheffield Wednesday 5

Portsmouth 2

It was a typical December day when Portsmouth made their first ever visit to Hillsborough for a league fixture, with the weather dull and bitterly cold and a light rain beginning to fall. Once before, back in 1909, they had travelled north for an FA Cup tie when they were still a Southern League club; however, by virtue of winning the Division Three (South) title six months earlier, for the first time Pompey were now able to meet the Owls as equals. Indeed the visitors watertight defence had conceded only sixteen goals in seventeen games, and this had contributed greatly to their impressive record of only two defeats to put them ahead of ninth place Wednesday in the Division Two table. The weather kept the crowd down at the start to around the 10,000 mark; and while the visitors were at full strength, the Owls were missing the influential Billy Marsden, his place being taken by Harold Hill. Extra interest centred around two ex-Pompey men, now in-situ at Hillsborough, with boss, Bob Brown and half-back, Fred Kean both having enjoyed spells at Fratton Park as manager and player respectively.

The Owls started well, twice going close before they quickly opened the scoring after just five minutes, when confusion in the Pompey defence allowed Jimmy Trotter to fire home with a well directed shot. With the crowd roaring them on it was all Wednesday in the early stages, and it was only a further seven minutes before the fans' heroes grabbed a second, again through Trotter. This time brilliant work from Harold Hill created the opportunity. He had drawn three defenders to him before squaring the ball to the unmarked number nine, allowing Trotter to promptly beat McColgan to drive the ball home to the delight of the crowd, which by now had swelled to 12,000. Soon after this Trotter was inches away from a quick-fire hat-trick, as his effort smacked against the crossbar, then was cleared to safety after an almighty goal-mouth scramble. Despite the Owls superiority, however, mid-way through the period their advantage was cut when Mackie headed past Teddy Davison from a superb centre by Beedie. The game was being contested at a furious pace, with Hill and Trotter a constant menace to the Pompey back line; however, the Southerners held firm to go in at the break only one goal in arrears.

The crowd, which had risen to almost 18,000 by the start of the second half, must have then been stunned, for, after seeing Sam Taylor shave the bar with a terrific drive, totally against the run of play, the visitors grabbed an equaliser, giving Watson his first goal of the season. Wednesday redoubled their efforts and seventeen minutes into the half, it was Trotter who headed home from Prince's corner to complete his first hat-trick in a blue and white shirt. This time there was no coming back for the Southerners, and, after Taylor had missed some proverbial sitters, it was that man again, as Trotter equalled the club's individual game scoring record; as, from another Prince corner kick, he netted his own and the Owls fourth goal. He thus became the fourth Wednesday player to achieve the feat, Sid Binks having last achieved the feat just under a year earlier. There were still fifteen minutes remaining, however, and now the home team were on fire against their punch-drunk visitors. Wednesday continued to press, and, with just three minutes remaining, it became a case where historians could rip up their record books. For just as Hill was about to shoot—after a mazy dribble had taken him into the box—Trotter almost took the ball off his toe to gleefully fire home and write his name in the club's history as the first man to score five times in a competitive encounter. This victory saw Wednesday move up to seventh in the league, and the team was cheered from the field of play. However, the fans would have to wait another season before the prolific Trotter would spearhead a successful promotion challenge.

Wednesday: Davison, Inglis, Felton, Kean, Froggatt, W. Powell, Prince, Hill, Trotter, S. Taylor, Richardson

Portsmouth: Kane, Probert, McColgan, Davies, Foxall, Martin, Meikle, Mackie, Haines, Watson, Beedie

Referee: Mr J.E. Head (West Bromwich)

Memory Match

Following the great escape of 1927–28, the Owls went into the following season full of confidence. Yet it must almost have been beyond the wildest dreams of most Wednesdayites to think that twelve months later their club would go into the last home game of the season needing a win to secure the League Championship. This was the reality, however, for the Owls held a three point lead over their nearest challengers, as they went into a Hillsborough meeting with Burnley in front of a crowd of over 33,000. The men from Turf Moor arrived with ten successive away defeats to their name and in deep relegation trouble; and so were fully expected to make Wednesday fight all the way for the points. There was a carnival atmosphere inside the ground before the kick-off, with many supporters dressed in blue and white and some carrying small stuffed Owls as mascots. Just in time for the scheduled start the sun came out on a pitch which was soft after heavy overnight rain.

Wednesday were at full strength for the vital encounter, and the opening exchanges were fairly even, until a snap shot from Hooper beat Down and struck the foot of the post before bouncing to safety. This near-miss sparked the Owls into a frenzy of action and for almost ten minutes they laid siege to the Burnley goal; however, the away team survived and Jack Brown in the Wednesday goal was forced to make his first save after twenty minutes had elapsed. As the game approached half time Burnley were again lucky to escape when the ball ricocheted around the penalty area; but at the break the champagne was still on ice, with neither side having troubled the official scorers.

Jack Allen

If the Owls had shaded the first period, then they totally dominated the opening twenty minutes of the second half and were exceptionally unlucky not to strike the first blow. Wednesday, it seemed, were tending to over elaborate, as the importance of the occasion prayed on their nerves. Yet, despite this, Hooper saw one effort strike the crossbar, before—in an amazing incident—Bob Gregg watched as his cross-shot struck the far post, to rebound for Mark Hooper, who could only strike the same post. Every time their side got near the goal the home fans roared their approval; though twenty five minutes into the half you could have heard a pin drop in the ground, when, out of the blue, Storer scored following a corner kick, after a hesitation in the Owls defence. With their Championship hopes hanging in the balance, Wednesday were visibly rattled and soon afterwards conceded another needless corner. Wednesdayites were not downhearted, however, and gave their side tremendous backing as the Owls again laid siege to the Burnley goal. With nine minutes remaining, the Owls won a corner and Ellis Rimmer swung the ball in for 34 goal, top scorer, Jack Allen, to soar at the near post and head the ball past the despairing goalie. Allen went mad and Hillsborough erupted with hats, scarves and umbrellas thrown into the arena to celebrate an absolutely vital goal. The last few minutes saw Burnley fight a rearguard action, hoofing the ball over the stands on several occasions in an attempt to save vital minutes. To Wednesday's frustration, the Lancashire side succeeded in gaining the point they required to guarantee them a First Division survival.

For Wednesday there was then an agonising wait, as both main rivals had kicked off fifteen minutes after they did. News came through that Aston Villa had lost at Maine Road, and the Hillsborough celebrations started in earnest when it was revealed that second club, Leicester City, could only draw at Huddersfield. Wednesday were therefore the Champions for the third time in their history. The crowd flooded onto the pitch and inspirational captain Jimmy Seed spoke to the massed ranks after one of the most dramatic afternoons of football seen at the old ground in its one hundred years.

Wednesday: Brown, Walker, Blenkinsop, Strange, Leach, Marsden, Hooper, Seed, Allen, Gregg, Rimmer

Burnley: Down, Knox, McCluggage, Parkin, Bowsher, Storer, Bruton, Stage, Beel, Devine, Page

Referee: Mr W. Walden (Derby)

Sheffield Wednesday
1
Burnley
1

Memory Match

Sheffield Wednesday v. Birmingham
Played at Hillsborough, Sheffield, SATURDAY, December 13th, 1930.

Sheffield Wednesday.

Right Wing. Left Wing.

Goal.
1
Brown
Backs.
2 3
Walker Blenkinsop
Half-Backs.
4 5 6
Strange Leach Wilson
Forwards.
7 8 9 10 11
Hooper Seed Ball Burgess Rimmer

Referee : Mr. J. Roscoe (Bolton).

Linesmen :
Messrs. J. Williams (Barnsley) & L. Heath (Sutton-in-Ashfield).
(Blue & White Flag) (Red & White Flag)

Forwards.
16 15 14 13 12
Curtis Briggs Fillingham Crosbie Horsman
Half-Backs.
19 18 17
Cringan Morrall Stoker
Backs.
21 20
Booton Liddell
Goal.
22
Hibbs

Left Wing. Right Wing.

Birmingham.

Sheffield Wednesday
9
Birmingham
1

With two consecutive Championships already under their belt Wednesday went into the 1930–31 season in full confidence that a hat-trick of titles could be achieved. In early December, and before the visit of Birmingham to Hillsborough, the feat looked more than a possibility, for the Owls stood in second position, just one point behind leaders, Arsenal. The club's chances of hitting the top spot for the first time in the season were also greatly enhanced, for the Gunners were without a fixture—while the fact that the visitors to Hillsborough had yet to win away and were missing two of their better players, Barkas and Bradford, all pointed towards a home victory.

The Owls were unchanged from the previous Saturday's win at Portsmouth; yet were almost behind in the first minute, as Birmingham, wearing vivid red jerseys, took advantage of a slip from Blenkinsop to create a chance for Briggs. However, Wednesday soon exerted their authority and after eighteen minutes the vital breakthrough came when Harry Burgess perfectly timed his dive to head home from Mark Hooper's pinpoint centre. The home team were now playing 'delightful' football and the crowd of just over 21,000 roared their approval, as Birmingham struggled to hold the Owls at bay. Unfortunately for the visitors they simply could not resist the Owls constant attacks, and in the fifteen minutes before the break they capitulated, conceding four times, to find themselves 5–0 in arrears at the interval. The Owls had doubled their lead on the half-hour, with the goal of the game; as Jack Ball brought the house down with a searing 30-yard drive which flew into the top corner of the net, with Hibbs rooted to the spot. It was 3–0 within a further two minutes, when a corner from star-man, Mark Hooper, was hit home at the near post by fellow winger, Ellis Rimmer. Wednesday were now in irresistible form and much to the crowd's delight it was Hooper who was next on the score sheet after forty minutes, netting at the second attempt after his first effort had been half parried by the goalie. The thirteen minute goal rush finally came to an end with two minutes of the half remaining, as Ball cleverly lobbed the ball over Hibbs to ensure the home fans could partake of their half-time refreshments with the two points already in the bag.

At the start of the second half the visitors had reshuffled their forward line, Briggs moving to the centre-forward position. The Owls began the half as they finished the first, on the attack, and within five minutes of the restart they added to the scoreline through popular captain, Jimmy Seed. The inside-forward started the move himself, and, after giving the ball to Hooper, he'd surged into the box where he sank to his knees to head home the winger's low cross from around a foot off the ground. The skipper's goal was tremendously popular, though the home fans then experienced a goal drought as the Owls failed to find the net for a full fourteen minutes! During this time the visitors had the cheek to break away and net through Briggs, though two minutes later the five goal margin was restored as Hooper went straight through the middle of the Reds defence to net his second. This heralded another rash of goals as Wednesday took their tally to nine, with twenty minutes left on the clock. Firstly, after 68 minutes, Jimmy Seed completed a personal brace of goals; before Mark Hooper recorded his hat-trick soon after, as his header crept past the England keeper, Harry Hibbs, via the inside of a post. The Owls had set a new club league goal scoring record, beating the 8–0 victory over Sunderland back in 1911. With the Wednesdayites baying for more, the visiting side were now a demoralised outfit, and desperate to hear the final whistle. The home fans desire to see double figures registered seemed to be on the cards, for in the last few minutes Ball was brought down in the area and the Owls awarded a penalty kick. However, Tom Walker fired straight at Hibbs and, with seconds remaining, Ball then missed a glorious chance. In the end Wednesday had to settle for single figures, after one of the most one-sided encounters ever seen at the ground.

Wednesday: Brown, Walker, Blenkinsop, Strange, Leach, Wilson, Hooper, Seed, Ball, Burgess, Rimmer

Birmingham: Hibbs, Liddell, Booton, Stoker, Morrall, Cringan, Horsman, Crosbie, Fillingham, Briggs, Curtis

Referee: Mr J. Roscoe (Bolton)

Memory Match

With Wednesday struggling to make an impact in the League, attention turned to the FA Cup. There, after beating Rotherham and Oldham, the Owls were paired against Manchester City at Hillsborough in the last sixteen. In this particular season Cup fever was almost out of control, and for this War of the Roses meeting Wednesday expected a crowd in excess of 60,000. As kick-off approached fans continued to pour into the ground, with the police and stewards doing their best to pack the crowd in. For a long time people were being rolled down the Spion Kop over the heads and shoulders of the spectators, right from the top to the bottom. The straw, which had been covering the pitch overnight, then became a very useful cushion for landing those fans who'd been passed over the railings. There were several stretcher cases and it later emerged one fan had been killed in the crush to accommodate what was a huge, record crowd of 72,841; with record gate receipts of over £5,500. The post-match boast of the club sounds quite astonishing to a modern perspective, for they stated that no barriers had been broken down, though several of the crush barriers on the Kop had been twisted! Police on horseback managed to keep the crowds under control, with one on a white horse bringing back memories of the chaos before the 1923 Cup Final.

There were still thousands locked out of the ground at the start, and these amazing scenes greeted the teams as they came out to a tremendous ovation. Wednesday lost the toss and had to kick down the slope, towards the Kop. After just eight minutes a miskick from Cowan allowed Ellis Rimmer to pounce and drill home the opening goal for the home side. The game then swayed from end to end, and after both sides had gone close, Herd scored for City to level the scores with a tremendous 25 yard shot—though questions were asked later as to why the inside-forward had not been closed down before he reached the edge of the box. The first half had been played at a furious pace and the teams went in at the break on level terms.

The fans were still struggling back from the refreshment bars when Wednesday re-took the lead just two minutes after the restart. It was Rimmer who was the creator, as he ran down the inside-lrft channel before driving in a shot towards the City goal. The Owls centre-forward saw his opportunity and just managed to get his foot to the ball to flick it over the onrushing Swift. Hillsborough exploded and even those fans perched on the house rooftops on Penistone Road celebrated the go-ahead goal, as the game continued to thrill the massed ranks. There must have been thousands of sore shoulders in Sheffield that night, for whenever the ball entered the penalty box, the crowd swayed to one side to try and catch a better view of the action. Wednesday missed several chances in the first twenty minutes of the second half and looked to have been denied a blatant penalty when Dale stopped Rimmer's centre with his hand. With the light fading fast, the visitors recovered their composure and the Manchester contingent in the crowd were celebrating when Herd's shot hit the underside of the bar before dropping into the back of the net. The Owls were made to rue their missed chances, for in the end City held on for a replay after a tremendous cup-tie which had matched the all-time Hillsborough crowd figure.

Wednesday: Brown, Walker, Catlin, Leach, Millership, Burrows, Hooper, Starling, Dewar, Burgess, Rimmer

Manchester City: Swift, Corbett, Dale, Busby, Cowan, McLuckie, Toseland, Marshall, Tilson, Herd, Brook

**FA Cup Fifth Round
Saturday 17th February 1934**

Sheffield Wednesday

2

Manchester City

2

Memory Match

Millership scores Wednesday's first goal

Sheffield Wednesday
3
FC Austria
0

Despite having embarked on several foreign tours after moving to Hillsborough, the Owls had yet to host Continental opposition. This was rectified, however, when FC Austria visited Sheffield for a Monday afternoon fixture. Arriving on the previous Friday, the Austrians watched Sheffield United play Hull City at Bramall Lane on the Saturday, then were taken by Wednesday officials on a sightseeing tour of Derbyshire on the Sunday. Meanwhile, the game had ruffled a few feathers among Wednesday shareholders and season ticket holders. They had protested to the club after a local press report announced that the match would be 'all pay'. The Owls were forced to issue a statement answering the criticism, explaining that in order for this game to be viable, this had to be arranged on Cup-tie terms. The club appealed to the sporting instincts of their supporters to waive their admission rights on this occasion, in order not to prejudice similar matches in the future.

The Austrians were so far unbeaten on their tour, having won at Liverpool and drawn at Fulham and Birmingham, and they now faced a Wednesday side who gave a rare start to amateur goalkeeper, Harold Hill, as well as experimenting with Ellis Rimmer at centre-forward. The Lord Mayor of Sheffield was introduced to the two teams, the Austrian National anthem was played, and the game finally kicked off in front of a healthy crowd of 12,445 who had paid total receipts of £740. Before the kick-off the clubs agreed there would be no charging of the goalkeepers. This meant the game would be missing that extra 'robustness' in the penalty box which generally prevailed in pre-war soccer. It quickly became apparent that the Owls had too much firepower for a visiting team who played some excellent passing football, but lacked a cutting edge. The Austrian running-off-the-ball impressed the Hillsborough faithful, but they needed goalkeeper, Havlieck, to save them on several occasions in the first half—with two stops from Sedley Cooper and Harry Burgess in particular drawing great applause. With their first attack, Stroh had actually fired against the crossbar for the Austrians; and even though Wednesday dominated, they couldn't break through, so the game remained goalless at the interval.

The second half was only eight minutes old when the breakthrough finally came, as Oxley's pin-point corner kick was headed in by the diving Walter Millership. Eight minutes later, the Owls' right-winger then set up a second when his cross was headed home by Ellis Rimmer, and this effectively finished the game as a contest. As they had in the first half, the Austrians continued to play a neat brand of attractive soccer, however, all their good approach play tended to break down on the edge of the Wednesday penalty box. The scoring was completed with seven minutes left on the clock, when Cooper was sandwiched in the box by two visiting defenders and Ellis Rimmer netted from the penalty spot. The consensus of opinion at the final whistle was that the European upstarts had listened well to those English coaches who had helped develop the game in Austria. However, the opinion of the countless managers and professional players who had travelled to watch the friendly was, that if FC Austria were placed in England's top division, they would not achieve any great measure of success. In the end, Wednesday were pleased at the response to the match and with the loyalty of the fans who had paid up despite having ground passes. In future years their loyalty would be rewarded by some truly memorable games against foreign opposition.

Wednesday: Hill, Nibloe, Walker, Sharp, Millership, Burrows, Oxley, Starling, Rimmer, Burgess, Cooper

FC Austria: Havlieck, Andritz, Seszta, Najemnick, Mock, Gall, Molzer, Adamek, Stroh, Nausch, Viertl

Referee: Mr L. Dale (Sheffield)

Memory Match

In November 1938, when Norwich City visited Hillsborough, the Owls' fortunes were at a fairly low ebb as they languished in fourteenth place following a 5–1 defeat seven days earlier at West Bromwich Albion. At this time there was no sign of the eventual promotion challenge that would emerge, and so manager, Jimmy McMullan decided it was time to make changes. Three players were omitted from the side who played at The Hawthorns, out went Bill Pickering, Harry Millership and Idris Lewis, with their places taken by Fred Lester, Harry Hanford and Len Massarella. A crowd of just under 17,000 filed into Hillsborough, not realising that within ninety minutes they would have witnessed history in the making; the likes of which will probably never be seen again at Hillsborough.

The visitors had, so far, failed to earn a point away from home. It quickly became apparent why, as Wednesday might well have scored at least three times in the opening ten minutes, with Hunt missing a proverbial sitter in the Owls first attack. However, the game's turning point probably came when the Norwich City defender, Peter Burke, was injured after quarter of an hour had been played. In those days, before substitutes, he was forced to retire to outside-left; where, with one good leg and one 'swinger' he proved to be of no more than nuisance value to his side. Burke had been the crucial defensive 'stopper' in the Norwich formation, and, once he departed, the Owls— and particularly Douglas Hunt—found acres of space at the heart of their opponents back line. In fact, within two minutes of his injury, Wednesday surged ahead when Hunt fired past Duke in the Norwich goal. After 25 minutes Hunt doubled his side's advantage, beating the Canaries offside trap to run on and coolly fire home. There were two further scores in the first half, with the goal of the game seeing Doug Hunt complete a personal treble with six minutes of the half remaining. He had picked up a pass from Jackie Robinson, beaten his man in a tackle and went on to crash the ball home from the edge of the penalty box. Soon after, he added his and Wednesday's fourth, to leave the Owls totally in control at the break.

Although Hunt would unsurprisingly grab the headlines after the game, it was the mercurial Jackie Robinson who was pulling the strings, giving one of his best displays in an Owls' shirt since making his debut three and a half years earlier. However, although Robinson created five of the Owls goals, he was not involved when Wednesday scored their fifth, as from Fallon's corner Hunt saw his effort strike a post before he was able to react quickly to score from the rebound. Hunt's fifth goal made him only the second Wednesday player this century to net five in a game, and with still twenty-five minutes to play a club record looked to be on the cards. The next goal fell not to Hunt, however, for Massarella's shot was tipped onto a post by Duke, only for Bill Fallon to be on hand to net Wednesday's sixth goal of the afternoon. With time starting to run out, it looked as if Hunt and Wednesday would have to be content with their haul; but then, with only three minutes remaining, the history books would be re-written as Douglas Hunt became the first and only Owls player to score a double hat-trick in a competitive game. The tremendous win put Wednesday up to mid-table; though the match will always be remembered as 'Hunt's game'.

Wednesday: Goodfellow, Ashley, Lester, Russell, Hanford, Burrows, Massarella, J. Robinson, Hunt, Napier, Fallon

Norwich City: Duke, Flack, Taylor, R. Robinson, Burke, Smalley, Church, Ware, O'Reilly, Furness, Manders

Referee: Mr W. Daly (Kent)

Douglas Hunt

Sheffield Wednesday
7
Norwich City
0

Soccer at War
1939–1946

WEDNESDAY IN WARTIME

With the political situation on mainland Europe deteriorating almost on a daily basis, thoughts throughout the summer of 1939 must rarely have turned to football. It was therefore probably no coincidence that boss, Jimmy McMullan was almost totally inactive in the transfer market, and though a handful of promising youngsters were signed, he failed to take on any new senior pros for the forthcoming campaign. The major transfer activity saw Fenwick sold to Reading, though it was also the end of an era, when, after over four hundred games and 136 goals, Mark Hooper moved to neighbours Rotherham United on a free transfer. The summer period also witnessed almost ten thousand tennis fans flock to Hillsborough in order to see an event dubbed 'Three hours of Wimbledon', with the Wednesday pitch marked out to allow four high ranking tennis professionals to provide an exhibition of the sport.

After losing to the Blades in a pre-season match, the Owls kicked off their Second Division campaign with a trip to Luton; but this proved a poor start to the season, for the Hatters triumphed 3–0. Wednesday were then hosts to Barnsley and then Plymouth. However, at eleven o'clock on the morning after the game with Plymouth, the country was plunged into crisis when Britain declared war on Hitler's Germany after they had failed to respond to Prime Minister, Neville Chamberlain's ultimatum to withdraw from Poland. The Government immediately banned all sporting events and all football ceased until the authorities could consider what action to take. The Football League eventually decided that soccer should continue, with games to be played on a regional basis because of travelling restrictions, and crowds limited to 8,000—or half of a ground's capacity—whichever was lowest.

Several emergency leagues were hastily set up, with the Owls entering the East Midlands League where they finished three off the bottom in an eleven team division. For Wednesday football restarted in late September with a friendly win at Barnsley. They then christened the new competition, with a 2–2 draw at Belle Vue, four weeks later (Hunt blazing over from a penalty with two minutes remaining). By now manager McMullan was only at the club on a part-time basis, having taken a full-time factory job once war had been declared. Many of the club's players had been called up to the forces, with playing contracts cancelled; though the clubs still retained the player's registration. The system of guest players came into being; which, as the war lengthened, probably stopped organised football from collapsing altogether. The Owls used only one such guest player in that first season— Sheffield born, Collett, of Arsenal. However, the public were fairly apathetic to the fare on offer, a situation which was

surely understandable given the circumstances, and crowds slumped to an all time low of only 752 for the Owls final home game of the season. The Owls struggled to continue in that first season, and, at the 1940 Annual General meeting, Mr Turner, the club Chairman, painted a bleak picture, for he reported that Wednesday would suffer a shortage of players in the coming campaign. However, the club was determined to continue with the help of local amateur players (eleven of whom signed, including future professionals Alf Rogers and Ron Thompson).

After one season the East Midlands League was scrapped, with Wednesday now taking their place in the newly formed North Regional League at the start of the 1940–41 campaign. They began with a home game against Huddersfield Town, in which the Terriers included seven of their pre-war side. Yet a Wednesday team containing three forwards straight from local football overcame their opponents to earn a splendid opening day victory. Nevertheless, it would prove to be a season of struggle for Wednesday, for they won only eight further games to finish third from bottom. This was in a 35-strong league in which the final position was decided on goal average because

games were played on a fairly *ad hoc* basis; with the likes of Bolton playing only sixteen times as opposed to the thirty eight games played by Bury. The Owls suffered some heavy losses during the season, conceding seven to both Newcastle and York on consecutive Saturdays, and with their defence being breached 78 times in only 30 games. The first leg of a War Cup tie defeat at Bootham Crescent stirred up controversy; for after Wednesday exited on aggregate they lodged a formal protest to the Football League that York had played Halton of Bury without Wednesday's permission, and that he was therefore ineligible. This proved to be a futile protest, for replays were not allowed because of a shortage of time. No action was taken, and the Minstermen were therefore allowed to progress into the next round. The campaign coincided with the height of the Sheffield blitz, and after Bramall Lane was severely damaged in December 1940, Sheffield United made Hillsborough their second home for several months.

When war was declared the Owls had 40 players on their books. However, by the start of the '41–'42 season, twenty-four of those were in the forces, and a further three amateurs

Eric Taylor

who'd played in '40–'41, had also been called into the Royal Air Force. Wednesday therefore started the new season devoid of almost all of the cream of their pre-war talent; yet, after two disappointing campaigns, the club were still optimistic that a better season would ensue. The Owls had fielded several guest players in the previous season, with certain of them, such as Joe Cockroft, George Drury and George Laking, becoming vital members of a side that finished in mid-table in a competition which ran until the end of the year. The home game with Lincoln was a perfect example of the problems wartime soccer faced, for the visitors struggled to obtain transport and were forced to use private cars to reach Hillsborough. The game finally kicked off seven minutes late with the Imps fielding only ten men; it was a full fifteen minutes into the match before their centre-forward took the field to complete the eleven. The first eight games of the second competition also counted as a War Cup qualifying competition. The Owls failed to even reach the knock-out stages this time, gaining only three miserable points from eight games (including an 8–2 thrashing at Bury) to finish way down in 51st place. With little more than pride left to play for, the season fizzled out somewhat. And Wednesday were not even officially placed in the Championship, for they had failed to play the requisite eighteen league games from the turn of the year.

The middle season of wartime football easily proved to be the best, as Wednesday came close to both League and Cup success, with a certain Jackie Robinson gaining national prominence because of his goal scoring exploits. This brought the brilliant inside-forward 35 goals in only 32 games. The Owls started the season with Eric Taylor effectively in charge, even though, officially, he was only the club secretary. This occurred because Wednesday decided not to re-engage Jimmy McMullan when his contract had expired. The ex-player, Billy Marsden, was also appointed to a part-time coaching role, while fellow ex-pros, Ernie Blenkinsop and Frank Froggatt were engaged as scouts. The summer also saw Alf Rogers sign professional forms for Wednesday; and, after impressing in a five-a-side competition, Sheffield YMCA inside-forward, Redfern Froggatt (son of the aforementioned Frank) joined on trial as a prelude to signing amateur forms.

Redfern Froggatt

The Owls made a tremendous start to the new season. Unbeaten in their first six games, they would lie amongst the leaders in the early tables. Hugh Swift was then signed on professional forms, and the Owls went goal-crazy against poor old Mansfield Town. After conceding nine at Hillsborough the Nottinghamshire side then proceeded to lose 10–2 at Field Mill a week later, with both Jackie Robinson and guest player, Maynell Burgin, helping themselves to hat-tricks. Wednesday were in truly unstoppable form, with the front pairing of Robinson and young centre-forward, Frank Melling, (better known for his 14 year stint as captain of the Sheffield United Cricket Club) starring, as the Owls swept all before them. This was particularly the case at Hillsborough, where the Owls won all nine games in the first competition,

completing their home programme with a 4–0 win over the Blades. This had produced the biggest crowd for a Wednesday home game since the start of hostilities. A week later, on Christmas Day, the Blades gained their revenge in front of the biggest crowd seen in wartime soccer, pushing Wednesday down to a final position of third, six points behind the champions, Blackpool.

This upturn in fortunes saw the crowds flock back to Hillsborough, with almost 20,000 attending the Boxing Day clash with Lincoln. Wednesday carried their good form into the New Year by qualifying for the knock-out stages of the League North Cup. One of the qualifying games came against the Blades at Hillsborough. This entered the annals of club history after a Robinson treble helped Wednesday to a landslide 8–2 win—the Owls biggest ever victory over their City rivals. Aggregate wins over Bradford and Nottingham Forest ensured Wednesday and United would clash again in the last eight of the competition. Robinson was once again the

Dated   3rd September   1942

THE

SHEFFIELD WEDNESDAY

Football Club

AND

HUMPHREY MILLS SWIFT,
63, City Road,
SHEFFIELD.2.

AGREEMENT
FOR HIRE OF A PLAYER

8. In consideration of the observance by the said player of the terms, provisions and conditions of this Agreement, the said E.W.TAYLOR - - - - - - - - on behalf of the Club hereby agrees that the said Club shall pay to the said Player the sum of £1-10-0------ per weekxxxx match, when playing or on reserve with the first team - - xxxxx xxxxxxxxxxx
xx

9. This Agreement (subject to the Rules of The Football Association) shall cease and determine on the cessation of hostilities - - unless the same shall have been previously determined in accordance with the provisions hereinbefore set forth.

Fill in any other provisions required.   SUBJECT to the War-time Regulations of the Football Association and The Football League.

As Witness the hands of the said parties the day and year first aforesaid

Signed by the said E.W.TAYLOR.
.... and ....
H.M.SWIFT.   H.M.Swift
In the presence of   (Player).
(Signature) CHenningfield
(Occupation) Departmental Manager,   Eric Taylor
(Address) 42, Trickett Road,   (Secretary).
SHEFFIELD.6.

hero, his brace in the first leg ensuring Wednesday would progress after holding United to a goalless draw at Bramall Lane. However, two days before the semi-final against York, the Owls plans were hit when keeper Albert Morton was called up. With no other senior keeper available, Wednesday—somewhat ironically—had to borrow Blades custodian, Jack Smith, for the two legged clash. Smith kept a clean sheet in the first leg, while a 1–1 draw at Bootham Crescent secured a 4–1 aggregate win. This meant that Wednesday had a first final appearance since their FA Cup victory eight years earlier. For the first leg of the final at Blackpool, goalkeeper Morton was back on leave and available. Goals from Joe Cockroft and Jackie Robinson suggested the Owls looked set for a superb 2–1 victory. However, the home team grabbed a last minute equaliser to put the sides on level terms for the Hillsborough meeting. A record wartime crowd of 47,657 packed into Hillsborough for the second leg, though the majority would go home disappointed, for Blackpool surged into a two goal lead, with only a late consolation from Robinson to cheer the home

fans. In the second League Championship, Wednesday again finished six points behind the winners, but were two places lower in fifth position, completing a fine season in which the club netted over a hundred times in competitive football.

Because of wartime unpredictability, and with Frank Melling unavailable and a limited number of appearances by Jackie Robinson, it perhaps came as no surprise that in the '43 –'44 campaign the Owls were unable to repeat the previous season's success; or that they effectively reverted to the poor form shown in the earlier war years. Six defeats were suffered in their opening nine league games, including a 3–1 defeat to the in-form side, Doncaster Rovers, whose success perhaps could be attributed to the fact they managed to field a side

'Jacky' Robinson

Clubs must send the results of League Matches with the Names of the Players competing therein to the League Secretary within three days of each Match.

THE FOOTBALL LEAGUE SEASON 1942-43

NORTH

Date of Match___13th February___1943

Home Club___SHEFFIELD WEDNESDAY___ Visiting Club___SHEFFIELD UNITED.___

Result :—Home Club___8___Goals ; Visiting Club___2___Goals.

Total No. of Matches Played___8___

Won___4___ Lost___1___ Drawn___3___

Total Goals for___22___ Goals Against___13___ Points___11___

Signed___ Secretary of___SHEFFIELD WEDNESDAY___

TEAM.

Notes.—The Surname, with Full Initials, must be given.
Add Name of Club after Guest Player.

Goal	A.MORTON.
Backs (Right)	J.A.ASHLEY.
„ (Left)	A.E.CATLIN.
Half-Backs (Right)	D.W.RUSSELL.
„ (Centre)	W.MILLERSHIP.
„ (Left)	J.COCKROFT (West Ham).
Forwards (Outside Right)	W.REYNOLDS (Rochdale). x
„ (Inside Right)	J.ROBINSON. xxx
„ (Centre)	F.MELLING. xx
„ (Inside Left)	J.THOMPSON. xx
„ (Outside Left)	H.K.SWIFT.

Joe Cockroft

consisting solely of guest players! As the season wore on, Wednesday were forced to field more and more youngsters, with their decline perhaps being typified when Mansfield won at Hillsborough, a year after having conceded nine in the same fixture. The Owls finished five points above bottom club, Crewe, in the opening Championship; with their hopes of better times in the New Year being hit by an event which occurred in early January. Charlie Napier, who had been banned *sine die* in 1941—only to have the decision reversed in August 1943—was again banned for life by the FA after a mystery incident reported by the referee in a home game against Grimsby, back in October 1943. The Owls appealed against the decision as their young side acquitted themselves well in the second half of the season, and qualified for the knock-out stages of the War League Cup. However, they exited this in the First round, losing 5–0 at Bradford Park Avenue; though they overcame the setback to eventually finish in a mid-table spot in the closing Championship.

In the summer of 1944, as the war in Europe started to swing the Allied powers way, the Owls' Chairman, W. Turner, announced his retirement at the age of 75, with William Fearnehough taking his place (Turner was elected President). The close season saw the Owls break new ground, when, for the first and only known occasion in their history, they competed in a five-a-side competition in an event held in Millhouses Park in South Sheffield. This was won against a local side, St Josephs, thanks to goals from Ibbotson, Caurton and Froggatt. Wednesday kicked off the 1944–45 fixture list with their first pre-season game since the beginning of hostilities, when Huddersfield Town were beaten at Hillsborough in a game for the Sheffield Telegraph War Fund. The new Football League North campaign started with a double-header against the Blades, and this saw the Owls take

three points off their rivals after winning at Bramall Lane for the first time since February 1933. The Owls included a new signing, Charlie Tomlinson, in those derby games. He had become the club's first fee-bearing signing since before the war, joining for a reputed £1,000 from Bradford Park Avenue. However, for the game at Notts County early in September, Wednesday arrived with only nine senior players. As a result, they were forced to field youngster, Reg Stewart at centre-forward, and goalkeeper, Harry Donaldson (who ironically had played seven times for the Owls in '43–'44 whilst on the books of County) at outside-right as they went down to a 2–0 defeat. The Owls league form was patchy in the first half of the season, with a shocking 6–1 home defeat to Mansfield being the definitive low point. Yet, overall, they won more than they lost and finished in a comfortable mid-table position. As

football started to return to normality, several new players who would form the backbone of Wednesday's post-war side joined during that period, including Dennis Woodhead, Keith Bannister and Cyril Turton. The Owls' attempts to then qualify for the knock-out stages of the War League Cup again floundered, for they won only one of ten designated games, a terrible start to the New Year that effectively ruined any chance of a high finish in the Second League competition. A thrilling 4–3 defeat at Leeds saw new centre-forward, Jack Lindsay, net twice—making such an impact that he was immediately signed after the final whistle. Lindsay's arrival brought back memories of earlier cross-border raids by secretary, Arthur Dickinson in the last century, for it was reported the Morton player was in such demand that he had been engaged in lengthy conversations at Glasgow Station, as several unknown individuals attempted to make him miss the train to Leeds! They failed, however, and Lindsay travelled to Yorkshire with his uncle, then came on to Sheffield after the game to sign for Wednesday. The month of May proved joyous for the Owls fans and the country at large, for on 8th May 1945 the

Action from 1943 War Cup Final at Hillsborough—Wednesday players Reynolds, Robinson and Melling fight for the ball

declaration of Victory in Europe sparked mass scenes of celebration on the streets of Sheffield. Twenty-four hours later the City's two sides met in a VE match at Bramall Lane. In front of the country's biggest crowd, the Blades won 2–0 in a match where, for once, the result was of little importance in comparison to that of the overall occasion. Soon after, however, Wednesday won 3–1 at Bramall Lane in the first leg of the Sheffield County Cup Final; and a week later they wrapped up their season by securing some silverware after completing a 7–2 aggregate win over the Blades.

With the war in Europe at an end, the Football League were keen to return to the pre-war status quo. This idea was actually vetoed by the clubs themselves, for they still believed it would not be possible because of a shortage of players and continuing problems with travel and accommodation. It was therefore decided to combine the pre-war First and Second Division clubs and then split them into two regional

*Wednesday v. Stoke FA Cup tie—
a rare photo of the Owls playing in hooped shirts*

groups—with the River Trent used as a dividing line. One pre-war competition that did return, however, was the FA Cup. At the request of the league clubs it was re-instated and played on a two-leg basis up to the semi-finals, as had been the case with the now defunct War League Cup. In preparation for this transitional season, the Owls added Alec Wands and Ron Thompson to their list of professionals, while they effectively gained a new player as the FA *sine die* suspension of Charlie Napier was lifted as part of the Victory in Europe celebrations. Unfortunately for Wednesday the inside-forward was back in Falkirk working as an electrical engineer, and it was in the hands of the Labour Ministry as to whether he would be allowed to return to Sheffield. The other major event of the summer came in July, when Eric Taylor, who had been secretary since 1942, was officially appointed to the position of Secretary-Manager; a position he would hold until 1958. The final change for the new 1945–46 season involved the Owls' kit. For the first time since the 1870s this would see Wednesday appear in blue and white hoops for the campaign.

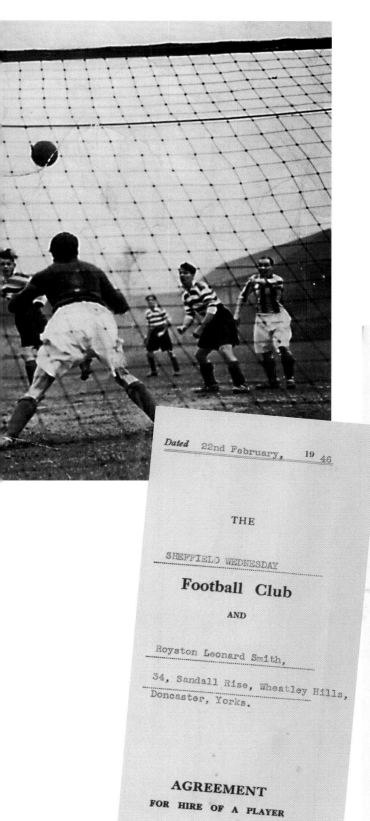

The Owls started the new season in goal scoring mood, with Sunderland hit for six. Despite losing the return game a week later at Roker Park, the Owls then recorded four consecutive wins, including a quickfire double over the Blades, to move into the top three. The second of the two meetings against United came at Hillsborough and saw Charlie Napier make his one and only appearance of the season before being sold to Falkirk a fortnight later. Other transfer news saw Joe Cockroft signed on a permanent basis from West Ham, while Vin Kenny joined as part time professional. The visit of Stoke to Hillsborough resulted in the season's biggest league crowd, but many were disappointed when the star attraction, a certain Corporal S. Matthews, failed to appear after encountering car trouble on his journey to the ground. The month of November saw Joe Cockroft appointed player-coach and Wednesday move to second in the league after a home win over

Dated 22nd February, 19 46

THE

SHEFFIELD WEDNESDAY

Football Club

AND

Royston Leonard Smith,

34, Sandall Rise, Wheatley Hills, Doncaster, Yorks.

AGREEMENT

FOR HIRE OF A PLAYER

8. In consideration of the observance by the said player of the terms, provisions and conditions of this Agreement, the said E.W. Taylor _____ on behalf of the Club hereby agrees that the said Club shall pay to the said Player the sum of £ 8-0-0------ per week from 22nd February, 1946 to 4th May, 1946 and £9-0-0-------------- per week from when playing in the First Team.

9. This Agreement (subject to the Rules of The Football Association) shall cease and determine on 4th May, 1946 unless the same shall have been previously determined in accordance with the provisions hereinbefore set forth.

Fill in any other provisions required.

As Witness the hands of the said parties the day and year first aforesaid

Signed by the said R.L. Smith

and

E.W. Taylor

In the presence of

(Signature) E. Street

(Occupation) Shorthand-typist

(Address) 325, Queen Mary Rd., Sheffield, 2.

(Player).

(Secretary).

Blackpool. The Owls subsequently went top of the table after a home draw with Blackburn; but this proved to be a false dawn, when only one win in their next seven league outings subsequently pushed Wednesday out of the title race.

The New Year brought the FA Cup and saw Wednesday cruise through to the last sixteen, after aggregate wins of 5–0 and 11–2 over Mansfield Town and York City respectively; setting up a mouth-watering clash with Stoke City. A huge crowd—almost double the gate for the league meeting—packed into Hillsborough. However, the match was something of an anti-climax, as City—who this time did include Stan Matthews—held Wednesday to a goalless draw. The second leg also proved a disappointment to the Owls, as a brace from Steele sent the Potteries side through to the quarter finals and left Wednesday to concentrate on the league. During the Cup run there was more transfer activity as James McCarter and Matt MacKenzie were signed. Half back, David Russell, then informed the club he had signed a three year contract to coach a Danish side and would be leaving for the Continent as soon as he was demobbed from the RAF. Doug Hunt, who before the war had set a club record by grabbing a double hat-trick in a home game with Norwich City, then left for Clapton Orient. Back in the league Wednesday had stopped the rot, and four victories in their final six games pushed the club up to a praiseworthy top six finish, twelve points behind the champions, Sheffield United. Meanwhile, the Owls reserve side lifted the Central League title for the second time in the club's history. Once the league fixtures had been completed, Wednesday had the satisfaction of retaining the County Cup, with a 2–1 aggregate win over Barnsley. They then ended the last official wartime season on tour in Scandinavia, where they drew two and lost one of their three games in Denmark, before putting nine goals past Swedish side Malmo.

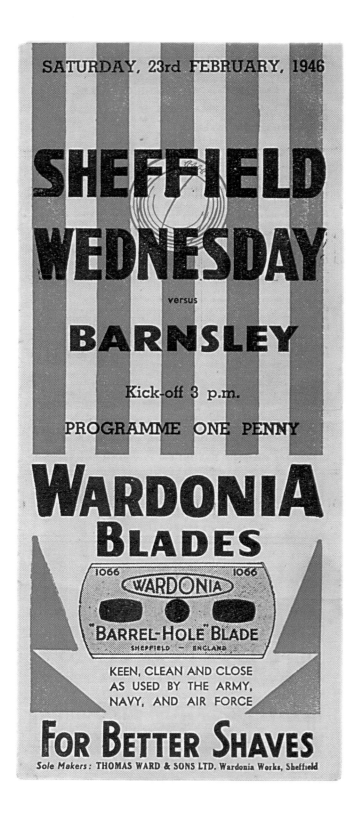

Chapter 5

The Yo-Yo Years
1946–1959

FOOTBALL ASSOCIATION CHALLENGE CUP

SEMI FINAL

Saturday,
26th March
1955

Kick-off
3 p.m.

HILLSBOROUGH, SHEFFIELD.

YORK CITY
versus
NEWCASTLE UNITED

Price 6d.

Official Programme

1946–47
ALMOST RELEGATED AS LEAGUE SOCCER RETURNS

In preparation for the first official season of post-war soccer the Owls were surprisingly quiet on the transfer front, and made only a handful of fairly low-key signings. Among the new arrivals were Jim Briscoe, Ivor Seemley and Alf Rogers; with three pre-war players, Harry Hanford, Bill Fallon and Jackie Thompson, leaving Hillsborough. Joining the administrative side was the future secretary, Eric England. He was appointed assistant to Eric Taylor, who retained the title of secretary-manager. The back room staff was completed by two pre-war players, Sam Powell and Tom Walker, who took up the posts of trainer and assistant trainer respectively. Before the season kicked off, Frank Slynn arrived on trial from local club, Batchelor Sports; and there was good news for the traditionalists amongst the Owls support, as Wednesday reverted to blue and white stripes after a season in hooped shirts.

The fixture list for the new season was a repeat of the aborted 1939–40 campaign and meant an opening-day trip to Luton. There, the turnover in players caused by the war became apparent, with Jackie Robinson the only remainder from the side which had run out at Kenilworth Road some seven years earlier. Unfortunately, the Owls didn't improve on the pre-war scoreline for they again lost by three goals, with Robinson netting Wednesday's first in post-war soccer. The Hillsborough campaign opened with a defeat to Barnsley; and only two wins in the first ten games, saw the Owls languishing just one place off the bottom of the table by mid-October. It quickly became apparent that Wednesday were not fully equipped for peacetime soccer, and their supporters were stunned when star-man, Jackie Robinson—who many believe to be the greatest player in Wednesday's history—was sold to First Division Sunderland for a record fee for the Owls. Allenby Driver then left for Luton Town; and, after being replaced by Roy Smith in the Wednesday goal, Derek Goodfellow was put on the transfer list at his own request.

Against this backdrop, the team not surprisingly struggled to gain enough points to pull themselves out of trouble. And it may be significant that in late October the Wednesday players became the last from a League club to join the Football Players Union. Soon after this, Jack Lindsay become the third attacker to leave in as many weeks when he signed for Bury; though the Owls would finally enter the transfer market themselves, and this helped steady the nerves of their fans. The two players who arrived would ultimately prove to be vital to the Owls relegation battle. Firstly, the experienced ex-England International, George Hunt, signed from Bolton and brought much needed experience to a relatively young side. Then, teenager Jimmy Dailey made an immediate goal scoring impact when he arrived from Scottish club, Third Lanark.

FA Cup action v. Preston

More Cup action—this time against Everton

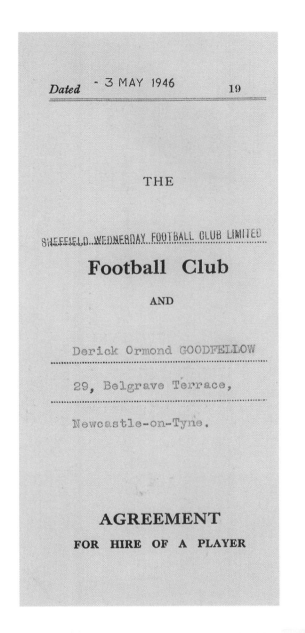

Dated - 3 MAY 1946   19

THE

SHEFFIELD WEDNESDAY FOOTBALL CLUB LIMITED

Football Club

AND

Derick Ormond GOODFELLOW

29, Belgrave Terrace,

Newcastle-on-Tyne.

AGREEMENT

FOR HIRE OF A PLAYER

Everton keeper, Sagar, denies Dailey

Indeed, the latter netted seven times in his first eight games to help the Owls out of the bottom two in time for the round of Christmas fixtures. The holiday period also saw John Logan arrive from neighbours, Barnsley, while the home game with Bury attracted over 41,000 to Hillsborough, Wednesday's biggest league crowd of the season. On the field, however, Wednesday were a side still lacking in confidence. A missed penalty by Lowes on New Year's Day saw further points dropped at home, before a heavy defeat at Plymouth increased the atmosphere of general despondency. The Owls reaction was to advertise the post of team-manager, with a brief that included the need to work alongside Eric Taylor. Unfortunately, this merely caused further problems for a beleaguered Wednesday, for after announcing the somewhat shock appointment of the Sheffield United trainer-coach, Dugland Livingstone, it later transpired that after several meetings with Wednesday he had, in fact, declined the post. The Owls then moved to Plan B and two weeks later, Huddersfield's experienced head-coach, William Knox was appointed to the position of trainer-coach; with Eric Taylor continuing in a managerial capacity.

Back on the field of play it was FA Cup time, with the Owls raising their game to knock out two First Division sides at Hillsborough on their way to a last sixteen home clash with Preston. However, one of the worst winters on record was severely disrupting the fixture list, and when the tie was finally played the Owls dreams of Wembley faded as they were outplayed on a snow covered Hillsborough surface. For several weeks matches were either postponed or played on snowbound pitches, and it was on such a surface that new record signing, Doug Witcomb, saw Dailey grab a treble as the Owls recorded their best win of the season. The 18-year-old, ex-Scunthorpe winger, Jackie Marriott, was also settling into the side, but couldn't help stop a heavy defeat at Coventry; a match played despite the tragic death of City's manager on the morning of the game. Walter Aveyard was another departure from Hillsborough; and, with the Owls flirting with the drop-zone, it wasn't until late in May that Wednesday finally knew their fate when a Tommy Ward goal in the home game with Manchester City 'brought the house down', and saved the club from the spectre of regional football. Even though they escaped the drop, Chairman William Fearnehough admitted it had been the worst season in the club's history. And despite media pressure, he declined to comment on anything that might have occurred behind the scenes to cause such a tumultuous season. Incidentally, Wednesday finally completed their programme at Chesterfield on June 7th, the latest ever finish to a season; and with the home side's, George Milburn entering the record books by netting a hat-trick of penalties in the Owls 4–2 defeat.

1947–48
REVERSAL IN FORTUNES

After the brush with relegation in that first season after the war, hopes were not high amongst Wednesday fans that a credible promotion challenge was even a possibility. Moreover, these feelings looked to have been reinforced during a close season, for no senior players were signed. The majority of the transfer activity was of an outgoing nature, with Alec Wands, Derek Goodfellow and Tommy Gale all departing. In retrospect, the most important moment of the summer came in June, when 'A' team forward, Derek Dooley, signed professional forms. Unbeknown to the supporters it had been a frustrating close season for Wednesday, with the club actually attempting to break their transfer record with swoops for three separate players; including the Derby centre-forward, Jack Stamps, and Rotherham's prolific forward, Walter Ardron. In each case, however, the respective clubs refused to sell. Eric Taylor thus went into the new campaign with what was basically an unchanged squad; although Jackie Marriott was unavailable after he crashed his motor cycle and fractured his ankle and wrist. The summer also saw a shareholders association created, and at the AGM, threaten to challenge for the four vacant seats. Ex-player, Ted Catlin become a scout for the club that summer, and the Owls installed one of those new fangled P.A. systems!

The Owls kicked off the new season with a welcome home win. But then three consecutive defeats pushed them into the lower reaches of the first published league tables. However, the home game with Barnsley saw Jimmy Dailey join a select band of Wednesday players when he netted all five in a confidence boosting derby victory. Soon after this, Joe Locherty signed from Scottish junior club, Lochee Harp; while the aforementioned victory against Barnsley triggered a run of six wins in eight games, and saw the club move into the top six. The revival was initially boosted by the arrival of goalie, Dave McIntosh from Scottish junior soccer; before the Owls long search for a quality attacker finally bore fruit when the Bury inside-forward, Eddie Quigley joined in a £12,000 club record transfer. The new man netted his first goals in a 2–2 draw at Elland Road, and a week later opened his home account against Fulham in a game tinged with sadness when the Blackpool Chairman, who was a guest of the club, collapsed and died just after the final whistle. The Owls went into the Christmas period just outside the promotion race, though the club minutes reveal there was crisis behind the scenes which shook the club to its very core! The problem concerned the secretary's office, from which supplies of whisky were found to have run out much too quickly on match days! A resolution was therefore passed that only the home and visiting directors, plus special guests, were to be served.

It proved to be an extremely happy Christmas for Wednesday, as a nine goal double over West Ham sent them into the New

Dennis Woodhead

Clarrie Jordan

Year in high spirits. The opening game of 1948 saw Spurs beaten at Hillsborough, and somewhat bizarrely saw the second period kick-off and continue for several seconds before anybody realised the referee was missing! The Owls progressed in the Cup with a victory at Cardiff; but were left to concentrate on the league after losing in round four at Filbert Street.

The club then entered the transfer market bringing Clarrie Jordan to Hillsborough from Doncaster for a fee, with Arnold Lowes going in the opposite direction. Three teenagers were then signed including the ABA Junior Boxing Champion, Doug Fletcher, who decided to pursue a career in football instead of the ring. Jordan made a goal scoring debut at home to Bradford Park Avenue, and then the forward line, which also contained Froggatt and Quigley, hit a purple patch in late March. This saw the side run off six consecutive wins to soar into third place just one point behind second club, Newcastle United, which sparked off an outbreak of promotion fever in the blue and white half of the City. However, the run was marred by the death of Wednesday director, Mr Johnson, who became the fourth board member—including ex-Chairman, W. Turner—to pass away inside twelve months. A couple of draws then ensued and meant the visit to St James' Park was a real 'four pointer', and a game that Wednesday simply could not afford to lose. An early Witcomb penalty put Wednesday ahead in front of a massive 66,480 crowd. The Geordies then hit back to go ahead, before a Marriott goal nine minutes from the end looked to have earned the Owls a vital point—they were two points behind with three games to play. Unfortunately it wasn't to be, for United scored twice in the last three minutes to win the crunch encounter 4–2, and leave Wednesday's promotion dreams in tatters. Although Wednesday could match Newcastle's points tally, the Geordies vastly superior goal average made it impossible for them to be

caught, and so the Owls had to be content with a final finishing place of fourth to earn £220 'talent money' for the club.

Meanwhile, a busy end to the season saw the signing of Chesterfield's highly rated centre-back, Raymond Parker, as the Owls player Joe Cockroft announced he would be spending his summer in Finland coaching for the FA. After a gap of eleven years, Wednesday then returned to Scunthorpe to regain the Hospital Cup. However, the campaign didn't finish with the final league game at West Brom, for after winning 4–1 at Rotherham to qualify for the County Cup Final, a hat-trick from Barnsley's Chilean attacker, George Robledo, won the tournament for the Tykes at Hillsborough. Finally, in mid-May, the City's two professional clubs broke new ground when they became the first league sides to face each other in Douglas on the Isle of Man, where an enthusiastic crowd of 8,000 saw the rivals share four goals.

Woodhead fires for goal

Scarecrow practice?

119

1948–49
PROMOTION CHALLENGE FAILS TO MATERIALISE

After the sudden upturn in fortunes experienced in 1947–48, and for the second consecutive summer, Wednesday's management again decided not to bring in any new first team players to Hillsborough. However, as with the situation twelve months earlier, the one signing they did make proved to be of long term benefit to the club's fortunes, when England schoolboy star, Albert Quixall signed his first professional contract. In total, the Owls transferred five players out of Hillsborough, with both Wilf Ibbotson and James McCarter going to Mansfield Town and William Pickering to Oldham. George Hunt, who'd been instrumental in helping the Owls avoid the drop just after the War, left the club, as did the long serving Tommy Ward, who attracted the highest fee of the quintet when Darlington paid £1,500 for his services. Three vacant places on the Board of Directors were filled during the close season; and plans to run a fourth side which would compete in the local Hatchard League in 1948–49 were announced at the annual dinner. Meanwhile, in late July, a unique event took place at Hillsborough when a healthy crowd attended a boxing bout between Hall and Armour.

The Owls had the dubious pleasure of conceding the earliest goal of the new season, when Tottenham's Ernest Jones netted after just ninety seconds at White Hart Lane, in a game that Wednesday lost by the odd goal in five. A comfortable win over West Ham opened the Owls' Hillsborough account. But Wednesday were inconsistent in the early weeks, and this set a pattern for the season which adversely affected any chances of promotion the club may have harboured before a ball had been kicked. This inability to string together a sequence of results saw Wednesday beat their Yorkshire rivals, Leeds United, and then twice succumb to Bury, the early pacesetters, in the space of five days. The Owls occasionally ventured into the top six, such as in late October when a Dennis Woodhead brace at Nottingham Forest secured the second of only three away wins that Wednesday would record in the whole campaign. A week later a controversial refereeing decision saw the Owls denied a point at home to Fulham. With the score at 2–1 to the Londoners, the official awarded a last minute penalty to Wednesday. The kick was taken by Witcomb, who netted. However, because several Fulham players were arguing with the ref and encroaching in the box, the man in black bizarrely ordered the kick to be retaken, and this was promptly missed by the unnerved Witcomb.

Early in November Roy Smith and the 37-year-old Joe Cockroft were both placed on the transfer list at their own request and in a surprise move, the latter went to First Division neighbours, United. The Owls received what was then the tremendous fee of £4,000 for the veteran defender, which, in retrospect, was a great sale by the club. For indeed,

Cockroft, who became the oldest player to make a First Division debut, struggled to cope with top flight football and within six months had moved on to Wisbech Town. Further transfer activity saw the Owls set a new club record when they paid £20,000 for the Bury right-winger, Eddie Kilshaw; while Smith earned the move he desired, signing for Notts County.

Back on the field of play the team had risen to the heady heights of fourth after a home win over Spurs, and the crowds flocked to Hillsborough as the countrywide post-war boom in attendances continued unabated, with the Owls average increasing to over 33,000 in this particular season. The FA Cup trail started with victory over Southampton, but promptly ended at their South coast rivals, Portsmouth. An astonishing crowd of almost 50,000 packed Hillsborough to see a home Cup tie with the Blades. And although this was only a County Cup tie, which saw the Blades four goals ahead at the interval, it firmly illustrated the depth of the public demand for football in Sheffield after the austerity of the War years. There was yet more transfer activity with Tony Conwell arriving from Bradford, and the superbly named, Herbert Higginbottom—who, in local football, revelled in the nickname of 'The

Cannonball Kid'—was signed as one for the future. Centre-forward, Jimmy Dailey, who had been competing with Clarrie Jordan for the number nine shirt, was then sold to Birmingham for a club record fee; and finally the Eire International, Eddie Gannon arrived for another big fee, as Wednesday broke the bank in an attempt to build a promotion winning side. One player that didn't arrive, however, was the Southampton and England International defender and future winning World Cup manager, Alf Ramsey. He stayed where he was when the Saints had the audacity to ask for Redfern Froggatt in exchange! New signing Gannon made his debut at Grimsby, but could do little as Wednesday finished the season with a terrible run of form, recording only one win in their final eight games to finish a massive thirteen points off the promotion places. If that wasn't bad enough the home game with Leicester not only saw the visitors grab a last minute winner but saw record buy, Eddie Kilshaw badly dislocate his knee. Tragically for Kilshaw, and Wednesday, the winger would never play again after having appeared only nineteen times in the blue and white shirt. For the Wednesday fans a season which had promised so much could not finish quickly enough, with the return to the big time still looking a long way off.

Goalkeeper Dave McIntosh leads the 'jump over the fence' training routine!

1949–50
PROMOTED—AND AT THE BLADES

For the fourth consecutive summer the Owls were relatively quiet in the transfer market, the only activity seeing several fringe players leave Hillsborough. These included the likes of Reg Stewart, Matt MacKenzie and Tony Collins, though key-man Eddie Quigley also seemed set to leave after handing in a transfer request, stating he wanted to be able to work part-time in addition to playing football. Wednesday, however, refused to accede and within six days he had seen the error of his ways and had withdrawn the transfer request! The club's 50th Annual General meeting took place at the Grand Hotel in Sheffield, and revealed that Wednesday had spent heavily in the previous campaign in order to try to secure promotion. The accounts revealed a deficit on transfer fees of over £17,000, with the report revealing the directors regretting that the playing season had not been not more successful. They also said 'it was found impossible to strengthen all the known weaknesses, determined efforts will again be made during the coming season to bring the team up to the required strength'.

The new season kicked off with a home win over Leicester but it was a bitter-sweet first Saturday for the club. Not only was Dennis Woodhead stretchered off at Hillsborough with a broken right leg, but, in a reserve game at Wolves, Wednesday goalie Albert Morton also fractured his leg. However, despite that double set back the Owls maintained their good start to the campaign and, after Quigley had set a club record by grabbing a hat-trick in just five minutes at home to Chesterfield, Wednesday sat comfortably in the top six. The Owls biggest crowd of the season then turned out for the Sheffield derby which went the way of the home side thanks to a great display from Eddie Quigley, and the club's tremendous form continued when Clarrie Jordan became the second man, in only five home games, to score four times as Hull City were overwhelmed at Hillsborough. The game at Grimsby in early October saw Wednesday concede three penalties, two of which were converted, but the subsequent 4-1 defeat was only the club's third loss of the season and would be the last until the New Year. After losing at Blundell Park, Wednesday embarked upon an unbeaten run which lasted for thirteen games to thrust them firmly into the promotion frame. Included in the run was a single-goal win at Preston where Charlie Tomlinson's strike after just 12 seconds is believed to be the quickest in the club's history, one second faster than a goal by John Pearson in the early 1980s. During that spell the Owls did actually finish on the losing side once but thankfully for them the match in question, at Coventry, was abandoned after just 63 minutes due to thick fog. Conditions were so bad in the first half that after City's Roberts had to go off with an injury it took him several minutes before he could get permission to return as he couldn't find the referee!

Walter Rickett

Off the field Wednesday signed ex-Sheffield United winger Walter Rickett from Blackpool, while their injury jinx struck again when reserve-forward Doug Fletcher became the third player to break his leg whilst playing in a representative game for the Army. However, the big transfer news involved Eddie Quigley who, in a new British record deal, signed for Preston with Wednesday receiving £26,000—over double what the Owls had paid for him two years earlier.

The New Year started badly for Wednesday, they were knocked out of the FA Cup at Arsenal, saw their undefeated run end against Plymouth, and suffered a burglary at the club offices, with £31 stolen. However, the Owls did strike gold in the transfer market, when Norman Curtis, who would play 324 times over the next decade, arrived from non-league Gainsborough Trinity. In the league, Wednesday failed to win for seven games, yet despite this they remained in the top three, even after a Tom Finney goal won the points for Preston in a game which saw a raw Derek Dooley make his Wednesday debut at Hillsborough. Off the field the Owls experienced one of the most incredible weeks in their history, as they strived to find a replacement for Quigley. The six day spell started tragically when their 44-year-old trainer, William Knox died suddenly at home. Wednesday then agreed a £25,000 fee with Newcastle for the Chilean, George Robledo. He declined the move, however, and it was the same story twenty-four hours later when Leicester's, Ken Chisholm rejected a move. The Owls weren't ready to give up though, and a day later they signed Gerry Henry from Bradford Park Avenue, followed a fortnight later by the capture of Hugh McJarrow. With transfer activity over it was

back to the business of winning promotion, and four wins in six games was completed with a home victory over Bury on Easter Monday. This put the Owls into second place, a point ahead of the Blades. However, Wednesday fans then saw their side contract a bad dose of the promotion jitters, and this allowed United to move into the last promotion spot. Luckily for Wednesday their City rivals finished their season early, and this left the Owls with the clear knowledge that a goalless draw (a 1–1 scoreline would have forced a play-off) at home to the champions, Spurs, would see them back in the big time on goal average. Over 50,000 packed into Hillsborough (the club averaged just over 40,000 in the season) for the decider, and fingernails were bitten to the quick as both sides missed chances in a game that eventually finished 0–0, sparking off wild scenes of celebration. The Owls had gained promotion over the Blades by a superior goal average of just 0.008, and a week later they sickened their rivals again by netting a last minute winner against them at Hillsborough in the County Cup Final. To round off a great season, Wednesday then toured Sweden and Denmark, recording two victories and a draw in the four games played. Back home, of course expectations were already growing as the countdown to the First Division started.

Gerry Henry

Ditchburn, of the Spurs saves from McJarrow, who is seen following up his shot

1950–51
GOAL AVERAGE TAKES REVENGE

It would be fair to say there had been a distinct change in the Owls' transfer policy in the post war years, moving away from a policy of summer signings to a system of purchases during the season; as once again, in the close season, Wednesday decided not to splash out on any big name players. In advance of their first season back in the top flight for fourteen years, Wednesday did, however, bring new blood into the club, with half-back, George Davies arriving from non-league Oswestry Town; and utility player, Peter Taylor signing from Gainsborough Trinity. Leaving Hillsborough were Frank Westlake to Halifax, Oscar Fox to Mansfield Town, plus the duo of Reg Stewart and Joe Locherty, who were signed by Football League new boys, Colchester United. Off the pitch the Owls agreed in principle to play a November friendly in Cologne, but this was eventually called off. Meanwhile, an offer of 200 guineas by the Maytime Ice Cream Company was accepted by the club for the forthcoming seasons 'Ice' franchise at Hillsborough.

Wednesday's re-introduction to top flight football was a harsh one, for on the opening day at Chelsea, on a tortuous afternoon, they conceded four without reply. Then forty-eight hours later, champions, Portsmouth, the first visitors to Hillsborough, provided one of the games of the season. Almost 47,000 saw Pompey go ahead with just eleven minutes remaining of an action packed encounter. Thankfully, within four minutes the Owls were level, and in the last minute Woodhead brought the house down when his cross hit the far post and bounced into the net to snatch a terrific victory. Unfortunately for Wednesday the match proved to be a false dawn, as three straight defeats saw the club slump to last place in the First Division table. After the win-less run had extended to seven games Eric Taylor decided it was time to bring in some new faces. Wednesday raided Oswestry again to sign Walter Thomas, before inside-forward, Johnny Jordan arrived from Birmingham City to go straight into the first team. A few weeks later another arrival proved to be vital for the future, with the winger Alan Finney signing for the Owls on his seventeenth birthday. However, the news of the new arrivals was tempered by the fact that the long serving Alf Rogers would be forced to retire early due to the onset of arthritis in a hip joint.

New signing Jordan made a winning debut at Huddersfield as the Owls scored twice in the last four minutes to earn a 4–3 first away win of the campaign. Wednesday then held the unbeaten league leaders, Newcastle, to a draw. However it was quickly becoming clear that the club were ill-equipped for First Division football, with an occasional victory insufficient to keep them out of the two relegation places. Wednesday were seemingly unable stop the flood of opposition goals, and suffered several heavy defeats on their travels. By the end of

the year the situation was serious, with the Owls bottom of the league despite two welcome wins over the Christmas period. The Cup run started and ended at Craven Cottage, and in January Wednesday lost every game, including a friendly at Leicester, leaving them three points adrift from the pack. The month finally saw the club replace the recently deceased Bill Knox, when future manager, Alan Brown, was appointed to the post of trainer-coach on an eighteen-month contract. Despite climbing off the foot of the table in February, the results were almost of secondary importance to one of the most sensational happenings ever seen in Sheffield football. This centred around Jimmy Hagan, arguably the greatest player ever to play for the Blades. It emerged that Wednesday had offered United a record transfer fee of £32,500 for the brilliant inside-right, and that United—to the fury of their fans—had accepted the massive offer from their city rivals. Unfortunately for the Owls, Hagan decided against the move, and so a transfer that would have rocked Sheffield football failed to happen. Wednesday then made an unpublicised, and ultimately unsuccessful, move for Bolton's Nat Lofthouse; but a month later the club again captured the national headlines when they tabled a double bid of over £50,000 for Wolves centre-forward, Jessie Pye, and Notts County inside-forward, Jackie Sewell. The former decided not to sign because his wife did not want to move North. Sewell did make the move, however, as Wednesday again broke the British transfer record by paying £35,000 for his services. Other transfer news saw Slynn sign for Bury and Charlie Tomlinson leave for Millmoor, while youngster, David Storrar signed professional forms.

STAFF
BANQUET

Held at the
GRAND HOTEL
SHEFFIELD

17th May, 1951

Souvenir Programme

1951

FESTIVAL OF BRITAIN

SHEFFIELD WEDNESDAY
v
FREM (Denmark)

WEDNESDAY, MAY 16th
Kick-off 6.15 p.m.

PRICE SIXPENCE

The country's most expensive footballer made a goal scoring debut at Anfield, his arrival sparking a significant Owls' rally as they went on to win four and draw two of their next eight games, to move out of the bottom two on goal average over Everton. A week later, however, a disastrous single goal defeat at Spurs saw Wednesday drop back to the bottom, level on points with Chelsea and two behind Everton. Unfortunately for the Owls, Chelsea had a superior goal average and Wednesday went into the final fixture knowing that whatever Chelsea did, the Owls would have to match this and net an additional four goals. Incredibly, in an astonishing game, Wednesday proceeded to crash six past Everton, to relegate their visitors. Hopes of survival proved to be in vain, however, for news came through that the Londoners had won 4–0, and Wednesday would have needed ten to stay up. In the end, and somewhat ironically, the Owls were down by a goal average of 0.044, only a year after an even smaller difference had elevated them to the top flight. Wednesday licked their wounds to retain the County Cup and completed the season with a game against the Danish side, Frem. This was one of a number of nation-wide friendlies (Sunderland v. Red Star, and Barnsley v. Rapid Vienna were two other games played on the same night) taking place under the banner of the Festival of Britain, and organised to promote British trade. A missed penalty from Dennis Woodhead ensured the game remained goalless to complete an eventful season that ultimately brought disappointment.

Wednesday on the attack against Fulham

1951–52
DOOLEY'S SEASON

Despite the disappointment of relegation on the final day, Owls fans saw enough in the final few weeks of the previous season to suggest their club was more than capable of bouncing back into Division One at the first attempt. The close season saw the Owls say good-bye to two senior pros forced to retire early through injury. One time record signing, Eddie Kilshaw was the first to leave after persistent injury problems. He was followed soon after by Hugh Swift. After making over 300 appearances in a Wednesday shirt, Swift hung up his boots but was retained as a scout on full wages. On the transfer scene, Doug Fletcher was sold to Bury, Brian Slater signed as a part-time pro, and Johnny Jordan was made available for transfer after rejecting Wednesday's offer of a new contract. Meanwhile, the club decided that from the new season a player who reached twenty appearances would be awarded 'club colours' in recognition of the achievement.

The Owls made a great start to the season, and with only one defeat in their opening half dozen games, Wednesday were in second place before they visited Bramall Lane for the first derby encounter of the campaign. Unfortunately, the wheels then fell off in spectacular style, when, despite the Owls being a goal up after just ninety seconds from Keith Thomas, the Blades proceeded to crush Wednesday 7–3. This was the club's largest ever defeat in a derby encounter, and was the prelude to a chronic loss of form which saw the Owls tumble down the division all the way to seventeenth; a position they held before the home game with local rivals, Barnsley. Meanwhile, during the time Wednesday had been struggling to amass points in Division Two, the club's reserve side had been experiencing no such problem. For their young centre-forward, Derek Dooley, was catching the eye with a run of thirteen goals in only nine games. Such displays persuaded Eric Taylor that it was perhaps time to give Dooley another chance in the first eleven, and he rewarded his boss by scoring both goals as the Tykes were overcome. It's history now that Dooley and the team never looked back, for in the ensuing weeks Wednesday hit a rich seam of form, moving to the top of the division in late December when Dooley hit all four as Everton were overwhelmed at Hillsborough. The tremendous run also included a five goal haul from Dooley at home to Notts County, followed by a club record 6–0 away win at West Ham. Some remarkable home attendances accompanied these games as supporters flocked to Hillsborough to see Wednesday's new goal scoring sensation—who incidentally set a new club record by netting in nine consecutive games. Away from the action, the Sheffield United centre-half, George Underwood was signed, as was Farsley Celtic youngster, Colin Whitaker. The Owls then raided Dundee junior football to bring brothers, Tom and Jim McAnearney to Sheffield. Departing Hillsborough was Gerry Henry, who, after requesting a transfer, was signed as

Derek Dooley

player-coach by Halifax Town, the Division Three (North) strugglers.

The Christmas and New Year period saw a hiccup in form, with defeats at Nottingham Forest, at Bradford Park Avenue in the Cup, and at home to the Blades in front of the Owls highest ever attendance for a league game. This beat the previous record, set in the 1930s against Arsenal, by just 39 spectators. However, a four goal salvo from Jackie Sewell at home to Cardiff soon restored the status quo; and over the next few weeks the Owls battled with several clubs for the leadership of the division. During this time the Owls were involved in some quite remarkable games, with two of the highlights being an action packed 5–4 defeat at Oakwell and another four goal haul from Dooley at home to Hull. The period also saw Hugh McJarrow leave for Luton Town; and a home friendly arranged with Manchester United duly postponed because of bad weather. The club also decided to investigate the possibility of installing floodlights at Hillsborough and a committee was formed to pursue the matter.

Back in the league, a mid-week home win over Luton took Wednesday to the top for the first time for almost two months. A second-half goal from Derek Dooley was, however, of greater significance for this was his 40th strike of the season, setting a new club goal-scoring record for a single campaign, and beating the previous mark jointly held by Jimmy Trotter and

Jack Allen. A win at Bury followed, and yet another Dooley hat-trick—his fifth of the season—brought victory at Brentford. At the summit, however, the teams were so closely matched that a home draw with Swansea allowed Birmingham to re-take the top spot from Wednesday. But on Easter Monday the Owls were back in pole position, and with only two games remaining, Wednesday knew that a victory at Coventry would clinch promotion. A brace from Dooley duly secured the Championship, after Birmingham's heavy defeat at Notts County. This ensured the final game of the season at home to West Ham was a celebratory match, and saw Wednesday issue a special souvenir match programme. Unfortunately, the visitors had failed to read the script and led 2–1 with only a minute remaining, before, who else but Derek Dooley popped up to equalise. This was his 47th goal of the season, scored in only 31 games. Moreover, the strike took the Owls' league goals tally to exactly one hundred, though their season wasn't over yet—for seven more games were played before the Wednesday players could put their feet up for the summer. The first of these came in the unlikely setting of the Lake District, where the Owls drew with Manchester City at Kendal before returning home to lose to the Blades for the third time in the season. Wednesday then undertook a mammoth five game tour of Switzerland where they faced the likes of Inter Milan, FC Nuremberg, and the Swiss national side. However, the season will always be remembered for the incredible goal scoring of Dooley, the likes of which will almost certainly never be repeated.

'Cheers—we're promoted!'

1952–53
DOOLEY TRAGEDY OVERSHADOWS RETURN TO THE TOP FLIGHT

Despite calls from their supporters Wednesday made no big signings during the summer of 1952, deciding instead on a policy of giving the members of their Second Division Championship winning squad the opportunity to show their worth in the top flight. Thus the only transfer activity of the close season was of an outgoing nature, with fringe player, Eric Kirby being the first of three departures when he signed for York City. He was followed by long serving, Edgar Packard, who after almost sixteen years at Wednesday dropped down the divisions to sign for Halifax Town. Walter Thomas completed the trio leaving Hillsborough. Meanwhile, the club reported record season ticket sales despite a price increase caused by a rise in a Government imposed 'entertainment tax', and the Owls looked set to match, if not better, the average of almost 42,000 which had been recorded in the previous campaign.

The Owls could not have asked for a more glamorous start to the season than a visit from the Cup holders, Newcastle United. The huge opening day crowd were thrilled when a late show from their side saw Wednesday grab a dramatic point, as four goals were shared. Unfortunately, Wednesdayites had little else to get excited about in those early weeks, for the point won against the Geordies proved to be the only one gained in their first five games, leaving the Owls firmly in last place. The period also saw the ex-player, John Logan appointed as assistant coach, as Wednesday attempted to bolster their side by making a large bid for Blackburn's England International left-back, Bill Eckersley. This, however, was turned down by the Lancashire side. Wednesday were thus forced to make do with what they already had and, thankfully, the first win of the season came soon after, at home to Spurs. This triggered a terrific unbeaten run of ten games to lift Wednesday into the top ten, and included a great win at Blackpool, with the seasiders losing for the first time at Bloomfield Road for over a year. It was also characterised by some quite astonishing Hillsborough crowds, and would see the club post their highest ever average attendance of any season in their history (42,530). Meanwhile, away from the first team picture, the Owls youth side made history when they played their first ever game in the new FA Youth Cup competition, losing 3–2 at home to Hull City.

After their unbeaten run ended in a seven goal thriller at home to Portsmouth, the Owls won only once more before the Christmas fixtures—an amazing 5–1 victory at Newcastle United. Off the field, Walter Rickett was sold to Rotherham, Barry Butler joined on part-time forms from non-league, South Bank; and another large bid—this time for Hancocks of Wolves—was unsuccessful. Behind the scenes, the secretary-manager, Eric Taylor was awarded a new contract, which

would take him through to June 1958. Back in the league, the Owls lost the lead four times in a dramatic Boxing Day defeat to West Brom, but redeemed themselves by winning the return game twenty-four hours later.

The New Year meant the Cup, and for the fourth season running Wednesday fell at the first hurdle as Blackpool gained revenge for their earlier home defeat. Soon after this, goalie Brian Ryalls signed from Grimesthorpe Colliery. Overall, however, the Owls had acquitted themselves well on their return to the top flight, and, after struggling initially, Derek Dooley started to climb the goal scoring charts—before the visit to Deepdale on 14th February 1953 he stood third in the league, with sixteen goals in 29 games. Fourteen minutes into the second half of the match it looked as if his season was over, for the big centre-forward collided with the Preston keeper, George Thompson, and broke his right leg. As Dooley was taken to the Preston Royal Infirmary his side conceded a winning goal from Tom Finney. However, the real drama unfolded on the following Monday, when Dooley's leg became infected with gas gangrene, probably caused by the soil from the Deepdale pitch. An SOS was sent out to Manchester Infirmary for a gangrene serum and police cars rushed to Preston. However, even after receiving the injections, Dooley's health slowly deteriorated. His surgeon, Mr Garden, took the momentous decision to amputate his patient's leg in order to save his life. Dooley remained critically ill after the operation, and it was several days before he started to recover, he then spent several weeks in hospital before returning to Sheffield. The unbelievable news that Dooley would never again terrorise opposition defences was almost too difficult for fans to take in, and the nation mourned a whirlwind career which had ended for the devastated Dooley at the tender age of 23 (ironically he'd made his first team debut for Wednesday against Preston three and a half years earlier). His loss was, of course, an immense one for Wednesday; and one can only speculate as to what Dooley and his club could have achieved were it not for the tragic events of February 1953.

The atmosphere at Hillsborough was sombre on the following Saturday, as Clarrie Jordan set out to replace the irreplaceable Dooley. However, Sewell hit the winner and this lifted the fans spirits somewhat. The following home game saw Arsenal's Cliff Holton net all of his side's four goals, and across the next few weeks Wednesday began to tumble down the table to the fringes of the relegation zone. During the slump in form there were major changes off the field, as James Longden become the new Chairman, following the death of William Fearnehough. Wednesday also splashed out to buy their first ever club car— a 'Humber Hawk' which cost the not inconsiderable sum of £1,200. Meanwhile, the club signed Sheffield born centre-forward, Ronnie Codd from Bolton. This, however, turned into something of a farce, for Codd returned from whence he came within a month, with the transfer cancelled because of a recurrence of a long term injury. On the field of play, the Owls went into the final day knowing a win would definitely secure First Division football, and they made no mistake by thrashing the visiting Sunderland side—with Jackie Sewell grabbing a treble. Before they could hang up their boots, however, the Owls players still had three games to play. These began with another trek to the Lake District, where a brace from future Wednesday centre-forward, Roy Shiner, helped Huddersfield to a 2–1 win in the 'Westmorland Invitation Cup'. Local disputes were then settled in the County Cup, where, after Doncaster had been defeated, the Owls promptly shocked their fans by crashing 7–0 in the next round at Rotherham. However, the Millmoor result probably only caused a ripple among the Wednesdayites, for this was a season which would be remembered for that one incident which altered the history of the club.

Dooley meets his double on Rag Day

Wednesday v. Wolves

1953–54
SAFETY AND A SEMI-FINAL

Following the traumatic events of 1952–53, the Summer of 1953 saw the Owls attempt to find a replacement for the stricken Dooley. To this end Wednesday raided their neighbours, Rotherham United, to bring their centre-forward, Jack Shaw to Hillsborough for a fee of £7,500. Keith Bannister and George Underwood departed the club, joining Chesterfield and Scunthorpe respectively; while amateur full-back, Don Megson joined the professional ranks at the beginning of a career which would see him become a fixture in Wednesday's first team for over a decade. Off the field the club appointed two new Directors, with Richard Gunstone and Robert Peasegood joining the Board. The club accounts reflected the record crowds of the previous campaign, with a gross profit of almost £23,000 declared. This, however, was accompanied by a similar increase in taxation, a situation which didn't go down so well in Sheffield 6.

A week before the big kick-off the Owls staged what would prove to be their last ever public practice match, sixty one years after the first trial game was held as a prelude to Wednesday's first season of league soccer. Four days later the Division One campaign got underway, and it was a winning start for Wednesday as they recorded a comfortable home success over Manchester City. Another home win put the Owls top of the first published tables, but the proverbial wheels then dropped off in the first away game of the season when Wednesday returned to Deepdale for the first time since the Dooley tragedy. After conceding a first minute goal the Owls then lost keeper McIntosh with a broken arm, forcing left-back Norman Curtis to play between the sticks. Incredibly, the stand-in goalie managed to save two penalties, but couldn't do anything about the other five goals that flew past him as Preston raced to a 6–0 win. The Owls gained revenge for the Deepdale debacle seven days later, and as autumn dawned, a comfortable mid-table position was being maintained; though, despite the relative success of the season, the absence of Derek Dooley looked to be the main contributory factor in an alarming 20 per cent drop in home attendances. Away from the action, both Vin Kenny and Doug Witcomb asked for transfers after failing to win back their first team places, with the latter moving to Newport County. Then, after several trial periods, the young winger Derek Wilkinson was signed from non-league soccer. The Owls then took a break from the rigours of league football to entertain a touring team of amateurs from South Africa. The difference in class was clearly revealed, for in the mid-week afternoon game (before the days of floodlights) Wednesday overwhelmed their visitors from the Southern Hemisphere to crash home nine goals.

Five days after the romp against the tourists the Owls took part in another friendly, this time at the Baseball Ground. To

Sheffield Wednesday Football Club Limited

FOOTBALL ASSOCIATION CHALLENGE CUP—6th ROUND

Sheffield Wednesday
versus
Bolton Wanderers

To be played on the Wednesday Ground
on SATURDAY, 13th MARCH, 1954
Kick-off 3.0 p.m.

Reserved Seat 7/6 (South Stand)

The Sheffield Wednesday Club does not guarantee that the proposed match will be played.

GANGWAY **6**

ROW **Q**

SEAT

Secretary and Manager.

THIS PORTION TO BE GIVEN UP AT
**ENTRANCE DOOR
(SOUTH STAND)**
(See plan at back)

ROW **Q**   SEAT

D

You are requested to take up your position not later than 2.30 p.m.

Gannon, Sewell, Seemley and their 'lucky' black cat

Owls in training: Ryalls, Curtis, Woodhead, Davies and Shaw

commemorate their UK debut under lights, Wednesday were dressed in what was described as a smart, all-blue, 'floodlight special' silk shirt, with white arms. The Owls lost 3–1 to Derby and recorded only one more victory before the New Year to slip down into the lower reaches of the First Division table—with a shock transfer request from Redfern Froggatt adding to their woes. The first month of the New Year proved an excellent one, with Wednesday winning two of the three league games played. This included a derby success against the Blades and progression in the FA Cup. A huge crowd assembled at Hillsborough for the Third Round tie, for Owls opponents happened to be Sheffield United. Despite drawing the first match at home, it was Wednesday who eventually came out on top after winning 3–1 in a stormy Bramall Lane replay, in which Vin Kenny became the first Owls player to be sent off in post-war football. The Owls were then handed another derby game and again needed a replay before overcoming Chesterfield at Saltergate to reach the last sixteen. The luck of the draw stayed with Wednesday as they were drawn at home in the next two rounds, and as Cup fever grew the club entered the transfer market to sign Ron Greensmith and John Martin from junior football—even as an unpublicised offer of £15,000 for Froggatt from Sheffield United was rejected. A late Bolton equaliser in the sixth round Hillsborough meeting, looked to have denied Wednesday a semi-final spot. However, for the third time in the Cup run the Owls won on opposition soil, and thus moved into the last four courtesy of a splendid 2–0 win at Burnden Park. Meanwhile, the Owls were treading water in the bread and butter of league football. Yet they had sufficient points not to worry about relegation, and all their energies could therefore be channelled towards the Maine Road semi-final meeting with Preston. Wednesday were to be disappointed, however, for in front of over 75,000 the eventual winners netted twice through Wayman and Baxter to win 2–0 and send the Owls tumbling out of the Cup after their best run for nineteen years. A Cup hangover then resulted in three straight defeats. But thankfully a late rally pushed Wednesday away from the danger zone, and they eventually finished a comfortable six points clear of the second relegation spot. After one season of abstinence the Owls again travelled to foreign shores at the season's end as they made a return visit to France as well as breaking new ground by also visiting Belgium. In Antwerp the Owls faced the crack Brazilian outfit, Portuguese Desportes. After being crushed 6–0, secretary-manager, Eric Taylor admitted the crowd had been treated to football at its finest, with every trick in the game revealed. A win in Paris against the Rio side, Bangu, restored some pride; but the final friendly of the tour against French club, Sedan, not only saw the unlucky McIntosh break his thumb, but witnessed four goals fly past his replacement.

1954–55
BACK TO DIVISION TWO

After a poor finish in the previous campaign it was perhaps surprising that the Owls failed to make any signings of note in the close season. The only transfer activity was of the outgoing variety, with Ron Capewell leaving for Hull City, and Norman Jackson signing for Bristol City. The major news of the summer came off the pitch, as firstly, Colonel Craig was appointed Chairman to replace James Longden. The future Chairman, Dr Andrew Stephen, was then seconded onto the board to fill the vacancy. Meanwhile, in addition to upgrading the Kop, Wednesday agreed plans to install floodlights at Hillsborough. This subsequently meant the cancellation of the scheduled practice matches, thus signalling the death knell for the annual pre-season warm-up game. There was one other departure just as the season kicked off, with trainer-coach Alan Brown leaving to take over as manager at Burnley after three and a half years at Hillsborough.

Within the first few weeks of the season it quickly became apparent to the supporters that the club's defensive frailties would cost them dear unless new players were quickly introduced. The Owls had slumped to the bottom three and conceded twenty-one goals in their first eight games, including three in a crazy 6–3 home win over Aston Villa. The opening run also saw a stormy match at Roker Park, in which Jack Shaw became the first Owls player since the end of the War to be dismissed in a league game, sent from the field along with Sunderland's Anderson following an altercation. Two wins in early October, including their only away success of the season at West Brom, pushed the club to the dizzy heights of eighteenth place. However, a visit to Deepdale, their new jinx ground, pushed them back down, as for the second consecutive season following the Dooley tragedy, Wednesday were thrashed 6–0—and reputedly were lucky to get nil. One of the biggest crowds of the season then packed into Hillsborough. The 40,000 school children had not come to see football, however, for Wednesday were being honoured by a visit from the newly crowned Elizabeth II. The young Queen, who was accompanied by various dignitaries on what was a rare visit by the sovereign to a football ground, signed the visitors book. When Eric Taylor was presented to Her Majesty, he was reported to have been asked about the origins of the club, with the Queen replying, 'it is a very nice name'. The eventful month of October also saw problems with the homesick Eddie Gannon, with the club coming to the somewhat bizarre agreement—to modern eyes—of allowing the Eire International to live and work in Ireland and travel over to Sheffield at the weekends.

As a prelude to hosting an FA XI v. The Army, representative game, the club played the former in a private practice match, with the Owls winning 3–1. However, points were becoming

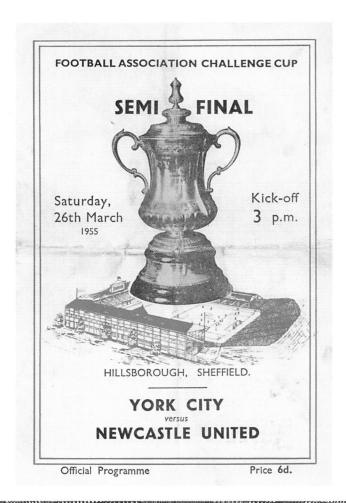

Queen Elizabeth II pays her first visit to Hillsborough

increasingly hard to come by in the league, and a heavy home defeat to Manchester City sent Wednesday tumbling to the bottom of the table, where sadly they would remain until the end of the campaign. In order to reinforce the back line, Wednesday then entered the transfer market to sign Peter Baker on a free transfer from Tottenham Hotspur, and the Huddersfield Town centre-back, Don McEvoy for £20,000. However, attempts to sign the Everton centre-forward, Dave Hickson failed to come to fruition. Wednesdayites had hoped the New Year would bring better fortune in both the league and cup, but after almost being embarrassed at home by Southern League, Hastings United, the Owls FA Cup fortunes hit the rocks in a replay at Meadow Lane. Behind the scenes Jack Marshall was appointed trainer-coach; though five days after arriving from Stoke City he might well have regretted his decision as he watched his new charges concede seven at Tottenham. The month of March did, however,

bring some good news, with the Owls using their new floodlights for the first time as 55,000 fans attended Derek Dooley's All-Star benefit match.

The situation looked hopeless for Wednesday and this was reflected in the Hillsborough attendances; and, for the second season running there was a massive slump in the average crowd size. At the close of the campaign this stood at 27,150, which compared drastically with an all-time high of over 42,000 just two seasons earlier. Mind you, the stay-away fans had good reason to withdraw their custom, for the '54–'55 campaign was such an horrendous season that a draw at Bolton on Good Friday saw the axe fall and the Owls relegated with still five games to play. A five goal mauling at Newcastle poured salt in the wounds, and, despite a surprise last match five goal home win watched by their lowest crowd for almost eight years, Wednesday finished a massive eleven points from the safety zone. The club then even lost at home to Rotherham United in the County Cup Final; with the only positive aspect to take from the season being the debut of Tony Kay and Derek Wilkinson, both of whom would serve the club admirably over the ensuing years.

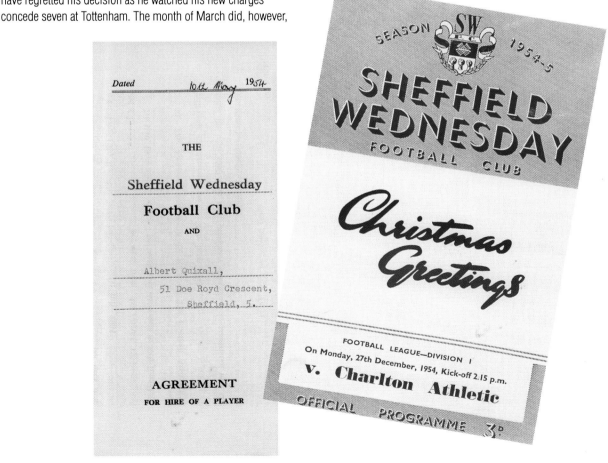

1955–56
JUST ON LOAN TO THE SECOND DIVISION

The first summer happening saw Wednesday agree to release Eddie Gannon from his contract in order for him to take over as player-manager to the Dublin side, Shelbourne, where he had started his playing career. The ever changing sands of the Boardroom then took centre stage yet again, as another reshuffle saw Chairman, Colonel Craig retire due to ill health, with Dr Andrew Stephen promoted from Vice Chairman to the vacant post. However, it might well have been prudent to issue new members of the board with a health warning, for the Owls board of twelve had seen eight deaths and three resignations since the war, with only two members remaining from the pre-war soccer days. In sharp contrast to previous years the summer of 1955 saw an explosion of transfer activity at Hillsborough, with ten players involved as Eric Taylor re-organised in advance of the hoped for promotion challenge ahead. The first arrivals were Walter Bingley from Bolton, and teenager, Gerry Young from Newcastle junior football. Manchester United defender, Don Gibson, was the first high profile arrival, costing the club £8,000. Notts County winger, Albert Broadbent then arrived shortly after at a fee of £6,500 (though strangely enough the local press reckoned the fee was twice as much). The current England full-back, Ron Staniforth then moved in from Huddersfield, along with Roy Shiner, in a deal that saw Jackie Mariott and Tony Conwell move to Leeds Road in exchange. The only other departures of note saw veteran Vin Kenny sign for Carlisle United and Ivor Seemley travel over the Pennines to join Stockport County.

Four of the new signings, Broadbent, Gibson, Shiner and Staniforth, all made their debut in the opening match of the season. This saw Jackie Sewell hit a hat-trick as Plymouth were overwhelmed at Hillsborough. A comfortable 3–0 win at Liverpool followed, to put Wednesday at the top as the first tables were published. During the early weeks of the season, however, the Owls were dogged by inconsistency. Though they only lost twice in their opening twelve league games, seven draws in the period ensured they occupied a mid-table position when the crack Hungarian side, Vasas, visited Hillsborough and gave the Owls a football lesson as they crushed the home side 7–1. As far as the Sheffield public were concerned, however, events behind a closed-doors friendly at Hillsborough between the two City sides was the main talking point of the day. Played to give both sides an advance taste of floodlit soccer before their scheduled County Cup meeting in the following month, Eric Taylor swore to secrecy the thirty or so people who attended the unannounced game, urging them not divulge the score. With the game in progress, a police car patrolled around the ground and one intrepid supporter was ordered off the roof of the stand. Despite the local press not breaking the silence, the result did eventually come out in what Taylor described as 'a shabby

INTERNATIONAL (under 23) MATCH

ENGLAND *versus* SCOTLAND

WEDNESDAY, 8th FEBRUARY, 1956, Kick-off 7.15 p.m.

BY FLOODLIGHT

Official Programme 3^D

This Ticket must be intact when presented at

SOUTH STAND ENTRANCE

D

——

PLEASE BE SEATED BEFORE 7.15 p.m.

HILLSBOROUGH, SHEFFIELD

BY FLOODLIGHT

SHEFFIELD WEDNESDAY versus

SAN LORENZO

(ARGENTINIA)

WEDNESDAY, 25th JANUARY, 1956. Kick-off 7.30 p.m.

The Sheffield Wednesday Football Club does not guarantee that the proposed match will be played.

Gangway **6**   Reserved Seat **7/6** (inc. tax)

Row **A**

Seat

Eric Taylor.

Secretary and Manager.

trick' by a national daily, for *The News Chronicle* revealed that the result of the secret match had been a 7–2 win for Wednesday! Wednesday fans were probably quite pleased the score had leaked out, though unfortunately it didn't do much good for the Owls, as four weeks later, when the Cup tie was played, they lost 5–2 at home to the Blades. The same period saw Dennis Woodhead leave for Chesterfield after scoring 75 times in 226 games during a decade at the club, while one-time record signing, Jackie Sewell was sold to Aston Villa, and Peter Howells signed full-time forms on his release from national service.

Back in the league the Owls were slowly starting to climb the table, and by early December they were just two points behind the leaders, Bristol City. A home win on Christmas Eve saw Wednesday hit the top spot, and they remained there as the New Year dawned with the FA Cup visit of First Division, Newcastle United. Two goals in the last three minutes saw the Geordies progress in the cup, though Wednesday were masters in the bread and butter world of the Second Division and maintained a one point advantage for six weeks before starting to pull clear in early February. Their early Cup exit gave Wednesday the opportunity to arrange a friendly against

a top Argentinian side, San Lorenzo, with the South Americans being totally outplayed in every department as Wednesday crashed in nine goals without reply. After beating Barnsley in the first floodlit league game held at Hillsborough, the Owls opened up a five point advantage at the top of the division, with Leicester and Liverpool struggling to keep pace. Two wins over the Easter period cemented their position, and, by the time Fulham arrived at Hillsborough, Wednesday only needed a win to clinch promotion. Unfortunately, the champagne had to be put on ice, for the Londoners won 3–2. Seven days later, however, it was promotion and the Championship, as Bury were thrashed 5–2 at Gigg Lane. The title was celebrated in style the following week, with Shiner grabbing a treble in the final home game. Two days later six goals were shared at Elland Road with Leeds United, in a friendly arranged to celebrate the promotion of both clubs to the top flight. To round off a great season, Wednesday planned games in both Bulgaria and Hungary. However, after failing to gain FA permission they reverted to Plan B and took the players on a mini-tour of Western Europe. This saw the Brazilian side, Vasco Da Gama, win 2–0 in Amsterdam, before the Owls again shared six goals with their hosts in the Wuppertal Zoo Stadium in Germany.

Wednesday finish their Hillsborough campaign as Champions

1956–57
COMFORTABLE RETURN TO TOP FLIGHT

The summer of 1956 was fairly low key, with only George Davies departing for Chester, and Wednesday receiving a king's ransom of £600 for his services! There were no transfers into Hillsborough, though Don Gibson was the next best thing when he returned to full fitness after being out of the game after suffering torn knee ligaments at Swansea, back in January. Incidentally, Gibson had married the daughter of Manchester United manager, Matt Busby during that summer, and was so keen to regain his fitness that he took his training kit with him on the honeymoon! There was also changes in Wednesday's back room staff, with Jack Marshall appointed as trainer-coach on a three year contract, and Jack Shaw—who was on the verge of being released—given a coaching role with the Owls Yorkshire League side instead. Meanwhile, regardless of the problems created by the previous season's private game between United and Wednesday, the former announced the arrangement of two such further matches. Within twenty four hours, however, these were unceremoniously called off by Eric Taylor.

The Owls had the advantage of playing three of their first four league games at Hillsborough, and pressed home this fixture abnormality in spectacular fashion by not only winning all three matches, but scoring four times in each game to sit comfortably in the top half of the table. This incredible start at home continued with five against Cardiff, a week after the team had lost a two goal advantage in a thrilling 4–4 draw at Charlton Athletic. The run had to end, however, and it was their old foes, Arsenal, who brought the winning run to a conclusion. The match with the Gunners also saw the home debut of left-winger, David Cargill, who'd arrived for a £5,000 fee from Burnley. However, he could do little as the Owls proceeded to lose five consecutive league games and slide down into the bottom six. An increasing number of clubs were installing floodlights, with the vogue of the time being to play friendlies against foreign opposition under these new fangled electric lights; Wednesday being one of the leading proponents. This saw two such games take place at Hillsborough, with top Rumanian side, CCA visiting, before the Yugoslavian (now Croatian) club, Zagreb, provided the opposition in a somewhat bad tempered friendly. The visitors perpetrated countless body checks during the match, causing a Wednesday fan to be moved to shout, 'Put out the lights and let them have a proper go'!

As Christmas approached Wednesday dropped to nineteenth, their lowest position of the season. Four consecutive away games then brought forth the only two successes on foreign soil in the whole season, and this steadied the ship somewhat. On the transfer front, Don Watson went to Lincoln City and Peter Howells to Hartlepool United, as goalkeeper,

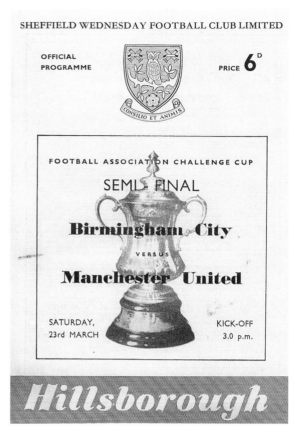

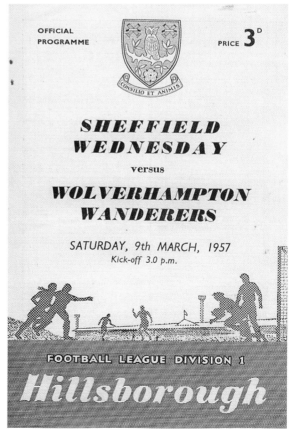

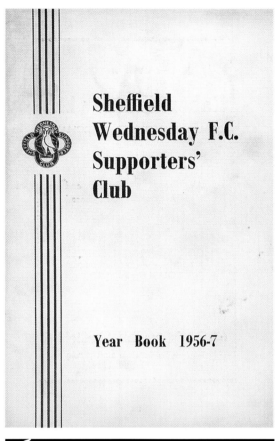

Sheffield Wednesday F.C. Supporters' Club

Year Book 1956-7

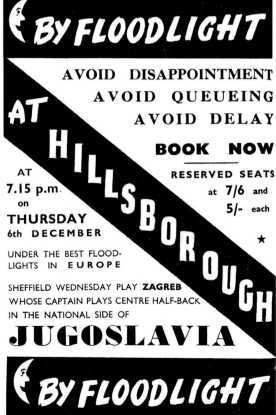

BY FLOODLIGHT

AVOID DISAPPOINTMENT
AVOID QUEUEING
AVOID DELAY

BOOK NOW

RESERVED SEATS
at **7/6** and
5/- each

AT
7.15 p.m.
on
THURSDAY
6th **DECEMBER**

UNDER THE BEST FLOOD-
LIGHTS IN **EUROPE**

SHEFFIELD WEDNESDAY PLAY **ZAGREB**
WHOSE CAPTAIN PLAYS CENTRE HALF-BACK
IN THE NATIONAL SIDE OF

JUGOSLAVIA

AT HILLSBOROUGH

★

BY FLOODLIGHT

Charlie Pllu (pronounced Ploo) was signed from non-league Scarborough. Meanwhile, at board level, the club started to discuss the possibility of building a new North Stand, and Eric Taylor was given a new five year contract. The two home games over the Festive period both fell victim to the weather, and so there was a five week gap between home fixtures before Wednesday welcomed Preston for an FA Cup replay, after having earned a goalless draw at Deepdale. When McIntosh saved a Tom Finney penalty kick in extra time to maintain Wednesday's 2–1 advantage, the Owls looked set to go into the next round. However, 'the Preston plumber' was not to be denied, and with four minutes remaining he drove home the equaliser to force a second replay. In those days such ties were usually held on a neutral ground, and so it was off to Goodison Park, where, despite a first minute goal from Albert Quixall, the Owls were then tumbled out of the old competition by conceding five times. The biggest league crowd of the season then saw a confidence boosting home win over Manchester United; although a poor away record kept the club on the fringes of the relegation zone. Meanwhile, another departure from Hillsborough was that of reserve-keeper, Leslie Williams, who dropped into Division Three (South) to sign for Swindon Town. Wednesday then announced plans to tour Spain in the close season, intending to play Valencia, Athletico Bilbao and Barcelona; however, the tour was later called off.

Despite their aforementioned barren away record, the Owls were relatively safe from the threat of relegation, and so attention turned to the club's Youth side. They had reached the FA Youth Cup semi-finals for the first time, after beating the Blades 1–0 in a Hillsborough quarter final which attracted over 18,000 fans. Wednesday were paired against West Ham in the last four; but it was not to be. For after a goalless home result, the Owls exited after losing 2–0 at Upton Park in the second leg. The team gained a reward of sorts, however, when the Owls entered their first ever youth tournament on foreign soil. The youngsters travelled to the Voelkingen in Germany, where goals from John Fantham and B. Finney were enough to secure a victory over MVV Maastricht in the Final. Back at first team level, the Owls ensured their first division future after beating Luton Town at Hillsborough. Once the pressure was off they then went out on a high note, and won their last two games to climb towards mid-table. The Owls had always seemed confident of pulling themselves into the safety zone, and the fact they had agreed to play three friendlies in April—at Norwich City, Grimsby Town and at Stocksbridge Works—probably illustrated that confidence. Overall, it was another season of consolidation, with Wednesday fans hoping that the addition of a few players in the summer would finally stop the tiresome cycle of promotion and subsequent relegation within two years.

1957–58
WHOOPS!—DOWN AGAIN

After a season of consolidation in the top flight, the big signings that the Wednesday fans hoped would arrive in the summer failed to materialise. And in one of the quietest close seasons in club history, the only transfer activity came just before the big kick-off, when Barry Butler was sold to Norwich City. The Owls did make several signings though, and these, with hindsight, would prove to be significant; with Peter Swan, Keith Ellis, Gerry Young, and Alan Finney all committing themselves to full-time contracts after completing their national service. There were also changes behind the scenes, with Robert Lyttle appointed as physiotherapist and ex-player, Ted Catlin as chief scout. Meanwhile, at the Annual General Meeting the Owls announced a profit of just over £2,000 for the year to 31st May 1957, with the Directors commenting that 'we are confident that the marked discrepancy in away performances can, and must be, corrected'. The big news though, was the announcement that a new stand would be built on the North side of the ground, in addition to a major development of the Leppings Lane end of the stadium. The summer was also witness to a unique event, when, in July, the famous New York Harlem Globetrotters brought their own particular brand of flamboyant basketball to Hillsborough, combining showmanship with dazzling ball control.

The fixture list handed Wednesday a home tie with Manchester City on the opening day of the season. The Owls, however, were unable to fulfil the fixture, as a flu epidemic had swept through the club, and for the first time ever the club was forced to postpone the opening match of the season. The outbreak first appeared when Jack Shaw reported sick, the influenza being of such a virulent strain that Hillsborough had to be totally shut down. Norman Curtis was perhaps the worst affected, and came within a whisker of contracting what, at that time, would have been a life threatening dose of pneumonia. The Owls were also given permission to call off their mid-week trip to Newcastle United, then a weakened side, still missing several key players, finally made a belated start as Nottingham Forest won at Hillsborough. Despite earning two points in their next fixture, it would perhaps be fair to say that Wednesday never really recovered from this problematic start, and they quickly slumped to the foot of the First Division table. Indeed, the Owls proceeded to lose nine of their next thirteen league games, yet surprisingly they were kept off the bottom rung by an equally deficient Leicester side. Before a glamorous friendly with Juventus, the Owls were boosted with a home win over Arsenal. The match against the Italian giants saw the crowd of just under 45,000 packed into Hillsborough treated to a thrilling game; which went the way of the Turin club, as the Welsh legend, John Charles grabbed the decisive goal in a seven goal spectacular. Off the pitch the Owls signed

Harry Clark on loan from Darlington, then allowed reserve defender Ralph O'Donnell to switch to part-time so he could start a teacher training course; and transferred Albert Broadbent to Millmoor—with Peter Johnson coming to Hillsborough as part of the deal.

The month of December saw a remarkable sequence of results which would contribute greatly to the Owls subsequent relegation. The period started with a County Cup romp against Barnsley. However, in the following six league games, and despite scoring fifteen times, Wednesday earned only a single point, as their generous defence parted like the Red Sea to concede 26 goals and leave the Owls three points adrift at the foot of the table as the New Year dawned. League troubles were then temporarily forgotten when a mini Cup run—starting with a win at Southern League, Hereford United—took the Owls to the last sixteen of the competition. Unfortunately for Wednesday, the draw then took them to Old Trafford for a game which no one in the country, bar Owls fans, wanted them to win. For this was the home side's first game following the Munich Air Disaster. On a night of high emotion (the United team line-up was poignantly left blank in the match programme) a scratch United team rose to the occasion and scored three without reply, leaving Wednesday to concentrate on their perilous league position.

During the Cup run further transfer activity took place, with both Walter Bingley and the long serving goalie, Dave McIntosh, leaving for pastures new. In March, hopes of signing the œ Park Rangers goalkeeper, Ron Springett looked to have floundered when he decided against the move. However, it was Eric Taylor to the rescue, as, in a last ditch effort, he managed to persuade Springett to change his mind and sign for the Owls, after it was agreed he could live and train in London. The future England keeper went straight into the side and a victory on his debut saw Wednesday move out of the bottom two for the first time since September. However, this was only on goal average, and within seven days they had slid back down onto the bottom rung of the ladder where they would stay for the majority of the remaining weeks of the season. Despite this, Wednesday went into their final game only twenty-four hours after selling Dave Cargill to Derby County, and still with a slim chance of surviving. A subsequent victory over Wolves proved irrelevant, however, results elsewhere ensured a third relegation in just seven years. The season ended with friendlies at King's Lynn, Hyde United and Bedford Town, but a home County Cup loss to the Blades didn't help the mood of the Wednesday support, for by this time, they must surely have been somewhat frustrated at their club's yo-yo existence between the top two divisions.

1958–59
OWLS BOUNCE BACK AGAIN

For the third time in the decade Wednesday found themselves back in Division Two, and, at a board meeting held in late June, the Directors decided it was time to split the job of secretary-manager held by Eric Taylor. The position of secretary would be retained by Taylor, for he was recognised nationally as one of the top administrators in the game. The job of club manager, however, was to be advertised for the first time since Jimmy McMullen was appointed in the 1930s. Before interviewing prospective candidates the Owls released ex-players, Tom Walker and Sam Powell from their assistant trainer roles, while the club's youth structure was shaken up when Wednesday were voted into the Northern Intermediate League. The identity of the first man interviewed for the manager's post was not released to the press. Though in retrospect, the fact that Tottenham Hotspur assistant manager, Bill Nicholson—who led Spurs to the double in 1961 as well as several other honours in the decade—was not appointed could well have indelibly altered the course of Wednesday's subsequent history. The club then turned their attentions across the Pennines, and just nine days before the start of the season, the Rochdale manager, Harry Catterick, took over at Hillsborough on a three year contract. Considering the upheaval behind the scenes it was perhaps not surprising there was no transfer activity whatsoever during those summer months, with the Owls probably having good reason to believe the players on their staff would again prove good enough to secure an immediate return to the big time.

Catterick's first game in charge was at home to Swansea Town, and he and the team experienced a good start thanks to a Redfern Froggatt second half winner. Defeat at Stoke followed, but then a tremendous unbeaten run of eleven games—including ten victories—saw the Owls top the table as the clocks went back. During this run, the Owls visited Sunderland. There, for the first time since the early 1900s, two brothers appeared together in a Wednesday league side, as Derek and Eric Wilkinson started the game. The Owls recorded a 6–0 victory in the return match with the Roker club, which proved to be the last appearance in a Wednesday shirt for 'Golden Boy', Albert Quixall. For after being chased by seven top clubs following his transfer request, Quixall signed for Manchester United for a British record fee of £45,000. Soon after this the Owls overcame the Blades in a derby encounter. This was tinged with sadness, however, as John Fantham's father collapsed and died outside the ground during the half-time break. Off the pitch, Wednesday agreed to release trainer, Jack Marshall in order that he could take over as boss at Rochdale; with Tom Eggleston filling the vacant role at Hillsborough. Meanwhile, Catterick made his first signing when he brought goalkeeper, Roy McLaren to Hillsborough for a £4,000 fee. The relatively unproven

SOUVENIR PROGRAMME

PRICE THREEPENCE

SATURDAY, 25th APRIL, 1959

SHEFFIELD WEDNESDAY v. BARNSLEY

League Division 2.   Kick-off 3 p.m.

APRIL '59 –BACK TO FIRST DIVISION

Hillsborough

Harry Catterick, Team Manager

Catterick had made such a good impression in his short time at Hillsborough that it was reported that Leicester City then tried to poach him by reputedly offering a huge pay rise. It then emerged that Catterick had yet to sign his Wednesday contract, though the fears of the Wednesday fans were put to rest when, twenty-four hours later, the club announced Catterick would not be going anywhere.

The Owls were setting a hot pace at the top of the Division and by the end of the old year, and after taking maximum points from their three Christmas fixtures, they had opened up a three point lead on their nearest challengers, Fulham. Incidentally, the club decided to award £20 Christmas boxes to all the first team players. The poor old reserve team players, however, only got a £10 gift! The New Year brought a home defeat in the Cup to First Division, West Bromwich Albion, and saw Don McEvoy sign for Lincoln City after one hundred and twelve games for the Owls. In late February, Sheffield United gained revenge for their Hillsborough defeat, thanks to a 'Doc' Pace strike, and then lost another derby game, this time at Millmoor. Thus, when the top two clashed on Good

Friday at Craven Cottage, the Owls only held a one point advantage over their Fulham rivals; but this disappeared when, after a disastrous ninety minutes, the Londoners won 6–2—with a certain Jimmy Hill grabbing a hat-trick. Wednesday, however, still had two games in hand, and although Fulham continued to win, so did the Owls. A mid-week home win over Liverpool then not only lifted Wednesday back to the summit but secured promotion back from whence they had come, with four games still to play. By this time the Everton centre-forward, Eric Kirby, had signed for a sizeable fee, but couldn't force his way into the team whose only ambition now was to hold off Fulham to clinch the Second Division Championship. Two days before the Owls final home game against Barnsley their nearest rivals lost at Charlton. This meant that a victory over the Tykes would secure the title for the Owls; and Wednesday made no mistake, putting five goals past Barnsley keeper Leeson in front of an ecstatic crowd—which, strangely, was the lowest of the season. At the time the Wednesday fans were unaware that this promotion would finally signal the end of the Owls yo-yo years; and so it was au revoir to the Second Division until the early 1970s.

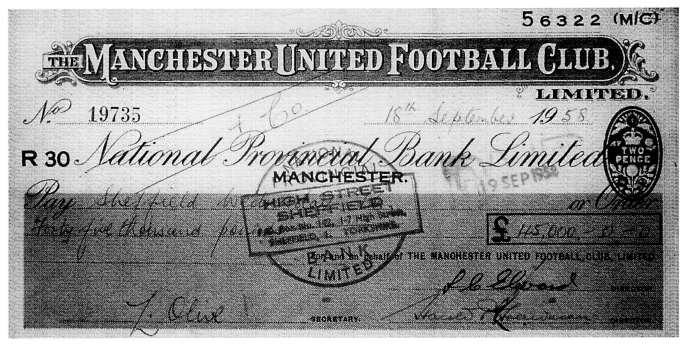

Manchester United's cheque paid to Sheffield Wednesday. The record-breaking fee of £45,000 was paid for Albert Quixall.

Memory Match

**Football League Division Two
Saturday 6th May 1950**

FOOTBALL LEAGUE   DIVISION II

SHEFFIELD WEDNESDAY
versus
TOTTENHAM HOTSPUR

At Wednesday Ground, Hillsborough, Saturday, 6th May, 1950
Kick-off 3 p.m.

Wednesday v. Coventry City   Photo by "Sheffield Telegraph" & "Star"

WATER LANE   PROPRIETOR:
SHEFFIELD   ERIC THORPE
Tel.: 23498   DONCASTER

Eric's Road-Cafes

TEAS
SUPPERS
BREAKFASTS
PRIVATE PARTIES   AND DINNERS
CATERED FOR   SEATING ACCOMM. 200
ALSO AT TINSLEY, SHEFFIELD ; CARBROOK, SHEFFIELD ; DONCASTER ROAD, BAWTRY

2d.   OFFICIAL PROGRAMME   2d.

Sheffield Wednesday
0
Tottenham Hotspur
0

The race to win promotion from the old Second Division in 1950 was one of the closest of all time. On the dawn of the season's final afternoon it was the Owls who arguably held the most slender of advantages, as three clubs attempted to finish in the second promotion spot, behind the Champions, Tottenham Hotspur. The Owls went into their home game lying just one point behind their City rivals, Sheffield United. The Blades, having already completed their fixtures, had to wait to see if Wednesday or fourth-placed Southampton would deny them promotion. The situation was further complicated by goal average (goals scored divided by goals conceded), with one of many permutations giving a possibility that all three clubs could actually finish in an unprecedented dead heat. The consensus of opinion was that a goalless draw would probably be enough, against a visiting team who came to Hillsborough on the back of five consecutive defeats, and who appeared to have certainly taken their foot off the Championship pedal. However, Spurs did boast two managerial greats of the future in their ranks, in Bill Nicholson and Alf Ramsey; and Wednesday were promised a tough afternoon.

A crowd of almost 51,000 packed into Hillsborough, and, on a pitch made greasy by showers, Swift won the toss and the Owls kicked off towards the Leppings Lane end. In an entertaining first half characterised by some superb passing and movement from both sides, it was the visitors who created the better chances, with the first real opportunity arriving midway through the period, when McIntosh was robbed on the edge of the area by Bennett. As Swift and company guarded the goal line, Bennett passed to Walters who fired just wide with the Owls keeper in no man's land. It then took a brilliant save from McIntosh to deny Bennett, as Spurs started to warm to the task in hand. McIntosh then came to the rescue again when, just before the interval, he got his finger tips to a spectacular drive from Bailey. Half time came with Wednesday grateful to be level, and thankful to both Dave McIntosh and their outstanding captain, Hugh Swift, who'd help to keep the Lilywhites at bay. The biggest cheer of the day so far, however, came during the interval when news filtered through that promotion rivals, Southampton were two goals down at home to West Ham.

Early in the second half, dangerman Dennis Woodhead caused Spurs problems, seeing one shot superbly tipped over by Ditchburn. In what had become an end-to-end game, Swift next cleared Bailey's effort from near the goal line, and as rain started to fall, the ineffective Hugh McJarrow spurned a good chance to settle everyone's nerves in the ground. As the game entered its final few minutes the Owls rallied for a winner, particularly as the Saints were now 3–2 ahead at the Dell. In the final minute the tension became almost unbearable, as Duquemin broke down the wing and sent a great cross into the penalty area. Medley came running in and Hillsborough held its collective breath as he headed goalwards—mercifully putting the chance just wide. Within seconds the final whistle had blown and Wednesday were up, having beaten United to promotion by a goal average of 0.008. Thousands of fans swarmed onto the pitch, and after they had carried the players from the field the massed ranks stood in front of the South Stand cheering until the players reappeared. After the players changed into their training suits they climbed onto a special platform which had been erected in front of the Director's Box, and captain Swift and Chairman Fearnehough addressed the delirious crowd to complete a memorable afternoon which ended with Wednesday back in the top flight, thirteen years after suffering relegation.

Wednesday: McIntosh, Kenny, Swift, Gannon, Packard, Witcomb, Rickett, Henry, McJarrow, Froggatt, Woodhead

Tottenham: Ditchburn, Ramsey, Willis, Nicholson, Clarke, Burgess, Walters, Bennett, Duquemin, Bailey, Medley

Referee: Mr S. Law (West Bromwich)

Memory Match

The 1951–52 season will always be associated with one man, for Derek Dooley cut a swathe through the opposition defences as the Owls steam-rollered their way out of the Second Division. However, as detailed elsewhere, Wednesday struggled in the early weeks of the season, and it wasn't until early October, when the big number nine was introduced, that results started to improve. By the time Notts County visited Hillsborough, the Owls had taken seven points out of the last eight and improved their league position to eighth. Both sides showed one change from the previous week's line-up, with County welcoming back their star man, Tommy Lawton. In order to combat the return of the prolific Lawton, Wednesday brought Edgar Packard back in place of Cyril Turton, with the half-back given the specific task of 'minding' the dangerous centre-forward.

The Magpies quickly had a taste of things to come when Dooley almost netted in the first minute, though considering the final scoreline the opening period was surprisingly even. Indeed, the best early chance fell to the visitors, with McPherson's low shot looking to be heading for the net before Dave McIntosh pounced near the post to bring off a clever save. The visitors were playing the more constructive football, with the main interest for those Wednesday fans in a bumper crowd of over 46,000 being the running battle between Dooley and County centre-half, Leon Leuty; a case of the moveable force meeting the immovable object. Just before the break, however, the home side were lucky not to concede a penalty, for Vin Kenny looked to have cleared the ball with his arm. It was Wednesday, though, who, in the final minute of the half made the vital break-through, as from Walter Rickett's corner kick, Jackie Sewell headed the Owls into a half-time lead against his old team mates.

Despite holding the advantage at the break, the game had been extremely close—with Derek Dooley apparently biding his time. Eight minutes into the second half, however, he dribbled between Deans and Leuty to hit an unstoppable shot past Smith. Soon after this, Jackie Sewell was reduced to half speed after receiving a crack on his leg. He was farmed out onto the right wing as Lawton finally shook off the attentions of Packard to force McIntosh into making a brilliant save. Mid-way through the second half, the visitors hopes of a comeback were dashed in spectacular style, as Dooley crashed in three goals inside a five minute period. A great pass from Eddie Gannon set Dooley up for the first, with the barnstorming centre-forward completing his hat-trick three minutes later, as he almost ran over the top of the now overworked Leuty to shoot past Smith at the second attempt. The legend was starting to be written when he headed his fourth within another two minutes, and then, with five minutes remaining, Dooley completed a personal nap hand after scoring from a low Alan Finney centre. This final strike wrapped up a remarkable six goal win which, in the first period, had looked virtually impossible as the teams fought for ascendancy. The difference, however, was a 6ft 2ins, Sheffield-born forward, who was soon to become the darling of Wednesday fans after becoming the second, and last, Owls' player to score five times in a competitive match since the end of the Second World War.

Wednesday: McIntosh, Bannister, Kenny, Gannon, Packard, Davies, Finney, Sewell, Dooley, Quixall, Rickett

Notts County: R. Smith, Southwell, Deans, Brunt, Leuty, Robinson, McPherson, Jackson, Lawton, Wylie, Crookes

Referee: Mr F. Gerrard (Preston)

Football League Division Two
Saturday 3rd November 1951

Sheffield Wednesday 6
Notts County 0

Memory Match

Derek Dooley Benefit Match
Wednesday 9th March 1955

OFFICIAL SOUVENIR, SIXPENCE

DEREK DOOLEY TRUST FUND

Floodlight Match

WEDNESDAY, 9th MARCH, 1955, Kick-off 7.30 p.m.

SHEFFIELD XI.
v.
INTERNATIONAL XI.

Sheffield XI
1
International XI
5

When Derek Dooley's soaring career was tragically cut short in February 1953, the football world at large was shocked—with Wednesday fans particularly distressed at the loss of their goal scoring hero. However, as 'big Derek' started to come to terms with his disability and the end of his career, the Sheffield public began to rally round to set up the Derek Dooley Trust Fund. Just over two years after that tragic afternoon at Deepdale this reached a climax, as Hillsborough staged his benefit match. An all-ticket crowd of 55,000 packed the stadium and were witness to an historic occasion as Wednesday used their new floodlighting system for the first time.

The game was a veritable who's-who of 1950's soccer talent, with the International side including the legendary Stanley Matthews; Busby Babe, Roger Byrne; 'Gentle Giant', John Charles; and 'The Preston plumber', Tom Finney. Ex-Owl, Eddie Quigley returned to Hillsborough, while the forward line boasted the incomparable talents of England centre-forward, Nat Lofthouse; and arguably Sheffield United's greatest ever player—Jimmy Hagan. Set against this line up was a Sheffield Select side made up of a Wednesday team which contained four guest players from the Blades. It was fairly obvious that the Sheffield players would have problems containing their star-studded opponents, and so it was no surprise when, after 15 minutes, Stanley Matthews crossed for Jimmy Hagan to fire past an unsighted Ted Burgin and put the International side ahead. With ten minutes of the half remaining, some wing wizardry from Matthews then led to a second goal, as he burst down the flank before drilling in a low cross which the unfortunate Don McEvoy could only turn into his own net. The crowd were being treated to a fabulous show from the Internationals, as they passed with superb accuracy, ran cleverly off the ball, and showed tremendous speed of thought. The audacity of Matthews also kept the crowd in good humour. On one occasion he received the ball well inside his own half and was then challenged by Graham Shaw; and although the defender was half his age, the 40-year-old winger easily outpaced the youngster. At times is seemed that Matthews was playing with Shaw like a cat plays with a kitten. It was therefore no surprise that when half time arrived the Internationals had stretched their lead to 3–0 through Hagan's second of the evening.

The second half saw the Sheffield eleven come into the proceedings, with Albert Quixall and Alan Finney prominent. And with eighteen minutes remaining, they were rewarded when Jackie Sewell fired home from close range. This only served to reawaken the Internationals, however, and they quickly reasserted their authority by netting twice in the last ten minutes. From Hagan's pass a Tommy Lawton pile-driver almost broke the net; before a rare trip into enemy territory from Bryne allowed him to set up Eddie Quigley, who scored on his old stamping ground to bring the curtain down on a dazzling night of football. This had more than matched the glare of the new floodlights, which the Manchester United boss, Matt Busby, had said were the best he'd seen since his visit to America. In the end the evening had been a marvellous success and brought the total of Dooley's benefit to around £15,000. In those days this was a considerable sum, considering the Owls total gate receipts for the 1954–55 season were just over £68,000. However, the overriding reason for the evening was to pay tribute to Wednesday's former centre-forward, who had given all his strength, ability and enthusiasm on behalf of the Owls in a brief but glorious career.

Wednesday: Burgin (Sheff. Utd.), Martin, G. Shaw (Sheff. Utd.), Jack Shaw, McEvoy, Joe Shaw (Sheff. Utd.), Finney, Quixall, Cross (Sheff. Utd.), Sewell, Marriott

International XI: Kelsey (Arsenal), Foulkes (Man. Utd.), Byrne (Sheff. Utd.), Farrell (Everton), Charles (Leeds), Forbes (Arsenal), Matthews (Blackpool), Quigley (Blackburn), Lawton (Arsenal), Hagan (Sheff. Utd.), Edlington (Everton)

Referee: Mr A. Ellis (Halifax)

Memory Match

In the early post-war years, England still considered themselves to be top dogs on the football field; and until 1953 no foreign side had visited these shores and returned home with a victory. However, this changed dramatically in October 1953 when Hungary visited London and stunned the English establishment by winning 6–3 at Wembley. If that wasn't bad enough, the Owls' Jackie Sewell was in an England side which was thrashed 7–1 in Budapest in May 1954, just before the Hungarians went all the way to the World Cup Final in Switzerland. This was without the doubt the golden period of Hungarian soccer, with the brilliant talents of Ferenc Puskas and Sandor Kocsis making them uncrowned 'World Champions'. Against this background, it was no surprise that Hungarian club football was also on a high, and the likes of Honved and Red Banner were a much sought after opposition across Western Europe. When Wednesday arranged for the Budapest side Vasas to visit Hillsborough, the interest in the game was therefore enormous; for the Hungarians were third in the league and had just won their domestic Cup after beating both Honved and Red Banner on the way to the trophy.

This was the first time a full Wednesday side had played under the new Hillsborough lights, and was the beginning of a plethora of glamorous friendlies against foreign opposition in the 1950s. The game was very much an experiment for Wednesday, though a crowd of over 45,000 rewarded the risk; and those fans who attended were treated to what was simply the most technically perfect display of football ever seen at Hillsborough. The Hungarians were superior in every department and seemingly had acres of space in which to attack the Owls. The visitors actually boasted only a handful of players who had earned full caps, yet everyone in their side seemed to be equally proficient with both feet. The biggest lesson learned by Wednesday was seeing how the visitors were able to hold off a challenge while still maintaining full control of the ball. At the start of the game it looked as if Wednesday might pull off a shock, for they played well and harassed Vasas. However, two goals inside three minutes opened the proverbial floodgates. First to net was Gyula Teleki, who drove home after trading passes with the outstanding Lajos Csordes. Soon after this Csordes doubled the Hungarians advantage, and after two Sewell headers had gone close, Albert Quixall scrambled a goal for Wednesday to lift hopes of a comeback as the whistle blew for half time.

Wednesday unfortunately spurned two chances that came their way early in the second half, and were soon made to pay when Teleki ran straight through the Owls' defence to restore a two goal cushion. Flying winger, Jozsef Raduly, then added a fourth before setting up another for Csordes, as Wednesday started to wilt under the Vasas onslaught. The rout was completed by substitute J. Szilagyi, and an own goal from Tony Kay. And though despite seeing their team concede seven, only a handful of fans in the bumper crowd failed to stay after the final whistle to pay tribute to a truly great side. At the end the Vasas players bowed to the crowd, as Wednesdayites realised they would not quickly forget the night the Hungarians gave their side a footballing lesson.

Wednesday: McIntosh, Staniforth, Bingley, Gibson, McEvoy, Kay, Froggatt, Sewell, Shiner, Quixall, Broadbent

Vasas: Kamaras, Sarosi, Kontha, Bodzsar, Bundzsak, Berendi, Raduly, Csordes (J. Szilagyi), G. Szilagyi, Teleki, Illovski

Referee: Mr G. McCabe (Sheffield)

Sheffield Wednesday
1
Vasas
7

Chapter 6

Rise and Fall
1959–1975

1959-60
TOP SIX FINISH FOR WEDNESDAY

It was Harry Catterick's first full summer as Wednesday boss, and his transfer activity in the period was fairly low key as the Owls again followed the somewhat risky policy of keeping faith with the side that had earned promotion. Although the club was criticised for their lack of big name signings, Catterick defended this inactivity, stating he had travelled thousands of miles in an attempt to secure the signings the fans craved, but for various reasons had been unable to do so. At the end of the previous season the Owls had given free transfers to several players, including Eric Wilkinson and Alan Hinchcliffe, who subsequently moved to Chesterfield and, after three years as player coach to the club's 'A' team, Jack Shaw was transferred to neighbours Denaby United. In total four new players arrived at Hillsborough, with Airdrie winger Willie McLean the first to sign on the dotted line. He was followed from over the border by Doug McMillan, from Scottish Junior club Woodhouse Rose; while John Quinn and Bill Lodge arrived from English non-league football.

The Owls were handed an unwelcome opening day fixture on their return to the top flight, having to visit Arsenal who had finished third in the last campaign. However, a John Fantham goal two minutes before the break proved to be the game's only score, as Wednesday got off to the proverbial flyer. Despite this success the Owls experienced an inconsistent opening few weeks to the season, which left them just below mid table after a dozen games. After losing at Sheffield United in a County Cup tie (Pace again proving to be the scourge of Wednesday with a brace), the Owls then let Ron Staniforth leave to become player coach at Division Three (North) club, Barrow.

As November dawned, Wednesday suddenly came alive and a win at Leeds was followed by a morale boosting success over the crack Russian side, Torpedo, in another floodlight friendly. However, what proved to be the turning point in Wednesday's season was the visit of league leaders West Ham, who travelled back to East London after having been sensationally beaten 7–0 by a rampant Owls side. This astonishing win was then followed by a 4–0 success at Chelsea, before the double was completed over the Gunners—thanks to a five goal Hillsborough haul. Among the scorers in that Arsenal romp was new signing Bobby Craig, who had joined from Scottish club Third Lanark after drawn out negotiations. There were also two departures, with Roy Shiner leaving for Hull City after 96 goals in only 160 games, and Eric Kirby ending a brief association with Wednesday by signing for Plymouth, after having started only three games in nine months since arriving from Goodison Park. Also following Kirby to Home Park was

Keith Ellis, fast car and beautiful girl

Jim McAnearney, with the Owls pocketing a combined fee of £10,000 for the twosome.

The New Year started badly, with a defeat at Manchester City. For the remainder of the month the Owls boasted a hundred percent record which saw them climb to the dizzy heights of fourth place, as well as reaching the last sixteen of the FA Cup. The crowds flocked to the Cup ties at Hillsborough, with over 50,000 watching the Midland League club, Peterborough United, go down fighting in the fourth round. Over 66,000 then saw a Tom McAnearney penalty earn a superb win at Manchester United in the next round, before a little local difficulty was overcome when a Derek Wilkinson brace won a sixth round derby clash at Bramall Lane. Back in the league, Wednesday had climbed to third place, and sat just one place lower when they faced Blackburn Rovers in the FA Cup semi-final at Maine Road. The Owls were favourites against a struggling Rovers side, but a goal in each half from Derek Dougan put the underdogs two goals ahead. Despite John Fantham pulling one back it wasn't enough, and dreams of a first Wembley appearance for twenty five years were broken. Left to concentrate on the league, Wednesday thankfully did not let the Cup disappointment adversely affect their form, and a post semi-final home win over Manchester United helped greatly. A top six position was maintained for the remainder of the season, although only one win in the Owls final five games meant a drop from third place down to fifth.

At the end of the season the club then undertook the most ambitious tour in their history, agreeing to play three games behind the Iron Curtain in the old Soviet Union. They kicked off in the Central Lenin stadium, Moscow, where, in front of 50,000, the CSKA (Soviet Army) won through a second-half goal from Mamikin. Wednesday then travelled thousands of miles south to Georgia, where, in Tiflis, they were beaten 1–0 by Dynamo through a dubious penalty; before finally going all the way back to Moscow where Locomotive beat them 3–2 to complete what must have been an exhausting schedule. Overall, it had been the Owls best season for a quarter of a century, and with crowds up fifteen percent to an average of almost 33,000 the immediate future looked rosy—with the pre-season criticism of the club thankfully proving to be unfounded.

1960–61
BEST POST WAR SIDE?

The major news of the Summer of 1960 centred around the club's decision to issue £150,000 of new debenture stock, the proceeds of which would be used to fund the construction of a new state of the art cantilever stand on the North side of the ground. This structure would seat 10,000 spectators and be the biggest of its kind in Europe. On the footballing side, manager Harry Catterick, in what proved to be indicative of his time at Hillsborough, again failed to enter the transfer market to bring additional talent to the club. This time, however, there was no criticism; probably due to the fact that in his short time at the club he had hardly put a managerial foot wrong, and in the process had turned Wednesday into one of the real forces in the game. His only signing was Maurice Lindley, who joined as coach; while Don Gibson went to Leyton Orient, and Norman 'Cannonball' Curtis joined Doncaster Rovers as player-manager after 324 games and almost ten years at Hillsborough.

Almost 35,000 saw an opening day home win over West Bromwich Albion; and in the club's best start to a campaign since their first season at Hillsborough they remained unbeaten in their opening twelve games to sit second to an outstanding Spurs side who were already starting to run away with the Championship. Goalscoring was not the Owls particular forté, but a defensive back line containing the likes of Ron Springett, Don Megson and Tony Kay ensured that only seven goals were conceded in those opening dozen games; leaving Wednesday four points adrift of a Tottenham side who had only dropped one point. The unbeaten tag finally went in late October at Wolves, but three weeks later came the clash of the top two, with a three-sided Hillsborough packed to the rafters for the visit of Spurs. The crowd were treated to a monumental encounter, which entered Hillsborough folklore after a second-half Fantham goal saw the dragon slain and the Spurs' lead at the top cut down to five points. It was definitely a case of 'After The Lord Major's Show' a week later, when defeat was suffered in thick fog at Leicester City; before Aston Villa became the first side to lower the Owls' colours at Hillsborough. By now Tottenham were an astonishing nine points clear and it looked like the only competition was to be for the runners-up spot. The Owls form was wavering, however, and by Christmas they had slipped to fifth spot. This was despite beating Blackburn 5–4 at Hillsborough, when the home fans had to be issued with tranquillisers at the end, after the Owls had tried their best to throw away a 5–1 half-time lead!

Boxing Day saw Wednesday earn a creditable draw at Highbury. On a freezing cold day, however, tragedy struck on the journey home when the Owls team bus failed to take a double right hand bend on the A1, near Huntingdon, and crashed off the road. The majority of the passengers escaped with cuts and bruises, although Peter Swan suffered a double fracture of his left shoulder. However, young professional Douglas McMillan was not so lucky, and was trapped in the wreckage to such an extent that in order to save his life the doctors had no choice but to amputate his right leg at the crash scene. Similarities with Derek Dooley were hard to ignore, and the events shocked the football world as McMillan had to come to terms with the end of his football career after having failed to play a first team game for the Owls. Five days later Wednesday were back in action; and, an hour before the kick off, McMillan phoned from his hospital bed and spoke to each player in turn to wish them luck. The least his team mates could do was win the game for the 19-year-old Scot, and this they duly did thanks to goals from Derek Wilkinson and John Fantham.

The first two months of the New Year saw Wednesday produce some of the most scintillating football their supporters had ever seen, winning eight and drawing two of the ten games played. It was not just the victories that impressed. however, but the manner of those wins—such as that at Fulham when

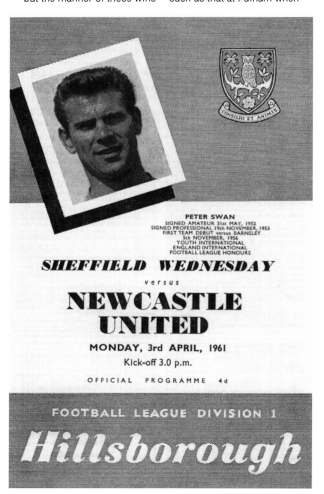

PETER SWAN
SIGNED AMATEUR 31st MAY, 1952
SIGNED PROFESSIONAL 19th NOVEMBER, 1953
FIRST TEAM DEBUT versus BARNSLEY
5th NOVEMBER, 1956
YOUTH INTERNATIONAL
ENGLAND INTERNATIONAL
FOOTBALL LEAGUE HONOURS

SHEFFIELD WEDNESDAY

versus

NEWCASTLE UNITED

MONDAY, 3rd APRIL, 1961

Kick-off 3.0 p.m.

OFFICIAL PROGRAMME 4d

FOOTBALL LEAGUE DIVISION 1

Hillsborough

the Owls hit six, with Alan Mullery incredibly scoring in his own net after just thirty seconds, without an Owls player having touched the ball. In a run of six consecutive wins, Preston were hit for five, and Wednesday scored four at Turf Moor. Yet it was the first game of that run that stunned the football community, when, in an FA Cup replay at Manchester United, a hat-trick from Keith Ellis spearheaded an astonishing 7–2 win to put the Owls into the last sixteen. Once there, they won at Leyton Orient, but then hopes of a second consecutive semi-final were dashed in a replay at Burnley. While the goals were flying in from all angles there were several new arrivals at Hillsborough, with St Mirren forward, John Frye, being the first newcomer, followed by John Meredith signed from Doncaster in exchange for John Ballagher plus a fee. Peter Baker also left for Queen's' Park Rangers, but these events paled into insignificance in early April, when, with Wednesday lying second in the table, Harry Catterick, arguably their best manager since Bob Brown, tendered his resignation. Catterick gave no reason for his shock decision, although it was suggested he was frustrated at a lack of cash available for transfers, and was unhappy at a high level of interference from the board. However, there was obviously more to the resignation, as ten days later he was appointed Everton boss.

The Owls fans were hugely disappointed at his departure, which meant the club was managerless for the game at Spurs which the Owls had to win to keep the Championship race open. Thousands were locked out at White Hart Lane as over 61,000 saw Megson put the Owls into a shock lead. However two goals in a minute put Spurs ahead and they held on to clinch the title and condemn Wednesday to the not inconsiderable prize of runners-up. In the end, Wednesday were left to reflect on the fact that their greatest post-war team unfortunately hit its peak in the Tottenham double season; as, frustratingly, their haul of 58 points would have been enough to win seven out of the fourteen Championships since the War. Nevertheless, the Owls had finished in their highest position since 1930. In addition the club's reserve side were Champions of the Central League, the Juniors finished runners up in the Northern Intermediate League, and a Wednesday Youth side travelled to Germany where they beat Hamburg in the Final of an International Youth Tournament. Finally, to round off a highly eventful season, the Owls outdid their visit to the Soviet Union a year earlier by undertaking a four game tour of Nigeria. Chalking up an 11–2 win in their opening game, before winning two and drawing the remainder, this was certainly an experience for the Wednesday party—with high temperatures and a local penchant for invading the pitch at every opportunity. This led to a mini riot in a bad tempered game against East Nigeria; and in retrospect it was perhaps not the most sensible foreign trip ever undertaken by the club.

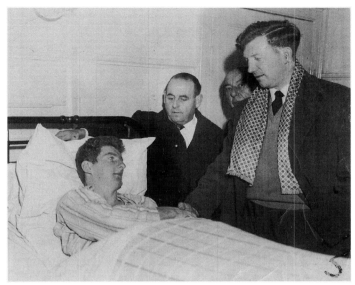

Bound by tragedy—Doug McMillan and Derek Dooley

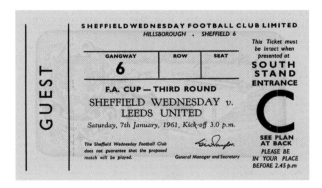

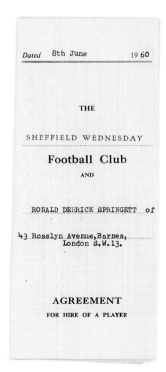

1961–62
FIRST TASTE OF EUROPEAN FOOTBALL

The first objective of the close season for the Owls' board of Directors was to replace the departed Catterick, and this problem was quickly solved when Ajax Amsterdam manager, Vic Buckingham, was appointed to the hot seat. His first task was to sell Bobby Lodge to Doncaster Rovers, but within a few weeks he had to start looking for his own backroom staff when Head Coach, Tom Eggleston, and assistant coach, Maurice Lindley, both resigned to take up other posts. The former eventually joined his old boss Catterick at Everton, while the latter went to Leeds United. The new man was unable to fill the vacancies until the season was underway, so his only other close-season activity was to transfer reserve team players Graham Beighton and Terry Whitham. Meanwhile, following the completion of the new North Stand, the Owls announced plans to cover the giant Spion Kop in the near future.

As a prelude to the big kick off, the Owls visited Buckingham's old club, Ajax, to play the first ever pre-season friendly in Wednesday's history. After recording a 2–1 win, it was back to Blighty to start the season with a win at West Bromwich Albion, before returning to Hillsborough where the home game with Bolton saw the new stand in use for the first time. Sir Stanley Rous, the secretary of the Football Association, officially opened the new £150,000 structure, and must have been impressed by the game that followed, as the Owls won an entertaining match by four goals to two. Three days later a Fantham hat-trick took Wednesday to the top of the league; then, after losing at Bolton, they returned to the summit following a superb 4–0 win at Everton. This must have been enjoyed by the Wednesday faithful who were still bristling over Catterick's departure.

Soon after this, the club made their first ever trip into Europe for a competitive match, visiting Lyon in France for the Fairs Cup clash with Olympique. A crowd of only 5,000 saw a terrible first half performance from Wednesday which left them trailing by three goals at the break. Thankfully, strikes from Young and Ellis pulled the tie around, only for a last minute breakaway goal from Combin leaving Wednesday with a hard task in the second leg. Before hosting the French side the Owls had four league games, but only picked up one solitary point to slide down the division into mid table. This mini slump included conceding a last minute winner to—who else but—Doc Pace, in the Bramall Lane derby; and also saw Division One new boys, Ipswich Town, romp to a 4–1 victory on their way to an unlikely Championship success. Despite this poor form, over 30,000 attended Hillsborough for their first taste of 'real' European football, where they watched another thrilling game which saw the aggregate scores tied at 6–6, with just five minutes left to play. And then, with a replay looking on the cards, it was John Fantham who dived in to head home from a free kick and send the Owls through.

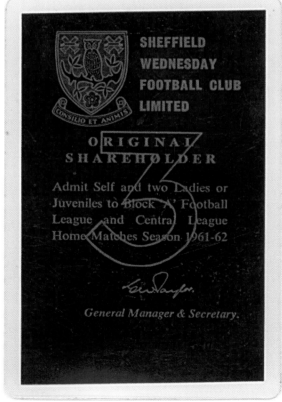

Soon after progressing in Europe, the Owls sold John Frye to Tranmere Rovers; and Vic Buckingham finally got his man, when Gordon Clark was appointed assistant manager. A good crowd turned out to support a Hillsborough benefit game for the unfortunate Douglas McMillan, in which the likes of Bobby Charlton and Billy Wright appeared for the select side. Incidentally, in the same month, the club's reserve side recorded their record league win against Barnsley in a Central League game at Hillsborough, when four different players grabbed hat-tricks in an amazing 14–0 win. Then, after slowly moving into the top eight in the league, it was back into Europe, with AS Roma providing the opposition, as well as that streak of cynicism which categorised the Italian game for several years. The latter showed itself when Lojacono was sent off by the Belgian referee for a crude tackle on Kay; yet, in pure footballing terms, the Owls were far superior, and a Gerry Young treble helped Wednesday to a comfortable win and eventual passage to the last eight, despite losing to a Peter Swan own goal in the return leg. That game in Rome was also the scene of a nasty incident after the final whistle, when Tony Kay was punched and kicked by a home player. All in all Wednesday were glad to get past the Italians and return to the bread and butter of league football where the Owls were seventh at the turn of the year.

An unblemished record in January took Wednesday through to the last sixteen of the Cup and into the First Division top six. The following month, though, saw a complete reversal, as they exited the FA Cup at the hands of Manchester United and lost the Sheffield derby to the Blades. There was one bright spot in February, and that came in the Fairs Cup when Spanish giants, Barcelona, visited Hillsborough and returned home after losing by the odd goal in five. The return match was watched by a crowd of 75,000, but goals from de Macedo and Kocsis were enough to send Wednesday crashing out after a great run in their first season of European football. Away from the action, Vic Buckingham made his first major signing when Eddie Holliday arrived from Middlesbrough; while, after earlier in the season turning down a move to Blackburn, Bobby Craig had a change of heart and joined the Ewood Park club. In the league Wednesday again slipped down into mid table, and this led directly to Buckingham earning front page headlines in the local paper when he launched an astonishing attack on his own players. However, the outburst seemed to have an effect, as Wednesday won their final four games to move back into the top six and round off another good season.

Wednesday run out before the game with Bolton Wanderers

Peter Johnson

1962–63
FA DENY WEDNESDAY EUROPEAN SPOT

The first act of the summer for Vic Buckingham was to announce the retained list. This heralded the end of an era, as Redfern Froggatt, after 536 games and 165 goals in all competitions, was released after twenty years at Hillsborough. Among the other departures were John Meredith and Jack Martin, both of whom had appeared in the Owls' first team; while the first new arrival was Bradford City's highly rated centre-forward, David Layne. Also signing professional forms was a young Howard Wilkinson, and, after initially refusing to re-sign, Peter Swan put pen to paper but then somewhat confusingly immediately asked for a transfer, saying he didn't think the terms offered were suitable! This request for a move was turned down, though one that did occur was Meredith's transfer to Chesterfield. The first signs of today's thriving commercial side to the club were also seen when Wednesday launched their first development fund draw, with tickets retailing at one shilling and a ceiling of fifteen thousand tickets set per draw. The Owls then added to their back room staff, appointing Jack Mansell as trainer coach from the Dutch side Blauw-Wit, while Red Froggatt signed for Cheshire League, Stalybridge Celtic. One player who did not come to Hillsborough was the prolific scorer, Brian Clough. Despite boasting a career record of almost a goal in every game, he was described in a Wednesday scouting report as 'lazy and a poor header but scores goals'.

The major talking point of the summer was the farcical intervention of the English Football Association which eventually led to the Owls being banned from competing in the Fairs Cup. Back in the early 1960s the competition was still an invitation event, and in July, the Cup committee announced that Wednesday, along with Everton and Birmingham City, were to be the English representatives. However the English FA and Football League had other ideas, and requested that Burnley and Sheffield United be substituted in place of the Owls and Birmingham. At the time, relations were somewhat strained between the two parties, as continental Europe started to a have a bigger say in World events. The Fairs Cup organisers were not impressed when the English authorities tried to dictate who should enter their competition, especially as they had asked three English clubs to take part—more than any other country. The draw went ahead with Wednesday paired with Victoria Cologne. Back home, however, the authorities would not budge, and both Birmingham and Wednesday were forbidden to enter the competition. Twenty four hours later the club held an emergency board meeting and agreed to appeal to the authorities. This was to no avail, and the stubbornness of the English administration not only ruined Wednesday's chances of European football but meant that only Everton entered the competition; for the Fairs Cup organisers refused to be

dictated to and promptly scrapped the two contentious invitations. To highlight the head-in-the-sand attitude of the English authorities. it emerged that when the situation arose the two Sheffield clubs had met with the Fairs Cup committee and agreed to compete in alternative years, with Wednesday entering that season!

While the Fairs Cup controversy raged, the Owls kicked off the new campaign with a defeat in their first outing in a friendly fixture at Ajax. The real action started six days later when the Owls, sporting a new strip consisting of narrow blue and white stripes, drew at home with Bolton. In the first four games they picked up only two points and sat near the foot of the early First Division table. A Hillsborough win over West Brom got the Owls off the mark, and, with new boy David Layne a regular scorer, they quickly started to climb the table, moving up to seventh place by the end of September. After losing out on competitive foreign opposition the Owls were then amply compensated when Santos, with Pele, visited to wow the Hillsborough faithful in front of a huge audience. The Owls then hit six in a testimonial at Bristol Rovers, before a home draw with Aston Villa was clouded in controversy when the newly nicknamed 'Bronco' Layne was sent off after clashing with McEwan. Several spectators ran onto the pitch to protest and cushions rained down from the stands in the worst case of crowd disorder seen for many years. The outcome was
that Layne was suspended for seven days and Wednesday escaped fairly lightly with a £100 fine for the events following the dismissal. Ironically, just before the crowd trouble, Hillsborough had been confirmed as one of the venues for the 1966 World Cup Finals. Back on the field of play, Wednesday's form was poor, and they ended 1962 having failed to win in twelve games, with defeat at Ipswich proving

Colin Dobson

to have far reaching implications. Meanwhile, there were two departures from the club, with Billy Griffin the first to leave for Bury, followed soon after by highly rated Tony Kay, who signed for Harry Catterick's Everton for a record fee for a wing half. Meanwhile, it was better late than never, when Wednesday were finally paid by the promoters who organised the tour of Nigeria way back in May 1961!

As the New Year dawned, one of the worst winters on record took an icy grip. It would be early March before the Owls were again in action at Hillsborough; although they did manage to play a handful of games away from home, including 3–0 romps on snow bound pitches at West Brom and Nottingham Forest, a draw in the Cup at Shrewsbury in a game postponed several times, and a friendly at Grimsby. The Owls returned to Sheffield to put Shrewsbury out of the FA Cup, and forty-eight hours later Bronco Layne hit his first hat-trick in a Wednesday shirt. Progress in the Cup was ended at Highbury, but the Owls Youth side went all the way to the last four in the FA Youth Cup, where a backlog of fixtures caused by the horrendous weather meant they were forced to play a one-off tie at Anfield, with the home side recording a comfortable 4–0 victory. At first team level Wednesday had to play their final twelve games in a forty day period, but eight wins in that period, including notable successes at Liverpool and Manchester United, plus a home over the Blades, ensured Wednesday finished in sixth place for the second consecutive season.

Colin Dobson opens the scoring against Manchester City

1963–64
BRIBES SCANDAL ROCKS WEDNESDAY

Compared to a year earlier, the summer of 1963 was relatively quiet. The first news of any note was the attempt by his old club, Ajax, to lure Vic Buckingham back to Holland. The Amsterdam club offered to double his wage at Hillsborough; but, after considering the offer the Owls manager decided to stay with Wednesday. For the third year running the Owls were invited to compete in the Fairs Cup. This time, thankfully, there was no interference whatsoever from home, and so Eric Taylor was able to travel to the Valencia draw, where Wednesday were paired with DOS Utrecht in the First Round. After one of the shortest close seasons on record the club travelled to the South Coast for their one and only pre season game, with both first team and reserves opposing Southampton; the former sharing six goals at the Dell.

A thrilling 3–3 draw with Manchester United opened the new league season; yet, despite a good home record, the Owls found themselves in the wrong half of the table after winning only a solitary point from their opening five away games. That poor form away from Hillsborough was ended in Holland against Utrecht in the Fairs Cup, when the Owls recorded a comfortable 4–1 win. This was after it had emerged that DOS intended to borrow three players from neighbouring clubs to bolster their team. Secretary Eric Taylor immediately stated that if they went ahead with the plan, he would appeal, and the Owls would go through by default. Not surprisingly Utrecht scrapped the plan and lost by the same score at Hillsborough to go out of the competition. The Owls then entered the transfer market to bring the Manchester United forward, Mark Pearson, to Hillsborough. He'd made his United debut against Wednesday in the first post Munich game. Soon after his arrival, the Owls were awarded four World Cup Final games by the organising committee. By the time Wednesday visited Cologne for their second round Fairs Cup tie, a mid table position had been achieved in the First Division. Their progress in Europe looked to be in jeopardy when the Owls found themselves three goals in arrears at half time in Germany. However, a double strike from Mark Pearson in the final seven minutes dramatically put Wednesday back in the tie to set up the return three weeks later. In the three intervening games the Owls hit a rich vein of goal scoring form, including four at Stoke when a John Ritchie treble put the home side 4–1 ahead ten minutes into the second half, only for Wednesday to storm back to grab an unlikely point. Five goals then followed at home to Wolves; but after Layne had levelled the aggregate scores against the Germans, the goals dried up, with Thielen and Overath netting in the second half to end Wednesday's European adventures until the early 1990s.

Unbeknown to the fans, Vic Buckingham then tried to sell John Fantham for a record fee, but thankfully the player stayed

and eventually won his place back from Pearson. In the bread and butter of the league, Wednesday had moved back into their usual sixth position, but were in for a shock early in the New Year when Third Division Newport County sent them tumbling out of the FA Cup, after winning 3–2 at Somerton Park. Seven days later Ipswich were hit by the backlash, with a Layne hat-trick helping Wednesday to a 4–1 success; before a win over Sheffield United took the Owls to fourth place. Centre-Forward Keith Ellis then moved to Scunthorpe before Ron Springett's transfer request was turned down by the board. Despite Wednesday's high league position there were mounting problems behind the scenes, and the month of April proved to be one of the most traumatic in the club's long history. Firstly, Vic Buckingham's contract was terminated after a complete breakdown in communications between him and the Wednesday board. Chief Coach Mansell then came into conflict with Buckingham, and the Board looked dimly on the fact that several players had appeared in court on motoring offences in recent weeks, culminating in Eddie Holliday being found guilty of drunk driving. Eric Taylor took temporary charge, and within days lost his right hand man when assistant manager Gordon Clark was released to take over as boss at Peterborough United.

As the fall out continued from the departures, the club prepared for the Monday evening home game with Spurs, but the preparations were sent into disarray when the Sunday People newspaper hit the streets. Within its pages was a sensational story alleging that the Ipswich versus Wednesday match at Portman Road in December 1962 was one of several games involved in a betting coup. It was alleged that Peter Swan, David Layne and Tony Kay (who had since been sold to Everton) were all involved in betting against Wednesday in the game, in a scam organised by Mansfield player Jimmy Gauld. All three denied betting against Wednesday, but Swan admitted he had placed bets on matches he knew to 'be bent'. The allegations rocked the club and its supporters, and both Layne and Swan were immediately suspended by Wednesday until an investigation could be made into the shocking allegations. Secretary Taylor described the allegations as 'horrifying' and the 'biggest blow the club has received'. The overriding feeling amongst Wednesdayites must have been 'why did it have to be arguably the club's two best players who were involved?' In one fell swoop the club lost the services of top scorer Layne and 19-cap England International Swan, a blow from which it could be said Wednesday never recovered. The shamed players went into hiding, with Derek Wilkinson and Vic Mobley replacing them for the final home game of the season against Tottenham. At half-time there was a stirring appeal from Taylor to the public to 'be patient with the club in its time of trouble', and the fans responded by roaring their side to a 2–0 win, after a wonderful display by Wednesday which would have overcome any side in the league. The fate of Swan and Kay would not be known for almost a year, and so Wednesday returned to some sort of normality to complete their season, with a draw at Blackpool and a 9–0 romp in a benefit match at Buxton. All in all, and despite another top six finish, Wednesday fans must have been glad to see the back of a season which had damaged their club's reputation and cast a black cloud over the immediate future.

STONES ALES
BREWED
WITH A
DIFFERENCE
FOR
YOU
CANNON BREWERY SHEFFIELD

SHEFFIELD WEDNESDAY
FIXTURE LIST
Season 1963-4

These Fixtures are the copyright of The Football League Limited and are printed by their permission under Licence No. 47. They must not be reproduced in whole or in part without permission from The Football League Limited.

SCHOLES CARAVAN CO., LTD.
YORK ROAD, WHINMOOR
LEEDS 14   TEL. 648940

N.C.C. APPROVED DISTRIBUTORS
FOR THE LEADING MAKES

Touring, Static Holiday and Residential Caravans
SITES EVERYWHERE.   Touring Caravans for hire

Wednesday v. West Ham United

1964–65
A TOUR OF EUROPE

After the drama of April 1964, the following summer was a busy one for Wednesday, as they searched for a new manager and dealt with the continuing controversy surrounding the bribes scandal. The former problem saw St Johnstone manager, Robert Brown, and Sunderland boss, Alan Brown, short listed for the position. The football world was somewhat surprised when it was announced the latter would be taking over, as he had just led Sunderland to promotion back to the First Division. It was a return to Hillsborough for Brown, as between 1951 and 1955 he'd held the position of trainer coach, before departing for Turf Moor. Soon after his arrival, Brown lost the services of his trainer coach, Jack Mansell, who moved to Ajax as manager-coach. However, he was quickly replaced by David Smith, who had been coaching in Libya. Robert Lyttle, the physio, also departed, though he soon returned in a part-time capacity; while reserve keeper Tony Read, and Graham Birks were the only players to leave. Wednesday then agreed a one-off £500 payment towards the legal costs of Layne and Swan, and told the disgraced duo to report for training. Soon after, however, the Attorney General announced charges of conspiracy against ten men involved in the scandal, with the duo amongst the roll of dishonour. This was effectively the end of the road for the players, and they would not pull on a Wednesday shirt for over eight years. Meanwhile the club announced plans to build an indoor training centre behind the North Stand.

Before the league season got underway, the Owls toured Germany, playing friendlies against Kaiserslautern and Werder Bremen. For three players it was a trip to forget. Firstly, young forward David Ford made his team debut in Bremen, but was stretchered off and subsequently missed the whole season through injury. Then, new manager Brown showed his disciplinarian streak, leaving Eddie Holliday and Mark Pearson behind in Germany after they had failed to show when the flight was called! The new boss had a winning start when Blackburn Rovers were beaten at Hillsborough, but Wednesday were inconsistent in those early weeks, and sat in mid table after ten games. The last game of that spell saw a 5–1 home win over Burnley, a bittersweet moment for Mark Pearson, as it later emerged he had played almost all of the game with a broken leg! It was a disastrous season for Pearson, when, on his first team comeback in January, at Liverpool, he broke the same leg for a second time. Following the aforementioned win over Burnley, the Owls beat Wolves to move into eighth place, but four days later they were severely embarrassed when they visited Denmark to play Aarhus as part of a British Week celebration. The Danish part-timers promptly beat the Owls 4–1, as a grim faced Alan Brown watched from the sidelines. Six days later, however, Wednesday made up for the poor display by earning a superb goalless draw in

Dusseldorf, against a German Select side which contained seven full Internationals. Meanwhile, off the field, the club agreed with Newton Chambers & Co. to rent their Thorncliffe Sports Ground at Chapeltown to use as a training facility five days a week.

In the league the Owls remained in mid table up until the New Year. This couldn't have started any better than with a derby win at Bramall Lane. It was also FA Cup time, with Wednesday seconds away from eliminating Everton at Goodison Park, when the Toffeemen grabbed a last gasp equaliser, before cruising to victory in the Hillsborough replay. The month of January also saw the fates of Swan and Layne decided when their trial took place at Nottingham Crown Court. Both were found guilty of throwing the game at Ipswich on December 1st 1962, after having placed a £50 bet for Wednesday to lose and collecting the £100 winnings from co-conspirator Gauld. They were jailed for four months, with mastermind Gauld being sentenced to four years in prison. Meanwhile there was

Fantham shoots just over against Liverpool

transfer activity occurring, with Robin Hardy moving to neighbours Rotherham United. Back on the field of play, goalkeeper Peter Wicks became the Owls youngest player when, aged just sixteen, he played at Anfield. As winter turned to spring, Wednesday climbed into the top six, with 'talent money' in sight. Then, after old foe, John Ritchie, had scored all four in a defeat at Stoke City, the Owls beat Spurs at Hillsborough in a game which saw referee Mr Bullough knocked unconscious by the ball. He was able to carry on after treatment, but to the crowds amusement was almost immediately hit again, but this time recovered to carry on. The game also saw the return of Gerry Young, who had spent four and a half months on the sidelines with thigh problems. A fixture anomaly then meant Wednesday had to play their final three games of the season away from home, and three defeats ensured a final place of eighth—the first finish outside the top six since returning to the First Division five years previously.

The month of April also saw the final act in the Bribes scandal, when, at an FA commission, Layne and Swan were banned *sine die* from playing or managing anywhere in the World. Wednesday then ended the season as they had begun, with a foreign tour. This time however they didn't just visit one country, but played in three. Two games were lost in Poland, the first watched by an astonishing 70,000 in Katowice. They then suffered a 3–0 defeat in Madrid against Valencia, before a busy finale ended with a win in Dublin against Shamrock Rovers.

A spectacular header from Fantham is just over against the Blades

1965–66
CUP FINAL AGONY

The summer of 1965 saw two Owls players forced to retire because of injury. Derek Wilkinson and Roy McLaren were the unfortunate duo. The loss of the former was certainly a major blow, as a persistent groin injury forced Wilkinson to hang up his boots at the tender age of 29, after over two hundred games for Wednesday. Also departing Hillsborough was Eddie Holliday, who returned to Middlesbrough, and Peter Johnson who signed for Peterborough United. There were several new arrivals, with both Colin Symm and Ian Branfoot signing from non-league soccer, while Brian Usher came from Sunderland. Among the players signed on schoolboy forms was future first teamer, Ken Burton. Major ground improvements started with the seating of the South stand enclosure, and the re-building of the West end of the Stadium. Finally, the traditionalists were outraged when the Owls launched a new stripe-free kit, with an all blue shirt with white arms, plus white shorts.

Bulgaria was the unlikely destination for the Owls pre-season tour, where all three games were lost. Returning to England to kick off the league campaign, the Owls began the season with a single goal defeat at Old Trafford; Wilf Smith being named as Wednesday's first ever substitute. However, success in the first two home games pushed Wednesday up into the top six, before Everton's Alex Young and West Brom's Jeff Astle both grabbed hat tricks in heavy away defeats. Away from the action, Wednesday, along with most other league clubs, symbolically resigned from the Football Association over a payments row, after they refused to sign an FA directive which said they should not pay amateur players on their books. Three weeks later the FA were again in the doghouse at Hillsborough after they helped organise a match with Inter Milan in the San Siro, as part of British week celebrations in the City. The Owls had booked the hotel and flights, but a week before the scheduled friendly the Italians suddenly called off the game, much to Wednesday's anger. The FA later apologised for the fiasco, by which time alternative plans had taken Wednesday to Dordrecht in Holland, where six goals were shared with a star-studded Dutch International XI.

With foreign assignments at an end for a few months, Wednesday restarted the league campaign with the first of several fiercely contested meetings during the 1960s against Leeds United. This particular Hillsborough clash ended goalless, with Peter Eustace receiving what, in those days of tolerant refereeing, was a rare booking after tangling with keeper Gary Sprake. Wednesday then entered the transfer market, bringing Jim McCalliog, Chelsea's highly rated Scottish Youth International, to Hillsborough; along with his brother Freddie, who had his apprentice contract at Stamford Bridge cancelled by mutual consent so he could move with his big brother to Sheffield. History was then made in the

home game with Sunderland when David Ford became the club's first substitute to be used, replacing the injured Don Megson after just eight minutes. Another player who looked set to join Wednesday, after his club Bolton had accepted the Owls' club record bid of £80,000, was Welsh International Wyn Davies. He declined the move, however, and so the search for a centre-forward continued. One departure occurred, with veteran Tom McAnearney leaving for Peterborough after the 382 games he'd played since joining from Scottish Junior football in the early 1950s.

The Owls were certainly keen to play a game in Italy, for in early November they arranged a friendly with AS Roma. However, they were foiled again as the English FA withheld permission for the game to take place. Back in the league, Liverpool ended the Owls' unbeaten home record, before a first away win of the campaign, somewhat ironically, was recorded at Tottenham seven days later. Despite that rare victory, the club's form away from Hillsborough was poor, and it needed a relatively good home record to keep Wednesday out of the bottom six places. The battle for points then took a distinct back seat as the road to Wembley started at Third Division Reading, where a brace from John Fantham set up a 3–2 win and a fourth round trip to Newcastle United. A week before the Cup meeting, the Geordies won 2–0 at St James' Park in the league, but Wednesday then turned the form book upside down by securing a 2–1 win, thanks to an own goal from United defender John McGrath. Cup fever was starting to grow, and, despite away draws in the next two rounds, the Owls went all the way to the semi-finals after winning 2–1 at both Huddersfield and Blackburn; the latter on a pitch which seemingly consisted of compacted mud. During this Cup run just enough points were accrued at home to banish relegation worries; and there was one significant departure. After a club post-war record of 504 games, Alan Finney left for Doncaster Rovers.

The FA Cup semi-final paired Wednesday with Chelsea at Villa Park, with the fashionable Londoners immediately installed as hot favourites. However, Wednesday had other ideas, and, ten minutes in to the second half, on another glue-pot of a pitch, they had the audacity to take the lead through Graham Pugh. A Fantham effort then struck a post before ex-Chelsea player, Jim McCalliog, wrapped up a terrific win in the last minute. This took Wednesday to Wembley for the first time since 1935. Before the Final date with Everton, the Owls had to cram six games into a twelve day period to complete their league programme. Two wins were secured, but defeat in their final three games saw them drop to a disappointing seventeenth position. However, Wednesdayites were surely not too concerned as they prepared to travel South to meet old

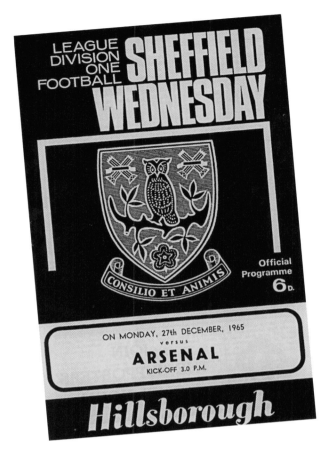

Hickton scores the Owls' 4th goal versus Arsenal

Cup rivals Everton and ex-manager Catterick. Owls fans in the 100,000 Wembley crowd were soon cheering when Jim McCalliog scored after just four minutes; and they were getting the Brasso ready when David Ford doubled the advantage. Unfortunately, little known Cornishman, Mike Trebilcock, then scored twice in five minutes to wipe out the advantage; and an agonising mistake from the normally reliable Gerry Young then gifted an opportunity to Derek Temple, which he didn't refuse. Alan Brown's young side had thus become the first to lose a two goal lead in a Cup Final, and at the final whistle became the first ever losing side to do a lap of honour, after a glorious defeat in one of the best Cup Finals ever seen.

Though manager Brown was immensely proud of his players, they were devastated after coming so close to winning a major honour. Five days later the team visited Belle Vue, to lose 6–5 in a testimonial match for Alan Finney, before embarking, with Fulham, on a three-week tour of the Far East. Six games were played at several venues, including Hong Kong and Singapore. Three of those were against the Londoners, and the remainder against local select sides. In the end, Wednesday finished their season in mid June, ten and a half months after kicking off in Bulgaria, after the longest season in their history.

Davies heads for goal (versus Chelsea)

1966–67
HILLSBOROUGH HOSTS WORLD CUP

The summer of 1966 was dominated by the World Cup, when, on home soil, England won the trophy for the first and only time. The Owls were privileged to host four games in the competition, with underdogs Switzerland playing all their three ties at Hillsborough; and the eventual finalists, West Germany, overcoming Uruguay in the Quarter Finals. Crowds flocked to the games, with England's eventual success over the Germans proving to be a massive lift for the domestic game. This would see the Owls average gate in 1966–67 increase by an astonishing 32% on the previous campaign. On tour in the Far East, the Owls had been invited to become the first ever English club to tour Japan; and considering their globe trotting exploits in the 1960s it was perhaps a surprise when they eventually declined the offer. Meanwhile, the Owls finally secured their own training facilities when Middlewood Road was purchased as Wednesday reported big profits on both their 1966 Cup run and the World Cup matches. On the playing side, Colin Dobson was transferred to Huddersfield Town and Howard Wilkinson to Brighton; while a large bid from Everton for John Fantham was turned down by Wednesday.

For their pre-season tour, Wednesday again ventured into Eastern Europe to visit Bulgaria for a second time. They managed to record three draws, although Sam Ellis had the misfortune to break his nose in the opening game against Spartak Varna. A Bulgarian select side then paid a reciprocal visit, before Wednesday kicked off the new season with a comfortable home success over Blackpool. It was the beginning of a great start to the campaign which saw the Owls go to the top of the First Division after remaining unbeaten in their opening seven league games. Last minute equalisers against Leicester and Arsenal had kept Wednesday at the summit; however, when Rotherham visited Hillsborough for the Owls first ever League Cup tie, it was the Millers who went through, thanks to a last minute strike from Frank Casper. Soon after, Eric Taylor was approached by the North American Soccer League, who offered him the staggering salary of £11,000 a year to organise their new professional league. After much deliberation over the Executive Secretary position Taylor decided to stay on at Hillsborough, much to Wednesday's relief—for they were faced with losing one of England's finest football administrators. The defeat by the Millers unfortunately triggered a slump in form, and within six weeks the Owls had slipped back into mid table after a six-game winless run. One defeat at the Dell was significant, for when the Birmingham referee pointed to the penalty spot with two minutes remaining, it was the first spot kick Wednesday had been awarded since December 1964—a run of 82 games! Peter Eustace scored from the spot, and it was he who scored first at West Brom, as Wednesday got back to winning ways in late October. By this time John Hickton had been sold to

Middlesbrough, and soon after Wednesday broke their transfer record when they paid £80,000 for Stoke City's prolific centre-forward, John Ritchie. As Christmas approached, however, the Owls failed to break into the top half of the table, and despite a tremendous 6–1 romp against Chelsea on New Year's Eve they went into 1967 down in 12th place.

The dawn of 1967 brought the usual hopes of FA Cup success. However, the competition didn't start until the final Saturday of January, and so four league games were played—along with a friendly to mark the opening of Hartlepool's floodlights—before the Cup visit of Third Division, Queen's Park Rangers. Cup exploits a year earlier, meant over 40,000 were packed into the ground, to see history made when goalkeeping brothers, Ron and Peter Springett, opposed each other for the first time. The game saw John Ritchie grab his only treble in a Wednesday shirt, while Ozzie Owl was hatched as the club took the opportunity to launch their first mascot, designed by the company who were responsible for World Cup Willie. The next round brought Mansfield Town to Hillsborough, with a sensation when the sides were announced. Sixteen-year-old Gary Scothorn in goal for Wednesday became the youngest player to appear in the Owls first team. The youngster subsequently kept a clean sheet as Wednesday cruised into the last sixteen, where a 3–1 win at Norwich City ensured further progress.

Off the pitch there were momentous changes as Alan Brown cut a swathe through his coaching staff. Trainer Coach, David Smith, was the first to be told his contract would not be renewed, and soon after, trainer, John Logan and part-time youth coaches, Hugh Swift and Keith Bannister, were all told their services were no longer required. Within two weeks, Jack Marshall returned as assistant manager, eight years after leaving; while Lawrie McMenemy completed the changes when he was appointed coach.

In the league, Owls' form was inconsistent, with a dismal home loss to Nottingham Forest contrasting greatly with a sparkling 5–0 home win over Sunderland just three days later. Back in the Cup, the Quarter Final draw took Wednesday to perennial opponents Chelsea, and over 52,000 saw a scrappy defence-dominated game which was goalless after ninety minutes. Unfortunately the referee then played two minutes of injury time, and this was just enough time for Baldwin to grab a late winner, and sicken the Owls travelling support. After having their Cup dreams shattered in London for the second year running, Wednesday rallied to complete the league programme. The penultimate home game against Burnley saw Jack Whitham become the first Owls' sub. to score, as his side romped to a stunning 7–0 victory. It was now almost tradition that at the season's close Wednesday would jet off on a foreign tour, and this season was no exception as they broke new ground by playing five games in Mexico. The famous Aztec Stadium in Mexico City was the venue for the hexagonal tournament and, in sweltering heat, crowds in excess of 40,000 saw Wednesday play the likes of the Spanish side, Deportivo, and Italian club, Bologna; as well as Mexican opposition. The Owls found it tough going and lost all but their final game against FC America, in which Coco Gomez and Wednesday's Sam Ellis were sent off in a fiercely contested clash. This time the playing season ended on the other side of the World in late June, eleven months after a friendly in Bulgaria had started another incredibly arduous campaign.

Leeds' Jack Charlton heads clear at Hillsborough

1967–68
CENTENARY SEASON SLUMP

The major transfer story in the summer of 1967 concerned a unique swap that brought Queen's' Park Rangers goalkeeper, Peter Springett, to Hillsborough, and took his brother Ron to Loftus Road. The Owls paid £40,000 for Springett Jnr., and received £16,000 for Ron, still the most capped England International in the club's history. Free transfers were given to five players, including Fred McCalliog, Andy Burgin and Brian Hill. The latter flew over to Belgium in June to play for Bruges against Anderlecht and eventually joined after a trial period. Five days after his brother was released, Jim McCalliog asked for and was granted a move, with the two events thought to be not unconnected.

Unusually, the Owls didn't play any pre season warm up games, and so went straight into the opening league game at Upton Park, where a Jim McCalliog goal, two minutes from time, secured a 3–2 success. As they had done twelve months earlier, the Owls then made a great start to the season, and topped the early league tables after winning five of their opening six games; including a derby win at Bramall Lane. It certainly couldn't have been more appropriate that, in the week that Wednesday celebrated their Centenary, the Owls sat atop the First Division table. A home game with Fulham was the designated celebration match, with the club cutting the cost of admission and handing out various Centenary gifts to the fans. Thankfully the West London visitors had read the script, losing 4–2, and despite dropping down to third, a week later, the Owls reclaimed top spot after putting four past top flight, new boys, Coventry City. Just after the Fulham game the club was again hit by tragedy, when David Ford crashed his car on Redmires Road. The highly rated inside-forward faced a ten week lay off because of injuries; but this must have mattered little to Ford, as his fiancee was killed in the accident.

Meanwhile, a first ever victory in the League Cup was secured at Stockport County, before minnows, Barrow, were beaten at Hillsborough to set up a last sixteen home meeting with Stoke City. Before this Cup tie, Wednesday won 2–0 at Chesterfield, in a match set up to officially open their floodlights. However, they couldn't find a way past Stoke's rearguard and were forced to replay at the Victoria Ground. The Owls were beaten in the Cup replay, and, after David Ford made his comeback in a testimonial at Barnsley, defeats started to pile up as Wednesday slipped down to mid table. The visit to Arsenal in early December looked like being another pointless journey, when McLintock netted for the Gunners. For once, however, the English weather came to the rescue, as heavy snow caused the match to be abandoned two minutes into the second half. Just before the Arsenal game, the Owls sold John Quinn to Rotherham United; and when Leeds became the first team to win at Hillsborough for nineteen games, hopes of a challenge for the title were finally extinguished.

OFFICIAL PROGRAMME   PRICE **9**^D

SHEFFIELD WEDNESDAY
FOOTBALL CLUB

FOOTBALL ASSOCIATION CUP—5th ROUND

CHELSEA
On Saturday, 9th March, 1968, kick-off 3.0 p.m.

at Hillsborough

The centenary cake

INTRODUCING HILLSBOROUGH'S NEW MASCOT...

Ozzie Owl

READ ALL ABOUT ME ON THE OPPOSITE PAGE!

Indeed, such was Wednesday's subsequent slump, that from December 23rd to the end of the season they recorded a miserly two league wins; both coming in a three-day period in March. Frustration grew among the perplexed Owls' support, and all was not well behind the scenes. In early February, manager Alan Brown sensationally resigned, vehemently denying he was set to take over as boss at Sunderland. The Wearsiders had dismissed manager Ian McColl earlier in the day, and no one was too surprised when, twenty-four hours later, Brown was appointed to the vacant Roker Park position. Assistant Jack Marshall became acting manager, with his first task being to prepare his charges for the Fourth Round home Cup clash with Third Division Swindon Town. Wednesday duly saw off the Wiltshire challenge, but must have been dismayed when the name of Chelsea came out of the hat immediately after that of the Owls. Almost 50,000 saw the Cup clash, when a second-half equaliser from Bobby Tambling meant a mid week trek to Stamford Bridge. There Wednesday's Cup dreams again hit the rocks as the Pensioners recorded a comfortable 2–0 win to reach the last eight.

The day before the replay Wednesday had given the manager's job to Marshall on a permanent basis, and within days he tried to sign his first player with the Owls agreeing a large fee for the Nottingham Forest winger, Barry Lyons. However Marshall's immediate attempt to strengthen the side was thwarted when Lyons decided to stay at the City Ground. The Cup exit therefore meant it was back to the league struggle for Wednesday supporters; but their spirits were lifted when the Owls won consecutive away games at Stoke City and Wolves, to move back into mid table. Two goals from youngster Brian Woodall contributed to the 3–2 win at Molineaux, but this was the last two point haul of the season for Wednesday, which saw them slide all the way down to nineteenth position by the time the last ball was kicked. It was now apparent that the Owls squad was becoming threadbare, and with the reserves also finishing fourth from bottom in the Central League, Marshall had a big task on his hands if he was to revive those Wednesday fortunes which, earlier in the decade, had looked so bright. Two games in Austria finished a season which had started so well, but fell away in alarming fashion to leave plenty of furrowed brows around Sheffield 6.

1968–69
GIANT KILLED—TWICE !

After the terrible conclusion to the previous campaign, Wednesdayites hoped to see several new faces arriving at the club in the summer of 1968. In the end they had to be content with just one arrival—Alan Warboys, who came from Fourth Division neighbours, Doncaster, in part exchange for Brian Usher. At least Owls' fans could drown their disappointments in the new Ozzie Owl social club which had opened in early May! One signing Wednesday almost made, which could have single handedly turned their fortunes around, was that of Fulham ace goal poacher, Allan Clarke. But their bid was unsuccessful, and the opportunity was lost. However, Marshall had more than enough problems in holding onto the squad he already had, for when Vic Mobley asked to be put on the transfer list, he joined Peter Eustace and Sam Ellis, who were both looking to leave. Meanwhile, Wednesday arranged a pre season tour of Germany where they would play Hamburg and Eintracht Frankfurt. This was quickly cancelled, however, and replaced by games in Northern Ireland against Ards and Glentoran.

The League season kicked off with a dull, goalless draw at West Bromwich Albion. Wednesday then made their now almost expected excellent start, and sat in the fifth place when European Champions, Manchester United, visited Hillsborough. The ninety minutes that followed is widely regarded as the best ever seen at the ground, as in an thrilling game Wednesday hit back from being 4–2 down, to win 5–4 in front of their best league crowd for almost eight years. The Owls' form, however, quickly went from the sublime to the ridiculous, when, on the following Wednesday, they visited Fourth Division minnows Exeter City in the League Cup, and promptly lost 3–1 to crash out at the first hurdle! The Owls then bounced back to beat Ipswich Town, but a plethora of draws meant a mid table position was their wont. Off the pitch there were again changes in staff, with ex-player Tom McAnearney returning to Hillsborough to become Chief Coach, just before Lawrie McMenemy was released so he could start his long managerial career by taking over as boss at Doncaster Rovers. He was replaced by Port Vale player, Bill Asprey, who retired from playing to take up the coaching role at Wednesday. There was also a snippet of transfer news, with Airdrie winger, Archie Irvine, signing from Scottish football. Back on the field of play, Wednesday made another mid week sortie into Europe, visiting Lille in France, where a representative side beat the Owls 3–1 in front of only 2,000 spectators. In the fight for points, Wednesday remained in mid table, but only one defeat in December left Owls fans looking upwards, with a top six finish looking a definite possibility. This optimism rose further in the New Year, when. after drawing at home to Leeds in the FA Cup, the Owls recorded a brilliant 3–1 win at Elland Road to set up a home tie with

John Ritchie

Action: Owls v. West Ham

Second Division, Birmingham City. Unfortunately that was as good as it got for Wednesday fans, as, in almost a carbon copy of the previous campaign, they watched in abject horror as their side completely lost the plot and crashed dramatically down the table. Almost unbelievably, after winning at Wolves on December 21st, the Owls managed to win only one league game to the end of the season—a record even worse than the one a year earlier, when only two wins were recorded! Part of the slump was a replay defeat at Birmingham in the Cup, and the only away win in the period was in a memorial match at Southern League, Hereford United. In a shocking 5–0 home loss to Arsenal, the ever widening gap between the Owls and the sides chasing honours was clearly shown; and with the natives restless, Wednesday trooped from the field to a chorus of boos. Ironically, the aforementioned single league win came in the next match, however, overall form was so poor that the club decided to act, and, after less than a year in the job, Jack Marshall was out of the door when Wednesday told him his contract would not be renewed in the summer. Tom McAnearney took over as caretaker manager, but the new man had no magic wand, and the Owls appalling goal scoring record continued. This would see Wednesday net only nine goals in the final nineteen games of another disappointing campaign.

However, just when the fans were starting to despair, their club made a shock entrance into the transfer market to make Tommy Craig, the highly rated Aberdeen midfielder, not only the costliest teenager in British football but also Wednesday's record signing at £100,000. Secretary Eric Taylor negotiated the deal for the managerless Wednesday, and Craig had turned twenty by the time he made his debut in Wednesday's last game of the season at home to Tottenham Hotspur. His first appearance impressed the watching fans, so perhaps the future did not look so bleak after all.

SHEFFIELD
WEDNESDAY
FOOTBALL CLUB

FOOTBALL LEAGUE—DIVISION I
LEEDS UNITED
On Tuesday, 1st April, 1969, kick-off 7.30 p.m.
OFFICIAL PROGRAMME - PRICE ONE SHILLING

at Hillsborough

Manager Jack Marshall

For the third time in eight years Wednesday went managerless into the summer break, with the continuity so vital to success again sadly missing. Still in temporary charge of the ship, Eric Taylor's first act of the off season was to release a total of six players; of whom only two, Gary Scothorn and Colin Symm, could boast first team appearances in their time at Hillsborough. Meanwhile, there were problems in Wednesday's forward line, as both Jim McCalliog and John Ritchie expressed a desire to leave; the former indicating his displeasure by refusing to put his name to a new contract. Soon after this, two players did depart, with David Mobley and Colin Symm signing for Grimsby Town and Sunderland respectively. There was some good news for the beleaguered acting boss, however, when Peter Eustace agreed to re-sign. And, in what proved to be his last act as manager, Taylor solved the Ritchie problem by letting Wednesday's record signing return to Stoke City; with the Owls having to accept a huge £52,000 loss on the deal, inside three years. Within ten days, however, Taylor was able to hand over the reigns when Swindon Town boss, Danny Williams, returned to his Yorkshire roots to become Wednesday's ninth manager. The new man's first act was to appoint ex-player, Albert Broadbent, to his coaching staff; while after a long drawn out saga Jim McCalliog was sold to Wolves for a record club fee of £70,000.

Although the Owls pre-season was relatively successful, winning three of the four friendlies played, the final game saw a shock home loss to the part-timers from Airdrie; and any confidence gained seemed to ebb away at the final whistle. The situation was not helped when Wednesday subsequently lost their opening three league games to slump to the foot of the table. A 4–1 opening day defeat at Manchester City set the tone, and it needed a single strike from Peter Eustace, in the home game with Newcastle, to give Wednesday their first points of the new season. The Owls were then embarrassed in the League Cup for the second year running, as Third Division Bournemouth and Boscombe won at Dean Court after having earned a draw at Hillsborough. In the league, Wednesday continued to struggle, with their home form a major cause for concern; so that, by mid September, three sides had already taken maximum points from their trip to North Sheffield. A huge crowd then saw a rather unlikely home win over Derby County, before a flurry of transfer activity resulted in two players arriving and the same number departing.

The newcomers were maverick winger, Tony Coleman, from Manchester City, and the virtually unknown Bill Lawson, who must have been surprised as anybody when he made the move from Scottish minnows, Brechin City. Vic Mobley left Hillsborough, incurring Wednesday's wrath after travelling to London to sign for Queen's Park Rangers without the Owls' knowledge, and then returning to Sheffield for the transfer forms to be countersigned by Wednesday. The other departure was a sad one for Wednesday fans, as John Fantham, the club's post-war record goalscorer, signed for neighbours Rotherham United after 166 goals for the Owls in 434 league and cup games. The same month saw the club host a testimonial for another one of their stalwart players, as in old-style fashion the Owls shared fourteen goals with an International side for the benefit of Don Megson. It was perhaps significant that in the season that the Owls said good-

Warboys fires in a shot against Burnley

bye to both Megson and Fantham, neither had been properly replaced. Nor had the likes of Ron Springett, Alan Finney or Derek Wilkinson; and this seemed to be a major factor in Wednesday's decline in the late 1960s.

After the confidence boosting win over Derby, the Owls then embarked on a disastrous twelve-game winless run which took them into the Christmas fixtures propping up the division. However, during the run up to the festive period, Williams had again been a busy man in the transfer market, operating with mixed fortunes. Several transfers did go through, with David Ford moving to Newcastle in exchange for Jackie Sinclair, and Harold Wilcockson arriving from Doncaster Rovers; with Archie Irvine and Ian Branfoot going to Belle Vue in another swap deal. Also arriving was unknown midfielder, Eric Potts, from Cheshire League, Oswestry Town, and Steve Downes. However, some of the biggest headlines surrounded the players that Wednesday didn't get. Firstly, a deal with Watford, for winger Stewart Scullion, collapsed at the last minute, when Archie Irvine decided against a move South as part of the deal. Wednesday then failed twice in as many days with big money bids for Rotherham United youngster and future England centre-half, Dave Watson, and for Charlton's highly rated midfielder, Alan Campbell. The manager's attempts to strengthen the side had met with mixed results, but a Boxing Day win over Sunderland lifted Wednesday briefly off the bottom, before a Cup success over West Brom boosted sagging confidence further. Unfortunately the win over the Baggies only led to further problems, as Wednesday were drawn against minnows, Scunthorpe United at Hillsborough in the next round, and were on the end of a major upset when a Kevin Keegan inspired United won 2–1.

The Owls had gone into the Scunthorpe match without the services of Peter Eustace, who had left for West Ham in a club record deal. Williams' wheeler-dealing continued soon after, when Nottingham Forest keeper, Peter Grummitt arrived, becoming the fourteenth player to be bought or sold by the new manager inside six months. However, despite the overwhelming change in personnel the results didn't improve, and Wednesday entered the final few weeks of the season still stranded in the two relegation places. One of Wednesday's greatest left backs, Don Megson, then left for Bristol Rovers, to be followed soon after by top scorer, Jack Whitham, who moved to Liverpool. Reserve goalie, Peter Wicks then uprooted to South Africa, and, finally, coach Bill Asprey left. A home defeat to Everton looked to have sealed the Owls' fate, but then a tremendous comeback at Old Trafford gave Wednesday a lifeline, when they came from two goals down to force a draw. The Owls went into the final game knowing victory would secure their first division safety; but it all went wrong on the night, as Wednesday just weren't good enough to overcome a lacklustre Manchester City, and so were

relegated after a ten year stay in the top flight. The players and fans probably wished the season could have ended there, but Wednesday had already committed themselves to the new Anglo–Italian competition; and, after earning a win and draw at home to Napoli and Juventus respectively, they travelled to Southern Italy where 30,000 saw Napoli put five past Wednesday before an action packed but ultimately disappointing season ended with defeat in Turin against Juventus.

Don Megson

1970–71
NO QUICK RETURN FOR WEDNESDAY

Despite relegation, boss Danny Williams continued to drastically change both playing and backroom personnel during the summer of 1970, in the hope of securing an immediate return to the top flight in his first full season as manager. The first player to arrive was Burnley's Irish International, Sammy Todd, who was willing to drop a division to join the Owls. Then, just as the pre season games kicked off, the protracted transfer of West Ham midfielder John Sissons was finally completed. Leaving Hillsborough were Tony Coleman and Brian Woodall, while coaches Albert Broadbent and Tom McAnearney also departed, with Manchester City trainer, Dave Ewing, being appointed to the role of Senior Trainer/Coach. The Owls played three pre season warm up games against Notts County, Huddersfield and Tranmere, with the game at Leeds Road resulting in a 5–0 defeat against a side who had replaced Wednesday in the First Division.

Despite opening the season with a victory, it soon became apparent to Wednesday fans that an imminent return to the big time was unlikely. For though they occupied eighth place after ten games, the Owls would fail to climb any higher during the season. The situation then took another turn for the worse, when Wilf Smith, one of the few players Wednesday had left on their books of 'First Division' quality, was transferred for a club record £100,000 fee, making him the costliest full-back in British football. After exiting the League Cup in a replay at First Division Chelsea, a Malcolm MacDonald hat trick for Luton helped his side to a stunning 5–1 win at Hillsborough. This prompted Williams to enter the market again, to bring Leicester City's right-back, Peter Rodrigues, to Wednesday. Back on the field of play, there was a slight improvement in fortunes, with a run of only one defeat in seven games lifting the Owls into the relative safety of a mid table position. However, over the next few weeks the club would again be in turmoil as their chief coach resigned, a flu epidemic struck, and manager Danny Williams was sacked. After only five months at Hillsborough, Dave Ewing was allowed to leave to sign a five year contract as Hibs' first ever coach; although, somewhat suspiciously, within a week the club's boss, Willie McFarlane, was sensationally sacked and Ewing was installed as manager! Around that time the Owls were struck by an influenza outbreak and unsuccessfully applied for a game at Birmingham City to be postponed, as seven senior players were victims of the outbreak. The Football League ordered the game to go ahead, which Wednesday lost by a single goal.

The Boxing Day encounter at Hull City then proved memorable for the wrong reasons, as Wednesday managed to throw away a 4–1 lead and only earned a solitary point. On Christmas Eve, Alan Warboys had been sold to Cardiff City,

F.A. CUP SEMI-FINAL

At Hillsborough, Sheffield
Saturday, 27th March, 1971

Kick-off 3 p.m.

ARSENAL

v

STOKE CITY

Official Programme . . . 10p

S. W. F. C.
Hillsborough, Sheffield

SOUTH STAND

Entrance H
Gangway 7

FRIDAY
4th JUNE
Kick-off 7-30 p.m.

Res. Seat £5·00
A 100

FOR FILE

S. W. F. C
Hillsborough, Sheffie

SOUTH STAND

Entrance H
Gangway 7

FRIDAY
4th JUNE
Kick-off 7-30 p.

Res. Seat £5·0
A 100

TO BE GIVEN UP

SHEFFIELD WEDNESDAY F.C.
Volume 2, Number 16

WEDNESDAY WORLD

SHEFFIELD WEDNESDAY v BIRMINGHAM CITY

Hillsborough, Saturday, February, 13th
1971, kick-off 3 p.m.   1/-

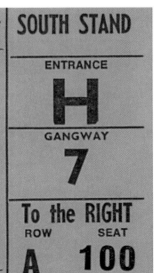

SHEFFIELD WEDNESDAY F.C. LTD.
HILLSBOROUGH, SHEFFIELD

SOUTH STAND

EUROPEAN CHAMPION CLUBS CUP

**FINAL
REPLAY**

ENTRANCE

H

Friday, 4th June, 1971
KICK-OFF 7-30 p.m.

GANGWAY

7

General Manager and Secretary

RESERVED SEAT £5·00

To the RIGHT
ROW   SEAT

A   100

Issued subject to the Rules, Regulations and
Bye-Laws of the Football Association
No Tickets exchanged nor money refunded
THIS PORTION TO BE RETAINED

YOU ARE REQUESTED TO
TAKE UP YOUR POSITION
THIRTY MINUTES BEFORE
KICK OFF

and problems behind the scenes became evident when record buy, Tommy Craig, handed in a transfer request early in the New Year. Unfortunately, in his reign as Wednesday boss, Williams had been unable to halt the club's decline; and in late January the almost inevitable axe fell when he was relieved of his duties by the Owls' board. Thankfully, Wednesday had a ready-made replacement on their doorstop, and the appointment of Development Fund manager, Derek Dooley, to the post of First Team boss on an eighteen month contract was a popular decision with the fans.

The new manager kicked off with a home draw to Swindon Town, but must have realised the depth of his task when, seven days later, the Owls were comprehensively outclassed at run-of-the-mill Watford. On being handed the job, Dooley had stated the climb back into the top flight would be a long and arduous one. This looked to be a gross understatement, as Wednesday had fallen so far in such a short space of time that avoiding relegation to the Third Division would seemingly have to be his first task. By now Spurs had knocked the Owls out of the FA Cup, but some pride was restored as six goals were shared with Birmingham City; for whom youngster Trevor Francis scored twice. Thankfully for Dooley, his arrival signalled a marked improvement in the Owls' home form, and a run of seven unbeaten games at Hillsborough ensured that a position just above the drop zone was maintained. This was vital, as Wednesday managed to lose all but one of their away games in the same period, where the chronic lack of a goalscorer was in evidence as the Owls failed to score in six of those games.

Meanwhile, away from the field of play, Dooley's first move in the transfer market was to let Willie Lawson leave for St Mirren, while he appointed Ron Staniforth to the post of Senior Coach and Gerry Young as reserve team coach. He then issued the club's retained list early, with the major surprise being the free transfer awarded to Harold Wilcockson and the listing of goalie Peter Springett. The club were then honoured when UEFA awarded Hillsborough any possible replay of the European Cup Final between Ajax and Panathinaikos, but the season ended on an acrimonious note, with the members of Wednesday's newly formed Rebel Shareholders Association furious that Matt Sheppard had been seconded onto the Board after neither of the Association's nominees were even considered. However, what must have worried the Board more than anything was the apparent loss of confidence in the club by their own supporters; for the 1970–71 season witnessed a truly worrying slump in attendances—over 40% down to an average of just over 16,000.

1971–72
THE RETURN OF PELE

You did not have to be a genius to know that the club's playing staff had to be radically altered if success was to return to Hillsborough in the foreseeable future, and Derek Dooley took several steps in the close season to try and stop the rot. His first foray into the transfer market saw experienced centre-half, John Holsgrove, arrive from First Division Wolves for £50,000; while teenagers Roger Wylde and Paul Taylor both signed their first professional contracts. The capture of Newcastle United player, Wynn Davies, also looked set to go through, but after a long drawn out saga he eventually decided to reject the move, and so the deal collapsed. This summer also signalled the end of a tradition, which, since the beginning of the century, had seen members of the local press travel, stay and dine with the team. The main reason seemed to be financial, as Wednesday footed the bill for the press men. With the Owls' accounts for the previous season showing a big loss, it was decided to start cutting costs where possible. Those accounts also revealed that Wednesday's loss of top flight status had been a financial disaster, with total income having plummeted by almost half, to just over £200,000. Had it not been for a large surplus on transfer activity, the overall loss would have been a record deficit. The club again came in for scathing criticism from the Shareholders Association. The Annual General Meeting was a stormy occasion, with the Board of Directors defending their position and the 'rebels' demanding changes. On a lighter note, an application from the Supporters Club to sell cushions in the ground was passed by Wednesday!

Following a three-game tour of Northern Ireland, the Owls returned to share four goals with the Blades in a Bramall Lane friendly, before the new Division Two campaign kicked off with a heavy defeat at Queen's' Park Rangers. Three days later progress was made in the League Cup with victory at Millmoor. However, the Owls' home programme couldn't have started in worse fashion, when Bristol City put five past Peter Grummitt to stun the Hillsborough faithful. This drove Dooley into the market again, and the Wednesday board seemingly went for broke by sanctioning a club record £100,000 swoop which secured the services of Coventry City duo, Brian Joicey and Dave Clements. The new boys went straight into the side but made little impact early on, as Wednesday sank to the foot of the table and crashed out of the League Cup with a shocking 5–0 loss at Carlisle United. Thankfully, Wednesday's new look side then slowly started to gel, and a four goal showing at home to Fulham took them off the bottom rung before consecutive home wins lifted them up into mid table. Brian Joicey was quickly becoming a big favourite with Owls fans, and a brace from him helped Wednesday to their biggest away win of the season at Orient. Suddenly the Hillsborough situation looked a lot brighter and there was genuine optimism when Wednesday moved into the top ten as Christmas dawned.

Manager Derek Dooley watches as Pele signs autographs

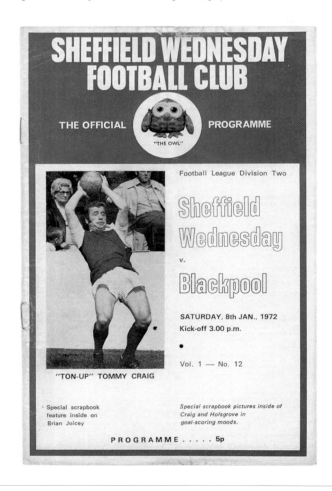

Unfortunately, the New Year started badly for the club, with the first two point haul not recorded until mid February; by which time Sunderland had knocked Wednesday out of the FA Cup and key forward Mick Prendergast's season was at an end through injury. The early Cup exit gave the Owls a free weekend. This was filled with a friendly defeat at Chesterfield, three days after having officially opened the floodlights of Welsh non-league side Rhyl. While those two exhibition games were fairly low key, the return to Hillsborough of Pele and Brazilian giants Santos, eleven years after their first visit, was arguably the highlight of the whole season. The friendly had to be played on a Wednesday afternoon and probably created the largest ever incidence of fictitious doctor's and dentist's appointments in the schools and workplaces of Sheffield! This was because the crowd, of almost 37,000, was more than 13,000 higher than the club's biggest attendance of the campaign; and was a great relief to Wednesday who needed a crowd of 25,000 to break even, after having paid Santos their match guarantee of £10,000. The game briefly saw the 'big time' return to Hillsborough, but on a bitterly cold afternoon Pele was subdued, reserving his quickest sprint for the final whistle when he fled to the tunnel to avoid the hundreds of Parka-wearing school kids who invaded the pitch to reach the great man. Moreover, the Brazilians were opposing a side which was inferior to the 1962 vintage and they waltzed to a comfortable 2–0 win thanks to goals from Nene and Ferreira, in a game which did not really match the occasion.

After the excitement of the Santos game, it was back to the humdrum of league football; although there was nothing dull about the visit to Turf Moor. John Sissons scored a hat trick for the Owls but still ended up on the losing side, in a game which also saw Tommy Craig sent off for two bookable offences. The following month saw Dooley take his squad for a five day break in Majorca, before entering the transfer market to sell Sam Ellis to Mansfield Town and Ken Johnson to Newcastle United, before signing Glentoran's Roy Coyle. In the league, Wednesday then suffered a goalkeeping crisis when both senior goalies were unavailable through injury. The Owls were, therefore, forced to call up nineteen-year-old part time keeper, Trevor Pearson, who stepped into the breach to play four times and gain what proved to be his only experience of league soccer. Injuries had certainly affected the second half of the season; and although Wednesday eventually finished in the bottom half of the table, the roots of a recovery were starting to show and hopes were genuinely high that a promotion challenge could be on the cards in the following campaign.

Wednesday v. Portsmouth. Prendergast and Joicey challenge for a header.

1972–73
WEDNESDAY LAUNCH PROMOTION CHALLENGE

For manager Derek Dooley the summer of 1972 was another busy time as he sought to find that elusive winning formula. His first slice of transfer activity proved to be a shock for Owls' fans, when Graham Pugh was sold to neighbours Huddersfield Town only days after he had withdrawn an earlier transfer request. Also leaving was Steve Downes, who eventually signed for Chesterfield after initially turning down a move to Peterborough United to fight for his place at Wednesday. There were four new arrivals, although three were familiar faces as Wednesday re-signed Peter Eustace on a three month loan from West Ham; and, after their lifetime bans were lifted by the FA, the Owls agreed to take back both David Layne and Peter Swan. Initially taken on trial, both players were eventually given one year deals, while a two year contract was given to ex-Rangers winger, Willie Henderson, who the Owls signed in something of a coup on a free transfer from South African club, Durban. Manager Dooley was also given a new two year deal, and the pre season optimism was heightened, as, for the first time since 1965, the Owls fans would see their team run out wearing the traditional blue and white stripes. The summer also saw the Wednesday Chairman become Sir Andrew Stephen when he was knighted in the Queen's Birthday Honours list. The other major news was the appointment by Wednesday of their first ever full-time physiotherapist, Geoff Eggerton, taking over from part-time incumbent, Bob Lyttle. However, there was also further worrying news on the financial state of the club, when the accounts were released to show a huge deficit of over £165,000. This had largely been caused by an ambitious transfer policy in the previous summer. However, although total income was again down, the Owls had enticed an extra 50,000 people through the turnstiles, and the Director's report was fairly upbeat about the coming campaign.

That faith was soon rewarded as the Owls made their best start to a season since the mid 1960s in topping the early league tables. Before the season had started, the Owls gained added confidence from three excellent wins north of the Border, against East Fife, St Johnstone and Dunfermline. And supporter optimism was shown on the opening day when a bumper crowd of over 23,000 cheered Wednesday to a comfortable home success over Fulham. With little Willie Henderson quickly becoming a crowd pleaser, and a forward line of Sunley and Joicey firing on all cylinders, the Owls played an entertaining brand of football and deservedly led the table until mid October; when, in a meeting of the top two at Hillsborough, the Owls lost to a single Leighton James strike for Burnley. Before the meeting with the Turf Moor club, the Owls had exited the League Cup in the Third Round at Wolves, while fringe player, Kevin Johnson, moved to Southend United on a free transfer. A poor run of league form

then resulted in a drop out of the top six, but by the end of the year Wednesday had rallied, and an injury time winner from Joicey in the final game of 1972 left the Owls in seventh place and very much in the promotion shake up. Before the old year was out Wednesday had made Eustace's transfer permanent; and, after it emerged that when the Owls signed Henderson he was still under contract, they agreed to pay £750 expenses to Durban United. Still in South Africa, Wednesday went on another shopping trip and came back with ex-Celtic full-back, Jim Craig, who had been appearing for Hellenic FC. Back home, David Layne, after failing to break back into the first team, joined Hereford United on loan.

Luton Town fan Eric Morecambe with Derek Dooley and John Hobgrove

The Wednesday Squad…'Don't give up the day job'

Orient keeper Goddard punches clear

'Lulu plays mother'

Swindon goalie Downsborough saves from Sunley

As usual the New Year meant the FA Cup, and, after overcoming Fulham at home, Wednesday were involved in a tremendous three game tussle with First Division, Crystal Palace. The Owls were held at home, before a last minute equaliser from Dave Sunley at Selhurst Park ensured the tie would go to a second replay at the neutral venue of Villa Park. What followed was a truly memorable evening, and one which Derek Dooley described as the 'greatest night of my life since my playing career ended'. In front of a crowd dominated by the travelling Owls fans, Wednesday twice came from behind, before, in extra time, up popped Brian Joicey to complete his hat-trick and send his delirious side into a home meeting with perennial foes Chelsea. Cup fever exploded, and a crowd of almost 47,000 were present to see Roy Coyle put Wednesday ahead, only for Chelsea to hit back and reach the quarter finals thanks to a second half winner from Peter Osgood.

While Cup football dominated the headlines, the Owls slipped in their promotion push. They were not helped when the home game with Bristol City became the only match ever to be abandoned at Hillsborough in peacetime soccer, with snow causing referee Mr Burns to call a halt to proceedings. After being dumped out of the Cup, the Owls results markedly improved. Four consecutive wins, including a tremendous success at league leaders Burnley, lifted Wednesday up to fourth place; although they still stood seven points behind the second promotion place. Before the promotion run-in began, both Jackie Sinclair and Ken Burton left on loan to Chesterfield and Peterborough United, while David Layne's attempted comeback ended on a sad note when he was forced to retire because of an ankle injury. Wednesday's attempt to climb nearer to the top two was then hindered by another goalkeeping crisis. This saw history made in the home game with Orient, when, at fifteen years and eight months, apprentice Peter Fox became the youngest ever player to appear in the Owls first team. He broke his toe, but kept a clean sheet as his side won 2–0. But now games were quickly running out, with the majority of the teams around Wednesday having games in hand. The Owls also had to cope with a worsening injury situation, and by early April the brave challenge from Dooley's new-look side was over. After a much improved season, Wednesday had slipped to sixth before their final home game, this must have been a bitter disappointment to the club, for only 8,895 fans attended—the Owls' smallest post-war crowd. In the final analysis it had been a season of progress, although Wednesday finished a massive seventeen points behind the promotion positions.

1973–74
SHOCK DOOLEY DEPARTURE OVERSHADOWS LAST DAY SURVIVAL

Despite the relative success of the 1972–73 season, Wednesday were still losing money, with the annual accounts showing yet another large trading loss recorded for the year to May 1973. Despite a large increase in gate receipts and season ticket sales, a big rise in the wage bill seemed to be at the root of the problem. Regardless of the financial problems, Derek Dooley was still able to trade in the transfer market, with Wolves defender Bernard Shaw, the first major signing of the close season. Within forty-eight hours, Colin Prophett had left for First Division Norwich City, with the Owls in profit by £5,000 on the two deals. In early July, Willie Henderson arrived back in Sheffield after an eight week loan spell with US club Miami Fusion, and he was joined by new signing from Hull City, Ken Knighton. Dooley had been trying to sign Knighton ever since he took over as Wednesday boss some thirty months earlier. The other major departure was Ken Burton, who joined Chesterfield; while several fringe players also moved to pastures new, with Ian Musson signing for Lincoln City, Paul Taylor for York City, and veteran Peter Swan going to Bury. The Owls also finally reached a settlement with ex manager, Danny Williams, to whom they agreed to pay a £10,000 'golden handshake' in order to end the protracted dispute which had rumbled on since his departure in January 1971.

As part of their pre season preparations the Owls, along with Crystal Palace, travelled to Sweden to compete in the VIF July Cup. Wednesday finished third in the tournament after winning two of the three games played, and even managed to fit in a friendly on the way home when Nörrkoping were beaten. The successful build up was completed with games at Southend and Gillingham, while the club's reserve team hit eleven goals in a friendly at Bridlington Town. Wednesday's youth team continued the theme by boasting a one hundred percent record to win a pre season tournament in Volendam, Holland. However, when the real action got underway, the Owls took only one point from their first three games; and despite straight consecutive wins, Wednesday soon found themselves in the lower reaches of the Second Division table. As gates continued to fall, the Owls' finances deteriorated rapidly, and as part of the drive to keep the payroll down, Dave Clements left for Everton for a large fee. Wednesday then beat off strong competition to sign Glentoran's highly rated goalkeeper, Alan Paterson, along with Mick Kent, who was signed after a trial period. Both Roy Coyle and David Sunley then submitted transfer requests which were subsequently accepted by the club.

If problems were already mounting for Dooley, they reached crisis point when a catalogue of injuries and a mystery stomach bug swept through the club and decimated his first team squad. The Owls actually appealed in late October to have their game against Notts County postponed because of the crisis. But, as

Sunley scores against Hull City

ACTION '74

Below (top): Brian Joicey scores No. 1 for Sheffield Wednesday against Bristol City.

Below (middle): Ray Cashley well beaten by Bernard Shaw for No. 3 for Wednesday.

Below (bottom): Ray Cashley punches the ball off Sunley's head.

usual, they got no joy from the Football League, and the game went ahead, finishing goalless. A few weeks earlier the situation had looked much rosier, when Mick Prendergast hit his only treble in Wednesday colours, as Crystal Palace were comprehensively beaten at Hillsborough. The Owls then overcame Bournemouth in the League Cup after three attempts, the first replay again setting a new record low crowd since the War. And, as events continued to conspire against him, Dooley could only watch as his patched up side were thrashed 8–2 at Queen's' Park Rangers in the next round of the League Cup. Incredibly, after winning at Cardiff in October, Wednesday would fail to win in the league until mid January; and this slump had repercussions both on and off the field.

The major changes behind the scenes were in the boardroom, where Chairman, Sir Andrew Stephen. resigned after almost twenty years in the position; and his vice chairman Keith Gardiner followed him out of the door. They were replaced by new Chairman, Matt Sheppard, while Chairman-elect Bert McGee, was seconded onto the board. Within days of being appointed Chairman, Sheppard presided over a marathon board meeting which discussed several topics, including team management, coaching, tactics, fitness, injuries, the virus, club spirit and the players' attitude. All had contributed to a haul of only fourteen points from twenty one games, but no action was taken until an emergency meeting was held on the day after the Owls earned a creditable draw at Crystal Palace. The decision was then made to relieve Dooley of his duties; though, in a major misjudgement, they only decided to tell Dooley of their decision the next day—Christmas Eve. The football world was stunned at the timing of the announcement, and it was almost twenty years before the Owls legendary ex centre-forward would set foot in Hillsborough again, such was his anger at the manner of his dismissal. The Owls' board had severely damaged the club's reputation, but the deed had been done and

Gerry Young was put in temporary charge until a successor could be found. Before any names entered the frame for the vacant post, Wednesday again sold players, with both John Sissons and Peter Grummitt leaving. The club then reeled further, with the news that, after 45 years at Hillsborough, secretary Eric Taylor had decided to retire at the end of the season. The Owls therefore not only needed a new manager, but a new secretary as well. The latter problem was the first to be solved, when Taylor's long time assistant, Eric England, was announced as the replacement for the almost irreplaceable Taylor. Looking back, it seems amazing that Ron Atkinson and a certain Brian Clough subsequently applied for the managerial vacancy, but the Owls board decided to give the post to Steve Burtenshaw—the 38-year-old chief coach of Queen's' Park Rangers, who had no managerial experience whatsoever! The new man soon appointed Young as his Chief Coach, but a Viv Busby hat-trick sent the Owls to a 4–0 defeat in Burtenshaw's first match in charge. Just over a week later, however, Wednesday staged their first ever game on a Sunday; and, with loanee goalkeeper Bobby Ferguson between the sticks, Bristol City were beaten to get the new manager off the mark.

Despite the win the Owls remained in the bottom four, and it took a remarkable sequence of three straight wins to push them up to the lofty heights of seventeenth. This was remarkable, because after struggling to find the net all season, Wednesday duly scored five at Notts County and another five at home to Orient, leaving their supporters aghast! However Wednesday were not out of the woods yet, and a calamitous 8–0 defeat at Jack Charlton's Middlesbrough, in the Owls' final away game, meant that to ensure their Second Division survival, Bolton would have to be beaten at Hillsborough. Thankfully, a late strike from captain Ken Knighton proved sufficient, and he was chaired off the field to bring the curtain down on one of the most eventful seasons in the club's long history.

Boss Steve Burtenshaw

Chairman Matt Sheppard

1974–75
WORST EVER SEASON

As soon as the traumatic season of 1973–74 ended, the Owls said good-bye to crowd favourite, Willie Henderson, who quit league soccer to move to Hong Kong Rangers. A further nine players were then released by the club, but only two, Mick Kent and Sammy Todd, had any senior experience, with the latter eventually moving into Northern Premier League football with Great Harwood Town. Manager Burtenshaw then made further changes to his back-room staff, with Jim McAnearney appointed second team coach, and another ex-player, Ron Staniforth, put in charge of the Owls' junior side. George McCabe arrived, and was put in charge of Youth development; while on the playing front, Chelsea's apprentice professional, Bobby Brown, was signed on a free transfer, and Glenavon defender, Hugh Dowd, also joined the ranks. In an attempt to cover their spiralling costs, Wednesday were then forced to announce large increases in the price of season tickets. By early July less than 2,000 had been sold, and this eventually rose to just over 3,000 for the start of the new season. The fans were then shocked when favourite, Eric Potts, asked for a move. Thankfully he changed his mind after being offered new terms, and, days later, a new squad member was added when ex-Sunderland player, Fred McIver, arrived on loan from Belgium side, Racing Jet Brussels. To begin their pre season build up Wednesday again travelled to Scotland and opened a three-game tour with a confidence boosting 4–0 win at Clyde. The Owls also played Kilmarnock and Dundee United, before returning south of the Border to compete their warm up games with a defeat at Port Vale.

The Division Two campaign kicked off at Oldham Athletic, where, despite leading at the break through a Tommy Craig penalty, the home side hit back to take the opening day points. The Owls then crashed out of the League Cup at Fourth Division minnows, Scunthorpe United, and depression quickly started to shroud Hillsborough as Wednesday won only once in their first fourteen games, leaving them firmly stranded in the bottom two. During that grim opening to the season, Wednesday had actually taken steps to stop the rot with the signing of classy Everton midfielder, Colin Harvey; a veritable coup. The transfer of Fred McIver was also made permanent for a fee of 500,000 Belgium francs (around £5,000); while Trevor Pearson and Roy Coyle both headed for the exit door. However, the saddest news came in late September, when, only two weeks after he retired, 'Mr Sheffield Wednesday', Eric Taylor, tragically passed away, aged just 62. Within four weeks the Owls staged a memorial match for their master administrator. Almost 12,000 fans attended and saw an England All Star team, containing the likes of Rodney Marsh, Tony Currie and Peter Shilton, cruise to a 5–0 victory in a fitting tribute to Taylor. If Taylor had been alive, however, he would no doubt have despaired at his old

club. For the first time ever, Wednesday's minute book also included a regular update on the club's financial position, and this was now reaching crisis point, as, in late 1974, their bank overdraft increased at an alarming rate.

With the Owls struggling desperately near the foot of the division, Burtenshaw then pulled off a masterstroke to obtain the services of Middlesbrough forward, Eric McMordie, on loan. Wednesday had only netted nine goals in thirteen league games before his arrival, but in the two months he was at Hillsborough, McMordie would net six times in only nine appearances, and lead the Owls out of the bottom two. One of his final appearances came in a stormy home game with leaders Manchester United. This ended in a thrilling 4–4 draw, but the match was overshadowed by events off the field, as several outbreaks of spectator violence dominated the Monday morning headlines. Just before the game against the Old Trafford club, the Owls had transferred Eddie Prudham to Carlisle United, on his return from a loan spell at Partick Thistle. But probably the key moment of the season then occurred, when Wednesday failed to persuade new goal scoring hero McMordie to move to Hillsborough on a permanent basis.

Just before the Christmas break, unsettled star man Tommy Craig finally got his move when First Division Newcastle United paid the Owls a record club fee of £120,000. On the pitch, Wednesday saw out the old year with a second away win of the season to boost survival hopes as 1975 dawned. However following a brave defeat at Chelsea in the Cup, where the Owls led 2–0 after an hour, the season quickly became a living nightmare for the rapidly dwindling hardcore of Wednesday fans; as their side not only failed to win any of the final seventeen games of the season, but, incredibly, scored only twice in the process. One of those goals came at Fulham in late February; but at Hillsborough, with crowds now down

Sheffield Wednesday match magazine·price 10p

to four figures, the faithful had long since given up hope of survival, and were now hoping just to see Wednesday score a goal. They finally got their wish in the home game with Oxford United, even though, eleven days earlier and with still five games to play, the Owls had been relegated to the Third Division for the first time in their long history. Such were the dire straits the Owls found themselves in, that, as the long term future of the club was called into question, the Sheffield Star launched a 'Save our Owls' campaign. It seems almost unbelievable that during this appalling run Manchester City midfielder, Phil Henson, actually agreed to join Wednesday; and directors Arthur Broomhead and Stan Ashton must have been glad to get out of the firing line when they stepped down from the board to be replaced by Cliff Woodward and Stanley Speight; while Bert McGee moved up to vice Chairman. Defeat at Hull City in the final game ensured Wednesday would post their lowest ever points tally; two less than the equally disastrous 1919–20 campaign. While the fact that Eric McMordie finished as the club's top scorer told its own story.

After the final league engagement, the Owls won at Worksop Town in a testimonial match; but it was perhaps apt that a truly horrendous season ended with Wednesday failing to beat non-league Goole Town in a benefit match.

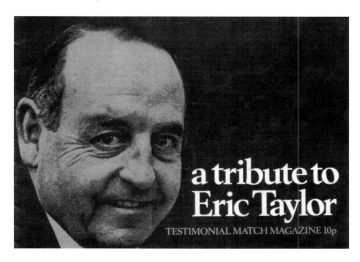

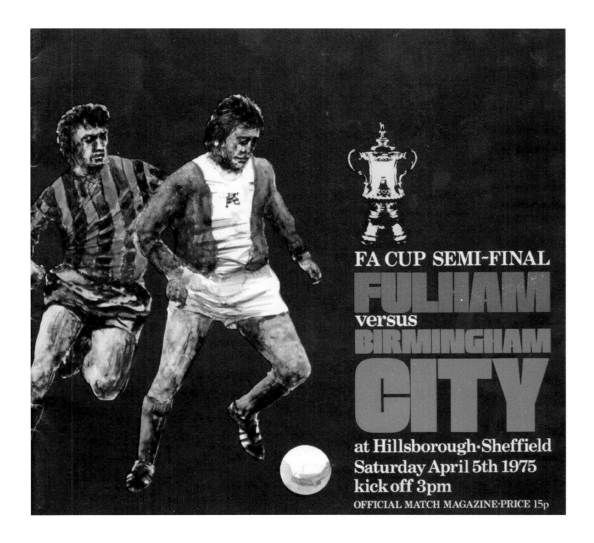

Memory Match

When the draw for the FA Cup third round paired the Owls with Second Division, Middlesbrough, they were fully expected to progress, which they duly did. The same opinion was expressed when Division Two side Rotherham United were drawn at home to the mighty Arsenal. There was huge interest in the Millmoor game, with an all-ticket crowd of just over 24,000 fans packed into the ground; and with only twenty minutes left it looked like the Millers were on their way out, as Arsenal led by two goals. However, this was the Cup, and Rotherham staged a remarkable comeback to net twice through Brian Sawyer and a Billy Myerscough penalty, to force a mid week replay at Highbury. On a frozen pitch the home side dominated, yet had only a single goal to show for their efforts at the break. The visiting supporters in a 57,598 crowd, the highest to ever watch the Millers, were then in raptures, when, on the hour, Barry Webster levelled the scores. The teams remained deadlocked after extra time to ensure a second replay. In those days the third match was always on a neutral ground, and, after Rotherham chairman Reg Cooper won the toss for choice of venue, he was wise enough to choose Hillsborough, with its huge capacity.

The bandwagon therefore rolled to Hillsborough, and all roads to the ground were jammed as another 56,000 plus crowd attended. The majority hoped to see the minnows progress, yet even they must have been surprised, as, in the first half, the Millers totally dominated their more illustrious opponents and raced to a two goal lead. United played a direct brand of fast football to which Arsenal had no answer, with the pacey Sawyer causing countless problems for Gunners centre halves, John Seddon and one Tommy Docherty. The Millers grabbed the lead after just eight minutes, with a superb move which ended with Brian Kettleborough firing past goalkeeper Standen into the Arsenal net. The build up had seen future Owls boss, Danny Williams, dribble the ball out of defence before supplying right-winger, Barry Webster, who evaded two tackles before sprinting away to centre for inside-right Kettlebrough to put the Millers ahead. After twenty minutes another tremendous goal then came the underdogs way. A cross field pass from Barry Webster found Kirkman on the opposite wing, and he headed the ball inside to centre-forward, Sawyer. However, he had his back to the goal, but in one movement, turned quickly to crack a fierce half-volley past the startled Arsenal keeper. At this point there was only one winner, with the Londoners struggling to create chances, and probably regretting their experiment of switching Mel Charles to centre-forward. They were to regret this tactical switch even more on the stroke of half time, when Charles missed the proverbial sitter to ensure the Millers two goal lead remained intact at the interval.

Within seconds of the restart the crowd were actually cheering a third goal for Rotherham, but somehow Standen scrambled back to his line to keep out a Myerscough effort. If Arsenal had failed to show much in the first period, then the second half was even worse; as they gained only one corner—while the Millers keeper, Roy Ironside, struggled to keep warm, such was his inactivity. Despite this, many supporters still expected the Gunners to stage some form of comeback. However, with Rotherham's back line a solid unit, they could simply find no way through and duly crashed out of the competition after being outplayed. Every player in the Millers side was a hero, with veteran 35-year-old half-back, Danny Williams, the pick in one of the greatest nights in Rotherham United's history. Incidentally the victory earned the Millers a home tie with Brighton, which also went to a third game. In the match, ironically staged at Highbury, United crashed out, losing 6–0. However this failed to tarnish the night that Rotherham dumped one of the game's aristocrats out of the Cup.

Arsenal: Standen, Magill, Wills, Docherty, Sneddon, Barnwell, Clapton, Julians, Charles, Bloomfield, Henderson

Rotherham: Ironside, Silman, Morgan, Lambert, Madden, Williams, Webster, Kettlebrough, Sawyer, Myerscough, Kirkman

Referee: Mr Clements (West Bromwich)

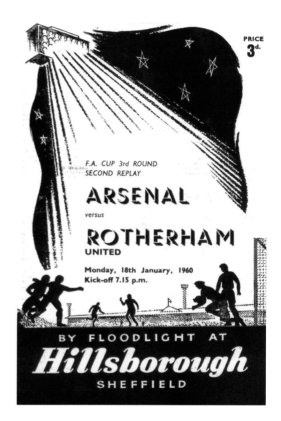

FA Challenge Cup 3rd Round—2nd Replay
Monday 18th January 1960

PRICE 3d.

F.A. CUP 3rd ROUND
SECOND REPLAY

ARSENAL
versus
ROTHERHAM
UNITED

Monday, 18th January, 1960
Kick-off 7.15 p.m.

BY FLOODLIGHT AT
Hillsborough
SHEFFIELD

Arsenal
0
Rotherham United
2

Memory Match

Sheffield Wednesday 2

Tottenham Hotspur 1

The 1960–61 season saw history made when Tottenham Hotspur, under the guidance of Bill Nicholson, became the first club since the 19th century to complete the elusive league and cup double. The North Londoners made a tremendous start to that season, and when they rolled into Sheffield in mid November they held a massive seven point advantage over the second placed club, having dropped only one point in their opening sixteen league games. Given Spurs imperious form, it was perhaps unfortunate that in this same season the Owls boasted their best side since the early 1930s; in any other campaign Wednesday's terrific record of ten wins in their opening fifteen games would have seen them top the division, instead of lying in second position. Not surprisingly there was huge interest in the clash, and if the North Stand had not been unusable due to its partial demolition, then a new record league attendance would surely have been set. As it was, the gates were closed before the start, with over 56,000 packed into a three-sided Hillsborough to witness the game of the season.

Both teams were at full strength, except that in the Wednesday goal Roy McLaren again stood in for first choice, Ron Springett, who had been injured in Milan twelve days earlier, playing for the Football League against the Italian League. The tension around the ground was palpable and in the early stages this affected both sides as they struggled to create clear cut chances in a scrappy opening. The first real opportunity came to the Owls when Bobby Craig saw his low shot caught by Spurs keeper Bill Brown. Soon after, McLaren made a magnificent flying save to turn over a terrific volley from Bobby Smith. The Owls then enjoyed a ten minute spell of dominance which had Spurs rocking for probably the first time that season, as Kay's effort was saved before Keith Ellis headed against the post. The old 'Wednesday roar' had made a welcome re-appearance and the fans were cheering to the rafters when, just before the break, a four man move ended with Billy Griffin putting Wednesday ahead with a low cross shot. However, hardly had the celebrations died down before Tottenham equalised, as a free kick from Spurs legendary hardman, Dave MacKay, was converted by Maurice Norman to send the teams in all square at the interval.

The Owls had so far failed to let Spurs settle into a rhythm. This ensured an open if not particularly entertaining match, with the result remaining in doubt for the whole of the second period. After the game the Tottenham manager commented somewhat bitterly that 'there was not enough football in the match for us'; though physically Spurs had given as much as they had received, and were obviously shocked that a team had refused to lie down and be walked over. Early in the second half Swan had to clear off the line from Smith, but the sixty-ninth minute proved to be the decisive moment, when, after the ball had ricocheted around the area, John Fantham was on hand to crash home what would prove to be the match winning strike for the Owls. The almighty roar which greeted the goal was said to have been heard at Bramall Lane, where United were playing a reserve game. The final twenty minutes reverted to type, with nerves frayed both on and off the pitch, before the referee brought the curtain down on a memorable afternoon which has duly entered Hillsborough folklore. After the final whistle, Spurs players, Smith and MacKay, stood in the centre circle reflecting sadly on their first defeat of the season, but were sporting enough to applaud their conquerors off the pitch. Meanwhile Griffin and Baker had other ideas and were engaged in something of a running battle as they left the field. This required the intervention of a linesman, and it was obvious that some in the visiting camp were none too happy that the northern upstarts had sent them to defeat. In the end Wednesdayites went home to their teas in high spirits, and briefly could dream about a possible tilt at the golden riches of the European Cup in the following season.

Wednesday: McLaren, Johnson, Megson, T. McAnearney, Swan, Kay, Griffin, R. Craig. K. Ellis, Fantham, Finney

Tottenham: Brown, Baker, Henry, Blanchflower, Norman, MacKay, Jones, White, Smith, Allen, Dyson

Referee: Mr R. Leafe (Nottingham)

Memory Match

Without doubt the definite highlight of the 1961–62 season for Sheffield Wednesday was their first foray into European football. This saw them progress all the way to the last eight of the Fairs Cup, now UEFA, after overcoming French and Italian opposition. On reaching this stage, they were rewarded with a home tie against the Spanish giants, Barcelona, and this started a tide of enthusiasm amongst supporters who eagerly awaited the visit of the Catalan club. As they are now, the Spanish club were then one of the greatest in World football, and their multi-national squad consisted of fifteen full Internationals from such countries as Hungary, Brazil, Paraguay, Uruguay and, of course, Spain. The visitors, along with their great rivals Real Madrid, had been among the pioneers of European club football; and by the time they visited Hillsborough, Barcelona had won not only the Fairs Cup in 1960, but had reached the final of the European Cup in 1961. The Spanish club had been dubbed the red millionaires by the local press, as it emerged their liabilities could be almost £1m (a huge sum in 1962). To balance this statistic, their Nou Camp stadium and star studded team were said to be worth at least twice that figure!

The Owls expected a 60,000 gate for the clash, but these hopes were badly hit when two inches of snow covered the Hillsborough pitch on the Tuesday before the tie. Barcelona were forced to train indoors at the Sheffield University gym even as Eric Taylor hoped the game would go ahead. Otherwise Wednesday would have to pay over half of Barca's £2,500 travel expenses, cutting greatly into the Owls' Fairs Cup revenue. Thankfully there was no deterioration in weather conditions and the tie went ahead twenty four hours later, although the icy conditions were a major contributory factor in a disappointing crowd of under 30,000. The Owls went into the game on the back of three straight home defeats, and were hit by injury problems which saw key men Tom McAnearney, Keith Ellis and Bobby Craig all missing; with Robin Hardy, Gerry Young and Derek Wilkinson taking their places. At the time the Spaniards were involved in a three way tussle with Real Madrid and Athletico Bilbao at the top of their domestic league, and this game proved to be a classic confrontation of Barcelona's superior skill and movement against British determination, enthusiasm and sheer work rate.

It was the continentals who were the first to strike, when, after fifteen minutes, Ramon Villaverde popped up to fire a right foot shot past Springett. In the opening twenty-eight minutes Wednesday had seemingly shown far too much respect for their famous opponents, however, this changed visibly when the Owls netted a superb equaliser through John Fantham. The move started with Colin Dobson drawing several defenders on the edge of the box before spraying the ball out to the now unmarked Young. He then cut inside Benetiz and crossed perfectly for Fantham to sprint into the box and score with a picture book diving header. From then on the Owls fought for every ball, but were rocked back when, after 35 minutes, Brazilian Evariste de Macedo noticed Springett was fractionally off his line and promptly sent a 20 yard dipping shot over the Wednesday keeper. The game was now end to end, and Wednesday were not to be denied an equaliser. This duly came on the stroke of half-time, when a string of short passes resulted in Alan Finney driving home a terrific left foot shot.

The second half couldn't match the high standard set in the first period, as the game became more of a rugged encounter. This saw a cynical side emerge in the Spaniards play, with Benetiz lucky not be sent off after an almost brutal tackle on Finney. However, shortly before this incident Hillsborough had erupted, when, five minutes into the second half, Hardy ran towards the area and tricked the Spanish defence by feigning to shoot, only to slip a great ball through for John Fantham to drive it past Coldran to put Wednesday ahead. The remainder of the half saw the Owls push for a fourth goal. This would make them favourites to go through on aggregate, but it was not to be: and Wednesday would have to go into the cauldron of the Nou Camp with just a one goal advantage after a tremendous night of European football.

Wednesday: Springett, Johnson, Megson, Hardy, Swan, Kay, Wilkinson, Dobson, Young, Fantham, Finney

Barcelona: Coldran, Benitez, Gracia, Segarra, Rodreguez, Garay, Pereda, Verges, de Maceda, Kocsis, Villaverde

Referee: Mr A. Dusch (West Germany)

Fairs Cup Quarter Final—1st Leg
Wednesday 28th February 1962

Sheffield Wednesday 3
Barcelona 2

Memory Match

Friendly
Monday 22nd October 1962

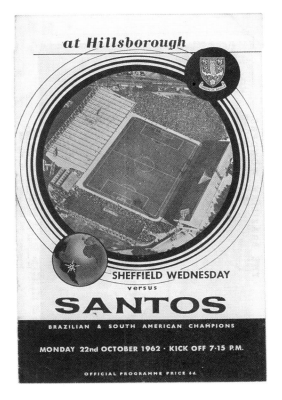

Of all the foreign clubs to have visited Hillsborough over the last one hundred years, it is almost certain that the best and most glamorous was the South American side, Santos. At the time of their visit the Brazilian club were not only Champions of their own country, but Champions of their continent. To complete an astonishing c.v., they had just been crowned World Champions, after having overcome Benfica 8–4 on aggregate; including a remarkable 5–2 second leg win in the Stadium of Light. If that was not enough to attract fans, then the inclusion in the Santos side of a player by the name of Edison Arantes de Nascimento surely would—the 21-year-old, better known by the nickname of Pele. An outstanding forward, Pele is widely recognised as the greatest player ever in the game; and in 1962 was at the height of his powers after helping Brazil to two World Cups in 1958 and 1962. Every major club in the world wanted to capture his signature, including Real Madrid and Juventus who were rumoured to be willing to pay an astonishing £500,000 for his services. However, the 'black pearl' remained loyal to Santos and the groans of disappointment in Europe were audible when he signed a new five year contract for the Rio de Janeiro side. At the tender age of 21, Pele had already starred in a film about his life and written his memoirs. These, when launched at his publishers, caused a mini riot in which he was mobbed and 257 people were injured. In addition to Pele, Santos also included Gilmar and Mauro, both of whom had played alongside Pele back in June, when Brazil had beaten Czechoslovakia in Chile to lift the Jules Rimet trophy for a second time. After Wednesday had been controversially kept out of the Fairs Cup, it would be fair to say that Eric Taylor had pulled off a rare coup in arranging for the star studded side to visit England for the first time ever. Indeed, the fixture had only been clinched at the last moment, and it took a herculean effort from Taylor and his staff to make the arrangements for an all-ticket game of such magnitude. However he was rewarded with a record Hillsborough crowd for a friendly fixture, when just under 50,000 responded to a game that game sparked enormous interest in Sheffield and the surrounding districts.

The fans who packed Hillsborough did so in eager anticipation of the night ahead, and were not to be disappointed as Santos produced a dazzling display of soccer which at times had the Owls spellbound. As Wednesday played the traditional all-action English game, so the Brazilians were cool and collected, and at times played at almost a walking pace before bursting into life to put the Owls goal under severe pressure. The actual game had a sensational start, when, after two minutes, Pele, from a seemingly innocuous position, fired a brilliant 40-yard pass straight down the middle of the pitch, where the ball bounced over the head of Swan for Coutinho to fire in the first goal. The Owls were stunned by this early set back, and looked to be out of the game when a sublime piece of skill from Pele after 28 minutes doubled the visitors advantage. The ball came to Pele just inside the box and he duly rode three tackles before sliding a perfect pass for Coutinho to net his second. However, Wednesday then fought back, and from a Holliday cross Billy Griffin reduced the arrears. Three minutes later, up popped Bronco Layne at the far post to net a shock equaliser from another Holliday centre. Soon after, Layne was forced to leave the field with a bad injury, and five minutes before the break another terrific goal put Santos back in the lead. This time the outstanding Coutinho needed no help as he beat two men on the edge of the box before crashing home his hat trick goal. The crowd were being richly entertained, and before the break would witness the most talked about penalty kick in Sheffield Wednesday's history. This was awarded when Kay tripped Pele, and it was the man himself who took the spot kick. The maestro walked up to the ball, pretended to take a shot with one foot, and in a flash did a little shuffle banging the ball into the corner of the net with the other foot. Wednesday keeper, Ron Springett, was literally rooted to the spot; the spectators had never seen anything like it in their lives, and for many years, Wednesday fans would still talk about the Pele penalty. Surprisingly there was no further scoring in the second half, although Colin Dobson did see his penalty kick saved by Gilmar. In the end the Brazilians were playing exhibition football and seemed to have so much in hand, with every man possessing terrific ball control and some sublime skills. The contrast between early 1960s English football and world football were vividly emphasised; but this mattered little to the paying public who had been present on one of greatest nights in the club's long history.

Wednesday: R. Springett, Johnson, Megson, T. McAnearney, Swan, Kay, Finney, Dobson, Layne (Young 35), Griffin, Holliday

Santos: Gilmar, Mauro, Dalmo, Olavo, Lima, Formiga (Carlos), Pagao, Mengalvio, Coutinho, Pele, Dorval

Referee: Mr M. Kitabdjian (France)

Memory Match

According to the local press, the build up to Sheffield's first full International for 42 years was blighted by 'the biggest administrative bungling that can have been known to football', with the major criticism levelled against the Football Association. Because Wembley was unavailable, they had transferred the game to Hillsborough, but then refused to lower the ticket prices, charging an exorbitant £2 for seat tickets. Instead of an attendance of between 50,000 and 60,000, Wednesday secretary, Eric Taylor, therefore reckoned the club would be lucky to pull a crowd of over 40,000. Admission to the terraces was more reasonable, but most of those tickets had been swallowed up to ensure that many empty seats would be on show come kick off time. The Football Association's pricing policy was also regarded as unwise, because, at the time, France was widely regarded as Western Europe's poorest side. As a result, manager Walter Winterbottom was to field an experimental England line up. The other major problem concerned the training arrangements for the two sides. These were thrown into chaos after everything had seemingly been arranged to the last detail. Abbeydale Park, the home of Sheffield FC, was to be used by the French for training. The club had altered their pitch to match the Hillsborough one, and had also refurbished their dressing rooms. However, the French did not turn up, for Henri Guerin, their coach, had a change of heart and took his players walking on the Derbyshire moors before retiring to the hotel to play skittles on the lawn. As for England, unexpectedly they turned up at Hillsborough, while reporters and photographers were seeking them at other grounds. Hopes were expressed that the match would not be as shambolic as the forty-eight hours that preceded it!

When the teams finally kicked off a crowd of just over 35,000 was in the stadium. The major interest locally centred on Wednesday goalie, Ron Springett, who, in winning his 26th cap, equalled the club record set by Ernest Blenkinsop between the wars. Hellawell, Crowe, Charnley and Hinton were all winning their first full caps for England; while the French team contained only two players who had played in their 1958 World Cup semi-final side. From the start it was obvious that whatever England was trying was not working, and these plans were wrecked anyway, after just nine minutes, when star man Raymond Kopa bamboozled the English defence to supply Yvon Goujon, who fired past Springett into the top corner of the net. The lambs to the slaughter were playing more like wolves. While England simply could not find any rhythm, with a glancing header from Roy Charnley being the closest they came in the opening half.

Matters did not improve much at the start of the second half and the crowd, who so far had been charitable to the experimental side, began to whistle derisively and slow hand clap a somewhat inept showing from their national side. Thankfully England saved their blushes after 56 minutes when Charnley was fouled in the box and the Danish referee pointed to the penalty spot. He was immediately submerged by protesting Frenchmen, and it was almost three minutes before the official could clear the penalty area so that Ron Flowers could equalise from the spot kick. This was as good as it got for England; and in the end they could count themselves fortunate not to be behind after the visitors had put England to shame with their superior play. The French also boasted the best player on the pitch, in centre-forward Kopa, and it was back to the drawing board for England after this particular experiment had obviously failed its first test run.

England: R. Springett (Sheff. Wed.), Armfield (Blackpool), Wilson (Huddersfield T.), Moore (West Ham United), Norman (Tottenham H.), Flowers (Wolves), Hellawell (Birmingham C.), Crowe (Wolves), Greaves (Tottenham), Hinton (Wolves)

France: Bernard (Nimes), Wendling (Rheims), Lerond (Stade Francais), Chorda (Bordeaux), Maryan (Sedan), Ferrier (St Etienne), Robushi (Bordeaux), Bonnel (Valencienne), Kopa (Rheims), Goujon (Rennes), Sauvage (Rheims)

Referee: Mr F. Hansen (Denmark)

OFFICIAL PROGRAMME PRICE SIXPENCE

ENGLAND v. FRANCE

EUROPEAN NATIONS CUP

WEDNESDAY 3rd OCTOBER 1962 · KICK-OFF 7-30 P.M.

Played at Hillsborough

England

1

France

1

Memory Matches

Argentina
Spain
Switzerland
Uruguay
West Germany

In 1962, as soon as Wednesday discovered they would be one of the host grounds for the 1966 World Cup Finals, arrangements began in earnest for the tournament. It is detailed elsewhere how Wednesday embarked on a massive upgrade of their Hillsborough ground in time for the Finals, with the West Stand being built, the South Stand enclosure seated, an electronic scoreboard installed, a gymnasium built and a restaurant opened at a total cost of almost £200,000. A development fund was started and various loans secured from the Football Association, but the club were of the opinion that once the competition was over the new facilities would be of benefit for years to come.

Thirty years later the City organised a cultural festival to run in conjunction with the Euro 96 tournament. Back in 1966, Sheffield attempted to do much the same, though some of the attractions seem somewhat quaint now to modern eyes. Among several exhibitions running for the whole of the tournament were obvious ones, such as that showing Sheffield cutlery and stainless steel. Alternatively, a collection of World Cup stamps, books and memorabilia was on view in the City Library. Meanwhile amongst places recommended to visit was the Abbeydale Industrial Hamlet and various fire stations. However, the absolute ultimate attraction was a half-hour conducted tour of the Park Hill Flats development! In addition, a programme of daily events was arranged, which included such items as Golf matches at Hillsborough Golf Club, a 'Swiss Night' at the Silver Blades Ice Rink, First Aid demonstrations by the Red Cross, and a series of football matches between Sheffield Boys and teams representing the nations who would play at Hillsborough. These games actually drew some excellent crowds, with over 5,000 fans watching the Swiss side, Berne, lose 5–0; while West Germany gained their only win over an English side in the tournament when a team from Sheffield's twin City of Bochum beat the City lads 4–1.

As soon as it became apparent that the Swiss would be based in Sheffield and play all their games at Hillsborough, they were immediately adopted by the City's supporters as their unofficial side. Switzerland were the underdogs of Group Two, and showed why in their opening match with the eventual finalists, West Germany. It quickly became apparent that the Swiss were neat but toothless, and once the Germans had got their measure they produced a highly disciplined performance which overwhelmed the clock makers. The first goal arrived to the Germans after 16 minutes through Siegfried Held. He netted at the second attempt, and by half time the game was effectively over as Helmut Haller and 'The Kaiser' Franz Beckenbauer scored twice more to put their side three goals ahead. The Swiss were struggling desperately to cope with the German runs from midfield and, with the classy Beckenbauer also surging forward from the back, it was one-way traffic. The plucky Swiss did not throw the towel in, however, and after Beckenbauer had scored a superb fourth goal they almost netted a consolation. But Richard Dürr could only watch as his shot beat Tilkowski to rebound to safety off a post. With thirteen minutes left, Haller scored from a penalty after Seeler had been brought down by Fuhrer, and at the final whistle the banner waving German supporters in a 36,000 crowd streamed from the ground chanting and singing, after their side had posted early notice that they would be a force to be reckoned with. For the Swiss it was a disastrous start and for one supporter it must have been a cruel ninety minutes. Window cleaner Emil Holliger had set off from his Zurich home on June 18th and walked the 810 miles to Sheffield, arriving in time for the opening game with cow bells jangling from his liberally decorated pram!

Switzerland: Elsener, Grobéty, Schneiter, Tacchella, Fuhrer, Bäni, Dürr, Odermatt, Künzli, Hosp, Schindelholz

West Germany: Tilkowski, Höttges, Schnellinger, Beckenbauer, Schulz, Weber, Brülls, Haller, Seeler, Overath, Held

Referee: Mr H. Phillips (Scotland)

After their hammering by West Germany, the Swiss made eight changes for the meeting with Spain. This included the recall of both Jakob Kuhn and Werner Leimgruber, who had made headlines for their off-the-field behaviour. On the night before the German game it emerged both men had returned 50 minutes late to the Hallam Tower Hotel and were accompanied by two mystery women! The Swiss officials were not amused and axed them from the team for the opening game; while back home in Zurich both the wives of the players in question were besieged by reporters and anonymous phone callers. In the end a Swiss pools company arranged for the angry spouses to fly to Sheffield, and the two guilty players had to face the music for their misadventures just hours before they took the field for the Spanish match. A Swiss official commenting on the scandal said: 'The trouble is there is a mouse and suddenly it becomes an elephant'! The Switzerland team which performed against Spain was far removed from the outfit that had met the Germans; and they came very close to creating an upset after holding the lead until well into the second period. Starting with a defensive 5–3–3 formation, the Swiss then realised the Spaniards were vulnerable and switched to a more orthodox formation. And Hillsborough exploded when Kuhn and Gottardi combined to set up a goal for Rene-Pierre Quentin after half an hour's play. The Spanish struggled to find their rhythm as their supporters whistled their disapproval, and the Swiss should have scored a second when Gottardi missed a great chance. However, twelve minutes into the second half, it was all square when a mistake by Bani in the Swiss midfield allowed Manuel Sanchis to grab his side's equaliser. The Swiss hit back and Quentin had the ball in the net; but it was disallowed after Zoco was deemed to have been impeded. Unfortunately for the underdogs, they then had to wave good-bye to World Cup glory, when, with fifteen minutes remaining, Spain scored a superb goal to send Switzerland tumbling to defeat. It was Real Madrid's Gento who created the goal, as he accelerated away from Fuhrer before pulling the ball back for Amancio Amaro to score with a spectacular diving header and keep alive the Spaniards hopes of qualification.

Spain: Iribar, Sanchis, Reija, J. Martinez, Fernandez, Zoco, Amaro, Del Sol, Peiró, Saurez, Gento

Switzerland: Elsener, Fuhrer, Brodmann, Leimgruber, Stierli, Bäni, Kuhn, Gottardi, Armbruster, Hosp, Quentin

Referee: Mr T. Balchramov (Russia)

World
Cup
Willie

Switzerland
0
West Germany
5

Spain
2
Switzerland
1

Tuesday 19th July 1966

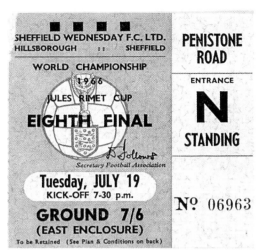

Argentina
2
Switzerland
0

With Switzerland now out of the competition, focus turned to their final opponents, Argentina, who required only a single point to qualify for the quarter finals. In order to guarantee progress, the South American team kicked off at Hillsborough with five men strung along their back line; and these players rarely ventured up field from their defensive position. This formation allowed Switzerland the majority of the possession, but once they reached the final third of the field they ran into an impregnable Argentinean wall. These tactics made for a frustrating afternoon for neutral fans, and no matter how much Switzerland's third captain in three games, Rene Brodmann, drove his side forward, they failed to create any clear cut chances in the first half. When Luis Artime scored off the inside of a post six minutes into the second half, it was very much a case of counting down the clock as Argentina's vice-like defence tightened. Once the South Americans had netted a second through Ermindo Onega's gentle lob ten minutes from the end, the Swiss finally gave up the ghost. In the final analysis, a masterful show of defensive play from the Argentineans had sent them through to a somewhat stormy last eight meeting with England at Wembley.

Argentina: Roma, Perfumo, Marzolini, Ferreiro, Calics, Rattin, Solari, Gonzalez, Artime, Onega, Mas

Switzerland: Eichmann, Fuhrer, Brodmann, Stierli, Armbruster, Bäni, Kuhn, Gottardi, Hosp, Künzli, Quentin

Referee: Mr J. F. Campos (Portugal)

Saturday 23rd July 1966

Uruguay
0
West Germany
4

The curtain came down on Hillsborough's involvement with the competition when West Germany returned to play their quarter final tie with Uruguay. The largest Hillsborough crowd of the tournament, 40,007, filled the stadium, and were treated to one of the stormiest games the old ground has seen in its hundred year history, as the Uruguayans tried to hack their way into the semi-finals with a disgraceful second-half display. The unfortunate aspect of the game was that Uruguay didn't really need to revert to strong-arm tactics, as in the first half, the South Americans had more than matched the Germans, with Cortes hitting a fierce fourth minute drive onto the crossbar, and Rocha's header being cleared off the line by Schnellinger. The ill-feeling that surfaced in the second half probably started with Rocha's shot, as the Uruguayans appealed in vain that the German defender had handled the ball away from the line. Their feelings of anger were heightened after twelve minutes, when West Germany took a fortunate lead as Held's shot was deflected past a wrong footed Mazurkieviez. As the half wore on the tackles started to fly in, forcing English referee, Jim Finney, to book both Cortes & Gonclavez. However, the game exploded four minutes into the second half, when Uruguay captain, Horatio Troche, punched Emmerich in the kidneys after an off-the-ball disagreement. The referee didn't see the incident, but his linesman did, and Finney had no choice but to send Troche from the field of play. Six minutes later all hell broke loose when Silva laid out Haller with a vicious tackle, and was sent off, reducing his side to only nine men. However, Silva wouldn't leave the field, and, as the Uruguayan team swarmed round the referee, Mr Finney was forced to call on the police to help Silva from the pitch. The boys in blue were then jostled on the touchline by the Uruguayans in disgraceful scenes. Completely losing their heads in this crazy six minute spell, the South Americans caused untold damage to their World Cup hopes as Germany took advantage of their two man advantage to net three more goals through Frank Beckenbauer, Uwe Seeler and Helmut Haller. According to the local Sheffield press the display was a typical example of 'Teutonic thoroughness', which would only be overcome a week later as the host nation enjoyed their finest moment in International football.

Uruguay: Mazurkieviez, Troche, Manicera, Ubinas, Gonclaves, Caetano, Cortes, Salva, Silva, Rocha, Perez

West Germany: Tilkowski, Höttges, Schenellinger, Beckenbauer, Schulz, Weber, Seeler, Haller, Held, Overath, Emmerich

Referee: Mr J. Finney (England)

Memory Match

Just a few short months after beating Benfica at Wembley to become the first English side to win the coveted European Cup, Manchester United visited Hillsborough for a Division One encounter. The 51,000 plus crowd which packed into the stadium were subsequently involved in a footballing version of utopia, for the Owls won a thrilling nine-goal spectacular in probably the most entertaining league game ever staged at the ground. The United side appearing at Hillsborough that day was packed with household names, including Bobby Charlton, Denis Law, Nobby Stiles, and the unique talent of George Best. Wednesday were classed as underdogs, although they had made a bright start to the season and sat inside the top six places at kick off. Three days earlier the Owls had surrendered their unbeaten record in a defeat at Chelsea; and manager Jack Marshall made two changes from that setback, with Gerry Young and John Ritchie coming into the side to replace Wilf Smith and Alan Warboys.

The match set off at a cracking pace and within ten minutes both sides had found the net, with Wednesday opening the score after just two minutes. A mistake from Dunne then allowed David Ford to supply Jack Whitham, and he found the net. After ten minutes United were level when Best beat Ellis before firing past the advancing Springett; and, a minute later as the crowd struggled for breath, they watched as the visitors took the lead. Wizardry from the feet of Best fooled Ellis, and after his close range shot had been parried by Springett, it was that supreme opportunist Denis Law who latched onto the loose ball to fire home before the Wednesday defence could react. Incredibly though, within four minutes the game was level again, as David Ford attacked down the right and sent in a perfect centre from which John Ritchie powerfully headed home the fourth goal: and all inside the first fifteen minutes. After this astonishing opening, the game became relatively quiet, with only three more goals coming before the referee blew for half time! The visitors scored the first two. After 26 minutes Law netted his second after a brilliant display of ball control, and then,

eleven minutes later came a stunning trademark goal from Bobby Charlton, blasting home from the edge of the penalty area after a deft flick from Law created the opportunity. The Owls were now two goals in arrears to the European Champions, and surely there was no way back. However, Wednesday weren't yet ready to wave the white flag, and after a splendid effort from Eustace was saved by Stepney, it was Jack Whitham who popped up on the stroke of half time to score this amazing game's seventh goal and send Wednesday into the break just one goal in arrears.

The huge crowd needed the ten minute half-time break just to digest the unprecedented first period; for within three minutes of the restart the goals started to flow again. Ford's curling free kick looked to be heading for the forehead of Whitham, only for Nobby Stiles to get there first—to nod the ball past a stunned Stepney into his own net. Ten minutes later, Don Megson crashed a 25 yard shot into the top corner, only to see his effort disallowed as John Fantham was in an offside position. Then, with twenty minutes left, Hillsborough went crazy as the home side surged ahead when Ford's effort was parried and Jack Whitham picked up the loose ball to gleefully crash home his first hat trick in senior football. The Wednesday fans were now in joyous mood, and chants of 'We want six' rose from the Kop as the Owls poured forward. Efforts from both Ritchie and Mobley almost granted the supporters their wish. United were still dangerous, however, and for once Best missed a great chance just before the referee called a halt to a game that will be talked about for generations to come. There are not enough superlatives to truly describe the entertainment on that Saturday afternoon, but a quote in the *Sunday People* aptly sums up a memorable ninety minutes: 'If you were not somewhere in Hillsborough on Saturday then you were under-privileged. This was not so much a football match—more a compendium of the delights of a thousand'.

Wednesday: P. Springett, Young, Megson, S. Ellis, Mobley, Eustace, Whitham, McCalliog, Ritchie, Ford, Fantham

Manchester United: Stepney, Brennan, Dunne (Burns 3), Fitzpatrick, Sadler, Stiles, Morgan, Kidd, Charlton, Law, Best

Referee: Mr W.S. Castle (Dudley)

Sheffield Wednesday 5

Manchester United 4

Memory Match

After a season-long struggle to maintain their First Division status, and, after gaining a surprise draw at Old Trafford a week earlier, the Owls went into the final match of the season with their fate in their own hands. Wednesday knew that if relegation was to be avoided they would have to beat Manchester City at Hillsborough to send Crystal Palace down instead. With both Palace and Sunderland having completed their fixtures, the Owls sat at the foot of the table at kick off, with only the two points for a win being enough to save them; and then on goal average. The general opinion among Wednesday fans was that City, who had a European Cup Winners Cup final against Gornik on the horizon, would take it easy, as they wouldn't want to sustain any injuries before the European tie: and given the choice, they'd prefer to see the Owls remain in the division rather than Crystal Palace. Whether Owls fans were right or wrong, however, it would matter little if Wednesday didn't perform well; and a record of nine home defeats did not instil confidence in that particular department. Wednesday were unchanged from the team that had won the heroic point at Manchester, and their mascot on the night was a young lad by the name of Colin Walker. Many years later he would make club history by becoming the only Wednesday substitute to score a hat-trick.

As is usually the case when a club is in serious danger of relegation the crowds come flooding back. Wednesday were no exception, and their best crowd of the season, 45,258, packed Hillsborough hoping to cheer their team to safety. The Owls were aided by the absence of star men, Franny Lee and Colin Bell, from the City line up, and were further boosted by the departure of the injured Mike Summerbee after only 23 minutes. Unfortunately his replacement, Ian Bowyer, would become the central figure on an emotional night. If the watching Wednesday fans were hoping to see their team attack from the first whistle, they were to be sadly disappointed; as in a distinctly lacklustre opening fifteen minutes the Owls were second best to a City side who themselves hardly moved out of first gear. In fact the visitors should have scored twice in that period, Towers coming closest when his shot wasn't held by Grummitt, who could only watch as the ball trickled goalwards and rebounded off the foot of a post. Despite the Owls poor play they did create a couple of chances, but both were

spurned before a late tackle from Colin Prophett ended Summerbee's night. Many still believe that when City's trainer, Dave Ewing, carried the centre-forward from the field, the Owls chances went with him. For the visitors felt aggrieved at Prophett's challenge, and seemingly doubled their efforts after previously having played with an almost indifferent attitude. Four minutes after Summerbee's departure City were awarded a penalty when Harold Wilcockson handled a Heslop header. The conspiracy theorists then had a field day when Doyle's feeble spot kick was almost passed to Grummitt. However, within four minutes City had scored, and it was substitute Bowyer who drilled home after a terrific cross from Neill Young found the youngster unmarked. Wilf Smith had limped off just before the goal, and the subsequent change of formation saw Jackie Sinclair switch into midfield, from which position he finally introduced a modicum of drive which had been non-existent up to that point. However, he couldn't inspire Wednesday to an equaliser and at half time their Division One lives were hanging by a thread, with Crystal Palace sharpening the scissors!

At least in the second half Wednesday had the majority of the possession. But as the period wore on, a feeling of resignation started to fill the air as the Owls searched in vain for the equaliser that would at least give them some hope. They did duly level the scores, thanks to a tremendous 20-yard drive from Tony Coleman which flew into the top corner: and with City's commitment waning, an unlikely escape began to seem possible. Unfortunately the Owls simply couldn't raise their game, and were put out of their misery in the last minute when Bowyer scored again with a close range header that condemned Wednesday to the Second Division. At the final whistle the team trooped off the field to some boos and whistles—an apt comment on their poor performance. According to the local press the Owls had been 'indifferent at the back, hapless in midfield and impotent in attack', but otherwise had given a good account of themselves! Wednesday secretary, Eric Taylor, said it was the unhappiest night of his 40 years at Hillsborough; while manager Danny Williams stated 'We shall just have to rebuild. I shall just have to get a good side and come back'- sadly it would be fourteen years before Wednesday could reclaim their first division place.

Wednesday: Grummitt, Wilcockson, Smith (Downes 30), S. Ellis, Prophett, T. Craig, Sinclair, G. Young, Warboys, Whitham, Coleman

Manchester City: Dowd, Book, Pardoe, Doyle, Booth, Oakes, Carrodus, Towers, Summerbee (Bowyer 23), N. Young, Heslop

Referee: Mr K. Howley (Teeside)

Sheffield Wednesday 1

Manchester City 2

SHEFFIELD WEDNESDAY FOOTBALL CLUB OFFICIAL MAGAZINE

WEDNESDAY WORLD
Volume 1
Number 25
1/-

WEDNESDAY, APRIL 22nd, 1970. Kick-off 7.30 pm.

SHEFFIELD WEDNESDAY v MANCHESTER CITY Teams on back page

Memory Match

It would be fair to say that Owls supporters have been frustrated in recent years, as their side has flirted with relegation from the Premiership. However, to the Wednesdayites who sat through the 1974–75 season, the experiences of the 1990s must have seemed like Shangri-la compared to what is officially the club's worst ever season in their long history. The situation was so dire, that when Oxford United visited Hillsborough in Wednesday's penultimate home game of a disastrous season, the long suffering Owls fans were met with the stark reality that their side had not scored a league goal since late February; and, almost unbelievably, had not scored a Division Two home goal since December 14th 1974. For the die-hard supporters it was now simply a case of blind loyalty and a perverse wish to say in future years that they had been there when Wednesday were at their lowest ebb. Not surprisingly, the crowds had dwindled as the season progressed, and this day saw the Owls down to their real hard core of support, as the crowd figure of 7,444 set a new post-war record low for the already relegated Wednesday.

Following the previous week's single goal defeat at Bristol City—the Owls fifth consecutive loss by that scoreline—Wednesday boss, Steve Burtenshaw, recalled both Brian Joicey and James Quinn. Early on, however, it was the same old story as United dominated; and after eight minutes future Owls' favourite Andy McCulloch put Wednesday into their usual position—a goal down. The Owls were actually down to ten men when Oxford scored. Hugh Dowd had hobbled off with an ankle injury and prospects looked bleak when Shaw almost turned the ball into his own net. However, the Owls then shocked their supporters by dominating the remainder of the half, and only a combination of poor finishing and excellent goal keeping from United custodian, Milkins, kept them out. A Joicey shot was cleared off the line by Light; and in an almighty goal-mouth melee, Sunley looked certain to score, before the ball somehow ricocheted into the keeper's grateful arms.

The second period continued in the same vein, as the Owls maintained their search for that elusive strike to end the goal famine. However, as the minutes ticked by hopes started to fade, and after Oxford scorer, McCulloch, had been stretchered off with concussion, a few fans started to drift out of the ground convinced that fate had decreed yet another loss for Burtenshaw's punch drunk outfit. But then, as the game entered the five minutes of injury time added on by referee Ken Walmsley, Wednesday attacked, and Jimmy Mullen swung in a high cross from the left wing. This wasn't properly dealt with by Milkins, allowing David Sunley to steer the ball towards the net with his head. As the ball headed for the net Brian Joicey made sure it was over the line. The roar that emanated from Hillsborough was truly deafening, with the fans who remained in the ground cheering as if their side had won the Championship. The basic facts were that this was the Owls first goal for 14 hours and 10 minutes, and their first at Hillsborough for a staggering 14 hours and 25 minutes—when, over four months earlier, Bobby Brown had scored against Oldham Athletic. The match has subsequently entered Hillsborough folklore as the day the goal famine ended. A comment from a happy supporter at the final whistle summed up the afternoon—'I was glad I was there to see that goal. I shall tell my grandchildren in years to come that I was there for that one...'

Wednesday: Fox, Cameron, Quinn, Mullen, Dowd (Wylde 9), Shaw, Potts, Harvey, Sunley, Henson, Joicey

Oxford United: Milkins, Light, Shuker, Lowe, C. Clarke, Jeffrey, McGrogan, Taylor, D. Clarke, McCulloch (Briggs 74), Aylott

Referee: Mr K. Walmsley (Fleetwood)

Football League Division Two
Saturday 19th April 1975

A goal that launched a thousand smile

. . . in the dying minutes of the Oxford game. Brian Joicey adds the finishing tou·
to the goal that Wednesdayites had been waiting for, for a long time.

Sheffield Wednesday
1
Oxford United
1

Chapter 7

The Road Back
1975–1984

1975–76
A POINT FROM DIVISION FOUR

After the disastrous campaign of 1974–75, the summer of 1975 was again dominated by the Owls' plight both on and off the pitch. The club faced mounting criticism in the press from the bitterly disappointed supporters, who were almost disbelieving at Wednesday's rapid fall from grace. If that were not bad enough, the financial problems continued to worsen and another reported huge deficit meant Wednesday had lost almost £500,000 since suffering relegation from the top flight in 1970. It was obvious that financially the Owls were bleeding to death, and to try to stem the flow the club's directors announced that from now on, Wednesday would concentrate their efforts on producing players through the club's youth policy, in addition to investigating ways in which extra revenue could be obtained. As part of their cost cutting measures, both chief scout, Fred Scott, and physiotherapist, Geoff Eggerton, were made redundant, and several players left, including Peter Eustace, Peter Springett, John Holsgrove and Peter Rodrigues. Two new faces arrived at the club, Neil Ramsbotton signing from Coventry City for £5,000 and Andy Proudlove coming in from non-league Buxton. Meanwhile, John Haselden was appointed as trainer. The month of June was set to see vital revenue flow into the coffers, when it was arranged for the famous American stunt motorcyclist, Evil Knievel, to appear at Hillsborough. However, it was typical of Wednesday's luck at the time that he had to cancel the show after being injured during his Wembley performance. Finally, at the club's Annual General Meeting Wednesday fans were not exactly joyous to hear Chairman, Matt Sheppard, announce that 'Wednesday are in serious trouble both from a financial and footballing point of view'. His comments probably did not help boost the season ticket sales, which stood at an all time low of only 2,050 when the league programme commenced.

Events on the field were almost secondary to problems off the pitch, and the pre-season warm up was problematic, with two friendly defeats suffered in Scotland before a win was secured at York and a heavy home loss suffered against the First Division side, Coventry City. The Owls first ever game in Division Three came at Southend, and though hundreds of Wednesday fans made the long trek they were to be disappointed, for despite holding a half-time lead, the Owls eventually lost 2–1. Three days later, however, Wednesday won 2–0 at Darlington in the League Cup but then rather carelessly managed to lose by the same score in the second leg, before losing their first ever penalty shoot-out after a third game finished goalless. Despite a terrific four goal showing at home to Grimsby, it was obvious that Wednesday would not be bouncing back to Division Two at the first attempt, for the Owls had quickly slipped into the bottom four relegation places. As the league struggles continued, a three week period beginning in late September

went a long way to securing Wednesday's long-term future, for a new Chairman was appointed and manager, Burtenshaw, departed, to be replaced by Len Ashurst. The new Chairman was Bert McGee, taking over from Matt Sheppard who resigned because of pressures of work. Within days McGee had presided over the departure of the boss, Steve Burtenshaw and the chief coach, Gerry Young. The Owls placed Jim McAnearney in temporary charge, and in his brief spell as caretaker he let David Sunley leave for Nottingham Forest on loan. Ron Atkinson was again one of the names linked to rumours about the post, but when the Owls made their choice it was the Gillingham manager, Len Ashurst, who was appointed—much to the Kent club's fury—with Tony Toms as his No. 2. The new man's first game in charge saw Wednesday lose at Cardiff; and, with the Owls' bank overdraft moving to within £5 of their agreed limit, Ashurst knew he could only rely on free transfers and youth players to turn the situation around.

After a game at Walsall was abandoned due to a waterlogged pitch, Ashurst gained his first win when, somewhat ironically, Gillingham fell to a Joicey goal at Hillsborough. That game saw new signing Neil O'Donnell make his debut after joining from Gillingham, though he did play in the aforementioned Walsall game. Aside from the FA Cup, the Owls then failed to win until the final day of January, leaving them in desperate trouble in the lower reaches of the division. The Cup saw the non-league teams, Macclesfield and Wigan, beaten at Hillsborough before defeat was suffered at the Valley against Second Division, Charlton Athletic. Off the pitch further measures were taken to cut costs, with the Youth Development Officer, George McCabe, being sacked and a sub-committee formed with the sole remit being to raise funds. Moreover, it certainly did not help matters

S. W. F. C. Hillsborough, Sheffield	S. W. F. C. Hillsborough, Sheffield
SOUTH STAND UNCOVERED	SOUTH STAND UNCOVERED
ENTRANCE E	ENTRANCE E
GANGWAY 13	GANGWAY 13
SATURDAY 3rd APRIL Kick-off 3.0 p.m.	SATURDAY 3rd APRIL Kick-off 3.0 p.m.
Res. Seat £3.50 incl. VAT	Res. Seat £3.50 incl. VAT
QQ FOR FILE	QQ TO BE GIVEN UP

much that Wednesday were still paying off a 1966 World Cup loan taken out to pay for ground improvements! The month of December saw Colin Harvey told to retire because of injury, and Ashurst stun the fans by putting favourites, Eric Potts, Jimmy Mullen, David Sunley and Roger Wylde on the transfer list. Ronnie Ferguson, was also released to join Darlington. In the end, the supporters were just glad for 1975 to come to a close, for it had seen the club win only four league games in their very own 'annus horribilis'.

The New Year started with Richard Walden arriving on a free transfer from Aldershot, before, in another cost-cutting measure, backroom boys, Jim McAnearney and Ron Staniforth were both sacked, leaving only Ashurst and Toms as full-time staff. Back on the field of play a win over Aldershot lifted Wednesday to the dizzy heights of 18th; though any hopes of building on that were hit when the home game with Chesterfield was postponed because of a serious flu outbreak at Hillsborough. To stop the disease spreading, the ground was then completely closed down, and the away game at Shrewsbury was also called off; a situation which saw the Owls slip back down the league. Before the outbreak, Ashurst had been busy in the transfer market, with goalie, Barry Watling arriving on trial; Sunley and Proudlove signing for Hull City and Norwich City respectively; and the Gillingham mid-fielder, Peter Feely, completing a protracted move to join his old boss; with the fringe player, Bobby Brown leaving for a loan spell at Aldershot. The period also saw Gillingham issue writs against Wednesday and Ashurst claiming that the former had made an illegal approach to the latter while he was still boss at the Gills.

The final weeks of another desperate season started with Danny Cameron leaving for Preston North End, while Ken Knighton was seconded onto the training staff with responsibility for the reserve and junior sides. However, all interest then switched to events on the field of play, for things looked critical after a home defeat to neighbours, Chesterfield, pushed Wednesday down to second from the bottom. In marked contrast to the finish of the previous campaign, the Owls then suddenly hit form at Hillsborough winning four crucial consecutive home games by a 1–0 scoreline to give hope of avoiding the dreaded drop into the basement of English soccer. A couple of hard fought draws were secured away from home, with the outcome being that when Southend visited Wednesday for the final game of the season, it was winner takes all, with the loser relegated. Thankfully, a huge crowd (by Third Division standards) turned out to support their fallen heroes, and the story had a happy ending as two first-half goals helped to secure a 2–1 win and stave off a second successive demotion from which they might never have recovered.

1976–77
THE GREAT SLUMP ENDS

The summer started with a mass clear out, which resulted in a total of nine players being given free transfers; including Allan Thompson, Brian Joicey and Bernard Shaw. The second named eventually joined Barnsley, with Thompson going to Stockport. Also departing was Neil Ramsbottom, who signed for Plymouth Argyle. Joining the Owls were Crystal Palace midfielders, Jeff Johnson and John Collins, along with a new chief scout, Dave Blakey, who had previously worked at Burnley. A well-known face returned as Peter Eustace came on trial after being released by Peterborough. However, he wasn't offered terms for a third spell and would have to wait a further seven years before returning in a rather different role. There was a groan from supporters when, after the club's worst ever season, they saw season ticket prices rise. Thankfully, however, the financial situation had eased slightly, and though the annual accounts again showed a big loss, it was almost half that of the previous season, with income from commercial activities showing a significant increase. The effect of the stringent cost cutting measures was revealed by the wage bill, which was cut by over fifty percent to only £12,734. Moreover, it was rumoured that mystery plans were being formulated to further boost the club's income.

In a what was welcome change, the Owls pre-season was a great success. They entered a four team mini-tournament called the Shipp Cup, and promptly won their games against Peterborough United, Lincoln City and Cambridge United to lift the trophy. This was a definite confidence booster and probably contributed to an excellent 3–0 League Cup win at Grimsby Town which opened the competitive season a week later. The Owls progressed in the Cup after a goalless home leg and then caused a major shock when, in the next round, goals from Potts and Wylde secured a terrific win at First Division, Wolves. In the league, Wednesday made a steady start and sat in mid-table when Watford were beaten to reach the last sixteen of the League Cup for the first time for nine years. By this time, the Hillsborough purse strings had been loosened somewhat to allow Ashurst to enter the transfer market and boost his squad by bringing several new players to Hillsborough; with Tommy Tynan the first to arrive from Liverpool. The Owls also paid a fee for Burnley's Sheffield-born winger, Paul Bradshaw, while the ex-West Brom player, Bobby Hope signed after returning from a spell in American football. Manchester United forward Ray Botham, and Derek Jefferson from Wolves came on loan, though the latter was the only one to make an impression on the first team before they returned to their respective clubs. Meanwhile, the rumoured 'mystery plan' to raise finance was revealed as being a new share issue which, the Owls hoped, would raise £400,000 and completely wipe out their debts. A total of 2,500 x £100 'B' shares, and 15,000 x £10 'C' shares were to be issued, with

supporters receiving various discounts on season tickets in return. The plans were eventually voted through at a special meeting, but not without the club being criticised by fans and shareholders—the head of the shareholders commenting: 'The directors have proved they don't know how to spend money. Why should we give them some more to throw away'. The Owls raised £27,500 within the first seven days, providing revenue that would help Wednesday turn the corner from a financial point of view.

On the field of play the Owls' star was in the ascendancy, and a hat-trick of wins lifted Wednesday into third place by mid-October. Though this was quickly followed by the same number of consecutive defeats and a league Cup exit at Millwall, after the seasons of decline, it was a welcome change for Wednesday fans to see their side in the top half of the table. The Owls then repeated their three-win trick and by the turn of the year they sat in the top six, with the idea of promotion actually being whispered around Sheffield 6.

The FA Cup hopes had bitten the dust at Darlington, where ex-Owl, Ronnie Ferguson came back to haunt Wednesday by

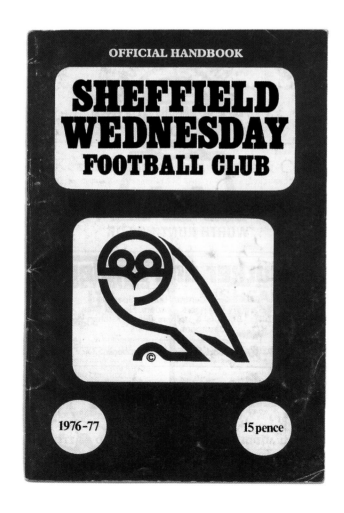

OFFICIAL HANDBOOK

SHEFFIELD WEDNESDAY FOOTBALL CLUB

1976-77

15 pence

netting the game's only goal: and early in 1977, both Dave Rushbury and Dennis Leman joined on loan as a prelude to signing on a permanent basis. The start of the Queen's Silver Jubilee year saw Dave Blakey promoted to assistant manager, David Barber appointed head groundsman, and the unfortunate Neill O'Donnell forced to retire due to a serious back injury—with the Owls agreeing to stage a testimonial match for him. Throughout the remainder of the season Wednesday remained in the top eight, and although never breaking into the three promotion places they remained in contention until mid-April thanks to some astute purchases from Ashurst, and the forty-goal forward partnership of Tommy Tynan and Roger Wylde—the latter contributing 25 goals to the double act. Further transfer activity culminated in John Davis and Bob Bolder arriving from Crystal Palace and non-league Dover, respectively; while Barnsley signed John Collins and Wednesday gave permission to Bobby Hope and Peter Fox to spend their summer playing in the North American Soccer League.

The Owls had a busy finish to their season. In the final week they played a select side at Denaby United as part of Mick

Prendergast's testimonial season, before hitting six at Hartlepool, twenty-four hours later in a fund-raising match for the ailing North East club. A final day home win over Oxford United sent Wednesdayites into the summer with hopes that the corner had finally been turned, after the first season for four years in which the word relegation had not loomed large on the horizon.

Roger Wylde scores against Walsall in the League Cup

1977–78
BIG JACK TO THE RESCUE

Manager Len Ashurst was obviously happy with his squad, for he retained all but two of his players following an encouraging season. He then strengthened his backroom staff by appointing the experienced ex-Sheffield United manager, John Harris to the post of Chief Scout, following the departure of Dave Blakey. On the playing front, the major signing of the close season was that of Sunderland Cup winner, Ian Porterfield, for £20,000; though the signing of Peter Shirtliff and Brian Cox on professional forms would be of longer term benefit to the club. Those leaving Hillsborough included Eric Potts to Brighton; while both Peter Feely and Phil Henson were transferred abroad, with the former signing a short term contract in Norwegian football, and the latter joining the Dutch side, Sparta Rotterdam. One vital signing was that of top scorer, Roger Wylde, to a three-year contract, while the dispute with Gillingham regarding Ashurst's appointment was resolved in an 'out of court settlement', with Wednesday agreeing to pay £5,000 compensation to the Kent club. The shock news of the summer was that the club accounts showed an astonishing profit of almost £130,000. This was largely due to the Owls trail-blazing lottery which had been introduced by the Commercial Manager, Dennis Woodhead. Indeed, such was its success that a second lottery was soon launched, which for some reason was named after the popular James Bond film, 'Moonraker'. The other news centred around the Middlewood Road training ground which the Owls had finally started to develop into a fully functional training facility, with the help of a large grant form Sheffield City Council.

The Owls again entered the Shipp Cup, but this time recorded only one win before they made a dream start to the season as Doncaster Rovers were beaten 8–0 on aggregate in the First Round of the League Cup. However, the Owls hopelessly failed to convert this form into their league soccer and after ten games they were rock bottom with only five points to their name. Strangely, they had no problem in dismissing Second Division Blackpool from the League Cup, but this was not enough for the Wednesday board, and, following a defeat at Preston, manager Len Ashurst was sacked after just over two years in the job. Ken Knighton was placed in temporary charge, though news then emerged that the former Middlesbrough boss, Jack Charlton, was in the frame for the vacant position; and despite Wednesday earning their first win of the season at home to Chesterfield, all eyes were turned away from the pitch to where Charlton was watching the game from the stands as he decided whether to take the job. The crowd's reaction to his appearance helped convince Big Jack of the club's potential, and immediately after the game he became the Owls' fifth manager inside seven years. His first task was to promote John Harris to his No. 2, before he

experienced a disappointing start to his tenure when the long trek to Exeter saw the Devonians grab a last minute winner.

Considered purely on a results basis, Charlton's early weeks at Hillsborough were difficult, and Wednesday remained bottom of the table until a victory at home to Hereford United, on New Year's Eve, moved them up one place. During this time Wednesday made further progress in the League Cup, and must have even surprised themselves when a huge crowd of over 36,000 packed Hillsborough to watch bottom of the Third Division, Wednesday, give a good account themselves before losing to top-flight Everton. That incredible crowd must have convinced Charlton he had made the right decision, and it must have hurt even harder when, just over three weeks later, his side crashed to an embarrassing FA Cup exit at Northern Premier League, Wigan Athletic. As the old cliché has it, the Owls were left to concentrate on their perilous league position, and this improved greatly early in 1978 when three wins in an unbeaten run of four games pushed Wednesday out of the bottom four for the first time in the season. The new boss quickly made sure that Wednesday became a difficult side to beat, and though several low scoring matches may not have

Tommy Tynan equalises against Everton

registered high in the entertainment stakes, this was almost irrelevant to the vital gathering of league points.

By the time winter had turned to spring the Owls were starting to pull clear of the relegation places, and Charlton had made his first big splash in the transfer market. After selling Mick Prendergast to Barnsley and reserve keeper, Peter Fox, to Stoke City, he used the proceeds to raid Shrewsbury Town and sign their star midfielder, Brian Hornsby for £45,000. From the transfer deadline day until the end of the season, the Wednesday fans were treated to a run of form which would have even tested the memories of the die-hard supporters, for in a dozen games the Owls lost only once, and won seven times to surge up to mid-table. The run included a spell of four consecutive wins which saw victory occur in a derby at Millmoor, and a win at Hereford where the pitch was so muddy that the scoring of Wednesday's winning goal was initially credited to Roger Wylde, but later was discovered to have been scored by a mud splattered, Ian Porterfield. The final day of the season saw the Champions, Wrexham, visit Hillsborough, where, in front of a higher than normal crowd, Wednesday went out on a high by winning 2–1, leaving fans to hope that this time, finally, the long awaited revival was about to begin.

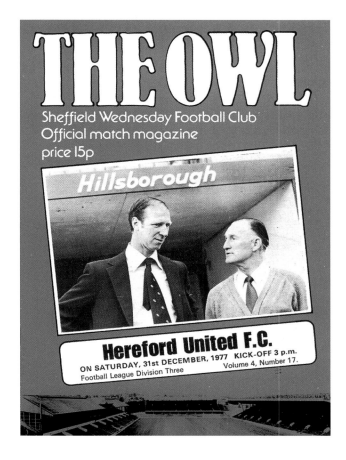

1978–79
THE ARSENAL CUP MARATHON

After the great finish to the 1977–78 season the Owls' fans eagerly awaited the new season but, if they also expected a flurry of transfer activity, they were to be sadly disappointed as only Newcastle United full-back Ray Blackhall was signed, and, among the new intake of apprentices were Mel Sterland and Charlie Williamson. Jack Charlton was furious with the actions of Richard Walden who walked out on the club just before his contract expired, to move to his newly purchased home in the south. As Walden had been ever present in the previous two seasons, his departure was a blow and this was accentuated when a subsequent transfer tribunal set his fee at a laughable £3,500, causing a stampede for his signature which was won by Len Ashurst, now boss at Newport County. The summer also saw Ian St John join the coaching staff, while the club's accounts were becoming more of a side issue now, as the financial turn around was confirmed when another small profit was reported.

For the second consecutive season the Owls were drawn against Doncaster Rovers in the League Cup and looked set to go through after a single-goal victory at Belle Vue. However, with only fifteen seconds left in the home leg, the Owls conceded a late winner and the teams returned to Doncaster for a third game which Wednesday won 1–0 to scramble through to the next round. The league campaign had started with a disappointing defeat at Peterborough United but Wednesday then earned some Brownie points as only a Gary Shelton goal for First Division Aston Villa separated the sides in the League Cup tie in Birmingham. The first two-point haul of the season came at Lincoln City and was followed seven days later by a Hillsborough win over Southend which put the Owls in mid table. Wednesday then sold Dave Cusack to their Hillsborough victims before lining up a transfer deal that would have shocked their Third Division rivals if it had succeeded. The player in question was Queen's Park Rangers' Welsh International, Leighton James. The Owls were willing to smash their club record and pay £165,000 for his services but they were in a two horse race with Second Division Burnley and it was the higher ranked club who eventually secured his signature. However, Charlton was not too discouraged, he re-entered the market to sell Tommy Tynan to Lincoln City and, to add experience to his defence, he captured the signature of Mick Pickering from First Division Southampton. Also arriving in Sheffield 6 was ex-Manchester United forward, John Lowey, who joined on trial after a spell with California Sunshine in the US. Yet another Owls' player was sadly forced to announce his premature retirement due to injury, 25-year-old Paul Bradshaw was the unfortunate player.

Following a draw in a testimonial game at Gainsborough Trinity, the Owls again won the derby game at Millmoor, Roger

Wylde scoring the late winner. However, the rather dull fare on offer in many of the home games contributed greatly to a drop in attendances which, at the end of the season, would result in the club's lowest ever average attendance of 10,643. The Owls' inconsistent form ensured they remained in mid table and with no relegation worries attention turned to the FA Cup. Draws were secured at both Scunthorpe United and Tranmere Rovers before the Owls could progress in the home replays. Then, following a thrilling 3–3 draw at Chesterfield on Boxing Day, the British winter took an icy grip on the fixture list, postponements abounded and the Owls would not appear again in Division Three action at Hillsborough until early March. As the country's fans were denied their football fix, the national press turned their attention to the FA Cup, particularly the game between Wednesday and Arsenal which had gone to a Highbury replay after over 33,000 had seen the teams draw 1–1 at Hillsborough. The Gunners were expected to brush the Owls aside in the replay but a Roger Wylde goal, just before the break, looked to have earned Wednesday a stunning win only for Liam Brady to net a last minute equaliser and force extra time. The sides remained deadlocked after the extra thirty minutes and, as Leicester City's Filbert Street was playable due to their investment in massive tarpaulins, the teams moved up the M1 to continue their struggle. This time a 25,000 crowd dominated by Owls' fans saw Arsenal ahead twice, but Wednesday hit back on both occasions through Brian Hornsby to force extra time again and then a fourth meeting. Forty-eight hours later the teams reconverged on Filbert Street and played out a classic Cup tie as Wednesday refused to bow down to their supposed superiors. Twice the

A jubilant Jeff Johnson after netting the equaliser at Hillsborough against Arsenal

Owls came from behind to share six goals as Rushbury, Lowey and a Hornsby penalty forced yet another game in a saga that had by now captured the nation's attention. By stretching to a fifth game the tie became the third longest in Cup history and over 30,000 filled Filbert Street for the next instalment. Unfortunately for Wednesday, this is where the marathon ended as they had no answer to two first-half goals from the Gunners who took the first step on their road to lifting the trophy in May. For the Owls the saga had earned them unquantifiable publicity, and the team spirit that was shown in the clashes was the first real sign that Wednesday were definitely on their way back.

Soon after the end of the Cup tie the Owls signed Aberdeen forward Ian Fleming while, due to the inactivity caused by the bad weather, Wednesday then spent a few days in Guernsey where Vale Recreation were beaten 5–0 in a friendly. The Owls were then thwarted by the Department of Employment when their number one transfer target, Yugoslavian, Mojas Radonjic, was refused a work permit as he wasn't a full International. However, a month later, Jack Charlton made a signing that would ignite the Owls' fortunes when, in a club record-equalling £100,000 transfer, Southampton's Terry Curran dropped down two divisions to sign for Wednesday. He quickly endeared himself to the faithful, scoring his first goal at Hull City where the Owls earned a draw despite having Lowey sent off after only nine minutes. Due to the weather and their Cup exploits,

the Owls ended their season with five consecutive home games in only fourteen days, and three wins ensured another mid table finish in a season where the green shoots of recovery were now starting to show as Jack Charlton formulated a promotion winning team.

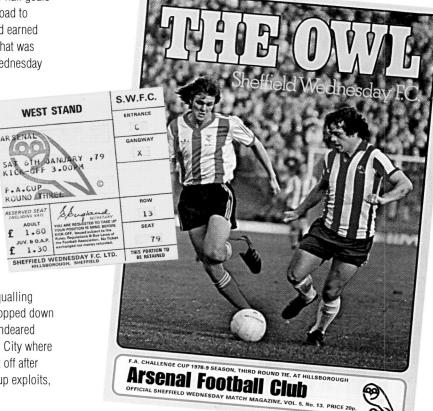

Jack Charlton and Ian St John meet transfer target Mojas Radonjic at the Midland Station

Roger Wylde celebrates scoring his second goal against Tranmere Rovers

1979–80
THE SLEEPING GIANT AWAKENS

The first news of the summer was that coach, Ian St John, was to leave in order to pursue a career at London Weekend Television. However, it was the transfer comings and goings that dominated the headlines, as Jack Charlton revamped his side by selling five senior pros and bringing three new faces to Hillsborough. The new signings all proved to be crucial in the forthcoming season, as Ian Mellor signed from Chester, Andy McCulloch from Brentford, and Jeff King from Walsall, for a total outlay of £160,000. Departing were Lindsay McKeown, who signed for the Irish side, Linfield, and Ian Nimmo who went to neighbouring Doncaster Rovers. The Owls then received a £90,000 fee from Sunderland for the out-of-favour keeper Chris Turner, before Hugh Dowd followed Nimmo to Belle Vue. The fifth and final departure saw a furious Charlton again slam the transfer tribunal system when they set Dave Rushbury's fee for his move to Swansea City at £30,000 less than Wednesday's valuation. The close season also saw the club finish the construction of the pavilion at their Middlewood Road training ground; and, after much deliberation, Ian Porterfield decided to accept Wednesday's offer of a player-coaching role at Hillsborough.

Pre-season preparations culminated in a solitary friendly being played at York City, before Wednesday kicked off the new season with a 3–2 aggregate victory over Hull City in the League Cup. The season would see derby games against Sheffield United, Rotherham United, Chesterfield and Barnsley, and it was at the latter venue that the Owls started their Third Division campaign. A large travelling support was sent into raptures as new boys McCulloch and Mellor were among the scorers as Wednesday soared to a 3–0 win. However, the Owls quickly came back down to earth after Blackburn won by the same score at Hillsborough. In the early weeks of the season, Wednesday struggled for consistency, and, after losing at Saltergate in late September, actually found themselves down in fifteenth position. By this time they had gone out of the League Cup to First Division, Manchester City, though the 3–2 aggregate defeat told only half of the story; for after a 1–1 draw at Hillsborough, a Mark Smith penalty put the Owls ahead on aggregate at Maine Road, with only ten minutes left to play. That was the scoreline with two minutes to go, but late goals are not a new phenomenon to Manchester football and City promptly scored twice in the remaining time, leaving Wednesday and their fans in a state of disbelief at their dramatic exit. The month of October would prove to be vital, as four wins in an unbeaten run of seven matches, including victory at Millmoor for a third consecutive season, and a thrilling 4–3 win at league new-boys, Wimbledon, lifted the Owls into the top six. With Terry Curran a regular scorer and Mark Smith proving to be deadly from the penalty spot, the Owls maintained a promotion push during the remaining weeks of 1979—although hopes of another lucrative FA Cup run ended in the Second Round with a defeat at Carlisle United. The promotion push seemingly

Jeff King celebrates after scoring against Lincoln City

moved into top gear on Boxing Day, when a bit of local difficulty was solved as Wednesday famously thrashed the Blades 4–0 at Hillsborough in front of a record crowd for the division.

Immediately following on from that Boxing Day massacre, frozen pitches became the norm, and Wednesday accepted an invitation from Coventry City to utilise their undersoil heating and play a friendly game. The return to league action saw a home defeat to Plymouth Argyle, however, Wednesday then hit such a rich vein of form that an unbeaten run of seventeen games effectively

Ian Mellor almost nets with a diving header against Sheffield United

clinched promotion to the Second Division. Included in the spell were five goal romps at home to both Bury and Rotherham United; and before the Wimbledon home game (who Wednesday defeated to move to the top of the table for the first time) Jack Charlton became the first ever Owls' manager to receive a Manager of the Month award.

Before Wednesday hit the front in the race for promotion, both Roger Wylde and Ian Fleming had departed, to Oldham Athletic and Dundee respectively; and the Owls released Ian Porterfield in order that he could take over the manager's job at Millmoor. After Terry Curran and Mark Smith were named in the PFA Division Three team, the side then visited Bramall Lane to play the return derby game with the Blades. Another huge crowd attended this Easter fixture and a wondrous goal from Terry Curran not only gained Wednesday another precious point, but elevated Curran from hero status to that of legend—and probably increased the demand for the *Sheffield Star's* collection of T.C. wall posters! Two days later, Mark Smith maintained his incredible 100 per cent success rate from the penalty spot, netting his 12th of the season to defeat Gillingham at Hillsborough. The Owls unbeaten run then ended at Bury, and nerves started to show as Grimsby Town moved four points clear at the top, with Chesterfield and Blackburn closing in. A win at home to Chester steadied the ship and meant that the midweek trip to promotion rivals, Blackburn Rovers, suddenly became the biggest game of the season. An Owls' support of around 10,000 travelled over the Pennines, though a Noel Brotherston goal put Rovers ahead at the break before Kevin Taylor grabbed a 63rd-minute equaliser. The score remained tied as the crunch game entered its final ten minutes. However, from a deep cross Ian 'Spiderman' Mellor then launched himself at the ball to score with a tremendous diving header, sending the Wednesday fans wild as the two points were clinched.

Promotion was now within touching distance and another large travelling army out-numbered the home fans at Exeter, where, after Mark Smith had missed his first penalty of the season, the Owls lost by the game's only goal. Their main rivals, Chesterfield, were playing at Millwall that same afternoon, and when news came through that they had lost, the party began as the Owls were promoted after five long years in the Third Division. The final game of the season attracted another massive crowd to Hillsborough, where, after a goalless draw, the joyous fans invaded the pitch. With all the players being treated to a heroes reception, it took fully fifteen minutes for the players to emerge, minus shirts, shorts, socks and boots. However, it was 24-goal top scorer, Terry Curran who took most of the plaudits—though the likes of Andy McCulloch, Ian Mellor and Mick Pickering were equally deserving in a memorable promotion season.

Curran scores against Colchester at a snowbound Hillsborough

An almighty goalmouth scramble against the Blades

Terry Curran salutes the kop after he scores Wednesday's second goal against the Blades

1980–81
HIGHLY PROMISING RETURN

After the joy of promotion, manager Jack Charlton decided to keep faith with the majority of the squad that had finally got the Owls out of the Third Division. Jimmy Mullen was the only player to leave, signing for Rotherham United, with Mike Pickering and Ray Blackhall signing new deals after initially turning down new contract offers. Big Jack's major summer target was the Nottingham Forest midfielder, Stan Bowles. However, after his club accepted Wednesday's bid of £110,000, the player declined the move to Hillsborough and Charlton instead turned his attention to the little known Yugoslavian, Ante Mirocevic, who spent a short period on trial in Sheffield. In a very quiet close season, the only other newsworthy event was the publication of the Owls' annual accounts which showed promotion had produced a record profit of almost £450,000; and that somehow Charlton had led Wednesday out of the Third Division yet had shown a surplus of £147,000 in his transfer dealings. With sales of season tickets reaching an all time high, comparison with the balance sheets of just a few short years earlier, clearly showed that the financial turn-round started by the arrival of cash-conscious Chairman, Bert McGee, had reached a peak.

On the field of play the Owls started their pre-season preparations with two games in Scotland, at Queen of the South and Kilmarnock, before returning to Hillsborough to draw with the Yugoslavian side, Olimpija Ljubljana. As new members of the Second Division, Wednesday still had to kick off their League Cup campaign at the first round stage, but could not have hoped for more attractive opposition than their neighbours, Sheffield United. Goals from Kevin Taylor and Jeff Johnson duly gave Wednesday a comfortable lead to take to Bramall Lane in the second leg, where, despite an early goal from Bob Hatton, a second-half leveller from Terry Curran ensured the Owls' passage into the next stage. On their return to Division Two soccer, Wednesday could not have asked for a better opening game than to entertain Newcastle United at home, and an excellent opening day crowd of over 26,000 saw the Owls make a flying start, netting two second-half goals without reply.

It would be their form at Hillsborough that would prove to be the key during the season, as Wednesday won their six opening games to maintain a top six position, despite only recording one win on their travels in the same period. One of these away trips took them over the Pennines to Boundary Park, where the afternoon's proceedings would see the Owls in the FA dock following crowd disturbances involving Wednesday's travelling supporters. It was a clash between Terry Curran and ex-Blade, Simon Stainrod, that caused the problems, for even as the referee was booking both players, Curran appeared to kick out at Stainrod, who, somewhat

theatrically, then fell to the floor, resulting in an early bath for T.C. After seeing their hero depart in such controversial circumstances, the Owls' fans rioted, and it was almost half an hour before play could be restarted. Nine days later Wednesday were called before an FA commission and informed that the Hillsborough terraces would be closed for four matches, with their next four away games made all-ticket. None of these were to be on sale to Wednesday fans and the Owls would have to pay £3,000 compensation to each of the four home clubs involved. From the Owls' point of view, the closing of the Hillsborough terraces was a financial money spinner, as attendances remained at the same level as before the ban, with the fans having to pay extra for seats—no doubt the FA had not banked on their measures boosting the Wednesday profits! As far as the away ban was concerned the majority of Wednesday supporters saw it as a challenge to gain entry (a similar situation occurred at Luton later in the decade) and when the Owls won at Swansea in the first 'ban' game, the roars that greeted the Wednesday goals led captain Mick Pickering to comment, 'They'll get where water won't'.

Soon after the Oldham riot, the Owls believed they had finally completed the protracted £250,000 record signing of Mirocevic from the Titograd club, Buducnost. Having been granted a work permit, though, did not mean he could play; for it emerged that Mirocevic had signed a contract with French club, Metz, back in May. He had done this, however, without the permission of his club or the Yugoslavian FA, and so the contract was deemed illegal and the move to Hillsborough could, at long last, be rubber-stamped. The newcomer made a

John Pearson celebrates after scoring against QPR in front of the empty kop

scoring debut in a home draw with Orient, and became a regular as the Owls reached the festive period still in the top four—with a consecutive promotion now a distinct possibility. By this time the Owls had sold John Lowey to Blackburn Rovers, Wednesday President and celebrated local farmer, Lord Netherthorpe, had passed away, and ex-England winger Frank Blunstone had been appointed coach after a month's trial.

The New Year brought an FA Cup exit at Newcastle United, and a last minute goal from Notts County's, Iain McCulloch, sent Wednesday tumbling to their first home defeat of the season. Despite these setbacks the Owls came back strongly in February, helped no doubt, by a mid-season break in Majorca, and a splendid win at Loftus Road by a ten-man Wednesday, following Blackhall's dismissal, which lifted Wednesday into the third promotion place. In the same month, youth product, Mark Smith, won his first England Under 21 Cap, while an unhappy Jeff King handed in his second transfer request of the season! However, it was too much to hope that the newly promoted side could remain in the top three, and in the final weeks they duly slipped out of contention, winning only one of their last six games—the solitary win was memorable for an Andy McCulloch hat-trick. A week later unseasonable weather forced the postponement of the April 25th clash with West Ham United, as Sheffield was covered by a thick blanket of snow. Three days later the conditions eased sufficiently for the home game with Grimsby to be played, and history was made when Peter and Paul Shirtliff became the first brothers to play in the same Owls' side since the McAnearneys 22 years earlier. The season ended with a visit from the runaway Champions, West Ham, and despite a narrow defeat it must have been a highly satisfying season for manager, Jack Charlton, who had seen his team consolidate in the higher league and never drop below tenth place throughout the campaign.

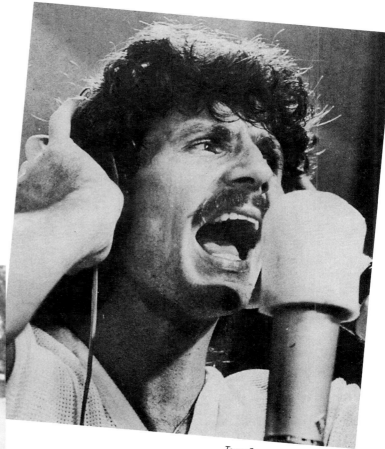

Terry Curran 'singing the blues'

Ante Mirocevic turns away after netting against Notts County

1981–82
AGONISINGLY CLOSE TO DIVISION ONE

The summer of 1981 was a fairly active one for manager Charlton, as he brought three new faces into the club and let three others depart. Youngsters Brian Strutt and Phil Campbell went to Matlock Town and Barnsley, and, when the experienced Jeff Johnson moved to Newport County for £60,000, he became the last of the players inherited by Jack Charlton back in 1977 to be sold. Two of the three newcomers would become vital players in the Owls' first team, but the first signing, ex-Manchester United centre-half, Jim Holton, failed to live up to his billing after being released by Coventry City. Wednesday had better luck with their second raid on Highfield Road, when striker Gary Bannister put pen to paper on a £100,000 deal. He was followed soon after this by Don Megson's flame-haired son, Gary, who signed for his boyhood club from Everton. Finally, Jeff King obviously thought Wednesday hadn't quite got the message yet, as he handed in his third transfer request of the year!

To start the build up to the new season, Wednesday organised a friendly with the Nigerian national side, who were on the brink of qualifying for the 1982 World Cup Finals. However, the term friendly seemed to have been lost on the Africans, for at half-time, Andy McCulloch had to be substituted after having been kicked from pillar to post. The second half was even worse, with Alloysius Atiebgu being sent off for punching Gary Megson to the floor, and two Nigerians were booked by a flustered Keith Hackett, as the Owls grabbed a 3–1 win thanks to two goals in the last nine minutes. Games were also played at Crewe and Wigan, the latter resulting in a shock 4–1 reverse, before First Division, Middlesbrough won by three clear goals at Hillsborough to complete a decidedly mixed set of warm up games. However, when the real action got underway there was simply no stopping the Owls, and they won their opening four games after a Terry Curran goal had given them an opening day win, with the first ever three-point haul (following summer changes in the points system) at Ewood Park, Blackburn. A fabulous 3–0 win at the eventual Champions, Luton Town, was achieved in front of the Match of the Day cameras, before the unbeaten start came to an end in a local derby at Oakwell, where a 40-yard snap-shot from Ian Banks caught Bob Bolder unawares to win the game for the Tykes. The Manager of the Month curse then struck, for after his acceptance of the award for September, Jack Charlton could only watch as Wrexham coasted to a 3–0 victory at Hillsborough to knock the Owls off the top of the league. One man who was not involved though was Jeff King, for he had left for Hibs on trial, only to return a few days later having picked up an injury—and surely poised to write out another transfer request! Meanwhile, after having four players sent off in the previous season, the club was fined £1,000 for their disciplinary record, and Brian Hornsby left for Chester on loan. After only a few weeks at Wednesday, Jim Holton was transfer listed, later going to Newcastle for an unsuccessful three-day trial.

The Second Round of the League Cup did not start until early October and, after a 1–1 draw at Blackburn, the Owls were confident of progressing. However, it was not be, as Rovers went through 3–2 on aggregate, with ex-Owl, John Lowey, netting

Kevin Taylor shoots for goal in the final home game against Norwich City

one of the visitors' goals. The Owls then drew 3–3 in a testimonial at Leeds United, before falling to a late defeat at Rotherham United in the final of the much maligned County Cup competition, which was then in its penultimate season. Meanwhile, back in the league, Wednesday were hit by a Simon Stainrod treble as Queen's Park Rangers won at Hillsborough. Then, after losing at Chelsea in early December, the Owls found themselves down in sixth place as David Pleat's Luton streaked away at the top. Following the Chelsea game, Wednesday would play only once more in five weeks, in an FA Cup defeat at Coventry City, as the English weather exerted an icy grip on the fixture list. During the enforced lay-off, Jeff King finally got his move, joining Sheffield United on a free transfer after his contract had been cancelled by mutual consent. The Owls then spent three days in Filey, hoping to play a friendly on grass against the Alliance Premier League team, Scarborough. Unfortunately, they were thwarted by the weather, which also claimed another scheduled friendly against Notts County, frustrating the Owls in their attempts to gain much needed match practice. When Wednesday did return to league action, they struck a rich vein of form which resulted in their rapid move up the table, to reach third place by the end of March. For sheer entertainment value the home game with Luton Town during that period would take some beating, for with only seven minutes left Gary Bannister scored to put the Owls 3–2 ahead in an end-to-end encounter. However, with two minutes left, Gary Megson was sent off for a second bookable offence, and in the 92nd minute Brian Stein grabbed a dramatic point for the visitors.

Promotion was certainly in the air following an Easter Monday home success over Newcastle, and despite a heavy defeat at second place, Watford, Wednesday stood six points clear in third place, with only six games to play. At this point Norwich City were down in tenth, a massive nine points behind, but they would emerge from the pack to challenge for the last promotion place. More transfer news saw Denis Leman, Brian Cox and Brian Hornsby all go out on loan to Wrexham, Huddersfield Town and the Canadian side, Edmonton Drillers, respectively; and, after initially joining on loan from Aston Villa, midfielder, Gary Shelton, was signed permanently after quickly becoming a favourite with the Owls' supporters. With three games remaining, the chase for the last promotion place was hotting up, with several clubs still in the hunt—including Leicester City and the aforementioned Norwich City. Two of the teams also in contention then met at Millmoor, with Rotherham and Wednesday both desperate for the three points. The game would finish 2–2, however, dashing the promotion ambitions of both sides, but this was not before referee, Ken Walmsley, had awarded the home side a highly dubious penalty, with twenty minutes left, which left manager, Charlton incensed. Four days later Wednesday visited Bolton for a game they simply had to win to keep their dreams alive. However, after Curran had scored an early goal, a youthful

Owls side fell away to a 3–1 defeat and to stinging criticism from their disappointed manager. Following a 6–3 win at Mansfield in a testimonial match, the final day of the season at Hillsborough produced a promotion party; though sadly it was the Norwich City fans who were celebrating—still gaining promotion even after losing to Wednesday. In the end, the lack of an experienced leader may have cost Wednesday promotion, but the biggest irony of all was that if the old system of two points for a win had still been in operation it would have been the Owls and not Norwich who would have been planning for First Division football.

Andy McCulloch salutes the crowd after heading the winning goal against Cardiff City

1982–83
CUP SEMI-FINALISTS BUT PROMOTION BID FALTERS

After the Owls' promotion dreams faded at the last moment in the previous season, manager, Jack Charlton, decided to the spend the summer overhauling his squad. Several players were released and some much needed experience was to be introduced into the side. The latter came in the shape of the inspirational centre-half and new captain, Mick Lyons, who arrived from Everton; and with the Middlesbrough left-back, Ian Bailey. Several players who had helped the Owls to promotion in 1980 left Hillsborough, including Ian Mellor, who signed on a free transfer for Bradford City. Ray Blackhall went to the Swedish club, Jankoping, and Dave Grant left for Scunthorpe United. Others who went in the clear-out were Jim Holton, Denis Leman and Brian Cox. However, the major transfer story of the period, without a doubt, involved the fans favourite, Terry Curran. In the previous December, Charlton had publicly criticised Curran, and an equally public row erupted which ended with Wednesday stating that T.C. would be going nowhere as he was still under contract. However, this agreement ended six months later, when, much to the disappointment of the Wednesday fans, he refused a new deal and signed for another club, the fee to be decided by tribunal. He did not sign for any old side, however, for in a sensational move he joined Sheffield United, with Charlton demanding £250,000 for his services. The large fee had seemed quite reasonable, but not for the first time Charlton was furious with a transfer tribunal when they ruled the Blades had to pay only £100,000, exactly what the Owls had paid Southampton for his services in March 1979. The fee still made the deal a record move between the city clubs, though when the Owls reported back for training Big Jack was said to be still seething over the whole sorry affair.

Hopes of another good start were raised when Wednesday put five goals past First Division, Notts County in a pre-season Hillsborough game. These hopes were fulfilled when, for the second consecutive season, the Owls were first out of the blocks to lead the early league tables. Their Division Two campaign started with a visit from newly relegated Middlesbrough, and a mini riot by the visiting fans could not spoil an excellent opening day win. This was quickly followed by a superb 3–0 result at Charlton, before John Pearson scored the quickest ever Hillsborough goal by an Owls player when he netted just 13 seconds into the home game with Bolton Wanderers. Another newly demoted side, Leeds United, ended Wednesday's 100 per cent record, though the Owls bounced back to win on the plastic pitch at Queen's Park Rangers; then following a win at Leicester in late October, they reclaimed the top spot. Meanwhile, Wednesday started their League Cup campaign (now known as the Milk Cup following sponsorship from the Milk Marketing board) somewhat inauspiciously. Following a 2–1 first leg win at Ashton Gate, the Owls then needed extra time at Hillsborough before squeezing past Bristol City to go through. The period also saw Mark Smith score the Owls 5,000th league goal in a defeat at Carlisle United;

then saw Brian Hornsby sign for the Cumbrian side, and Andy McCulloch lucky to escape with only cuts and bruises after having written off his car in Worksop returning home from a game of golf.

In the Milk Cup, Wednesday reached the last sixteen following a win at Crystal Palace, and then entered the quarter finals for the first time in their history when, in a hard fought local derby, the Owls overcame Barnsley thanks to a solitary Andy McCulloch strike. The club were then forced to deny rumours that they would be joining a proposed new Super League in the following season, while Charlton was named Manager of the Month for October, and Gordon Owen joined Doncaster on loan. The Owls' boss was then secretly cursing Terry Curran again as he indirectly thwarted Charlton's attempts to bring Bolton's highly rated midfielder, Peter Reid, to Hillsborough. Reid had agreed to move to Wednesday but, after Sheffield United refused to make Curran's loan deal at Goodison Park permanent, the Everton boss, Howard Kendall, made an eleventh-hour bid for Reid which proved to be successful—and so the future England International joined the growing list of top performers who have almost joined the Owls! Charlton had probably entered the market because he had seen his side's form dip to such an extent in the December, that Wednesday gained only three points from three draws and slid out of the promotion positions. One of the two defeats came at home to Rotherham, when, in an incident which has reached legendary status with the Millers followers, a long punt forward from Gerry Gow hit a divot as Bolder bent down to pick the ball up and promptly flew straight

Hillsborough by night

to Joe McBride who scored into an empty net! New Year's Day brought a heavy defeat at Burnley, and two days later Hillsborough was witness to a remarkable game against Charlton, which saw the visitors 3–1 ahead at the break. The Owls quickly pulled level, however, and despite Athletic going back in front within a minute, a crazy own goal from Steve Gritt and a header from Mick Lyons secured the points in a nine goal pantomime of a game.

Cup football then dominated the remainder of the month, as a Tony Woodcock goal, for old foes Arsenal, knocked the Owls out of the Milk Cup. However, Wednesday reached the last sixteen of the FA Cup, following victories over Southend United and Torquay United. The Southend game went to three matches, with Megson and Stead sent off at Roots Hall in a goalless first tie, before Gary Bannister received his marching orders in the second home replay, as Wednesday eventually saw off the plucky Third Division challenge. Basement club, Torquay, were then beaten 3–2 at Plainmoor, and progression was made to the quarter-finals after a Megson brace took Wednesday to a 2–1 win at Second Division, Cambridge United. Further transfer activity saw Pat Heard sign from Aston Villa, Gavin Oliver go on loan to Tranmere Rovers, and David Mills arrive for a cut-price fee from West Brom—where his career had stalled following a British record transfer move. Back in the league the Owls promotion challenge was slowly fading, though Cambridge were beaten at Hillsborough in a game in which Andy McCulloch was denied a hat-trick when his last minute penalty was saved. An eventful game then took place at Molineux, with

the Owls losing 1–0 after Bannister twice had penalty kicks saved, and Lyons was distraught after being controversially sent off for the only time in his distinguished career.

All attention now switched to the Cup, and a kind draw took them to struggling Division Two side, Burnley, where, after Bob Bolder had saved Steve Taylor's early spot kick, a first half Gary Bannister goal was enough to force a Hillsborough replay. On an unforgettable Hillsborough night, the Turf Moor side were then put to the sword, as Wednesday stormed to a Highbury meeting with Brighton in the semi-final following a 5–0 romp. In the run up to the semi, the Owls' form was distinctly patchy, with a 3–0 win at Millmoor being the highlight. However, tragedy struck in the last game before the meeting with Brighton, when key defender, Ian Bailey was stretchered off with a broken left leg. The English weather produced a red hot day for the semi-final, with the massed Wednesday fans on the North Bank stunned as a 30-yard pile-driver from Jimmy Case put Albion ahead after 14 minutes. Despite not really performing on the day, the Owls fought back to equalise through Ante Mirocevic's close range goal; however, it was to be a bitterly disappointing journey back up the M1, as Michael Robinson scored the winner for Brighton just thirteen minutes from the end. Three days later, Hillsborough was a depressing place when, on a night of torrential rain, the Kopites were soaked to the skin and the lowest crowd of the season were 'treated' to a dismal home defeat to Queen's Park Rangers. To the Owls' credit they did rally in the final few weeks to secure a top six finish in a season which was certainly memorable if not ultimately successful.

David Mills challenges for the ball against Cambridge United

1983–84
CHARLTON OUT, WILKINSON IN, WEDNESDAY UP!

It was the end of an era in the summer of 1983 when, after almost six years in the job, Jack Charlton surprisingly announced he was taking a break from football altogether, and was to resign his position as the Owls' boss. In his time at Hillsborough, Charlton had taken Wednesday from the bottom of Division Three to the verge of the top flight, and Wednesday fans were sad to see him depart after he had played such a major part in reversing the club's fortunes. Before his departure Charlton had to deal with the disturbing news that several players, including Bob Bolder, Mark Smith and Andy McCulloch, had all failed to agree new contracts. And just before going with his players on a club holiday to Majorca, Big Jack's final task as Wednesday manager was to put Ante Mirocevic, and a bottle of champagne, on a plane home to Yugoslavia, after he had been given a free transfer by Wednesday.

Following Charlton's resignation, the Owls No.1 target was said to be Watford's Graham Taylor, but, after his club refused Wednesday permission to speak to him, the Owls' attentions turned to ex-player and Notts County manager. Howard Wilkinson. Within three days, Wilkinson was installed as manager, to be followed soon after by Peter Eustace, who left a coaching position at Sunderland to become his assistant, with physiotherapist Alan Smith arriving from Blackpool. Before the new manager's arrival, in a back room clear out, Wednesday dispensed with the services of coach, Frank Ashton, fitness expert, Tony Toms, and part-time physio, John Honey. As soon as Wilkinson was appointed, a whirlwind of transfer and contract signing activity ensued, starting with Peter Shirtliff agreeing to sign a new deal. Soon after this Wilkinson persuaded Kevin Taylor, Trevor Matthewson, Paul Shirtliff and Gavin Oliver to put pen to paper on new contracts, while Charlie Williamson and Mark Smith soon did likewise. The new boss then turned to the transfer market, and, after Gordon Owen was sold to Cardiff City, Wilkinson made his first signing when the England Under 21 keeper, Iain Hesford,

The new backroom line-up: Wilkinson, Blunstone, Smith and Eustace

arrived from Blackpool. There were then two more departures, with Andy McCulloch going to Crystal Palace and Bob Bolder signing for League Champions, Liverpool. After Bolder's sale, Wilkinson then took Everton keeper, Martin Hodge, on a month's loan as back up to Hesford; though the eventual outcome was somewhat different as the loan player started the season between the sticks and Hesford never played a first team game for the Owls. Just before the kick off, Lawrie Madden—after a month's trial—and Imre Varadi from Newcastle United, were added to the playing rosta. Following four pre-season games, at Mexborough, Chesterfield, Lincoln City and Hull City, the Owls final warm-up game saw First Division, West Brom held to a draw at Hillsborough. For these friendlies Wilkinson used as many as twenty-two players in each game, and in two of the matches the Finnish International keeper, Olli Huttunen, made an appearance while on trial.

As happens with any new boss, the Wednesday fans were unsure how the side would gel early in the season. However, they soon received their answer, and in spectacular fashion, for the Owls set a new club record by remaining unbeaten in 18 league and cup games from the start of the season. The new manager's brand of exciting, direct soccer did not win many plus-points with football purists, but Wednesday fans were in raptures as the Owls quickly shot to the top of the table—a position they maintained until New Year's Eve. Wilkinson's side, trained to the peak of fitness, had a workrate that other sides were simply unable to match, and Wednesday boasted

Gary Megson in action v. Chelsea

Gary Bannister shows his dribbling skills against Barnsley

genuine quality in their ranks which made them the team to fear. There were many highlights in the opening unbeaten run, including a 25-yard Megson free kick to beat Chelsea, though the meeting with Newcastle United at Hillsborough was the game that really stood out. Over 41,000 packed into the ground to see a somewhat remorseless Varadi net twice against his old club, as Wednesday went six points clear at the

top after an action packed 4–2 success. The same period also saw the team progress in the Milk Cup, as Darlington and Preston were overcome. The last eight was reached after a 1–0 win at First Division, Stoke City, four days after the Owls unbeaten tag had been lost at Crystal Palace. Wilkinson was also busy in the transfer market, as Hodge's move from Goodison Park was made permanent, and Madden was given a new improved 18-month contract. Matthewson left for Newport County and Tony Simmons for QPR, while Mike Pickering, who'd completed a hat-trick of loan spells at Norwich City, Bradford City and Barnsley, finally got a permanent move to Rotherham United early in the New Year. One newcomer to Hillsborough was the Barnsley forward, Tony Cunningham; and, after 47 years at the club (as secretary since 1974), Eric England announced his retirement, with the ex-Sheffield United, Chief Executive, Dick Chester taking over the reins.

Following the defeat at Crystal Palace, Wednesday visited Maine Road for a crunch promotion clash with Manchester City, where the hordes of Owls' fans who travelled over the Pennines saw a Varadi double secure a thoroughly deserved 2–1 win. The Christmas period saw Wednesday stutter, as Grimsby won at Cleethorpes, Middlesbrough sent the Owls to their only home defeat of the season, and a last minute equaliser was conceded in a match ruined by gale-force winds at Carlisle. By that time Chelsea had emerged as the major threat to Wednesday's title aspirations, and the big two would battle it out at the top until the last day of the season. The New Year brought even more drama for Wednesdayites, when Swansea were hit for six in a snow blizzard at Hillsborough, First Division Coventry City were sent tumbling out of the FA Cup, and the Owls played two games against the invincibles from Anfield. The meetings with Liverpool came in the fifth round of the Milk Cup, where, after almost winning at home, the abiding memory of the 3–0 replay defeat at Anfield was the singing of 'We'll Be Back' by the 12,000 defiant travelling Wednesdayites. The fans had struggled through snow blizzards to reach Anfield, and the overwhelming opinion was that indeed they would be back.

Attention then switched to the other cup, as the Third Division high-flyers, Oxford United were well beaten at the Manor Gound, to set up a quarter-final home tie with Southampton. The match was switched to Sunday to become the first Owls match ever to be televised live from Hillsborough. However, the viewing public probably reached for the off-switch well before the end, as the teams cancelled each other out in a dull, goalless draw. Before their TV debut, Wednesday announced that Crosby Kitchens would be their first ever shirt sponsor, in a deal lasting until the end of the season. In the previous month, Nigel Worthington had arrived at Hillsborough from Wilkinson's old club, Notts County. A story then emerged that a player, who remained nameless to save his embarrassment, got hopelessly lost during one of Wilkinson's infamous cross-country runs, eventually being found by a farmer, wet and miserable, and just a little bit confused. In the replay at Southampton, Wednesday started well and led through Peter Shirtliff's 21st-minute goal. However, a disastrous three minute spell before the break saw the home side score twice, before eventually going on to end the Owls' dreams of Wembley with a 5–1 win. Wednesday were now left to concentrate on clinching promotion, and a Gary Shelton overhead kick won a crunch promotion clash at Newcastle United. A win at Middlesbrough would then have secured promotion, but the home side became the only team to do the double over Wednesday and keep the champagne on ice.

After a fourteen year absence, the Owls were to clinch promotion back to the top flight on the following Saturday, when a Mel Sterland penalty was enough to beat Crystal Palace and trigger off a celebration party. The final task now was to clinch the Championship. A victory at Huddersfield lifted the Owls five points clear with only three games to play, but defeat at the jinx side, Shrewsbury Town, hit their hopes. A disappointing home draw with Manchester City then resulted in Chelsea moving to the top, and, despite a win on the final day at Cardiff, it was the Londoners who lifted the title, on goal difference, in an anti-climactic end to the season. This was only a minor disappointment, however, for this had been a glorious season which finally laid to rest the ghost of 1970, the year when Wednesday had tumbled from the big time.

Memory Match

Sheffield Wednesday

2

Southend United

1

Just ten years after Alan Brown's promising young side agonisingly lost to Everton in the 1966 FA Cup Final, the Owls were staring oblivion in the face as they battled to avoid relegation to the bottom division of English soccer. The early 1970s were a time of bitter disappointment for Wednesday fans, as, following the horror season of 1974–75, hopes of a revival were quickly dashed as the Owls slumped to the lower reaches of the Third Division, and stayed there for the remainder of the season. As the campaign reached its climax, a run of home wins meant that Wednesday went into their final game of the campaign with their destiny firmly in their own hands. The simple fact of the matter was that if 21st placed Wednesday could avoid defeat against 23rd placed Southend United, they would then be safe; with Aldershot—who had already completed their fixtures—going down instead. Relegation could well have meant the end for Wednesday at this time, and as they sank deeper into the financial mire, Chairman, Bert McGee, must surely have had this in mind when he commented: 'We are still in the trenches [but] there will be 11 good men out on the pitch fighting for this club; that I promise the supporters'.

The Owls team was unchanged from the one which had drawn at Brighton the previous week, in a game in which Wednesday had conceded a last minute equaliser. Again, for the umpteenth time, the lapsed Wednesday fans in the City rallied round their ailing side, and at the kick-off over 25,000 hopefuls filled Hillsborough to cheer their side to safety. In contrast to the final game of the 1970 season, the Owls tore into their Southern opponents from the kick-off, with Potts, Nimmo and Prendergast prominent. As the visitors struggled to keep a tigerish Wednesday at bay, their defence was finally breached in the 16th minute—only for Mick Prendergast to see his header turned on to the post by the United keeper, Sean Rafter. However, the moment the Hillsborough crowd had been waiting for came thirteen minutes later, when Wylde sent Neil O'Donnell clear to drill in a low cross. Eric Potts got a touch, before the ground erupted as Mick Prendergast pounced on the loose ball, gleefully driving it into the net. The Owls were now totally dominant and effectively secured their Third Division status thanks to a tremendous strike from Eric Potts. A Phil Henson free kick was headed down by Ian Nimmo, allowing the diminutive left-winger to crash home a stunning volley which befitted the importance of the occasion. The Shrimpers only response was a Parker effort that clipped the top of the bar; and, after Prendergast did likewise, the Owls received a standing ovation as the whistle blew for half-time.

After the tempo of the first period the second half was a quieter affair, with a few worried brows around the ground when Alan Moody scored a scrappy goal for United after 61 minutes. As the tension inside the stadium started to rise, manager, Len Ashurst, repeatedly jumped from his dug-out to tell his side not to play possession football, but to continue attacking instead. He need not have worried, however, for Wednesday's opponents simply did not perform like a side who needed a win to save themselves from the drop; and the Owls held on, fairly comfortably, to complete the rescue act. At the final whistle the delirious Wednesday fans flooded onto the Hillsborough turf and sang 'We are the Champions' as they celebrated in front of the South Stand. The scenes were more akin to the winning of a trophy, as the massed ranks called on the players to show themselves for a salute, after the Owls had stepped back from the precipice.

Wednesday: Fox, Walden, Shaw, Mullen, Cusack, O'Donnell, Wylde, Henson, Nimmo, Prendergast, Potts

Southend United: Rafter, Worthington, Ford, Little, Hadley, Moody, Foggo (Pountney ht), Nicholl, Parker, Silvester, Taylor

Referee: Mr E. Garner (Liverpool)

Memory Match

No publication on Sheffield Wednesday would be complete if the story of what became known as 'The Boxing Day Massacre' was not recounted. Hundreds of paragraphs have been written about the game over the ensuing twenty years, each detailing the remarkable scoreline and the record divisional attendance of 49,309—a figure which will almost certainly never be bettered. The players who pulled on a blue and white shirt on that Boxing Day morning will always be remembered with the utmost fondness by Wednesdayites, and when the club recently held two reunion dinners in their honour, the five hundred or so Wednesday fans who attended gave the players a rapturous welcome. It is now perhaps forgotten that when the game was played the Owls were the actual underdogs, for United led the division, with Wednesday down in sixth place following a win at Reading on the previous Friday evening. That victory had seen 17-year-old, Charlie Williamson make his first appearance, replacing the injured Dave Grant; and he would remain in an unchanged side to make a truly unforgettable Hillsborough debut. On the morning of the game the scenes round the ground were more reminiscent of a Cup semi-final than a Third Division game, for the match had captured the imagination of the Sheffield public and ensured that Hillsborough hosted its biggest attendance for a league game since the two old foes had met back in 1971.

Few had dared to predict the outcome before the game, and the opening half hour failed to provide any clues, as, in an exciting tussle, neither side stamped their authority on the proceedings. As befitted the league leaders, United set out to play the more cultured football, but were taken by surprise as the Wednesday players rose to the cup-tie atmosphere generated by the huge crowd. As the half wore on, the home side slowly started to edge the contest, and, after 29 minutes, Andy McCulloch saw his glancing header cleared off the line by Tony Kenworthy. With five minutes to half-time, the majority in Hillsborough erupted as Ian 'Spiderman' Mellor unleashed a spectacular 25-yard shot which had Richardson clawing thin air as it flew past him into the top corner. The deadlock had been broken, though the Blades should have equalised almost immediately when Bob Bolder performed heroics to turn Bourne's shot onto the crossbar and MacPhail scuffed the rebound straight at the prone Owls' keeper.

It had been a superb first half, yet Wednesday fans could not, in their wildest dreams, have imagined what was to occur in the second half; for Harry Haslam's Blades were to be put to the sword. As the Owls attacked the heart of the Blades defence, the Wednesday trio of Jeff Johnson, Jeff King and Brian Hornsby began creating a midfield superiority over a somewhat lightweight United threesome; with the aforementioned trio's willingness to distribute the ball quickly becoming a key to the home side's eventual success. After the game the United coach, Danny Begara, (who would join the Owls in a similar capacity under David Pleat) said the Blades had played into Wednesday's hands by allowing them to break quickly from defence; a tactic which allowed both Mellor and King to fire against the woodwork in the early stages of the second half. The game was effectively settled as the Owls continued to pour forwards, for Wednesday scored twice in as many minutes to send the home fans into dreamland. The first of the two came after 63 minutes when McCulloch burst from the Owls' midfield. As Richardson rushed out to narrow the angle, McCulloch unselfishly crossed for Terry Curran to fling himself at the ball and score with a spectacular flying header, the darling of the fans sank to his knees in front of the Kop to milk the applause. Then before the cheers had died down, it was 3–0, as Curran sprinted down the wing before pulling the ball back for the onrushing Jeff King to smash the ball past an exposed Richardson from 15 yards out. The period immediately after this third goal saw the Blades lose their discipline somewhat, with MacPhail receiving a booking for his tackle from behind on McCulloch. Wednesday, however, would have the last word, when, with three minutes remaining, Curran was pulled down by Richardson and penalty king, Mark Smith scored his seventh spot kick of the season. To beat their rivals was the best Christmas present any Owls fan could have wished for, but to record the highest ever peacetime win over the Blades made sure that the roast turkey tasted even better on this particular Boxing Day.

Wednesday: Bolder, Blackhall, Williamson, Smith, Pickering, Hornsby, King, Johnson, McCulloch, Mellor, Curran

United: Richardson, Speight (Cutbush 57), Tibbott, Kenworthy, MacPhail, Matthews, de Goey, Bourne, Butlin, Garner, Sabella

Referee: P. Partridge (Bishop Auckland)

Mellor celebrates his goal

Sheffield Wednesday 4
Sheffield United 0

Memory Match

Gary Shelton scores his second goal

Sheffield Wednesday 5
Burnley 0

After reaching the quarter final of the FA Cup for the first time for sixteen years, the draw was kind to the Owls with an away tie against fellow Division Two side, Burnley, coming out of the hat. A goal from top scorer, Gary Bannister, was enough to bring the teams back to Hillsborough after a 1–1 draw. However, for the replay Wednesday were without Bannister and their captain, Mike Lyons, the latter starting a suspension after an unfortunate sending off at Wolves. Their places, on a memorable evening, were taken by Kevin 'Ticker' Taylor and Peter Shirtliff, who would both play their parts in front of the biggest Hillsborough crowd since the 'Boxing Day massacre'. On the Sunday morning following the draw, large queues began to form as the replay tickets went on sale. Cup fever again swept the city, for in that season the Owl fans were spoilt for Cup-tie football, as in addition to the run in the FA Cup, Wednesday had also reached the last eight of the League Cup, while the club's junior side followed the trend by reaching the semi-finals of the FA Youth Cup.

Considering the final scoreline it is perhaps surprising to learn that although Wednesday set off at a blistering pace, it was Burnley who settled first and were the better of the two sides; to the extent it needed a superb sliding tackle from Peter Shirtliff to deny Hamilton after only six minutes. The Owls were showing big match nerves, but these were to disappear after seventeen minutes, when, after a terrible blunder from Brian Flynn, they were handed the opening goal on a plate. There seemed to be no danger as the diminutive Welsh International aimed a back pass at his goalkeeper, however, he woefully underhit the pass and Gary Shelton seized on the error to take the ball round Stevenson and begin the Hillsborough celebrations. Soon after this, Peter Shirtliff again proved himself to be a more than able deputy for Lyons, as another last-ditch tackle on Steve Taylor denied the Lancastrians a quickfire leveller. The Owls, however, had one foot in the semi-final after twenty eight minutes, when the persistence of Gary Shelton led to a second goal. The midfielder first shook off two challenges to feed Pat Heard on the left-wing, then surged into the area to be on hand to score from eight yards out as David Mills knocked down Heard's subsequent centre. The Owls confidence had now gone through the roof, and, with five minutes of the half remaining, Wednesday scored again after being awarded a rather dubious penalty, as Donachie bundled Andy McCulloch over in the box. With Bannister, their regular penalty taker injured on the sidelines, it was left to Gary Megson to send Stevenson the wrong way from the spot, and give Wednesday an unassailable half time lead—though they had only managed four shots in the whole forty-five minutes.

At the interval, Frank Casper, the Burnley manager, threw on striker Terry Donovan in an attempt to salvage something from the game. However, any thoughts they might have had of staging a comeback were put to rest ten minutes into the half, when, from Taylor's pinpoint cross, Andy McCulloch rose majestically to head home a fourth goal. Both teams and the fans now knew the Owls were through, and it was simply a case of how many a rampant Wednesday would score before Burnley were put out of their misery by the final whistle. The remainder of the game was played in almost a carnival atmosphere; and, after Heard and McCulloch had gone close, Shelton spurned a glorious chance to record his hat-trick, as he slid the ball wide when it seemed easier to score. With the visitors now a spent force, the icing was put firmly on the cake with six minutes left, as big Andy 'Mac' found acres of space in the Burnley defence to chest down Megson's cross and stroke the ball consummately past a shell-shocked Stevenson. By now the fans were dancing with delight on the Kop, for they had savoured one of the greatest Cup nights in Hillsborough history and the biggest home win in the competition since Mansfield Town were hit for six way back in 1946—next stop Highbury.

Wednesday: Bolder, Sterland, Bailey, Smith, Pet. Shirtliff, Shelton, Megson, S. Mills, K. Taylor, McCulloch, Heard

Burnley: Stevenson, Laws, Donachie, Phelan, Dobson (Donavon ht), Flynn, Scott, Steven, Hamilton, S. Taylor, Young

Referee: G. Tyson (Sunderland)

Memory Match

The 1983–84 season contained many memorable matches, for new manager, Howard Wilkinson, made a perfect start to his Hillsborough career by leading the Owls back to the promised land after a fourteen-year absence. In addition to their league success, Wednesday also experienced a great time in Cup football, reaching the quarter finals in the Milk Cup and the FA Cup; where they exited to First Division sides, Liverpool and Southampton respectively. However, it was the home meeting with the Anfield club that was arguably the match of the season, for at the time Liverpool were the dominant force in English football, and they arrived at Hillsborough as the reigning League Champions and holders of the Milk Cup. Against such a backdrop, the Owls were considered rank outsiders. Interest in the tie was immense, however, and at the kick-off a crowd of over 49,000 was packed into the ground to give the Owls their biggest attendance since the legendary game with Manchester United back in August 1968.

After scoring as a sub, in a 6–1 win over Swansea City on the previous Saturday, Imre Varadi was recalled to the starting eleven, with John Pearson stepping down. One other change resulted in Gary Shelton replacing Pat Heard. The visiting team almost constituted an International eleven, with the likes of Rush, Hansen and Souness being household names. On a very soft pitch there was an early worry for Wednesday when, after a clumsy challenge from Robinson, their inspirational leader, Mick Lyons, had to have treatment off the pitch for three minutes. Thankfully he returned, driving his side on to almost take the lead after 19 minutes when Gary Shelton's terrific 20-yard shot was acrobatically turned over by Bruce Grobbelaar. However, within two minutes it was the visitors who scored the first goal, as Graeme Souness supplied future Owl, Steve Nicol, and he superbly chipped the ball over the advancing Martin Hodge. The Owls were now up against it, though Hillsborough was celebrating eleven minutes later when man-of-the-match, Gary Megson, scored a superb equaliser. The goal originated with a burst down the wing by Varadi, who, after the ball had come back to him off Mark Lawrenson, crossed a second time for Megson to score with a delightful glancing header. The Merseyside giants were looking vulnerable now and the Owls—who were tending to use the long ball more than usual because of the muddy conditions— gained a measure of supremacy which should have given them a penalty; with the TV replay later showing Hansen handling Megson's chip inside the area. Just before the break, a Lyons goal was ruled out because of a doubtful foul by Bannister, and at the whistle Wednesday went off to a terrific ovation after having more than matched their illustrious visitors.

Within seven minutes of the re-start the Owls had forged ahead, when, after Lyons had turned on Sterland's throw-in, Gary Bannister ran on into the box to score past Grobbelaar, thanks to a deflection off Lawrenson. However, the defining moment of the game came on the hour as Wednesday attacked the Kop end and Sterland whipped in a terrific low cross which found Gary Shelton just six yards from an open goal. Unfortunately, Shelton made a real mess of the glorious opportunity and the Owls paid dearly for their carelessness. Liverpool broke way, Ian Rush burst into the area, and Hodge took his legs away to give the Reds a penalty. Full-back, Phil Neal duly sent Hodge the wrong way from the spot and Liverpool were rather fortuitous to be back on level terms. The equaliser took the wind from the Owls' sails somewhat, but with seven minutes left Bannister almost grabbed the glory when he volleyed over from just outside the penalty box. The Anfield club thus managed to hang on to a draw, though Wednesday could be proud, for a tremendous Cup-tie had thrilled the massive crowd, and, perhaps more importantly, had shown that the Owls could live with top flight opposition.

Wednesday: Hodge, Sterland, Pet. Shirtliff, Smith, Lyons, Madden, Megson, Bannister, Varadi, Pearson, Shelton

Liverpool: Grobbelaar, Neal, Kennedy, Lawrenson, Nicol, Hansen, Robinson, Lee, Rush, Johnston, Souness

Referee: Mr M. Scott (Nottingham)

The equaliser from Gary Megson

Sheffield Wednesday
2
Liverpool
2

Chapter 8

Back in Division One
1984–92

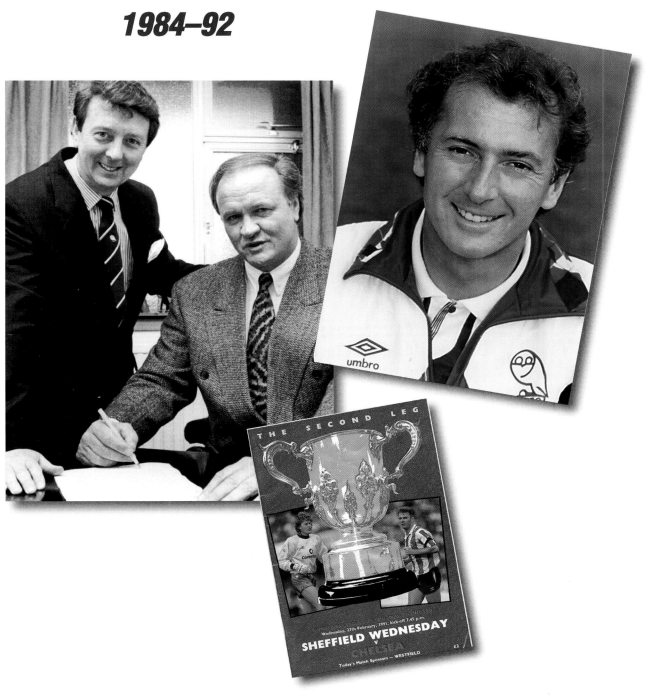

1984–85
EVENTFUL FIRST SEASON BACK IN THE BIG TIME

In preparation for the club's return to top flight football, manager Howard Wilkinson spent the summer months restructuring his side for the higher grade of football. However, one transfer he could have done without was that of top scorer, Gary Bannister. Much to the fans disappointment, Bannister decided to sign for Queen's Park Rangers for a club record £200,000, tribunal-set fee, after refusing a new deal at Hillsborough. Gary Megson also left, for Nottingham Forest, Tony Cunningham went to Manchester City, Paul Shirtliff to Northampton, and Kevin Taylor signed for Derby County. New arrivals included Hull City's highly rated winger, Brian Marwood; the Scottish midfielder Andy Blair, who came in from Villa; and Lee Chapman from Sunderland, who had been labelled a 'misfit' after failing to make an impression at both Highbury and Roker Park. Other news and activity saw 'Zico' Sterland sign a new four-year deal, Mick Lyons sign a 2-year contract which gave him a secondary role as a youth coach, a bid for Brighton's Danny Wilson being turned down, and the ex-Blades keeper, Alan Hodgkinson, appointed to coach the club's custodians.

The Owls pre-season began in bizarre circumstances, as Wilkinson took his side to Keswick in the Lake District. There, in a friendly for the NSPCC, Wednesday beat the Royal Hotel 25–1, with thirteen different players scoring for the Owls and the home goal coming when Mick Lyons, who was in the net at the time, had his hands tied together by the cheerleaders! More conventional friendlies followed at Grimsby, York and Notts County, before an attractive opening home game with Brian Clough's Nottingham Forest launched the club's league season. The Owls had sold almost 9,000 season tickets for the new campaign, and over 31,000 attended that first game, with the majority delighted as, early on, a Sterland penalty put Wednesday ahead. The visitors soon levelled the scores, but thirteen minutes into the second half, Imre Varadi scored one of the most memorable goals ever seen at Hillsborough when he picked the ball up just outside his own box and proceeded to run fully 70 yards before lashing the ball past Steve Sutton in the Forest goal. That strike was good enough to win any game, and a third goal from John Pearson secured a joyous return to the top flight. In the early weeks of the season, Wednesday's home form ensured the club maintained a top six position; though they really made the country sit up and take notice when their first away win came at the unlikely setting of Anfield, home of the Champions, Liverpool. Nine months after the Wednesdayites had defiantly sung 'We'll be back', the same fans were now in raptures as Imre Varadi—thanks to a certain Mr Grobbelaar—and Gary Shelton netted in a landmark 2–0 win. A few days later the Owls travelled to Sweden where they drew with Halmstads BK in a game to

mark the 80th birthday of the country's FA. Meanwhile, just before the visit to Liverpool, Wednesday announced a £150,000 shirt sponsorship deal with the Barnsley company, MHS, and completed the signing of Newcastle United's John Ryan, with Pat Heard moving to the North East as part of the transfer.

The Owls great start to the season peaked in mid-October, when a Varadi hat-trick helped beat Leicester City 5–0, lifting Wednesday to the dizzy heights of second place. However, they couldn't really expect to maintain that lofty position, and by the end of the Boxing Day game with Villa they had slipped down to ninth place. In the intervening period the club won through to the last eight of the Milk Cup for the third consecutive season, making history in the home game with Luton Town when Andy Blair became the first and only man to score a hat-trick of penalties in the competition. The home win over Arsenal then entered the record books, for this was the club's first ever live televised league game. Meanwhile, off the pitch, and following the demise of the Canadian club, Vancouver Whitecaps, for which he had played, there was an unsuccessful trial for David O'Leary's brother, Pierce. The transfer to Sheffield of the Cologne forward, Vic Mannie, then broke down when the respective club's failed to agree on a fee, and Spalding United manager, Mick Hennigan, was appointed Youth Coach. Finally, the Icelandic teenage wonderkid, Siggi Jonsson, signed for the club, but had to wait in the wings over five weeks before securing a work permit.

The early stages of the new year were dominated by Cup football, with Wednesday involved in a three-game Milk Cup marathon with their old foes, Chelsea; and then exiting the FA Cup in controversial circumstances at Ipswich Town. The Milk

Andy Blair in action versus Newcastle

Cup ties began with a draw at Stamford Bridge, before Wednesday somehow managed to lose a three goal half-time lead in the replay, to eventually draw 4–4, thanks to a late leveller from Mel Sterland. Arch nemesis, Mickey Thomas then broke the Owls' hearts with a last minute winner in the second replay. In the FA Cup, after Wednesday had cruised through to the last sixteen, they were again hit by a late goal at Portman Road. That game was played on a Monday evening because of bad weather, and Wednesday looked to be heading for a deserved replay, as the game was tied at 2–2 with only two minutes remaining. However, the home player, Mich D'Avray, then received the ball in what was a blatant offside position. To the consternation and anger of the Wednesday fans there was no whistle, and he ran on to cross for Alan Sunderland to score a bitterly contested winner. Back in the league, the Owls had returned to the top six, with Wilkinson winning the Manager of the Month award for January. Soon after this, Wednesday broke their club transfer record in bringing the striker, Simon Stainrod, from Queen's Park Rangers for £250,000. Strangely, the record buy would not make his debut for almost six weeks, by which time several players had left on loan, including Charlie Williamson and David Mossman, and third choice keeper, David Redfern. Ian Bailey then left on a permanent basis, with his contract being cancelled by mutual consent. Meanwhile, after a highly successful trial spell in the club's reserve side, the unknown Spalding United forward, Carl Shutt signed his first professional contract.

A good run of form in April hoisted Wednesday up to fourth position, with a UEFA Cup place now being a distinct possibility. The same month also saw manager, Wilkinson turn down a reported £1m managerial offer from the Saudi Arabian oil sheik who owned the Aittihad Club of Jeddah. The club's Euro hopes were then hit by a home defeat to the Champions, Everton, followed by another at Chelsea. A victory in the last home game left Wednesday needing to win at Spurs in their final match to have any chance of playing UEFA Cup football, but they lost 2–0 to finish eighth. However, subsequent events at Heysel made the issue somewhat irrelevant, as a five year European ban on English clubs was enforced. Overall it had been a successful season back in the First Division. A rejuvenated Chapman had contributing 20 goals to a 41 goal partnership with Imre Varadi, and Wednesday wound up the campaign with a testimonial at Chesterfield, and a game with Watford in the unusual surroundings of Bangkok, with the Owls winning the Cup 3–2 in a penalty shoot-out to at least put some silverware in the trophy cabinet.

Imre Varadi against his old club Newcastle

1985–86
OWLS HIT BY EURO BAN AND SEMI-FINAL DEFEAT

After a promising first campaign back in the big-time the close season again saw Howard Wilkinson busy in the transfer market, when, for the second summer running he was forced to find a replacement for the club's top scorer. This time it was Imre Varadi who left, signing for West Bromwich Albion when his contract ended. The tribunal was again called in, and awarded Wednesday a record £285,000—though the Owls wanted closer to £400,000, plus a third of any future transfer fee. His direct replacement, for a club record of £450,000, was the bustling forward, Gary Thompson, who somewhat ironically arrived from Varadi's new employers. Other newcomers included John Cooke, Glynn Snodin, the Doncaster Rovers utility player, and the vastly experienced centre-half Paul Hart. Meanwhile, Simon Mills signed for York City, Charlie Williamson left for neighbours, Chesterfield, and John Ryan went to Oldham. And, although not actually signing a new five year contract, Wilkinson agreed to one, following speculation in the media about his future. The Heysel ban then hit Wednesday's pre-season preparations, with the club forced to cancel their plans for an early August match in their twin city of Bochum.

The Owls were therefore restricted to pre-season games in the UK, and kicked off with a comprehensive 6–2 win at Scunthorpe United, before Goole Town, Barnsley and Derby were all beaten as a prelude to Chelsea holding Wednesday to an opening day Hillsborough draw. Wednesday then proceeded to win their next four games to set up a clash of the top two, as the leaders, Everton travelled to Sheffield. The Owls looked to be heading for the top spot when a Brian Marwood penalty put them

ahead; however, the roof then caved in as a Gary Lineker brace helped the Toffeemen race to a 5–1 win, leaving the home fans somewhat shell-shocked. A few days later the club re-entered the transfer market signing ex-England winger, Mark Chamberlain from Stoke City; though they refused to pay the inflated asking price of £750,000, and eventually paid less than half of that figure at a transfer tribunal. On the same day, Wednesday were drawn to play Huddersfield Town in the new Full Members Cup competition. Some seventy-two hours later, however, they pulled out—along with their scheduled opponents—putting the tournament's future into doubt even before it started. Meanwhile, Simon Stainrod's brief spell at Hillsborough came to a close, when, after a move to Terry Venables' Barcelona broke down, he signed for Aston Villa. In the league, Wednesday subsequently recovered from the Everton defeat, and then slipped down the league standings to reach third place by late October. At this juncture, a two week period provided Owls' fans with the low point of the season, then followed this with the definitive high point. The former moment came in the Milk Cup, when Wednesday crashed out in an embarrassing defeat at Fourth Division, Swindon Town. The latter then occurred in the shape of a visit from the unbeaten league leaders, Manchester United. This attracted over 48,000 to Hillsborough and saw a fiercely fought encounter won by a Lee Chapman header, with only six minutes remaining. Soon after this Mick Lyons left to take over as player-manager at Grimsby Town, while Gavin Oliver signed for Bradford City. The Owls were then voted runners-up in the Fiat Team of the Year Award, with £500 going to a local boys club. And, eighteen months after leaving the club, Gary Megson returned on loan from Manchester City. A hat-trick of pre-Christmas home wins not only saw Martin Hodge at the peak of his powers, taking him to the verge of an England call-up, but saw Wednesday placed comfortably in the top six, with another high league finish on the cards. And, as the Old Year ended and 1986 dawned, Wilkinson, Eustace and the physio, Alan Smith, all signed new five year contracts to ensure back room continuity.

The New Year started with a creditable draw at Anfield, Shutt scoring only 44 seconds after the kick-off. The FA Cup campaign then began with a delayed home draw against West Brom. The replay highlighted the major change that has now occurred in the English game in the 1990s. When ITV *asked* for the game to be moved so that the tie could be televised live, the clubs *refused* permission! The replay went the Owls' way thanks to a late winner from the perennial substitute, Mark Chamberlain. Over the season Chamberlain played 27 times but started in only three matches—a situation much to his own and the Wednesday fans frustration. Before the fourth round clash with Orient, Gary Megson completed a permanent transfer, and after the Division Four side were summarily despatched by five goals to nil, the Owls' teenage starlet, Siggi Jonsson, went to Oakwell on a month's loan. A series of postponements and general poor form then resulted in Wednesday slipping down the table, though this was soon rectified in the month of March when the virtually unknown, Carl Shutt, hit the national headlines by netting seven times in as many games. This tally included a hat-trick at home to Birmingham City, and propelled Wednesday into the semi-finals of the FA Cup. As Cup fever grew, the club called a press conference and announced plans to finally put a roof over the Kop. Andy Blair then re-signed for Aston Villa, and Wednesday agreed a sponsorship deal until the end of the season with the Finnish electronics company, Finlux Limited, which was worth £40,000.

On the first Saturday in April all roads led to Villa Park, where a semi-final crowd of just over 47,000 saw the old foes Everton score first through the future Wednesday player, Alan Harper. Carl Shutt's fairy tale story continued though, as he headed the Owls level within two minutes. However, the Wembley dream

died for another year when Graeme Sharp crashed an unstoppable shot past Hodge, just eight minutes into the first period of extra time. Following the Cup disappointment, Wilkinson rallied his troops to such an extent that they won five and drew two of their final seven matches of the season, the best finish by a Wednesday side since the 1951–52 Second Division Championship team. The run included a televised win at Old Trafford, a home win over Aston Villa in which talented youngster, Ian Knight, made his debut, and a last day home victory over Ipswich, which sent the Suffolk side down and proved to be the last game played at Hillsborough in front of an uncovered Kop. The club eventually finished fifth, though the final position was a somewhat bitter-sweet one, for had the Heysel ban had not been in place, then Wednesday would have been playing UEFA Cup football in 1986–87. Unfortunately, many English sides experienced similar emotions in the 1980s, and, for Wednesday, three testimonials in as many days, at Sheffield United, Matlock Town and Frickley Athletic brought to an end another season of progress.

Carl Shutt's fairytale season continues as he scores in the FA Cup tie versus Derby at Hillsborough

1986–87
THE QUEEN VISITS HILLSBOROUGH

The summer of 1986 again saw the usual flurry of transfer activity which characterised Howard Wilkinson's managerial reign at Hillsborough. However, his first foray into the transfer market was unsuccessful, for the Aberdeen centre-half, Neale Cooper, rejected a move to Wednesday, and eventually signed for Aston Villa. Joining him at Villa Park was the Owls' record signing, Gary Thompson, who, somewhat surprisingly, left after less than a year at Hillsborough, with Wednesday recouping all of the £450,000 originally paid for his services. There was only one other departee, as Peter Shirtliff joined Charlton Athletic. Meanwhile, Wilkinson scoured the lower leagues, bringing in Ken Brannigan from the amateur Scottish outfit, Queen's Park, and David Reeves from the West Cheshire League minnows, Heswell. Colin Walker, who somewhat infamously counted the role of dustman among his previous occupations, then signed a two-year contract after impressing during a trial period; and the highly rated Barnsley teenager, David Hirst, was secured for an initial fee of £200,000. The off-season also saw Wednesday sign a new £100,000 sponsorship deal with Finlux. Meanwhile, soon after agreeing terms, Brannigan was sent out on loan to Stockport County, and a similar fate befell the reserve goalie, Iain Hesford, who signed for Sunderland.

For the first time since the early 1970s the Owls began their pre-season friendly engagements

on foreign soil. Three games were played in Finland, with HJK Helsinki winning the inaugural Finlux Cup in the opening match of the tour. On their return home, Wednesday won at Notts County and drew at Hull City, before a Gary Shelton goal earned the Owls an opening day 1–1 scoreline at Charlton Athletic. The initial home game of the season, against Everton, was memorable for two reasons, as the new roofed Kop was used for the first time, and the Wednesday fans started a love affair with David Hirst—after coming on as a substitute, he scored in front of the packed home end with his first touch. A home success over Chelsea and a last-minute winning goal from Carl Shutt at St James' Park lifted Wednesday into the top ten, before the club made a mid-week trek to Kuwait, where the national side were beaten 5–2 in a friendly game. On their return from the desert, Wednesday sold Hesford to Sunderland, and the club's 'club-call' telephone information line was launched. The trialist, Andy Kiwomya then signed for the Owls, but within a month he was hospitalised with a back injury after a training ground accident cut short his career before it had really begun. In the First Division, Wednesday were again riding high as Oxford were hit for six at Hillsborough. And in the newly sponsored Littlewoods Cup, Stockport were thrashed 10–0 on aggregate, with Colin Walker entering the record books as he scored a hat-trick in the 7–0 second-leg romp at Maine Road after entering the fray as a half-time substitute.

SHEFFIELD WEDNESDAY v
HELSINGIN JALKAPALLOKLUBI

AN INTERNATIONAL FRIENDLY GAME
FOR THE FINLUX CHALLENGE CUP
TUESDAY, 31st MARCH, 1987, KICK-OFF 7.30 p.m.

Queen Elizabeth II meets Owls' boss Howard Wilkinson as the roofed kop is given royal approval

The Cup run ended, however, with a heavy defeat at Everton; and then, after scoring nine in a testimonial at fog-bound Grimsby Town, the Hillsborough fans witnessed one of the rarest sights in football, as the Coventry keeper, Steve Ogrizovic hoisted a long clearance up the field and scored past a stunned Martin Hodge.

Wednesday finally made their bow in the somewhat ill-conceived Full Members Cup, a year after pulling out of a competition which was created to compensate for the lack of European football. Less than 8,000 saw them slump to a truly dismal home defeat to Portsmouth. A week later, the Luton Town secretary, Graham Mackrell, arrived to take over from the departing Dick Chester. Her Majesty the Queen then visited Hillsborough, where, in front of over 40,000 spectators she officially cut the ribbon on the new Wednesday Kop. It had been a tremendous year for Wednesday, though a slump over the festive period saw them tumble from fifth to tenth place; and, in a surprise move, Paul Hart was sold to Birmingham City on the final day of 1986. The mini-crisis continued into the New Year, when a depleted Wednesday side, in which Ken Brannigan and David Tomlinson made their only first team appearances in an Owls shirt, crashed to a 6–1 reverse at Leicester City. Incredibly, Wednesday would not win again in the league until late March, when an outrageous injury-time goal from David Hirst beat

Manchester United at Hillsborough. This poor league form was masked somewhat by the club's progression to the quarter-finals of the FA Cup, a run starting with a stormy home win over Derby County in which Lee Chapman was sent off by George Courtney (who was to be roundly booed on every subsequent visit!). The fourth round meeting with Chester would not be remembered because of the Owls 3–1 replay victory, or even for Martin Hodge's record breaking 190th consecutive appearance (overtaking Mark Hooper's record from the 1930s); rather it would stay in the mind because of the horrific 'over-the-top' tackle by Gary Bennett. This effectively ended the career of the England Under 21 International, Ian Knight, for the sickening crack was distinctly heard in the stands as Bennett made contact with the youngster's leg. Knight's injury was said to be so severe that the shattered leg was compared to that of a road crash victim. The shocking incident was seen by Match of the Day viewers, with the Owls physio, Alan Smith stating he had never encountered such a serious football injury. Knight could only watch from the sideline as his side won 2–0 at West Ham in a fifth round replay that would set up a last eight meeting with Coventry City at Hillsborough. Incidentally, during the Cup run, Wednesday signed the Barnsley captain, Larry May, some two days after a deal to acquire him and the Glasgow Rangers forward, Colin West, had seemingly collapsed. Meanwhile, a scheduled home friendly with the crack Yugoslavian side, Red Star Belgrade, was called off because of bad weather.

The tie with the eventual Cup winners, Coventry, generated enormous interest, especially in the Midlands; and 15,000 fans travelled north to swell the attendance to over 48,000. It was the Sky Blues supporters who celebrated first, as Regis put them ahead. However, a Gary Megson second-half equaliser revived the home fans dreams of a second successive semi-final appearance. Unfortunately, it was not to be, and a Keith Houchen double in the final eleven minutes sent City through, leaving Wednesday to salvage what was left of their league campaign. The aforementioned dramatic win over Manchester United helped raise spirits seven days later, but then, despite another win at West Ham, Wednesday tumbled all the way down to seventeenth following an Easter Saturday defeat at Carrow Road. They still had enough points in the bag, however, not to worry about being dragged into the relegation zone; and the highlight of a five-game unbeaten run that duly followed was the seven goal bonanza in the home game with Queen's Park Rangers. The perennial 'party-poopers', Wimbledon then spoilt the Owls final game of a season in which Lee Chapman was again the top scorer, this time with 22 league and cup goals. However, the squad still had four games to play as the season ended, for Wednesday then undertook a four-game tour of Canada which saw three games played against Team Canada and a goalless encounter with the Calgary Kickers.

1987–88
SUMMER OF FRUSTRATION FOR WILKINSON

Despite a late end-of-season flurry, the Wednesday boss, Howard Wilkinson, decided that the poor form shown in mid-season was indicative of his team's true ability and he therefore decided to spend the close season attempting to add quality to his squad. This was easier said than done, however, and the summer period saw Wilkinson frustrated at almost every turn. Two big name players rejected moves at the last moment, and one signed, only to change his mind within a week! The first 'nearly man' was Nottingham Forest's, Chris Fairclough. On the verge of a club record move to Hillsborough, he then tried to delay the signing so he could talk to another club, at which an angry Wilkinson called the whole deal off. The other one that got away was Southampton's highly rated, Mark Wright. After rejecting a record £750,000 move, apparently because his wife did not want to move to the North, he, in almost comic fashion, signed for those 'deep southerners' at Derby County! The one player Wednesday did apparently sign from the south coast club, was David Armstrong. However, within three days he quit the Owls, giving as his reason the fact that he 'did not want to move his son out of his school'. Wednesday also missed out with bids for Mick McCarthey and Ray Houghton, yet, despite getting more rejections than a talentless author, Wilkinson did manage to bring three new faces into the club,

with the purchase of Ipswich Town full-back, Steve McCall, being the major outlay. The arrival of Gary Owen from the Greek club Panionios, and Boston United's, Greg Fee were fairly low-key events, while Wednesday fans said good-bye to several old favourites, such as Glynn Snodin, Chris Morris, Mark Smith and Gary Shelton, who all left for pastures new. Away from the club's problems in the transfer market, a new sponsorship deal was agreed with Finlux, while the launch of the club's new pin-stripe home shirt outraged the traditionalists, and went down like a 'lead balloon' amongst the supporters. Finally, as a result of increasing football related violence, Wednesday fell into line with Football League demands, and made the North Stand a members-only area.

Wednesday began their pre-season preparations with a four match tour of Germany, with David Armstrong playing his only game in a blue and white shirt against Armenia Bielefeld. The Owls then won the Finlux Cup from HJK in Finland, before beating the Blades 3–0 at Bramall Lane in a fund raising match for the forthcoming World Student Games. League newcomers, Scarborough, were then beaten, before the league season got underway with a disappointing defeat at Chelsea, followed by a poor quality home draw with Oxford

Southampton's goal remains intact as Lee Chapman and Mark Proctor try to force the ball over the goal-line

United. The early weeks were becoming a struggle as Wednesday slipped to third from bottom of the new 20-club division after a shocking 3–0 home loss to Coventry City, in which Steve McCall was stretchered off with a broken leg. Wilkinson realised he needed to re-enter the transfer market, and within a week had brought three new faces into the club, signing Eire International, Tony Galvin, from Tottenham, Mark Procter from Sunderland, and Colin West from Glasgow Rangers. Though Wednesday hardly set the league alight with this influx of new blood, they did at least manage to pull themselves out of the bottom four, climbing up to 17th as they went into the festive fixtures. The main excitement for the fans in the first half of the season had come in the Littlewoods Cup, where, after Shrewsbury Town were beaten (a certain Nigel Pearson impressing to the extent that Wednesday immediately signed him) a late David Hirst winner sealed a fierce tie at Oakwell. The next round took Wednesday to Villa Park, where, in a controversial tie, Gary Megson was sent off for allegedly lashing out at Mark Lillis. In what was arguably the display of the season, Wednesday kept the home side at bay, however, and went through 2–1 thanks to a Colin West winner. The run would end early in the New Year, though, when a Martin Hodge gaff gave Arsenal a safe passage at Hillsborough. In the preceding weeks Carl Shutt had left for

Bristol City and Colin Walker moved to the New Zealand club, Gisborne City.

A splendid run of three consecutive wins over Christmas moved the Owls into the top half of the table for the first time, and, after finally managing to overcome their bogey side, Everton, at Hillsborough on New Year's Day, the club went into the FA Cup tie full of optimism against the same side. What followed was a classic Cup marathon that stretched to four games before the tie was settled in a somewhat spectacular style in the third replay at Hillsborough. Two days after earning a second 1–1 draw at Goodison Park, Wednesday brought their opponents back onto home territory. The loss of key defender, Lawrie Madden, proved to be crucial, however, and by half-time the pubs round the ground were packed with the disconsolate fans, for a Graeme Sharp treble was a major factor as Wednesday found themselves five goals in arrears, and still with forty-five minutes to play! The second half saw no further scoring, and embarrassingly Wednesday crashed out after one of the worst cup nights in their long history. The Owls were therefore left to try to pick up the pieces. However, five defeats in their next six games, including losing on a return visit to Kuwait, failed to cheer supporters. In the transfer deadline week they said good-bye to Brian Marwood, Larry May and Wayne Jacobs, and welcomed the arrival of the Ipswich Town centre-half, Ian Cranson. Actually, the Larry May transfer collapsed four days later on medical grounds, and he returned to Sheffield to play in Wednesday's final four games of the season. These followed some impressive displays at Wembley in the Mercantile Credit Festival, a competition organised to celebrate the Football League Centenary. The Owls were one of the teams which qualified to the play in the 11-a-side, 40 minute games, beating Crystal Palace, Wigan and Manchester United to reach the final. There, after a 60-minute goalless encounter, they lost 3–2 on penalties to Nottingham Forest, in a tournament that singularly failed to catch the public imagination. Six days later Wednesday were back in London, becoming the last team to play QPR on their plastic pitch. Back in Sheffield, the 100th league meeting between Arsenal and the Owls was a thriller, with Mel Sterland running almost 70 yards to fire Wednesday into a third minute lead. The advantage soon increased to three, though the Gunners stormed back with an injury time goal from Alan Smith winning them a point, much to the frustration of the home fans. But if the fans were frustrated by this surrender of a three goal lead, then the mood following the final home game of the season was much worse, for the Champions, Liverpool, won by five goals to one to bring the curtain crashing down on a generally disappointing campaign which highlighted the need for further team strengthening.

1988–89
DISASTER OVERSHADOWS A SEASON OF THREE MANAGERS

The 1988–89 season will be remembered for one reason only; the tragic events of April 15th in the crush at the Leppings Lane end resulting in the loss of 96 lives. This occurred at the beginning of the Liverpool v. Nottingham Forest FA Cup semi-final; with questions as to how and why this terrible event took place having been well documented over the ensuing ten years and are still being debated. Suffice to say, that from that day forward the game was irrevocably changed, with the subsequent Taylor Report ensuring that all the top grounds in England and Wales are now all-seater stadia. A memorial to the tragedy now stands on the south side of the ground in remembrance.

Back in the summer of 1988, the new signings that the Wednesday fans had hoped for simply did not materialise, and this triggered serious doubts about the club's ability to compete in the top flight. The only newcomers were Alan Harper, and free transfer signing, David Hodgson. Meanwhile, as if to compound the fears, top scoring Lee Chapman, with 79 goals in 187 games, signed for little known French club, Niort, with the fee to be decided by UEFA tribunal. Also leaving were Gary Owen, Des Hazel and Mark Chamberlain, while Manager, Wilkinson, again turned down a lucrative job offer—this time from the Greek side, PAOK Salonika.

The opening friendly game gave every indication of the season of struggle that would follow, as a desperately poor goalless draw played out with Exeter City left the small band of travelling Owls' fans wishing they had stayed on the beach. Two days later, however, there came a victory at Torquay, and with Mel Sterland in use as a makeshift striker, Wednesday somewhat surprisingly started the season well; and, after winning at Southampton in late October, found themselves in fifth position in a very tight league. That game saw the home side field three brothers, the Wallace brothers, the first time since the War that this had occurred. More importantly it saw Peter Eustace take charge of Wednesday in a caretaker capacity following the departure of Howard Wilkinson. Before resigning to take over at Leeds United, Wilkinson had been busy in the transfer market, with Chris Turner and Imre Varadi both arriving for second spells with the club, and a large bid for Liverpool's, Nigel Spackman being rejected. Carl Bradshaw, Martin Hodge and Larry May all left Hillsborough, before good news came with the return of Ian Knight, as he made his comeback in the reserves after 20 months out of the game. The other event of note concerned the summer move of Lee Chapman. This had turned to farce when his new side, ordered to pay £290,000 for his signature, couldn't afford the fee; and so promptly sold him to Nottingham Forest at a large profit! Howard Wilkinson had tendered his resignation two days before the Littlewoods Cup tie with Blackpool, and, with Peter Eustace in temporary charge, Wednesday won 3–1, but

then crashed out of the competition on away goals. Over the next two weeks the Owls tried to obtain the managerial services of Graham Turner, Ray Harford, Lou Macari, Steve Coppell and, finally, Jim Smith. But, in the end, Eustace was given the role, with Frank Barlow promoted from Youth Coach to be Eustace's No. 2. This was to be the start of the worst and shortest career record of any Wednesday manager.

Across the 109 days of Eustace's reign Wednesday failed to win one league game, and slumped to the bottom three. As the weeks passed, problems mounted behind the scenes, reaching a peak in early January when five players asked for moves; these included Mel Sterland, who, two months earlier became the first Wednesday player to be capped by England for 22 years. 'Zico' had been stripped of his captaincy, and like Kevin Pressman, he then saw his transfer request turned down by Eustace. On the field of play a disastrous 5–0 defeat at Coventry, in which Jonsson was red carded, worsened the situation; while the signings of Wilf Rostron and Darren Wood did little to ease the pressure. During his short reign Eustace also sold Gary Megson; but the straw that would break the camel's back came in the shape

New manager Peter Eustace on his appointment—he would last only 109 days

of the home game with Manchester United. This was lost 4–2, and most famously saw Mrs Imre Varadi call in to a local radio station to express her husband's dissatisfaction with Eustace. The Owls' forward was immediately suspended, but within the week the Wednesday board put Eustace out of his misery, and to great media coverage, Ron Atkinson breezed in to take over as the club's third manager of the season.

Big Ron's first game in charge saw him thankful that a last minute Mark Procter goal would salvage a point in the home draw with Southampton. Within a fortnight, however, Atkinson had broken the club's transfer record, signing Carlton Palmer from West Bromwich for £550,000, with Colin West, rated at £200,000, leaving for West Brom as part of the deal. He also recruited Richie Barker as his assistant. Steve Whitton then arrived, as Sterland left in a record club move to Rangers. This was followed soon after by the shock transfer of Procter to Middlesbrough. The new boss then recorded his first win at home to Charlton Athletic, and a Hirst special at Luton took Wednesday out of the bottom three for the first time in over two months. Deadline-day in the transfer market saw the winger,

Dave Bennett, sign from Coventry City, and the West Bromwich keeper, Tony Godden, arrive on loan, though Atkinson lost out to Leeds United in the chase for Gordon Strachan. Another spectacular Hirst strike then sealed a victory at Newcastle in a proverbial six pointer, so that by mid-April the Owls were seemingly out of relegation danger.

Following the tragic semi-final events at Hillsborough, however, the Owls would play only one league game in a five week period; and this resulted in a slide back into the relegation waters. To gain vital match practice during this time of inactivity, Atkinson took his side to play friendly matches at Kettering and in Guernsey. But in the first home game since the disaster, West Ham won 2–0, setting the scene for a 'winner takes-all' encounter with the next visitors, Middlesbrough. A win for Wednesday was needed to keep them up and send Boro down; a task they achieved, when, after a flurry of corners, Steve Whitton headed home in front of a delirious Kop. The Owls were safe and at their final home game, to a standing ovation, Atkinson signed a new one year contract, thus ending perhaps the most traumatic season in Wednesday's history.

Floral tributes laid at the Leppings Lane entrance of Hillsborough reflecting the public's sorrow at the tragedy of 15th April 1989

1989–90
TOO GOOD TO GO DOWN?

Following the brush with relegation, manager Ron Atkinson spent the close season wheeling and dealing in the transfer market, with a total of nine players involved in his activities. The first move of the summer resulted in the Ipswich Town forward, Dalian Atkinson arriving for £450,000. He was followed by the Walsall duo, Craig Shakespeare and Mark Taylor, while Peter Shirtliff arrived, for a second spell at Hillsborough, from Charlton Athletic. David Hodgson headed for the exit door and moved to Japanese football, and Ian Cranson left Hillsborough, along with David Reeves, Tony Galvin and Siggi Jonsson. The ex-Aston Villa player, Gary Shaw, signed on a two month loan period from the Austrian club, Klagenfut; meanwhile Nigel Worthington signed a new contract after turning down the Champions, Arsenal. Wednesday then signed a new £100,000 shirt sponsorship deal with VT Plastics, and then returned to a traditional striped shirt to complete the preparations for the new season.

The Owls experienced a fairly gentle build up to the new season, opening with a three game winning salvo against non-league opposition, followed by a 2–1 win at the Belfast based club, Glentoran. However, their final game at Bramall Lane in United's centenary match, caused problems for Ron Atkinson, for in a goalless encounter the key midfielder, Carlton Palmer, managed to get himself sent off and suspended from league duty in the crucial early weeks of the season. Wednesday opened the new season at home to Norwich City, where, despite the presence of Palmer, the Canaries flew home with the three points to immediately burst the Owls pre-season optimism. Any hopes that the bad start was a blip also disappeared, as Wednesday then proceeded to gain only one point, and one goal in their first five matches, as they slipped to the foot of the table. Thanks to a Dalian Atkinson drive and a Kevin Pressman penalty save, the first win of the season came at home to Aston Villa; but there was to be no revival, and for once Big Ron was left speechless as his side were cut adrift in bottom spot. Further misery came when the minnows, Aldershot, then held a shot-shy Wednesday to a draw in the Rumbelows League Cup. To the astonishment of the fans, however, Wednesday proceeded to win 8–0 in the second leg, setting a new club record away victory, with Whitton netting four and Atkinson three. The next round saw a dramatic exit at Derby, where, despite taking the lead with only four minutes remaining, the Rams then scored twice to leave Wednesday to concentrate on rectifying their perilous league position.

That twentieth league position was to remain until Atkinson entered the transfer market, making a trio of outstanding signings which would totally turn the season around and trigger off a tremendous run of form which would hoist Wednesday towards a mid-table spot. The outstanding playmaker, John Sheridan, was the first to arrive from Nottingham Forest, followed by full-backs, Phil King and IFK Gothenburg's, Roland Nilsson. All three quickly became favourites, with the first two making winning starts in a surprise success at Forest. After several weeks of struggle the Owls were suddenly playing a highly entertaining brand of football, and with Sheridan at the heart of matters, Wednesday moved out of the bottom three in time for Christmas. Shortly before the Boxing Day defeat at Anfield, which saw Franz Carr play his first game in a three month loan, Wilf Rostron had joined Sheffield United on a free transfer, and Alan Harper left for Manchester City. The only other game of note at this time came in the Full Members Cup which was now sponsored by Zenith Data Systems, and for which the Blades visited Hillsborough, with over 30,000 creating a crowd record for the much maligned competition. With the teams locked at 2–2 in extra time, John Sheridan scored one of the most memorable goals seen at the ground in recent years, ensuring that 'Shezza' would attain hero status even before the subsequent events of April 1991!

The club's revival produced hopes of an FA Cup run, and this was heightened when Wolves were overcome to set up a fourth round clash with those old Cup foes, Everton. However, a high-noon Sunday clash went the Merseyside club's way through a Norman Whiteside double, and Cup glory was again put on ice. The month of January saw the first

John Sheridan in action v. Liverpool

appearance of John Harkes, who arrived on trial with goalie Tony Meola; while ex-England International, Trevor Francis signed on a free transfer from Queen's Park Rangers. Despite the Cup exit, Wednesday were still one of the form teams in the division, and an outstanding 4–1 win at Coventry City, plus a home success over Manchester United had the supporters looking with confidence towards a top ten finish. Around this same time, Atkinson sold Craig Shakespeare and the unfortunate Ian Knight. Then, to everyone's surprise, Franz Carr turned down the opportunity to join Wednesday on a permanent basis, returning instead to fight for his place at the City Ground. There was also a major change off the field, when, in a surprise move, 46-year-old Dave Richards was elected Chairman to replace the departing Bert McGee, whose belt tightening in the 1970s had effectively saved the club from extinction. McGee retired after holding the post since September 1975, with his successor, Richards seemingly as surprised as anyone at his elevation, having only been elected onto the board of directors at the AGM in October 1989. The new incumbent promised increased investment and exciting times ahead in the 1990s, though he and the Wednesday fans were in for a nasty shock in the remaining weeks of the season.

It is often said that football is a fickle mistress, and after victories in friendly games at Ryde Sports and in Sweden against Malmo, a couple of defeats caused a ripple amongst the Owls fans. However, no one really expected Wednesday to then be sucked back into the relegation danger area, though that is exactly what happened as the team proceeded to lose four consecutive games. A victory in the final away trip of the season was therefore of vital importance, and a Hirst brace helped beat Charlton 2–1, triggering celebratory scenes as the final whistle blew and the news came over the tannoy that relegation foes, Luton Town, had drawn—meaning that Wednesday were safe. The cruel reality for the thousands of travelling fans came later, when it was revealed that, in fact, Luton had hit a late winner, and meant that Wednesday still needed a point from their last home game against Nottingham Forest. The events at Hillsborough that final afternoon quickly became irrelevant, as Forest cruised to a 3–0 victory, so that all attention switched to Derby, where the visitors, Luton, had to win to send Wednesday down. At half-time the Hatters were holding Derby to a 2–2 draw after having led 2–0. However, gloom then descended back in Sheffield when Kingsley Black restored their lead; though this was dispelled and the ground exploded when the news came in that Derby had equalised, and this was confirmed on the Owls' scoreboard. However, as with events a week earlier, this was also found to be incorrect, and, at the final whistle, the Wednesday fans stood in total disbelief. Their team had suffered relegation after a season in which the quality of football on offer had been the best for several years. To compound matters, on the same day Sheffield United earned the right to take the Owls' place in the top flight, so that for the first time in eleven seasons the Blades would be playing in the higher grade.

Dave Richards on his appointment as Wednesday Chairman

1990–91
DOUBLE GLORY

In the immediate aftermath of a relegation there is usually speculation surrounding the future of the demoted club's manager. But such was the rapport that Ron Atkinson had built with the Wednesday fans, that even relegation could not put his position under pressure, and he rewarded that loyalty by vowing to get Wednesday back at the first attempt. Overall, the summer was relatively quiet, with Big Ron obviously confident that the side that had suffered relegation would be good enough for the task ahead. The major transfer activities of the close season all came in the same week in early August, when, in a shock move, Dalian Atkinson was sold to Real Sociedad for a huge new club record fee of £1.7m; with the Charlton Athletic forward, Paul Williams arriving to become Hirst's new attacking partner. The midfielder, Danny Wilson signed for the club, while other moves saw Tony Gregory sign for Halifax Town, Steve Whitton join the Swedish club, Halmstad, on loan, and the Preston winger, Brian Mooney arrive on loan—with a permanent transfer fee already agreed.

The pre-season started with a friendly against the Western League minnows, Dawlish Town. After putting eight past the Devon club, Wednesday then won comfortably at Torquay, before jetting off for two games in Italy. Optimism for the new season then soared as the top flight newcomers, Sheffield United, were well beaten in Lawrie Madden's testimonial, before, amazingly, the Owls hit eight again, this time at Crewe.

A huge travelling army of fans then followed their side to the opening league fixture at Ipswich, in which another tremendous display saw a superb 2–0 win get the season off to a flying start. A week later a fabulous individual display from David Hirst saw him net four times as Hull City were put to the sword, and a series of swashbuckling displays made Wednesday the team to watch as they remained unbeaten until late October, scoring four at Leicester City and at Brighton in the process. 'Old Timer' Trevor Francis then played his best game in a Wednesday shirt, as his home town club Plymouth were overwhelmed at Hillsborough, and Brentford were eventually overcome in the Rumbelows Cup, thanks to a brace of 2–1 wins. Off the pitch, John Harkes returned on trial, signing on a permanent basis a week later; Atkinson then signed a new 3-year contract and injury-hit Brian Mooney returned to Preston.

There was a double blow as the unbeaten start came to an end at Millwall, for in addition to the defeat, Roland Nilsson was stretchered off with an injury that would keep him out of action until early April. Thankfully for Wednesday, the newly signed Harkes slipped into the vacant spot, and made his debut as Swindon held the Owls to a home draw in the Rumbelows Cup; before a Nigel Pearson goal in the replay took Wednesday into the last sixteen. A tremendous match with the leaders, Oldham Athletic, followed, as a sell-out crowd witnessed a Wednesday comeback from two down to earn a deserved point. After netting seven in Mel Sterland's testimonial game at Leeds United, the Owls scored a sensational late win at West Bromwich, before the home fans witnessed the strange sight of Wednesday wearing their away kit for the home game with Notts County, when the visitors found their two strips clashed. The name of John Harkes then became well-known after an incredible 40-yard strike put Wednesday through in the League Cup at Derby County (a certain Mr Tango also earning his first dose of notoriety). And although they were not hitting the heights of their early season form, the Owls remained in the top three over the festive and New Year period. Cup football dominated the early weeks of 1991, with progress being made in both major competitions, as first, Mansfield, and then Millwall (after a thrilling 4–4 away draw) were beaten in the FA Cup. This handed Wednesday a fifth round tie with the Third Division high flyers, Cambridge United; the Owls never got started at the Abbey Stadium, however, and subsequently crashed 4–0. Wednesday were still in the Rumbelows Cup, though, after yet another Pearson goal had sealed the quarter-final tie at Coventry City. The club was therefore through to the semi-finals for the first time in their history, and had one foot in Wembley when goals from Hirst and Shirtliff secured a 2–0 first leg win at top flight Chelsea. The second leg provided one of those unforgettable Hillsborough nights, as the Owls completed a 5–1 aggregate win to guarantee a trip to Wembley for the first time since 1966.

Thankfully these Cup exploits were not having any detrimental effect on Wednesday's promotion push, and, with new signings Viv Anderson and Steve MacKenzie on board, the Owls became involved in a three horse race for the title, alongside Oldham and West Ham. This period also saw several comings and goings at Hillsborough, with Steve Whitton, Dean Barrick and Greg Fee all departing, as Michael Williams arrived from non-league Maltby, and Gordon Watson came in from Charlton Athletic. A run of three consecutive defeats over the Easter period then suddenly cast doubts over the Owls' chances of automatic promotion (three clubs would be promoted in this season), though a return to form steadied the nerves somewhat. A bumper home crowd then saw promotion rivals, Middlesbrough, beaten in Wednesday's final home game before the Cup Final meeting with Manchester United. Unfortunately, Carlton Palmer missed the final after being sent off in the game at Portsmouth two weeks earlier; but if he was missed, then Wednesday did not show it, for on a glorious afternoon every player gave one hundred per cent as they beat the hot favourites thanks to a 38th-minute strike by John Sheridan. Without doubt the man of the match was the Wednesday captain, Nigel Pearson, though all the Owls' players were equally deserving of praise after bringing the first major trophy to the club for 56 years. The Cup was paraded round the Wednesday pitch three days later, before the goalless home draw with Leicester City. The task now was to clinch promotion back to Division One, and two consecutive home wins kept the rapidly closing Notts County at bay; a draw at Port Vale meant that victory at home to Bristol City would then be required to clinch a famous double. A brace from Hirst secured the three points and one almighty promotion party started at the final whistle. A last minute

defeat at Oldham on the last day denied Wednesday the chance of the 'runners up' spot, but this was of little importance after an outstanding season which not only saw the first team claim the two honours, but also saw the reserves win the Central League for the first time since 1961, and the Juniors reach their first ever Youth Cup Final. Ron Atkinson won the Manager of the Month award on three occasions, and the campaign was rounded off nicely in mid-May, when 32-goal top scorer David Hirst was called into the full England squad following one of the greatest seasons in Wednesday's long history.

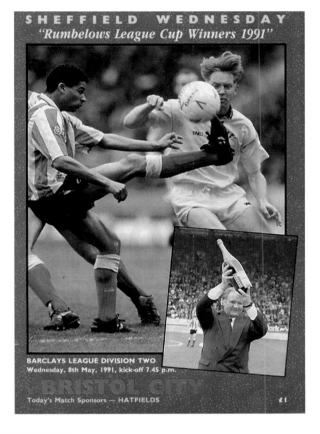

Wembley glory

1991–92
ATKINSON DEPARTS BUT OWLS STILL CLINCH A EURO SPOT

One event dominated the close season of 1991–92, with the fans running the gamut of emotions as boss Ron Atkinson left, returned, and then left again—to the bitter disappointment of Wednesdayites. There was no sign of the drama that was to come when Atkinson's first task of the summer was to give new contracts to Jon Newsome and Michael Williams. With hindsight, however, the surprise cut-price sale of Newsome and fellow defender, David Wetherall, to Leeds United for only £300,000, probably indicated that Atkinson had other things on his mind. Three days later, on the day of the club's civic reception, the shock news emerged that Atkinson was set to join his boyhood club, Aston Villa. However, the Owls fans were soon celebrating, for after hours of talks, Dave Richards apparently persuaded Big Ron to stay on. Atkinson's popularity then increased still further, when, after the Rumbelows Cup had been paraded through the streets of Sheffield, he stood on the Town Hall balcony and said 'I must have been barmy to think of leaving here'. That statement only succeeded in increasing the eventual fury of the fans, when a week later he quit; sparking off cries of 'Judas' from the distressed Wednesdayites. As the dust settled on the acrimonious split, the Owls were left searching for a new boss, and, after Ray Harford had spurned their advances, Trevor Francis was appointed as the club's first-ever player-manager. His first signing was the Oldham Athletic defender, Paul Warhurst, and, just before the new season started, he then smashed the club transfer record by paying £1.2m to Glasgow Rangers for the England keeper, Chris Woods.

Pre-season, the Owls broke new ground when they visited the United States for the first time. There, after beating Maryland Bays, they lost 2–0 to the US national side in Philadelphia, watched by almost 45,000 fans in a sweltering 94 degrees Fahrenheit. The slightly less glamorous setting of Belfast then saw Glentoran hit for six, before a visit to Portsmouth completed the warm up for the return to the big time. The fixture computer in use for this particular season must have had an 'irony chip' fitted, for on the opening day at Hillsborough, Wednesday were paired with Aston Villa and a 'certain ex-manager'. The ground was sold out, and on a sweltering day revenge was in the air as an outstanding goal from David Hirst, and a second from Danny Wilson, put Wednesday in command. Unfortunately though, it wasn't to be, and a flap from Woods at a corner got Villa back into the game just before the break. Second half strikes from ex-Owl, Dalian Atkinson, and future Blade, Dean Saunders, went on to give the visitors the points. In the week that followed, the veteran defender, Lawrie Madden, signed for Wolves, and the club signed a deal with Presto Tools for the sponsorship of the West Stand. Wednesday got off the mark with a point at Leeds and then never looked back, surging up the table into the top six with a series of tremendous displays. These included the unlikely event of

Trevor Francis

Carlton Palmer scoring a first-half hat-trick in the home game with Queen's Park Rangers, and a memorable home win over Manchester United. After having a £1m bid for Andy Sinton turned down, Trevor Francis then switched his attentions to the Forest striker, Nigel Jemson; and, after selling Mark Taylor to Shrewsbury Town, he made Jemson his third signing. Also arriving at Hillsborough was the outstanding Leyton Orient teenager, Chris Bart-Williams, who, to everyone's surprise— including his own—was given an immediate debut at home to Arsenal and performed like a seasoned top-flight player. Incidentally, in early October the Owls became part of an unwanted record when, despite travelling support of 1,000 fans, the attendance at Wimbledon numbered only 3,121, the lowest top flight crowd since the War. By Christmas the Owls had moved into third place, although their grip on the Rumbelows Cup had ended in a replay at Southampton; and what proved to be their last ever game in the Full Members Cup came at Notts County.

As 1992 dawned, bouts of illness and injury severely depleted the Wednesday squad and was a major reason behind the televised 6–1 home defeat to the eventual Champions, Leeds United. This shocking loss was, at the time, the club's heaviest home defeat in its history. Just before the Leeds debacle, Wednesday had signed a new sponsorship deal with the German confectionery firm,

Hosta Schokolade, and would have the name of their chewy bar 'Mr Tom' emblazoned across their shirts for the rest of the season. The month of January also saw the club miss out on the chance to sign Eric Cantona, when, after playing in a six-a-side game at Sheffield Arena, he refused Francis's request for a further trial period and signed instead for Leeds. Wednesday's hopes of FA Cup success then ended at home to Middlesbrough, after Preston had been beaten in the third round; and an astonishing game then took place at Arsenal in which Wednesday conceded six times in the final eighteen minutes to lose by an unbelievable 7–1. Phil King was then fined two weeks wages for refusing to play in the home game with West Ham United, after a bust up with Richie Barker; Julian Watts then signed from Rotherham United, and both Steve McCall and Steve MacKenzie moved to pastures new. Back in the league, the Owls remained in third spot, despite the Blades completing a costly double over them. A late run of form, though, suddenly gave Wednesday an outside

chance of pinching the title from under the noses of Leeds and Manchester United; with a victory in the final away game at Crystal Palace not only giving Wednesday the chance to temporarily sit at the top of the division, but to also clinch a UEFA Cup spot. The thousands of travelling fans were therefore in raptures when a rare Paul Williams header put the Owls ahead; however, a late equaliser from Mark Bright dashed those hopes—though the celebrations continued when news came through that Arsenal had drawn to ensure Wednesday would be back in Europe for the first time in almost twenty years. The first season under the management of Francis could not really have gone any better, as Wednesday continued to produce an exciting brand of soccer which saw the average crowd almost reach the 30,000 mark. The player of the season was Phil King, and, once again, the England regular, David Hirst, top-scored with 21 goals, in a season in which he passed the landmark of a century of goals for Sheffield Wednesday.

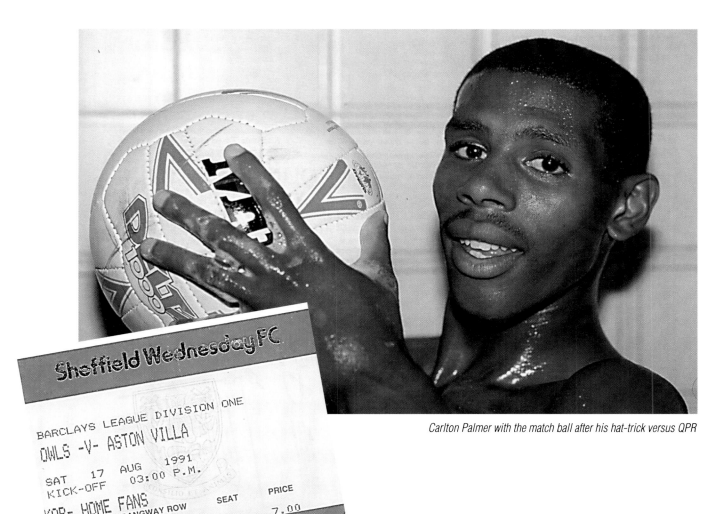

Carlton Palmer with the match ball after his hat-trick versus QPR

Memory Match

When Chelsea and Wednesday were drawn together in the quarter finals of the Milk Cup it meant a continuation of the rivalry which had built between the sides in the previous season when the two clubs had fought for the Second Division Championship. Several barbed comments by the outspoken Chelsea Chairman, Ken Bates, regarding Wednesday's style of play helped fan the flames, so there was little doubt that Bates would have been somewhat frustrated when the Owls held his side to a draw at Stamford Bridge in the first match. A goal from Lawrie Madden was enough to force a replay for Wednesday, although they had to thank the outstanding Martin Hodge for saving a penalty from the country's leading goalscorer, Kerry Dixon; as in a thrilling tie the home club also struck the post twice.

If the first game was considered to have been a tremendous Cup tie, then the replay must surely go down as one of the greatest Cup games ever to have been staged on British soil. Because the original game had been delayed, the replay took place only 48 hours later; and although the Owls were unchanged, the Londoners brought Jasper in to replace Pates. A crowd of over 36,000 packed Hillsborough, the majority hoping to see Wednesday finally progress into the last four for the first time. They were then witness to a totally one-sided first half, which finished with Wednesday three goals ahead and seemingly on their way to the semi-finals. The goal feast started as early as the eighth minute when Mick Lyons headed in Andy Blair's free kick. That lead was doubled after 21 minutes when trickery from Blair allowed Lee Chapman to head home at the far post. Wednesday's fans were in dreamland, and on the stroke of half-time the route to Wembley was being checked after a superb solo run from Brian Marwood ended with him striking a curling shot into the top corner. At this point Chelsea looked to be a well beaten side that had totally lost the plot. They'd already had four players booked, and Wednesday fans had been incensed when Micky Thomas had flattened Blair out of the sight of the referee.

It was fully expected Wednesday would press home their advantage in the second half against a bedraggled visiting side. In retrospect, however, it was an injury to Colin Lee on the stroke of the interval that was to totally change the direction of the match, for within ten seconds of the restart his replacement, Paul Canoville, ran straight through the middle of a sleeping home defence to reduce the arrears. From that point on the Owls seemed to totally lose confidence and cohesion, and mid-way through the period, Kerry Dixon ran on to a Thomas pass and rounded Hodge for his 28th goal of the season. The home fans could hardly believe what they were seeing, as the situation worsened nine minutes later. Sloppy play from Varadi gifted the ball to Spackman, who started a counter-attack which ended with Mickey Thomas curling in an equaliser from the edge of the box. With four minutes remaining, Hillsborough fell silent as Canoville completed the incredible transformation in fortunes. At this point many of the fans made for the exits, no doubt shaking their heads at how their side could throw away the chance of glory. However, those who left early missed the final twist in this remarkable match, for with just 22 seconds left in normal time, Mel Sterland surged into the opposition area and was clearly upended by Rougvie. The referee pointed to the spot and it was Sterland who took the responsibility to gleefully fire home to take the game into extra time. The excitement continued unabated in the extra thirty minutes, with chances coming at both ends. With five minutes left, Canoville ran clean through only for Hodge to make a crucial block to ensure the teams would return to Stamford Bridge a week later, after Bert McGee had lost the toss for choice of venue. The result eventually went the way of the Pensioners, but the tie will always be remembered for the match which was, without doubt, one of the most sensational games seen at Hillsborough in its one hundred years.

Wednesday: Hodge, Sterland, Peter Shirtliff, Madden, Lyons, Worthington, Marwood, Blair, Varadi, Chapman (Oliver 109), Shelton

Chelsea: Niedzwiecki, K. Jones, Rougvie, Lee (Canoville ht), McLoughlin, Jasper, Nevin, Spackman, Speedie, Dixon, Thomas

Referee: G. Tyson (Sunderland)

Milk Cup 5th Round Replay
Wednesday 30th January 1985

A breather before extra-time

Lee Chapman scores no. 2

Sheffield Wednesday 4
Chelsea 4

Memory Match

Dalian Atkinson in full flow

Carlton Palmer celebrates his late strike

Sheffield Wednesday 3

Sheffield United 2

Many people probably do not even recall the Full Members Cup which was introduced in 1985 following the European ban imposed by UEFA after the Heysel stadium disaster. The competition was sponsored by the likes of Simod, and Zenith Data in its time, but was constantly dogged by poor crowds, with even a Wembley final sometimes failing to catch the public imagination. The Owls won only three ties in the seven years the trophy was played for, but the competition did provide one of the greatest Hillsborough nights in recent history when the draw meant the two Sheffield teams met for their first competitive encounter in nine years. An all-ticket Hillsborough crowd of over 30,000 set a tournament record for a game outside of the Wembley final, and provided a sharp contrast in styles—with Dave Bassett's United preferring a direct route, while the Owls tended to play a more cultured brand of football.

It was United who created a flurry of early chances, with Ian Bryson missing the best of these when he shot straight at Pressman. Hirst was then guilty of missing a gilt edged chance for Wednesday. However, the first goal came to the Owls, and it was a superb strike from Dalian Atkinson after 19 minutes that broke the deadlock. The Wednesday forward had already caused problems for the Blades with his pace, and they could do little when he latched onto a long pass from Madden, turned inside United's two central defenders, and then crashed home a fierce low shot on the run past a bemused Simon Tracey. Despite falling behind, the visitors continued to create chances, though it needed a mistake from Kevin Pressman to allow them to find an equaliser, as the goalkeeper failed to hold a low drive from Bryson and Brian Deane was quickly in to force the ball home.

The first half was a thrilling spectacle for the big crowd, generating a typical derby atmosphere, and it was the team whose fans sported the blue and white favours that dominated the second half, as United were unable to rediscover their earlier form. The Wednesday dangerman, Dalian Atkinson, went close twice, and the Owls' fans were celebrating what looked to be the winning goal when, with only four minutes remaining, the United defence was caught napping to allow Carlton Palmer to sidefoot home a Nigel Worthington pass. The Blades then poured every man forward and fingernails were bitten to the quick on the Kop as Wednesday tried to withstand the late flurry. Unfortunately, the task was beyond them, and in the final minute Deane drove in a low ball which flew in off Bob Booker, the United cult favourite, to force extra time. In retrospect the Wednesday fans were probably grateful to Booker, for if he had not scored that late equaliser they would have been denied one of the greatest goals seen at Hillsborough. With the first period of extra time only four minutes old, the man of the match, John Sheridan, won the ball just inside his own half outside the centre circle, and proceeded to run at the United defence down the left hand channel. No challenge came from the back-pedalling Blades defence, and when 'Shezza' reached the edge of the box he effortlessly cut inside two defenders before joyously firing a right foot shot into the roof of the net. That wonder goal deserved a bigger stage than that of the little Zenith Cup, but this mattered little to the Wednesday fans, for their only interest was that the tremendous goal proved enough to beat the near neighbours and reaffirm Wednesday's position as top dogs in the City.

Wednesday: Pressman, Pearson, King, Palmer, Peter Shirtliff, Madden, Bennett (Shakespeare 105), Sheridan, Hirst, Atkinson, Worthington (Unused sub—Lycett)

United: Tracey, Hill, Barnes, Booker, Stancliffe, Morris, Bradshaw (Francis 75), Gannon, Agana (Webster 81), Deane, Bryson

Referee: Mr J. Worrall (Warrington)

Memory Match

Wednesday went into the home leg with Chelsea knowing that a visit to the twin towers was within their reach. Four days earlier they had recorded a stunning 2–0 win at Stamford Bridge, and, unsurprisingly, were now the hot favourites to reach their first major final since 1966. The scene was therefore set, with Hillsborough a sell-out and an unchanged Wednesday side desperate to complete the job which had began so well in West London.

Only those who were there on the actual night can fully comprehend the incredible atmosphere generated by 30,000 home fans on one of the most emotional occasions in the club's history. The constant singing and general din caused by the Wednesday fans made for a truly memorable evening which started before the game kicked off and continued until well after the final whistle. On the field of play the visitors pushed forward in the early stages, but Nigel Pearson and Peter Shirtliff were a rock at the back. Wednesday, who had become the dominant force, then looked to have scored when Pearson bundled the ball home following a corner. Unfortunately, the goal was disallowed, though eleven minutes before half time the Hillsborough party began as Pearson leapt to send a classic header past Beasant. The whole ground burst into song with 'Que Sera, Sera, Whatever will be, will be, we're going to Wembley'. The noise level increased even further, when, eight minutes later, Danny Wilson scored a classic second. A long ball from Shirtliff was headed down by David Hirst to Carlton Palmer. He nudged it back to Wilson, who crashed an unstoppable volley into the top corner, to send the Wednesday fans into raptures. With the Owls effectively four goals ahead at the break, even the fans who had been at Hillsborough seven years earlier must have known that this time there was no way back for Chelsea.

Though the Londoners tried to salvage some pride in the second half, the Owls were in no mood to surrender possession and they performed in a totally professional manner with 'Captain Fantastic', Nigel Pearson, the leading light on a night when every player was a hero. With twenty-five minutes remaining, a ripple of doubt did spread round the ground when Graham Stuart pulled one back for Chelsea, but the visitors simply could not create the requisite chances to make a game of the tie. As the match entered its final ten minutes the Wednesdayites celebrations increased and were even unaffected when a Townsend shot was turned onto a post by Chris Turner. A glorious night was completed in the final minute when the sub, Paul Williams, ran onto McCall's pass to neatly lob the ball into the net to wrap up a 3–1 victory, and ensure Wednesday reached the promised land after a comprehensive 5–1 aggregate win. At the final whistle Hillsborough erupted and the fans swarmed onto the pitch to celebrate a day that many thought they would never see. A tannoy announcement cleared the playing surface, and to chants of 'We want Ron', Manager Atkinson responded with a clenched fist salute. The players then did a lap of honour and renditions of 'We Love you Wednesday' and 'High Ho Sheffield Wednesday' rounded off a night when both supporters and team gave their all.

Wednesday: Turner, Harkes, King, Palmer, Shirtliff, Pearson, Wilson (McCall 86), Sheridan, Hirst, Francis (Williams 69), Worthington

Chelsea: Beasant, Clarke, Dorigo, Townsend, Cundy, Monkou, Stuart, Dickens, Dixon, Durie, Wise (Unused subs—McAllister, Lee)

Referee: Mr R. Milford (Bristol)

Rumbelows Cup Semi-final—2nd Leg
Wednesday February 27th 1991

Sheffield Wednesday
3
Chelsea
1

Chapter 9

The Premiership
1992–99

1992–93
SO NEAR BUT YET SO FAR

After achieving their best league finish for over thirty years, the Owls and their fans were confident that a repeat was on the cards in the following season. The first task of Manager, Francis, was to release four players, including Darren Wood and the long-time, reserve full-back, Scott Cam. Within a few weeks, though, he'd secured one of the best signings in the club's history, when the ex-England International, Chris Waddle, was persuaded to join from Marseilles, in a £1m deal. Waddle was the only major signing made by the club in the summer months, but for once this did not attract criticism, as the squad at Wednesday's disposal was, without doubt, one of the best in the League. It was of equal importance that John Sheridan, Viv Anderson and Nigel Worthington had all put their names to new contracts, along with David Hirst, who signed a new lucrative four-year deal amid rumours that Manchester United were poised to make a record offer. The Owls refused to entertain offers, however, and were themselves rumoured to be entering the race for a certain Alan Shearer. These were indeed heady days for Wednesday supporters, and their club were amongst the favourites for the inaugural FA Premier League, which kicked off the season after BSkyB had signed a £304m deal for the exclusive TV rights. Unfortunately for the Premier League club supporters, the statement made by a Wednesday director that this deal would end the situation where fans had to pay high entrance fees did not quite run true! Meanwhile, one of the most exciting days of the whole close season came in mid July, when the European Competition draw took place in Geneva. The Owls were seeded 43 out of the 64 teams in the UEFA Cup, and were quite pleased when the Luxembourg minnows, 63rd seeded, Spora, came out of the hat.

Wednesday's pre-season preparations started with two games in Ireland, before Waddle made his debut in a draw at West Bromwich. Local rivals, Rotherham United, then won at Millmoor, before the Owls were thrashed 4–0 at AEK Athens in a match organised with the UEFA cup in mind, and to give Wednesday an experience of a hostile European environment. The first game for the club in the new Premier League ended in a 1–1 draw at Everton, with the travelling fans dismayed to see their new hero, Chris Waddle stretchered off just before half-time. He would be out for four games, but in that time the Owls—and especially David Hirst—experienced mixed fortunes. A crude tackle by Arsenal's, Steve Bould, at Highbury broke Hirst's ankle; this not only helped the Gunners end the Owls' unbeaten record, but started a catalogue of injuries that would stop Hirsty from ever reaching the heights that looked to be his destiny. That loss in North London was the start of three successive defeats, with the pre-season optimism looking to have been misplaced as Wednesday surprisingly languished in the bottom six. Steps were then taken to rectify the matter, with the prolific forward, Mark Bright, being signed from Crystal Palace for £500,000, with the £375,000 rated Paul Williams going in the opposite direction. The new man made a winning start at Nottingham Forest, though

it was a goal by Paul Warhust which proved a sign of things to come, as boss Francis experimented with a forward role for the defender. The pacey Warhust impressed to the extent that he retained the forward role for the home leg of the UEFA Cup game versus Spora; where, despite scoring twice, all the post-match headlines focused on his near-death after he collided with the opposition goalie. In the collision Warhust swallowed his tongue, and only the prompt action of the Owls' physio, Alan Smith, saved his life. Warhust, who was unconscious for 20 minutes, spent several days in hospital before making a full recovery. The same week also saw Wednesday sign a club record sponsorship deal with the Sheffield Computer firm, Sanderson, while a proposed swap involving Nottingham Forest's, Kingsley Black, and the Owls' Nigel Jemson finally collapsed. The club's first appearance on Sky saw Spurs beaten at Hillsborough, though Wednesday were then in the middle of a major injury crisis, which, at one point, resulted in ten first team players being out of action. The club rode the storm, however, and there was good news in Luxembourg when the returning Paul Warhurst fittingly scored with a header as an under-strength Wednesday completed a comfortable 10–1 aggregate win.

After a draw at Hartlepool secured Wednesday's progress in the League Cup (now sponsored by Coca Cola) two games were played in South Africa, with Government pressure causing a change of heart after the original plans had been abandoned. In the league, the club still remained in the bottom half, though Cup football kept the spirits high as Wednesday cruised through to the last eight of the Coca Cola Cup, and played two titanic games with Kaiserslautern which ended in a controversial aggregate defeat. Off the pitch, Wednesday angrily rejected two Manchester United bids for the services of Hirst, while the £3m offer for Waddle by the French club, Toulon, was also turned away. A seven match winless run finally ended at home to QPR, then in front of Hillsborough's best crowd of the season, the Boxing Day encounter with Manchester United saw the visitors come back from three down to share six goals. The New Year proved to be the launching pad for Wednesday's season, for in the ensuing weeks the Owls recorded an incredible thirteen wins in a sixteen game unbeaten run which took them all the way up to fourth place, as well as seeing them reach the semi-finals of the Coca Cola Cup and the last eight of the FA Cup. The football on show in this period was without doubt the most entertaining to be played by the club in the 1990s, and for many, the apex was reached at Blackburn Rovers in the first leg of the Coca Cola Cup. There, in a sensational thirty minute period, the Owls crashed in four goals to effectively clinch a Wembley appearance with a 4–2 victory. Meanwhile, in the

Premier Cup competition, Cambridge, Sunderland and Southend fell by the wayside before Wednesday drew 3–3 at Derby, in yet another sensational game in a season of unforgettable matches. The City of Sheffield then experienced what was arguably the greatest week in its history, as the Cup draw then paired United and Wednesday together in the semi-final, if both could win their replays. The Blades duly earned their place, and twenty-four hours later a Warhurst goal set up an all-Sheffield semi-final, which was to be played at Elland Road. However, the other semi-final was an all North London affair, and after it had been switched to Wembley, the FA was bombarded by indignant Sheffield football fans who demanded equal rights. The governing body eventually bowed to public pressure and the meeting between the sides proved to be one of the greatest occasions in the history of both clubs. In the end the tie went Wednesday's way, thanks to Waddle's goal and an extra-time winner from Mark Bright. All the headlines, however, were grabbed by the defender-turned-striker, Paul Warhurst, who became the first man since Redfern Froggatt, in 1958, to score in six consecutive games for Wednesday. Such was his form that he even received a call-up to the full England side, and his eighteen goals helped the Owls to become the first side to reach both domestic Cup finals. Unfortunately, both finals were against a dour Arsenal side and despite an early goal from John Harkes, the Coca Cola Cup Final was lost as the Gunners came back to score twice. By this time, the Owls had signed a new two-year, £800,000 deal with Sanderson; and Mick Mills had been appointed chief scout, with Clive Baker moving to Youth development.

No doubt a whole book could be written about the 1992–93 season, for as the final weeks approached, Chris Waddle was voted the 'Football Writers Player of the Year'—the first and only time a Wednesday player has received the honour in its 45-year existence. Near the end of the season the sheer volume of games resulted in the Owls slipping out of the top six, as many inexperienced players such as Ryan Jones and Simon Stewart were given their chance to shine. The campaign finally ended on a Thursday in late May, when the FA Cup Final was replayed following David Hirst's equaliser in the first game. This time a Chris Waddle second-half leveller took the game into extra time, and in the very last minute of the 63rd and last game of the season Arsenal won a corner. The season had been the most remarkable in the club's history, the Wednesday fans had been treated to some magnificent displays, and so no one could now bring themselves to believe that the football gods would deny them at least one trophy. However, Andy Linighan was on the end of the corner kick, and despite sending a seemingly weak header goalwards, keeper Woods could only help it into the roof of the net, as total despair engulfed a disbelieving Wednesday support.

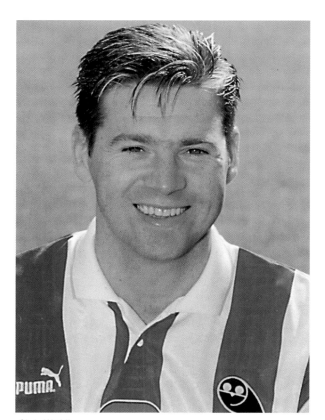

Chris Waddle

1993–94
OWLS SPLASH OUT BUT SUCCESS IS ELUSIVE

So far, the 1990s had seen the Owls up with the leading clubs in the English game, and this position was seemingly strengthened in the summer of 1993 as Wednesday invested heavily in a bid to be among the search for honours. For the second year running the Owls secured the signature of an outstanding ex-England International as Des Walker signed from Italian club, Sampdoria, for a club record £2.75m fee. Coventry City's giant centre-half, Andy Pearce, also signed for the club, while the long-serving Peter Shirtliff ended a 359 game association with the Owls when he moved to Wolves. However, it was the transfer deal that didn't take place that made all the headlines, as the shock sale of Paul Warhurst to Blackburn Rovers for £3m was called off when it emerged that Wednesday had failed in a sensational bid to secure Sheffield United's prize asset, Brian Deane; sparking off memories of a similarly audacious but unsuccessful bid that Wednesday made in the late 1940s for the United star man, Jimmy Hagan. The close season also saw Viv Anderson and Danny Wilson join Barnsley as manager and coach respectively, while both Warhurst and Carlton Palmer signed lucrative new contracts; though one player who spurned a new contract offer was John Harkes. Finally, not only did Wednesday announce a £1m kit deal with Puma, but also announced record season ticket figures in both monetary and numerical terms.

Everything was therefore geared for another successful season, with the optimism heightened for those fans who travelled to the South West for the start of the pre-season warm up, as Bodmin Town, Plymouth Argyle and then Exeter City were ruthlessly despatched, with the Owls crashing in 20 goals in the process. The Irish side, Glentoran were then hit for seven, and a draw at Glasgow Celtic and victory at Bramall Lane were the final away games before the new season kicked off in glorious sunshine at Anfield. Somewhat typically, when

Des Walker

everyone expected a great start, the absolute opposite then occurred, for the Owls won only a single point and failed to score in their opening four games! During this terrible start there was a flurry of transfer activity, with, firstly, Warhust finally signing for Blackburn Rovers. Owls fans were then highly delighted to beat rivals, Arsenal, for the signature of the England International winger, Andy Sinton, who joined in a club record equalling big-money move. There was also some sadness at the departure of the popular John Harkes to Derby County, while the sale of the reserve striker, David Johnson completed a busy first few weeks of the season for Trevor Francis. Off the field, the club's search for honours was reflected in the annual accounts which not only showed an increase of a third in the wage bill to £4.7m, but highlighted a massive four year rise in turnover, from £2.7m to £12.8m. The first goal of the new campaign finally came from Mark Bright at Chelsea, but there would be no immediate revival, and in late October Wednesday still languished in the bottom three. However, a 6–1 friendly win at Enfield seemed to boost confidence, and three days later Carlton Palmer scored one of the goals of the season as Ipswich Town were routed 4–1 at Portman Road. Victories over Middlesbrough and at Queen's Park Rangers, courtesy of a Ryan Jones spectacular late

diving header, took the Owls through to the last eight of the Coca Cola Cup; as by the end of the old year, Wednesday had moved up to tenth spot in the league. Other events saw the little-known Australian, Adam Poric, signing from Sydney Budapest, whilst injuries and player unrest beset Francis as Wednesday struggled to live up to their pre-season billing. Both Nigel Pearson and Michael Williams suffered broken legs, and after Phil King quit Hillsborough only to return seven days later, the biggest bombshell was dropped by the outstanding full-back, Roland Nilsson, who asked to be released to return home to Sweden. A compromise was eventually reached whereby 'Rolo' would be given a free transfer at the end of the season, but could play only for Helsingborg for the remaining two years of his Wednesday contract. The one piece of good news in this period came from the FA, who officially confirmed Hillsborough as being one of the venues for the 1996 European Championship Finals.

A great start to 1994 resulted in Wednesday progressing in both Cups, with a rare long-range special from Mark Bright earning a tremendous Coca Cola Cup quarter final victory at Wimbledon. A win at Nottingham Forest put Wednesday through in the FA Cup, while in the Premier League, Spurs were beaten in monsoon conditions at Hillsborough, and Owls fans were in raptures when short-term, cult hero, Andy

Pearce, was one of the scorers in a derby win over Sheffield United. Boss, Francis, was then named Manager of the Month, though injuries still dogged his side's progress, with Waddle, Worthington and Nilsson all in plaster. One player on his way back, however, was David Hirst; and such was the affection in which he was held by Owls' fans, that around 10,000 packed Hillsborough for his return in a Central League game against Sheffield United. Unfortunately, within a few weeks Hirst was injured again, missed the rest of the season, and was joined on the sidelines by Andy Sinton who suffered a stress fracture of his foot. Meanwhile, off the field, there was general surprise when the long serving physio, Alan Smith, quit the club to concentrate on his private practice; with Dave Galley taking his place. Following a draw at Chelsea, the Owls then disappointingly crashed out of the FA Cup in the Hillsborough replay; and there was more home Cup misery in the Coca Cola competition, when, despite only losing 1–0 in the first leg at Old Trafford, visitors Manchester United then coasted to a 5–1 aggregate win, much to the embarrassment of Wednesday fans. The season had turned somewhat sour by now and a greatly under-strength side were thrashed at Old Trafford during a winless run of eight league and cup games. Thankfully though, a midweek trip to 'Sunny Spain' to play a friendly against Real Madrid in Cordoba, seemed to do the squad the world of good, and Wednesday then embarked on a nine-game unbeaten run up to the end of the season. This lifted them into a respectable seventh place after a season fraught with problems both on and off the pitch.

1994–95
FRANCIS DEPARTS AS WEDNESDAY FLIRT WITH RELEGATION

Wednesday prepared for the new season hoping that the problems encountered in the previous campaigns, both on and off the field, would not be repeated. Boss, Trevor Francis, was certainly a busy man in the transfer market as he radically overhauled his squad. This resulted in the departure of many of the players who contributed to the successes of the early 1990s. The first to leave was the midfield dynamo, Carlton Palmer, who signed for Leeds United. Within a week, the long serving full-back, Nigel Worthington, had followed him to Elland Road after rejecting a new contract. Incidentally 'Irish' moved only weeks after becoming the first Wednesday player to earn 50 caps for his country. Phil King also left, and on the plus side, the club then spent just short of £5m attempting to replace the old heroes—with Port Vale's highly rated midfielder, Ian Taylor, being the first capture. He was followed into Hillsborough by Peter Atherton, with the Rumanian World Cup star, Dan Petrescu, being the next to put pen to paper. Throughout the close season Francis also tracked the Tranmere Rovers defender, Ian Nolan—even though, almost by the week, his price rose—before finally, Wednesday paid somewhat over-the-odds for a player who had no top flight experience.

The opening match of Wednesday's pre-season fixture list saw new ground broken on two counts, not only did the Owls pay a first ever visit to Japan, but also played an indoor, 11-a-side match for the first time, when Yomiuri Verdy were faced in the Tokyo Dome. The same venue saw Shimizu S-Pulse beaten 4–3 in front of another near 45,000 crowd, before friendlies against Dundalk, Glenavon, Sunderland, Hibs, Sheffield United and Mansfield Town completed a somewhat congested 25 days of warm up games. The debut of the Spurs new signing, Jørgen Klinsmann, ensured that the opening game of the season would attract not only a sell-out crowd, but would draw the national media to Hillsborough. The German duly scored in a thrilling game, with Wednesday almost grabbing a draw after a seven goal bonanza. A Gordon Watson strike was enough to eventually give Wednesday their first win of the season at Wimbledon, though the team that Francis had built was failing to gel, and only a handful of players still remained from Atkinson's time. Now, as in the previous campaign, the Owls found themselves in the lower reaches of the Premier League, and left the fans looking for a Christmas revival. Despite purchasing the PSV Eindhoven midfielder, Klas Ingesson, problems mounted off the field for Francis—a Sunday newspaper ran a story from a Hillsborough 'mole' which slated his tactics. The name of the mole was never revealed, Francis was supported by several of the players, and this ensured that the story would prove to be a storm in a tea cup. One of the handful of victories that the Owls did manage to record in the early months of the season came at Ipswich Town, where, following a last minute winner from Hirst, the travelling

Wednesday fans and watching Sky viewers were witness to an unprecedented sight, as the usually unflappable Des Walker was red-carded after the final whistle, following the 'minor misdemeanour' of head-butting the Ipswich player, Simon Milton. Indeed, the Owls had four players sent off in the season, with Kevin Pressman twice making the 'early walk', a situation which perhaps gives some indication of the frustrations that were starting to show on the field of play as Wednesday struggled to pull out of danger.

With hindsight, one single signing was all that was needed to effectively save the Owls from relegation, for after the arrival of the striker, Guy Whittingham, the club embarked on a ten game unbeaten run, which included successive victories in the ex-Army man's first three appearances. Whittingham, who arrived from Aston Villa for a fee of £700,000 (with the £1m rated, Ian Taylor, going in the opposite direction) could not have wished for a better start, scoring twice on his debut as Wednesday recorded a stunning 4–1 victory at Everton on Boxing Day. Two days later, Chris Waddle, now back from long term injury, helped Whittingham to score another brace, as Coventry City were well beaten at Hillsborough; before a long range effort from Graham Hyde completed a fabulous festive period with the only goal at

Chris Bart-Williams

Filbert Street. The New Year brought a series of league draws, plus a victory at Gillingham in the FA Cup, where Lance Key made an heroic substitute appearance following Pressman's red card just before the interval. Unfortunately, the next Cup match brought First Division Wolves to Hillsborough, and, after Chris Bart-Williams had missed a late penalty, the replay at Molineaux was lost in such unbelievable circumstances that the confidence of the team was badly affected for the remainder of the season. After the tie had been drawn 1–1, the outcome was decided by penalties; and, after leading 3–0 in the shoot-out, Wednesday then somehow managed to lose 4–3 after a dozen spot kicks. Three straight defeats immediately followed this Cup debacle, with only a Waddle inspired win at Leeds United lifting the spirits of Owls' fans, as their side lost all the ground that had been gained in the earlier unbeaten run. The situation came to a head at Hillsborough on April Fool's Day, when Nottingham Forest inflicted the biggest home defeat in the club's history. The 7–1 trouncing sparked calls for the manager's head, though Francis weathered the storm. However, the slump continued to such an extent that, on the last day of the season, at least a point was required to guarantee Premier League football in the following term. Thankfully for the Wednesdayites, the danger of relegation disappeared when Whittingham netted in the opening minutes,

and in the end a comfortable 4–1 win brought a huge sigh of relief from everyone concerned. During their losing run Wednesday had spent £50,000 on Doncaster Rovers, O'Neill Donaldson, though a considerably greater amount was recouped when Gordon Watson was sold to Southampton. Within a month 'Flash' was facing his old team as he guested at the Valley for Charlton Athletic in Bob Bolder's testimonial game. Meanwhile the Club expressed their sadness when their previous Chairman, Bert McGee, passed away at his home. However, the season still had a late twist in the tail, for on Cup Final day the news was released that manager, Trevor Francis had parted company by 'mutual consent' and the search was on for Wednesday's 15th post-war boss.

SHEFFIELD
WEDNESDAY
FOOTBALL
CLUB Plc

Sample the
Wednesday
atmosphere
any day
of the week

1995–96
PLEAT ARRIVES BUT FORTUNES DETERIORATE FURTHER

It quickly became apparent that the Luton Town manager, David Pleat, was the board's number one choice to replace Francis. However, Pleat's Chairman, David Kohler, was not so enthusiastic about the idea, and after Pleat left to join Wednesday, Kohler obtained a court injunction to stop his old manager taking up his new post. It was therefore, not until late June that the two clubs agreed to go to FA arbitration, and another month before the issue was finalised, with Wednesday paying £150,000 compensation in an out-of-court settlement. Before the new man had been appointed, the Owls agreed to be one of the English representatives in UEFA's newly revamped Intertoto Cup. However, the timing of the first game was such that the Youth Coach, Clive Baker, was temporarily in charge when the Owls travelled to Switzerland to face Basel. With several players still on holiday, the Owls were forced to field a scratch side containing several unknown faces; however, they battled gamely before losing 1–0 to the experienced home side. The Owls two home games were played at Millmoor, with the Polish side Gornik Zabrze, and Aarhus from Denmark both being beaten. Despite achieving a draw in Germany against Karlsruher, the Owls then just missed out on qualifying for the next stage. During the time Wednesday were attempting to battle through to the

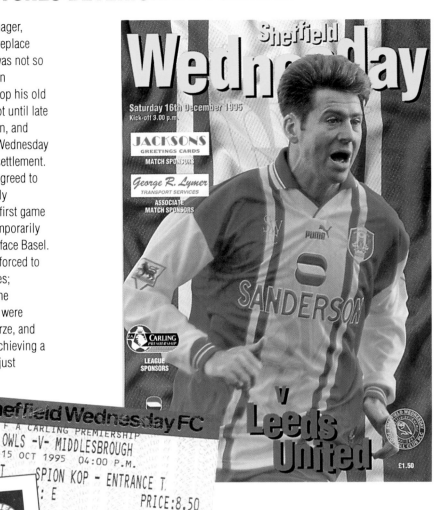

UEFA Cup, new boss, Pleat, was making changes both on and off the field of play. The first of these saw Danny Begara appointed as Head Coach, with Ritchie Barker moving to a newly created position as 'Director of Football Development'. Chris Bart-Williams then left for Nottingham Forest, with Wednesday subsequently receiving a record tribunal fee of £2.5m. The Owls then launched their new Ajax-style home kit, and Pleat's first signings proved to be Anderlecht's Belgium captain, Marc Degrsye, and the Derby County midfielder, Mark Pembridge. The new manager also tried unsuccessfully to persuade Roland Nilsson to return to Sheffield, while Chris Waddle turned down the chance of a coaching role at Hillsborough to concentrate on playing.

Despite having played four competitive games in Europe, Wednesday still played the same number of pre-season games, and the fans were optimistic for the new season after

Dan Petrescu

Birmingham City, Rotherham United, Sheffield United and Kettering Town were all beaten away from home. Warm-up games, however, are a notoriously bad indicator of a side's true form; and despite beating the Champions, Blackburn Rovers in their first home game, the Owls would find themselves in the lower reaches of the new 20-club Premier League for the whole of a disappointing first season under Pleat's reign. Highlights were few and far between in the first half of the campaign, with the televised 4–3 home victory over Coventry City and an astonishing 6–2 home win over their Yorkshire rivals, Leeds United, being the only matches to stand out. Wednesday did progress in the Coca Cola Cup though, beating Crewe 5–2 on aggregate and winning 2–0 at Millwall. However, a trip to Highbury in the Fourth Round proved fruitless, as usual. By this time, Dan Petrescu had engineered a transfer to Chelsea and Klas Ingesson had moved to Italian football. Andy Pearce signed for

Wimbledon, and the veteran, Steve Nicol, arrived for a nominal fee. The biggest transfer move during Pleat's tenure saw the Owls pay £4.5m for the talents of the Red Star Belgrade duo, Darko Kovacevic and Dejan Sefanovic. The deal almost collapsed, however, because of red tape, fully seven weeks after the twosome had been signed, they still had not been issued with work permits by the Department of Employment. The club was on the verge of aborting the transfer, when, thankfully, the permits were granted and Kovacevic scored twice on his full home debut, instantly endearing himself to the Hillsborough faithful—unfortunately the goals proved to be the high spot of a disappointingly short Wednesday career.

The New Year brought an unhappy FA Cup exit at the hands of First Division Charlton Athletic, leaving Wednesday with the task of ensuring their Premiership status would be maintained for another year. Andy Sinton then left the club for Tottenham, while the loan of John Sheridan to Birmingham City was see by many of the fans as being just short of a criminal act. To boost his struggling side, Pleat then acquired the services of the dreadlocked winger, Regi Blinker, in a cut price deal with Feyernoord, in one of the first cases of a Bosman influenced transfer. Pleat then spent £1.6m to bring Jon Newsome back to Hillsborough, almost five years after he had left. The Dutch winger made a quite remarkable start to his English league career, netting two sparkling goals on his debut in a 3–2 defeat at Aston Villa. However, despite a rash of 'Regi wigs' quickly appearing in the Owls' shop, there was no sudden surge up the table—although consecutive wins at home to Villa and away at Southampton did ease the pressure somewhat. The form of Marc Degryse was arguably the one major plus in a poor season, and it was he who scored the winner at home to Arsenal in a vital Easter Monday meeting that blew away some of the relegation clouds which had been forming over the club. The victory over the Gunners certainly proved to be important, for Wednesday then failed to win any of their final four games; and were embarrassed when a devastating Andrei Kanchelskis hat-trick led Everton to a 5–2 win in Wednesday's final home outing of the season. That heavy defeat meant Wednesday travelled to West Ham on the final Sunday knowing that a point was required to guarantee safety. However, the scores which were being reported from elsewhere in the country made the requirement somewhat academic, and even a Dicks goal for the Hammers did not unduly worry the noisy travelling support. A comeback by relegation rivals, Manchester City, then caused quite a few flutters, until a last-minute headed equaliser from Jon Newsome took Wednesday to the traditional forty point safety mark; which on this occasion proved to be enough as the Owls finished two points away from the dreaded drop.

1996–97
GREAT START HELPS PUSH FOR EUROPE

On his arrival as Manager, David Pleat said it would take three years for him to bring success to the club, and, after a poor showing first time out, he realised major surgery was required to stop the rot. His first action was to sell Chris Woods to NASL club, Denver, and, within the week the backroom staff of Frank Barlow (Reserve Team Manager), Mick Mills (Chief Scout), and Arvel Lowe (Fitness Trainer) had all left to link up with their old boss, Trevor Francis, at Birmingham City. Within a few dramatic days Ritchie Barker also departed, and, after less than a year in the job, the Head Coach, Danny Begara, was also told his contract would not be renewed. With the backroom cull completed, David Pleat moved to fill the many vacancies, firstly appointing the experienced Peter Shreeves to fill Begara's shoes. Albert Phelan was then promoted to the post of Reserve Team Manager, while newcomers Ricky Hill and Bobby Smith were to be Youth Coaches, with Martin Hodge becoming the club's first full time goalkeeping coach, replacing part-timer Jim Barron. Probably of more interest to the supporters, though, were the Owls' dealings in the transfer market, and they were in for a few surprises as two recently acquired big-money signings departed the scene. The first to go was the unsettled Darko Kovacevic who signed for Spanish club, Real Sociedad, in a 'get-your-money-back' deal. Perhaps the more surprising departure, however, was that of Marc Degryse who left for PSV Eindhoven after a successful one-and-only season in English soccer. Also leaving for pastures new were Simon Stewart, Lance Key and Richard Barker. Pleat then re-invested the majority of the transfer income to bring several new faces to Hillsborough, but missed out on what would have been the club's record deal. Those players that did sign included Andy Booth, Matt Clarke, Wayne Collins and Scott Oakes, with the club's foreign quota boosted when midfielder Orlando Trustfull signed from Feyenoord (after memorably playing a trial game at Stocksbridge under the bizarre pseudonym of Ryan Twerton!). The big transfer story of

the summer, however, surrounded Juventus' follically challenged winger, Attililo Lombardo, which seemingly dragged on for several weeks after a record fee had been agreed with his club. Eventually Wednesday were forced to pull out of the deal when Lombardo demanded an astronomical £1.7m annual pay packet—only £500,000 more than world record signing Alan Shearer was being paid at Newcastle United!

The Owls outdid themselves in pre-season, playing nine warm up games which included a six-match tour of Holland following practice games at Brighton, Peterborough and Rotherham United. The Dutch tour started with a 12–0 romp at Gouda and had a significant ending when the emerging Ritchie Humphreys scored a spectacular late winner at Utrecht. The teenagers form on tour convinced Pleat to give him his first Premiership start when it became clear that David Hirst would not be fit for the opening game of the new season at home to Aston Villa. It was Humphreys who grabbed all the headlines, when, in a sensational opening, Wednesday won their first four games to top the table for the first time since 1967. Early victories at Leeds and Newcastle were especially sweet; though, after losing their first game of the season at home to Chelsea, the Owls form slumped to such an extent that they failed to win in ten league and cup outings, and were sent crashing out of the Coca Cola Cup by First Division,

Oxford United. Off the pitch Chris Waddle signed for Scottish minnows, Falkirk, on a month to month contract, while, at a stormy AGM, the board had to defend fierce criticism from the shareholders concerning their transfer policy. Meanwhile, 17-year-old Steve Haslam, and Mark Platts were elevated to professional status, as Wednesday then hit the headlines when they set a new club transfer record to sign the Italian midfielder, Benito Carbone, from Inter Milan for a £3m fee. Meanwhile the Owls fell foul of FIFA, who banned Regi Blinker pending an investigation into claims by the Italian club, Udinese, that the winger had earlier in the year signed a declaration of intent to join them. FIFA eventually ruled that the Italians had acted improperly and, after Blinker was fined £35,700, the ban was lifted. There was, however, one significant departure, when the scorer of the goal that won the Owls their only major trophy in 64 years, John Sheridan, was sold to Bolton Wanderers.

On the whole the season was very much a roller-coaster ride for the Wednesday fans. After a great start and then the subsequent run of poor form, the Owls embarked on a remarkable mid-season run which saw them beaten only once in 21 games—although eleven of those ended in a draw. The run included a great win at Liverpool, and, in winning 3–2 at Southampton, the Owls came back from two goals down for the first time since 1963! Progress was also made in the FA Cup, as Grimsby Town, Carlisle United and Bradford City were overcome to reach the last eight for the first time for four seasons. The Owls then ran into more trouble with mainland Europe, for after Mark Bright had been sold to the Swiss club, Sion, they failed to pay any of the transfer fee and Bright was refused International clearance. Wednesday were eventually forced to sue the Swiss club, though, in a farcical turn, Bright was back in Blighty by this time, having signed for Charlton Athletic. The run in the FA Cup ended with a hugely disappointing home defeat to those perennial 'party poopers', Wimbledon; though on this occasion Wednesday still had a lot to play for in the Premiership, with a place in Europe being a distinct possibility. However, before the run in for a UEFA Cup place began in earnest, the club announced a major change behind the scenes, with the City of London investment company, Charterhouse Development Capital Funds apparently set to take a 20 per cent share in the club, with the Owls receiving £17m in return. The deal, which was later rubber stamped by the club's shareholders at an extraordinary general meeting, valued Wednesday at £42.5m, with the board stating that the money raised would be used to purchase players, improve the training ground, add more catering and leisure facilities to the stadium, and reduce bank borrowing. The day after the news of the share scheme broke, Wednesday paid Peterborough United £1m for the two young Eire starlets,

David Billington and Mark McKeever; and with the Owls sitting just outside the top six, new contracts up to June 2000 were signed with the manager, David Pleat, and the shirt sponsors, Sanderson. Unfortunately for Pleat there was precious little else to smile about in the final weeks of the season. With a European place tantalisingly close, his side then completely ran out of steam, losing three consecutive games, conceding a total of nine goals on visits to Blackburn and West Ham, and blowing any chance of European football returning to Hillsborough. Despite missing out on a top six place, a sell-out crowd still attended Wednesday's final home game of the season. There they not only saw a female streaker but O'Neill Donaldson grab a rare goal, and also witnessed Matt Clarke make his long awaited debut, only to be sent off—somewhat harshly—by referee David Elleray, eight minutes after replacing the injured Kevin Pressman. Forward, Andy Booth took over between the sticks and memorably saved one shot with his face, so earning the Owls a point as a much improved campaign finished on an entertaining note.

1997–98
BIG RON TO THE RESCUE AFTER PLEAT DEPARTS

The summer of 1997 was one of the quietest for many years at Sheffield 6. David Pleat was seemingly happy with a playing squad which had finished seventh in the previous campaign; and so by the time Wednesday kicked off their first pre-season friendly at Exeter City, only the Monaco defender, Patrick Blondeau had been added to the ranks—though a club record bid for Crystal Palace's play-off hero, David Hopkin had hit the rocks after the Welshman decided to sign for Leeds. The Ukranian winger, Serguy Nahornyak, from the superbly named Dnipro Dnipropetrovsk, joined for a trial period, but failed to impress and was soon heading back east. Despite little in the way of incoming transfer activity, Pleat did persuade several first-teamers to commit to new long-term contracts, including Kevin Pressman, Des Walker and Peter Atherton, while Brian Linighan and Mike Williams were the only two to depart from Hillsborough. The club also launched a new home strip, reverting back to a traditional striped shirt. Then, in the last few days of pre-season, Pleat smashed the club's transfer record when he paid £3m to Glasgow Celtic for Paulo Di Canio, with the £1.5m rated Regi Blinker moving to Celtic Park as part of the deal. On the same day, the club's second Dutchman departed, as Orlando Trustfull returned home to sign for Vitesse Arnhem.

The club's pre-season fixture list incorporated three games in Devon and Holland, plus a friendly at Huddersfield. However, the Owls failed to really convince in any of the matches and, for once, this form carried over into the season proper, for despite a 'wonder goal' from Benny Carbone, the side lost 2–1 at Newcastle United on the opening day. A poor first home showing saw Leeds United then take the three points, before the wheels really fell off as Sky TV viewers watched Carbone net twice and get himself sent off as the Owls crashed to a humiliating 7–2 defeat at Ewood Park. The first victory finally came in game five, but was an unconvincing performance which persuaded Pleat to re-enter the market to bring Southampton midfielder, Jim Magilton, to Hillsborough, along with fading star, Nigel Clough, who joined on loan from Manchester City. Both newcomers played, as Second Division Grimsby Town embarrassed Wednesday in the Coca Cola Cup at Blundell Park, and the situation deteriorated further a few days later when Blondeau was sent off as Derby County put five past Matt Clarke at Hillsborough. Soon after this, the little known midfielder, Petter Rudi arrived from the Norwegian club, Molde, and Bruce Grobbelaar signed on a short term contract. It was then the end of an era when, after eleven years and 128 goals, David Hirst was sold to Southampton for a £2m fee. The departure of the popular striker meant there was now no player left at the club out of those who had started in the 1993 Cup Final; and it was clear that the quality of that team had not been adequately replaced, for after a six goal mauling at Manchester United, the Owls slumped to the bottom of the table for first time since October 1989. Manager, David Pleat, paid the ultimate price as he was 'relieved of his

duties', with his assistant, Peter Shreeves, being put in temporary charge until a successor could be found.

As the board decided on Pleat's replacement, Paulo Di Canio was fined a laughable £1,000 for baring his buttocks, at Wimbledon, after scoring in a 1–1 draw in August. With Shreeves in charge the Owls then welcomed Bolton Wanderers to Hillsborough, and astonished everyone when an Andy Booth hat-trick helped Wednesday to an almost unbelievable 5–0 half-time lead. There was no further scoring in the second half, and the points were enough to lift Wednesday off the foot of the table in advance of the new appointee. The new manager proved to be an old one; as, to the surprise of many, Ron Atkinson returned to Hillsborough six years after his acrimonious departure from the scene, and signed a contract to the end of the season. The return of Atkinson brought a mixed reaction, though much of the bad feeling quickly evaporated as he led Wednesday to three straight victories, which included an outrageous winning goal from Di Canio at Southampton, and a derby win at home to Barnsley. Atkinson's first signing was that of the Eire Under 18 International, Alan Quinn, followed soon after by IFK Gothenburg's, Niclas Alexandersson. A swap deal involving Mark Pembridge and Coventry City's, David Burrows, then collapsed when the former turned down the move; and in true Atkinson fashion, the club's reserve side was then flooded with numerous foreign trialists— though it would be a few months yet before a certain Mr Thome arrived on the scene! Big Ron's next signing was the Macedonian international, Goce Sedloski; with Patrick Blondeau's unhappy

a relegation dogfight had been dispelled, thanks to a crucial win at struggling Everton which was again sealed by an outstanding individual goal from Di Canio. The season did end on a sour note, however, with two extremely disappointing performances sandwiching a testimonial win at Luton Town. These ensured a significant fall in the league standings, and probably influenced the decision that the Wednesday board was about to make.

Kevin Pressman scores the decisive penalty in the shoot out against Watford— he is then mobbed by his team-mates

stay in Sheffield being mercifully cut short when he returned to France to sign for Bordeaux. Atkinson's wheeler-dealing continued unabated, with the Austrian forward, Christian Mayrleb signed on loan for the rest of the season, Wayne Collins moving to Fulham, Adem Poric's contract cancelled by mutual consent, and the England International, Andy Hinchcliffe, signing for £2.75m from Everton. Back on the field of play, 1998 started well with a Cup win over Watford as Kevin Pressman scored the winning penalty in the shoot-out. This was followed by arguably the best home display of the season as Newcastle United were beaten. The Owls remained just below mid-table for several weeks and then boosted their squad still further as Earl Barrett signed on a free transfer, and the completely unknown, Emerson Augusto Thome, put his signature to a contract to the end of the season. On deadline day, Wednesday also signed goalie, Stuart Jones from Western League football, and a third Italian in the shape of Francesco Sanetti. The latter made his debut as the Owls drew 2–2 in a testimonial game at Glasgow Rangers. By this time any worries of being dragged into

1998–99
WILSON RETURNS TO REPLACE HIS OLD BOSS

Ron Atkinson's first act of the close season was to award free transfers to several players, including Christian Mayrleb and Steve Nicol. However, this proved to be his final act as Wednesday boss, for the surprise news broke that he would not be offered a new contract, and his second spell as Owls' boss had came to a somewhat abrupt end. It would be almost six weeks before the search for a new manager came to fruition, and during this time Mark Pembridge departed on a 'Bosman' free transfer, while the Owls appointed Youth Development Officer, Clive Baker, as the director of their newly created Youth Academy. The search for a new boss looked to be at an end when the ex-Rangers manager, Walter Smith seemed set to sign. However, the Owls' attempts to secure his signature were thwarted at the last moment when he refused a contract, and, instead, crossed the Pennines to join Everton. Within a week, however, the Barnsley boss, Danny Wilson became a popular 18th post-war manager, returning five years after he had left Hillsborough to become player coach at Oakwell. Unfortunately for the new incumbent, he only had five weeks before the new season kicked off, but in that time he did manage to secure the services of the Dutch World Cup midfielder, Vim Jonk, from PSV Eindhoven, plus Juan Cobian from Argentinean club, Boca Juniors. Emerson Thome was given a new extended contract, and Youth Coach, Mick Walker, departed when his contract was not renewed.

The Owls played a total of eight pre-season games against a diverse selection of lower league opposition. This produced a mixed bag of results, ranging from a 4–0 mauling at Birmingham City, to a comfortable 3–0 win at Lincoln City. During this time the Owls became one of the last ever opponents for Reading at Elm Park before the bulldozers moved in. At Sincil Bank, Benny Carbone made a re-appearance after he had looked set to move on after delaying his return to the UK for personal reasons. The Owls then became the first team from outside the county to contest the Shropshire Cup, when a mixed eleven lost 1–0 to Shrewsbury Town. However, these warm-up matches are no more than the starter to the main course, and the fixture list determined that the Wilson years would start at Hillsborough with a visit from West Ham United. In a game of few chances it was the Londoners who sneaked a 1–0 win, though a week later Wednesday visited crisis club, Tottenham, and recorded an outstanding 3–0 success to kick-start the season. Before visiting White Hart Lane, the Owls had been hit by the news that Dejan Stefanovic's appeal against the refusal of a work permit had been rejected and that he was now unable to play in English football (a month later a second appeal was successful). After Aston Villa had also won 1–0 at Hillsborough, Wednesday then parted company with coach, Peter Shreeves, and the process of bringing Frank Barlow

back from Birmingham City to become Wilson's assistant began in earnest. It would be over a month, however, before Barlow was able to take up his new position, during which time Wednesday had settled into a mid-table slot. In that time, they had also lost the unpredictable talents of Paulo Di Canio after his infamous one round bout with referee, Paul Alcock. Following the well publicised clash in the game with Arsenal, the Italian was immediately suspended by the club, subsequently fined £10,000 and banned for eleven matches by an FA disciplinary committee. Unfortunately for Wednesday, it was just the start of their problems with the Roman, for in the ensuing months he sent in a plethora of sick notes before the Owls finally lost patience with their AWOL striker, and cut their losses by agreeing to his 'January Sale Price' transfer to West Ham.

The early part of the season showed that, defensively, Wednesday had improved greatly on the previous campaign, with the central pairing of Thome and Walker ensuring the 'Goals Against' column stayed at an impressively low level. However, the main problem was at the other end, as Wednesday scored in only three of their opening eleven league games, and slid down into the bottom five. There was also embarrassment in the Coca Cola Cup when, for the third consecutive season, a minnow sent them tumbling out at the first stage, as the 'basement side' Cambridge United won at Hillsborough, in the definite low point of the '98–'99 campaign. After the heaviest defeat of the season, by 4–0 at Middlesbrough, Wilson entered the transfer market to sign the virtually unknown, Danny Sonner, from Ipswich Town for a knock-down fee. Sonner subsequently proved to be one of the bargains of the season, and within a month, the ex-Newcastle United keeper, Pavel Srnicek, put pen to paper on a two-year contract after his move from Banik Ostrava. The Czech's debut at St James' Park was the start of a mini revival, as Petter Rudi's first goal for the club earned Wednesday a draw. This was followed by a ten-point haul out of the next available twelve, and included a confidence boosting home win over Manchester United. After experiencing an unhappy Christmas, Wednesday hit the ground running in the New Year, and won through to the last sixteen of the FA Cup in comfortable style. They also recorded a stunning 4–0 win at Upton Park, where the on-form Carbone was almost unplayable. The little Italian had been at the forefront of Wednesday's general improvement in mid-season, but when his goal scoring talents dried up, then so did the points for the side. Following a disappointing Cup exit to Chelsea, the Owls suddenly became outsiders for a UEFA Cup berth, for after Middlesbrough had been beaten Wednesday moved into tenth place. As soon as the dreaded Europe word was whispered, however, Wednesday proceeded to lose five consecutive games to plunge them right back into relegation trouble. Meanwhile, off the pitch, Graham Hyde, Mark Platts, Goce Sedloski and Jim Magilton all moved to pastures new, while Chris Waddle returned to Hillsborough in a coaching capacity. Wednesday then had Bosman to thank for three of their four subsequent captures, as the Celtic duo, Simon Donnelly and Phil O'Donnell, signed pre-contract agreements with the Owls, and the St Johnstone midfielder, Philip Scott, arrived in a Bosman influenced cut price £75,000 deal. Scott signed on deadline day, and, with only minutes before the 5 pm deadline, Wilson raided Bootham Crescent to sign the York City forward, Richard Cresswell, for a fee approaching £1m.

After the flurry of transfer activity it was back to the struggle in the league for Wednesday. As was the case twelve months earlier, a saviour was on hand in the shape of Everton FC, for two defensive howlers by the Toffeemen gifted Carbone a brace as the Owls won 2–1 at Goodison Park. The three points on Merseyside effectively dispelled any fears of the drop, and two consecutive home draws were enough to mathematically guarantee safety. It had not been an easy first season for Wilson, but victory in the last two games pushed Wednesday up to a respectable 12th position and gave the new manager breathing space to rebuild in the summer, and hopefully bring back some of the glory he experienced when he was a player at Hillsborough.

The first 100 hundred years at Hillsborough have provided fans with their fair share of drama and despite what happens in the Millennium season, future generations of supporters will no doubt experience the same highs and lows in following one of the oldest clubs in the English game.

Memory Match

In their first European adventure for almost thirty years, Wednesday experienced a gentle re-introduction with a first round tie against the Luxembourg minnows, Spora. However, the draw for the next round was an altogether different story as Wednesday were sent into the cauldron that is the Fritz Walter Stadium, home of the German side, Kaiserslautern. An early goal from David Hirst put the Owls in command, but then a series of dubious refereeing decisions and play-acting from the home side resulted in Hirst being controversially sent off, and the Germans scoring three without reply, to make Wednesday the underdogs in the return game in Sheffield. Incidentally, the French referee, Joel Quiniou, whose dismissal of Hirst had seemed to be based purely on the reaction of the home crowd, was withdrawn from the second leg, with a Hungarian official appointed in his place.

The club appealed for the fans to get behind their team for the second leg, with the sense of injustice felt by supporters after the first match manifesting itself in what was arguably the best atmosphere at any game played at Hillsborough in living memory. Wednesday fans created such an intimidating atmosphere that it fell not far short of the white-hot reception that greeted Wednesday in Germany. With the theme tune from 'Dambusters' playing over the tannoy, and Marco Harber identified as Public Enemy No.1 (it was he who 'dived' to get Hirst sent off in the first match) the scene was set for a classic night of European soccer, and one that will live long in the memory of the many fans in the 27,597 crowd. If the task ahead was not hard enough already, Wednesday were also handicapped by the fact that their first choice attack of Hirst and Bright were both absent; the former, of course, because of his red card in Germany, and the latter being ineligible having signed after the UEFA deadline for the second round. Wednesday drafted Gordon Watson and Paul Warhurst to fill the vacancies, and almost grabbed a sensational lead inside the first minute when John Sheridan's shot was deflected just wide. As expected it was Wednesday who did all the early attacking, with the breakthrough the Owls fans hoped for finally coming after 27 minutes, when Harkes long throw-in was flicked on by Nigel Pearson for Danny Wilson to crash a glorious volley into the roof of the net. Hillsborough exploded and the noise level increased still further as the home fans urged their team on; for a 2–0 result would be enough to send Wednesday through to the last sixteen. However, Kaiserslautern were a potent threat, and such was their command down the left hand side—with future Chelsea player, Bjarne Goldaek, being one of the main problems—that Trevor Francis took the decision to replace John Harkes with Roland Nilsson, after Woods had touched over Marin's long range effort and Nigel Worthington cleared Hotic's header off the line. The Owls makeshift forward line had failed to make an impression on the tie so far, but at the break the job was half complete, with Wednesday now just one goal in arrears on aggregate.

Ten minutes into the second half a Viv Anderson goal was disallowed for offside. Then, seven minutes later disaster struck, when Marcel Witeczek took a long ball from Miroslav to outpace Pearson and round Anderson, before firing home the equaliser. The Owls would need a quick reposte if their European dream was to be kept alive, and this thankfully occurred within three minutes when Warhurst won a free kick 25 yards out, from which John Sheridan curled in a glorious shot past Serr in the visiting goal. Another goal was still needed to take the game into extra time, however, with the defining moment of the tie probably coming three minutes later, as Warhurst ran onto Shezza's chipped pass, but his first-time shot was parried by the keeper. Wednesday's rhythm was then interrupted, when in typical European fashion, the visiting goalie was treated for a mystery injury and play was held up. Then, with fourteen minutes remaining, you could have heard a pin drop on the Kop when hesitancy in the Owls defence allowed the substitute, Michael Zeyer the time and space to crack a low 25-yard shot into the bottom corner of the net. This second equaliser killed the game off totally for Wednesday, as they now needed three goals and this proved to be an impossible task. They exited the competition after an unforgettable, if ultimately disappointing night of European football.

Wednesday: Woods, Harkes (Nilsson 33), Worthington, Palmer, Pearson (Bart-Williams 77), Anderson, Wilson, Waddle, Watson, Warhurst, Sheridan (Unused subs—Shirtliff, Jemson, Pressman)

Kaiserslautern: Serr, Goldbaek, Richter, Ritter, Kadlec, Dooley, Hotic (Zeyer 62), Haber, Witeczek (Lieberknecht 83), Shafer, Marin (Unused subs—Antes, Lelle, Winkler)

Referee: Sandor Puhl (Hungary)

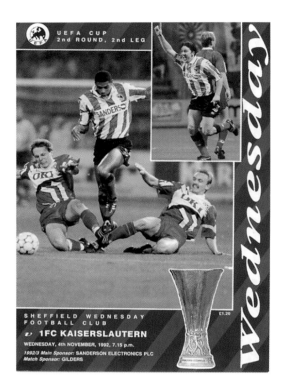

**UEFA Cup 2nd Round—2nd Leg
Wednesday 4th November 1992**

Sheffield Wednesday
2
Kaiserslautern
2

Memory Match

FA Carling Premiership
Saturday 18th December 1993

Sheffield Wednesday 5

West Ham United 0

After the excitement of the double Cup Final season which had gone before, the first half of the 1993–94 season was, without doubt, a great disappointment to Wednesday fans. However, with the Owls languishing in fifteenth position, following a sickening injury-time defeat at Highbury on the previous Sunday, the home game with West Ham would prove to be the showcase for one of the greatest individual displays ever seen from a Wednesday player. The man in question was Chris Waddle, who, over the ninety minutes, proceeded to produce such a display of consummate brilliance, that the Hammers—and especially their hapless full-back, David Burrows—simply had no answer; with the awe-inspiring Waddle having a hand in three goals and scoring himself in a particularly one-sided encounter.

The only change in the team that suffered a narrow defeat at Highbury the week before, saw Andy Pearce replace Simon Coleman. However, despite the fact that Wednesday dominated the game early on, the scoresheet remained blank until ten minutes before the break, when, from Waddle's short corner, Andy Pearce rose to see his header come back off the crossbar and deflect into the net off the West Ham defender, Mike Marsh. At this point Waddle had played only a bit part in the proceedings, but in the second half he was simply unplayable, with the opposition's left-back, Dave Burrows, being teased and tormented. There was an element of the matador and the bull here, as time and again Waddle drew Burrows into the challenge before slipping the ball past him, with one trademark shimmy from the 'Waddler' memorably leaving the humiliated Burrows on his backside. The Hammers were rarely out of their own half in the second period, and once Waddle had laid on a simple tap-in for Mark Bright, there was only one winner—with the player the fans simply referred to as 'God' then adding a third with a divine 30-yard drive. Poor old Burrows then experienced the indignity of Waddle playing a one-two off his shin to set up a fourth goal for Nigel Jemson, but Burrows then lost any sympathy the Owls' fans might have had for him, when, with fifteen minutes left, his frustration saw him earn a yellow card after scything down his tormentor. The rout was completed with a late strike from Carlton Palmer, though this time Waddle did not play a part; with the victory becoming the trigger Wednesday needed to move up the table over the Christmas and New Year period.

All the post-match talk centred on Chris Waddle, with increasing calls being made for him to be recalled to the International scene. Superlatives abounded, for such was his display that Hillsborough had its first ever unanimous result in the match sponsors poll, as all thirty groups voted for the dazzling winger. Leading the praise was his 'victim' David Burrows, who commented: 'There's no stopping him in that mood. Whoever comes in as England Manager will have to take a look at him, 33 or not'. The TV pundit, Alan Hansen, said 'The worst thing that can happen to you in professional football is to have Waddle coming at you with the ball', while West Ham's experienced defender, Tony Gale, went further, saying that 'Waddle was world class. I haven't seen a better performance in my years in the top flight'. The mob of young autograph hunters Waddle encountered after the game provided a greater obstacle to him than the Hammers defence had produced all afternoon, and, after being swamped by the gentlemen of the press, he could bask in the glory of a game that will go down in Wednesday folklore as 'Waddle's game'.

Wednesday: Pressman, Nilsson, Worthington, Pearce, Walker, Waddle, Hyde, Palmer, Bart-Williams, Jemson, Bright (Unused subs—Watson, Poric, Woods)

West Ham: Miklosko, Breacker, Burrows, Potts, Gale, Marsh, Butler, Bishop (M. Allen 76), Holmes (Boere 68), Chapman, Morley (Unused sub—Peyton)

Referee: Mr D. Frampton (Poole)

Memory Match

Thirty years after Hillsborough staged matches in the World Cup Finals, the Euro 96 bandwagon rolled into Sheffield for three games in the continent's premier International competition. As was the case in 1966, a cultural festival ran parallel with the tournament; though in the 1990s, the programme of events was far greater and diverse than had been the case three decades earlier. The celebrations began with a parade through the city streets, and on the first weekend Tudor Square rang out to the sounds of a world music festival. Other events on show included a football exhibition at Kelham Island Museum, a Jazz and Blues festival at Victoria Quays, and a three team International triangular football tournament involving the world's two oldest clubs, Hallam FC. and Sheffield FC, plus Hvidovre FC from Denmark.

Sunday 9th June

The opening Group D game paired the 1992 winners, Denmark with the dark horses from Portugal. Well over 10,000 Danish fans crossing the North Sea to make the pilgrimage to follow their national side, Sheffield became buried under a sea of red flags. Before the game those Wednesday fans who ventured into Hillsborough Park found thousands of beer-swilling Danes, who, throughout the evening would remain good natured and friendly. Inside the ground the Kop was another blanket of red, creating a truly amazing sight as the fans swayed from side to side in opposite directions to create a wave effect. The smaller band of Portuguese fans also contributed to a noisy atmosphere and the ninety minutes that followed saw a clash of two distinct styles, as the more workmanlike Danish team had to survive a thrillingly skilful assault from Portugal. The one touch play on offer from Portugal was, at times, breathtaking, and in Fiorentina star, Rui Costa, they possessed the game's outstanding individual, who, in the first half, was at the heart of many attacks that eventually floundered on the rock of Denmark's packed defence. However, Portugal did create several opportunities in the first period and it needed excellent goalkeeping from Peter Schmeichel to keep the scoresheet blank. The somewhat ineffective Brian Laudrup then switched to the left wing, and after 22 minutes, against the run of play, he capitalised on a defensive mix up to fire an angled drive past Baia's right hand. The overworked Schmeichel then saved bravely at the feet of Joao Pinto, though somewhat incredibly, at the break Denmark still led despite having clearly been second best. Justice was seen to be done seven minutes into the second period, however, when the live-wire striker, Sa Pinto, brought the Portuguese level; and though they continued to have the upper hand, Denmark still posed a danger on the break. In the end many saw the ensuing 1–1 draw as being a fair result, though the fact that all the creative invention came from Portugal would suggest that they were probably disappointed to earn only a single point from their opening fixture.

Denmark: Schmeichel, Helveg, Hogh, Reiper, Risager, B. Laudrup, Larsen (Vilfort 89), Thomsen (Piechnik 63), Steen, Nielsen, M.Laudrup, Beck

Portugal: Vitor Baia, Paulinho Santos, Fernanado, Couto, Helder, Dimas, Sa Pinto, Rui Costa, Oceano (Folha 36), Paulo Sousa (Tavares 79), Joao Pinto, Luis Figo (Domingos 62)

Referee: Van der Ende (Holland)

Sunday 16th June

A week later the Viking hordes again invaded Sheffield, but would return home downhearted after their Croatian opponents matched them on a physical level, and at the end of ninety minutes proved themselves to be a class act, superior in every department to Denmark. The fledgling Croatian side, for whom Euro 96 was their first major Championship, were accompanied to Hillsborough by a small army of bare chested (the men anyway!) and noisy supporters, who kept the stewards and police busy in the West Stand as they gave their side vociferous support. The Danes started the game without a recognised striker, Michael Laudrup and Larsen alternating between attack and midfield. This proved to be a costly mistake, especially after they had fallen behind to Davol Suker's 52nd-minute penalty, which was awarded for a rather dubious Schmeichel foul on Mario Stanic.

Denmark 1
Portugal 1

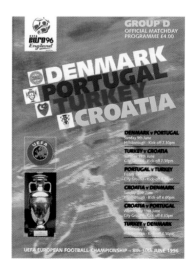

Memory Match

Croatia
3

Denmark
0

The first half had been fairly even, with neither side conceding much ground, although Suker had been the major attacking threat. Soon after the Croatians had forged ahead, Brian Laudrup stabbed a close range effort against the foot of the post, however such opportunities would need to be taken against impressive opponents, and the Danes were made to pay in the final fifteen minutes as Croatia scored twice more and came close to scoring one of the greatest goals of all time. Goal number two arrived after 77 minutes, when, Man of the Match, Suker, escaped his marker and fired square across the six yard box for AC Milan's, Zvonimir Boban, to stab the ball home. Confidence was now soaring in the Croatian ranks, and the highlight of the match came with six minutes left when Suker spotted Schmeichel out of his goal, and memorably tried to lob him from inside his own half. Schmiechel, who dashed back, just got his fingertips to the ball to keep it out, but it was a sublime piece of skill from the Seville player, and said everything about the confidence of the Croats. Suker was not to be denied, however, and in the last minute he scored what was arguably the goal of the tournament. After running fully fifty yards with the ball, from a left field angle he chipped it over Schmeichel, who was desperately trying to regain his position after a foray up-field. Neutral fans in the North West corner of the ground certainly enjoyed seeing the Manchester United goalie made to look foolish, and the goal nicely rounded off the best game of Hillsborough's allocation of Euro 96 ties.

Croatia: Ladic, Bilic, Jerkan, Stimac, Stanic, Asanovic, Boban (Soldo 81), Prosinecki (Mladenovic 87), Jarni, Vlaovic (Jurcevic 81), Suker

Denmark: Schmeichel, Thomsen, J. Hogh, Reiper, Helveg (Laursen ht), Vilfort (Beck 58), Larsen (Tofting 68), Steen Nielsen, Schjonberg, B.Laudrup, M.Laudrup

Referee: M.Batta (France)

Denmark
3

Turkey
0

Wednesday 19th June

Hillsborough's final game of the European Championships was billed as a wooden spoon encounter, as neither side could realistically qualify for the next stage. In that sense it proved a disappointment to neutral supporters, for the pre-tournament stories had suggested that wherever the Turkish team would play, a huge army of fans would follow, creating an atmosphere to remember. However, the reality was that the support for Turkey almost totally disappeared leaving a half-empty ground containing the ever loyal Danish 'Roligan' army, and a few thousand English fans. All that was at stake for both sides was pride, though any hopes of an open contest quickly receded, as a dour first-half finished goalless—with the Danes refusing to come out of their defensive shell and Turkey not having the guile to break them down. At the break the news that Portugal were 2–0 ahead against Croatia convinced Denmark that their grip on the Henri Delauney trophy was at an end, and paradoxically they stepped up a gear to dominate the second period. Only five minutes after the re-start, the Rangers players, Bo Anderson and Brian Laudrup, combined for the latter to round Rustu to put Denmark ahead—and from this point it was one-way traffic. The Danes then proceeded to miss several chances before, with twenty minutes left, Michael Laudrup set up the second goal for Allan Neilsen. The rout was completed six minutes from time when the Scandinavian star man, Brian Laudrup, again combined with Bo Anderson to net a third. In the end it had been 'too little too late' for the departing Danish coach, Richard Moller Nielsen; but at least the fabulous travelling support had returned home with a victory to show for their loyalty as the sun set on Hillsborough's involvement in Euro 96.

Denmark: Schmeichel, Helveg, Rieper, J. Hogh, Schjonberg (Larsen ht), Steen Nielsen, Thomsen, M. Laudrup, B. Laudrup, Bo Anderson, Nielsen

Turkey: Rustu, Recep(Saffet 67), Alpay, Vedat, Tugay, Hami, Ogun, Hakan (Arif ht), Orhan (K.Bulent 67), Tayfun, Abdullah

Referee: N. Levnikov (Russia)

Memory Match

When the Champions, Arsenal, visited Hillsborough, the Owls were looking for a lift after having just exited the Coca Cola Cup at the hands of the basement club, Cambridge United, in mid week. However, there was no intimation that by the end of the afternoon events both on and off the pitch would bring world-wide publicity for all the wrong reasons. Boss, Danny Wilson, had made three changes from the Abbey Stadium debacle, with Juan Cobian, Niclas Alexandersson and Petter Rudi all returning, and Newsome, Briscoe and Carbone making way.

The first real opportunity of the game fell to Anelka, though a brilliant recovery tackle from Des Walker ensured the Frenchman could not test Pressman. Pressman then saved brilliantly from a fierce low drive from Ray Parlour, before Alexandersson missed a great chance to break the deadlock when he swung and missed a looping ball which had come back off the post from Rudi's dipping cross. However, after 44 minutes the incident that would make all the headlines occurred, when 'all-hell' broke loose following an altercation between Viera and Jonk. The Owls' Dutch player had pulled the Arsenal midfielder back, at which point Viera retaliated by throwing Jonk to the floor. What followed was nothing less than a mass brawl, which worsened as Paulo Di Canio charged in to aim a kick at Martin Keown. When the situation calmed down, the referee called Di Canio over— and the rest, as they say, is history! In the years to come supporters will remember the moment when the fiery Italian pushed over referee, Paul Alcock, after he had brandished the red card in his direction. For a moment the ground was stunned as the supporters took in what had just happened. However, as Di Canio stormed past Danny Wilson on the touch line, his manager must have realised that his top scorer might never again pull on a Wednesday shirt. After Alcock had recovered from the shock he also dismissed Keown, and soon after this blew the whistle for half time—during which period both teams could try to comprehend what had happened. Viera was only booked for his part in the incident, and the home fans became involved in angry exchanges with the Arsenal player as he left the pitch at half-time. During the second half he was booed every time he touched the ball, and at the final whistle he was confronted by the police after making gestures to the public.

It was an extraordinary game on an afternoon when many players did not enhance their reputations, but for Lee Briscoe it was a game to remember. This was because in the second half the Owls shaded the play, and, after he had missed an absolute sitter, Briscoe proceeded to score the winner for Wednesday in the very last minute. A great ball from Jonk released Briscoe down the left-hand channel, and though he was marked by two defenders and was near the corner of the penalty box, he looked up and promptly sent a stunning chip over Manninger into the top corner—his first league goal in an Owls' shirt, and right in front of the home Kop! Unfortunately for Briscoe his tremendous strike was destined to be totally overshadowed by other matters, for Arsenal's first defeat for 27 games produced little in the way of column inches, the afternoon produced only the one story, one which would effectively end the Wednesday career of the club's record signing, and prove to be a very expensive tumble for the Owls.

Wednesday: Pressman, Cobian, Thome, Walker, Hinchcliffe, Alexandersson (Briscoe 59), Atherton, Jonk (Magilton 90), Rudi, Di Canio, Booth (Humphreys 20) (Unused subs—Barrett, Clarke)

Arsenal: Manninger, Vivas, Keown, Adams, Winterburn, Parlour (Ljungberg 78), Viera, Petit (Hughes 78), Overmars (Bould ht), Bergkamp, Anelka (Unused subs—Garde, Taylor)

Referee: P. Alcock (Halstead)

Sheffield Wednesday
1
Arsenal
0

Chapter 10

Hillsborough
– the Ground

There is no doubt that in 1899 when Wednesday took the decision to purchase a ten acre plot of land on the North side of the River Don, at High Bridge, Owlerton, they took an almighty risk. At the time, although it is difficult to imagine now, Owlerton was a thinly populated district, poorly served by public transport, and contained very little in the way of amenities. The supporters would have had to make the trip to the new ground on foot, though, thankfully, Wednesday's fans at the time were a resilient and loyal bunch, to the extent that the early crowd figures for Owlerton did not differ greatly from those in the final days at Olive Grove. As mentioned in an earlier chapter, when they realised that they were to lose Olive Grove, Wednesday explored several options. Eventually, however, the finance was put in place to pay £4,500 for the meadowland belonging to James Dixon's the famous firm of Sheffield silversmiths. The cost of purchasing the plot, including the various disbursements, came to a grand total of £4,783. This was broken down into £1,483 in cash, and a mortgage for £3,300 made out in the name of director, Charles Clegg, and payable on a monthly basis at an interest rate of 3 per cent.

In June 1899, as soon as the land was secured, work began in earnest to try to turn the field into a football ground fit for league soccer. Over the following weeks some 70 or 80 men employed by the contractor J. Mastin & Sons, who had been responsible for most of the building work undertaken at Olive Grove, worked to bring Owlerton to a reasonable condition. Wednesday paid out around £730 for the 'laying out' of the ground, and by the time the club played their first practice match at the nearby Niagara Grounds in late August, the work had progressed significantly. Those fans who called in to

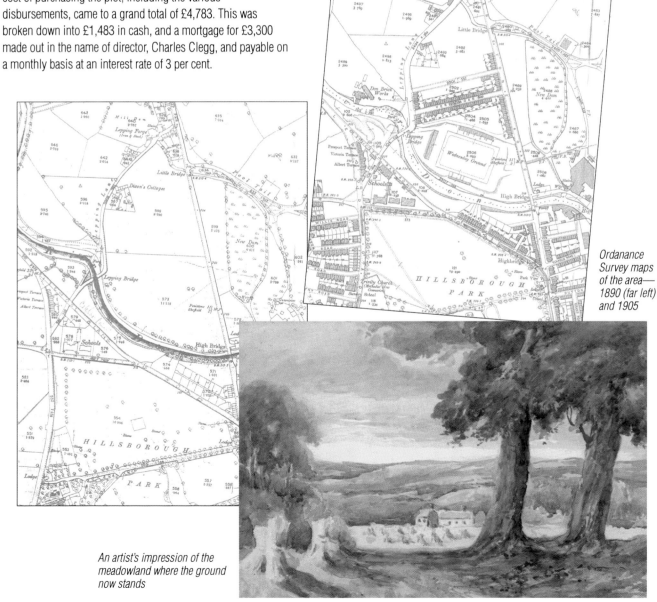

Ordanance Survey maps of the area— 1890 (far left) and 1905

An artist's impression of the meadowland where the ground now stands

witness developments would have found that the old Olive Grove stand, which had been dismantled four weeks earlier, had now been re-erected on the river side of the new ground, and was ready for occupation. The pitch was in place and ready and was now virtually level—rising slightly to the Leppings Lane entrance and the right hand corner of the Penistone Road end—after having been raised by as much as two feet. The surface measured 115 x 75 yards, and in the centre there were two 'plugs' in which a hose could be attached to refresh all those parts of the pitch that other hoses could not reach! The fencing was completed all along the river side, from bridge to bridge, the only unfenced area being the corner of Leppings Lane and the Penistone Road side of the ground. Rails now surrounded the playing surface, except for a gap left for the excavation of a new stand on the Wadsley Bridge side, with the 11 yard space between the rail and the touch line providing a much greater gap than at Olive

Grove. Entrances had been constructed for the new North Stand, one at the corner of Leppings Lane, and a block of 8 to 10 turnstiles on Penistone Road. At this time the club had no plans for stands behind the goals, these ends would be banked up; and when Wednesday officially christened the enclosure 'Wednesday Football Club, Owlerton', the ground was open for business. In the intervening hundred years since then, all four sides of the ground have undergone huge changes—and it is perhaps suitable to look individually at the subsequent developments on each side of the ground.

Hillsborough c.1953

Wednesday's at home—don't forget your cap!

THE SOUTH / RIVERSIDE

When Owlerton staged its first game on 2nd September 1899 it was a three sided ground, with the only accommodation available being in the old Olive Ground stand on the river side. The 1,000 seater stand had originally been erected at Olive Grove in 1892 in preparation for the club's first season of league football, and at the time was considered to be one of the best in the country. The stand was constructed by Mastin & Sons, and was 197ft wide, by 18ft deep. Dressing rooms, bathrooms, committee and refreshment rooms were contained in the interior, as well as a front standing enclosure. The club paid just over £1,000 to have the whole structure dismantled and moved to Owlerton, brick by brick, where, on its arrival it was painted blue and white. Erected on the banks of the River Don, it was very much seen as a stop gap measure, to the extent that when the new North Stand was eventually built the Olive Grove stand was downgraded to rate as a threepenny

WEDNESDAY FOOTBALL CLUB.

THE COMING SEASON:—ALTERATIONS AT OLIVE GROVE

THE NEW PAVILION.

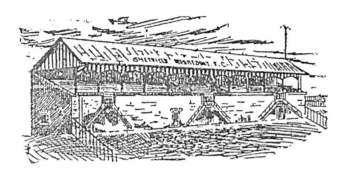

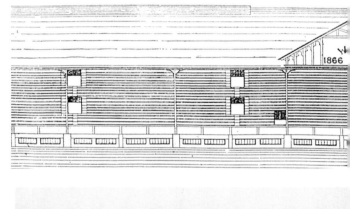

Workmen who helped construct the South Stand in 1913

stand to which admission could be gained after having paid the ground entrance fee. The underneath of the stand was later converted into a gym, and this remained its function until the summer of 1913, when Wednesday decided to greatly enhance their enclosure by building a state-of-the-art South Stand.

The 'Olive Grove' stand, as it was christened by supporters after it was transposed to Owlerton, was subsequently sold to the builders, Freckingham & Sons for £65 and was demolished. However, Wednesday were allowed to keep half of the roof, the gable ends, and the uprights, in order to build a refreshment room. To take its place Archie Leitch, the famous architect of football stadia, designed the South Stand, 'one of

Promotion, 1950

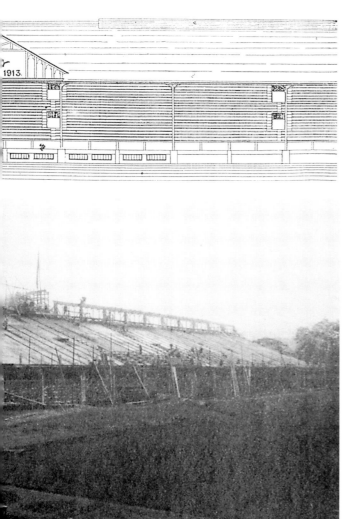

the greatest structures on any football ground' which was then constructed along the whole of the river side of the ground. The magnificent new stand seated 5,600, with some 11,000 fans reckoned to be able to be fitted into the enclosure at its front. Wednesday stretched themselves to the financial limit to pay for the new building—the final cost being calculated at the enormous figure of £17,884. The architect, Leitch, received £500; the builders, Freckingham & Sons, £4,969; the Glasgow steel company, Clyde & Son, £1,395; and the contractors, Hodkin & Jones, £5,850. The new stand boasted luxury dressing rooms, offices and even a billiards room; but when it was opened for the first time on 6th September 1913, it was unable to boast a roof—though this did not seem to matter to the hundreds of fans who sat there as the rain came down in order to be able say they had watched from the great new stand. On that day only 3,000 seats were available to the public, yet when Derby County visited on Ist November 1913 the stand was in full use. A month later the words 'The Wednesday Football Club Ltd.' appeared, with the cherry on the cake being a decorative football bearing the date 1866; which, at the time, was thought to be the year of the club's formation. After waiting several months for the internal rooms to 'thoroughly dry', the team and officials moved across from the North Stand on 10th January 1914, and, after the game the stand was voted by both sides to be the 'swellest' in the country.

Overall, the stand was so well built, that over the decades that followed Wednesday have only had to undertake routine maintenance. It was not until 1965 that the face of the stand

designed before the First World War. Phase One of a massive redevelopment programme started straight after the home game with Liverpool on 2nd May 1993, when workmen from Ackroyd & Abbott moved onto the site. This eventually resulted in a huge new roof supported by a single-span girder weighing 500 tonnes towering over the old structure, and, thanks to modern technology, the stand now offered an uninterrupted view of the pitch—the new roof stretching all the way back to the edge of the river. Other work included the replacement of all the wooden seats in the stand with the new plastic tip-up variety. The bill for first part of the work came to £1.8m, with the club receiving a grant from the Football Trust of £960,000. Phase Two was completed during the 1995–96 season, when, for a cost of around £5m, Wednesday received an extra 3,000 seats, in what is now called the Grandstand, with 30 executive boxes a multitude of hospitality suites and other offices. This multi-million pound transformation has totally obliterated any trace of the old South Stand, although the decorative ball that adorned the 1913 construction has thankfully been retained, and the 'new stand' now rivals any structure built since the Taylor report was published.

was changed, when, in preparation for the World Cup, the enclosure was seated. A total of 3,356 seats were installed at a cost of £27,600 and the new fully-seated stand was used for the first time on 6th November 1965, when Liverpool visited Hillsborough. Following the Bradford fire in 1985, the wooden floors in the stand were replaced, and by the 1990s the structure had undergone such a remarkable development that Archie Leitch would be unable to recognise the stand he

CURRENT CAPACITY: 11,354

The South Stand, 1999

EAST / KOP

Considering that the Kop is now strictly the 'home end', it seems remarkable that the Penistone Road end of Hillsborough was the last area to be developed and the last to be covered; and that this did not occur until the mid 1980s. When the ground was first opened there was only a small bank behind the goal. This saw a handful of crush barriers subsequently erected during the early years of the 20th century, with the first major change occurring in the summer of 1914, when Wednesday first extended the area and then installed concrete terracing at a total cost of £800. Across the subsequent decades the 'Spion Kop'—a name originating from a hill in the Natal, South Africa, which became famous in 1900 during the Boer War—was gradually upgraded, with extensive work being undertaken in July 1954; which meant that the traditional pre-season practice game had to cancelled. In February

when the greatly extended Kop was opened for the first time for the home game with Everton. The capacity of the uncovered Kop had been 16,850; however, once the roof had been completed the capacity rose to an astonishing 22,000, making it the largest covered standing area in Europe. Over 17,500 packed the area for that opening game with Everton, with the fans delighted to see that their loyal support in all weathers had finally been rewarded with

1986 plans were finally announced to roof the Kop, with the architects Eastwood & Partners designing the structure, and Ackroyd & Abbott contracted to put a roof over the terracing. The Football Trust eventually provided £500,000 towards the total cost of £850,000. Various fund-raising events were also undertaken, including a 'Raise The Roof Fun Run' in April which was attended by thousands of supporters. The big day arrived in August 1986,

the long promised roof. The newly roofed Kop was officially opened by Her Majesty the Queen on Friday 12th December 1986, but the extended capacity was only in use for three years, for after the Hillsborough disaster, the allocated numbers allowed on the terracing were significantly slashed, and the Kop capacity dropped to below the pre-roof era figure. With all-seater stadia now just around the corner, it was only a matter of time before the famous

Kop was seated, and in the summer of 1993, a year earlier than had been expected, the club decided to go ahead with the project. The usual contractors at that time, Ackroyd & Abbott, were again engaged for the job which cost £750,000 to complete, and the new 11,210 capacity home-end was opened for the Premiership encounter with Aston Villa in August 1993. Over 8,500 season tickets were sold on the Kop in the first season that it was seated and, despite the installation of the seating, it has remained the staunch and spiritual home of Wednesday's hard core support.

CURRENT CAPACITY: 11,210

The Kop, 1999

WEST LEPPINGS LANE

The Leppings Lane end of the ground was actually the first to be developed following the move from Olive Grove, when in October 1899 the club announced plans to erect a covered stand which would have a standing capacity for 3,000 spectators. When the £315 structure was completed, it was 240 ft wide by 33ft deep, with a corrugated iron roof, and was at the back of a grassy bank, about fifty feet from the railings which surrounded the playing surface. This stand was eventually extended to join up with the new North Stand. However, in the 1920s this area of the ground was totally transformed as two new stands were built. The first change occurred in 1927, when, at a cost of £2,373, a small stand was erected in the north west corner. A year later, the old Leppings Lane covered stand was demolished to make way for a splendid new stand which boosted the capacity of the ground by 12,000 to

The north west corner

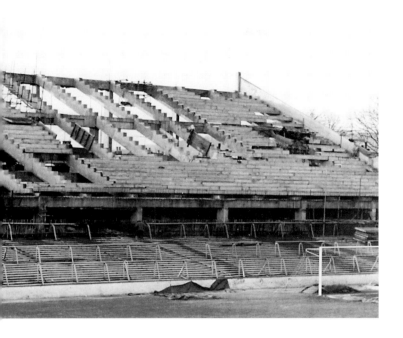

an estimated figure of between 80,000 and 85,000. The impressive new edifice, which cost Wednesday £7,233, was designed by Frank Bradshaw (the architect behind the old Olive Grove stand) of Chapman & Jenkinson; with the regular contractors Freckingham & Sons employed to undertake the construction work. The stand, which was opened in September 1928, provided covered terracing for 7,000, plus a further 5,000 uncovered, and consisted of 90 tonnes of steelwork and 20,000 roof slates. Underneath the imposing new accommodation were store rooms, conveniences and a 40ft refreshment area; and the new stand was eventually completed when a large scoreboard was erected on the roof. On this board were twenty large letters of the alphabet, which, with the aid of a match programme, kept spectators informed of the half- and full-time scores around the country for almost forty years. The new stand took Hillsborough's covered accommodation to 20,000, which, at the time, was the highest of any ground in the UK. Incidentally, at the outbreak of the Second World War, in September 1939, the Leppings Lane end of the ground saw several air raid shelters erected.

Civil Engineering, were charged with the task of constructing the 240ft long stand, which boasted a 75ft cantilevered roof, designed by Husband & Co., who were now Wednesday's consulting engineers and architects. There was also a terraced enclosure at the stand's base and the whole area, which cost a total of £109,036, was first opened when Switzerland faced Germany on 12th July 1966 in the World Cup Finals. Seven months later the new north west terrace was opened at a cost of £29,000, following the dismantling of the small stand built in 1927. This completed a flurry of building work, which, inside five years, had seen Wednesday spend over £200,000 to make Hillsborough arguably the best ground in Britain. Little changed at the Leppings Lane end for over two decades, but the tragic events of April 1989 meant that the terracing was closed for just over two years. When it re-opened in August 1991, it contained 2,494 blue tip-up plastic seats. In fact, that whole end of the ground was restructured in line with the Taylor report, with a new stand roof which extended to cover the new seating, new turnstiles, and a police room was added. The bill for these improvements totalled £800,000. The final alteration came in the summer of 1993 when 1,382 seats were installed in the north west corner increasing the Hillsborough capacity to an all-seater 35,726. Finally, in the summer of 1997, all the old wooden seats in the top tier were replaced with the plastic variety, completing a 98-year metamorphosis of the west end of the stadium.

Without doubt, the West end of Hillsborough has been witness to the greatest number of changes since the ground was opened. In advance of the 1966 World Cup Finals the 1928 stand was razed to the ground in order that a new 4,471-seater West Stand could rise from the ashes. This time the Rotherham company, Tarmac

CURRENT CAPACITY: 8,040

The West Stand, 1999

NORTH

The Wadsley Bridge side of Wednesday's stadium has seen only two structures built in a hundred years, with the first serving the club for well for over sixty of those. The original North Stand was erected during the club's first season at Owlerton, and was 'an elaborate structure embodying all the arrangements for the comfort and convenience of the football spectator which experience and ingenuity can suggest'. The stand was constructed by J. Mastin & Sons, to the design of Sheffield architects W. H. Lancashire & Sons, while the Glasgow company, A. J. Main provided the steelwork, T. Lees the joinery skills, and J. B. Corrie the plumbing. The structure was 290ft long, seated 3,000 fans and was built 'with a tendency to the crescent formation in order to afford a free and uninterrupted view from all vantage points'. The seats were in 13 tiers, with a 'promenade' at the rear. The centre portion was for ticket holders and those supporters who were willing to pay the extra shilling on top of the entrance fee. For an extra sixpence you could gain admission to the seating on either side of the centre section, while at the front was a banked enclosure which accommodated around 2,500 extra supporters. The new stand was revolutionary, for in contrast to the norms of the day all the entrances to the seats were at the rear (Chesterfield's main stand, which was built around the same time, is one of last remaining examples in the Football League of a stand with front stairways) while stairs at the end of each section ensured an equal distribution of spectators, and greatly facilitated their entrance and exit. There was also a separate entrance to a special press area in the front of the middle section, which accommodated between 40 and 50 journalists. It was without doubt the most up-to-date structure in the country, underneath the seating area there were roomy dressing rooms (26ft 6ins x 24ft),

and bathrooms which not only contained baths, showers, and hot and cold water, but even a 'wave attachment'. There was also a refreshment room below run by a Mr & Mrs Donohue (who paid the club £70 for the privilege). The stand also contained a tea and coffee room which was equipped 'cafe style', lavatories for both sexes, various offices, and even a cycle room for those fans who did not travel to Owlerton by tram. The sub-structure was brick and timber with a roof of galvanised iron. This was supported by several steel pillars, 28ft apart—which somewhat ruined the aforementioned uninterrupted view! To complete the work, new turnstiles and a large door were erected on Penistone Road in order to gain entrance to the new stand. The total cost to Wednesday came to £2,674. The new structure was partially opened for the home game with Luton Town in December 1899, and was fully operational on 27th January 1900. This prompted the secretary, Arthur Dickinson, to comment 'they have not spoilt the ship for a ha'p'orth of tar'. Just before it was opened the name of would-be advertisers, 'Bass', was painted out on the gable ends of the stand, and replaced by the club's name. The stand was effectively completed in the summer of 1903 when the grassy bank was replaced by terracing.

The Owls were again at the forefront of stand construction in 1960 when demolition work started on the old stand and the erection, in its place, of the state-of-the-art 10,008 seater, cantilever, new North Stand. In order to finance the building of England's best stand since Arsenal's East Stand was built in the 1930s, Wednesday issued £150,000 worth of 6 per cent debenture stock, which was available to the public in £100 blocks (roughly six times the average weekly wage). The major appeal in this was the healthy debenture rate offered, and the fact that the stock also gave a supporter the right to purchase the same seat for any game played at Hillsborough, regardless of whether

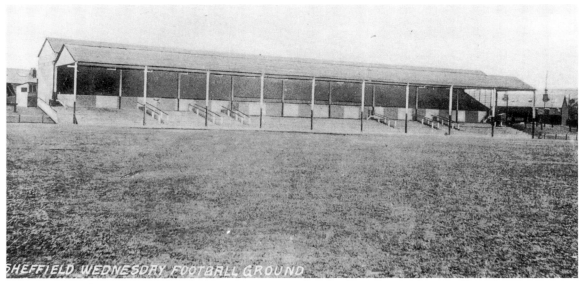

The original North Stand

Wednesday were involved or not. The magnificent new stand was opened by the Chairman of the FA, Sir Stanley Rous, before the home game with Bolton Wanderers on 23rd August 1961, and consisted of 48 rows of tip-up seats in a structure that measured 362ft in width, was 124ft deep, and incorporated a rise of 51ft from front to back. The huge roof was supported by steel girders cantilevered from the back of the stand which projected 16ft. beyond the front row to provide protection from driving rain. The terraces supporting the seats consisted of 3 miles of pre-cast concrete, while other ingredients included: 508 tonnes of steelwork, 4,000 tonnes of reinforced concrete, 115,000 bricks, and 30 miles of beechwood seating. A unique feature was that the stand contained two entrance

Chairman of the FA, Sir Stanley Rous, officially opens the new North Stand

levels, with one entrance 12ft higher accessed via spiral rampways. All round, it was considered to rival any structure built by the giants of European club football. The stand obviously remains in place today, though the capacity dropped to 9,882 in the mid 1980s, and was subsequently reduced further to its current mark. The stand received a facelift in the summer of 1997 when the somewhat uncomfortable wooden seats were replaced with plastic ones, in which SWFC was spelt out by the strategic placing of a number of white seats amongst the blue.

CURRENT CAPACITY: 9,255; TOTAL GROUND CAPACITY FOR THE 1999–2000 SEASON: 39,859

The North Stand, 1999

OTHER DEVELOPMENTS

CLUB SHOP

The club's merchandising operation really began with the launch of the Ozzie Owl mascot in 1967, and this resulted in several booths appearing around the ground which offered various Ozzie souvenirs for sale, such as the ever popular enamel badges. The early 1970s saw the first club shop opened on the south side of the ground, towards the Penistone Road entrance and between the gates and the Commercial office. The small shop shared space with the Supporters Club, where fans could book away trips in the days before Wednesday arranged match travel. However, in the summer of 1977, the Supporters Club moved out, and the Owls extended the club shop into the vacant space, doubling its size. This shop remained the main outlet for Wednesday souvenirs until the early 1990s and was extended in the process, before, in September 1994, the club's two-floor 'Owls Superstore' opened behind the North Stand. Part of the Sports Hall was demolished to make way for this new sales outlet, which remains one of the club's major sources of income.

RESTAURANT

The 1966 World Cup Finals were again the catalyst for this particular development, as on the 12th July 1966 Wednesday opened their first club restaurant. Measuring 120ft x 27ft, it was constructed by the Sheffield firm of William Monks Limited, and was built on stilts behind the South Stand. The Owls restaurant was refitted and reopened as the 'Tavern at Hillsborough' on 9th November 1978, and was later renamed 'The Steps Restaurant' in the 1980s. The massive redevelopment of the South Stand meant the end for the restaurant, but a phoenix rose from the ashes in the shape of 'Dooleys' which opened on 21st November 1997, bearing the name of Wednesday's legendary centre-forward.

Derek Dooley is possibly the greatest centre-forward ever to play for Sheffield Wednesday.

Dooleys Restaurant is now open to give arguably the finest eating-out experience anywhere in Sheffield.

A superb menu and a wide selection of drinks in an atmosphere of open friendliness mixed with intimate ambience.

Lunches		Evenings	
Tues	12-2pm	Tues	6-10pm
Wed	12-2pm	Wed	6-10pm
Thur	12-2pm	Thur	6-10pm
Fri	12-2pm	Fri	6-10pm
Sun	12-3pm (Carvery)	Sat	6-10pm

NOW OPEN SIX DAYS A WEEK

Reserve your table for this unique dining experience - telephone 0114 221 2310/2121 • fax 0114 221 2122.

ELECTRONIC SCOREBOARD

Yet again it was the World Cup that provided Wednesday fans with their first sight of this particular item, as a large scoreboard was installed at the rear of the Kop to keep the fans informed of scores from the other World Cup matches being played. Wednesday retained the scoreboard for the following season and it remained in full working use until the mid 1970s, when it fell into disrepair. The years without an electronic scoreboard ended in early 1983, when Wednesday paid £25,000 for a one line GEC scoreboard to be installed in the south west corner of the ground. This tended to have a bad habit of 'going on the blink', and was replaced in the summer of 1991 with the current one which stands in the same position.

OZZIE OWL CLUB

The Ozzie Owl Social Club was opened on 3rd May 1968 in the South Stand car park above the sight of the old club shop, and it quickly became a popular haunt for Wednesday fans. After Wednesday let the premises to the Mansfield Brewery in September 1970, the social club was converted into the 'Ozzie Nite Owl' which provided wining, dining, dancing and cabaret until 2 am. Further name changes occurred, until, in May 1976, the club allowed the brewery to sub-let the club to J. Baldwin, who subsequently renamed it the 'Hillsborough Suite', and offered match-day hospitality and various evening functions. The premises were finally vacated in the early 1980s, but many fans still have happy memories of the early days of the Ozzie Club.

Actress Diana Dors opens the 'Ozzie Owl Club'

GYM

The month of June 1965 saw work start on Wednesday's own gymnasium situated behind the North Stand. The project was yet another that was linked to the World Cup Finals, the Owls spending the not inconsiderable sum of £45,150 to build the 180ft x 80ft structure, which was used as a temporary press centre and restaurant during the Finals. After the excitement of 1966 passed, the gym was used by the club for its intended purpose, and also, under the guise of the Sports Hall—which was managed for a six-year period by the ex-player, Keith Bannister—it has been available for many years to the general public for five-a-side, badminton, and for other recreational sports.

FLOODLIGHTS

The contractors Husband & Co. were the company who liaised with Eric Taylor throughout the 1950s and 1960s to turn the latter's great vision for Hillsborough into reality. It has been mentioned earlier that the summer of 1954 saw the Kop upgraded, but, at the same time, Husband & Co. were paid around £15,000 to install the club's first floodlighting system.

The lights were, of course, used for the first time in the famous Derek Dooley benefit match, in March 1955, and they continued to illuminate Hillsborough until 1977, when a new floodlighting system was installed. As the Owls have reconstructed the ground across the last fifteen years, the old lights slowly started to become obsolete when lights were installed on the new stand roofs. However, they remained in place until the mid 1990s when one of the traditional sights at any football ground disappeared into the history books for ever.

TICKET OFFICE

The club's first proper ticket office was situated underneath the old restaurant. However, it was only a one-window operation and soon led to the short move to a new ticket office site underneath the walkway that linked the restaurant to the back of the South Stand. This was slowly extended over the years before a move came to the new spacious ticket office which, of course, is now situated behind the Owls Superstore.

The gym

Floodlight generators in the 1950s

Chapter 11

The Hillsborough Record
1899–1999

Date	Opponents	Competition	Score	Scorers	Att.
02 Sep. 1899	Chesterfield	Division 2	5–1	Millar 2(64, 78), Spiksley (33), Ferrier(38), Brash (81)	12000
Massey, Earp, Langley, Ferrier, T.Crawshaw, Ruddlesdin, Brash, Pryce, Millar, Wright, Spiksley					
16 Sep. 1899	Bolton Wanderers	Division 2	2–1	Spiksley(27), Millar (32)	12000
Massey, Layton, Langley, Ferrier, T.Crawshaw, Ruddlesdin, Lee, Pryce, Millar, Wright, Spiksley					
30 Sep. 1899	Newton Heath	Division 2	2–1	Wright(42), Langley(65)	8500
Massey, Layton, Langley, Ferrier, T.Crawshaw, Ruddlesdin, Lee, Pryce, Millar, Wright, Spiksley					
21 Oct. 1899	Small Heath	Division 2	4–0	Wright 2(10, 38), Millar(28), Spiksley(33)	13500
Massey, Layton, Langley, Ferrier, T.Crawshaw, Ruddlesdin, Lee, Pryce, Millar, Wright, Spiksley					
02 Dec. 1899	Luton Town	Division 2	6–0	Spiksley 3, Pryce 2(10, 52), Wright(40)	8000
Massey, Layton, Langley, Ferrier, T.Crawshaw, Ruddlesdin, Brash, Pryce, Millar, Wright, Spiksley					
16 Dec. 1899	Walsall	Division 2	2–0	Spiksley(5), Millar(76)	4000
Massey, Layton, Langley, Ferrier, T.Crawshaw, Ruddlesdin, Brash, Pryce, Millar, Wright, Spiksley					
01 Jan. 1900	Grimsby Town	Division 2	2–1	Langley(68), Wright(83)	15000
Massey, Layton, Langley, P.Crawshaw, T.Crawshaw, Ruddlesdin, Brash, Pryce, Millar, Wright, Spiksley					
06 Jan. 1900	Gainsborough Trinity	Division 2	5–1	Millar 4(16, 60, 75, –), Brash(78)	3000
Massey, Layton, Langley, Ferrier, T.Crawshaw, Ruddlesdin, Brash, Pryce, Millar, Wright, Spiksley					
20 Jan. 1900	Loughborough	Division 2	5–0	Wright 2(25, 70), Millar(2), Topham(–), Langley(89)pen.	4000
Massey, Layton, Langley, Ferrier, T.Crawshaw, Ruddlesdin, Simmons, Pryce, Millar, Wright, Topham					
27 Jan. 1900	Bolton Wanderers	F.A.Cup 1	1–0	Wright(49)	12390
Massey, Layton, Langley, Ferrier, T.Crawshaw, Ruddlesdin, Brash, Pryce, Millar, Wright, Topham					
19 Feb. 1900	Sheffield United	F.A.Cup 2R	0–2		23000
Mallinson, Layton, Langley, Ferrier, T.Crawshaw, Ruddlesdin, Brash, Pryce, Lee, Wright, Topham					
27 Feb. 1900	Barnsley	Division 2	5–1	Wright 3, Brash(5), Davis(11)	3000
Mallinson, Layton, Langley, Ferrier, T.Crawshaw, Ruddlesdin, Brash, Pryce, Davis, Wright, Topham					
03 Mar. 1900	New Brighton Tower	Division 2	4–0	Wright 2(30, 39), Pryce(60), Brash(70)	5000
Mallinson, Layton, Langley, Ferrier, T.Crawshaw, Ruddlesdin, Brash, Pryce, Davis, Wright, Topham					
12 Mar. 1900	Burton Swifts	Division 2	6–0	Topham(35), Wright(40), Ferrier(60), Ruddlesdin(62), Crawshaw(–), Earp(75)	3000
Bolsover, Layton, Earp, Ferrier, T.Crawshaw, Ruddlesdin, Brash, Davis, Millar, Wright, Topham					
17 Mar. 1900	Woolwich Arsenal	Division 2	3–1	Davis 2(14, 89), Ruddlesdin(21)	4500
Bolsover, Earp, Layton, Ferrier, T.Crawshaw, Ruddlesdin, Brash, Davis, Millar, Wright, Spiksley					
31 Mar. 1900	Leicester Fosse	Division 2	2–0	Beech(48), Wright(77)	13500
Massey, Earp, Layton, Ferrier, T.Crawshaw, Ruddlesdin, Davis, Pryce, Beech, Wright, Topham					
14 Apr. 1900	Burslem Port Vale	Division 2	4–0	Wright 3(8, 54, 62), Davis(2)	5000
Massey, Layton, Langley, Ferrier, T.Crawshaw, Ruddlesdin, Brash, Pryce, Millar, Wright, Davis					
17 Apr. 1900	Lincoln City	Division 2	1–0	Ruddlesdin(21)	6000
Massey, Layton, Langley, Ferrier, T.Crawshaw, Ruddlesdin, Brash, Pryce, Millar, Wright, Davis					
28 Apr. 1900	Middlesbrough	Division 2	3–0	Davis 2(7, –), Pryce(46)	4000
Massey, Layton, Langley, Ferrier, T.Crawshaw, Ruddlesdin, Brash, Pryce, Millar, Wright, Davis					

OTHER GAMES AT HILLSBOROUGH

16 Apr. 1900	Sunday School Final	Wycliffe 1	Meadow Hall 2	n/k
21 Apr. 1900	Stores Cup	Star(Cole Brothers) 1	Alliance(Cockaynes) 2	n/k
07 May 1900	Wednesday Shield s/f	Central Board 2	Hillsborough 3	n/k
07 May 1900	Wednesday Shield s/f	Duchess Road 2	Pyebank 1	n/k
12 May 1900	Wednesday Shield Fnl	Hillsborough 6	Duchess Road 0	n/k
12 May 1900	Clegg Shield Final	Blue Coat 3	Central School 1	n/k
		Charity School		

Date	Opponents	Competition	Score	Scorers	Att.
08 Sep. 1900	Bolton Wanderers	Division 1	1–0	Wright(77)	18000
Massey, Layton, Langley, Ferrier, T.Crawshaw, Ruddlesdin, Davis, Pryce, A.Wilson, Wright, Malloch					
22 Sep. 1900	Notts County	Division 1	4–1	Wilson 2, Wright(1), Crawshaw(89)	17500
Massey, Layton, Langley, Ferrier, T.Crawshaw, Ruddlesdin, Davis, Pryce, A.Wilson, Wright, Malloch					
06 Oct. 1900	Preston North End	Division 1	0–1		10000
Massey, Layton, Langley, Ferrier, T.Crawshaw, Ruddlesdin, Davis, Pryce, A.Wilson, Wright, Malloch					
03 Nov. 1900	Aston Villa	Division 1	3–2	Wilson(25), Wright(60), Davis(62)	20000
Massey, Layton, Langley, Ferrier, T.Crawshaw, Ruddlesdin, Spiksley, Davis, A.Wilson, Wright, Malloch					
17 Nov. 1900	Liverpool	Division 1	3–2	Wilson 2(17, 33), Crawshaw(15)	12000
Massey, Layton, Langley, Ferrier, T.Crawshaw, Ruddlesdin, McWhinnie, Davis, A.Wilson, Wright, Malloch					
01 Dec. 1900	Newcastle United	Division 1	2–2	Malloch(–), Ferrier(82)	10000
Massey, Layton, Langley, Ferrier, T.Crawshaw, Ruddlesdin, McWhinnie, Davis, A.Wilson, Wright, Malloch					
22 Dec. 1900	Derby County	Division 1	2–1	Malloch(20), Wright(57)	6000
Massey, Layton, Langley, Ferrier, T.Crawshaw, Ruddlesdin, Davis, Pryce, A.Wilson, Wright, Malloch					
28 Dec. 1900	The Casuals	Langley Benefit	4–2	Chapman 2(10, 15), Tivey og., Simpson	3000
Stubbs, Cole, Langley, P.Crawshaw, Thackeray, Fish, McWhinnie, Millar, H.Simpson, Chapman, Spiksley					
29 Dec. 1900	Manchester City	Division 1	4–1	Wilson(48), Pryce(60), Malloch, Davis(82)	15000
Massey, Layton, Langley, Ferrier, T.Crawshaw, Ruddlesdin, Davis, Pryce, A.Wilson, Wright, Malloch					
01 Jan. 1901	Wolverhampton W.	Division 1	2–0	Wright(40), Pryce(57)	25000
Massey, Layton, Langley, Ferrier, T.Crawshaw, Ruddlesdin, Davis, Pryce, A.Wilson, Wright, Malloch					
12 Jan. 1901	Bury	Division 1	1–2	Wilson(22)	10000
Massey, Layton, Langley, Ferrier, T.Crawshaw, Ruddlesdin, Davis, Pryce, A.Wilson, Wright, Malloch					
09 Feb. 1901	Bury	F.A.Cup 1	0–1		27000
Massey, Layton, Langley, Ferrier, T.Crawshaw, Ruddlesdin, Spiksley, Pryce, A.Wilson, Wright, Malloch					
16 Feb. 1901	Blackburn Rovers	Division 1	1–1	Chapman(44)	7000
Stubbs, Layton, Langley, Ferrier, T.Crawshaw, Ruddlesdin, McWhinnie, Pryce, A.Wilson, Chapman, Spiksley					
02 Mar. 1901	Stoke	Division 1	4–0	Wright(5), Davis(44), Wilson(51), Chapman(57)	4000
Stubbs, Layton, Langley, Ferrier, T.Crawshaw, Ruddlesdin, Davis, Chapman, A.Wilson, Wright, Spiksley					
16 Mar. 1901	West Bromwich Albion	Division 1	2–1	Millar(39), Davis(70)	10000
Stubbs, Layton, Langley, Ferrier, T.Crawshaw, Ruddlesdin, Davis, Chapman, Millar, Wright, Malloch					
30 Mar. 1901	Everton	Division 1	3–1	Chapman 2(–, 65), Spiksley(66)	4500
Stubbs, Layton, Gosling, Ferrier, Thackeray, Fish, Davis, Chapman, A.Wilson, Wright, Spiksley					
09 Apr. 1901	Nottingham Forest	Division 1	4–1	Wilson(9), Langley(54)pen., Layton(68), Crawshaw(75)	18000
Stubbs, Layton, Langley, Ferrier, T.Crawshaw, Ruddlesdin, Davis, Chapman, A.Wilson, Wright, Spiksley					
13 Apr. 1901	Sunderland	Division 1	1–0	Wilson(65)	14000
Stubbs, Layton, Langley, Ferrier, T.Crawshaw, Ruddlesdin, Davis, Chapman, A.Wilson, Wright, Spiksley					
29 Apr. 1901	Sheffield United	Division 1	1–0	Wilson(48)	11000
Stubbs, Layton, Langley, Ferrier, T.Crawshaw, Ruddlesdin, Davis, Chapman, A.Wilson, Wright, Spiksley					

OTHER GAMES AT HILLSBOROUGH

20 Aug. 1900	Public Trial Match	Stripes 1	Whites 4	3000
22 Aug. 1900	Public Trial Match	Stripes 4	Whites 1	n/k
27 Aug. 1900	Public Trial Match	Stripes v. Whites – score n/k		n/k
02 Jan. 1901	Boys	Sheffield 0	Nottingham 0	3000
20 Feb. 1901	Representative	Royal Artillery 0	4th Yorkshire Regiment 4	n/k
20 Apr. 1901	Sunday School Final	Wycliffe 0	Heeley Friends 0	n/k
25 Apr. 1901	S.School Final – Rep.	Wycliffe 2	Heeley Friends 1	n/k
04 May 1901	Wednesday Shield Fnl	Duchess Road 0	Central Board 0	n/k
04 May 1901	Clegg Shield Final	Gleadless Board 2	Hillsborough 2	n/k
11 May 1901	W. Shield Final – Rep.	Duchess Road 2	Central Board 1	n/k
11 May 1901	C. Shield Final – Rep.	Gleadless Board 2	Hillsborough 0	n/k

Date	Opponents	Competition	Score	Scorers	Att.
07 Sep. 1901	Grimsby Town	Division 1	3–1	Wilson 2(80, 89), Crawshaw(82)	17500
Stubbs, Layton, Langley, Ferrier, T.Crawshaw, Ruddlesdin, Davis, Chapman, A.Wilson, Wright, Spiksley					
21 Sep. 1901	Bolton Wanderers	Division 1	5–1	Chapman 2(4, 78), Wilson(1), Brown(64)og., Davis(81)	7000
Lyall, Layton, Langley, Ferrier, T.Crawshaw, Ruddlesdin, Davis, Chapman, A.Wilson, Wright, Spiksley					
05 Oct. 1901	Wolverhampton W.	Division 1	1–1	Wilson(30)	7500
Lyall, Layton, Langley, Ferrier, T.Crawshaw, Ruddlesdin, Davis, Chapman. A.Wilson, Wright, Spiksley					
19 Oct. 1901	Newcastle United	Division 1	0–0		16000
Lyall, Layton, Langley, Ferrier, T.Crawshaw, Ruddlesdin, Davis, Chapman, A.Wilson, Wright, Spiksley					
02 Nov. 1901	Sheffield United	Division 1	1–0	Wilson(20)	27500
Lyall, Layton, Langley, Ferrier, T.Crawshaw, Ruddlesdin, Dryburgh, Chapman, A.Wilson, Wright, Malloch					
16 Nov. 1901	Bury	Division 1	4–1	Malloch 2(36, 41), Dryburgh(27), Spiksley(50)	10000
Lyall, Layton, Langley, Ferrier, T.Crawshaw, Ruddlesdin, Dryburgh, Chapman, A.Wilson, Malloch, Spiksley					
30 Nov. 1901	Stoke	Division 1	3–1	Malloch(15), Chapman(30), Spiksley(83)	8500
Lyall, Layton, Langley, Ferrier, T.Crawshaw, Ruddlesdin, Dryburgh, Chapman, A.Wilson, Malloch, Spiksley					
14 Dec. 1901	Sunderland	Division 1	1–1	Chapman(78)	5500
Lyall, Layton, Langley, Ferrier, T.Crawshaw, Fish, Davis, Chapman, A.Wilson, Malloch, Spiksley					
26 Dec. 1901	Manchester City	Division 1	2–1	Wright(75), Spiksley(85)	20000
Lyall, Layton, Langley, Ruddlesdin, T.Crawshaw, Fish, Davis, Wright, A.Wilson, Malloch, Spiksley					
30 Dec. 1901	The Corinthians	Crawshaw Benefit	3–4	Wilson, Malloch, Spiksley	8000
Lyall, Layton, Langley, P.Crawshaw, T.Crawshaw(Moralee), Fish, Dryburgh, Wright, A.Wilson, Malloch, Spiksley					
11 Jan. 1902	Notts County	Division 1	4–0	Spiksley(18), Chapman(45), Wright(54), Moralee(56)	9000
Lyall, Layton, Langley, P.Crawshaw, Moralee, Fish, Davis, Wright, Hutton, Chapman, Spiksley					
25 Jan. 1902	Sunderland	F.A.Cup 1	0–1		30,096
Lyall, Layton, Langley, Fish, T.Crawshaw, Ruddlesdin, Dryburgh, Wright, A.Wilson, Malloch, Spiksley					
22 Feb. 1902	Aston Villa	Division 1	1–0	Davis(4)	10500
Lyall, Layton, Langley, Ferrier, T.Crawshaw, Ruddlesdin, Davis, Dryburgh, A.Wilson, Wright, Malloch					
08 Mar. 1902	Nottingham Forest	Division 1	0–2		9000
Lyall, Layton, Langley, Ferrier, T.Crawshaw, Ruddlesdin, Davis, Chapman, A.Wilson, Wright, Malloch					
17 Mar. 1902	Derby County	Division 1	2–0	Dryburgh 2(75, –)	4500
Lyall, Layton, Langley, Ferrier, T.Crawshaw, Ruddlesdin, Dryburgh, Chapman, A.Wilson, Wright, Malloch					
22 Mar. 1902	Blackburn Rovers	Division 1	0–1		8000
Lyall, Layton, Langley, Ferrier, T.Crawshaw, Ruddlesdin, Davis, Chapman, A.Wilson, Dryburgh, Malloch					
01 Apr. 1902	Liverpool	Division 1	1–1	Wilson(38)	17000
Lyall, Layton, Langley, Ferrier, T.Crawshaw, Ruddlesdin, Davis, Chapman, A.Wilson, Beech, Spiksley					
05 Apr. 1902	Everton	Division 1	1–1	Beech(70)	2500
Lyall, Layton, Langley, Ferrier, T.Crawshaw, Ruddlesdin, Davis, Chapman, V.Simpson, Beech, Spiksley					
19 Apr. 1902	Small Heath	Division 1	1–2	Spiksley (30secs.)	13500
Lyall, Layton, Langley, Ferrier, T.Crawshaw, Ruddlesdin, Davis, Chapman, V.Simpson, Beech, Spiksley					
03 May 1902	Sheffield United	Friendly	3–0	Beech, Wilson, Spiksley	4747
Lyall, Layton, Ruddlesdin, Ferrier, T.Crawshaw, Fish, Davis, Chapman, A.Wilson, Beech, Spiksley					

OTHER GAMES AT HILLSBOROUGH

21 Aug. 1901	Public Trial Match	Stripes 1	Whites 2		3000
28 Aug. 1901	Public Trial Match	Stripes 2	Whites 0		2000
18 Jan. 1902	F.A.Amateur Cup 1	Sheffield F.C. 7	Stanley United 3		400
15 Mar. 1902	Clegg Shield	Crookesmoor 1	Duchess Road 3		n/k
15 Mar. 1902	Clegg Shield s/f	Hillsborough Board 2	All Saints 2		n/k
15 Mar. 1902	Clegg Shield s/f	Duchess Road 2	Crookesmoor 1		n/k
31 Mar. 1902	Sunday School s/f	Shiregreen 1	Wycliffe 1		n/k
12 Apr. 1902	Sunday School s/f – Rep	Shiregreen 1	Wycliffe 1		n/k
12 Apr. 1902	Sunday School s/f – Rep	Heeley Friends 0	Thorpe Hesley 0		n/k
14 Apr. 1902	Sunday School s/f – 2R	Shiregreen 1	Wycliffe 2		n/k
19 Apr. 1902	Sunday School s/f – 2R	Heeley Friends 2	Thorpe Hesley 1		n/k
28 Apr. 1902	Sunday School Final	Heeley Friends 5	Wycliffe 0		n/k
29 Apr. 1902	Wednesday Shield s/f	Duchess Road 4	Neepsend 1		n/k
08 May 1902	Wednesday Shield Final	Duchess Road 3	Central Board 0		n/k
12 May 1902	Clegg Shield Final	Hillsborough Board 4	Duchess Road 1		n/k

Date	Opponents	Competition	Score	Scorers	Att.
13 Sep. 1902	Middlesbrough	Division 1	2–0	Wilson(77), Davis(85)	20000
Lyall, Layton, Langley, Ferrier, T.Crawshaw, Ruddlesdin, Davis, Chapman, A.Wilson, Malloch, Spiksley					
27 Sep. 1902	Wolverhampton W.	Division 1	1–1	Chapman(27)pen.	15000
Lyall, Layton, Langley, Ferrier, T.Crawshaw, Ruddlesdin, Davis, Chapman, A.Wilson, Malloch, Spiksley					
11 Oct. 1902	Sheffield United	Division 1	0–1		21500
Lyall, Layton, Langley, Ferrier, Moralee, Ruddlesdin, Davis, Chapman, A.Wilson, Malloch, Spiksley					
08 Nov. 1902	Bury	Division 1	2–0	Wilson(–), Chapman(65)	8000
Lyall, Layton, Langley, Ferrier, T.Crawshaw, Ruddlesdin, Davis, Chapman, A.Wilson, Malloch, Spiksley					
22 Nov. 1902	Sunderland	Division 1	1–0	Chapman(6)	12500
Lyall, Layton, Langley, Ferrier, T.Crawshaw, Ruddlesdin, Davis, Chapman, A.Wilson, Malloch, Spiksley					
06 Dec. 1902	Everton	Division 1	4–1	Wilson 3(25, 40, –), Spiksley(70)	10000
Lyall, Thackeray, Langley, Ferrier, T.Crawshaw, Ruddlesdin, Davis, Chapman, A.Wilson, Malloch, Spiksley					
13 Dec. 1902	Derby County	Division 1	0–1		14000
Lyall, Layton, Langley, Ferrier, T.Crawshaw, Ruddlesdin, Davis, Chapman, A.Wilson, Beech, Malloch					
27 Dec. 1902	Notts County	Division 1	2–0	Davis(3), Chapman(52)	30000
Lyall, Layton, Langley, Ferrier, T.Crawshaw, Ruddlesdin, Davis, Chapman, A.Wilson, Malloch, Spiksley					
29 Dec. 1902	The Corinthians	Ferrier Benefit	5–3	G.Simpson 2, Bartlett, Davis, V.Simpson	7000
Lyall, Layton, Burton, Ferrier, R.Hoyland, Bartlett, Davis, Chapman, V.Simpson, G.Hoyland, G.Simpson					
01 Jan. 1903	Aston Villa	Division 1	4–0	Ruddlesdin 2(65, 89), Wilson(7), Malloch(20)	28000
Lyall, Layton, Langley, Ferrier, T.Crawshaw, Ruddlesdin, Davis, Chapman, A.Wilson, Malloch, Spiksley					
03 Jan. 1903	Bolton Wanderers	Division 1	3–0	Davis 3(20, –, 70)	10500
Lyall, Layton, Langley, Ferrier, T.Crawshaw, Ruddlesdin, Davis, Chapman, A.Wilson, Malloch, Spiksley					
17 Jan. 1903	Newcastle United	Division 1	3–0	Chapman 2(27, 68), Spiksley(85)	10000
Lyall, Layton, Langley, Ferrier, T.Crawshaw, Ruddlesdin, Davis, Chapman, A.Wilson, Malloch, Spiksley					
31 Jan. 1903	Liverpool	Division 1	3–1	Chapman 2(20, 67pen.), Davis(–)	16000
Lyall, Layton, Langley, Ferrier, T.Crawshaw, Ruddlesdin, Davis, Chapman, A.Wilson, Malloch, Spiksley					
12 Feb. 1903	Blackburn Rovers	F.A.Cup 1R	0–1		25410
Lyall, Thackeray, Langley, Ferrier, T.Crawshaw, Ruddlesdin, Davis, Chapman, A.Wilson, Malloch, Spiksley					
14 Feb. 1903	Grimsby Town	Division 1	1–1	Langley(36)pen.	9000
Lyall, Thackeray, Langley, Ferrier, T.Crawshaw, Ruddlesdin, Chapman, Beech, A.Wilson, Stewart, Spiksley					
28 Feb. 1903	Nottingham Forest	Division 1	1–0	Langley(42)pen.	12500
Lyall, Layton, Langley, Ferrier, T.Crawshaw, Ruddlesdin, Davis, Chapman, A.Wilson, Malloch, Spiksley					
14 Mar. 1903	Blackburn Rovers	Division 1	0–0		9000
Lyall, Layton, Langley, Ferrier, T.Crawshaw, Ruddlesdin, Ryalls, Chapman, A.Wilson, Malloch, G.Simpson					
28 Mar. 1903	Stoke	Division 1	1–0	Marrison(65)	8000
Lyall, Thackeray, Langley, Ferrier, T.Crawshaw, Ruddlesdin, Davis, Marrison, A.Wilson, Malloch, Spiksley					
18 Apr. 1903	West Bromwich Albion	Division 1	3–1	Wilson(8), Langley(–)pen., Spiksley(85)	15500
Lyall, Layton, Langley, Ferrier, T.Crawshaw, Ruddlesdin, V.Simpson, Chapman, A.Wilson, Malloch, Spiksley					

OTHER GAMES AT HILLSBOROUGH

22 Aug. 1902	Public Trial Match	Stripes 0	Whites 2		4000
27 Oct. 1902	Inter City	Sheffield 0	Glasgow 2		n/k
24 Jan. 1903	F.A. Amateur Cup	Sheffield F.C. 3	Scarborough 0		n/k
07 Feb. 1903	Boys	Sheffield 2	Derby 0		3000
21 Mar. 1903	Boys	Sheffield Manual 0 Training School	Grimsby St. Johns 5		n/k
04 Apr. 1903	All Saints Jnr lge s/f	All Saints 4	Owlerton Reform 1		n/k
13 Apr. 1903	Clegg Shield Final	Charity School 2	Crookesmoor 1		n/k
13 Apr. 1903	Sunday School s/f	Oxford Street 2	Heeley Friends 4		n/k
14 Apr. 1903	Sunday School s/f	South Street N.C. 1	Wycliffe 3		n/k
15 Apr. 1903	Wednesday Shield s/f	Crookesmoor 0	Hillsborough 1		n/k
15 Apr. 1903	Wednesday Shield s/f	Charity School 5	Alma Board 3		n/k
23 Apr. 1903	Thursday Lge. Final	Castlefords 1	Whitworths 0		n/k
02 May 1903	Wednesday Shield Fnl	Hillsborough 7	Charity School 2		n/k

Date	Opponents	Competition	Score	Scorers	Att.
05 Sep. 1903	Middlesbrough	Division 1	4–1	Malloch(15), Wilson(37), Chapman(55), Simpson(75)	18000
Lyall, Layton, Langley, Ferrier, T.Crawshaw, Ruddlesdin, Davis, Chapman, A.Wilson, Malloch, G.Simpson					
19 Sep. 1903	Bury	Division 1	1–1	Wilson(40)	18000
Lyall, Layton, Langley, Ferrier, T.Crawshaw, Ruddlesdin, Davis, Chapman, A.Wilson, Malloch, G.Simpson					
03 Oct. 1903	Nottingham Forest	Division 1	2–1	Wilson(15), Henderson(31)og.	30000
Lyall, Layton, Langley, Ferrier, T.Crawshaw, Ruddlesdin, Davis, Chapman, A.Wilson, Stewart, G.Simpson					
24 Oct. 1903	West Bromwich Albion	Division 1	1–0	Chapman(1)	12000
Lyall, Layton, Burton, Ferrier, T.Crawshaw, Ruddlesdin, Davis, Chapman, A.Wilson, Malloch, G.Simpson					
07 Nov. 1903	Everton	Division 1	1–0	Chapman(38)	15500
Lyall, Layton, Burton, Ferrier, T.Crawshaw, Ruddlesdin, Davis, Chapman, A.Wilson, Malloch, G.Simpson					
21 Nov. 1903	Derby County	Division 1	1–0	Simpson(3)	6000
Lyall, Layton, Burton, Ferrier, T.Crawshaw, Ruddlesdin, Davis, Chapman, A.Wilson, Malloch, G.Simpson					
19 Dec. 1903	Newcastle United	Division 1	1–1	Langley(65)pen.	8500
Lyall, Layton, Langley, Ferrier, T.Crawshaw, Ruddlesdin, Davis, Chapman, A.Wilson, V.Simpson, Malloch					
29 Dec. 1903	The Corinthians	Layton Benefit	1–1	G.Hoyland(65)	4815
Jarvis, Burton, Langley, P.Crawshaw, J.Hoyland, Ruddlesdin, Hemmingfield, G.Hoyland, A.Wilson, V.Simpson, Spiksley(G.Simpson 5)					
01 Jan. 1904	Wolverhampton W.	Division 1	4–0	Simpson 2(46, 49), Chapman(28)pen., Malloch(50)	18000
Lyall, Layton, Burton, Ferrier, T.Crawshaw, Ruddlesdin, Davis, Chapman, A.Wilson, V.Simpson, Malloch					
09 Jan. 1904	Liverpool	Division 1	2–1	Crawshaw(46), Stewart(–)	12000
Lyall, Layton, Burton, Ferrier, T.Crawshaw, Ruddlesdin, Davis, Chapman, A.Wilson, Stewart, Malloch					
23 Jan. 1904	Blackburn Rovers	Division 1	3–1	Chapman 2(40, 70), Crawshaw(49)	13000
Lyall, Layton, Burton, Hemmingfield, T.Crawshaw, Ruddlesdin, Davis, Chapman, A.Wilson, V.Simpson, Malloch					
10 Feb. 1904	Plymouth Argyle	F.A.Cup 1R	2–0	Davis(41), Chapman(70)pen.	18845
Lyall, Layton, Burton, Ferrier, T.Crawshaw, Ruddlesdin, Davis, Chapman, A.Wilson, V.Simpson, Malloch					
13 Feb. 1904	Sunderland	Division 1	0–0		8500
Lyall, Layton, Burton, Ferrier, T.Crawshaw, Ruddlesdin, Davis, Chapman, Beech, Stewart, Malloch					
20 Feb. 1904	Manchester United	F.A.Cup 2	6–0	V.Simpson 3(1, 75, 89), Davis 2(17, 59), G.Simpson(–)	22051
Lyall, Layton, Burton, Ferrier, T.Crawshaw, Ruddlesdin, Davis, Chapman, Beech, V.Simpson, G.Simpson					
22 Feb. 1904	Notts County	Division 1	2–0	G.Simpson 2(43, –)	7000
Lyall, Layton, Burton, Ferrier, T.Crawshaw, Bartlett, Davis, Chapman, V.Simpson, Stewart, G.Simpson					
27 Feb. 1904	Small Heath	Division 1	3–2	Chapman(7), Davis(20), Hemmingfield(35)	7000
Lyall, Layton, Burton, Ferrier, T.Crawshaw, Ruddlesdin, Davis, Chapman, Hemmingfield, Stewart, G.Simpson					
09 Mar. 1904	Tottenham Hotspur	F.A.Cup 3R	2–0	Davis(57), Chapman(88)	30011
Lyall, Layton, Burton, Ferrier, T.Crawshaw, Ruddlesdin, Davis, Chapman, Hemmingfield, V.Simpson, G.Simpson					
12 Mar. 1904	Stoke	Division 1	1–0	Chapman(87)	12000
Lyall, Layton, Burton, Ferrier, Hemmingfield, Bartlett, Davis, Chapman, Eyre, Malloch, G.Simpson					
26 Mar. 1904	Manchester City	Division 1	1–0	Chapman(6)	25000
Lyall, Layton, Burton, Ferrier, T.Crawshaw, Ruddlesdin, Davis, Chapman, G.Hoyland, Beech, G.Simpson					
09 Apr. 1904	Sheffield United	Division 1	3–0	Chapman 2(1, 30), Simpson(80)	17500
Lyall, Layton, Burton, Ferrier, T.Crawshaw, Ryalls, Chapman, A.Wilson, Stewart, G.Simpson					
23 Apr. 1904	Aston Villa	Division 1	4–2	Wilson(6), Chapman(12), Davis(35), Simpson(67)	15000
Lyall, Layton, Burton, Ferrier, T.Crawshaw, Bartlett, Davis, Chapman, A.Wilson, Malloch, G.Simpson					

OTHER GAMES AT HILLSBOROUGH

22 Aug. 1903	Public Trial Match	Stripes 3	Whites 3	7000
24 Sep. 1903	Friendly	Sheffield Bankers 3	Leicester Bankers 2	n/k
06 Feb. 1904	Boys	Sheffield 0	Manchester 5	5000
04 Apr. 1904	Sunday School s/f	Wycliffe 3	Oxford Street 2	n/k
27 Apr. 1904	Sunday School Fnl–Rep	Wycliffe 4	Heeley Friends 0	n/k
04 May 1904	Wednesday Shield s/f	Duchess Road 3	Netherthorpe 0	n/k
04 May 1904	Wednesday Shield s/f	Crookesmoor 0	Hillsborough 2	n/k
07 May 1904	Clegg Shield Final	Duchess Road 2	Charity School 2	n/k
09 May 1904	Wednesday Shield Final	Hillsborough 2	Duchess Road 1	n/k
16 May 1904	Clegg Shield Fnl–Rep.	Duchess Road 1	Charity School 2	n/k

1900–01
Frith (trainer), Ruddlesdin, Langley, Massey, T. Crawshaw, Layton, Millar;
McWhinnie, Pryce, Wilson, Wright, Malloch;
Davis, Ferrier.

1901–02
Frith (trainer), Ruddlesdin, Layton, Langley, Massey, Millar, Ferrier;
McWhinnie, Davis, Pryce, Wilson, Wright, Malloch, T. Crawshaw.

1902–03
Eyre, Ryalls, Hemmingfield, Beech, Stewart, Bartlett, Thackeray,
Moralee, P. Crawshaw, W. Ruddlesdin;
Davis (trainer), Marrison, H. Ruddlesdin, Ferrier, Layton, Lyall,
T. Crawshaw, Stubbs, Burton, Cawley (staff), Frith (trainer);
V.S. Simpson, Davis, Chapman, Wilson, Malloch, Spiksley, G.
Simpson.

1904–05
Hemmingfield, Stewart, Jarvis, Bartlett;
Davis (ass. trainer), Ferrier, Langley, Lyall, T. Crawshaw, Layton,
Burton, Ruddlesdin, Frith (trainer);
Davis, Chapman, Wilson, Malloch, G. Simpson

Date	Opponents	Competition	Score	Scorers	Att.
10 Sep. 1904	Wolverhampton W.	Division 1	4–0	Wilson 2(57, 60), Davis(47), Chapman(87)	18000
Lyall, Layton, Burton, Ferrier, T.Crawshaw, Bartlett, Davis, Chapman, A.Wilson, Malloch, G.Simpson					
24 Sep. 1904	Aston Villa	Division 1	3–2	Davis(61), Chapman(62), Simpson(75)	15500
Lyall, Layton, Burton, Ferrier, T.Crawshaw, Bartlett, Davis, Chapman, A.Wilson, Malloch, G.Simpson					
03 Oct. 1904	Sheffield United	Charity	0–2		7991
Lyall, Layton, Langley, Ferrier, T.Crawshaw, Bartlett, Davis, Chapman, A.Wilson, Malloch, G.Simpson					
08 Oct. 1904	Nottingham Forest	Division 1	2–0	Simpson(9), Davis(74)	14000
Lyall, Layton, Burton, Ferrier, T.Crawshaw, Bartlett, Davis, Chapman, A.Wilson, Malloch, G.Simpson					
15 Oct. 1904	Stoke	Division 1	3–0	Wilson(7), Chapman(16), Simpson(44)	15000
Lyall, Layton, Burton, Ferrier, Hemmingfield, Bartlett, Davis, Chapman, A.Wilson, Malloch, G.Simpson					
29 Oct. 1904	Woolwich Arsenal	Division 1	0–3		13500
Lyall, Layton, Burton, Ferrier, T.Crawshaw, Bartlett, Davis, Chapman, A.Wilson, Malloch, G.Simpson					
12 Nov. 1904	Everton	Division 1	5–5	Davis(10), Stewart(63), G.Simpson(68), V.Simpson(80), Ferrier(89)	12500
Jarvis, Layton, Burton, Ferrier, T.Crawshaw, Ruddlesdin, Davis, Stewart, A.Wilson, V.Simpson, G.Simpson					
26 Nov. 1904	Manchester City	Division 1	2–1	Wilson 2(15, 18)	15000
Lyall, Slavin, Burton, Ferrier, T.Crawshaw, Ruddlesdin, Davis, V.Simpson, A.Wilson, Malloch, G.Simpson					
10 Dec. 1904	Sheffield United	Division 1	1–3	Wilson(30)	16000
Lyall, Layton, Burton, Ferrier, T.Crawshaw, Ruddlesdin, V.Simpson, Stewart, A.Wilson, Malloch, G.Simpson					
27 Dec. 1904	Sunderland	Division 1	1–1	V.Simpson(72)	20000
Jarvis, Slavin, Burton, P.Crawshaw, T.Crawshaw, Ruddlesdin, Davis, Marrison, A.Wilson, V.Simpson, G.Simpson					
31 Dec. 1904	Middlesbrough	Division 1	5–0	Stewart 2(40, 89), Wilson 2, Chapman(20)	12000
Jarvis, Slavin, Burton, P.Crawshaw, T.Crawshaw, Ruddlesdin, Davis, Chapman, A.Wilson, Stewart, G.Simpson					
02 Jan. 1905	Preston North End	Division 1	2–0	Wilson(12), Chapman(22)	17500
Jarvis, Slavin, Burton, Ruddlesdin, Hemmingfield, Bartlett, Davis, Chapman, A.Wilson, Stewart, G.Simpson					
14 Jan. 1905	Bury	Division 1	4–0	Stewart 3(14pen., 53, 74), Hemmingfield(29)	16000
Lyall, Slavin, Burton, Ruddlesdin, T.Crawshaw, Bartlett, Davis, Brittleton, Hemmingfield, Stewart, G.Simpson					
28 Jan. 1905	Blackburn Rovers	Division 1	1–2	Davis(18)	15000
Lyall, Slavin, Burton, Ruddlesdin, T.Crawshaw, Bartlett, Davis, Brittleton, A.Wilson, Stewart, Malloch					
18 Feb. 1905	Portsmouth	F.A.Cup 2	2–1	Stewart(28), Davis(88)	36413
Lyall, Slavin, Burton, Ruddlesdin, T.Crawshaw, Bartlett, Davis, Chapman, Hemmingfield, Stewart, Malloch					
09 Mar. 1905	Preston North End	F.A.Cup 3R	3–0	Simpson(–), Stewart(30), Wilson(38)	24848
Lyall, Slavin, Burton, Ruddlesdin, T.Crawshaw, Bartlett, Davis, Chapman, A.Wilson, Stewart, G.Simpson					
18 Mar. 1905	Small Heath	Division 1	3–1	Hemmingfield(20), Stewart(85), Wilson(87)	12000
Lyall, Layton, Burton, Ruddlesdin, T.Crawshaw, Bartlett, Davis, Hemmingfield, A.Wilson, Stewart, G.Simpson					
01 Apr. 1905	Notts County	Division 1	1–0	Davis(24)	8000
Jarvis, Layton, Burton, Ferrier, T.Crawshaw, Bartlett, Davis, Brittleton, A.Wilson, Stewart, Malloch					
03 Apr. 1905	Derby County	Division 1	1–1	Stewart(67)	3000
Lyall, Eaton, Burton, Ruddlesdin, T.Crawshaw, Bartlett, Davis, Brittleton, A.Wilson, Stewart, Malloch					
26 Apr. 1905	Newcastle United	Division 1	1–3	Simpson(25)	11000
Lyall, Layton, Slavin, Ferrier, T.Crawshaw, Bartlett, Davis, Brittleton, A.Wilson, Stewart, G.Simpson					

OTHER GAMES AT HILLSBOROUGH

24 Aug. 1904	Public Trial Match	Stripes 3	Whites 0	*30 mins. each way	4000
29 Aug. 1904	Public Trial Match	Stripes 0	Whites 2		2000
04 Feb. 1905	Boys (EST 2)	Sheffield 6	Hull 1		n/k
11 Feb. 1905	S.Challenge Cup s/f	Rotherham Main 1	Sheffield United Reserves 2		n/k
04 Mar. 1905	Boys	Sheffield 3	London 1		n/k
11 Mar. 1905	S.Challenge Cup Final	Sheffield United Res. 3	The Wednesday Res. 1		6000
15 Apr. 1905	Sunday School s/f	Wycliffe 5	Oxford Street 2		n/k
24 Apr. 1905	Sunday School Final	Wycliffe 1	Heeley Friends 1		2010
27 Apr. 1905	Thursday League Final	Whitworths 1	Doncaster Thursday 0		n/k
06 May 1905	Clegg Shield Final	Duchess Road 1	All Saints 1		n/k
08 May 1905	Wednesday Shield Final	Charity School 1	Hillsborough 1		n/k
09 May 1905	W. Shield Final – Rep.	Charity School 0	Hillsborough 1		n/k
09 May 1905	Clegg Shield Fnl– Rep.	Duchess Road 3	All Saints 0		n/k

Date	Opponents	Competition	Score	Scorers	Att.
02 Sep. 1905	Manchester City	Division 1	1–0	Stewart(65)	20000
Lyall, Layton, Burton, Ruddlesdin, T.Crawshaw, Bartlett, Davis, Chapman, A.Wilson, Stewart, G.Simpson					
16 Sep. 1905	Middlesbrough	Division 1	3–0	Wilson(38), Stewart(44), Brittleton(70)	18000
Lyall, Layton, Burton, Ruddlesdin, T.Crawshaw, Bartlett, Davis, Brittleton, A.Wilson, Stewart, G.Simpson					
30 Sep. 1905	Newcastle United	Division 1	1–1	Crawshaw(77)	15000
Lyall, Layton, Burton, Ruddlesdin, T.Crawshaw, Bartlett, Davis, Brittleton, A.Wilson, Stewart, G.Simpson					
14 Oct. 1905	Liverpool	Division 1	3–2	Ruddlesdin(3), Stewart(25), Chapman(35)	12000
Lyall, Layton, Burton, Ruddlesdin, T.Crawshaw, Bartlett, Davis, Chapman, A.Wilson, Stewart, G.Simpson					
28 Oct. 1905	Notts County	Division 1	3–1	Wilson(25), Simpson(40), Stewart(85)	10000
Lyall, Layton, Slavin, Ruddlesdin, T.Crawshaw, Bartlett, Davis, Chapman, A.Wilson, Stewart, G.Simpson					
11 Nov. 1905	Bolton Wanderers	Division 1	1–2	Brittleton(69)	7000
Lyall, Layton, Burton, Ruddlesdin, T.Crawshaw, Bartlett, Davis, Brittleton, A.Wilson, Stewart, G.Simpson					
25 Nov. 1905	Blackburn Rovers	Division 1	0–1		12000
Lyall, Layton, Burton, Ruddlesdin, T.Crawshaw, Bartlett, Davis, Chapman, Brittleton, Stewart, Malloch					
09 Dec. 1905	Birmingham	Division 1	4–2	Wilson 2(25, 75), Chapman(35), Simpson	12000
Lyall, Slavin, Burton, Ruddlesdin, T.Crawshaw, Bartlett, Davis, Chapman, A.Wilson, Stewart, G.Simpson					
23 Dec. 1905	Derby County	Division 1	1–0	Ruddlesdin(56)	8000
Lyall, Layton, Burton, Ruddlesdin, T.Crawshaw, Bartlett, Davis, Chapman, A.Wilson, Stewart, G.Simpson					
26 Dec. 1905	Wolverhampton W.	Division 1	5–1	Stewart 4(2, 41, 55, 78), Wilson(4)	18000
Lyall, Layton, Burton, Ruddlesdin, T.Crawshaw, Bartlett, Davis, Chapman, A.Wilson, Stewart, Malloch					
27 Dec. 1905	Nottingham Forest	Division 1	1–0	Stewart(14)	15500
Lyall, Layton, Burton, Brittleton, T.Crawshaw, Ruddlesdin, Davis, Chapman, A.Wilson, Stewart, Malloch					
06 Jan. 1906	Bury	Division 1	1–1	Davis(39)	4500
Lyall, Layton, Burton, Brittleton, T.Crawshaw, Ruddlesdin, Davis, Chapman, A.Wilson, Stewart, Malloch					
13 Jan, 1906	Bristol Rovers	F.A.Cup 1	1–0	Simpson(41)	15661
Lyall, Layton, Burton, Ruddlesdin, T.Crawshaw, Bartlett, Davis, Chapman, A.Wilson, Stewart, G.Simpson					
27 Jan. 1906	Preston North End	Division 1	1–1	Chapman(55)	15000
Lyall, Layton, Burton, Ruddlesdin, T.Crawshaw, Bartlett, Davis, Chapman, A.Wilson, Stewart, Malloch					
03 Feb. 1906	Millwall	F.A.Cup 2	1–1	Stewart(57)	21511
Lyall, Layton, Burton, Ruddlesdin, T.Crawshaw, Bartlett, Davis, Brittleton, A.Wilson, Stewart, Malloch					
10 Feb. 1906	Aston Villa	Division 1	2–2	Davis(50)pen., Stewart(71)	10000
Lyall, Layton, Burton, Ruddlesdin, T.Crawshaw, Bartlett, Davis, Chapman, A.Wilson, Stewart, G.Simpson					
24 Feb. 1906	Nottingham Forest	F.A.Cup 3	4–1	Wilson(12), Simpson(30), Chapman(47), Stewart(71)	36363
Lyall, Layton, Burton, Ruddlesdin, T.Crawshaw, Bartlett, Davis, Chapman, A.Wilson, Stewart, G.Simpson					
24 Mar. 1906	Woolwich Arsenal	Division 1	4–2	Stewart 3(5, –, 80), Chapman(13)	11000
Lyall, Layton, Burton, Ruddlesdin, T.Crawshaw, Bartlett, Davis, Chapman, V.Simpson, Stewart, G.Simpson					
07 Apr. 1906	Sunderland	Division 1	3–3	Wilson 2(40, 65), Simpson(89)	9000
Lyall, Layton, Burton, Ruddlesdin, T.Crawshaw, Bartlett, Reynolds, Brittleton, A.Wilson, Stewart, G.Simpson					
09 Apr. 1906	Stoke	Division 1	2–0	Wilson(57), Simpson(75)	4500
Lyall, Layton, Burton, Brittleton, T.Crawshaw, Bartlett, Davis, Chapman, A.Wilson, Stewart, G.Simpson					
18 Apr. 1906	Sheffield United	Division 1	1–0	Davis(80)pen.	12000
Lyall, Layton, Burton, Brittleton, T.Crawshaw, Bartlett, Davis, Hemmingfield, A.Wilson, Stewart, Malloch					
23 Apr. 1906	Everton	Division 1	3–1	Bradshaw 2(43, 52), Tummon(84)	5000
Lyall, Layton, Crapper, Brittleton, T.Crawshaw, Bartlett, Davis, Bradshaw, A.Wilson, Stewart, Tummon					

OTHER GAMES AT HILLSBOROUGH

24 Aug. 1905	Public Trial Match	Stripes 0	Whites 1		2000
18 Jan. 1906	Representative	Sheffield Tramways 0	Manchester Tramways 5		n/k
13 Feb. 1906	S.Challenge Cup s/f	Denaby United 2	Sheffield United Reserves 2		n/k
16 Apr. 1906	Sunday School Final	All Saints Mission 0	Oxford Street 2		2000
17 Apr. 1906	Free Churches Final	Darnall Congregational 1	Stephen Hill Wesleyens 0		1500
21 Apr. 1906	Bible Class Final	All Saints Mission 1	Lopham Street U.M. 3		800
28 Apr. 1906	Wednesday Shield S/F	Burgoyne Road 0	Gleadless Road 2		n/k
28 Apr. 1906	Hatchard Cup Fnl–Rep.	Parkgate Athletic 4	Tinsley Club 1		n/k
01 May 1906	Clegg Shield S/F	All Saints 4	Charity School 1		n/k
07 May 1906	Clegg Shield Final	All Saints 1	Gleadless 0		n/k

Date	Opponents	Competition	Score	Scorers	Att.
03 Sep. 1906	Newcastle United	Division 1	2–2	Brittleton(10), Tummon(60)	8000
Lyall, Layton, Burton, Hemmingfield, T.Crawshaw, Bartlett, Davis, Brittleton, A.Wilson, Stewart, Tummon					
08 Sep. 1906	Manchester City	Division 1	3–1	Stewart 2(48, 89), Wilson(36)	10000
Lyall, Layton, Burton, Ruddlesdin, T.Crawshaw, Bartlett, Davis, Brittleton, A.Wilson, Stewart, Malloch					
22 Sep. 1906	Preston North End	Division 1	2–1	Stewart 2(43, 80)	16000
Lyall, Layton, Burton, Ruddlesdin, T.Crawshaw, Bartlett, Davis, Bradshaw, A.Wilson, Stewart, G.Simpson					
01 Oct. 1906	Sheffield United	Charity	3–0	Wilson(23), Tummon(33), Davis(75)pen.	6500
Lyall, Layton, Burton, Brittleton, T.Crawshaw, Bartlett, Davis, V.Simpson, A.Wilson, Tummon, Malloch					
06 Oct. 1906	Aston Villa	Division 1	2–1	Wilson(37), Chapman(40)	18000
Lyall, Layton, Burton, T.Crawshaw, Bartlett, Davis, Chapman, A.Wilson, Tummon, Malloch					
20 Oct. 1906	Bristol City	Division 1	3–0	Davis(22, 82), Wilson(89)	20000
Lyall, Layton, Burton, Brittleton, T.Crawshaw, Bartlett, Davis, V.Simpson, A.Wilson, Malloch, Tummon					
03 Nov. 1906	Sheffield United	Division 1	2–2	Wilson 2(44, 53)	12000
Lyall, Layton, Burton, Brittleton, T.Crawshaw, Bartlett, Davis, V.Simpson, A.Wilson, Stewart, Tummon					
17 Nov. 1906	Manchester United	Division 1	5–2	Wilson 2, G.Simpson(3), Crawshaw, Stewart(75)	8500
Lyall, Layton, Burton, Brittleton, T.Crawshaw, Bartlett, Tummon, V.Simpson, A.Wilson, Stewart, G.Simpson					
01 Dec. 1906	Blackburn Rovers	Division 1	3–1	Stewart(40), Wilson(50), G.Simpson(85)	12000
Lyall, Layton, Burton, Brittleton, T.Crawshaw, Bartlett, Tummon, V.Simpson, A.Wilson, Stewart, G.Simpson					
15 Dec. 1906	Birmingham	Division 1	0–1		10000
Lyall, Layton, Burton, Brittleton, T.Crawshaw, Bartlett, Tummon, Chapman, A.Wilson, Stewart, G.Simpson					
25 Dec. 1906	Derby County	Division 1	1–1	Tummon(10)	17500
Lyall, Layton, Burton, Ruddlesdin, Brittleton, Bartlett, Tummon, Chapman, A.Wilson, Rollinson, G.Simpson					
29 Dec. 1906	Bury	Division 1	1–2	Wilson(22)	10000
Lyall, Layton, Slavin, Brittleton, T.Crawshaw, Bartlett, Davis, Lloyd, A.Wilson, Stewart, G.Simpson					
01 Jan. 1907	Woolwich Arsenal	Division 1	1–1	Wilson(50)	14500
Lyall, Layton, Slavin, Brittleton, T.Crawshaw, Bartlett, Tummon, Bradshaw, A.Wilson, Malloch, G.Simpson					
12 Jan. 1907	Wolverhampton W.	F.A.Cup 1	3–2	Tummon(58), Stewart(67), G.Simpson(70)	21938
Lyall, Layton, Burton, Brittleton, T.Crawshaw, Ruddlesdin, Tummon, V.Simpson, A.Wilson, Stewart, G.Simpson					
19 Jan. 1907	Middlesbrough	Division 1	0–2		10000
Lyall, Layton, Slavin, Brittleton, T.Crawshaw, Proud, Tummon, V.Simpson, A.Wilson, Stewart, G.Simpson					
07 Feb. 1907	Southampton	F.A.Cup 2R	3–1	Wilson 2(5, 15), Stewart(68)	27367
Lyall, Layton, Slavin, Brittleton, T.Crawshaw, Bartlett, Davis, Chapman, A.Wilson, Stewart, G.Simpson					
16 Feb. 1907	Liverpool	Division 1	2–3	Davis(–)pen., V.Simpson(89)	10000
Lyall, Layton, Burton, Brittleton, Holbem, Bartlett, Davis, Chapman, A.Wilson, V.Simpson, G.Simpson					
23 Feb. 1907	Sunderland	F.A.Cup 3	0–0		36324
Lyall, Layton, Slavin, Brittleton, T.Crawshaw, Bartlett, Davis, Chapman, Bradshaw, Stewart, G.Simpson					
02 Mar. 1907	Notts County	Division 1	1–3	Wilson(45)	8000
Lyall, Layton, Burton, Brittleton, Holbem, Bartlett, Ruddlesdin, Bradshaw, A.Wilson, Stewart, G.Simpson					
09 Mar. 1907	Liverpool	F.A.Cup 4	1–0	Chapman(51)	37830
Lyall, Layton, Burton, Brittleton, T.Crawshaw, Bartlett, V.Simpson, Chapman, A.Wilson, Stewart, G.Simpson					
16 Mar. 1907	Bolton Wanderers	Division 1	2–0	Wilson 2(48, –)	10000
Lyall, Slavin, Burton, Brittleton, Holbem, Bartlett, Tummon, Chapman, A.Wilson, Bradshaw, G.Simpson					
30 Mar. 1907	Stoke	Division 1	0–1		10000
Lyall, Layton, Burton, Brittleton, Holbem, Bartlett, Reynolds, Bradshaw, A.Wilson, Stewart, G.Simpson					
13 Apr. 1907	Sunderland	Division 1	2–1	Foxall(1), Maxwell(3)	3000
Lyall, Slavin, Burton, Lloyd, T.Crawshaw, Hemmingfield, Maxwell, Chapman, A.Wilson, Foxall, G.Simpson					
27 Apr. 1907	Everton	Division 1	1–1	Bradshaw(–)	7000
Lyall, Layton, Slavin, Brittleton, T.Crawshaw, Bartlett, Maxwell, Bradshaw, A.Wilson, Stewart, Foxall					

OTHER GAMES AT HILLSBOROUGH

Date	Competition	Home	Away	Note	Att.
23 Aug. 1906	Public Trial Match	Stripes 0	Whites 4	*30 mins. each way	n/k
25 Aug. 1906	Public Trial Match	Stripes 1	Whites 1		7000
15 Oct. 1906	Inter City	Sheffield 3	Glasgow 2		4500
09 Feb. 1907	S.Challenge Cup s/f	Sheff. United Res. 4	South Kirkby Colliery 2		n/k
14 Mar. 1907	Representative	Sheffield University 2	Durham University 1		n/k
18 Mar. 1907	S.Challenge Cup Final	Sheff. United Res. 2	The Wednesday 2		4000
01 Apr. 1907	Sunday School Final	Brunswick Mission 3	Heeley Friends 0		2500
02 Apr. 1907	"Pub Cup" Final	Bellefield Inn 2	Great Britain 0		6800
02 Apr. 1907	Free Churches s/f	Darnall Congregrational 0	Millhouses Wesleyans 0		1200
27 Apr. 1907	Bible Class Final	Lopham Street 2	Birley Carr 2		n/k
29 Apr. 1907	Free Churches Final	Millhouses Wesleyans 3	Stephen Hill Wesleyans 2		1000
30 Apr. 1907	Bible Class Final – Rep.	Lopham Street 3	Birley Carr 1		n/k
04 May 1907	Wednesday Shield s/f	Crookesmoor 1	Newhall Road 1		n/k
07 May 1907	Clegg Shield Final	Duchess Road 0	Burgoyne Road 0		n/k
11 May 1907	Clegg Shield Fnl– Rep.	Duchess Road 0	Burgoyne Road 1		n/k
11 May 1907	Wednesday Shield Final	Crookesmoor 5	Charity School 4		n/k

Date	Opponents	Competition	Score	Scorers	Att.
07 Sep. 1907	Newcastle United	Division 1	3–1	Stewart(20), Bradshaw(57), Wilson(72)	18000
Lyall, Layton, Burton, Brittleton, T.Crawshaw, Bartlett, Maxwell, Bradshaw, A.Wilson, Stewart, G.Simpson					
21 Sep. 1907	Notts County	Division 1	2–0	Wilson(2), Brittleton(65)	14000
Lyall, Layton, Slavin, Brittleton, T.Crawshaw, Bartlett, Maxwell, Chapman, A.Wilson, Stewart, G.Simpson					
23 Sep. 1907	Bristol City	Division 1	5–3	Wilson 2(49, 84), Stewart 2(58, 63), Chapman(10)	8500
Lyall, Layton, Burton, Brittleton, T.Crawshaw, Bartlett, Maxwell, Chapman, A.Wilson, Stewart, G.Simpson					
05 Oct. 1907	Preston North End	Division 1	1–0	Brittleton(82)	10000
Lyall, Slavin, Burton, Brittleton, Holbem, Bartlett, Chapman, Bradshaw, A.Wilson, Stewart, G.Simpson					
19 Oct. 1907	Aston Villa	Division 1	2–3	Chapman(35), Wilson(60)	16000
Lyall, Slavin, Burton, Brittleton, T.Crawshaw, Ruddlesdin, Chapman, Bradshaw, A.Wilson, Stewart, G.Simpson					
02 Nov. 1907	Middlesbrough	Division 1	3–2	Chapman(8), Simpson(11), Stewart(25)	14000
Lyall, Layton, Burton, Brittleton, T.Crawshaw, Bartlett, Chapman, Bradshaw, A.Wilson, Stewart, G.Simpson					
16 Nov. 1907	Chelsea	Division 1	3–1	Simpson(30), Wilson(82), Chapman(88)	13500
Lyall, Layton, Burton, Brittleton, T.Crawshaw, Bartlett, Chapman, Bradshaw, A.Wilson, Stewart, G.Simpson					
30 Nov. 1907	Manchester United	Division 1	2–0	Bartlett(52), Stewart(83)	40000
Lyall, Layton, Burton, Brittleton, T.Crawshaw, Bartlett, Chapman, Bradshaw, A.Wilson, Stewart, G.Simpson					
14 Dec. 1907	Bolton Wanderers	Division 1	5–2	Stewart 2(59, 69), Bradshaw(79), Brittleton(81), Wilson(85)	2000
Lyall, Slavin, Burton, Brittleton, Chapman, Bartlett, Maxwell, Bradshaw, A.Wilson, Stewart, G.Simpson					
26 Dec. 1907	Sunderland	Division 1	2–3	Napier(13), Stewart(53)	20000
Lyall, Layton, Burton, Brittleton, Napier, Bartlett, Chapman, Bradshaw, A.Wilson, Stewart, G.Simpson					
28 Dec. 1907	Everton	Division 1	1–2	Napier(69)	13500
Lyall, Layton, Burton, Brittleton, Napier, Bartlett, Maxwell, Bradshaw, A.Wilson, Stewart, Foxall					
31 Dec. 1907	Woolwich Arsenal	Division 1	6–0	Bradshaw 3(18, 38, 62), Wilson(40), Brittleton(49)pen., Chapman(62)	9500
Lyall, Layton, Burton, Napier, Brittleton, Taylor, Chapman, Bradshaw, A.Wilson, Stewart, G.Simpson					
25 Jan. 1908	Manchester City	Division 1	5–1	Bradshaw 2(4, 62), Stewart 2(41, 80), Chapman(35)	12000
Lyall, Layton, Burton, Napier, Brittleton, Bartlett, Maxwell, Chapman, Bradshaw, Stewart, Bolland					
08 Feb. 1908	Bury	Division 1	2–0	Maxwell(10), Bolland(89)	8000
Lyall, Layton, Slavin, Napier, T.Crawshaw, Bartlett, Maxwell, Chapman, Bradshaw, Stewart, Bolland					
07 Mar. 1908	Sheffield United	Division 1	2–0	Wilson(57), Maxwell(–)	20000
Lyall, Layton, Burton, Brittleton, T.Crawshaw, Bartlett, Maxwell, Bradshaw, A.Wilson, Stewart, G.Simpson					
09 Mar. 1908	Liverpool	Division 1	1–2	Simpson(20)	3500
Lyall, Layton, Holbem, Napier, Brittleton, Bartlett, Maxwell, Bradshaw, A.Wilson, Stewart, G.Simpson					
21 Mar. 1908	Nottingham Forest	Division 1	2–1	Wilson(30), Simpson(83)	7500
Lyall, Jameson, Burton, Brittleton, Bradshaw, Bartlett, Maxwell, Chapman, A.Wilson, Stewart, G.Simpson					
04 Apr. 1908	Blackburn Rovers	Division 1	2–0	Simpson(43), Maxwell(80)	4000
Crinson, Layton, Slavin, Brittleton, Hibbett, Bartlett, Maxwell, Chapman, Miller, Rollinson, G.Simpson					
18 Apr. 1908	Birmingham	Division 1	1–4	Wilson(45)	6500
Lyall, Layton, Slavin, Lloyd, Hibbett, Bartlett, Bolland, Chapman, A.Wilson, Stewart, Foxall					

OTHER GAMES AT HILLSBOROUGH

24 Aug. 1907	Public Trial Match	Stripes 1	Whites 2	*30 mins. each way	5000
14 Mar. 1908	S.Challenge Cup Final	South Kirkby Colliey 0	Sheff. United Res. 1		n/k
26 Mar. 1908	Representative	Sheffield Tramways 0	Manchester Tramways 2		n/k
13 Apr. 1908	Wednesday Shield s/f	Hillsborough 5	Morley Street 0		n/k
20 Apr. 1908	Sunday School Final	Heeley Friends 2	Owlerton New Congregrational 1		2000
21 Apr. 1908	"Pub Cup" Final	Bellefield Inn 2	Sawmill 0		5000
21 Apr. 1908	Free Churches Final	Darnall Cong. 0	Martin St. Primitives 2		n/k
25 Apr. 1908	Minor Cup Final	Nelson 3	Handsworth Rovers 1		n/k
27 Apr. 1908	Wednesday Shield Final	Hillsborough School 7	Newhall Road 0		n/k

1905–06
Davis (ass. trainer), Brittleton, Layton, Ruddlesdin, T. Crawshaw, Lyall, Burton, Bartlett, Frith (trainer);
Reynolds, Davis, Chapman, Wilson, Stewart, G. Simpson, Malloch.

1906–07
Lloyd, Chapman, Layton, Malloch;
Frith (trainer), Brittleton, Ruddlesdin, Burton, Crawshaw, Lyall, Bartlett, J. Davis (ass. trainer);
Tummon, H. Davis, Wilson, Sewart, G. Simpson.

1907–08
Davis (ass. trainer), Bradshaw, Brittleton, Layton, Lyall, Bartlett, Slavin, Burton, Maxwell;
Foxall, Chapman, Wilson, T. Crawshaw, Stewart, G. Simpson.

1908–09
Foxall, Caterer, Davison, Napier, Simpson, Spoors, Rollinson;
Davis (ass. trainer), Jameson, McConnell, Slavin, Layton, Lyall, Burton, Holbem, Burns, Tummon, Parramore (trainer);
Cook, Lloyd, Brittleton, Armstrong, Chapman, Wilson, Bradshaw, Bartlett, Bolland, Taylor.

Date	Opponents	Competition	Score	Scorers	Att.
12 Sep. 1908	Notts County	Division 1	2–0	Chapman(57), Brittleton(–)	15000
Lyall, Layton, Holbem, Brittleton, McConnell, Bartlett, Armstrong, Chapman, A.Wilson, Bradshaw, Foxall					
26 Sep. 1908	Newcastle United	Division 1	2–0	Bradshaw 2(70, 77)	30000
Lyall, Layton, Holbem, Brittleton, McConnell, Bartlett, Armstrong, Chapman, A.Wilson, Bradshaw, G.Simpson					
05 Oct. 1908	Sheffield United	Charity	0–0		7306
Davison, Holbem, Burton, Brittleton, McConnell, Taylor, Lloyd, Chapman, A.Wilson, Bradshaw, Foxall					
10 Oct. 1908	Bristol City	Division 1	2–0	Rollinson(9), Lloyd(27)	14000
Davison, Layton, Holbem, Brittleton, McConnell, Bartlett, Lloyd, Chapman, A.Wilson, Rollinson, Foxall					
24 Oct. 1908	Preston North End	Division 1	1–0	Chapman(10)	10000
Lyall, Layton, Holbem, Brittleton, McConnell, Bartlett, Lloyd, Chapman, A.Wilson, Bradshaw, G.Simpson					
07 Nov. 1908	Middlesbrough	Division 1	3–2	Brittleton(20), Bradshaw(26), Wilson(–)	10500
Lyall, Layton, Burton, Brittleton, Spoors, Bartlett, Lloyd, Chapman, A.Wilson, Bradshaw, G.Simpson					
21 Nov. 1908	Manchester City	Division 1	3–1	Chapman 3(30, 40, 70)	10500
Lyall, Layton, Burton, Brittleton, McConnell, Bartlett, Lloyd, Chapman, A.Wilson, Bradshaw, Foxall					
05 Dec. 1908	Liverpool	Division 1	2–3	Wilson(18), Lloyd(85)	10000
Lyall, Layton, Burton, Brittleton, Spoors, Bartlett, Lloyd, Chapman, A.Wilson, Bradshaw, Bolland					
19 Dec. 1908	Bury	Division 1	4–3	Bradshaw 2(12, 70), Lloyd(30), Wilson(89)	5500
Davison, Layton, Burton, Brittleton, McConnell, Bartlett, Lloyd, Chapman, A.Wilson, Bradshaw, Bolland					
25 Dec. 1908	Sheffield United	Division 1	1–0	Simpson(38)	30000
Lyall, Layton, Burton, Brittleton, McConnell, Bartlett, Lloyd, Chapman, A.Wilson, Bradshaw, G.Simpson					
28 Dec. 1908	Arsenal	Division 1	6–2	Wilson 3(6, 33, 38), Tummon 2(2, 67), Lloyd(30)	8000
Lyall, Holbem, Burton, Napier, McConnell, Taylor, Lloyd, Brittleton, A.Wilson, Bradshaw, Tummon					
01 Jan. 1909	Leicester Fosse	Division 1	3–1	Wilson 2(3, 25), Bradshaw(1)	13000
Lyall, Jameson, Holbem, Brittleton, Spoors, Taylor, Lloyd, Chapman, A.Wilson, Bradshaw, Tummon					
02 Jan. 1909	Aston Villa	Division 1	4–2	Brittleton(23), Wilson(66), Tummon (74), Chapman(85)	17000
Lyall, Holbem, Burton, Spoors, Taylor, Lloyd, Chapman, A.Wilson, Bradshaw, Tummon					
16 Jan. 1909	Stoke	F.A.Cup 1	5–0	Wilson 2(35, 45), Bradshaw 2(43, –), Chapman(20)	7893
Lyall, Layton, Burton, Brittleton, McConnell, Bartlett, Lloyd, Chapman, A.Wilson, Bradshaw, Tummon					
23 Jan. 1909	Nottingham Forest	Division 1	3–0	Wilson 2(30, 70), Bradshaw(55)	9500
Lyall, Layton, Burton, Brittleton, McConnell, Bartlett, Tummon, Chapman, A.Wilson, Bradshaw, Foxall					
11 Feb. 1909	Portsmouth	F.A.Cup 2R	3–0	Brittleton(1), Lloyd(22), Wilson(55)	26066
Lyall, Layton, Burton, Brittleton, McConnell, Bartlett, Lloyd, Chapman, A.Wilson, Rollinson, Tummon					
20 Feb. 1909	Glossop North End	F.A.Cup 3	0–1		35019
Lyall, Layton, Burton, Brittleton, McConnell, Bartlett, Lloyd, Chapman, A.Wilson, Bradshaw, G.Simpson					
20 Mar. 1909	Bradford City	Division 1	0–2		15000
Lyall, Layton, Burton, Brittleton, Spoors, Bartlett, Stringfellow, Chapman, A.Wilson, Rollinson, Bolland					
22 Mar. 1909	Chelsea	Division 1	5–1	Rollinson 2(11, –), Lloyd(50), Wilson(80), Brittleton(89)	6000
Davison, Holbem, Burton, Brittleton, Spoors, Bartlett, Lloyd, Stringfellow, A.Wilson, Rollinson, Foxall					
29 Mar. 1909	Sunderland	Division 1	2–5	Bradshaw(35), Simpson(–)	6000
Lyall, Layton, Holbem, Brittleton, Spoors, Taylor, Hunter, Chapman, Bradshaw, Rollinson, G.Simpson					
03 Apr. 1909	Manchester United	Division 1	2–0	Bradshaw 2(20, 51)	10000
Davison, Layton, Holbem, Lloyd, McConnell, Bartlett, Hunter, Chapman, A.Wilson, Bradshaw, Foxall					
17 Apr. 1909	Everton	Division 1	2–0	Bradshaw(25), Foxall(–)	6000
Kinghorn, Slavin, Holbem, Lloyd, McConnell, Taylor, Hunter, Stringfellow, A.Wilson, Bradshaw, Foxall					
19 Apr. 1909	Blackburn Rovers	Division 1	1–2	Bradshaw(7)	2000
Kinghorn, Brittleton, Holbem, Lloyd, Spoors, Bartlett, Hunter, Stringfellow, A.Wilson, Bradshaw, Rollinson					

OTHER GAMES AT HILLSBOROUGH

22 Aug. 1908	Public Trial Match	Stripes 2	Whites 2	*35 mins. each way	4000
27 Jan. 1909	Representative	Sheffield University 0	Durham University 4		n/k
06 Feb. 1909	Boys	Sheffield 6	Rotherham 0		n/k
15 Mar. 1909	S.Challenge Cup Final	Rotherham County 2	Sheff. United 2		3384
03 Apr. 1909	Boys – EST R4 *	Sheffield 1	Birkenhead 0		8000
12 Apr. 1909	Sunday School Final	Sharrow Lane 0	Sharrow Reform 1		3000
13 Apr. 1909	"Pub Cup" Final	Bellefield Hotel 1	Great Britain 0		5000
15 Apr. 1909	Boys – EST R4	Sheffield 1	Birkenhead 0		4500
01 May 1909	Boys – EST S/F	Sheffield 4	Sunderland 2		5000
04 May 1909	Wednesday Shield Final	Hillsborough 3	Morley Street 0		n/k
04 May 1909	Clegg Shield s/f	Lydgate 1	Carlisle Street 2		n/k
08 May 1909	Boys – EST FINAL	Sheffield 2	Aston Manor 0		6000
10 May 1909	Clegg Shield Final	Hillsborough 2	Carlisle Street 0		n/k

*replay ordered after a protest by Birkenhead

Date	Opponents	Competition	Score	Scorers	Att.
04 Sep. 1909	Middlesbrough	Division 1	1–5	Chapman(42)	10000
Davison, Layton, Holbem, Brittleton, Spoors, Taylor, Hunter, Chapman, A.Wilson, Bradshaw, Foxall					
18 Sep. 1909	Bury	Division 1	1–4	Kirkman(48)	8000
Davison, Layton, Holbem, Brittleton, Spoors, Bartlett, Kirkman, Chapman, Bradshaw, Rollinson, Tummon					
20 Sep. 1909	Everton	Division 1	1–3	Rollinson(45)	8000
Davison, Layton, Slavin, Brittleton, Spoors, Taylor, Kirkman, Chapman, A.Wilson, Rollinson, Tummon					
02 Oct. 1909	Preston North End	Division 1	4–1	Rollinson 2(28, 62), Kirkman, Foxall	12000
Davison, Spoors, Holbem, Brittleton, McConnell, Taylor, Kirkman, Chapman, A.Wilson, Rollinson, Foxall					
16 Oct. 1909	Newcastle United	Division 1	3–1	Rollinson 3(32, 45, –)	19000
Davison, Spoors, Holbem, Brittleton, McConnell, Taylor, Kirkman, Bradshaw, A.Wilson, Rollinson, Foxall					
30 Oct. 1909	Aston Villa	Division 1	3–2	Rollinson 2(6, 52), Wilson(–)	15000
Davison, Spoors, Holbem, Brittleton, McConnell, Taylor, Kirkman, Bradshaw, A.Wilson, Rollinson, Foxall					
13 Nov. 1909	Woolwich Arsenal	Division 1	1–1	Wilson (–)	7000
Davison, Spoors, Warren, Brittleton, McConnell, Taylor, Kirkman, Chapman, A.Wilson, Rollinson, Tummon					
27 Nov. 1909	Chelsea	Division 1	4–1	Wilson(–), Brittleton(17)pen., Foxall (55), Kirkman(56)	8000
Davison, Spoors, Holbem, Brittleton, McConnell, Bartlett, Kirkman, Chapman, A.Wilson, Rollinson, Foxall					
11 Dec. 1909	Nottingham Forest	Division 1	4–3	Wilson 2(21, 38), Foxall(24), Rollinson(43)	7000
Davison, Spoors, Holbem, Brittleton, McConnell, Bartlett, Kirkman, Bradshaw, A.Wilson, Rollinson, Foxall					
27 Dec. 1909	Manchester United	Division 1	4–1	Wilson 2(36, –), Tummon(34), Kirkman	33000
Davison, Spoors, Holbem, Lloyd, Brittleton, Bartlett, Kirkman, Chapman, A.Wilson, Bradshaw, Tummon					
20 Jan. 1910	Northampton Town	F.A.Cup 1R	0–1		13533
Davison, Spoors, Holbem, Brittleton, McConnell, Bartlett, Kirkman, Chapman, A.Wilson, Rollinson, Tummon					
22 Jan. 1910	Bristol City	Division 1	2–0	Rollinson(30), Chapman(–)	6000
Davison, Spoors, Holbem, Lloyd, McConnell, Bartlett, Kirkman, Chapman, Hamilton, Rollinson, Tummon					
19 Feb. 1910	Notts County	Division 1	0–0		9000
Kinghorn, Spoors, Holbem, Lloyd, McConnell, Weir, Kirkman, Brittleton, Hamilton, Bradshaw, Tummon					
05 Mar. 1910	Liverpool	Division 1	3–0	Brittleton 2(19, 42), Lloyd(47)	10000
Kinghorn, Spoors, Holbem, Lloyd, McConnell, Weir, Kirkman, Stringfellow, Brittleton, Hamilton, Tummon					
14 Mar. 1910	Tottenham Hotspur	Division 1	1–1	Foxall(86)	3500
Kinghorn, Spoors, McSkimming, Lloyd, O'Connell, Bartlett, Kirkman, Stringfellow, A.Wilson, Hamilton, Foxall					
19 Mar. 1910	Sheffield United	Division 1	1–3	Brittleton(24)	16000
Kinghorn, Spoors, Holbem, Lloyd, O'Connell, Bartlett, Chapman, Stringfellow, Brittleton, Rollinson, Foxall					
28 Mar. 1910	Bradford City	Division 1	2–1	Murray, Robertson	15500
Kinghorn, Spoors, McSkimming, Weir, McConnell, Lloyd, Kirkman, Chapman, Murray, A.Wilson, Robertson					
02 Apr. 1910	Bolton Wanderers	Division 1	0–0		6000
Kinghorn, Spoors, McSkimming, Lloyd, McConnell, Weir, Hunter, Chapman, Murray, A.Wilson, Robertson					
16 Apr. 1910	Blackburn Rovers	Division 1	2–1	Hunter 2(28, 62)	3000
Kinghorn, Spoors, McSkimming, Lloyd, Brittleton, Weir, Hunter, Chapman, Murray, A.Wilson, Robertson					
30 Apr. 1910	Sunderland	Division 1	1–0	Chapman(52)	6500
Kinghorn, Spoors, McSkimming, Lloyd, Brittleton, Weir, Hunter, Chapman, Murray, A.Wilson, Robertson					

OTHER GAMES AT HILLSBOROUGH

28 Aug. 1909	Public Trial Match	Stripes 0	Whites 1	4000
28 Mar. 1910	Sunday School Final	All Saints 1	Owlerton UM 0	2000
29 Mar. 1910	"Pub Cup" Final	Prospect View 3	Industry Inn 2	4500
29 Mar. 1910	Free Churches Lge Finl	Croft House Settlement 1	Oak Street 0	n/k
07 Apr. 1910	Thursday League s/f	Whitworths 2	Tramways 1	n/k
09 Apr. 1910	Wednesday Shield Final	Hillsborough 10	Hunters Bar 3	n/k
11 Apr. 1910	Wharncliffe Charity Fnl.	Barnsley Reserves 4	Sheffield United Reserves 1	n/k
18 Apr. 1910	Amateur Lge. s/f– rep.	Rotherham Amateurs 4	Tinsley Park 0	n/k
25 Apr. 1910	Clegg Shield s/f	Hillsborough 7	Crookesmoor 0	n/k
28 Apr. 1910	Amateur Lge. Fnl – Rep	Tinsley Church 3	Rotherham Amateurs 0	n/k
05 May 1910	Friendly	Sheffield Indepenent 4	Sheffield Telegraph 3	n/k
07 May 1910	Clegg Shield Final	Whitby Road 0	Hillsborough 7	n/k

Date	Opponents	Competition	Score	Scorers	Att.
10 Sep. 1910	Middlesbrough	Division 1	1–1	Chapman	16000
Kinghorn, Spoors, Holbem, Brittleton, McSkimming, Weir, Kirkman, Chapman, Murray, A.Wilson, Robertson					
24 Sep. 1910	Notts County	Division 1	1–3	Murray	12000
Kinghorn, Spoors, Holbem, Brittleton, McSkimming, Weir, Dowling, Chapman, Murray, A.Wilson, Robertson					
03 Oct. 1910	Sheffield United	Charity	2–0	Dowling(42), Wilson	5000
Davison, Spoors, McSkimming, Lloyd, Brittleton, Weir, Kirkman, Chapman, Dowling, A.Wilson, Robertson					
08 Oct. 1910	Liverpool	Division 1	1–0	Robertson(7)	14500
Davison, Spoors, McSkimming, Lloyd, Brittleton, Weir, Kirkman, Chapman, Dowling, A.Wilson, Robertson					
22 Oct. 1910	Sheffield United	Division 1	2–0	Chapman 2(40, 41)	25000
Davison, Spoors, Holbem, Lloyd, McSkimming, Weir, Kirkman, Chapman, Brittleton, A.Wilson, Robertson					
05 Nov. 1910	Sunderland	Division 1	1–1	Brittleton	20000
Davison, Spoors, Holbem, Lloyd, McSkimming, Rollinson, Kirkman, Chapman, Brittleton, A.Wilson, Robertson					
19 Nov. 1910	Bradford City	Division 1	0–1		6000
Davison, Spoors, Holbem, Lloyd, McSkimming, Weir, Chapman, Brittleton, O'Connell, A.Wilson, Rollinson					
03 Dec. 1910	Nottingham Forest	Division 1	5–2	Chapman 2(7, –pen.), Rollinson, Kirkman, Wilson	5000
Davison, Spoors, Warren, Lloyd, O'Connell, Weir, Kirkman, Chapman, A.Wilson, Rollinson, Robertson					
17 Dec. 1910	Everton	Division 1	0–2		7000
Davison, Spoors, Warren, Lloyd, O'Connell, Weir, Kirkman, Chapman, A.Wilson, Rollinson, Robertson					
27 Dec. 1910	Newcastle United	Division 1	0–2		25000
Kinghorn, Spoors, Holbem, Lloyd, O'Connell, Weir, Kirkman, Chapman, A.Wilson, Rollinson, Robertson					
31 Dec. 1910	Tottenham Hotspur	Division 1	2–1	Stringfellow(35), Glennon(48)	10000
Kinghorn, Spoors, Holbem, Brittleton, O'Connell, Weir, Kirkman, Stringfellow, Glennon, A.Wilson, Robertson					
02 Jan. 1911	Bristol City	Dvision 1	2–1	Glennon 2(5, 10)	6000
Davison, Spoors, Holbem, Brittleton, O'Connell, Weir, Kirkman, Stringfellow, Glennon, A.Wilson, Robertson					
14 Jan. 1911	Coventry City	F.A.Cup 1	1–2	Wilson(45)	19603
Davison, Spoors, Holbem, Lloyd, O'Connell, Weir, Kirkman, Stringfellow, Glennon, A.Wilson, Robertson					
21 Jan. 1911	Preston North End	Division 1	0–0		4000
Davison, Worrall, Holbem, Brittleton, McSkimming, Weir, Kirkman, Stringfellow, Glennon, A.Wilson, Robertson					
18 Feb. 1911	Bury	Division 1	1–0	Spoors(35)	14000
Davison, Spoors, McSkimming, Brittleton, Weir, Campbell, Dowling, Paterson, McLean, A.Wilson, Robertson					
04 Mar. 1911	Aston Villa	Division 1	1–0	Paterson(12)	14000
Davison, Spoors, McSkimming, Brittleton, Weir, Campbell, Kirkman, Paterson, McLean, A.Wilson, Robertson					
18 Mar. 1911	Woolwich Arsenal	Division 1	0–0		6000
Davison, Spoors, McSkimming, Brittleton, Weir, Campbell, Kirkman, Paterson, McLean, A.Wilson, Robertson					
01 Apr. 1911	Blackburn Rovers	Division 1	1–0	Kirkman(40)	8000
Davison, Spoors, McSkimming, Brittleton, Weir, Campbell, Kirkman, Paterson, McLean, A.Wilson, Robertson					
15 Apr. 1911	Manchester City	Division 1	4–1	Campbell, Stringfellow, Paterson, Robertson	10000
Davison, Spoors, McSkimming, Brittleton, Weir, Campbell, Kirkman, Stringfellow, Paterson, A.Wilson, Robertson					
17 Apr. 1911	Manchester United	Division 1	0–0		20000
Davison, Spoors, McSkimming, Brittleton, Weir, Campbell, Kirkman, Stringfellow, Paterson, A.Wilson, Robertson					
29 Apr. 1911	Oldham Athletic	Division 1	2–0	Robertson, Wilson	6000
Davison, Spoors, Warren, Brittleton, Weir, Campbell, Kirkman, Paterson, McLean, A.Wilson, Robertson					

OTHER GAMES AT HILLSBOROUGH

Date					Att.
27 Aug. 1910	Public Trial Match	Stripes 3	Whites 0	*40mins. each way	4500
17 Oct. 1910	Inter City	Sheffield 2	Glasgow 2		n/k
25 Feb. 1911	Wednesday Shield s/f	Hillsborough 3	Hunters Bar 1		n/k
25 Feb. 1911	Wednesday Shield s/f	Lowfields 2	Charity School 1		n/k
03 Apr. 1911	Clegg Shield s/f	Walkley 3	Firshill 2		n/k
10 Apr. 1911	Wednesday Shield Final	Lowfields 1	Hillsborough 0		n/k
17 Apr. 1911	Sunday School Final	Heeley St. Peter's 1	Owlerton U.M. 1		n/k
18 Apr. 1911	"Pub Cup" Final	Industry Inn 1	Douglas 0		3000
20 Apr. 1911	Early Closing Lge. Final	Sheaf Markets 0	Whitworths 0		n/k
22 Apr. 1911	Friendlies Lge. Final	Hillsborough & Wadsley Ath. 1	Sharrow Old Boys 1		n/k
26 Apr. 1911	Inter Guild	Sheffield 0	Rotherham 0		n/k
01 May 1911	Clegg Shield Final	Hillsborough 4	Walkley 0		n/k

Date	Opponents	Competition	Score	Scorers	Att.
02 Sep. 1911	Preston North End	Division 1	0–1		14000
Davison, Spoors, McSkimming, Brittleton, Weir, Campbell, Kirkman, Paterson, McLean, A.Wilson, Robertson					
16 Sep. 1911	Middlesbrough	Division 1	0–2		16000
Davison, Spoors, Warren, Lloyd, Weir, Campbell, Kirkman, Paterson, McLean, A.Wilson, Robertson					
30 Sep. 1911	Tottenham Hotspur	Division 1	4–0	McLean(30), Burkinshaw(55), Wilson (70), Glennon(76)	11000
Davison, Spoors, McSkimming, Brittleton, Weir, Campbell, L.Burkinshaw, Glennon, McLean, A.Wilson, Robertson					
14 Oct. 1911	Liverpool	Division 1	2–2	Glennon(65), Wilson(85)	13000
Davison, Spoors, McSkimming, Brittleton, Weir, Campbell, L.Burkinshaw, Glennon, McLean, A.Wilson, Robertson					
28 Oct. 1911	Newcastle United	Division 1	1–2	McLean(82)pen.	14000
Davison, Spoors, McSkimming, Brittleton, Weir, Campbell, Kirkman, Paterson, McLean, A.Wilson, Robertson					
11 Nov. 1911	Oldham Athletic	Division 1	1–0	Robertson(80)	12000
Davison, Worrall, McSkimming, Brittleton, Weir, Campbell, Kirkman, Glennon, McLean, A.Wilson, Robertson					
25 Nov. 1911	Bradford City	Division 1	4–2	McLean 2(15, 55), Kirkman(44), Robertson(49)	12000
Davison, Worrall, Spoors, Brittleton, Weir, Campbell, Kirkman, Glennon, McLean, A.Wilson, Robertson					
09 Dec. 1911	Manchester City	Division 1	3–0	McLean 2(17, 57), Glennon(25)	12000
Davison, Worrall, Spoors, Brittleton, Weir, Campbell, Kirkman, Glennon, McLean, A.Wilson, Robertson					
23 Dec. 1911	West Bromwich Albion	Division 1	4–1	McLean 2(20, 89), Robertson(11), Glennon(38)	17000
Davison, Worrall, Spoors, Brittleton, Weir, Campbell, Kirkman, Glennon, McLean, A.Wilson, Robertson					
26 Dec. 1911	Sunderland	Division 1	8–0	McLean 4(30, 37, 43, 55), Kirkman 2(4, 25), Glennon 2(36, 40)	33000
Davison, Worrall, Spoors, Brittleton, Weir, Campbell, Kirkman, Glennon, McLean, A.Wilson, Robertson					
25 Jan. 1912	Middlesbrough	F.A.Cup 1R	1–2	McLean(41)	30468
Davison, Worrall, Spoors, Brittleton, O'Connell, Campbell, Kirkman, Glennon, McLean, A.Wilson, Robertson					
27 Jan. 1912	Notts County	Division 1	3–0	McLean 2(21, 75), Robertson(46)	10000
Davison, Worrall, Spoors, Lloyd, McSkimming, Campbell, Kirkman, Glennon, McLean, A.Wilson, Robertson					
10 Feb. 1912	Manchester United	Division 1	3–0	McLean(48), Wilson(80), Glennon(89)	20000
Davison, Worrall, Spoors, Weir, McSkimming, Campbell, Kirkman, Glennon, McLean, A.Wilson, Robertson					
24 Feb. 1912	Aston Villa	Division 1	3–0	Kirkman(15), Wilson(30), McLean(67)	15000
Davison, Worrall, Spoors, Brittleton, McSkimming, Campbell, Kirkman, Glennon, McLean, A.Wilson, Robertson					
09 Mar. 1912	Sheffield United	Division 1	1–1	Glennon(60)	30000
Davison, Worrall, Spoors, Brittleton, McSkimming, Campbell, Kirkman, Glennon, McLean, A.Wilson, Robertson					
18 Mar. 1912	Bury	Division 1	2–1	Glennon 2(15, 50)	6500
Davison, Worrall, Spoors, Brittleton, Weir, Campbell, Kirkman, Glennon, McLean, A.Wilson, Robertson					
23 Mar. 1912	Bolton Wanderers	Division 1	0–1		7000
Davison, Worrall, Spoors, Lloyd, McSkimming, Campbell, Kirkman, Paterson, Glennon, Wright, Robertson					
06 Apr. 1912	Woolwich Arsenal	Division 1	3–0	Wilson(17), Brittleton(20), Glennon(67)	5500
Davison, Worrall, Spoors, Brittleton, McSkimming, Campbell, Kirkman, Glennon, McLean, A.Wilson, Robertson					
08 Apr. 1912	Blackburn Rovers	Division 1	1–1	McLean(2)	12000
Davison, Worrall, Spoors, Brittleton, McSkimming, Campbell, Kirkman, Glennon, McLean, A.Wilson, Robertson					
20 Apr. 1912	Everton	Division 1	1–3	Wilson(70)	10000
Davison, Worrall, Spoors, Brittleton, McSkimming, Campbell, Kirkman, Glennon, McLean, A.Wilson, Robertson					

OTHER GAMES AT HILLSBOROUGH

26 Aug. 1911	Public Trial Match	Stripes 2	Whites 3	7000
30 Mar. 1912	Bible Class s/f	Attercliffe Church 1	Attercliffe Zion 1	n/k
30 Mar. 1912	Bible Class s/f	Heeley Friends 1	Owlerton 0	n/k
03 Apr. 1912	F.A.Cup S/F Replay	West Bromwich Albion 1	Blackburn Rovers 0	20050
08 Apr. 1912	Sunday School Final	St.John's Institute 1	Heeley Friends 0	2000
09 Apr. 1912	"Pub Cup" Final	Industry Inn 2	Bird in Hand 1	3000
09 Apr. 1912	Free Churches Final	Valley Road 1	Malin Bridge 1	n/k
10 Apr. 1912	Clegg Shield s/f	Walkley 7	Manor 0	n/k
10 Apr. 1912	Clegg Shield s/f	Hillsborough 2	Abbeydale 2	n/k
16 Apr. 1912	Clegg Shield s/f – Rep.	Hillsborough 1	Abbeydale 2	n/k
18 Apr. 1912	Early Closing Lge. Fnl.	Barnsley Amateurs 1	Mortimer's 0	n/k
04 May 1912	Clegg Shield Final	Walkley 3	Abbeydale 1	n/k
04 May 1912	Wednesday Shield Fnl.	Tinsley Park 2	Hunters Bar 1	n/k

1909–10
Miller, Hamilton, Rollinson, Davison, Spoors, Kinghorn, Warren, Taylor, O'Connell, Cook;
Lloyd, Brittleton, Layton, Wharler, Slavin, Napier, Bartlett, Holbern, Parramore (trainer);
Weir, Kirkman, Hunter, Chapman, Wilson, Bradshaw, Foxall, Stringfellow.

1910–11
Dowling, Brittleton, Spoors, Kinghorn, McSkimming, Rollinson, Weir, O'Connell;
Lloyd, Kirkman, Chapman, Murray, Robertson, Holbem.

1911–12
Wilson, Lloyd, Tyler, Cawley, Clarke, Miller, Beech, Brelsford, Pickering, Bentley;
Davis (ass trainer), Nicholson, Brittleton, Lamb, Worrall, Davison, Spoors, McSkimming, Wright, Campbell, Kinnear (trainer);
Armitage, Burkinshaw, Kirkman, Glennon, McLean, Wilson, Robertson, Hemstock, Siddall, Dawson.

1912–13
Miller, McSkimming, Brelsford, Davison, Spoors, J. Davis (ass. trainer), Campbell;
Kirkman, Glennon, L. Burkinshaw, Wilson, Wright.

Date	Opponents	Competition	Score	Scorers	Att.
02 Sep. 1912	Blackburn Rovers	Division 1	2–1	McLean 2(7, 17)	15000
Davison, Worrall, Spoors, Brittleton, McSkimming, Campbell, Kirkman, Glennon, McLean, A.Wilson, Robertson					
14 Sep. 1912	Middlesbrough	Division 1	3–1	McLean 2(33, 70), Kirkman(20)	22000
Davison, Worrall, Spoors, Brittleton, McSkimming, Campbell, Kirkman, Glennon, McLean, A.Wilson, Robertson					
28 Sep. 1912	Manchester United	Division 1	3–3	McLean(47)pen., Kirkman(75), Wilson(85)	27000
Davison, Worrall, Spoors. Brittleton, McSkimming, Campbell, Kirkman, Glennon, McLean, A.Wilson, Robertson					
07 Oct. 1912	Sheffield United	Charity	3–0	Wright 2(21, 60), Lloyd(75)	7566
Davison, Worrall, Spoors, Brittleton, McSkimming, Campbell, Kirkman, Lloyd, A.Wilson, Wright, Robertson					
12 Oct. 1912	Liverpool	Division 1	1–0	Wright(37)	20000
Davison, Worrall, Spoors, Brittleton, McSkimming, Campbell, Kirkman, Wright, McLean, A.Wilson, Robertson					
26 Oct. 1912	Sheffield United	Division 1	1–0	Glennon(17)	15500
Davison, Worrall, Spoors, Brittleton, McSkimming, Campbell, Kirkman, Glennon, McLean, A.Wilson, Wright					
09 Nov. 1912	Oldham Athletic	Division 1	5–0	Kirkman 2(44, 63), McLean 2(67pen., –), Glennon(11)	16000
Davison, Worrall, C.Brelsford, Brittleton, McSkimming, Campbell, Kirkman, Glennon, McLean, A.Wilson, Robertson					
23 Nov. 1912	Woolwich Arsenal	Division 1	2–0	McLean(2), Wilson(47)	16000
Davison, Worrall, Spoors, Brittleton, McSkimming, Campbell, Kirkman, Glennon, McLean, A.Wilson, Robertson					
07 Dec. 1912	Manchester City	Division 1	1–0	Wilson(52)	26000
Davison, Worrall, Spoors, Brittleton, McSkimming, Campbell, Kirkman, Glennon, McLean, A.Wilson, Robertson					
21 Dec. 1912	Everton	Division 1	1–2	McLean(42)	14500
Davison, Worrall, C.Brelsford, Brittleton, McSkimming, Campbell, Kirkman, Glennon, McLean, A.Wilson, Robertson					
25 Dec. 1912	Sunderland	Division 1	1–2	Robertson(30secs.)	37000
Davison, Worrall, Spoors, Brittleton, McSkimming, Campbell, Kirkman, Glennon, McLean, A.Wilson, Robertson					
28 Dec. 1912	Tottenham Hotspur	Division 1	2–1	Robertson(59), Burkinshaw(66)	18000
Davison, Worrall, Spoors, Brittleton, McSkimming, Campbell, L.Burkinshaw, Glennon, McLean, A.Wilson, Robertson					
01 Jan. 1913	Derby County	Division 1	3–3	McLean 2(75, 84), Kirkman(85)	40000
Davison, Worrall, Spoors, Brittleton, McSkimming, Campbell, Kirkman, Glennon, McLean, A.Wilson, Robertson					
16 Jan. 1913	Grimsby Town	F.A.Cup 1	5–1	McLean 4(36, 46, –, –), Brittleton(44)	26442
Davison, Worrall, Spoors, Brittleton, McSkimming, Campbell, Kirkman, Glennon, McLean, A.Wilson, Robertson					
18 Jan. 1913	Notts County	Division 1	3–1	McLean(15), Wilson(44), Glennon(64)	14000
Davison, Worrall, Spoors, Brittleton, McSkimming, Campbell, L.Burkinshaw, Glennon, McLean, A.Wilson, Wright					
05 Feb. 1913	Chelsea	F.A.Cup 2R	6–0	McLean 3(3pen., 55, 83), Wilson 2(35, 60), Kirkman(10)	35860
Davison, Worrall, Spoors, Brittleton, McSkimming, Campbell, Kirkman, Glennon, McLean, A.Wilson, Robertson					
08 Feb. 1913	Aston Villa	Division 1	1–1	Wilson(30)	41000
Davison, Worrall, Spoors, Miller, Brittleton, Campbell, Kirkman, Glennon, McLean, A.Wilson, Robertson					
24 Feb. 1913	Bolton Wanderers	Division 1	2–2	McLean(7)pen., Glennon(48)	10000
Davison, Worrall, Spoors, Brittleton, McSkimming, Campbell, Kirkman, Glennon, McLean, A.Wilson, Robertson					
22 Mar. 1913	Chelsea	Division 1	3–2	Wilson(20), Robertson(25), Kirkman(86)	6000
Davison, Worrall, Spoors, Miller, McSkimming, Campbell, Kirkman, Glennon, McLean, A.Wilson, Robertson					
05 Apr. 1913	Bradford City	Division 1	6–0	McLean 2(31, 60), Glennon(8), Kirkman(25), Burkinshaw(58), Wright(59),	8000
Davison, Worrall, Spoors, Miller, McSkimming, Campbell, Kirkman, Glennon, McLean, L.Burkinshaw, Wright					
14 Apr. 1913	Newcastle United	Division 1	1–2	McLean(75)pen.	10000
Davison, Brittleton, Spoors, Miller, McSkimming, Campbell, Kirkman, L.Burkinshaw, McLean, A.Wilson, Robertson					
19 Apr. 1913	West Bromwich Albion	Division 1	3–2	McLean 2(30, 40), Glennon(6)	10000
Davison, Brittleton, Spoors, Miller, McSkimming, Campbell, Kirkman, Glennon, McLean, A.Wilson, Robertson					

OTHER GAMES AT HILLSBOROUGH

Date	Match	Home		Away		Att.
24 Aug. 1912	Public Trial Match	Stripes	1	Whites	0	8000
24 Mar. 1913	Sunday School s/f	Heeley Friends	2	Owlerton Wesleyans	0	n/k
25 Mar. 1913	"Pub Cup" Final	Beehive Inn	1	Bird In Hand	5	n/k
07 Apr. 1913	Wednesday Shield s/f	Lydgate	3	Malin Bridge	1	n/k
10 Apr. 1913	Thursday Lge. s/f	Wild & Son	4	Sheffield Post Office	1	n/k
17 Apr. 1913	Thursday Lge. Final	Wild & Son	1	Excelsior	1	n/k
21 Apr. 1913	Clegg Shield s/f	Hillsborough	3	Hunters Bar	2	n/k
28 Apr. 1913	Vitulers Final	Industry Inn	2	Beehive Inn	0	n/k
05 May 1913	Clegg Shield Final	Hillsborough	0	Coleridge Road	1	n/k

Date	Opponents	Competition	Score	Scorers	Att.
06 Sep. 1913	Manchester United	Division 1	1–3	Burkinshaw(38)	29000
Davison, Worrall, Spoors, Brittleton, McSkimming, Campbell, Kirkman, Glennon, J.Burkinshaw, A.Wilson, Robertson					
20 Sep. 1913	Preston North End	Division 1	2–1	Wilson(20), Spoors(50)pen.	20000
Davison, Worrall, Spoors, Miller, McSkimming, Campbell, Kirkman, Glennon, J.Burkinshaw, A.Wilson, Robertson					
22 Sep. 1913	Oldham Athletic	Division 1	1–2	Glennon(10)	16000
Davison, Worrall, Spoors, Miller, Lamb, Campbell, Kirkman, Glennon, J.Burkinshaw, A.Wilson, Robertson					
04 Oct. 1913	Liverpool	Division 1	4–1	Wilson, Burkinshaw, Robertson, Kirkman	20000
Davison, Worrall, Spoors, Miller, McSkimming, Campbell, Kirkman, Glennon, L.Burkinshaw, A.Wilson, Robertson					
18 Oct. 1913	Middlesbrough	Division 1	2–0	Robertson(8), Burkinshaw(12)	20000
Davison, Brittleton, Spoors, Miller, McSkimming, Campbell, Kirkman, J.Burkinshaw, Glennon, A.Wilson, Robertson					
01 Nov. 1913	Derby County	Division 1	1–3	Spoors(85)	25000
Davison, Brittleton, Spoors, Miller, McSkimming, Campbell, Kirkman, J.Burkinshaw, Glennon, A.Wilson, Pickering					
15 Nov. 1913	Bradford City	Division 1	1–3	Wilson(74)	15000
Davison, Brittleton, Spoors, Miller, McSkimming, Campbell, Kirkman, J.Burkinshaw, Glennon, A.Wilson, Pickering					
29 Nov. 1913	Sunderland	Division 1	2–1	Robertson(44), Wilson(–)	25000
Davison, Worrall, Spoors, Brittleton, McSkimming, Campbell, Kirkman, Glennon, Miller, A.Wilson, Robertson					
13 Dec. 1913	West Bromwich Albion	Division 1	1–4	Robertson(38)	20000
Davison, Worrall, Spoors, Brittleton, McSkimming, Campbell, Monaghan, J.Burkinshaw, Miller, A.Wilson, Robertson					
26 Dec. 1913	Chelsea	Division 1	3–0	J.Burkinshaw(7), L.Burkinshaw(63), Campbell(68)	38000
Davison, Worrall, Spoors, Brittleton, McSkimming, Campbell, L.Burkinshaw, J.Burkinshaw, McGregor, Miller, Wright					
29 Dec. 1913	Bolton Wanderers	Division 1	1–1	McGregor(35)	8000
Davison, Worrall, C.Brelsford, Brittleton, McSkimming, Miller, Kirkman, J.Burkinshaw, McGregor, L.Burkinshaw, Wright					
03 Jan. 1914	Burnley	Division 1	2–6	Brittleton(58), McGregor(–)	25000
Streets, Worrall, Spoors, Brittleton, McSkimming, Nicholson, L.Burkinshaw, J.Burkinshaw, McGregor, Miller, Wright					
10 Jan. 1914	Notts County	F.A.Cup 1	3–2	J.Burkinshaw(7), L.Burkinshaw(38), Brittleton(48)	27579
Davison, Worrall, Spoors, Brittleton, McSkimming, Campbell, L.Burkinshaw, J.Burkinshaw, A.Wilson, Miller, Wright					
24 Jan. 1914	Newcastle United	Division 1	0–0		25000
Davison, Worrall, Spoors, Brittleton, McSkimming, Campbell, Kirkman, J.Burkinshaw, McLean, A.Wilson, Robertson					
04 Feb. 1914	Wolverhampton W.	F.A.Cup 2R	1–0	Kirkman(50)	43050
Davison, C.Brelsford, Spoors, Brittleton, McSkimming, Campbell, Kirkman, Glennon, McLean, A.Wilson, Gill					
14 Feb. 1914	Aston Villa	Division 1	2–3	Wilson 2(44, 89)	25000
Davison, Worrall, Spoors, Miller, McSkimming, Campbell, Kirkman, J.Burkinshaw, McLean, A.Wilson, Gill					
21 Feb. 1914	Brighton & Hove Alb.	F.A.Cup 3	3–0	McLean(53), Gill(75), Burkinshaw(84)	38997
Davison, Worrall, Spoors, Brittleton, McSkimming, Campbell, Kirkman, J.Burkinshaw, McLean, A.Wilson, Gill					
28 Feb. 1914	Sheffield United	Division 1	2–1	Glennon(39), McLean(59)	39000
Davison, Worrall, Spoors, Brittleton, McSkimming, Campbell, Kirkman, Glennon, McLean, A.Wilson, Gill					
07 Mar. 1914	Aston Villa	F.A.Cup 4	0–1		56991
Davison, Worrall, Spoors, Brittleton, McSkimming, Campbell, Kirkman, Glennon, McLean, A.Wilson, Gill					
14 Mar. 1914	Manchester City	Division 1	2–2	Burkinshaw(25), McLean(80)pen.	15000
Davison, Worrall, Spoors, Brittleton, Parkes, Campbell, Kirkman, Glennon, McLean, J.Burkinshaw, Robertson					
28 Mar. 1914	Blackburn Rovers	Division 1	3–1	Burkinshaw(28), Wilson(40), McLean(89)	17500
Davison, McSkimming, Spoors, Brittleton, Parkes, Campbell, L.Burkinshaw, Glennon, McLean, A.Wilson, Robertson					
11 Apr. 1914	Everton	Division 1	2–2	McLean 2(–, –)	16000
Davison, McSkimming, Spoors, Nicholson, Parkes, Campbell, L.Burkinshaw, J.Burkinshaw, McLean, A.Wilson, Robertson					
25 Apr. 1914	Tottenham Hotspur	Division 1	2–0	Wilson(49), McLean(67)	10000
Davison, Worrall, Spoors, Brittleton, Parkes, McSkimming, L.Burkinshaw, J.Burkinshaw, McLean, A.Wilson, Robertson					
30 Apr. 1914	Sheffield United	Charity	0–2		5000
Davison, Worrall, Spoors, Brittleton, Parkes, McSkimming, L.Burkinshaw, J.Burkinshaw, Platts, A.Wilson, Robertson					

OTHER GAMES AT HILLSBOROUGH

Date	Competition	Home	Away		Att.
23 Aug. 1913	Public Trial Match	Stripes 5	Whites 4		12000
02 Apr. 1913	Thursday Lge. s/f	Whitworth's 6	R.F.A. 0		n/k
13 Apr. 1914	Sunday School s/f	Owlerton 0	St. John's Institute 0		n/k
13 Apr. 1914	Bible Class Final	Grimethorpe U.M. 3	St.Alban's Church 0		n/k
14 Apr. 1914	Free Churches S/F	Upperthorpe Unitarians 2	Woodburn Road 0		n/k
15 Apr. 1914	Wednesday Shield Fnl.	Tinsley 8	High Wincobank 0		n/k
16 Apr. 1914	Thursday Lge. Final	Whitworth's 2	Barnsley Amateurs 1		n/k
18 Apr. 1914	Boys Brigade Final	All Saints 0	St. John's Institute 3		n/k
28 Apr. 1914	Clegg Shield s/f	Hillsborough 2	Coleridge Road 1		n/k
29 Apr. 1914	Sun. School Fnl. – Rep.	Grenoside B.C. 0	Owlerton 0		n/k
02 May 1914	Boys (EST FINAL)	Sheffield 1	West Ham 0		16000

Date	Opponents	Competition	Score	Scorers	Att.
01 Sep. 1914	Middlesbrough	Division 1	3–1	Wilson 2(–, 60), Kirkman(31)	12000
Davison, Worrall, Spoors, Brittleton, Parkes, McSkimming, Kirkman, Glennon, McLean, A.Wilson, Robertson					
12 Sep. 1914	Aston Villa	Division 1	5–2	McLean 3(3, 22, 80), Glennon(10), Wilson(31)	12000
Davison, Worrall, Spoors, Bentley, Parkes, McSkimming, Kirkman, Glennon, McLean, A.Wilson, Gill,					
26 Sep. 1914	Bradford Park Avenue	Division 1	6–0	McLean 3(77pen., 80, 82), Kirkman(39), Glennon(40), Capper(89)	20000
Davison, Spoors, Blair, Bentley, Parkes, McSkimming, Kirkman, Glennon, McLean, A.Wilson, Capper					
05 Oct. 1914	Sheffield United	Charity	2–0	Glennon(75), McLean(82)	6000
Davison, Spoors, Blair, Bentley, Parkes, McSkimming, Kirkman, Glennon, McLean, A.Wilson, Capper					
10 Oct. 1914	Manchester United	Division 1	1–0	Glennon(73)	20000
Davison, Spoors, Blair, Bentley, Parkes, McSkimming, Kirkman, Glennon, McLean, A.Wilson, Capper					
24 Oct. 1914	Blackburn Rovers	Division 1	1–1	McLean(26)	24000
Davison, Spoors, Blair, Bentley, Parkes, McSkimming, Kirkman, Glennon, McLean, A.Wilson, Capper					
07 Nov. 1914	Sunderland	Division 1	1–2	Capper(12)	22000
Davison, Spoors, Blair, Bentley, Parkes, McSkimming, Kirkman, Glennon, McLean, A.Wilson, Capper					
14 Nov. 1914	Manchester City	Division 1	2–1	Glennon 2(16, 64)	20000
Davison, Spoors, Blair, Bentley, Parkes, McSkimming, Kirkman, Glennon, McLean, A.Wilson, Capper					
28 Nov. 1914	Everton	Division 1	1–4	McLean(49)	14000
Davison, Worrall, Spoors, Bentley, Parkes, McSkimming, Kirkman, Glennon, McLean, A.Wilson, Capper					
12 Dec. 1914	Bradford City	Division 1	3–3	Wilson(22), Brittleton(75), McLean(80)	8000
Davison, Worrall, Spoors, Brittleton, Parkes, Bentley, Kirkman, Glennon, McLean, A.Wilson, Robertson					
25 Dec. 1914	Tottenham Hotspur	Division 1	3–2	Burkinshaw(3), McLean(15), Wilson(79)	25000
Davison, Worrall, Spoors, Brittleton, McSkimming, Bentley, Kirkman, J.Burkinshaw, McLean, A.Wilson, Robertson					
01 Jan. 1915	Newcastle United	Division 1	2–1	McLean(62), Bentley(80)	12000
Davison, Worrall, Spoors, Brittleton, McSkimming, Bentley, Kirkman, Glennon, McLean, A.Wilson, Robertson					
02 Jan. 1915	Sheffield United	Division 1	1–1	Wilson(30)	28000
Davison, Worrall, Spoors, Brittleton, McSkimming, Bentley, Kirkman, Glennon, McLean, A.Wilson, Robertson					
09 Jan. 1915	Manchester United	F.A.Cup 1	1–0	Wilson(71)	23248
Davison, Blair, Spoors, Brittleton, Parkes, Bentley, Kirkman, Glennon, McLean, A.Wilson, Robertson					
23 Jan. 1915	Liverpool	Division 1	2–1	McLean(22), Kirkman(82)	11000
Davison, Spoors, Blair, Brittleton, Parkes, Bentley, Kirkman, Glennon, McLean, A.Wilson, Robertson					
30 Jan. 1915	Wolverhampton W.	F.A.Cup 2	2–0	Robertson(17), Glennon(40)	22919
Davison, Blair, Spoors, Brittleton, Parkes, McSkimming, Kirkman, J.Burkinshaw, Glennon, A.Wilson, Robertson					
06 Feb. 1915	Oldham Athletic	Division 1	2–2	Wilson(35), Capper(38)	20000
Davison, Spoors, Blair, Brittleton, Parkes, McSkimming, Capper, J.Burkinshaw, Glennon, A.Wilson, Robertson					
20 Feb. 1915	Newcastle United	F.A.Cup 3	1–2	McLean(61)	25971
Davison, Worrall, Spoors, Bentley, Parkes, McSkimming, Capper, Glennon, McLean, A.Wilson, Robertson					
01 Mar. 1915	Bolton Wanderers	Division 1	7–0	Parkes(15), Glennon(32), Gill(36), Robertson(61), Wilson (66), Capper(73), Bentley(80)	7000
Davison, Spoors, McSkimming, Brittleton, Parkes, Bentley, Capper, Gill, Glennon, A.Wilson, Robertson					
06 Mar. 1915	Notts County	Division 1	0–0		11000
Davison, Spoors, McSkimming, Brittleton, Parkes, Bentley, Capper, Gill, Glennon, A.Wilson, Robertson					
27 Mar. 1915	West Bromwich Albion	Division 1	0–0		12000
Davison, Spoors, McSkimming, Brittleton, Parkes, Bentley, Kirkman, Capper, McLean, A.Wilson, Gill					
10 Apr. 1915	Chelsea	Division 1	3–2	McLean 2(–, 67), Wilson(–)	10000
Davison, Spoors, Blair, Brittleton, McSkimming, Bentley, Capper, Glennon, McLean, A.Wilson, Robertson					
24 Apr. 1915	Burnley	Division 1	0–0		5000
Davison, Spoors, Blair, Brittleton, Parkes, McSkimming, Capper, J.Burkinshaw, McLean, A.Wilson, Robertson					

OTHER GAMES AT HILLSBOROUGH

22 Aug. 1914	Public Trial Match	Stripes 5	Whites 3		15652
26 Oct. 1914	Inter City	Sheffield 2	Glasgow 1		n/k
13 Feb. 1915	S.Challenge Cup s/f	Worksop Town 3	Rotherham Town 0		n/k
27 Feb. 1915	Boys (EST)	Sheffield 3	Hull 1		n/k
08 Apr. 1915	Thursday Lge. s/f	Barnsley Amateurs 3	Heeley 0		n/k
15 Apr. 1915	Thursday Lge. s/f	Eccleshall Amateurs 0	Sheffield Tramways 1		n/k
22 Apr. 1915	Thursday Lge. Final	Barnsley Amateurs 0	Sheffield Tramways 2		n/k
08 May 1915	Wednesday Shield Final	Hillsborough R.C. 2	Carbrook 0		n/k
08 May 1915	Clegg Shield Final	Coleridge Road 0	Duchess Road 3		n/k

Date	Opponents	Competition	Score	Scorers	Att.
04 Sep. 1915	Bradford Park Avenue	Midland	2–4	Wilson(4), Goodwin(–)	5000
Streets, Worrall, Womack, Brittleton, Harrop, Bentley, Capper, Glennon, Goodwin, A.Wilson, Tasker					
18 Sep. 1915	Hull City	Midland	2–4	Goodwin(8), Wilson(89)	3000
Streets, C.Brelsford, Womack, Brittleton, Harrop, Bentley, Capper, Glennon, Goodwin, A.Wilson, T.Brelsford					
02 Oct. 1915	Barnsley	Midland	1–4	Brittleton(3)	5000
Causer, Worrall, Stapleton, Brittleton, Harrop, Bentley, Capper, J.Burkinshaw, Glennon, A.Wilson, Watson					
16 Oct. 1915	Sheffield United	Midland	0–0		11000
Davison, Ball, Womack, Brittleton, Harrop, Bentley, Capper, Glennon, J.Burkinshaw, A.Wilson, Watson					
30 Oct. 1915	Huddersfield Town	Midland	2–1	Harrop(68)pen., Hatton(85)	4000
Streets, Brittleton, Stapleton, T.Brelsford, Harrop, Clarke, McGregor, Reed, Glennon, A.Wilson, Hatton					
13 Nov. 1915	Notts County	Midland	4–1	Cawley 2(40, 80), Glennon(30), Wilson(88)	4000
Streets, Stapleton, Womack, Brittleton, Harrop, Bentley, Capper, Glennon, A.Wilson, Cawley, Hatton					
27 Nov. 1915	Lincoln City	Midland	4–1	Wilson 2(15, 86), Glennon(21), Hatton(73)	3000
Streets, Stapleton, Womack, Brittleton, Harrop, Bentley, Capper, Glennon, A.Wilson, Cawley, Hatton					
11 Dec. 1915	Leeds City	Midland	0–0		2000
Davison, Stapleton, C.Brelsford, Brittleton, Harrop, T.Brelsford, Capper, Glennon, A.Wilson, Cawley, Hatton					
25 Dec. 1915	Nottingham Forest	Midland	0–1		18000
Streets, Stapleton, C.Brelsford, Brittleton, Harrop, T.Brelsford, J.Burkinshaw, Glennon, A.Wilson, Cawley, Hatton					
08 Jan. 1916	Leicester Fosse	Midland	3–1	Wilson(30), Burkinshaw(48), Cawley(85)	5000
Davison, Stapleton, Womack, Brittleton, Harrop, T.Brelsford, Capper, J.Burkinshaw, A.Wilson, Cawley, Hatton					
22 Jan. 1916	Bradford City	Midland	1–0	Burkinshaw(20)pen.	5000
Streets, Stapleton, C.Brelsford, Brittleton, Glennon, T.Brelsford, Lloyd, J.Burkinshaw, A.Wilson, Cawley, Hatton					
05 Feb. 1916	Grimsby Town	Midland	2–1	Hatton(62), Wilson(75)	3000
Davison, Brittleton, C.Brelsford, J.Burkinshaw, Harrop, T.Brelsford, Capper, Islip, A.Wilson, Cawley, Hatton					
19 Feb. 1916	Derby County	Midland	5–0	Wilson 2(37, 88), Hatton(21), Islip(63), Harrop(75)	4000
Davison, Brittleton, C.Brelsford, J.Burkinshaw, Harrop, T.Brelsford, Capper, Islip, A.Wilson, Cawley, Hatton					
04 Mar. 1916	Lincoln City	Subsidiary	2–2	Glennon 2(60, 70)	4000
Davison, Brittleton, C.Brelsford, J.Burkinshaw, Harrop, T.Brelsford, Capper, Glennon, A.Wilson, Cawley, Islip					
25 Mar. 1916	Hull City	Subsidiary	0–2		6000
Streets, Brittleton, Stapleton, Bentley, Glennon, T.Brelsford, Johnson, J.Burkinshaw, A.Wilson, Cawley, Islip					
15 Apr. 1916	Grimsby Town	Subsidiary	2–1	Burkinshaw(25)pen., Wilson(64)	3000
Streets, Stapleton, C.Brelsford, Brittleton, Glennon, T.Brelsford, Johnson, J.Burkinshaw, Capper, A.Wilson, Islip					
22 Apr. 1916	Rotherham County	Subsidiary	3–2	Islip 2(36, 43), Burkinshaw(32)	10000
Streets, Stapleton, C.Brelsford, Brittleton, Glennon, T.Brelsford, Johnson, J.Burkinshaw, A.Wilson, Islip, Jones					
24 Apr. 1916	Sheffield United	Subsidiary	0–1		14000
Streets, Stapleton, Brittleton, J.Burkinshaw, Glennon, Clarke, T.Brelsford, Islip, Brown, A.Wilson, Jones					

OTHER GAMES AT HILLSBOROUGH

28 Aug. 1915	Public Trial Match	Stripes 3	Whites 2	4000
18 Mar. 1916	Bible Class s/f	Carbrook Reform 2	St. John's Wesleyans 2	n/k
08 Apr. 1916	Free Churches s/f	Hartshead 2nd Section 2	Valley Road 1	n/k
17 Apr. 1916	Clegg Shield Final	Coleridge Road 0	Duchess Road 5	n/k
29 Apr. 1916	Friendlies Final	Gas Co. 1	Hillsborough & Walkley 2	n/k

Date	Opponents	Competition	Score	Scorers	Att.
09 Sep. 1916	Bradford Park Avenue	Midland	1–3	Jones(5)	6000
Lyall, Thorpe, C.Brelsford, Brittleton, Harrop, T.Brelsford, J.Burkinshaw, Islip, Glennon, A.Wilson, Jones					
23 Sep. 1916	Hull City	Midland	2–1	Islip(59), Glennon(–)	6000
Lyall, Brittleton, C.Brelsford, J.Burkinshaw, Harrop, T.Brelsford, Kirkman, Glennon, Islip, Cawley, Robertson					
07 Oct. 1916	Barnsley	Midland	3–0	Glennon 2(–, –), Cawley(47)	5000
Lyall, Brittleton, C.Brelsford, J.Burkinshaw, Harrop, T.Brelsford, Capper, Glennon, A.Wilson, Cawley, Robertson					
21 Oct. 1916	Sheffield United	Midland	2–2	Islip(35), Kirkman(70)	16000
Lyall, Brittleton, C.Brelsford, J.Burkinshaw, Spoors, T.Brelsford, Kirkman, Capper, Islip, Watson, Glennon					
04 Nov. 1916	Leicester Fosse	Midland	3–0	T.Brelsford(12), Glennon(–), Cawley(–)	5000
Lyall, Spoors, C.Brelsford, Brittleton, Harrop, T.Brelsford, Capper, Glennon, Islip, Cawley, Jones					
18 Nov. 1916	Notts County	Midland	2–0	Kirkman(–), Wilson(82)	3000
Lyall, Brittleton, C.Brelsford, J.Burkinshaw, Glennon, T.Brelsford, Kirkman, Capper, A.Wilson, Cawley, Islip					
02 Dec. 1916	Huddersfield Town	Midland	0–0		4000
Lyall, Brittleton, C.Brelsford, J.Burkinshaw, Harrop, T.Brelsford, Capper, Glennon, A.Wilson, Cawley, Islip					
09 Dec. 1916	Chesterfield	Midland	3–1	Oldacre 2(10, 40), Glennon(–)	3500
Lyall, Brittleton, C.Brelsford, A.Wilson, Harrop, T.Brelsford, Capper, Glennon, Oldacre, Cawley, Islip					
23 Dec. 1916	Birmingham	Midland	0–2		2000
Lyall, Thorpe, C.Brelsford, Bingham, Glennon, Clarke, Brittleton, Gill, A.Wilson, T.Brelsford, Smith					
01 Jan. 1917	Rotherham County	Subsidiary	2–3	Spoors(–)pen., Wilson(76)	12000
A.Cooper, Thorpe, C.Brelsford, Firby, Spoors, Clarke, Kirkman, Grayson, A.Wilson, T.Brelsford, Islip					
06 Jan. 1917	Nottingham Forest	Midland	1–4	Wilson(17)	5000
A.Cooper, Thorpe, C.Brelsford, Glennon, Harrop, T.Brelsford, Cowham, Batiste, Oldacre, A.Wilson, Islip					
20 Jan. 1917	Leeds City	Midland	2–2	Glennon(26), Kirkman(81)	4500
Lyall, Brittleton, C.Brelsford, Lamb, Harrop, T.Brelsford, Kirkman, A.Wilson, Glennon, Cawley, Watson					
03 Feb. 1917	Bradford City	Midland	1–0*	Glennon(8)	5000
Lyall, Thorpe, C.Brelsford, Brittleton, Glennon, T.Brelsford, Cowham, Capper, A.Wilson, Cawley, Jones					
17 Feb. 1917	Grimsby Town	Midland	3–1	Edwards(7)pen., Butler(78)og., Capper(89)	3000
A.Cooper, C.Brelsford, Thorpe, Brittleton, Edwards, T.Brelsford, Kirkman, Capper, Buddery, Cawley, Cowham					
03 Mar. 1917	Rotherham County	Midland	1–0	Wilson(53)	9000
Birch, Thorpe, C.Brelsford, Roulson, Brittleton, T.Brelsford, Capper, A.Wilson, Glennon, Islip, Cawley					
31 Mar. 1917	Barnsley	Subsidiary	2–2	Brittleton(8), Wilson(70)	3000
Birch, Thorpe, C.Brelsford, Brittleton, Harrop, T.Brelsford, J.Burkinshaw, Glennon, Buddery, A.Wilson, Jones					
14 Apr. 1917	Sheffield United	Subsidiary	2–1	Brittleton(6), Glennon(30)	10000
Birch, Thorpe, C.Brelsford, Brittleton, Harrop, J.Burkinshaw, Capper, Glennon, A.Wilson, Islip, Robertson					
28 Apr. 1917	Lincoln City	Midland	7–1	Burkinshaw 3, Bell 2, Glennon, Kirkman	5000
Birch, Thorpe, C.Brelsford, Brittleton, Glennon, Helliwell, Kirkman, J.Burkinshaw, Buddery, Bell, Harrop					

*Match abandoned after 87 mins. – result stood

OTHER GAMES AT HILLSBOROUGH

17 Mar. 1917	Bible Class s/f	Grenoside 4	St. John's 1		n/k
07 Apr. 1917	Minor Cup s/f	Craven's Sports 4	Hallam 1		n/k
07 Apr. 1917	Charity	Shrewsbury 3	G.C.R. Loco 2		n/k
09 Apr. 1917	Sunday School s/f	Grenoside 4	Hollinsend 0		n/k
09 Apr. 1917	Bible Class Final	Carbrook Reform 3	Grenoside 2		n/k
10 Apr. 1917	Minor Cup Final	Craven's Sports 1	Treeton 0		2000
21 Apr. 1917	Sunday School s/f	Hartshead 1	Heeley 2		n/k

Date	Opponents	Competition	Score	Scorers	Att.
01 Sep. 1917	Leeds City	Midland	0–1		6000
Cooper, Thorpe, C.Brelsford, Brittleton, Harrop, Roulson, Cowham, Clarke, Glennon, Bell, Jones					
15 Sep. 1917	Nottingham Forest	Midland	0–3		4000
Cooper, Thorpe, C.Brelsford, Brittleton, Harrop, Roulson, J.Burkinshaw, Glennon, A.Wilson, Bell, McGregor					
29 Sep. 1917	Leicester Fosse	Midland	1–3	Glennon(61)	4000
Cooper, Thorpe, C.Brelsford, Brittleton, Harrop, Roulson, Capper, Glennon, J.Burkinshaw, Bell, McGregor					
20 Oct. 1917	Hull City	Midland	4–3	Glennon 2(57, 69), Burkinshaw(58), Bell(65)	7000
Davison, Stapleton, C.Brelsford, Brittleton, Harrop, Roulson, Capper, J.Burkinshaw, Glennon, Bell, Maw					
17 Nov. 1917	Barnsley	Midland	4–2	Burkinshaw 2(14pen, –), Wilson, Kay og.	7000
Cooper, Stapleton, C.Brelsford, Brittleton, Glennon, Bentley, J.Burkinshaw, L.Armitage, A.Wilson, Toulson, Capper					
01 Dec. 1917	Bradford Park Avenue	Midland	3–1	Brittleton(56), Armitage(62), Burkinshaw(78)pen.	n/k
Cooper, Thorpe, C.Brelsford, Brittleton, Glennon, Stapleton, Capper, J.Burkinshaw, L.Armitage, Hinchliffe, Spratt					
08 Dec. 1917	Bradford City	Midland	3–0	Hinchliffe 2(57, 59), Armitage(16)	4000
Cooper, Stapleton, C.Brelsford, Brittleton, Harrop, Glennon, Capper, J.Burkinshaw, L.Armitage, Hinchliffe, Spratt					
22 Dec. 1917	Rotherham County	Midland	3–3	Spratt(49), Armitage(56), Capper(86)	3000
Cooper, Roulson, C.Brelsford, Brittleton, Glennon, Harrop, Capper, J.Burkinshaw, L.Armitage, Hinchliffe, Spratt					
26 Dec. 1917	Sheffield United	Midland	3–1	McLean, Armitage, Glennon	20000
Cooper, McSkimming, Blair, Brittleton, Glennon, Roulson, Capper, L.Armitage, McLean, A.Wilson, Spratt					
05 Jan. 1918	Lincoln City	Midland	7-2	Spratt2(35,_),Capper(13),Glennon(14), Armitage(15), Buddery(27), Brittleton(62)	n/k
Summers, Stapleton, C.Brelsford, Brittleton, Harrop, Glennon, Capper, Buddery, L.Armitage, Hinchliffe, Spratt					
09 Feb. 1918	Birmingham	Midland	0-2		3000
Streets, Stapleton, C.Brelsford, Brittleton, Harrop, Glennon, Capper, Buddery, L.Armitage, Donaldson, Spratt					
23 Feb. 1918	Notts County	Midland	2-1	Glennon(12), Spratt(58)	3000
Summers, Stapleton, C.Brelsford, Brittleton, Harrop, Whitchurch, Pearson, J.Burkinshaw, Glennon, Hinchliffe, Spratt					
09 Mar. 1918	Huddersfield Town	Midland	3-1	Glennon 3(41,54,70)	5000
Summers, Stapleton, C.Brelsford, Brittleton, Harrop, Hinchliffe, Pearson, J.Burkinshaw, Godfrey, Glennon, Hibbert					
23 Mar. 1918	Sheffield United	Subsidiary	2-1	Glennon 2(16,25)	15000
Summers, Stapleton, C.Brelsford, Brittleton, Harrop, Hinchliffe, Capper, Thompson, J.Burkinshaw, Glennon, Spratt					
01 Apr. 1918	Barnsley	Subsidiary	6-2	Salt 3(8,36,_), Burkinshaw 2(35,_pen.), Pearson	10000
Summers, Stapleton, C.Brelsford, Brittleton, Parkes, J.Burkinshaw, Pearson, Salt, Buddery, Glennon, Spratt					
06 Apr. 1918	Rotherham County	Subsidiary	1-1	Burkinshaw(80)	2000
Summers, Stapleton, Roulson, Brittleton, Harrop, Hinchliffe, J.Burkinshaw, Buddery, Thompson, Salt, Ford					
13 Apr. 1918	Sheffield United	Friendly	2-0	Salt(65), Capper(_)	6000
Summers, Stapleton, C.Brelsford, Brittleton, Harrop, Hinchliffe, Pearson, Salt, Capper, Glennon, Spratt					
27 Apr. 1918	Grimsby Town	Midland	1-1	Brittleton(17)	3000
Summers, Stapleton, Spoors, Brittleton, Harrop, Peach, Pearson, Hibbert, Ford, Smith, Spratt					
11 May 1918	Liverpool	Charity	3-1	Glennon 2(15,50), Lamb(60)	6000
Summers, Stapleton, C.Brelsford, Brittleton, Harrop, Smith, Pearson, J.Burkinshaw, Salt, Glennon, Lamb					

OTHER GAMES AT HILLSBOROUGH

20 Apr. 1918	Minor Cup s/f	Simplex Sports 2	Treeton 1		n/k
04 May 1918	Representative	Wycliffe Boys Club 1	Rest of League 3		n/k
18 May 1918	Charity	Hadfield's 1	Vickers 2		2000
21 May 1918	Clegg Shield Final	Hillsborough Boys Club 13	Crookesmoor 0		n/k
21 May 1918	United Shield Final	Hillsborough R.C. 2	Walkley 0		n/k

Date	Opponents	Competition	Score	Scorers	Att.
14 Sep. 1918	Bradford Park Avenue	Midland	2–3	Glennon 2(–, 78)	4000
Summers, Thorpe, Stapleton, Brittleton, Harrop, Hinchcliffe, Pearson, Capper, J.Burkinshaw, Glennon, Spratt					
28 Sep. 1918	Hull City	Midland	3–1	Glennon(33), Ford(57), Burkinshaw(60)	7000
Summers, Stapleton, C.Brelsford, Brittleton, Harrop, Hinchcliffe, Pearson, J.Burkinshaw, Ford, Glennon, Maw					
12 Oct. 1918	Coventry City	Midland	3–0	J.Burkinshaw(13), Glennon(–), Ford(85)	10000
Summers, Stapleton, Brittleton, Campbell, Harrop, Hinchcliffe, Pearson, J.Burkinshaw, R.Burkinshaw, Glennon, Ford					
19 Oct. 1918	Barnsley	Midland	2–0	J.Burkinshaw(40), Glennon(75)	8000
Davison, Stapleton, Hill, Brittleton, Harrop, Hinchcliffe, Spratt, J.Burkinshaw, R.Burkinshaw, Glennon, S.Lamb					
02 Nov. 1918	Leicester Fosse	Midland	0–2		7000
Thorpe, Stapleton, Hill, Brittleton, Harrop, J.Burkinshaw, Pearson, Spratt, R.Burkinshaw, Glennon, S.Lamb					
16 Nov. 1918	Nottingham Forest	Midland	1–2	Ford(10)	8000
Birch, Rutledge, Thorpe, Brittleton, Glennon, Hill, Capper, J.Burkinshaw, R.Burkinshaw, Pearson, Ford					
30 Nov. 1918	Leeds City	Midland	0–2		10000
Birch, Thorpe, Hill, Brittleton, Glennon, Hinchcliffe, Pearson, J.Burkinshaw, Ford, R.Burkinshaw, S.Lamb					
21 Dec. 1918	Bradford City	Midland	1–0	Roe(58)	7500
Birch, Thorpe, Blair, Brittleton, Harrop, Hinchcliffe, Pearson, Roe, Andrews, J.Burkinshaw, S.Lamb					
25 Dec. 1918	Sheffield United	Midland	4–0	Burkinshaw(20), Brittleton(29), Pearson(–), McLean(74)	20000
Birch, Thorpe, Blair, Brittleton, Glennon, Hinchcliffe, Pearson, Roe, McLean, J.Burkinshaw, S.Lamb					
01 Jan. 1919	Rotherham County	Subsidiary	4–2	Glennon 2, Brittleton(4), Godfrey	3000
Birch, Thorpe, Deans, Brittleton, Harrop, Hinchcliffe, Pearson, Roe, Godfrey, Glennon, S.Lamb					
18 Jan. 1919	Lincoln City	Midland	4–2	Burkinshaw 3(15pen., 30, –), Roe(–)	9000
Summers, Stapleton, Thorpe, Frith, Harrop, Hinchcliffe, Pearson, Salt, Roe, J.Burkinshaw, S.Lamb					
01 Feb. 1919	Rotherham County	Midland	0–0		7000
Birch, Stapleton, Thorpe, Brittleton, Harrop, Nicholson, Pearson, Capper, Roe, J.Burkinshaw, S.Lamb					
08 Feb. 1919	Birmingham	Midland	0–1		15000
Birch, Stapleton, C.Brelsford, Brittleton, Harrop, Hinchcliffe, Capper, Pearson, Buddery, Roe, S.Lamb					
22 Feb. 1919	Notts County	Midland	2–2	Capper(13), Burkinshaw(–)	8500
Summers, Thorpe, Sanders, Brittleton, Harrop, Hinchcliffe, Pearson, Capper, Glennon, J.Burkinshaw, S.Lamb					
08 Mar. 1919	Huddersfield Town	Midland	1–3	Lamb(15)	9000
Birch, Stapleton, C.Brelsford, Brittleton, Parkes, Harrop, Pearson, Glennon, Buxton, Wood, S.Lamb					
22 Mar. 1919	Sheffield United	Subsidiary	0–2		18000
Birch, Stapleton, Brittleton, J.Lamb, Parkes, Campbell, Pearson, Capper, Glennon, J.Burkinshaw, S.Lamb					
12 Apr. 1919	Sheffield United	Friendly	0–1		8000
Johnson, Stapleton, Spoors, Brittleton, J.Lamb, Campbell, Kirkman, Capper, Glennon, Gill, S.Lamb					
22 Apr. 1919	Grimsby Town	Midland	5–2	Glennon 2, Burkinshaw 2, Gill	n/k
Birch, Stapleton, Spoors, Brittleton, Harrop, Campbell, Kirkman, J.Burkinshaw, Glennon, Gill, Baker					
26 Apr. 1919	Barnsley	Subsidiary	4–3	Bentley 2(58, 62), Gill 2(8, 89)	7000
Birch, Stapleton, Spoors, Brittleton, J.Lamb, Campbell, Kirkman, Bentley, Reed, Gill, Elshaw					
03 May 1919	Rotherham County	Charity	3–1	Gill 2(43, 82), Glennon(25)	5000
Johnson, Stapleton, Spoors, Brittleton, Clarke, Campbell, Reed, Bentley, Glennon, J.Burkinshaw, Gill					
24 May 1919	Everton	Friendly	1–4	Glennon(48)	8000
Davison, Stapleton, Spoors, Brittleton, Harrop, Campbell, Pearson, Bentley, Glennon, Kirkman, Gill					

OTHER GAMES AT HILLSBOROOUGH

27 Mar. 1919	Wednesday Shield s/f	Manor Social 2	Hillsborough 2		n/k
27 Mar. 1919	Wednesday Shield s/f	Malin Bridge 2	Hunters Bar 0		n/k
05 Apr. 1919	Minor League s/f	Cammell's Sports 2	Kimberwoth Old Boys 1		n/k
10 Apr. 1919	United Shield s/f– replay	Wadsley CE 4	Duchess Road 0		n/k
10 Apr. 1919	Wednesday Shield s/f–r	Manor Social 0	Hillsborough 0		n/k
21 Apr. 1919	Sunday School Final	Heeley Friends 2	Mosborough 0		n/k
29 Apr. 1919	Wed.Shield s/f – 2r	Manor Social 2	Hillsborough 1		n/k
01 May 1919	Wednesday Shield Final	Manor Social 0	Malin Bridge 1		n/k
01 May 1919	Clegg Shield Final	Hillsborough 8	Coleridge Road 1		n/k

Date	Opponents	Competition	Score	Scorers	Att.
30 Aug. 1919	Middlesbrough	Division 1	0–1		25000
Birch, Stapleton, Spoors, Brittleton, McSkimming, Campbell, Kirkman, Burkinshaw, McLean, Bentley, Gill					
08 Sep. 1919	Manchester United	Division 1	1–3	Bentley(47)	8000
Birch, Brittleton, Spoors, Bentley, McSkimming, Campbell, Capper, Stapleton, Burkinshaw, Gill, Robertson					
13 Sep. 1919	Notts County	Division 1	0–0		14000
Birch, Stapleton, Spoors, Brittleton, McSkimming, Reed, Capper, Bentley, Gill, Burkinshaw, E.Harvey					
27 Sep. 1919	Sheffield United	Division 1	2–1	Campbell(30), Gill(48)	30000
Birch, Stapleton, Spoors, Burkinhaw, McSkimming, Reed, Capper, Brittleton, Gill, Campbell, Alf.Cooper					
11 Oct. 1919	Blackburn Rovers	Division 1	0–0		15000
Birch, McSkimming, Spoors, Bentley, Lamb, Campbell, Capper, Brittleton, Armitage, Burkinshaw, Reed					
01 Nov. 1919	Manchester City	Division 1	0–0		12000
Davison, Stapleton, Blair, Brittleton, McSkimming, Bentley, W.Harvey, Burkinshaw, Edmondson, Price, Capper					
15 Nov. 1919	Derby County	Division 1	2–0	Gill(7), Spoors(49)pen.	14000
Birch, McSkimming, Blair, Brittleton, Spoors, Campbell, Kirkman, Binney, Edmondson, Price, Gill					
29 Nov. 1919	West Bromwich Albion	Division 1	0–3		30000
Birch, Spoors, Blair, Brittleton, Reed, Campbell. W.Harvey, Burkinshaw, Edmondson, Price, Gill					
13 Dec. 1919	Sunderland	Division 1	0–2		30000
Davison, Spoors, Blair, Bentley, O'Neill, Campbell, W.Harvey, Capper, Edmondson, Gill, Robertson					
26 Dec. 1919	Bradford City	Division 1	1–0	McKay(75)	35000
Birch, Stapleton, Blair, Burkinshaw, Parkes, Campbell, W.Harvey, Binney, McKay, Price, Gill					
27 Dec. 1919	Arsenal	Division 1	1–2	Harvey(35)	30000
Birch, Stapleton, Blair, Burkinshaw, Parkes, Campbell, W.Harvey, Binney, McKay, Price, Gill					
17 Jan 1920	Everton	Division 1	1–0	Welsh(79)	30000
Birch, McSkimming, Blair, Brittleton, Parkes, Hinchliffe, Capper, Binney, Welsh, McKay, Gill					
19 Jan 1920	Darlington	F.A.Cup 1r	0–2		52388
Birch, McSkimming, Blair, Brittleton, Reed, Campbell, Capper, Binney, Bretnall, McKay, Gill					
24 Jan 1920	Burnley	Division 1	3–1	Welsh 2(70, 75), Gill(3)	20000
Davison, Stapleton, Blair, Brittleton, Parkes, Campbell, Capper, Binney, Welsh, McKay, Gill					
31 Jan 1920	Derby County	Friendly	2–1	McKay(5), Taylor(24)	5000
Davison, Stapleton, Parkes, Binney, Spoors, Eggo, Kirkman, W.Taylor, Welsh, McKay, Shelton					
07 Feb. 1920	Preston North End	Division 1	0–1		14000
Davison, Stapleton, Blair, Brittleton, Parkes, Campbell, Kirkman, C.Taylor, Welsh, McKay, Gill					
13 Mar. 1920	Liverpool	Division 1	2–2	McKay(12), Welsh(38)	15000
Davison, Brittleton, O'Neill, Brelsford, G.Wilson, Sykes, Capper, C.Taylor, Welsh, McKay, Shelton					
22 Mar. 1920	Newcastle United	Division 1	0–1		10000
Davison, Brittleton, Blair, Brelsford, G.Wilson, Price, W.Harvey, Capper, Gill, McIntyre, Shelton					
05 Apr. 1920	Bolton Wanderers	Division 1	0–2		16000
Davison, Spoors, Blair, Brittleton, Brelsford, McIntyre, W.Harvey, Whalley, Gill, Capper, Shelton					
06 Apr. 1920	Chelsea	Division 1	0–2		12000
Davison, Bentley, O'Neill, Capper, Brelsford, McIntyre, W.Harvey, Whalley, McKay, Gill, Shelton					
19 Apr. 1920	Bradford Park Avenue	Divison 1	0–1		5000
Davison, Stapleton, Blair, Brelsford, G.Wilson, McIntyre, Capper, Whalley, Edmondson, C.Taylor, E.Harvey					
29 Apr. 1920	Aston Villa	Division 1	0–1		15000
Davison, Brittleton, O'Neill, Eggo, G.Wilson, McIntyre, Capper, C.Taylor, Welsh, W.Taylor, E.Harvey					
01 May 1920	Oldham Athletic	Division 1	1–0	W.Taylor(89)	18000
Kite, Stapleton, Brittleton, Eggo, G.Wilson, Price, Kirkman, C.Taylor, Welsh, W.Taylor, E.Harvey					

OTHER GAMES AT HILLSBOROUGH

23 Aug. 1919	Public Trial Match–	Stripes 2	Whites 1	7000
14 Feb. 1920	S.Challenge Cup s/f	Rotherham County 0	Sheff. United Res. 1	n/k
10 Apr. 1920	International	England 5	Scotland 4	25536
23 Apr. 1920	Police	Sheffield 1	Hull 0	n/k
10 May 1920	Wednesday Shield Final	Owler Lane 2	Manor Social 0	n/k

Date	Opponents	Competition	Score	Scorers	Att.
30 Aug. 1920	Nottingham Forest	Division 2	0–0		18000
Davison, Dunn, Blair, Eggo, G.Wilson, McIntyre, Capper, Kean, Welsh, W.Taylor, Lofthouse					
04 Sep. 1920	Barnsley	Division 2	0–0		25000
Davison, Dunn, Blair, Eggo, G.Wilson, McIntyre, Reed, Kean, Welsh, W.Taylor, Lofthouse					
11 Sep. 1920	Stoke	Division 2	1–3	McIntyre (78)	25000
Davison, Dunn, Blair, Eggo, G.Wilson, Sykes, Shelton, Kean, McIntyre, W.Taylor, Lofthouse					
25 Sep. 1920	Coventry City	Division 2	3–0	McIntyre 3(16, 53, 59)	25000
Davison, Dunn, Blair, Eggo, G.Wilson, Sykes, Capper, Binney, McIntyre, Price, Lofthouse					
09 Oct. 1920	Leeds United	Division 2	2–0	McIntyre 2(33, 61)	25000
Davison, Bellas, Blair, Eggo, G.Wilson, Sykes, Shelton, Binney, McIntyre, Price, Lofthouse					
23 Oct. 1920	Birmingham	Division 2	1–2	McIntyre (13)pen.	25000
Davison, Bellas, Blair, Eggo, O'Neill, Sykes, Shelton, Binney, McIntyre, Price, Lofthouse					
06 Nov. 1920	West Ham United	Division 2	0–1		20000
Davison, O'Neill, Blair, Eggo, Reed, Price, Reilly, Binney, McIntyre, T.Brelsford, Lofthouse					
20 Nov. 1920	Fulham	Division 2	3–0	McIntyre(10), Dent(53), Binney(62)	18000
Davison, Bellas, O'Neill, Eggo, G.Wilson, Sykes, Capper, Binney, McIntyre, Dent, Lofthouse					
04 Dec. 1920	Cardiff City	Division 2	0–1		12000
Davison, Bellas, O'Neill, Eggo, G.Wilson, Price, Binney, Capper, McIntyre, Dent, Lofthouse					
18 Dec. 1920	Leicester City	Division 2	0–0		15000
Davison, Bellas, O'Neill, Eggo, G.Wilson, Price, Binney, Dent, Hall, McIntyre, E.Harvey					
25 Dec. 1920	Notts County	Division 2	1–1	Kean(19)	27000
Davison, Bellas, O'Neill, T.Brelsford, G.Wilson, Price, Capper, Kean, Hall, McIntyre, W.Taylor					
08 Jan. 1921	West Ham United	F.A. Cup 1	1–0	Price(8)	49125
Davison, Bellas, O'Neill, T.Brelsford, G.Wilson, Price, Capper, Kean, McIntyre, W.Taylor, Shelton					
22 Jan. 1921	Port Vale	Division 2	1–0	McIntyre(13)	20000
Davison, Bellas, O'Neill, T.Brelsford, G.Wilson, Levick, Capper, Hall, S.Taylor, McIntyre, Shelton					
03 Feb. 1921	Everton	F.A.Cup 2R	0–1		62407
Davison, Bellas, Kell, T.Brelsford, G.Wilson, Price, Reed, Kean, S.Taylor, McIntyre, Lofthouse					
07 Feb. 1921	Blackpool	Division 2	0–1		10000
Davison, Kell, Bellas, T.Brelsford, G.Wilson, Price, Kean, Hall, S.Taylor, McIntyre, Lofthouse					
19 Feb. 1921	South Shields	Division 2	1–1	Taylor(20)	20000
Davison, Kell, Bellas, T.Brelsford, G.Wilson, Price, Smelt, Hall, S.Taylor, McIntyre, Lofthouse					
21 Mar. 1921	Hull City	Division 2	3–0	McIntyre 2(56, 65), Wilson(90)	12000
Davison, Bellas, O'Neill, T.Brelsford, G.Wilson, Price, Smelt, Hall, S.Taylor, McIntyre, Lofthouse					
26 Mar. 1921	Stockport County	Division 2	2–1	McIntyre 2(1pen., 53pen.)	25000
Davison, Bellas, O'Neill, T.Brelsford, G.Wilson, Price, Smelt, Hall, S.Taylor, McIntyre, Lofthouse					
28 Mar. 1921	Rotherham County	Division 2	2–0	McIntyre(40), Taylor(75)	25000
Davison, Bellas, O'Neill, T.Brelsford, G.Wilson, Price, Smelt, Hall, S.Taylor, McIntyre, Lofthouse					
09 Apr. 1921	Clapton Orient	Division 2	1–1	Taylor(65)	15000
Davison, Bellas, O'Neill, T.Brelsford, Kean, Price, Smelt, Hall, S.Taylor, McIntyre, Lofthouse					
11 Apr. 1921	Wolverhampton W.	Division 2	6–0	Taylor 2(42, 75), McIntyre(21), Price(31), Lofthouse(59), Smelt(85)	14000
Davison, O'Neill, Bellas, T.Brelsford, G.Wilson, Price, Smelt, Hall, S.Taylor, McIntyre, Lofthouse					
23 Apr. 1921	Bury	Division 2	2–0	Taylor(27), McIntyre(57)	15000
Davison, Bellas, O'Neill, T.Brelsford, G.Wilson, Price, Smelt, Hall, S.Taylor, McIntyre, Lofthouse					
02 May 1921	Bristol City	Division 2	2–2	Smelt(5), McIntyre(40)	15000
Davison, Armitage, O'Neill, T.Brelsford, G.Wilson, Price, Smelt, Hall, S.Taylor, McIntyre, Lofthouse					
14 May 1921	Rotherham County	County Cup s/f	1–0	Taylor(12)	15000
Davison, Kell, O'Neill, T.Brelsford, G.Wilson, Price, Smelt, S.Taylor, Hall, McIntyre, Lofthouse					
21 May 1921	Sheffield United	County Cup final	1–2	Taylor(75)	21203
Davison, Kell, O'Neill, T.Brelsford, Kean, Price, E.Thompson, Binney, S.Taylor, McIntyre, Lofthouse					

OTHER GAMES AT HILLSBOROUGH

12 Feb. 1921	S.Challenge Cup s/f	Barnsley Res. 2	Doncaster Rovers 1	n/k
02 Mar. 1921	Junior Cup Final Rep.	Bird In Hand 0	Grenoside 2	n/k
19 Mar. 1921	F.A.Cup Semi–Final–	Tottenham Hotspur 2	Preston North End 1	44668
31 Mar. 1921	Boys	Sheffield 6	Castleford 0	6000
18 Apr. 1921	Bible Class Final	Attercliffe Wesleyans 1	Birley Carr 0	n/k
22 Apr. 1921	Wednesday Shield s/f	Newhall 1	Walkley 0	n/k
22 Apr. 1921	Wednesday Shield s/f	Manor 6	Abbeydale 0	n/k
25 Apr. 1921	Sunday School Final	Owlerton U.M. 1	St.Micheals 1	n/k
26 Apr. 1921	Amateur League Final	Malin Bridge 2	Grenoside 0	n/k
29 Apr. 1921	Clegg Shield Final	Manor 4	Hunter's Bar 0	2500
04 May 1921	Ladies	Dick Kerr's 4	Atalanta (Yorkshire) 0	22000
11 May 1921	Wednesday Shield Final	Manor 0	Newhall 0	n/k
16 May 1921	Yorks. Shield Fl(Boys)	Sheffield 0	York 0	n/k
19 May 1921	W. Shield Final–Rep	Manor 2	Newhall 1	n/k

Date	Opponents	Competition	Score	Scorers	Att.
27 Aug. 1921	Barnsley	Division 2	2–3	McIntyre(6)pen., Ratcliffe(80)	20000
Davison, Prior, O'Neill, Brelsford, G.Wilson, Price, Smelt, S.Taylor, Ratcliffe, McIntyre, Lofthouse					
05 Sep. 1921	Derby County	Division 2	1–1	Lofthouse(75)	18000
Davison, Prior, O'Neill, Brelsford, G.Wilson, Price, Hall, Armstrong, S.Taylor, W.Taylor, Lofthouse					
17 Sep. 1921	Notts County	Division 2	0–0		15000
Davison, Holmes, O'Neill, Brelsford, G.Wilson, Price, Thompson, McIntyre, S.Taylor, W.Taylor, Lofthouse					
01 Oct. 1921	Crystal Palace	Division 2	1–0	W.Taylor(83)	22000
Davison, Holmes, O'Neill, Brelsford, G.Wilson, Price, Thompson, McIntyre, S.Taylor, W.Taylor, Lofthouse					
08 Oct. 1921	Rotherham County	Division 2	1–0	Lofthouse(48)	20000
Davison, Holmes, O'Neill, Brelsford, G.Wilson, Price, Thompson, McIntyre, S.Taylor, Armstrong, Lofthouse					
22 Oct. 1921	Bradford Park Avenue	Division 2	2–1	Ratcliffe(11), McIntyre(44)	12000
Davison, Holmes, O'Neill, Brelsford, F.Froggatt, Price, Thompson, McIntyre, Ratcliffe, Armstrong, Lofthouse					
05 Nov. 1921	Fulham	Division 2	1–4	McIntyre(46)	20000
Davison, Holmes, O'Neill, Brelsford, G.Wilson, Price, Thompson, McIntyre, Ratcliffe, Armstrong, Lofthouse					
26 Nov. 1921	Blackpool	Division 2	5–1	Lofthouse 2(22, 84), Brelsford(6), Ratcliffe(28), McIntyre(–)pen.	12000
Davison, Holmes, O'Neill, Kean, G.Wilson, Price, Hall, Brelsford, Ratcliffe, McIntyre, Lofthouse					
03 Dec. 1921	Clapton Orient	Division 2	0–0		18000
Davison, Gray, Holmes, Kean, G.Wilson, Price, Thompson, Brelsford, Ratcliffe, McIntyre, Lofthouse					
27 Dec. 1921	Leeds United	Division 2	2–1	Lofthouse(23), Wilson(65)	25000
Davison, Gray, Ramsbottom, Kean, G.Wilson, Brelsford, Hall, S.Taylor, Ratcliffe, Price, Lofthouse					
14 Jan. 1922	Stoke	Division 2	0–1		8000
Davison, Holmes, Ramsbottom, Kean, G.Wilson, Brelsford, Thompson, S.Taylor, Lunn, W.Taylor, Lofthouse					
04 Feb. 1922	Nottingham Forest	Division 2	0–4		14000
Davison, Gray, Ramsbottom, Kean, G.Wilson, Brelsford, Thompson, Lowdell, S.Taylor, Bellas, Lofthouse					
13 Feb. 1922	Wolverhampton W.	Division 2	3–1	Trotter(47), Petrie(65), Brelsford(63)pen.	16000
Davison, Holmes, Ramsbottom, Kean, G.Wilson, Brelsford, Thompson, Lowdell, Trotter, Petrie, Lofthouse					
18 Feb. 1922	Bristol City	Division 2	1–0	Petrie(46)	20000
Davison, Holmes, Prior, Kean, G.Wilson, Brelsford, Thompson, Lowdell, Trotter, Petrie, Lofthouse					
04 Mar. 1922	South Shields	Division 2	0–3		15000
Davison, Holmes, Ramsbottom, Sykes, G.Wilson, Brelsford, Thompson, Lowdell, Trotter, Petrie, Lofthouse					
13 Mar. 1922	Coventry City	Division 2	3–2	Binney 3(3, 34, 80)	10000
Birch, Prior, Holmes, Kean, G.Wilson, Brelsford, Binney, S.Taylor, Hall, Petrie, Lofthouse					
03 Apr. 1922	Port Vale	Division 2	2–0	Brelsford(70)pen., Lowdell(87)	10000
Davison, Gray, Prior, Kean, G.Wilson, Brelsford, Binney, Lowdell, Lunn, Price, Lofthouse					
08 Apr. 1922	West Ham United	Division 2	2–1	Lunn(2), Lofthouse(52)	6000
Davison, Gray, Prior, Kean, Froggatt, Brelsford, Binney, Lowdell, Lunn, Price, Lofthouse					
17 Apr. 1922	Hull City	Division 2	0–0		15000
Davison, Gray, Prior, Kean, G.Wilson, Brelsford, S.Taylor, Lowdell, Lunn, Price, Lofthouse					
22 Apr. 1922	Bury	Division 2	4–1	Lunn 2(6, 46), Kean(77), Lowdell(87)	7000
Davison, Gray, Prior, Kean, G.Wilson, Levick, S.Taylor, Lowdell, Lunn, Petrie, Lofthouse					
24 Apr. 1922	Rotherham County	County Cup s/f	1–0	Lofthouse(25)	6000
Davison, Gray, Prior, Kean, Froggatt, Levick, S.Taylor, Lowdell, Lunn, Petrie, Lofthouse					
06 May 1922	Leicester City	Division 2	1–0	Petrie(60)	12000
Davison, Gray, Prior, Kean, G.Wilson, Brelsford, S.Taylor, Lowdell, Lunn, Petrie, Lofthouse					

OTHER GAMES AT HILLSBOROUGH :

20 Aug. 1921	Public Trial Match	Stripes 1	Whites 1		8000
23 Feb. 1922	S.Challenge Cup s/f	Barnsley Res. 2	Eckington Works 1		n/k
02 Mar. 1922	Junior Cup Final–Rep	Evesborough 1	Grenoside 3		n/k
25 Mar. 1922	F.A.Cup Semi Final	Preston 2	Tottenham 1		50095
27 Mar. 1922	Boys	Sheffield 11	Doncaster 0		n/k
04 Apr. 1922	City League s/f	Malin Bridge O.B. 1	Birley Carr 0		n/k
13 Apr. 1922	Y.Shield s/f (boys)	Sheffield 4	Rotherham 0		n/k
04 May 1922	Amateur League Final	Norton Woodseats 0	Darnall O.B. 1		n/k
17 May 1922	Wednesday Shield Final	Newhall 2	Crookesmoor 0		5000
18 May 1922	Clegg Shield Final	Newhall 1	Crookesmoor 2		5000
20 May 1922	Yorks. Shield Final	Sheffield 5	Hull 1		n/k

1920–21
Eggo, Bellas, Davison, Blair, Jackson, Sykes;
Shelton, Binney, Prior, Wilson, McIntyre, E. Harvey.

1921–22

1922–23
Kean, Gray, Davison, Prior, Binks, T. Brelsford;
R. Williams, Lowdell, G. Wilson, Petrie, Lofthouse.

1922–23
Davison, Swan, Betts (ass. trainer), Fletcher, Birch, Frogatt, Sykes;
Brown (sec-manager), Wolfe, Trotter, Prior, Gray, Matthewson,
Pennington, Jackson;
Williams, Brelsford, Binks, Lowdell, Lofthouse, Bellas, Binney,
Ramsbottom;
Taylor, Wright, Dickinson, Randle.

Date	Opponents	Competition	Score	Scorers	Att.
28 Aug. 1922	Manchester United	Division 2	1–0	Binks(16)	20000
Davison, Gray, Prior, Kean, G.Wilson, Brelsford, Williams, Lowdell, Binks, Petrie, Lofthouse					
02 Sep. 1922	Rotherham County	Division 2	1–0	Evans(50)og.	30000
Davison, Gray, Prior, Kean, G.Wilson, Brelsford, Williams, Lowdell, Binks, Petrie, Lofthouse					
09 Sep. 1922	Derby County	Division 2	0–0		20000
Davison, Gray, Prior, Kean, G.Wilson, Brelsford, Williams, Lowdell, Binks, S.Taylor, Lofthouse					
23 Sep. 1922	Notts County	Division 2	0–1		20000
Davison, Gray, Prior, Kean, G.Wilson, Brelsford, Williams, Lowdell, Binks, Trotter, Lofthouse					
07 Oct. 1922	Fulham	Division 2	1–0	Binks(35)pen.	15000
Davison, Gray, Prior, Kean, G.Wilson, Brelsford, S.Taylor, Lowdell, Binks, Binney, Lofthouse					
28 Oct. 1922	Clapton Orient	Division 2	4–1	Taylor 3(18, 56, 58), Lofthouse(61)	15000
Davison, Gray, Bellas, Kean, G.Wilson, Brelsford, Williams, S.Taylor, Binks, Smailes, Lofthouse					
04 Nov. 1922	Crystal Palace	Division 2	3–1	Taylor(46), Smailes(80), Binks(87)	15000
Davison, Gray, Prior, Kean, G.Wilson, Brelsford, Williams, S.Taylor, Binks, Smailes, Lofthouse					
25 Nov. 1922	Hull City	Division 2	1–0	Taylor(68)	15000
Davison, Prior, Dickinson, Kean, G.Wilson, Brelsford, Williams, S.Taylor, Binks, Smailes, Lofthouse					
09 Dec. 1922	Leicester City	Division 2	2–1	Williams(49), Smailes(70)	20000
Davison, Bellas, Dickinson, Kean, G.Wilson, Brelsford, Williams, S.Taylor, Binks, Smailes, Henshall					
23 Dec. 1922	Barnsley	Division 2	2–3	Smailes(21), Taylor(51)	30000
Davison, Bellas, Dickinson, Kean, G.Wilson, Brelsford, Williams, S.Taylor, Binks, Smailes, Henshall					
25 Dec. 1922	Bradford City	Division 2	2–2	Smailes 2(30, 54)	25000
Davison, Bellas, Prior, Kean, G.Wilson, Brelsford, Williams, S.Taylor, Trotter, Smailes, Henshall					
01 Jan. 1923	Southampton	Division 2	0–0		30000
Birch, Bellas, Felton, Kean, G.Wilson, Brelsford, Williams, S.Taylor, Binks, Smailes, Henshall					
06 Jan. 1923	Blackpool	Division 2	2–3	Binks(9), Smailes(65)	20000
Birch, Bellas, Felton, Kean, G.Wilson, Brelsford, Williams, S.Taylor, Binks, Smailes, Henshall					
13 Jan. 1923	New Brighton	F.A.Cup 1	3–0	Binks 2(72, 75), Smailes(20)	36082
Davison, Bellas, Dickinson, Kean, G.Wilson, Brelsford, Williams, S.Taylor, Binks, Smailes, Henshall					
20 Jan 1923	Bury	Division 2	2–0	Smailes(14), Binks(65)	20000
Davison, Dickinson, Felton, Kean, Wilson, Levick, Williams, S.Taylor, Binks, Smailes, Henshall					
03 Feb. 1923	Barnsley	F.A.Cup 2	2–1	Smailes(50), Binks(56)	66103
Davison, Bellas, Blenkinsop, Kean, G.Wilson, Sykes, Williams, Lowdell, Binks, Smailes, Henshall					
10 Feb. 1923	Stockport County	Division 2	4–1	Binks 3(25, 60, 66), Henshall(55)	15000
Davison, Bellas, Blenkinsop, Kean, G.Wilson, Sykes, Williams, Lowdell, Binks, Smailes, Henshall					
10 Mar. 1923	The Corinthians	Friendly	3–2	Binks 2(11, 66), Taylor(23)	12000
Davison, Felton, Blenkinsop, Kean, G.Wilson, Sykes, Williams, S.Taylor, Binks, Smailes, Henshall					
17 Mar. 1923	South Shields	Division 2	2–0	Harron(30), Binks(40)	15000
Davison, Felton, Blenkinsop, Kean, G.Wilson, Sykes, Henshall, S.Taylor, Binks, Smailes, Harron					
19 Mar. 1923	Leeds United	Division 2	3–1	Binks(10)pen., Brelsford(50), Smailes(63)	11000
Davison, Felton, Blenkinsop, Brelsford, Froggatt, Sykes, Williams, S.Taylor, Binks, Smailes, Harron					
31 Mar. 1923	Wolverhampton W.	Division 2	1–0	Brelsford(14)	10000
Davison, Felton Blenkinsop, Kean, G.Wilson, Brelsford, Williams, S.Taylor, Binks, Smailes, Harron					
14 Apr. 1923	Coventry City	Division 2	3–0	Sykes(47), Binks(51), Petrie(56)	10000
Davison, Felton, Blenkinsop, Sykes, Froggatt, Levick, Lowdell, S.Taylor, Binks, Petrie, Harron					
28 Apr. 1923	Port Vale	Division 2	2–0	Smailes(55), Harron(64)	12000
Davison, Felton, Blenkinsop, Kean, G.Wilson, Froggatt, Lowdell, S.Taylor, Smailes, Petrie, Harron					
30 Apr. 1923	West Ham United	Division 2	0–2		10000
Davison, Felton, Blenkinsop, Kean, G.Wilson, Froggatt, Lowdell, S.Taylor, Smailes, Petrie, Harron					

OTHER GAMES AT HILLSBOROUGH

19 Aug. 1922	Public Trial Match	Stripes 2	Whites 2		9283
25 Jan. 1923	F.A.Cup 3–2r	Sheffield United 1	Nottingham Forest 0		31982
03 Apr. 1923	Amateur Lge. s/f	Grenoside 3	Norton Woodseats 4		n/k
05 Apr. 1923	Boys	Sheffield 6	Newcastle 0		n/k
07 Apr. 1923	Amateur League Final	Hallam 3	Norton Woodseats 0		n/k
16 Apr. 1923	Boys	Sheffield 7	Dearne Valley 0		5000
26 Apr. 1923	Attercliffe All. Lge. Fnl	King's Head 0	Gatefield Inn 0		n/k
01 May 1923	Bible Class Final	High Green P.M. 0	Heeley St. Peter's 4		n/k
04 May 1923	Sheffield Corp. Final	City Treasurers 3	Education 0		n/k
09 May 1923	Wednesday Shield Fnl	Duchsss Road 2	Crookesmoor 3		n/k
10 May 1923	Clegg Shield Final	Abbeydale 1	Newhall Road 5		n/k

Date	Opponents	Competition	Score	Scorers	Att.
25 Aug. 1923	Bradford City	Division 2	0–0		25000
Brown, Felton, Blenkinsop, Kean, G.Wilson, Levick, R.Williams, S.Taylor, Binks, Smailes, J.Wilson					
03 Sep. 1923	Port Vale	Division 2	2–1	S.Taylor(30)pen., Trotter(61)	12000
Brown, Felton, Blenkinsop, Kean, G.Wilson, Levick, R.Williams, S.Taylor, Trotter, Petrie, Harron					
08 Sep. 1923	Southampton	Division 2	1–1	Petrie(9)	20000
Brown, Felton, Blenkinsop, Kean, G.Wilson, Levick, R.Williams, S.Taylor, Trotter, Petrie, Harron					
22 Sep. 1923	Fulham	Division 2	2–1	Binks(49), Harron(52)	15000
Brown, Felton, Blenkinsop, Kean, G.Wilson, Smailes, R.Williams, S.Taylor, Binks, Petrie, Harron					
06 Oct. 1923	Blackpool	Division 2	2–2	Harron(57), Petrie(64)	15000
Brown, Felton, Blenkinsop, Kean, G.Wilson, Froggatt, R.Williams, S.Taylor, Binks, Petrie, Harron					
27 Oct. 1923	Nelson	Division 2	5–0	Walker 2(10, 61), S.Taylor 2(33, 38pen.) Petrie(3)	18000
Davison, Felton, Blenkinsop, Kean, G.Wilson, Brelsford, R.Williams, S.Taylor, Walker, Petrie, Harron					
10 Nov. 1923	Barnsley	Division 2	1–0	Petrie(10)	20000
Davison, Felton, Blenkinsop, Kean, G.Wilson, Brelsford, R.Williams, S.Taylor, Binks, Petrie, Harron					
17 Nov. 1923	Hull City	Division 2	1–0	Petrie(15)	15000
Davison, Felton, Blenkinsop, Kean, G.Wilson, Brelsford, R.Williams, S.Taylor, Binks, Petrie, Harron					
08 Dec. 1923	Stoke	Division 2	3–0	Petrie 2(46, 51), Kean(40)	18000
Davison, Felton, Blenkinsop, Kean, G.Wilson, Brelsford, R.Williams, S.Taylor, Binks, Petrie, Harron					
22 Dec. 1923	Crystal Palace	Division 2	6–0	Binks 4(4, 43, 60, 68), Petrie 2(35, 65)	18000
Davison, Felton, Blenkinsop, Kean, G.Wilson, Brelsford, R.Williams, Walker, Binks, Petrie, Harron					
26 Dec. 1923	Coventry City	Division 2	2–0	Kean(55), Binks(63)	30000
Davison, Felton, Blenkinsop, Kean, G.Wilson, Froggatt, R.Williams, S.Taylor, Binks, Petrie, Harron					
31 Dec. 1923	Barnsley	County Cup s/f	5–1	Walker 3(38, 41, –), S.Taylor(55), Binks(–)	15419
Davison, Felton, Blenkinsop, Kean, Levick, Froggatt, R.Williams, S.Taylor, Binks, Walker, Harron					
05 Jan. 1924	Derby County	Division 2	1–0	Binks(67)	28000
Davison, Felton, Blenkinsop, Kean, G.Wilson, Froggatt, R.Williams, S.Taylor, Binks, Petrie, Harron					
12 Jan. 1924	Leicester City	F.A.Cup 1	4–1	S.Taylor 2(37, 44), Petrie(11), Binks(33)	39127
Davison, Felton, Blenkinsop, Kean, G.Wilson, Froggatt, R.Williams, S.Taylor, Binks, Petrie, Harron					
19 Jan. 1924	Leeds United	Division 2	0–0		20000
Davison, Felton, Blenkinsop, Kean, G.Wilson, Froggatt, R.Williams, S.Taylor, Binks, Petrie, Harron					
02 Feb. 1924	Bristol City	F.A.Cup 2	1–1	Harron(32)	38238
Davison, Felton, Blenkinsop, Kean, G.Wilson, Froggatt, R.Williams, S.Taylor, Binks, Petrie, Harron					
11 Feb. 1924	Leicester City	Division 2	2–1	Binks 2(13, 70)	5000
Davison, Felton, Blenkinsop, L.Williams, Sykes, Brelsford, R.Williams, Walker, Binks, Trotter, J.Wilson					
16 Feb. 1924	Clapton Orient	Division 2	1–0	Petrie(38)	14000
Davison, Felton, Blenkinsop, Kean, G.Wilson, Brelsford, R.Williams, S.Taylor, Binks, Petrie, Harron					
01 Mar. 1924	Stockport County	Division 2	3–0	Walker(44), Binks(68), Petrie(72)	10000
Davison, Felton, Blenkinsop, Kean, G.Wilson, Brelsford, R.Williams, Walker, Binks, Petrie, Harron					
22 Mar. 1924	Oldham Athletic	Division 2	1–2	Taylor(80)	15000
Davison, Felton, Blenkinsop, Kean, Froggatt, Levick, Lowdell, Walker, Eyre, S.Taylor, Harron					
05 Apr. 1924	South Shields	Division 2	5–0	S.Taylor 3(25, 40, 83), Walker(26), Harron(84)	15000
Brown, L.Williams, Blenkinsop, Kean, G.Wilson, Levick, R.Williams, Walker, Binks, S.Taylor, Harron					
19 Apr. 1924	Bury	Division 2	1–1	Petrie(6)	15000
Brown, Felton, Blenkinsop, Kean, G.Wilson, Froggatt, R.Williams, S.Taylor, Walker, Petrie, Harron					
21 Apr. 1924	Bristol City	Division 2	1–0	Taylor(62)	7000
Brown, Felton, Blenkinsop, Kean, G.Wilson, Levick, R.Williams, S.Taylor, Trotter, Petrie, Harron					
03 May 1924	Manchester United	Division 2	2–0	Walker(62), Ayres(67)	10000
Brown, Felton, Blenkinsop, Kean, G.Wilson, Levick, Chapman, S.Taylor, Ayres, Walker, Harron					
10 May 1924	Sheffield United	County Cup Fl	0–2		15000
Brown, Felton, Blenkinsop, Kean, G.Wilson, Froggatt, R.Williams, S.Taylor, Binks, Ayres, Harron					

OTHER GAMES AT HILLSBOROUGH

Date	Competition	Home	Away	Att.
18 Aug. 1923	Public Trial Match	Stripes 3	Whites 4	6000
10 Sep. 1923	Inter City	Sheffield 1	Glasgow 2	n/k
08 Nov. 1923	Representative	Sheffield University 6	Leeds University 3	n/k
27 Dec. 1923	Boys	Yorkshire 2	Lancashire 1	3000
01 Apr. 1924	Friendly	Sheffield Independent 1	Sheffield Telegraph 2	n/k
22 Apr. 1924	Bible Class Final	High Green P.M. 1	Wycliffe 1	n/k
24 Apr. 1924	Boys	Sheffield 0	Birmingham 3	n/k
01 May 1924	Thursday Lge. Final	Wild's 3	Mexborough Thursday 1	n/k
01 May 1924	City League Final	Birley Carr 2	Shiregreen P.M. 0	n/k
12 May 1924	Clegg Shield Final	Newhall Road 2	Hillsborough 0	n/k
12 May 1924	Wednesday Shield Fnl	Duchess Road 3	Woodhouse East 2	n/k

Date	Opponents	Competition	Score	Scorers	Att.
01 Sep. 1924	Derby County	Division 2	0–1		30000
Davison, Felton, Blenkinsop, Kean, G.Wilson, Collier, R.Williams, Marsden, Binks, Ayres, Prince					
06 Sep. 1924	Southampton	Division 2	1–0	Williams(71)pen.	30000
Davison, Felton, Blenkinsop, Kean, G.Wilson, Collier, R.Williams, Marsden, Binks, Petrie, Harron					
20 Sep. 1924	Stockport County	Division 2	3–0	Ayres 3(35, 77, 80)	22000
Davison, Inglis, Felton, Kean, G.Wilson, Collier, R.Williams, S.Taylor, Binks, Ayres, Harron					
04 Oct. 1924	Leicester City	Division 2	1–4	Trotter(70)	18000
Davison, Felton, Blenkinsop, Kean, G.Wilson, Toone, Prince, Lowdell, Trotter, Ayres, Harron					
16 Oct. 1924	Royal Air Force	Friendly	3–0	Trotter 2(60, 89), Weaver(84)	5000
Carr, Inglis, Blenkinsop, Kean, G.Wilson, Collier, R.Williams, Weaver, Trotter, Ayres, Prince					
18 Oct. 1924	Coventry City	Division 2	2–0	Hill(17), Trotter(30)	25000
Davison, Inglis, Felton, Kean, G.Wilson, Collier, Chapman, Hill, Trotter, Ayres, Harron					
01 Nov. 1924	Bradford City	Division 2	3–3	Trotter(19), Williams(50)pen., Ayres(63)	15000
Davison, Inglis, Felton, Kean, G.Wilson, W.Powell, R.Williams, Hill, Trotter, Ayres, Prince					
15 Nov. 1924	Middlesbrough	Division 2	2–0	Trotter 2(4, 42)	13983
Davison, Inglis, Felton, Kean, G.Wilson, W.Powell, R.Williams, Hill, Trotter, S.Taylor, Prince					
29 Nov. 1924	Wolverhampton W.	Division 2	2–0	Marsden(50), Hill(61)	16668
Davison, Inglis, Felton, Kean, Froggatt, W.Powell, Prince, Hill, Trotter, Marsden, Richardson					
13 Dec. 1924	Portsmouth	Division 2	5–2	Trotter 5(5, 12, 62, 75, 88)	17255
Davison, Inglis, Felton, Kean, Froggatt, W.Powell, Prince, Hill, Trotter, S.Taylor, Richardson					
25 Dec. 1924	Blackpool	Division 2	2–6	Hill 2(46, –)	35000
Brown, Felton, Blenkinsop, Kean, G.Wilson, W.Powell, R.Williams, Hill, Trotter, S.Taylor, Richardson					
27 Dec. 1924	Crystal Palace	Division 2	0–1		15500
Brown, Inglis, Felton, Toone, G.Wilson, Froggatt, R.Williams, Hill, Trotter, Ayres, Prince					
01 Jan. 1925	Oldham Athletic	Divison 2	1–0	Hill(70)	15300
Brown, Inglis, Felton, Toone, Froggatt, W.Powell, Lowdell, Hill, Weaver, Ayres, Prince					
10 Jan. 1925	Manchester United	F.A.Cup 1	2–0	Hill 2(34, 62)	35079
Brown, Inglis, Felton, Toone, G.Wilson, Froggatt, Lowdell, Hill, Trotter, W.Powell, Richardson					
17 Jan. 1925	Chelsea	Division 2	2–1	Trotter 2(1, 75)	18000
Brown, Inglis, Blenkinsop, Toone, G.Wilson, Froggatt, Lowdell, Hill, Trotter, W.Powell, Richardson					
14 Feb. 1925	Stoke	Division 2	2–1	Ayres(50), Hill(68)	12000
Brown, Inglis, Felton, Toone, G.Wilson, W.Powell, Lowdell, Hill, Marsden, Ayres, Richardson					
23 Feb. 1925	Manchester United	Division 2	1–1	Weaver(9)	8000
Brown, Inglis, Felton, Toone, G.Wilson, Collier, R.Williams, Hill, Ayres, Weaver, Prince					
28 Feb. 1925	South Shields	Division 2	0–1		15000
Brown, Inglis, Felton, Toone, G.Wilson, Froggatt, Lowdell, Hill, Ayres, Weaver, Prince					
14 Mar. 1925	Port Vale	Division 2	0–1		12000
Brown, Inglis, Felton, Toone, G.Wilson, Collier, Lowdell, R.Williams, Trotter, Hill, Prince					
28 Mar. 1925	Barnsley	Division 2	1–0	S.Powell(53)	28000
Brown, Felton, Blenkinsop, Toone, Froggatt, W.Powell, R.Williams, Hill, S.Powell, Barrass, Prince					
11 Apr. 1925	Fulham	Division 2	3–1	S.Powell 3(25, 40, 80)	20000
Brown, Felton, Blenkinsop, Kean, Froggatt, W.Powell, R.Williams, Barrass, Trotter, S.Powell, Prince					
25 Apr. 1925	Hull City	Division 2	5–0	Trotter 2(28, 35), Barrass(51), Marsden(–), Hill(85)	14000
Brown, L.Williams, Blenkinsop, Lowdell, Froggatt, Marsden, Hill, Barrass, Trotter, S.Powell, Prince					
02 May 1925	Clapton Orient	Division 2	0–0		14000
Brown, Felton, Blenkinsop, Lowdell, Froggatt, Marsden, Hill, Barrass, Trotter, S.Powell, Prince					

OTHER GAMES AT HILLSBOROUGH

23 Aug. 1924	Public Trial Match	Stripes 2	Whites 3	10352
13 Apr. 1925	Amateur League Final	Atlas & Norfolk 1	Malin Bridge O.B. 2	n/k
15 Apr. 1925	Boys	Sheffield 2	Grimsby 2	n/k
07 May 1925	Boys (EST S/F)	Sheffield 7	East Northumberland 1	n/k
08 May 1925	Wednesday Shield Fnl	Malin Bridge 1	Owler Lane 2	n/k
09 May 1925	County Cup Final	Barnsley 1	Rotherham County 0	6500

Date	Opponents	Competition	Score	Scorers	Att.
29 Aug. 1925	Fulham	Division 2	3–0	Lowdell(4)pen., Bedford(47), Powell(78)	21173
Brown, Felton, Blenkinsop, Lowdell, Froggatt, Marsden, R.Williams, Barrass, Trotter, S.Powell, Bedford					
12 Sep. 1925	Preston North End	Division 2	5–1	Trotter 4(2, 34, 50, 51), Blenkinsop(45)	24967
Brown, Felton, Blenkinsop, Kean, Froggatt, Marsden, R.Williams, Barrass, Trotter, S.Powell, Bedford					
21 Sep. 1925	Stockport County	Division 2	6–2	Trotter 5(36, 38, 42, 44, 67), Ayres(24)	12761
Brown, Felton, Blenkinsop, Kean, Froggatt, Marsden, R.Williams, Barrass, Trotter, Ayres, Bedford					
26 Sep. 1925	Portsmouth	Division 2	4–2	Ayres 2(35, 62), Barrass(17), Trotter(70)	22966
Brown, Felton, Blenkinsop, Kean, Froggatt, Marsden, R.Williams, Barrass, Trotter, Ayres, Bedford					
10 Oct. 1925	Swansea Town	Divison 2	3–1	Barrass(20), Bedford(49), Kean(87)	27992
Brown, Felton, Blenkinsop, Kean, Froggatt, Marsden, R.Williams, Barrass, Trotter, Ayres, Bedford					
17 Oct. 1925	Derby County	Divison 2	1–4	Trotter(20)	31445
Brown, Felton, Blenkinsop, Kean, Froggatt, Marsden, R.Williams, Barrass, Trotter, Ayres, Bedford					
31 Oct. 1925	Barnsley	Division 2	3–0	Hill 2(30, 61), Trotter(26)	23920
Brown, Felton, Blenkinsop, Kean, Froggatt, Marsden, Lowdell, Barrass, Trotter, Hill, Prince					
09 Nov. 1925	Barnsley	County Cup s/f	3–2	Prince(15), Whitworth(22), Marsden(24)	6000
Brown, Felton, Blenkinsop, Lowdell, Froggatt, Marsden, R.Williams, Barrass, Whitworth, Hill, Prince					
14 Nov. 1925	Darlington	Division 2	4–0	Trotter 3(20, 31, 59), Blenkinsop(89)pen.	19726
Brown, Felton, Blenkinsop, Lowdell, Froggatt, Marsden, R.Williams, Barrass, Trotter, Hill, Prince					
28 Nov. 1925	Chelsea	Division 2	4–1	Hill 3(17, 30, 46), Trotter(72)	23827
Brown, Felton, Blenkinsop, Lowdell, Froggatt, Marsden, R.Williams, Barrass, Trotter, Hill, Prince					
12 Dec. 1925	Southampton	Division 2	2–1	Trotter(3), Hill(12)	20628
Brown, Felton, Blenkinsop, Lowdell, Froggatt, Marsden, R.Williams, Barrass, Trotter, Hill, Prince					
26 Dec. 1925	Bradford City	Division 2	5–1	Trotter 2(63, 79), Hill 2(30, 38), Barrass(76)	37409
Brown, Felton, Blenkinsop, Lowdell, Froggatt, Marsden, R.Williams, Barrass, Trotter, Hill, Prince					
28 Dec. 1925	Oldham Athletic	Division 2	5–1	Trotter 2(44, 62), Hill 2(42, 74), Barrass(25)	25933
Brown, Felton, Blenkinsop, Lowdell, Froggatt, Marsden, R.Williams, Barrass, Trotter, Hill, Prince					
16 Jan. 1926	South Shields	Division 2	1–0	Barrass(80)	19555
Brown, Felton, Blenkinsop, Lowdell, Froggatt, Marsden, R.Williams, Barrass, Trotter, Hill, Prince					
13 Feb. 1926	Wolverhampton W.	Division 2	2–1	Barrass(15), Hill(32)	29398
Brown, Felton, Blenkinsop, Lowdell, Froggatt, Marsden, R.Williams, Barrass, Trotter, Hill, Prince					
22 Feb. 1926	Middlesbrough	Division 2	2–0	Trotter 2(7, 20)	20684
Brown, Felton, Blenkinsop, Lowdell, Froggatt, Marsden, R.Williams, Barrass, Trotter, Hill, Prince					
06 Mar. 1926	Kilmarnock	Friendly	6–1	S.Powell 2(15, 55), Barrass 2(42, –), Trotter(57), Lowdell(87)	12000
Brown, Walker, Blenkinsop, Lowdell, Froggatt, W.Powell, R.Williams, Barrass, Trotter, S.Powell, Prince					
20 Mar. 1926	Port Vale	Division 2	0–2		24965
Brown, Felton, Blenkinsop, Lowdell, Froggatt, Marsden, R.Williams, Barrass, Trotter, Hill, Prince					
22 Mar. 1926	Nottingham Forest	Division 2	2–0	Trotter(2), Prince(74)	29975
Brown, Felton, Blenkinsop, Lowdell, Froggatt, Marsden, R.Williams, Barrass, Trotter, Hill, Prince					
03 Apr. 1926	Hull City	Division 2	2–0	Trotter(9), Wilkinson(83)	29075
Brown, Walker, Blenkinsop, Kean, Froggatt, Marsden, R.Williams, Fletcher, Trotter, Barrass, Wilkinson					
06 Apr. 1926	Stoke City	Division 2	2–0	S.Powell(14), Wilkinson(81)	28679
Brown, Walker, Blenkinsop, Kean, Froggatt, Marsden, R.Williams, Barrass, Trotter, S.Powell, Wilkinson					
17 Apr. 1926	Clapton Orient	Division 2	3–0	Wilkinson(38), Williams(49), Trotter(88)	21227
Brown, Walker, Blenkinsop, Kean, Froggatt, Marsden, R.Williams, Lowdell, Trotter, Barrass, Wilkinson					
01 May 1926	Blackpool	Division 2	2–0	Trotter(9), Lowdell(35)	20575
Brown, Walker, Blenkinsop, Kean, Froggatt, Marsden, R.Williams, Lowdell, Trotter, S.Powell, Wilkinson					

OTHER GAMES AT HILLSBOROUGH

22 Aug. 1925	Public Trial Match	Whites 4	Stripes 4		10594
08 Apr. 1926	Boys	Sheffield 0	Newcastle 1		n/k
26 Apr. 1926	Bible Class Final	Grimesthorpe 3	St. Micheals 1		n/k
29 Apr. 1926	Boys	Sheffield 6	Ardsley 0		n/k

Date	Opponents	Competition	Score	Scorers	Att.
28 Aug. 1926	Sheffield United	Division 1	2–3	Trotter 2(42,62)	43282
Brown, Walker, Blenkinsop, Kean, Froggatt, Burridge, R.Williams, Anstiss, Trotter, Marsden, Wilkinson					
06 Sep. 1926	West Ham United	Division 1	1–0	Trotter(22)pen.	18602
Brown, Felton, Blenkinsop, Lowdell, Kean, Marsden, R.Williams, Hill, Trotter, S.Powell, Wilkinson					
11 Sep. 1926	Everton	Division 1	4–0	Trotter 3(20,70,79), Anstiss(17)	22889
Brown, Felton, Blenkinsop, Lowdell, Kean, Marsden, R.Williams, Hill, Trotter, Anstiss, Wilkinson					
25 Sep. 1926	Huddersfield Town	Division 1	1–1	Trotter(60)	32493
Brown, Felton, Blenkinsop, Lowdell, Kean, Marsden, R.Williams, Hill, Trotter, Anstiss, Wilkinson					
09 Oct. 1926	West Bromwich Albion	Division 1	2–1	Trotter(38), Hill(81)	15508
Brown, Walker, Blenkinsop, Lowdell, Froggatt, Marsden, R.Williams, Hill, Trotter, Anstiss, Wilkinson					
16 Oct. 1926	Liverpool	Division 1	3–2	Anstiss(13), Wilkinson(53), Hill(60)	24535
Brown, Walker, Blenkinsop, Lowdell, Kean, Marsden, R.Williams, Hill, Trotter, Anstiss, Wilkinson					
30 Oct. 1926	Derby County	Division 1	2–1	Wilkinson(50), Trotter(74)	29805
Brown, Walker, Blenkinsop, Lowdell, Kean, Marsden, R.Williams, Hill, S.Powell, Trotter, Wilkinson					
13 Nov. 1926	Bolton Wanderers	Division 1	2–1	Trotter(34), Wilkinson(60)	21033
Brown, Walker, Blenkinsop, Lowdell, Kean, Marsden, R.Williams, Hill, Trotter, Burridge, Wilkinson					
29 Nov. 1926	Cardiff City	Division 1	3–0	Hill 2(67,89), Kirkwood(35)	16986
Brown, Walker, Blenkinsop, Lowdell, Kean, Marsden, R.Williams, Kirkwood, Trotter, Hill, Wilkinson					
11 Dec. 1926	Newcastle United	Division 1	3–2	Trotter 2(12,60), Hill(38)	38422
Brown, Walker, Blenkinsop, Lowdell, Kean, Marsden, R.Williams, Kirkwood, Trotter, Hill, Wilkinson					
28 Dec. 1926	Tottenham Hotspur	Division 1	3–1	Trotter 2(26,89), Hill(3)	35529
Brown, Walker, Blenkinsop, Lowdell, Kean, Marsden, R.Williams, Kirkwood, Trotter, Hill, Wilkinson					
01 Jan. 1927	Bury	Division 1	1–3	Hill(40)	35367
Brown, Walker, Blenkinsop, Lowdell, Kean, Marsden, R.Williams, Kirkwood, Trotter, Hill, Wilkinson					
08 Jan. 1927	Brighton & Hove Alb.	F.A.Cup 3	2–0	Hill(35), Trotter(54)	24945
Brown, Walker, Blenkinsop, Lowdell, Kean, Marsden, R.Williams, Kirkwood, Trotter, Hill, Wilkinson					
22 Jan. 1927	Leicester City	Division 1	2–2	Hill(56), S.Powell(58)	19796
Brown, Walker, Blenkinsop, Lowdell, Kean, Marsden, Hooper, Hill, Trotter, S.Powell, Wilkinson					
29 Jan. 1927	South Shields	F.A.Cup 4	1–1	Trotter(54)	33471
Brown, Walker, Blenkinsop, Lowdell, Kean, Marsden, R.Williams, Hill, Trotter, S.Powell, Wilkinson					
05 Feb. 1927	Blackburn Rovers	Division 1	0–3		16708
Brown, Walker, Blenkinsop, Lowdell, Kean, Marsden, R.Williams, Leach, Trotter, Marson, Hooper					
19 Feb. 1927	Sunderland	Division 1	4–1	Trotter 3(10,21,74), Hooper(16)	24851
Brown, Walker, Blenkinsop, Leach, Kean, Marsden, Hooper, Kirkwood, Trotter, Strange, Wilkinson					
12 Mar. 1927	Arsenal	Division 1	4–2	Trotter 3(7,25,85), Leach(59)	21252
Brown, Walker, Felton, Leach, Kean, Marsden, Hooper, Kirkwood, Trotter, Strange, Wilkinson					
26 Mar. 1927	Manchester United	Division 1	2–0	Trotter 2(40,83)	11997
Brown, Walker, Blenkinsop, Lowdell, Kean, Marsden, Hooper, Kirkwood, Trotter, Hill, Wilkinson					
09 Apr. 1927	Aston Villa	Division 1	3–1	Trotter(12), Hooper(66), Strange(80)	9020
Brown, Felton, Blenkinsop, Leach, Kean, Marsden, Hooper, Strange, Trotter, Allen, Wilkinson					
19 Apr. 1927	Birmingham	Division 1	4–4	Trotter 2(18,32), Strange(15), Hill(34)	17720
Brown, Walker, Blenkinsop, Leach, Kean, Marsden, R.Williams, Strange, Trotter, Hill, Wilkinson					
23 Apr. 1927	Burnley	Division 1	2–1	Kean(70), Strange(81)	16721
Brown, Felton, Blenkinsop, Leach, Kean, Marsden, Hooper, Strange, Trotter, Allen, Wilkinson					
07 May 1927	Leeds United	Division 1	1–0	Trotter(77)	12027
Brown, Felton, Blenkinsop, Leach, Kean, Marsden, Hooper, Strange, Trotter, Allen, Wilkinson					
14 May 1927	Barnsley	County Cup Fnl	4–1	Trotter 2(43,89), Strange(10), Kean(–)	15856
Brown, Felton, Blenkinsop, Leach, Kean, Marsden, Hooper, Strange, Trotter, Allen, Wilkinson					

OTHER GAMES AT HILLSBOROUGH

14 Apr. 1927	Boys	Sheffield 8	Dearne 0		n/k
21 Apr. 1927	Thursday League Final	Barnsley Amateurs 3	Thursday Amateurs 1		n/k
21 Aug. 1926	Public Trial Match	Stripes 2	Whites 5		

Date	Opponents	Competition	Score	Scorers	Att.
29 Aug. 1927	Manchester United	Division 1	0–2		17944
Brown, Felton, Blenkinsop, Leach, Kean, Burridge, R.Williams, Seed, Trotter, Strange, Wilkinson					
03 Sep. 1927	Cardiff City	Division 1	3–3	Hooper(14), Trotter(36)pen., Allen(50)	19218
Mellors, Felton, Blenkinsop, Burridge, Froggatt, Marsden, Hooper, Seed, Trotter, Allen, Marson					
17 Sep. 1927	Bolton Wanderers	Division 1	3–0	Trotter 2(60, 79), Marsden(6)	19111
Mellors, Felton, Blenkinsop, Burridge, Kean, Marsden, Hooper, Strange, Trotter, Allen, Marson					
08 Oct. 1927	Birmingham	Division 1	2–3	Allen(28), Trotter(30)	19974
Mellors, Felton, Blenkinsop, Burridge, Kean, Marsden, Hooper, Seed, Trotter, Allen, Marson					
22 Oct. 1927	Arsenal	Division 1	1–1	Hooper(66)	12698
Mellors, Felton, Blenkinsop, Leach, Kean, Burridge, Hooper, Seed, Trotter, Allen, Wilkinson					
05 Nov. 1927	Bury	Division 1	4–0	Hill(18), Trotter(47), Seed(65), Wilkinson(–)	16808
Brown, Walker, Blenkinsop, Burridge, Kean, Marsden, Hooper, Hill, Trotter, Seed, Wilkinson					
14 Nov. 1927	Huddersfield Town	Friendly	1–6	Gilmour(75)	4000
Brown, Walker, Felton, Burridge, Kean, Marsden, Hooper, Strange, Gilmour, Seed, Wilkinson					
19 Nov. 1927	Leicester City	Division 1	1–2	Trotter(65)	15969
Brown, Walker, Blenkinsop, Burridge, Kean, Marsden, Hooper, Hill, Trotter, Seed, Wilkinson					
28 Nov. 1927	Sheffield United	County Cup s/f	3–1	Strange 2(7, 40), Hill(13)	10339
Brown, Walker, Blenkinsop, Leach, Kean, Marsden, Hooper, Hill, S.Powell, Strange, Wilkinson					
03 Dec. 1927	West Ham United	Division 1	2–0	Hooper(9), Harper(88)	22796
Brown, Walker, Blenkinsop, Leach, Kean, Marsden, Hooper, Hill, Harper, Seed, Wilkinson					
17 Dec. 1927	Sunderland	Division 1	0–0		19755
Brown, Walker, Blenkinsop, N.Smith, Kean, Marsden, Hooper, Hill, Harper, Seed, Wilkinson					
27 Dec. 1927	Huddersfield Town	Division 1	0–5		41824
Brown, Walker, Felton, N.Smith, Leach, Seed, Hooper, Hill, Harper, Strange, Wilkinson					
31 Dec. 1927	Everton	Division 1	1–2	Marsden(28)	18354
Brown, Walker, Blenkinsop, Leach, Kean, N.Smith, Hooper, Marsden, Trotter, Strange, Wilkinson					
14 Jan. 1928	Bournemouth & Boscombe	F.A.Cup 3	3–0	Harper 2(66, 80), Seed(33)	26797
Brown, Walker, Blenkinsop, N.Smith, Kean, Marsden, Hooper, Hill, Harper, Seed, Wilkinson					
21 Jan. 1928	Blackburn Rovers	Division 1	4–1	Harper 2(12, 30), Hill(5), Hooper(83)	36094
Brown, Walker, Blenkinsop, N.Smith, Kean, Marsden, Hooper, Hill, Harper, Seed, Wilkinson					
04 Feb. 1928	Sheffield United	Division 1	3–3	Wilkinson 2(29, 83), Harper(47)	41646
Brown, Walker, Blenkinsop, N.Smith, Kean, Marsden, Hooper, Trotter, Harper, Seed, Wilkinson					
11 Feb. 1928	Middlesbrough	Division 1	2–3	Hooper 2(35pen., 57)	15631
Brown, Walker, Blenkinsop, N.Smith, Kean, Marsden, Hooper, Kirkwood, Harper, Seed, Wilkinson					
18 Feb. 1928	Sheffield United	F.A.Cup 5	1–1	Wilkinson(48)	57076
Brown, Walker, Blenkinsop, N.Smith, Kean, Marsden, Hooper, Strange, Harper, Seed, Wilkinson					
25 Feb. 1928	Newcastle United	Division 1	0–0		25462
Brown, Walker, Blenkinsop, N.Smith, Kean, Burridge, Hooper, C.Wilson, Harper, Seed, Rimmer					
10 Mar. 1928	Burnley	Division 1	5–0	Wilson 2(7, 34), Rimmer 2(69, 87), Trotter(76)	12401
Brown, Hodgkiss, Walker, N.Smith, Leach, Burridge, Hooper, Seed, Trotter, C.Wilson, Rimmer					
24 Mar. 1928	Liverpool	Division 1	4–0	Seed(1), Hooper(13), Trotter(36), Rimmer(45)	12255
Brown, Walker, Blenkinsop, Kean, Leach, Marsden, Hooper, Seed, Trotter, Allen, Rimmer					
07 Apr. 1928	Derby County	Division 1	2–2	Trotter(48), Seed(56)	28566
Brown, Walker, Blenkinsop, N.Smith, Leach, Marsden, Hooper, Seed, Trotter, Strange, Rimmer					
10 Apr. 1928	Tottenham Hotspur	Division 1	4–2	Hooper 3(27pen, 30, 52), Seed(36)	15900
Brown, Walker, Blenkinsop, Kean, Leach, Strange, Hooper, Seed, Trotter, Allen, Rimmer					
21 Apr. 1928	Portsmouth	Division 1	2–0	Trotter(38), Allen(78)	14536
Brown, Walker, Blenkinsop, N.Smith, Leach, Strange, Hooper, Seed, Trotter, Allen, Rimmer					
25 Apr. 1928	Rotherham United	County Cup Fl	5–2	Allen 3(1, 15, 40), Hill(–), Wilkinson(79)	7000
Brown, Walker, Blenkinsop, Strange, Leach, Marsden, Hooper, Hill, Harper, Allen, Wilkinson					
05 May 1928	Aston Villa	Division 1	2–0	Allen(47), Trotter(75)	36636
Brown, Walker, Blenkinsop, Strange, Leach, Marsden, Hooper, Seed, Trotter, Allen, Rimmer					

OTHER GAMES AT HILLSBOROUGH

22 Aug. 1927	Public Trial Match	Stripes 4	Whites 4		5000
19 Sep. 1927	Inter City	Sheffield 4	Glasgow 1		n/k
12 Apr. 1928	Boys	Sheffield 2	Newcastle 1		1421
01 May 1928	Association Lge. Final	Ecclesfield United 1	Norton Woodseats 3		n/k
07May 1928	Wednesday Shield	Tinsley 3	Woodburn 1		n/k
07 May 1928	Clegg Shield s/f	Carfield Intermediate 4	Heeley Bank 1		n/k
21 May 1928	Boys (EST3–Rep.)	Sheffield 3	York 3		n/k

Date	Opponents	Competition	Score	Scorers	Att.
25 Aug. 1928	Arsenal	Division 1	3–2	Hooper 2(43, 68), Marsden(63)	23684
Brown, Walker, Blenkinsop, Strange, Leach, Marsden, Hooper, Seed, Trotter, Allen, Rimmer					
03 Sep. 1928	Everton	Division 1	1–0	Seed(8)	24322
Brown, Walker, Blenkinsop, Strange, Kean, Marsden, Hooper, Seed, Trotter, Allen, Wilkinson					
08 Sep. 1928	Sunderland	Division 1	2–1	Trotter(20), Strange(62)	25716
Brown, Walker, Blenkinsop, Strange, Kean, Marsden, Hooper, Seed, Trotter, Gregg, Wilkinson					
22 Sep. 1928	Sheffield United	Division 1	5–2	Allen 2(8, 70), Hooper 2(11, 50), Rimmer(57)	44699
Brown, Walker, Felton, Strange, Leach, Marsden, Hooper, Seed, Harper, Allen, Rimmer					
29 Sep. 1928	Bolton Wanderers	Division 1	0–0		25098
Brown, Walker, Blenkinsop, Strange, Leach, Marsden, Hooper, Seed, Harper, Allen, Rimmer					
13 Oct. 1928	Birmingham	Division 1	3–0	Allen 3(4, 68, 80)	21677
Brown, Walker, Blenkinsop, Strange, Leach, Marsden, Hooper, Seed, Allen, Gregg, Rimmer					
27 Oct. 1928	Cardiff City	Division 1	1–0	Hooper(37)	20116
Brown, Walker, Blenkinsop, Strange, Burridge, Marsden, Hooper, Seed, Allen, Gregg, Rimmer					
10 Nov. 1928	Manchester United	Division 1	2–1	Hooper(31), Gregg(61)	18113
Brown, Walker, Blenkinsop, Strange, Leach, Marsden, Hooper, Seed, Allen, Gregg, Wilkinson					
24 Nov. 1928	Liverpool	Division 1	3–2	Allen 2(49, 75), Rimmer(19)	14624
Brown, Walker, Blenkinsop, Strange, Leach, Marsden, Hooper, Seed, Allen, Gregg, Rimmer					
26 Nov. 1928	Barnsley	County Cup s/f	3–0	Allen 3(25, 70, –)	4500
Brown, Walker, Felton, Strange, Leach, Marsden, Hooper, Trotter, Allen, Hill, Rimmer					
08 Dec. 1928	Newcastle United	Division 1	3–1	Allen 2(28, 79), Hooper(82)	23835
Brown, Walker, Blenkinsop, Strange, Leach, Marsden, Hooper, Gregg, Allen, C.Wilson, Rimmer					
22 Dec. 1928	Aston Villa	Division 1	4–1	Seed 2(17, 90), Hooper(2), Allen(33)	24822
Brown, Walker, Blenkinsop, Strange, Leach, Marsden, Hooper, Seed, Allen, Gregg, Rimmer					
25 Dec. 1928	Manchester City	Division 1	4–0	Allen 2(6, 84), Hooper(7), Gregg(–)	45093
Brown, Walker, Blenkinsop, Strange, Leach, Marsden, Hooper, Seed, Allen, Gregg, Rimmer					
01 Jan. 1929	Huddersfield Town	Division 1	1–1	Gregg(82)	57143
Brown, Walker, Blenkinsop, Strange, Leach, Marsden, Hooper, Seed, Allen, Gregg, Rimmer					
05 Jan. 1929	Blackburn Rovers	Division 1	1–0	Allen(83)	28136
Brown, Walker, Blenkinsop, Strange, Leach, Marsden, Hooper, Seed, Allen, Gregg, Rimmer					
18 Feb. 1929	Derby County	Division 1	5–0	Harper 3(10, 86, 87), Gregg(1), Strange(21)	16026
Brown, Walker, Blenkinsop, Strange, Leach, Marsden, Hooper, Seed, Harper, Gregg, Rimmer					
02 Mar. 1929	Bury	Division 1	3–1	Whitehouse(49), Harper(57), Seed(70)	23826
Brown, Walker, Blenkinsop, Strange, Leach, Marsden, Hooper, Seed, Harper, Whitehouse, Rimmer					
04 Mar. 1929	Portsmouth	Division 1	2–1	Hooper(12), Wilson(14)	13705
Brown, Walker, Blenkinsop, Strange, Leach, Marsden, Hooper, Seed, C.Wilson, Whitehouse, Rimmer					
16 Mar. 1929	Leicester City	Division 1	1–0	Allen(12)	30176
Brown, Walker, Blenkinsop, Strange, Leach, Marsden, Hooper, Seed, Allen, Whitehouse, Hargreaves					
30 Mar. 1929	Leeds United	Division 1	4–2	Rimmer 3(13, 42, 84), Seed(47)	30655
Brown, Walker, Blenkinsop, Strange, Leach, Marsden, Hooper, Seed, Allen, Gregg, Rimmer					
13 Apr. 1929	West Ham United	Division 1	6–0	Strange 2(33pen., 43), Hooper 2(38, 68), Rimmer(42), Allen(70)	22596
Brown, Walker, Hatfield, Strange, Leach, Marsden, Hooper, Seed, Allen, Gregg, Rimmer					
27 Apr. 1929	Burnley	Division 1	1–1	Allen(81)	33314
Brown, Walker, Blenkinsop, Strange, Leach, Marsden, Hooper, Seed, Allen, Gregg, Rimmer					
06 May 1929	Sheffield United	County Cup Final	2–0	Whitehouse(20), Hooper(40)	11800
Brown, Walker, Blenkinsop, Strange, Leach, Marsden, Hooper, Whitehouse, Allen, Gregg, Rimmer					

OTHER GAMES AT HILLSBOROUGH

Date					Att.
18 Aug. 1928	Public Trial Match	Stripes 1	Whites 1		9000
04 Feb. 1929	International Trial	England 4	The Rest 3		n/k
02 Apr. 1929	Boys	Yorkshire 2	Kent 2		n/k
25 Apr. 1929	Thursday Lge. Final	Tramways 2	Sheffield Amateurs 1		n/k
09 May 1929	Clegg Shield Final	Crookesmoor 6	Coleridge Road 4		n/k
09 May 1929	Wednesday Shield Final	Shiregreen 3	Woodburn 2		n/k

Date	Opponents	Competition	Score	Scorers	Att.
02 Sep. 1929	Bolton Wanderers	Division 1	1–0	Allen(85)	26480
Brown, Walker, Blenkinsop, Strange, Leach, Marsden, Hooper, Whitehouse, Allen, Gregg, Rimmer					
07 Sep. 1929	Arsenal	Division 1	0–2		38735
Brown, Walker, Blenkinsop, Strange, Leach, Marsden, Hooper, Whitehouse, Allen, Gregg, Rimmer					
21 Sep. 1929	Leeds United	Division 1	1–2	Seed(67)	21353
Brown, Walker, Blenkinsop, Strange, Leach, Marsden, Hooper, Seed, Allen, Burgess, Rimmer					
12 Oct. 1929	Sunderland	Division 1	1–1	Burgess(5)	23158
Brown, Walker, Blenkinsop, Strange, Leach, Marsden, Hooper, Seed, Allen, Burgess, Rimmer					
19 Oct. 1929	Huddersfield Town	Division 1	3–1	Burgess(17), Allen(39), Rimmer(85)	25998
Mellors, Walker, C.Wilson, Strange, Leach, Marsden, Hooper, Seed, Allen, Burgess, Rimmer					
21 Oct. 1929	Rotherham United	County Cup s/f	5–2	Burgess 4(10, 57, –, 83), Jackson(22)og.	3000
Mellors, Walker, C.Wilson, Strange, Leach, Marsden, Jones, Seed, Allen, Burgess, Rimmer					
02 Nov. 1929	Leicester City	Division 1	4–0	Allen 3(50, 57, 70), Burgess(12)	19159
Brown, Beeson, C.Wilson, Strange, Leach, Burridge, Hooper, Seed, Allen, Burgess, Rimmer					
16 Nov. 1929	Manchester United	Division 1	7–2	Allen 4(33, 43, 73, 87), Rimmer 2(23, 55), Hooper(38)	14264
Brown, C.Wilson, Blenkinsop, Strange, Leach, Marsden, Hooper, Seed, Allen, Burgess, Rimmer					
30 Nov. 1929	Liverpool	Division 1	2–1	Strange(4), Hooper(20)	19701
Brown, C.Wilson, Blenkinsop, Strange, Leach, Marsden, Hooper, Seed, Allen, Burgess, Rimmer					
14 Dec. 1929	Blackburn Rovers	Division 1	4–0	Allen 2(42, 66), Seed(3), Burgess(64)	19278
Brown, Walker, Blenkinsop, Strange, Leach, Marsden, Hooper, Seed, Allen, Burgess, Rimmer					
26 Dec. 1929	Everton	Division 1	4–0	Leach 2(49, 69), Burgess(11), Allen(88)	45559
Brown, Walker, Blenkinsop, Strange, Leach, Marsden, Hooper, Seed, Allen, Burgess, Rimmer					
28 Dec. 1929	Portsmouth	Division 1	1–1	Strange(79)	23548
Brown, Walker, Blenkinsop, Strange, Burridge, Marsden, Hooper, Seed, Burgess, Gregg, Rimmer					
11 Jan. 1930	Burnley	F.A.Cup 3	1–0	Allen(57)	31794
Brown, Walker, Blenkinsop, Strange, Leach, Marsden, Hooper, Seed, Allen, Burgess, Rimmer					
18 Jan. 1930	Aston Villa	Division 1	3–0	Rimmer(40), Marsden(85), Hooper(88)	34911
Brown, Walker, Blenkinsop, Strange, Leach, Marsden, Hooper, Seed, Allen, Burgess, Rimmer					
01 Feb. 1930	Sheffield United	Division 1	1–1	Burgess(27)	54459
Brown, Walker, Blenkinsop, Strange, Leach, W.Smith, Hooper, Seed, Allen, Burgess, Rimmer					
08 Feb. 1930	Burnley	Division 1	4–1	Rimmer 2(59, 88), McCluggage(20)og., Seed(40)	23864
Brown, Walker, Blenkinsop, Strange, Leach, Marsden, Hooper, Seed, Allen, Burgess, Rimmer					
15 Feb. 1930	Bradford Park Avenue	F.A.Cup 5	5–1	Seed(10), Rimmer(30), Allen(60), Bentley(78)og., Hooper(83)	53268
Brown, Walker, Blenkinsop, Strange, Leach, Marsden, Hooper, Seed, Allen, Burgess, Rimmer					
05 Mar. 1930	Nottingham Forest	F.A.Cup 6R	3–1	Seed(16), Allen(71)pen., Burgess(88)	59205
Brown, Walker, Blenkinsop, Strange, Leach, Marsden, Hooper, Seed, Allen, Burgess, Rimmer					
15 Mar. 1930	Newcastle United	Division 1	4–2	Rimmer 2(20, 35), Allen(45), Burgess(56)	9350
Brown, Walker, Blenkinsop, Strange, Leach, Marsden, Hooper, Seed, Allen, Burgess, Rimmer					
29 Mar. 1930	West Ham United	Division 1	2–1	Hooper(16), Burgess(54)	25092
Brown, Walker, Blenkinsop, Strange, Leach, Marsden, Hooper, Seed, Allen, Burgess, Rimmer					
12 Apr. 1930	Middlesbrough	Division 1	1–0	Rimmer(38)	23087
Brown, Walker, Blenkinsop, Strange, Leach, Marsden, Hooper, Millership, Allen, Burgess, Rimmer					
22 Apr. 1930	Derby County	Division 1	6–3	Allen 3(10, 53, 60), Millership(40), Rimmer(51), Hooper(57)	41218
Brown, Walker, Blenkinsop, Strange, Leach, W.Smith, Hooper, Millership, Allen, Burgess, Rimmer					
26 Apr. 1930	Grimsby Town	Division 1	1–0	Jacobson(46)og.	22524
Brown, Walker, Blenkinsop, Strange, Leach, W.Smith, Hooper, Seed, Allen, Burgess, Rimmer					
28 Apr. 1930	Birmingham	Division 1	1–1	Strange(17)	9310
Brown, Walker, Blenkinsop, Strange, Mackey, Marsden, Hooper, Seed, Allen, Burgess, Rimmer					
03 May 1930	Manchester City	Division 1	5–1	Hooper 3(21, 65, 85), Allen(14), Seed(34)	22293
Brown, Beeson, Blenkinsop, Strange, Leach, Marsden, Hooper, Seed, Allen, Burgess, Rimmer					

OTHER GAMES AT HILLSBOROUGH

24 Aug. 1929	Public Trial Match	Stripes 10	Whites 3	7000
16 Sep. 1929	Inter City	Sheffield 2	Glasgow 0	n/k
01 Mar. .1930	Minor Lge. s/f	Grenoside 1	Greenhead 1	n/k
21 Apr. 1930	Schools	England 3	Scotland 1	n/k
29 Apr. 1930	Wharncliffe C.Cup Final	Rotherham United 3	Sheffield United Res. 6	n/k
30 Apr. 1930	Wednesday Shield Final	Crookesmoor 3	Newhall 2	n/k
30 Apr. 1930	Clegg Shield Final	Wadsley Bridge 2	Ann's Road 0	n/k

Date	Opponents	Competition	Score	Scorers	Att.
30 Aug. 1930	Newcastle United	Division 1	2–1	Burgess(52), Weaver(89)og.	23673
Brown, Walker, Blenkinsop, Strange, Leach, W.Smith, Hooper, Seed, Allen, Burgess, Rimmer					
08 Sep. 1930	Chelsea	Division 1	1–1	Rimmer(29)	21282
Mellors, Walker, Blenkinsop, Strange, Leach, Peacock, Hooper, Gregg, Ball, Burgess, Rimmer					
20 Sep. 1930	Manchester United	Division 1	3–0	Ball 2(22, 74), Rimmer(63)	18705
Brown, Walker, Blenkinsop, Strange, Leach, C.Wilson, Hooper, Seed, Ball, Burgess, Rimmer					
04 Oct. 1930	Bolton Wanderers	Division 1	1–0	Burgess(83)pen.	21310
Brown, Walker, Blenkinsop, Strange, Leach, C.Wilson, Hooper, Seed, Allen, Burgess, Rimmer					
18 Oct. 1930	Manchester City	Division 1	1–1	Ball(39)	20750
Brown, Walker, Blenkinsop, Strange, Leach, C.Wilson, Hooper, Seed, Ball, Burgess, Rimmer					
01 Nov. 1930	Sunderland	Division 1	7–2	Ball 3(44, 61, 80), Rimmer(16), Burgess(35), Hooper(50), Wilson(74)	19299
Brown, Walker, Blenkinsop, Strange, Leach, C.Wilson, Hooper, Seed, Ball, Burgess, Rimmer					
03 Nov. 1930	Sheffield United	County Cup s/f	1–2	Ball(15)	5000
Brown, Walker, Blenkinsop, Robson, Leach, C.Wilson, Hooper, Seed, Ball, Burgess, Rimmer					
15 Nov. 1930	Arsenal	Division 1	1–2	Ball(13)	43671
Brown, Walker, Blenkinsop, Strange, Leach, C.Wilson, Hooper, Seed, Ball, Burgess, Rimmer					
29 Nov. 1930	Blackpool	Division 1	7–1	Hooper 3(11, 12, 21), Seed(17), Ball(65), Rimmer(83), Burgess(89)	17393
Brown, Walker, Blenkinsop, Strange, Leach, C.Wilson, Hooper, Seed, Ball, Burgess, Rimmer					
13 Dec. 1930	Birmingham	Division 1	9–1	Hooper 3(38, 63, 73), Ball 2(29, 41), Seed 2(49, 70), Burgess(16), Rimmer(31)	21226
Brown, Walker, Blenkinsop, Strange, Leach, C.Wilson, Hooper, Seed, Ball, Burgess, Rimmer					
29 Dec. 1930	Middlesbrough	Division 1	3–2	Ball 2(14, 21), Rimmer(–)	18530
Breedon, Walker, Blenkinsop, Strange, Leach, C.Wilson, Hooper, Millership, Ball, Burgess, Rimmer					
01 Jan. 1931	Huddersfield Town	Division 1	2–1	Burgess(9), Rimmer(33)	39631
Breedon, Walker, Blenkinsop, Strange, Leach, C.Wilson, Hooper, Millership, Ball, Burgess, Rimmer					
03 Jan. 1931	Sheffield United	Division 1	1–3	Ball(6)	33322
Breedon, Walker, Blenkinsop, Strange, Mackey, C.Wilson, Hooper, Millership, Ball, Burgess, Rimmer					
17 Jan. 1931	Grimsby Town	Division 1	4–1	Rimmer(12), Allen(40), Burgess(44), Ball(60)pen.	19729
Breedon, Walker, Blenkinsop, Strange, C.Wilson, W.Smith, Hooper, Burgess, Ball, Allen, Rimmer					
31 Jan. 1931	West Ham United	Division 1	5–3	Rimmer 2(49, 75), Wade(5)og., Burgess(16), Hooper(72)	16796
Breedon, Walker, Blenkinsop, Strange, Mackey, C.Wilson, Hooper, Seed, Ball, Burgess, Rimmer					
14 Feb. 1931	Liverpool	Division 1	3–5	Ball 2(22, 46), Stephenson(67)	21675
Breedon, Walker, Blenkinsop, Strange, Davison, C.Wilson, Hooper, Stephenson, Ball, Burgess, Rimmer					
14 Mar. 1931	Leeds United	Division 1	2–1	Menzies(20)og., Rimmer(70)	14562
Brown, Beeson, Blenkinsop, Strange, Davison, C.Wilson, Hooper, Seed, Ball, Burgess, Rimmer					
28 Mar. 1931	Leicester City	Division 1	4–0	Rimmer 2(26, 77), Ball 2(30, 55)	10525
Brown, Walker, Catlin, Robson, Leach, C.Wilson, Hooper, Seed, Ball, Stephenson, Rimmer					
11 Apr. 1931	Portsmouth	Division 1	2–2	Stephenson(14), Hooper(59)	13400
Brown, Walker, Blenkinsop, Strange, Leach, C.Wilson, Hooper, Stephenson, Ball, Burgess, Rimmer					
20 Apr. 1931	Derby County	Division 1	3–2	Hooper(31), Ball(36), Rimmer(67)	5141
Brown, Beeson, Blenkinsop, Strange, Leach, C.Wilson, Hooper, Burgess, Ball, Stephenson, Rimmer					
25 Apr. 1931	Blackburn Rovers	Division 1	1–3	Rimmer(30)	5101
Brown, Beeson, Blenkinsop, Strange, Leach, C.Wilson, Hooper, Burgess, Ball, Stephenson, Rimmer					
02 May 1931	Aston Villa	Division 1	3–0	Stephenson 2(5, 15), Rimmer(57)	12419
Breedon, Walker, Blenkinsop, Strange, Leach, W.Smith, Hooper, Burgess, Ball, Stephenson, Rimmer					

OTHER GAMES AT HILLSBOROUGH

23 Aug. 1930	Public Trial Match	Stripes 5	Whites 2		3973
15 Apr. 1931	Boys	Sheffield 1	Edinburgh 2		n/k
12 May 1931	Wednesday Shield Final	Woodburn 4	Crookesmoor 2		n/k

1925–26
Kean, Lowdell, Felton, Brown Frogatt, Blenkinsop, Marsden;
R. Williams, Barrass, Trotter, Hill, Prince.

1928–29
Strange, Allen, Felton, Brown, Craig (trainer), Blenkinsop, Burridge, Marsden;
Hooper, Seed, Harper, Gregg, Rimmer, Leach.

1929–30
Hopkins, Francis, Flint, Nixon, Dickinson (officials);
Turner, Hodgkiss, Webster, Johnson, Neale, Brown, Dodds, Hargreaves, Mellors, Mills, Fearnhough, Rhind;
Wardley, Jones, Hooper, Harston, Whitehouse, Leach, Blenkinsop, Burgess, Smith, Bardson, Trotman, Gunstone, Blanchard;
B. Brown (manager), Hooper, Strange, Walker, W.C. Clegg, C. Clegg, Allen, Rimmer, Gregg, C. Wilson, W. Smith, Dean, Stephenson;
Craig, Beeson, Seed, Marsden, Hatfield, Goddard, Burridge.

1932–33
Strange, Leach, Beeson, Brown, Blenkinsop, Malloch, Craig (trainer);
Hooper, Starling, Ball, Burgess, Rimmer.

Date	Opponents	Competition	Score	Scorers	Att.
31 Aug. 1931	Grimsby Town	Division 1	4–1	Rimmer 2(59, 65), Ball(13), Stephenson(70)	16734
Brown, Walker, Blenkinsop, Strange, Leach, W.Smith, Hooper, Burgess, Ball, Stephenson, Rimmer					
05 Sep. 1931	Bolton Wanderers	Division 1	7–1	Rimmer 2(42, 83pen.), Burgess 2(18, 60), Ball(43), Leach(50), Stephenson(52)	14544
Brown, Walker, Blenkinsop, Strange, Leach, W.Smith, Hooper, Burgess, Ball, Stephenson, Rimmer					
19 Sep. 1931	Huddersfield Town	Division 1	4–1	Millership 2(41, 71), Rimmer 2(43pen., 76)	24326
Brown, Walker, Blenkinsop, Strange, Leach, W.Smith, Hooper, Burgess, Ball, Millership, Rimmer					
21 Sep. 1931	Chelsea	Division 1	2–2	Ball(8), Burgess(17)	11809
Brown, Walker, Blenkinsop, Strange, Leach, W.Smith, Hooper, Burgess, Ball, Millership, Rimmer					
03 Oct. 1931	Aston Villa	Division 1	1–0	Burgess(10)	28798
Brown, Beeson, Blenkinsop, Strange, Davison, W.Smith, Hooper, Wright, Ball, Burgess, Rimmer					
12 Oct. 1931	Sheffield United	County Cup s/f	4–1	Burgess(26), Rimmer(–), Jones(55), Ball(80)	6000
Brown, Beeson, Catlin, Robson, Davison, W.Smith, Jones, Burgess, Ball, Millership, Rimmer					
24 Oct. 1931	Derby County	Division 1	3–1	Stephenson(1), Hooper(29), Ball(89)	12901
Brown, Beeson, Blenkinsop, Strange, Davison, W.Smith, Hooper, Burgess, Ball, Stephenson, Rimmer					
07 Nov. 1931	Birmingham	Division 1	5–1	Rimmer 2(11, 52), Ball 2(59, 80), Hooper(20)	17438
Brown, Beeson, C.Wilson, Strange, Davison, W.Smith, Hooper, Burgess, Ball, Stephenson, Rimmer					
21 Nov. 1931	Sheffield United	Division 1	2–1	Ball(25), Stephenson(43)	25823
Brown, Beeson, Blenkinsop, Strange, Davison, C.Wilson, Hooper, Burgess, Ball, Stephenson, Rimmer					
05 Dec. 1931	Arsenal	Division 1	1–3	Ball(5)	23265
Brown, Walker, Blenkinsop, Strange, Mackey, W.Smith, Hooper, Millership, Ball, Stephenson, Rimmer					
19 Dec. 1931	Manchester City	Division 1	1–1	Ball(44)	7431
Brown, Walker, Blenkinsop, Robson, Davison, Strange, Hooper, Millership, Ball, Burgess, Rimmer					
26 Dec. 1931	Liverpool	Division 1	1–1	Stephenson(60)	34705
Brown, Walker, Blenkinsop, Strange, Leach, Malloch, Hooper, Stephenson, Ball, Burgess, Rimmer					
02 Jan. 1932	Blackburn Rovers	Division 1	5–1	Millership 3(9, 32, 48), Stephenson(69), Leach(82)	12792
Brown, Walker, Blenkinsop, Strange, Leach, Malloch, Hooper, Stephenson, Millership, Burgess, Rimmer					
13 Jan. 1932	Tottenham Hotspur	F.A.Cup 3R	3–1	Millership(5), Rimmer(66), Stephenson(69)	30000
Brown, Walker, Blenkinsop, Strange, Leach, C.Wilson, Hooper, Stephenson, Millership, Burgess, Rimmer					
23 Jan. 1932	Bournemouth & Bosc'e	F.A.Cup 4	7–0	Millership 4(21pen., 49, 53, 82), Burgess 3(17, 62, 74)	32600
Brown, Walker, Blenkinsop, Strange, Leach, Malloch, Hooper, Stephenson, Millership, Burgess, Rimmer					
25 Jan. 1932	Middlesbrough	Division 1	1–1	Hooper(67)	9525
Brown, Walker, Blenkinsop, Strange, Leach, Malloch, Hooper, Ball, Millership, Burgess, Rimmer					
06 Feb. 1932	Newcastle United	Division 1	2–0	Millership 2(38pen, 54)	16270
Brown, Walker, Blenkinsop, Strange, Davison, Malloch, Hooper, Stephenson, Millership, Burgess, Rimmer					
13 Feb. 1932	Chelsea	F.A.Cup 5	1–1	Stephenson(9)	39600
Brown, Walker, Blenkinsop, Strange, Davison, Malloch, Hooper, Stephenson, Millership, Burgess, Rimmer					
20 Feb. 1932	Leicester City	Division 1	3–1	Ball 2(38, 62), Rimmer(32)	11391
Brown, Walker, Blenkinsop, Strange, Leach, Malloch, Hooper, Stephenson, Ball, Jones, Rimmer					
27 Feb. 1932	Everton	Division 1	1–3	Stephenson(72)	24279
Brown, Walker, Blenkinsop, Strange, Leach, Malloch, Hooper, Stephenson, Ball, Burgess, Rimmer					
12 Mar. 1932	West Bromwich Albion	Division 1	2–5	B.Richardson(30)og., Rimmer(63)	15110
Brown, Walker, Blenkinsop, Strange, Leach, Malloch, Hooper, Stephenson, Ball, Millership, Rimmer					
26 Mar. 1932	Blackpool	Division 1	3–0	Ball(15), Jones(43), Rimmer(85)pen.	13101
Breedon, Walker, Blenkinsop, Strange, Leach, Malloch, Jones, Hooper, Ball, Burgess, Rimmer					
28 Mar. 1932	West Ham United	Division 1	6–1	Hooper 2(39, 50), Jones 2(47, 75), Strange(60), Leach(67)	14848
Breedon, Walker, Blenkinsop, Strange, Leach, Malloch, Jones, Hooper, Ball, Burgess, Rimmer					
09 Apr. 1932	Portsmouth	Division 1	3–1	Rimmer(35), Hooper(50), Burgess(58)	8037
Breedon, Walker, Catlin, Gowdy, Leach, Malloch, Hooper, Jones, Ball, Burgess, Rimmer					
23 Apr. 1932	Sunderland	Division 1	3–2	Ball(7), Hooper(19), Jones(56)	7908
Breedon, Walker, Blenkinsop, Strange, Leach, Malloch, Hooper, Jones, Ball, Burgess, Rimmer					

OTHER GAMES AT HILLSBOROUGH

Date	Game	Home	Away	Att.
22 Aug. 1931	Public Trial Match	Stripes 3	Whites 3	5724
14 Sep. 1931	Inter City	Sheffield 7	Glasgow 2	n/k
28 Sep. 1931	Billy Marsden Benefit	Sheffield XI 1	F.A.XI 0	9613
04 Jan. 1932	Boys	Sheffield 3	York 0	1000
09 Jan. 1932	Representative	Sheffield & 3 Hallamshire F.A.	West Riding County F.A. 2	n/k
01 Feb. 1932	F.A.Cup 4–2R	Newcastle United 9	Southport 0	19350
05 May 1932	Wednesday Shield Final	Coleridge Road 2	Hillsborough C.S. 0	n/k

Date	Opponents	Competition	Score	Scorers	Att.
27 Aug. 1932	Blackpool	Division 1	4–1	Burgess 2(50, 59), Hooper(20), Ball(71)pen.	15152
Breedon, Walker, Blenkinsop, Strange, Leach, Malloch, Hooper, Starling, Ball, Burgess, Rimmer						
05 Sep. 1932	Everton	Division 1	3–1	Leach(9), Ball(57), Rimmer(89)	14890
Breedon, Walker, Blenkinsop, Strange, Leach, Malloch, Hooper, Starling, Ball, Burgess, Rimmer						
10 Sep. 1932	Blackburn Rovers	Division 1	1–1	Ball(45)pen.	14454
Breedon, Walker, Blenkinsop, Strange, Leach, Malloch, Hooper, Starling, Ball, Burgess, Rimmer						
24 Sep. 1932	Sheffield United	Division 1	3–3	Ball(25), Rimmer(35), Hooper(59)	24804
Breedon, Beeson, Blenkinsop, Strange, Leach, Malloch, Hooper, Starling, Ball, Burgess, Rimmer						
01 Oct. 1932	West Bromwich Albion	Division 1	3–1	Ball(1), Leach(28), Hooper(37)	10775
Breedon, Beeson, Catlin, Strange, Leach, Malloch, Hooper, Starling, Ball, Burgess, Rimmer						
15 Oct. 1932	Sunderland	Division 1	3–1	Ball(7), Murray(41)og., McDougall(53)og.	11799
Brown, Beeson, Blenkinsop, Strange, Leach, Malloch, Jones, Starling, Ball, Burgess, Rimmer						
29 Oct. 1932	Newcastle United	Division 1	2–0	Rimmer(25), Ball(67)	9496
Brown, Beeson, Blenkinsop, Strange, Leach, Malloch, Hooper, Starling, Ball, Burgess, Rimmer						
12 Nov. 1932	Portsmouth	Division 1	2–1	Strange(30), Leach(89)	10319
Brown, Walker, Blenkinsop, Strange, Leach, Malloch, Hooper, Starling, Ball, Burgess, Rimmer						
26 Nov. 1932	Huddersfield Town	Division 1	2–1	Hooper(38), Ball(45)pen.	17890
Brown, Beeson, Blenkinsop, Strange, Leach, Malloch, Hooper, Starling, Ball, Burgess, Rimmer						
10 Dec. 1932	Middlesbrough	Division 1	2–1	Ball(34)pen., Strange(69)	11651
Brown, Beeson, Blenkinsop, Strange, Leach, Malloch, Hooper, Starling, Ball, Burgess, Rimmer						
24 Dec. 1932	Liverpool	Division 1	3–0	Burgess(10), Ball(74), Starling(76)	14948
Brown, Beeson, Catlin, Strange, Leach, Malloch, Hooper, Starling, Ball, Burgess, Rimmer						
27 Dec. 1932	Manchester City	Division 1	2–1	Rimmer(57), Hooper(75)	37589
Brown, Beeson, Catlin, Strange, Leach, Burrows, Hooper, Starling, Ball, Burgess, Rimmer						
02 Jan. 1933	Arsenal	Division 1	3–2	Ball 2(62pen., 72), Leach(43)	65345
Brown, Beeson, Catlin, Strange, Leach, Malloch, Jones, Starling, Ball, Burgess, Rimmer						
07 Jan. 1933	Derby County	Division 1	0–0		20565
Brown, Beeson, Catlin, Strange, Leach, Malloch, Jones, Starling, Ball, Burgess, Rimmer						
14 Jan. 1933	Chesterfield	F.A.Cup 3	2–2	Ball 2(10, 15)	30178
Brown, Beeson, Catlin, Strange, Leach, Malloch, Hooper, Starling, Ball, Burgess, Rimmer						
28 Jan. 1933	The Corinthians	Friendly	3–1	Leach(55), Jones(69), Millership(79)	2831
Brown, Walker, Malloch, Strange, Leach, Burrows, Jones, Starling, Ball, Millership, Rimmer						
08 Feb. 1933	Leeds United	Division 1	2–0	Ball 2(15pen., 20pen.)	9585
Brown, Beeson, Catlin, Strange, Leach, Malloch, Jones, Starling, Ball, Stephenson, Rimmer						
04 Mar. 1933	Wolverhampton W.	Division 1	2–0	Starling(44), Ball(84)	12982
Brown, Beeson, Catlin, Strange, Leach, Malloch, Hooper, Starling, Ball, Burgess, Rimmer						
18 Mar. 1933	Leicester City	Division 1	4–1	Ball 3(4, 55, 76), Burgess(22)	13964
Brown, Beeson, Blenkinsop, Strange, Bratley, Malloch, Hooper, Starling, Ball, Burgess, Rimmer						
01 Apr. 1933	Chelsea	Division 1	2–2	Jones(25), Rimmer(33)	10121
Brown, Beeson, Catlin, W.Smith, Millership, Malloch, Hooper, Jones, Ball, Burgess, Rimmer						
05 Apr. 1933	Birmingham	Division 1	1–1	Ball(21)	6088
Brown, Beeson, Blenkinsop, Strange, Millership, Malloch, Hooper, Starling, Ball, Burgess, Rimmer						
15 Apr. 1933	Aston Villa	Division 1	0–2		16700
Brown, Beeson, Catlin, Strange, Leach, Burrows, Hooper, Starling, Ball, Burgess, Rimmer						
29 Apr. 1933	Bolton Wanderers	Division 1	2–0	Burgess 2(27, 68)	4810
Breedon, Beeson, Blenkinsop, Strange, Leach, Burrows, Hooper, Starling, Ball, Burgess						

OTHER GAMES AT HILLSBOROUGH

Date	Opponents				Att.
20 Aug. 1932	Public Trial Match	Stripes 6	Whites 4		4000
18 Feb. 1933	Representative	Sheffield & 0 Hallamshire F.A.	West Riding Assoc. 1		500
18 Apr. 1933	Sunday School s/f	Heeley Friends 5	Owlerton U.M. 3		n/k
20 Apr. 1933	Boys	Sheffield 0	Edinburgh 1		5000

Date	Opponents	Competition	Score	Scorers	Att.
28 Aug. 1933	Aston Villa	Division 1	1–2	Burgess(20)	19362
Breedon, Beeson, Blenkinsop, Strange, Leach, Burrows, Hooper, Starling, Ball, Burgess, Rimmer					
02 Sep. 1933	Arsenal	Division 1	1–2	Burgess(42)	22377
Breedon, Beeson, Blenkinsop, Strange, Leach, Burrows, Hooper, Starling, Ball, Burgess, Rimmer					
16 Sep. 1933	Middlesbrough	Division 1	3–0	Hooper(15), Rimmer(25), Ball(65)	12670
Brown, Beeson, Blenkinsop, Strange, Millership, Burrows, Hooper, Starling, Ball, Burgess, Rimmer					
30 Sep. 1933	Newcastle United	Division 1	3–1	Ball 2(44pen., 82), Rimmer(66)	14278
Brown, Beeson, Blenkinsop, Strange, Millership, Burrows, Hooper, Starling, Ball, Burgess, Rimmer					
14 Oct. 1933	Derby County	Division 1	1–1	Millership(46)	14780
Brown, Walker, Blenkinsop, Brolly, Leach, Burrows, Hooper, Starling, Millership, Jones, Rimmer					
21 Oct. 1933	Sheffield United	Division 1	0–1		27951
Brown, Beeson, Blenkinsop, Strange, Leach, Burrows, Hooper, Starling, Ball, Burgess, Rimmer					
04 Nov. 1933	Chelsea	Division 1	2–1	Burrows(50), Burgess(80)	10830
Brown, Beeson, Catlin, Strange, Leach, Burrows, Hooper, Starling, Ball, Burgess, Cooper					
18 Nov. 1933	Portsmouth	Division 1	1–2	Starling(80)	8810
Brown, Beeson, Blenkinsop, Strange, Leach, Burrows, Hooper, Starling, Ball, Burgess, Cooper					
02 Dec. 1933	Leicester City	Division 1	1–1	Strange(14)	10313
Brown, Beeson, Blenkinsop, Leach, Millership, Burrows, Hooper, Strange, Ball, J.Thompson, Cooper					
16 Dec. 1933	Tottenham Hotspur	Division 1	2–1	Hooper(43), Law(55)	17232
Brown, Beeson, Blenkinsop, Leach, Millership, Burrows, Jones, Hooper, Law, Burgess, Rimmer					
26 Dec. 1933	West Bromwich Albion	Division 1	3–1	Hooper(26), Law(27), Rimmer(56)	33675
Brown, Walker, Blenkinsop, Leach, Millership, Burrows, Hooper, Starling, Law, Burgess, Rimmer					
30 Dec. 1933	Manchester City	Division 1	1–1	Starling(9)	27074
Brown, Walker, Blenkinsop, Leach, Millership, Burrows, Hooper, Starling, Dewar, Burgess, Rimmer					
02 Jan. 1934	Birmingham	Division 1	2–1	Burgess 2(23, 75)	12754
Brown, Walker, Blenkinsop, Leach, Millership, Burrows, Hooper, Starling, Law, Burgess, Rimmer					
20 Jan. 1934	Everton	Division 1	0–0		23393
Brown, Walker, Blenkinsop, Leach, Millership, Burrows, Jones, Starling, Dewar, Burgess, Rimmer					
31 Jan. 1934	Oldham Athletic	F.A.Cup 4R	6–1	Dewar 3(8, 43, 57), Hooper(21), Rimmer(74), Burgess(76)	41311
Brown, Walker, Blenkinsop, Leach, Millership, Burrows, Hooper, Starling, Dewar, Burgess, Rimmer					
03 Feb. 1934	Blackburn Rovers	Division 1	4–0	Dewar 2(26, 60), Burgess(10), Hooper(75)	19303
Brown, Walker, Blenkinsop, Leach, Millership, Burrows, Hooper, Starling, Dewar, Burgess, Rimmer					
17 Feb. 1934	Manchester City	F.A.Cup 5	2–2	Rimmer(8), Dewar(47)	72841
Brown, Walker, Catlin, Leach, Millership, Burrows, Hooper, Starling, Dewar, Burgess, Rimmer					
26 Feb. 1934	Leeds United	Division 1	0–2		6771
Brown, Walker, Catlin, Strange, Millership, Burrows, Hooper, Starling, Dewar, Burgess, Rimmer					
10 Mar. 1934	Wolverhampton W.	Division 1	2–1	Hooper(18), Walker(24)pen.	5182
Brown, Walker, Blenkinsop, Brolly, Millership, Burrows, Hooper, Starling, Law, Burgess, Rimmer					
19 Mar. 1934	St. Johnstone	Friendly	3–0	Rimmer(15), Leach(27), Law(61)	1688
Breedon, Beeson, Catlin, Burrows, Leach, Malloch, Hooper, Strange, Law, Burgess, Rimmer					
24 Mar. 1934	Huddersfield Town	Division 1	1–2	Cooper(44)	17278
Breedon, Beeson, Catlin, Burrows, Millership, Malloch, Hooper, Starling, Law, Burgess, Rimmer					
07 Apr. 1934	Sunderland	Division 1	2–0	Cooper(6), Dewar(15)	11799
Breedon, Walker, Catlin, Burrows, Millership, Malloch, Jones, Starling, Dewar, Burgess, Cooper					
21 Apr. 1934	Liverpool	Division 1	1–2	Starling(25)	13633
Breedon, Walker, Catlin, Burrows, Millership, Malloch, Hooper, Starling, Dewar, Burgess, Rimmer					
05 May 1934	Stoke City	Division 1	2–2	Oxley(3), Dewar(55)	9235
Breedon, Walker, Catlin, Burrows, Millership, Malloch, Hooper, Starling, Dewar, Oxley, Rimmer					
12 May 1934	Doncaster Rovers	County Cup Final	3–0	Dewar(9), Cooper(14), Hooper(40)	3100
Breedon, Walker, Catlin, Burgess, Millership, Malloch, Cooper, Starling, Dewar, Hooper, Rimmer					

OTHER GAMES AT HILLSBOROUGH

15 Aug. 1933	Private Trial Match	Stripes 5	Whites 2	n/k
19 Aug. 1933	Public Trial Match	Stripes 7	Whites 3	3239
26 Apr. 1934	Thursday Lge. s/f rep	Sheffield Police 2	Central Thursday 2	n/k
30 Apr. 1934	Thursday Lge. s/f 2rep	Sheffield Police 2	Central Thursday 1	n/k

Date	Opponents	Competition	Score	Scorers	Att.
25 Aug. 1934	Stoke City	Division 1	4–1	Dewar(27), Hooper(50), Turner(55)og., Rimmer(60)	17657
Brown, Nibloe, Catlin, Burrows, Millership, Malloch, Hooper, Starling, Dewar, Burgess, Rimmer					
03 Sep. 1934	Chelsea	Division 1	3–1	Burrows(29), Dewar(54), Rimmer(67)	13696
Brown, Walker, Nibloe, Burrows, Millership, Malloch, Hooper, Starling, Dewar, Burgess, Rimmer					
08 Sep. 1934	Middlesbrough	Division 1	3–3	Dewar(1), Burgess(54), Rimmer(85)	16103
Brown, Walker, Nibloe, Burrows, Millership, Malloch, Hooper, Starling, Dewar, Burgess, Rimmer					
22 Sep. 1934	Arsenal	Division 1	0–0		25334
Brown, Nibloe, Catlin, Burrows, Millership, Nicholls, Oxley, Starling, Dewar, Burgess, Rimmer					
06 Oct. 1934	Liverpool	Division 1	4–1	Hooper 2(70, 84), Burgess(19), Rimmer(53)	17935
Brown, Nibloe, Catlin, Burrows, Millership, Malloch, Hooper, Starling, Dewar, Burgess, Rimmer					
20 Oct. 1934	Wolverhampton W.	Division 1	3–1	Rimmer 2(38, 52), Hooper(2)	14646
Brown, Nibloe, Catlin, Burrows, Millership, Malloch, Hooper, Starling, Dewar, Burgess, Rimmer					
03 Nov. 1934	Derby County	Division 1	1–0	Burgess(12)	19401
Brown, Walker, Nibloe, Nicholls, Millership, Burrows, Hooper, Starling, Oxley, Burgess, Rimmer					
17 Nov. 1934	Preston North End	Division 1	2–1	Rimmer(28), Burgess(61)	16000
Brown, Nibloe, Baird, Burrows, Millership, Malloch, Hooper, Dewar, Starling, Burgess, Rimmer					
01 Dec. 1934	Sunderland	Division 1	2–2	Dewar(14), Starling(47)	22880
Brown, Walker, Nibloe, Burrows, Millership, Malloch, Oxley, Starling, Dewar, Burgess, Rimmer					
10 Dec. 1934	FC Austria	Friendly	3–0	Rimmer 2(61, 83pen.), Millership(53)	12445
Hill, Walker, Nibloe, Sharp, Millership, Burrows, Oxley, Starling, Rimmer, Burgess, Cooper					
15 Dec. 1934	Everton	Division 1	0–0		19266
Brown, Walker, Nibloe, Sharp, Millership, Burrows, Oxley, Starling, Palethorpe, Burgess, Rimmer					
25 Dec. 1934	Birmingham	Division 1	2–1	Burgess(28), Oxley(–)	24090
Brown, Walker, Nibloe, Sharp, Millership, Burrows, Oxley, Surtees, Palethorpe, Burgess, Cooper					
01 Jan. 1935	West Bromwich Albion	Division 1	2–1	Surtees(68), Millership(86)	30055
Brown, Walker, Catlin, Sharp, Millership, Burrows, Oxley, Surtees, Palethorpe, Starling, Rimmer					
05 Jan. 1935	Manchester City	Division 1	1–0	Oxley(87)	31356
Brown, Walker, Catlin, Sharp, Millership, Burrows, Oxley, Surtees, Palethorpe, Starling, Rimmer					
12 Jan. 1935	Oldham Athletic	F.A.Cup 3	3–1	Palethorpe(6), Rimmer(65), Surtees(72)	26662
Brown, Walker, Catlin, Sharp, Millership, Burrows, Hooper, Surtees, Palethorpe, Starling, Rimmer					
28 Jan. 1935	Blackburn Rovers	Division 1	2–2	Crook(18)og., Rimmer(48)	8043
Brown, Walker, Catlin, Sharp, Millership, Burrows, Hooper, Surtees, Smith, Starling, Rimmer					
09 Feb. 1935	Portsmouth	Division 1	3–0	Palethorpe(5), Surtees(6), Cooper(51)	17396
Brown, Nibloe, Catlin, Sharp, Millership, Burrows, Cooper, Surtees, Palethorpe, Starling, Rimmer					
23 Feb. 1935	Leeds United	Division 1	1–0	Rimmer(50)	19591
Brown, Nibloe, Catlin, Sharp, Millership, Burrows, Hooper, Surtees, Palethorpe, Starling, Rimmer					
02 Mar. 1935	Arsenal	F.A.Cup 6R	2–1	Hooper(33), Rimmer(71)	66945
Brown, Nibloe, Catlin, Sharp, Millership, Burrows, Hooper, Surtees, Palethorpe, Starling, Rimmer					
09 Mar. 1935	Huddersfield Town	Division 1	1–1	Rimmer(51)	19819
Brown, Nibloe, Catlin, Sharp, Millership, Burrows, Hooper, Surtees, Palethorpe, Starling, Rimmer					
23 Mar. 1935	Aston Villa	Division 1	2–1	Starling(16)pen., Dewar(35)	12495
Brown, Nibloe, Catlin, Sharp, Millership, Burrows, Hooper, Surtees, Dewar, Starling, Rimmer					
03 Apr. 1935	Sheffield United	Craig Benefit	0–0		1500
Brown, Wright, Catlin, Leyland, Millership, Burrows, Hooper, Starling, Palethorpe, Walker, Cooper					
06 Apr. 1935	Tottenham Hotspur	Division 1	4–0	Law 2(34, 87), Palethorpe(37), Rimmer(89)	12158
Hill, Nibloe, Catlin, Sharp, Millership, Burrows, Law, Surtees, Palethorpe, Starling, Rimmer					
20 Apr. 1935	Leicester City	Division 1	1–1	Sharp(85)	15654
Brown, Nibloe, Catlin, Sharp, Millership, Burrows, Hooper, Surtees, Palethorpe, Starling, Rimmer					
04 May 1935	Grimsby Town	Division 1	1–0	Rimmer(80)	21046
Brown, Nibloe, Catlin, Sharp, Millership, Burrows, Hooper, Surtees, Palethorpe, Starling, Rimmer					

OTHER GAMES AT HILLSBOROUGH

18 Aug. 1934	Public Trial Match	Stripes 3	Whites 0	4675
12 Dec. 1934	Universities Trial	The Whites 2	The Colours 2	500
12 Feb. 1935	Public Trial Match	Sripes 1	Whites 4	7000
06 Mar. 1935	Representative	Sheffield City Police 2	Royal Ulster Constabulary 4	3000
03 May 1935	Wragg League Final	St. Philips 1	Lopham Street 0	n/k

Date	Opponents	Competition	Score	Scorers	Att.
04 Sep. 1935	Glasgow Rangers	Friendly	1–1	Dewar(34)	23986
Brown, Nibloe, Catlin, Sharp, Millership, Burrows, Hooper, Surtees, Dewar, Starling, Rimmer					
07 Sep. 1935	Wolverhampton W.	Division 1	0–0		21381
Brown, Nibloe, Catlin, Sharp, Millership, Burrows, Hooper, Surtees, Palethorpe, Starling, Rimmer					
09 Sep. 1935	Bolton Wanderers	Division 1	2–2	Hooper(10), Palethorpe(20)	12912
Brown, Nibloe, Catlin, Sharp, Millership, Burrows, Hooper, Bargh, Palethorpe, Starling, Rimmer					
16 Sep. 1935	Huddefield Town	Division 1	1–2	Rimmer(28)	14164
Brown, Nibloe, Catlin, Sharp, Millership, Burrows, Hooper, Surtees, Palethorpe, Starling, Rimmer					
28 Sep. 1935	Preston North End	Division 1	1–0	Hooper(26)	17106
Brown, Nibloe, Catlin, Sharp, Millership, Burrows, Hooper, Starling, Palethorpe, Bargh, Rimmer					
12 Oct. 1935	Derby County	Division 1	1–0	Hooper(36)	34646
Brown, Nibloe, Catlin, Sharp, Millership, Burrows, Hooper, Starling, Dewar, Bruce, Rimmer					
19 Oct. 1935	Birmingham	Division 1	3–1	Millership(26), Dewar(54), Rimmer(87)	13840
Brown, Nibloe, Catlin, Rhodes, Millership, Burrows, Hooper, Starling, Dewar, Bruce, Rimmer					
02 Nov. 1935	West Bromwich Albion	Division 1	2–5	Dewar(6), Hooper(90)	22597
Brown, Nibloe, Catlin, Rhodes, Millership, Burrows, Hooper, Starling, Dewar, Bruce, Rimmer					
16 Nov. 1935	Grimsby Town	Division 1	3–0	Dewar(25), Surtees(69), Starling(80)	20241
Brown, Nibloe, Catlin, Sharp, Millership, Burrows, Hooper, Surtees, Dewar, Starling, Rimmer					
18 Nov. 1935	Sparta & Slavia Select	Friendly	4–1	Dewar 2(67, –), Hooper(11), Rimmer(68)	3241
Brown, Nibloe, Catlin, Bargh, Millership, Burrows, Hooper, Surtees, Dewar, Starling, Rimmer					
30 Nov. 1935	Chelsea	Division 1	4–1	Dewar 2(32, 48), Hooper(73), Burrows(82)pen.	16014
Brown, Nibloe, Catlin, Sharp, Millership, Burrows, Hooper, Robinson, Dewar, Starling, Rimmer					
14 Dec. 1935	Stoke City	Division 1	0–1		14070
Brown, Nibloe, Catlin, Sharp, Burrows, Malloch, Hooper, Robinson, Dewar, Starling, Rimmer					
28 Dec. 1935	Aston Villa	Division 1	5–2	Starling(18), Hooper(21), Dewar(54), Rimmer(73), Surtees(88)	25371
Brown, Nibloe, Catlin, Sharp, Millership, Burrows, Hooper, Surtees, Dewar, Starling, Rimmer					
15 Jan. 1936	Crewe Alexandra	F.A.Cup 3R	3–1aet	Dewar(92), Rimmer(100), Surtees(118)	15995
Brown, Nibloe, Catlin, Sharp, Millership, Burrows, Hooper, Surtees, Dewar, Starling, Rimmer					
18 Jan. 1936	Arsenal	Division 1	3–2	Dewar(23), Rimmer(37), Hooper(89)	35576
Brown, Nibloe, Catlin, Sharp, Millership, Burrows, Hooper, Surtees, Dewar, Starling, Rimmer					
27 Jan. 1936	Newcastle United	F.A.Cup 4	1–1	Dewar(39)	25355
Brown, Nibloe, Catlin, Sharp, Millership, Burrows, Hooper, Surtees, Dewar, Starling, Rimmer					
03 Feb. 1936	Everton	Division 1	3–3	Rimmer 3(28, 57, 75)	5938
Brown, Nibloe, Catlin, Bargh, Millership, Burrows, Hooper, Surtees, Dewar, Starling, Rimmer					
08 Feb. 1936	Brentford	Division 1	3–3	Starling 2(52, 79), Dewar(57)	21470
Brown, Nibloe, Wright, Sharp, Millership, Burrows, Hooper, Starling, Dewar, Surtees, Rimmer					
12 Feb. 1936	Portsmouth	Division 1	0–1		6135
Brown, Nibloe, Wright, Hull, Millership, Burrows, Bargh, Surtees, Dewar, Starling, Rimmer					
29 Feb. 1936	Leeds United	Division 1	3–0	Rimmer(51), Dewar(72), Luke(73)	6589
Brown, Nibloe, Catlin, Millership, Hanford, Burrows, Luke, Grosvenor, Dewar, Starling, Rimmer					
14 Mar. 1936	Sunderland	Division 1	0–0		32450
Brown, Nibloe, Catlin, Millership, Hanford, Malloch, Luke, Grosvenor, Dewar, Starling, Rimmer					
28 Mar. 1936	Manchester City	Division 1	1–0	Luke(87)	21540
Brown, Nibloe, Catlin, Millership, Hanford, Burrows, Luke, Grosvenor, Dewar, Starling, Rimmer					
11 Apr. 1936	Blackburn Rovers	Division 1	0–0		15569
Brown, Nibloe, Catlin, Millership, Hanford, Burrows, Luke, Grosvenor, Dewar, Starling, Rimmer					
14 Apr. 1936	Middlesbrough	Division 1	0–0		21157
Brown, Nibloe, Catlin, Rhodes, Millership, Burrows, Hooper, Grosvenor, Dewar, Starling, Rimmer					
25 Apr. 1936	Liverpool	Division 1	0–0		7630
Brown, Nibloe, Catlin, Rhodes, Hanford, Burrows, Luke, Robinson, Grosvenor, Starling, Rimmer					

OTHER GAMES AT HILLSBOROUGH

24 Aug. 1935	Public Trial Match	Stripes 2	Whites 2		4431
23 Sep. 1935	Inter City	Sheffield 3	Glasgow 1		5000
09 Apr. 1936	Representative	Sheffield City Police 3	Glasgow Police 2		n/k

1933–34
Burrows, Nibloe, Catlin, Brown, Millership, Malloch;
Hooper, Starling, Dewar, Burgess, Rimmer.

1934–35
Irwin (trainer), Nibloe, Brown, Walker (manager), Catlin,
Millership, Burrows;
Sharp, Hooper, Surtees, Palethorpe, Starling, Rimmer.

1935–36
Irwin (trainer), Sharp, Millership, Nibloe, Brown, Catlin,
Burrows, Walker (manager);
Hooper, Thompson, Palethorpe, Starling, Rimmer.

1936–37
Nibloe, Millership, Catlin, Brown, Hanford, Burrows;
Luke, Robinson, Ashley, Thompson, Roy.

Date	Opponents	Competition	Score	Scorers	Att.
29 Aug. 1936	Sunderland	Division 1	2–0	Hooper(54), Starling(67)	27016
Brown, Nibloe, Catlin, Rhodes, Hanford, Burrows, Luke, Starling, Dewar, Hooper, Rimmer					
10 Sep. 1936	Everton	Division 1	6–4	Dewar 3(6, –, –), Rimmer 2(21, –), Luke(47)	16677
Brown, Ashley, Catlin, Rhodes, Hanford, Burrows, Luke, Starling, Dewar, Hooper, Rimmer					
12 Sep. 1936	Derby County	Division 1	2–3	Dewar(25), Hooper(34)	25921
Brown, Ashley, Catlin, Rhodes, Hanford, Burrows, Luke, Starling, Dewar, Hooper, Rimmer					
17 Sep. 1936	Huddersfield Town	Division 1	2–2	Starling(55), Luke(78)	18452
Goodfellow, Nibloe, Catlin, Hanford, Millership, Burrows, Luke, Starling, Dewar, Hooper, Rimmer					
26 Sep. 1936	Portsmouth	Division 1	0–0		20312
Goodfellow, Nibloe, Catlin, Rhodes, Millership, Burrows, Luke, Starling, Dewar, Hooper, Rimmer					
28 Sep. 1936	Doncaster Rovers	County Cup Pr	3–0	Surtees 2(32, 46), Robinson(78)	1443
Goodfellow, Ashley, Catlin, Rhodes, Hanford, Burrows, Luke, Surtees, Starling, Robinson, Rimmer					
03 Oct. 1936	Preston North End	Division 1	0–1		18090
Goodfellow, Nibloe, Catlin, Rhodes, Hanford, Burrows, Luke, Starling, Surtees, Robinson, Rimmer					
24 Oct. 1936	Stoke City	Division 1	0–0		22169
Brown, Nibloe, Catlin, Rhodes, Millership, Burrows, Luke, Hooper, Starling, J.Thompson, Rimmer					
07 Nov. 1936	Grimsby Town	Division 1	2–1	Robinson(17), Dewar(87)	19636
Brown, Nibloe, Catlin, Rhodes, Millership, Burrows, Drury, Robinson, Dewar, Hooper, Rimmer					
21 Nov. 1936	Leeds United	Division 1	1–2	Drury(24)	18411
Goodfellow, Nibloe, Ashley, Moss, Millership, Burrows, Drury, Robinson, Dewar, Hooper, Rimmer					
05 Dec. 1936	Middlesbrough	Division 1	1–0	Hooper(56)	18826
Brown, Nibloe, Catlin, Moss, Millership, Burrows, Drury, Robinson, Starling, Hooper, Green					
19 Dec. 1936	Manchester City	Division 1	5–1	Robinson 2(6, 52), Drury 2(28, 65), Hooper(54)	19821
Brown, Ashley, Catlin, Moss, Millership, Burrows, Drury, Robinson, Starling, Hooper, Rimmer					
28 Dec. 1936	Brentford	Division 1	0–2		20374
Brown, Ashley, Catlin, Moss, Millership, Burrows, Drury, Robinson, Starling, Hooper, Rimmer					
02 Jan. 1937	Wolverhampton W.	Division 1	1–3	Shelley(13)	17819
Brown, Ashley, Catlin, Moss, Millership, Burrows, Drury, Robinson, Shelley, Starling, Rimmer					
16 Jan. 1937	Port Vale	F.A.Cup 3	2–0	Robinson(10), Drury(30)	27450
Brown, Nibloe, Catlin, Moss, Millership, Burrows, Drury, Robinson, Dewar, Hooper, Rimmer					
23 Jan. 1937	Manchester United	Division 1	1–0	Millership(9)	9021
Brown, Ashley, Catlin, Millership, Hanford, Burrows, Luke, J.Thompson, Dewar, Hooper, Rimmer					
13 Feb. 1937	Arsenal	Division 1	0–0		35813
Brown, Nibloe, Catlin, Millership, Hanford, Burrows, Luke, Robinson, Ashley, Hooper, Roy					
20 Feb. 1937	Chelsea	Division 1	1–1	Ashley(46)	16459
Brown, Nibloe, Catlin, Moss, Millership, Burrows, Drury, Robinson, Ashley, J.Thompson, Roy					
06 Mar. 1937	Charlton Athletic	Division 1	3–1	Ashley(9), Luke(10), Robinson(27)	17586
Brown, Nibloe, Catlin, Moss, Hanford, Millership, Luke, Robinson, Ashley, J.Thompson, Roy					
20 Mar. 1937	Liverpool	Division 1	1–2	Thompson(38)	19918
Brown, Nibloe, Catlin, Moss, Hanford, Millership, Luke, Robinson, Ashley, J.Thompson, Roy					
29 Mar. 1937	Bolton Wanderers	Division 1	2–0	Thompson 2(61, 85)	30859
Smith, Ashley, Catlin, Moss, Hanford, Grosvenor, Hooper, Drury, J.Thompson, Robinson, Rimmer					
03 Apr. 1937	Birmingham	Division 1	0–3		21555
Smith, Ashley, Catlin, Moss, Hanford, Grosvenor, Hooper, Drury, Millership, Robinson, Rimmer					
17 Apr. 1937	West Bromwich Alb.	Division 1	2–3	Millership(74), Dewar(85)	12002
Smith, Ashley, Catlin, Moss, Hanford, Rhodes, Drury, Millership, Robinson, Dewar, Rimmer					

OTHER GAMES AT HILLSBOROUGH

22 Aug. 1936	Public Trial Match	Stripes 2	Whites 1		4812
15 Mar. 1937	F.A.Cup 6–2R	Sunderland 4	Wolves 0		48960
19 Apr. 1937	Association Lge. s/f	Norton Woodseats 2	Hall Sports 2		n/k
23 Apr. 1937	Association Lge. s/f–r	Norton Woodseats 1	Hall Sports 3		n/k
26 Apr. 1937	Association Lge. Final	Thurnscoe Victoria 3	Hall Sports 3		n/k

Date	Opponents	Competition	Score	Scorers	Att.
02 Sep. 1937	Fulham	Division 2	2–1	Drury(2), Robinson(33)	16511
Goodfellow, Ashley, Catlin, Rhodes, Hanford, Moss, Chedgzoy, Robinson, Ware, Drury, Rimmer					
04 Sep. 1937	Swansea Town	Division 2	1–1	Ware(29)	18739
Goodfellow, Ashley, Catlin, Rhodes, Hanford, Moss, Chedgzoy, Robinson, Ware, Drury, Rimmer					
16 Sep. 1937	Tottenham Hotspur	Division 2	0–3		13263
Goodfellow, Ashley, Catlin, Rhodes, Hanford, Walker, Chedgzoy, Drury, Matthews, Hooper, Green					
18 Sep. 1937	Aston Villa	Division 2	1–2	Matthews(5)	20565
Goodfellow, Ashley, Catlin, Moss, Hanford, Rhodes, Luke, Hooper, Matthews, Curry, Rimmer					
02 Oct. 1937	West Ham United	Division 2	1–0	Rimmer(66)	19987
Goodfellow, Ashley, Nibloe, Ware, Millership, Rhodes, Hooper, Robinson, Matthews, Roy, Rimmer					
11 Oct. 1937	Barnsley	County Cup	0–2		1086
Goodfellow, Ashley, Nibloe, Fenwick, Millership, Burrows, Chedgzoy, Robinson, Matthews, Ware, Rimmer					
16 Oct. 1937	Sheffield United	Division 2	0–1		52523
Goodfellow, Ashley, Nibloe, Ware, Millership, Rhodes, J.Thompson, Robinson, Matthews, Drury, Rimmer					
30 Oct. 1937	Stockport County	Division 2	3–3	Rimmer 2(22, 35), Robinson(6)	14272
Goodfellow, Nibloe, Lester, Ashley, Millership, Drury, Roy, Robinson, J.Thompson, Ware, Rimmer					
13 Nov. 1937	Luton Town	Division 2	4–0	Robinson(40), Luke(50), Rimmer(60), Thompson(78)	16815
Goodfellow, Ashley, Catlin, Drury, Millership, Burrows, Luke, Walker, J.Thompson, Robinson, Rimmer					
27 Nov. 1937	Nottingham Forest	Division 2	0–2		17133
Goodfellow, Ashley, Catlin, Drury, Millership, Burrows, Luke, Walker, J.Thompson, Driscoll, Rimmer					
11 Dec. 1937	Bury	Division 2	2–0	Roy(20), Driscoll(48)	10492
Goodfellow, Nibloe, Catlin, Rhodes, Millership, Burrows, Roy, Robinson, Ashley, Driscoll, Rimmer					
27 Dec. 1937	Plymouth Argyle	Division 2	1–1	Matthews(24)	20560
Goodfellow, Nibloe, Catlin, Rhodes, Millership, Burrows, Roy, J.Thompson, Matthews, Drury, Rimmer					
01 Jan. 1938	Chesterfield	Division 2	1–0	Driver(24)	43199
Goodfellow, Nibloe, Catlin, Rhodes, Millership, Burrows, Roy, Driver, Matthews, Drury, Rimmer					
08 Jan. 1938	Burnley	F.A.Cup 3	1–1	Millership(80)	33006
Goodfellow, Nibloe, Catlin, Rhodes, Millership, Burrows, Roy, Driver, Ashley, Drury, Rimmer					
22 Jan. 1938	Norwich City	Division 2	1–0	Burrows(6)pen.	12690
Goodfellow, Ashley, Catlin, Rhodes, Millership, Burrows, Massarella, Driver, Matthews, Drury, Rimmer					
05 Feb. 1938	Bradford Park Avenue	Division 2	1–0	Matthews(87)	24838
Goodfellow, Nibloe, Catlin, Ashley, Millership, Burrows, Massarella, J.Thompson, Matthews, Drury, Rimmer					
19 Feb. 1938	Southampton	Division 2	0–0		17781
Goodfellow, Ashley, Catlin, Rhodes, Millership, Burrows, Massarella, Driver, Matthews, Drury, Rimmer					
05 Mar. 1938	Manchester United	Division 2	1–3	Massarella(76)	37156
Goodfellow, Ashley, Catlin, Rhodes, Millership, Burrows, Massarella, Robinson, D.Hunt, Drury, Matthews					
19 Mar. 1938	Barnsley	Division 2	0–1		34629
Goodfellow, Ashley, Catlin, Rhodes, Millership, Burrows, Massarella, Robinson, D.Hunt, Napier, Fallon					
02 Apr. 1938	Coventry City	Division 2	2–1	Robinson(49), Hunt(66)	25956
Smith, Ashley, Catlin, Walker, Millership, Burrows, Massarella, Robinson, D.Hunt, Napier, Fallon					
16 Apr. 1938	Newcastle United	Division 2	3–0	Massarella 2(52, 70), Robinson(17)	30137
Smith, Ashley, Catlin, Walker, Millership, Burrows, Massarella, Robinson, D.Hunt, Napier, Fallon					
19 Apr. 1938	Blackburn Rovers	Division 2	1–1	Walker(9)	28207
Smith, Ashley, Catlin, Walker, Millership, Burrows, Massarella, Robinson, D.Hunt, J.Thompson, Fallon					
30 Apr. 1938	Burnley	Division 2	2–1	Hunt 2(1, 22pen.)	19553
Goodfellow, Nibloe, Catlin, Walker, Millership, Burrows, Massarella, Robinson, D.Hunt, Napier, Fallon					

OTHER GAMES AT HILLSBOROUGH

21 Aug. 1937	Public Trial Match	Stripes 6	Whites 3		3782
16 Mar. 1938	Universities	Sheffield 2	Leeds 0		n/k
12 Apr. 1938	Senior Cup Final	Norton Woodseats 2	Lopham Street UM 1		n/k
21 Apr. 1938	Boys	Sheffield 2	Doncaster 4		n/k

Date	Opponents	Competition	Score	Scorers	Att.
20 Aug. 1938	Sheffield United	Friendly	4–1	Hunt 3, Lewis	14917
Goodfellow, Ashley, Catlin, Russell, Hanford, Burrows, Lewis, Robinson, D.Hunt, Napier, Fallon					
27 Aug. 1938	Bury	Division 2	2–0	Hunt(25), Robinson(57)	24568
Goodfellow, Ashley, Catlin, Russell, Hanford, Burrows, Lewis, Robinson, D.Hunt, Napier, Fallon					
08 Sep. 1938	Blackburn Rovers	Division 2	3–0	Fallon(33), Robinson(44), Napier(89)	23036
Goodfellow, Ashley, Catlin, Russell, Hanford, Burrows, Lewis, Robinson, D.Hunt, Napier, Fallon					
10 Sep. 1938	Tranmere Rovers	Division 2	2–0	Lowes(60), Lewis(75)	32600
Goodfellow, Ashley, Catlin, Russell, Hanford, Burrows, Lewis, Robinson, Lowes, Napier, Fallon					
24 Sep. 1938	Swansea Town	Division 2	1–1	Robinson(33)	23632
Goodfellow, Ashley, Catlin, Russell, Hanford, Burrows, Lewis, Robinson, Lowes, Napier, Fallon					
08 Oct. 1938	Manchester City	Division 2	3–1	Robinson(23), Fallon(50), Hunt(87)pen.	25372
Goodfellow, Ashley, Lester, Russell, Hanford, Burrows, Massarella, Robinson, D.Hunt, Napier, Fallon					
22 Oct. 1938	Coventry City	Division 2	2–2	Driver(35), Lewis(55)	24007
Goodfellow, Ashley, Lester, Russell, Hanford, Burrows, Massarella, Driver, D.Hunt, Napier, Lewis					
05 Nov. 1938	Newcastle United	Division 2	0–2		25358
Goodfellow, Ashley, Pickering, Russell, Millership, Burrows, Dillon, Robinson, D.Hunt, Napier, Fallon					
07 Nov. 1938	Rotherham United	County Cup s/f	4–1	Hunt 4(9, 28, 32, 55)	n/k
Goodfellow, Ashley, Pickering, Russell, Millership, Packard, Dillon, Driver, D.Hunt, Lowes, Fallon					
19 Nov. 1938	Norwich City	Division 2	7–0	Hunt 6(17, 25, 39, 44, 65, 87), Fallon(80)	16963
Goodfellow, Ashley, Lester, Russell, Hanford, Burrows, Massarella, Robinson, D.Hunt, Napier, Fallon					
03 Dec. 1938	Plymouth Argyle	Division 2	1–2	Hanford(83)	22144
Goodfellow, Ashley, Lester, Russell, Hanford, Burrows, Massarella, Robinson, D.Hunt, Napier, Fallon					
17 Dec. 1938	Burnley	Division 2	4–1	Robinson(20), Massarella(59), Fallon(76), Hunt(80)pen.	12259
Goodfellow, Ashley, Lester, Russell, Hanford, Burrows, Massarella, Robinson, D.Hunt, Napier, Fallon					
27 Dec. 1938	Fulham	Division 2	5–1	Lewis 2(38, 51), Millership(9), Keeping(85)og., Robinson(88)	46743
Goodfellow, Ashley, Lester, Russell, Hanford, Burrows, Massarella, Robinson, Millership, Napier, Lewis					
31 Dec. 1938	West Ham United	Division 2	1–4	Millership(31)	29070
Goodfellow, Ashley, Lester, Russell, Hanford, Burrows, Massarella, Robinson, Millership, Napier, Lewis					
07 Jan. 1939	Yeovil & Petters Utd.	F.A.Cup 3	1–1	Robinson(41)	24466
Smith, Ashley, Lester, Russell, Hanford, Burrows, Massarella, Robinson, Millership, Napier, Lewis					
21 Jan. 1939	Chester	F.A.Cup 4	1–1	Millership(18)	29237
Smith, Ashley, Lester, Russell, Hanford, Burrows, Massarella, Robinson, Millership, Napier, Fallon					
04 Feb. 1939	Bradford Park Avenue	Division 2	2–0	Hunt(53), Robinson(55)	25261
Smith, Ashley, Catlin, Russell, Hanford, Burrows, Dillon, Robinson, D.Hunt, Napier, Fallon					
13 Feb. 1939	Chelsea	F.A.Cup 5R	0–0		47549
Smith, Ashley, Catlin, Russell, Hanford, Burrows, Lewis, Robinson, D.Hunt, Napier, Fallon					
18 Feb. 1939	Southampton	Division 2	2–0	Hunt 2(30, 39)	26329
Smith, Ashley, Catlin, Russell, Hanford, Burrows, Dillon, Robinson, D.Hunt, Napier, Lewis					
04 Mar. 1939	Sheffield United	Division 2	1–0	Fallon(78)	48983
Smith, Ashley, Catlin, Russell, Hanford, Burrows, Dillon, Robinson, D.Hunt, Napier, Fallon					
18 Mar. 1939	West Bromwich Albion	Division 2	2–1	Robinson(9), Fallon(16)	31061
Smith, Ashley, Catlin, Russell, Hanford, Burrows, Toseland, Robinson, Millership, Napier, Fallon					
20 Mar. 1939	Chesterfield	Division 2	0–0		18823
Smith, Ashley, Catlin, Russell, Hanford, Burrows, Toseland, Robinson, D.Hunt, Napier, Fallon					
01 Apr. 1939	Luton Town	Division 2	4–1	Hunt(3)pen., Fallon(–), Robinson(52), Toseland(–)	27646
Smith, Ashley, Catlin, Russell, Hanford, Burrows, Toseland, Robinson, D.Hunt, Napier, Fallon					
10 Apr. 1939	Millwall	Division 2	3–1	Napier 2(30, 57), Millership(52)	34804
Smith, Ashley, Catlin, Russell, Hanford, Burrows, Toseland, Robinson, Millership, Napier, Fallon					
15 Apr. 1939	Nottingham Forest	Division 2	1–1	Davies(2)og.	24747
Smith, Ashley, Catlin, Russell, Hanford, Burrows, Toseland, Robinson, Millership, Napier, Fallon					
29 Apr. 1939	Tottenham Hotspur	Division 2	1–0	Napier(68)	27639
Smith, Ashley, Catlin, Russell, Hanford, Burrows, Toseland, Lowes, D.Hunt, Napier, Fallon					

OTHER GAMES AT HILLSBOROUGH

13 Aug. 1938	Public Trial Match	Stripes 4	Whites 2	4841
18 Feb. 1939	F.A.Cup 5–2nd replay	Blackburn Rovers 1	Sunderland 0	30217
07 Apr. 1939	Representative	Sheffield City Police 2	Royal Ulster Constabulary 1	n/k
11 Apr. 1939	Boys	Sheffield 1	South London 2	7500

Date	Opponents	Competition	Score	Scorers	Att.
19 Aug. 1939	Sheffield United	Friendly	2–4	Napier(57), Toseland(89)	11378
Smith, Ashley, Catlin, Russell, Hanford, Burrows, Toseland, Robinson, D.Hunt, Napier, Massarella					
28 Aug. 1939	Barnsley	Division 2	3–1	Napier 2(14, 80), Hunt(55)	23810
Smith, Ashley, Catlin, F.Walker, Hanford, Burrows, Toseland, Robinson, D.Hunt, Napier, Lewis					
02 Sep. 1939	Plymouth Argyle	Division 2	0–1		12079
Smith, Ashley, Catlin, F.Walker, Hanford, Burrows, Toseland, Driver, D.Hunt, Napier, Fallon					
14 Oct. 1939	Huddersfield Town	Friendly	5–4	Millership 2, Ward, Hunt, Massarella	3669
Smith, Ashley, Lester, Russell, Hanford, F.Walker, Toseland, Ward, D.Hunt, Millership, Massarella					
28 Oct. 1939	Notts County	E.Midlands	1–1	Driver	4000
Smith, Ashley, Catlin, Packard, Burrows, Toseland, Driver, D.Hunt, Lowes, Massarella					
18 Nov. 1939	Barnsley	E.Midlands	1–1	Ward(32)	4005
Smith, Ashley, Catlin, Russell, Packard, Burrows, Toseland, Driver, D.Hunt, Ward, Massarella					
02 Dec. 1939	Sheffield United	E.Midlands	2–3	Driver, Millership	5500
Smith, Ashley, Lester, Russell, Packard, Burrows, Toseland, Driver, D.Hunt, Millership, Ward					
16 Dec. 1939	Stoke City	Friendly	1–2	Ward(65)	2708
Smith, Ashley, Lester, Russell, Hanford, F.Walker, Massarella, Robinson, Hunt, Millership, Ward					
23 Dec. 1939	Mansfield Town	E.Midlands	2–0	Ward(30), Millership(–)	2000
Smith, Ashley, Catlin, Russell, Packard, F.Walker, Massarella, Driver, Lowes, Millership, Ward					
26 Dec. 1939	Chesterfield	E.Midlands	2–1	Massarella(35), Driver(67)	5200
Smith, Ashley, Catlin, Russell, Packard, Burrows, Massarella, Driver, D.Hunt, Millership, Ward					
13 Jan. 1940	Rotherham United	E.Midlands	0–1		1700
Smith, Ashley, Lester, Russell, Millership, Burrows, Dillon, Lowes, Hoyle, J.Thompson, Ward					
09 Mar. 1940	Bolton Wanderers	Friendly	3–3	Massarella 2, Millership	2686
Smith, Ashley, Pickering, Russell, Packard, Collett, Ward, Driver, Millership, J.Thompson, Massarella					
23 Mar. 1940	Grimsby Town	E.Midlands	2–1	Thompson 2(33, 44)	3975
Morton, Ashley, Pickering, Russell, Collett, Burrows, Mulrenan, Ward, Hoyle, J.Thompson, Massarella					
06 Apr. 1940	Nottingham Forest	E.Midlands	2–1	Ward(46), Thompson(85)pen.	4641
Morton, Ashley, Pickering, Russell, Collett, Burrows, Mulrenan, J.Thompson, Hoyle, Millership, Ward					
27 Apr. 1940	Leeds United	War North Cup	3–2	Napier 3(15, 30, 77pen.)	9506
Morton, Ashley, Catlin, Russell, Collett, Burrows, Toseland, Robinson, J.Thompson, Napier, Massarella					
04 May 1940	Doncaster Rovers	E.Midlands	1–3	Ward(22)	2000
Morton, Ashley, Catlin, Russell, Collett, Burrows, Massarella, Ward, Hoyle, Millership, Ellison					
09 May 1940	Lincoln City	E.Midlands	2–3	Scholfield(35), Hoyle(70)	752
Morton, Ashley, Catlin, Ward, Packard, Collett, Rogers, Driver, Hoyle, Lowes, Scholfield					

OTHER GAMES AT HILLSBOROUGH

14 Aug. 1939	Public Trial Match	Stripes 2	Whites 1	1857
13 Apr. 1940	Junior Cup Final	Davy Sports 0	Hoyland Law 0	n/k

1939–40
*Millership, Hanford, Ashley,
Smith, Catlin, Burrows;
Robinson, Hunt, Napier,
Fallon, Powell (trainer);
Russell, Lowes.*

Date	Opponents	Competition	Score	Scorers	Att.
31 Aug. 1940	Huddersfield Town	N.Regional	1–0	Wynn(20)	3197
Morton, Russell, Pickering, Ward, Millership, Burrows, Roebuck, Rogers, Wynn, J.Thompson, Scholfield					
04 Sep. 1940	Army XI	Friendly	4–2	Thompson 3, Rogers	n/k
Morton, Bentley, Pickering(Bannister), Lavender, Burgin, Gill, Roebuck, Rogers, J.Thompson, Robinson, Scholfield					
14 Sep. 1940	Notts County	Friendly	3–1	Ward 3(1, 34, 49)	2052
Morton, Westlake, Pickering, Herbert, Millership, Burrows, Roebuck, R.Thompson, Ward, J.Thompson, Scholfield					
28 Sep. 1940	Chesterfield	N.Regional	0–5		3898
Morton, Gill, Pickering, Lowes, Packard, Burrows, Ward, Burgin, Millership, J.Thompson, Scholfield					
12 Oct. 1940	Barnsley	N.Regional	2–2	Thompson 2(4pen., 21)	3525
Turner, Ashley, Pickering, Herbert, Millership, Burrows, Roebuck, Robinson, Ward, J.Thompson, Scholfield					
19 Oct. 1940	Halifax Town	N.Regional	4–2	Thompson 2(35, 68), Scholfield, Millership	2075
Turner, Ashley, Pickering, Russell, Millership, Burrows, Roebuck, Ward, Burgin, J.Thompson, Scholfield					
02 Nov. 1940	Middlesbrough	N.Regional	6–3	J.Thompson 2(38, 48), Robinson 2(13, 29), Ward(44), R.Thompson(89)	1163
Turner, Ashley, Pickering, Gill, Millership, Burrows, R.Thompson, Robinson, Ward, J.Thompson, Scholfield					
16 Nov. 1940	Rotherham United	N.Regional	1–1	Ward(78)	3440
Morton, Ashley, Pickering, Gill, Millership, Burrows, R.Thompson, Rogers, Ward, J.Thompson, Scholfield					
30 Nov. 1940	Bradford Park Avenue	N.Regional	4–3	Robinson 2(35,–), J.Thompson(8), Scholfield(67)	2234
Morton, Ashley, Pickering, Gill, Millership, Burrows, Roebuck, Robinson, Ward, J.Thompson, Scholfield					
25 Dec. 1940	Sheffield United	N.Regional	0–0*		6757
Morton, Ashley, Pickering, Cockroft, Millership, Burrows, Massarella, Rogers, Ward, Curry, Scholfield					
04 Jan. 1941	Rotherham United	N.Regional	4–2	Ward 3(58, 68, 80), Curry(14)	1000
Morton, Ashley, Pickering, Cockroft, Millership, Burrows, Massarella, Curry, Ward, J.Thompson, Scholfield					
15 Mar. 1941	Newcastle United	N.Regional	2–0	Massarella(49), Scholfield(88)	1371
Morton, Gill, Pickering, Cockroft, Millership, Burrows, Massarella, R.Thompson, J.Thompson, Davis, Scholfield					
29 Mar. 1941	Burnley	N.Regional	0–2		1257
Morton, Ashley, Pickering, Cockroft, Millership, Burrows, Massarella, Robinson, Drury, J.Thompson, Scholfield					
12 Apr. 1941	Chesterfield	N.Regional	3–1	Drury(4), Lowes(14), Thompson(36)	4071
Morton, Gill, Pickering, Cockroft, Packard, Davis, Drury, Starling, Lowes, J.Thompson, Massarella					
14 Apr. 1941	Sheffield United	N.Regional	3–1	Starling 2(15, 25), Drury(89)	7606
Morton, Westlake, Pickering, Cockroft, Packard, Herbert, Massarella, Starling, Drury, J.Thompson, Scholfield					
19 Apr. 1941	Nottingham Forest	N.Regional	1–1	Thompson(8)	2378
Smith, Westlake, Pickering, Cockroft, Johnson, Davis, Massarella, Rogers, Drury, J.Thompson, Scholfield					

*Away game switched to Hillsborough due to Blitz damage at Bramall Lane
Note : War League Cup home tie v. York City on 08/02/41 switched to Scunthorpe (2–1 win for Wednesday)

OTHER GAMES AT HILLSBOROUGH

18 Jan. 1941	Representative	Football League 5	British All Stars 3	4409
15 Feb. 1941	League War Cup 1	Sheffield United 2	Rotherham United 3	2214
08 Mar. 1941	League War Cup 2	Sheffield United 3	Hull City 1	1644
22 Mar. 1941	League War Cup 3	Sheffield United 3	Barnsley 1	4776
05 Apr. 1941	League War Cup 4	Sheffield United 2	Newcastle United 0	5745
10 May. 1941	Representative	Army 2	Royal Air Force 5	4836

SEASON 43   1941–42   *Football League North (1st Competition–16th)*

(2nd Competition–not placed as failed to play min. number of games)

Date	Opponents	Competition	Score	Scorers	Att.
30 Aug. 1941	Rotherham United	League North	1–0	Thompson(70)pen.	3679
Morton, Ashley, Catlin, Cockroft, Millership, Herbert, Rogers, Drury, Lowes, J.Thompson, Roebuck					
08 Sep. 1941	Army XI	Friendly	5–2	Ward 2, Drury 2, Cockroft pen.	n/k
McCabe, Laking, Pickering, Cockroft, Millership, Herbert, Rogers, Drury, Hanks, Ward, Roebuck					
20 Sep. 1941	Grimsby Town	League North	0–2		3534
Morton, Ashley, Laking, Cockroft, Millership, Gill, Wynn, Drury, Hanks, J.Thompson, Roebuck					
27 Sep. 1941	Lincoln City	League North	1–1	Melling	3959
R.Smith, Ashley, Pickering, Cockroft, Millership, Herbert, Rogers, Drury, Melling, J.Thompson, Roebuck					
18 Oct. 1941	Doncaster Rovers	League North	5–2	Drury 2(65, 87), Roebuck(40), Lowes(46), Melling(75)	940
R.Smith, Ashley, Laking, Cockroft, Packard, Herbert, Drury, Lowes, Melling, J.Thompson, Roebuck					
25 Oct. 1941	Sheffield United	League North	1–3	Millership(67)	8907
R.Smith, Ashley, Laking, Cockroft, Millership, Herbert, Drury, Robinson, Melling, J.Thompson, Roebuck					
15 Nov. 1941	Mansfield Town	League North	2–0	Melling 2(2, 13)	2305
Morton, Laking, Pickering, Cockroft, Millership, Herbert, Rogers, Drury, Melling, J.Thompson, Roebuck					
22 Nov. 1941	Chesterfield	League North	1–1	Robinson(75)	3591
Morton, Gill, Pickering, Cockroft, Millership, Herbert, Driver, Robinson, Melling, J.Thompson, Scholfield					
13 Dec. 1941	Barnsley	League North	3–0	Melling 2(35, –), Burgin	2806
McCabe, Laking, Pickering, Cockroft, Millership, Herbert, Rogers, C.Walker, Melling, Burgin, Roebuck					
20 Dec. 1941	Newcastle United	League North	4–2	Herbert pen., Rogers, Melling, Drury(64)	3375
Morton, Gill, Pickering, Cockroft, Millership, Herbert, Rogers, Driver, Melling, Burgin, Drury					

2nd Competition

Date	Opponents	Competition	Score	Scorers	Att.
27 Dec. 1941	Everton	League North	0–3*		11721
Morton, Laking, Pickering, Cockroft, Packard, Herbert, Drury, Robinson, Melling, Millership, Scholfield					
10 Jan. 1942	Bradford City	League North	0–1*		3884
Morton, Ashley, Pickering, Cockroft, Millership, Herbert, Howsam, Robinson, Melling, Lowes, Drury					
21 Feb. 1942	Burnley	League North	3–1*	Thompson, Rogers, Melling	1472
Morton, Laking, Pickering, Cockroft, Millership, Herbert, Rogers, Padgett, Melling, J.Thompson, Drury					
21 Mar. 1942	Bury	League North	2–2*	Burgin(60), Thompson(79)	2850
Morton, Ashley, Pickering, Cockroft, Millership, Herbert, Rogers, Padgett, Burgin, J.Thompson, A.Smith					
11 Apr. 1942	Leicester City	League North	4–1	Melling 2, Nelson, Howsam	3416
Morton, Laking, Pickering, Cockroft, Millership, Herbert, Rogers, Burgin, Melling, Nelson, Howsam					
09 May 1942	Nottingham Forest	League North	3–1	Burgin(25), Driver(30), Thompson	2402
McCabe, Westlake, Pickering, Cockroft, Millership, Herbert, Rogers, Driver, Burgin, J.Thompson, Swift					

*War Cup qualifying competition

OTHER GAMES AT HILLSBOROUGH

Date	Opponents	Competition	Score	Scorers	Att.
04 Apr. 1942	Representative	England 4	Scotland 1		28657

Date	Opponents	Competition	Score	Scorers	Att.
05 Sep. 1942	Doncaster Rovers	League North	3–2	Thompson 2, Melling	3817
Morton, Laking, Catlin, Herbert, Millership, Cockroft, Reynolds, Burgin, Melling, J.Thompson, Swift					
12 Sep. 1942	Rotherham United	League North	4–1	Melling 3(40, –, 75), Cockroft pen.	5070
Morton, Westlake, Catlin, Herbert, Millership, Cockroft, Reynolds, R.Thompson, Melling, Burgin, Swift					
26 Sep. 1942	Bradford Park Avenue	League North	1–0	Cockroft(80)pen.	5870
Morton, Ashley, Catlin, Russell, Millership, Cockroft, Reynolds, Robinson, Melling, J.Thompson, Swift					
17 Oct. 1942	Grimsby Town	League North	2–0	Vincent(26)og., Melling(65)	7703
Morton, Ashley, Catlin, Gill, Millership, Herbert, Reynolds, Robinson, Melling, J.Thompson, Swift					
24 Oct. 1942	Barnsley	League North	5–1	Robinson 2(15, 40), Thompson 2(–, 66) Melling(55)	7550
Morton, Ashley, Catlin, Herbert, Millership, Cockroft, Reynolds, Robinson, Melling, J.Thompson, Swift					
07 Nov. 1942	Mansfield Town	League North	9–1	Burgin 4(30, 47, 64, 70), Robinson 3(20, 48, 51) Thompson(63), Swift(78)	9569
Morton, Ashley, Catlin, Herbert, Millership, Cockroft, Reynolds, Robinson, Burgin, J.Thompson, Swift					
28 Nov. 1942	Notts County	League North	3–1	Robinson 3(2, 44, 45)	9776
Morton, Ashley, Catlin, Herbert, Millership, Cockroft, Reynolds, Robinson, Melling, J.Thompson, Swift					
12 Dec. 1942	Chesterfield	League North	6–0	Melling 3, Swift 2, Reynolds	10876
Morton, Ashley, Catlin, Russell, Millership, Cockroft, Reynolds, Robinson, Melling, Herbert, Swift					
19 Dec. 1942	Sheffield United	League North	4–0	Robinson 2, Reynolds(19), Melling(82)	18942
Morton, Ashley, Catlin, Herbert, Millership, Cockroft, Reynolds, Robinson, Melling, Rogers, Swift					

2nd Competition

Date	Opponents	Competition	Score	Scorers	Att.
26 Dec. 1942	Lincoln City	League North	4–3*	Robinson 3(–, 10, 80), Reynolds(35)	19787
Morton, Ashley, Catlin, Gill, Millership, Cockroft, Reynolds, Robinson, Melling, J.Thompson, Swift					
16 Jan. 1943	Nottingham Forest	League North	1–1*	Thompson(17)	9983
Morton, Ashley, Catlin, Herbert, Millership, Cockroft, Reynolds, Robinson, Melling, J.Thompson, Swift					
23 Jan. 1943	Rotherham United	League North	3–2*	Robinson 3(35, –, 80)	10068
Morton, Ashley, Catlin, Gill, Millership, Cockroft, Reynolds, Robinson, Melling, J.Thompson, Swift					
13 Feb. 1943	Sheffield United	League North	8–2*	Robinson 3(12, 20, 67), Melling 2(25, 69), Thompson 2(15, 40), Reynolds(35)	18232
Morton, Ashley, Catlin, Russell, Millership, Cockroft, Reynolds, Robinson, Melling, J.Thompson, Swift					
20 Feb. 1943	Grimsby Town	League North	2–2*	Melling, Cockroft pen.	12852
Morton, Ashley, Catlin, Russell, Millership, Cockroft, Reynolds, Froggatt, Melling, J.Thompson, Swift					
06 Mar. 1943	Bradford City	Lge/War Cup1	1–0	Reynolds(77)	17588
Morton, Ashley, Catlin, Gill, Millership, Cockroft, Reynolds, Melling, Everitt, J.Thompson, Swift					
27 Mar. 1943	Nottingham Forest	Lge/War Cup2	5–1	Melling 4, Robinson	23518
Morton, Ashley, Catlin, Russell, Millership, Cockroft, Reynolds, Robinson, Melling, J.Thompson, Swift					
03 Apr. 1943	Sheffield United	Lge/War Cup3	3–2	Robinson 2(25, 67), Melling(81)	37550
Morton, Ashley, Catlin, Russell, Millership, Cockroft, Reynolds, Robinson, Melling, J.Thompson, Swift					
17 Apr. 1943	York City	Lge/W. Cup s/f	3–0	Robinson 2(6, 23), Hodgson og.	35253
Smith, Westlake, Catlin, Russell, Millership, Cockroft, Reynolds, Robinson, Ardron, J.Thompson, Swift					
08 May 1943	Blackpool	War Cup Final	1–2	Robinson	47657
Morton, Ashley, Gadsby, Russell, Millership, Cockroft, Reynolds, Robinson, Melling, J.Thompson, Swift					

*League Cup qualifying competition

_1943_
Taylor (sec. manager), Russell, Ashley, Millership, Morton, Gadsby, Cockroft, Catlin; Reynolds, Robinson, Melling, Thompson, Swift, Powell (trainer).

Date	Opponents	Competition	Score	Scorers	Att.
04 Sep. 1943	Barnsley	League North	3–1	Ward(13), Robinson, Thompson	10252
Morton, Ashley, Catlin, Russell, Herbert, Cockroft, Reynolds, Robinson, Ward, J.Thompson, Swift					
11 Sep. 1943	Doncaster Rovers	League North	2–2	Ward(7), Millership(87)	8365
Wiseman, Ashley, Pickering, Russell, Millership, Herbert, Reynolds, Robinson, Ward, J.Thompson, Swift					
02 Oct. 1943	Bradford Park Avenue	League North	2–3	Ward(2), Swift(67)	10120
Morton, Ashley, Catlin, Russell, Millership, Herbert, Fox, Ward, Beddows, J.Thompson, Swift					
16 Oct. 1943	Rotherham United	League North	1–1	Beddows	9846
Drury, Ashley, Catlin, Herbert, Millership, Cockroft, Fox, Robinson, Beddows, Hinsley, Driver					
23 Oct. 1943	Grimsby Town	League North	2–3	Ward(14), Robinson(40)pen.	11806
Morton, Ashley, Catlin, Herbert, Millership, Cockroft, Fox, Robinson, Ward, Napier, Swift					
13 Nov. 1943	Mansfield Town	League North	2–3	Wright(–), Rogers(50)	9721
Drury, Ashley, Catlin, Herbert, Millership, Cockroft, Fox, Rogers, Wright, Froggatt, Swift					
20 Nov. 1943	Notts County	League North	1–0	Wright(81)	8251
Morton, Ashley, Catlin, Russell, Millership, Cockroft, Reynolds, Rogers, Wright, Froggatt, Barton					
04 Dec. 1943	Chesterfield	League North	5–0	Robinson 2, Ashley, Barton, Rogers	8872
Wilkinson, Westlake, Catlin, Russell, Millership, Cockroft, Barton, Robinson, Ashley, Rogers, Woodhead					
18 Dec. 1943	Sheffield United	League North	0–2		12855
Wilkinson, Ashley, Catlin, Russell, Herbert, Cockroft, Burton, Robinson, Wright, Rogers, Froggatt					
01 Jan. 1944	Chesterfield	League North	3–1*	Russell(19), Ashley(32), Rogers(34)	12195
Wilkinson, Westlake, Catlin, Russell, Herbert, Cockroft, Reynolds, Rogers, Ashley, Wright, Froggatt					
08 Jan. 1944	Nottingham Forest	League North	0–0*		11137
Wilkinson, Westlake, Catlin, Russell, Herbert, Cockroft, Reynolds, Rogers, Ashley, Wright, Froggatt					
22 Jan. 1944	Derby County	League North	3–1*	Reynolds(8), Wright(33), Froggatt(–)	8482
Gadsby, Westlake, Catlin, Russell, Herbert, Cockroft, Reynolds, Rogers, Ashley, Wright, Froggatt					
12 Feb. 1944	Leicester City	League North	0–3*		19320
Morton, Westlake, Catlin, Russell, Millership, Cockroft, Rogers, Robinson, D.Hunt, Wright, Froggatt					
19 Feb. 1944	Notts County	League North	2–0*	Cockroft(17)pen., Wright(62)	10070
Curnow, Westlake, Catlin, Russell, Millership, Cockroft, Reynolds, Rogers, Robinson, Wright, Froggatt					
11 Mar. 1944	Bradford Park Avenue	League North	1–2	Rogers	12830
Curnow, Westlake, Catlin, Russell, Herbert, Cockroft, Reynolds, Rogers, Millership, Wright, Lowes					
25 Mar. 1944	Rotherham United	League North	0–0		10213
Curnow, Ashley, Catlin, Herbert, Millership, Cockroft, Massarella, Rogers, Ibbotson, Ward, Froggatt					
08 Apr. 1944	Lincoln City	League North	2–0	Driver(53), Massarella(80)pen.	8000
Donaldson, Swift, Catlin, Herbert, Millership, Cockroft, Massarella, Rogers, Driver, R.Thompson, Froggatt					
10 Apr. 1944	Huddersfield Town	League North	2–2	Massarella 2(21, 75pen.)	10555
Donaldson, Swift, Brown, Goodson, Ashley, Pickering, Massarella, Rogers, Ibbotson, R.Thompson, Froggatt					
15 Apr. 1944	Huddersfield Town	League North	2–1	Rogers(3), Massarella(85)	9230
Donaldson, Ashley, Swift, Goodson, Millership, Pickering, Massarella, Rogers, Ibbotson, Fox, Froggatt					
29 Apr. 1944	York City	League North	2–1	Froggatt(13), Rogers(–)	5180
Donaldson, Westlake, Swift, Cockroft, Herbert, Pickering, Massarella, Rogers, Ibbotson, Froggatt, McCarter					

*League Cup qualifying competition

OTHER GAMES AT HILLSBOROUGH

29 Jan. 1944	Senior Cup s/f	Frickley Colliery 3	Royal Army Signal Corps 3	n/k
22 Apr. 1944	Junior Cup Final	Atlas & Norfolk 2	Thorncliffe Welfare 4	n/k

SEASON 46   1944–45   Football League North (1st Competition–23rd) (2nd Competition–33rd)

Date	Opponents	Competition	Score	Scorers	Att.
19 Aug. 1944	Huddersfield Town	Friendly	3–2	Froggatt 2, Tomlinson	3767
Gadsby, Swift, Catlin, Goodson, Millership, Cockroft, Froggatt, Lowes, Ibbotson, J.Thompson, Tomlinson					
26 Aug. 1944	Sheffield United	League North	1–1	Ward(17)	17888
Gadsby, Swift, Catlin, Goodson, Millership, Cockroft, Massarella, Robinson, Ward, Froggatt, Tomlinson					
16 Sep. 1944	Notts County	League North	6–1	Massarella 2, Thompson 2, Froggatt, Catlin	9430
Gadsby, Swift, Catlin, Goodson, Millership, Cockroft, Massarella, Froggatt, Ibbotson, J.Thompson, Tomlinson					
23 Sep. 1944	Chesterfield	League North	0–1		10459
Gadsby, Swift, Catlin, Herbert, Millership, Cockroft, Massarella, Froggatt, Driver, J.Thompson, Tomlinson					
14 Oct. 1944	Mansfield Town	League North	1–6	Massarella	7908
Donaldson, Westlake, Catlin, Cockroft, Turton, Pickering, Massarella, Driver, Ibbotson, Fox, Tomlinson					
21 Oct. 1944	Rotherham United	League North	1–0	Robinson(49)	16321
White, Swift, Pickering, Ward, Millership, Cockroft, Fox, Robinson, Wright, J.Thompson, Tomlinson					
11 Nov. 1944	Lincoln City	League North	2–1	Massarella(52), Cockroft(–)	9332
Wakley, Swift, Pickering, Ward, Millership, Cockroft, Massarella, Rogers, Wright, Fox, Tomlinson					
02 Dec. 1944	Nottingham Forest	League North	2–1	Hawkswell(7), Tomlinson(42)	8092
Wakley, Swift, Pickering, Ward, Millership, Cockroft, Rogers, Robinson, Hawkswell, Fox, Tomlinson					
23 Dec. 1944	Barnsley	League North	5–0	Tomlinson 2, Rogers, Hawkswell, Robinson	10000
Wakley, Catlin, Pickering, Ward, Turton, Cockroft, Massarella, Rogers, Hawkswell, Robinson, Tomlinson					
25 Dec. 1944	Sheffield United	League North	1–2*	Hawkswell(80)	18580
Wakley, Swift, Pickering, Ward, Turton, Cockroft, Kippax, Robinson, Hawkswell, Fox, Tomlinson					
13 Jan. 1945	Grimsby Town	League North	2–2*	Hawkswell(4), Scholfield(70)	5539
White, Swift, Pickering, Turton, Millership, Cockroft, Froggatt, Fox, Hawkswell, Tomlinson, Scholfield					
20 Jan. 1945	Rotherham United	League North	1–4*	Thompson	6501
White, Swift, Pickering, Turton, Millership, Cockroft, Froggatt, Robinson, J.Thompson, Fox, Tomlinson					
10 Feb. 1945	Doncaster Rovers	League North	1–6*	Herbert	13804
White, Swift, Pickering, Ward, Millership, Cockroft, Massarella, Robinson, Herbert, J.Thompson, Tomlinson					
24 Feb. 1945	Lincoln City	League North	1–3*	Lowes(21)	5859
Wakley, Beach, Pickering, Turton, Herbert, Cockroft, Fox, Rogers, Lowes, J.Thompson, Tomlinson					
10 Mar. 1945	Doncaster Rovers	League North	1–0**	Froggatt	8827
Parkin, Swift, Pickering, Goodson, Turton, Cockroft, Fox, Herbert, Lindsay, Froggatt, Tomlinson					
17 Mar. 1945	Leeds United	League North	1–1	Rogers(11)	7941
Parkin, Swift, Pickering, Goodson, Turton, Cockroft, Bates, Rogers, Lindsay, Froggatt, Tomlinson					
31 Mar. 1945	Blacburn Rovers	League North	2–0	Lindsay, Thompson	9178
Parkin, Ashley, Pickering, Goodson, Hanford, Cockroft, Bates, R.Thompson, Lindsay, Froggatt, Tomlinson					
14 Apr. 1945	Halifax Town	League North	7–0	Lindsay 3, Tomlinson 2, Turton, Rogers	4819
Parkin, Swift, Pickering, Turton, Gale, Cockroft, Bates, Rogers, Lindsay, Froggatt, Tomlinson					
21 Apr. 1945	Bradford Park Avenue	League North	3–1	Robinson 2, Tomlinson	10237
Parkin, Swift, Pickering, Turton, Gale, Cockroft, Rogers, Robinson, Lindsay, Froggatt, Tomlinson					
12 May 1945	Barnsley	League North	4–1**	Lindsay 2, Rogers, Froggatt	9155
Smith, Ashley, Swift, Turton, Gale, Cockroft, Bates, Rogers, Lindsay, Froggatt, Tomlinson					
26 May 1945	Sheffield United	League North	4–2**	Tomlinson 2(15, –), Robinson(3), Lindsay	15464
Medhurst, Ashley, Swift, Turton, Gale, Cockroft, Rogers, Robinson, Lindsay, Froggatt, Tomlinson					

*League Cup qualifying competition
**Sheffield County Cup
Note: League North home game v. Grimsby Town on 25/11/44 switched to Doncaster (3–2 defeat for Wednesday)

OTHER GAMES AT HILLSBOROUGH

25 Nov. 1944	Representative	Scotland 7	Royal Air Force 1	40172

1944–45
Swift, Goodson, Catlin, Gadsby, Millership, Cockroft; Massarella, Robinson, Ward, Froggatt, Tomlinson.

Date	Opponents	Competition	Score	Scorers	Att.
25 Aug. 1945	Sunderland	League North	6–3	Robinson 3(6pen, 35, 60), Rogers 3(30, 44, 46)	19219
Morton, Swift, Pickering, Turton, Gale, Cockroft, Rogers, Robinson, Lindsay, Froggatt, Tomlinson					
15 Sep. 1945	Sheffield United	League North	2–1	Robinson 2(66, 80)	32512
Morton, Swift, Pickering, Turton, Gale, Cockroft, Froggatt, Robinson, Lindsay, Napier, Tomlinson					
22 Sep. 1945	Middlesbrough	League North	2–1	Froggatt(30), Lindsay(55)	20334
Morton, Swift, Pickering, Turton, Gale, Cockroft, Ward, Robinson, Lindsay, Froggatt, Tomlinson					
13 Oct. 1945	Stoke City	League North	1–0	Lindsay(15)	33389
Morton, Swift, Pickering, Turton, Gale, Cockroft, Rogers, Robinson, Lindsay, Froggatt, Tomlinson					
20 Oct. 1945	Grimsby Town	League North	4–1	J.Thompson 2(39, 50), Lindsay(60), Rogers(85)pen.	18000
Morton, Swift, Pickering, Turton, Gale, Cockroft, Rogers, R.Thompson, Lindsay, J.Thompson, Tomlinson					
10 Nov. 1945	Blackpool	League North	3–2	Robinson 2(41, –), Lindsay(16)	25619
Morton, Swift, Pickering, Turton, Packard, Cockroft, Rogers, Robinson, Lindsay, Froggatt, Tomlinson					
17 Nov. 1945	Liverpool	League North	2–3	Rogers(7), Froggatt(27)	23514
Morton, Swift, Pickering, Turton, Gale, Cockroft, Rogers, R.Thompson, Lindsay, Froggatt, Tomlinson					
08 Dec. 1945	Bury	League North	2–0	Cockroft(74)pen., Lindsay(–)	16963
Morton, Swift, Pickering, Turton, Gale, Cockroft, Fox, R.Thompson, Lindsay, Froggatt, Tomlinson					
15 Dec. 1945	Blackburn Rovers	League North	1–1	Cockroft(80)	17768
Goodfellow, Swift, Pickering, Turton, Gale, Cockroft, Fox, Robinson, Lindsay, Lowes, Tomlinson					
26 Dec. 1945	Bradford Park Avenue	League North	3–0	Robinson 2(47, –pen.), Froggatt(50)	32078
Goodfellow, Swift, Pickering, Turton, Gale, Wands, Ward, Robinson, Lindsay, Froggatt, Tomlinson					
29 Dec. 1945	Manchester City	League North	1–1	Tomlinson(30)	24684
Goodfellow, Swift, Pickering, Turton, Gale, Wands, R.Thompson, Lindsay, Froggatt, Tomlinson					
10 Jan. 1946	Mansfield Town	F.A.Cup 3–L2	5–0	Thompson(35), Ward(60), Froggatt(68), Aveyard(69), Tomlinson(77)	22208
Goodfellow, Swift, Pickering, Cockroft, Stewart, Wands, Ward, J.Thompson, Aveyard, Froggatt, Tomlinson					
19 Jan. 1946	Burnley	League North	1–1	Hunt(2)	15109
Goodfellow, Swift, Pickering, Cockroft, Gale, Wands, Ward, J.Thompson, Aveyard, D.Hunt, Tomlinson					
26 Jan. 1946	York City	F.A.Cup 4–L1	5–1	Driver 2(7, 75), Thompson, Aveyard, Froggatt	33363
Goodfellow, Swift, Pickering, Cockroft, Gale, Wands, Driver, J.Thompson, Aveyard, Froggatt, Tomlinson					
04 Feb. 1946	Huddersfield Town	League North	3–0	Lindsay(7), Froggatt(85), Tomlinson(89)	10090
Wakley, Westlake, Swift, Cockroft, Gale, Wands, Driver, Ward, Lindsay, Froggatt, Tomlinson					
11 Feb. 1946	Stoke City	F.A.Cup 5–L2	0–0		62728
Goodfellow, Swift, Pickering, Cockroft, Gale, Wands, Driver, Robinson, Aveyard, Froggatt, Tomlinson					
16 Feb. 1946	Chesterfield	League North	1–0	Tomlinson(9)	31304
Goodfellow, Swift, Westlake, Turton, Gale, Cockroft, Tomlinson, Driver, D.Hunt, Froggatt, McCarter					
23 Feb. 1946	Barnsley	League North	0–3		24657
Goodfellow, Swift, Westlake, Turton, Gale, Cockroft, Tomlinson, Driver, D.Hunt, Froggatt, McCarter					
16 Mar. 1946	Everton	League North	0–0		27301
Goodfellow, Swift, Pickering, Cockroft, Gale, Wands, Kippax, J.Thompson, Ward, Froggatt, Tomlinson					
01 Apr. 1946	Bolton Wanderers	League North	0–0		13500
Goodfellow, Swift, Pickering, Turton, Packard, MacKenzie, Kippax, Robinson, Ward, Froggatt, Tomlinson					
13 Apr. 1946	Preston North End	League North	2–0	Robinson 2(6, –)	16804
Goodfellow, Westlake, Swift, Cockroft, Packard, Wands, Kippax, Driver, Ward, Robinson, Tomlinson					
15 Apr. 1946	Sheffield United	County Cup	1–0	Robinson(40)	18060
Goodfellow, Westlake, Swift, Cockroft, Packard, Wands, Kippax, Driver, Ward, Robinson, Tomlinson					
23 Apr. 1946	Leeds United	League North	2–0	Wands(10), Robinson(77)pen.	14000
Goodfellow, Westlake, Swift, Cockroft, Packard, Wands, Fox, Froggatt, Lindsay, Robinson, Tomlinson					
27 Apr. 1946	Manchester United	League North	1–0	Robinson(48)	12000
Goodfellow, Westlake, Swift, Cockroft, Packard, Wands, Kippax, Froggatt, Lindsay, Robinson, Tomlinson					
04 May 1946	Newcastle United	League North	2–3	Kippax(50), Robinson(67)pen.	20000
Goodfellow, Westlake, Swift, Cockroft, Packard, Wands, Kippax, Froggatt, Lindsay, Robinson, Tomlinson					
11 May 1946	Barnsley	C. Cup Final	1–0	Kippax(76)	18249
Goodfellow, Sanders, Swift, Cockroft, Turton, Wands, Kippax, Driver, Ward, Robinson, Tomlinson					

OTHER GAMES AT HILLSBOROUGH :

23 Mar. 1946	F.A.Cup Semi Final	Birmingham City 1	Derby County 1		65013

Date	Opponents	Competition	Score	Scorers	Att.
02 Sep. 1946	Barnsley	Division 2	2–4	Ward(45), Lindsay(48)	30028
Goodfellow, Westlake, Swift, Cockroft, Packard, Lowes, Ward, Robinson, Lindsay, Froggatt, Tomlinson					
07 Sep. 1946	Plymouth Argyle	Division 2	2–1	Robinson(11), Aveyard(30)	27326
Goodfellow, Westlake, Swift, Cockroft, Packard, Lowes, Ward, Robinson, Aveyard, Froggatt, Tomlinson					
16 Sep. 1946	Fulham	Division 2	1–1	Robinson(51)	21000
Smith, Westlake, Swift, Cockroft, Turton, Wands, Froggatt, Robinson, Ward, Lowes, Tomlinson					
21 Sep. 1946	Chesterfield	Division 2	0–1		28476
Smith, Swift, Kenny, Cockroft, Turton, Wands, Froggatt, Robinson, Ward, Lowes, Tomlinson					
05 Oct. 1946	Bradford Park Avenue	Division 2	1–2	Froggatt(73)	20590
Smith, Swift, Kenny, Cockroft, Turton, Wands, Rogers, Lowes, Aveyard, Froggatt, McCarter					
19 Oct. 1946	Burnley	Division 2	1–2	Briscoe(70)	22083
Smith, Swift, Kenny, Packard, Stewart, Wands, Froggatt, Lowes, Briscoe, Cockroft, McCarter					
02 Nov. 1946	Swansea Town	Division 2	3–0	Lowes 2(78, 82), Briscoe(51)	22793
Smith, Swift, Kenny, Packard, Stewart, Cockroft, Fox, Lowes, Briscoe, Froggatt, McCarter					
16 Nov. 1946	West Bromwich Albion	Division 2	2–2	Lowes(79)pen., Dailey(85)	23964
Smith, Swift, Kenny, Packard, Stewart, Cockroft, Froggatt, G.Hunt, Dailey, Lowes, Tomlinson					
30 Nov. 1946	Coventry City	Division 2	4–2	Dailey 2(3, 48), Hunt(60), Ward(77)	24590
Smith, Swift, Kenny, MacKenzie, Packard, Lowes, Froggatt, G.Hunt, Dailey, Ward, Tomlinson					
09 Dec. 1946	Copenhagen Combination	Friendly	2–3	Ward 2(15, 22)	7000
Smith, Swift, Kenny, MacKenzie, Packard, Lowes, Froggatt, G.Hunt, Dailey, Ward, Slynn					
14 Dec. 1946	Southampton	Division 2	3–0	Ward 2(9, 88), Dailey(80)	15404
Smith, Westlake, Swift, MacKenzie, Packard, Lowes, Froggatt, G.Hunt, Dailey, Ward, Slynn					
26 Dec. 1946	Bury	Division 2	2–5	Dailey(60), Hunt(73)	41183
Smith, Westlake, Kenny, Lowes, Packard, Bannister, Froggatt, G.Hunt, Dailey, Ward, Slynn					
28 Dec. 1946	Luton Town	Division 2	1–1	Ward(87)	29495
Goodfellow, Westlake, Swift, Logan, Packard, Wands, Froggatt, Ward, G.Hunt, Lowes, Slynn					
01 Jan. 1947	West Ham United	Division 2	1–1	Wands(–)	31192
Goodfellow, Westlake, Swift, Logan, Packard, Wands, Froggatt, G.Hunt, Lowes, Ward, Slynn					
11 Jan. 1947	Blackpool	F.A.Cup 3	4–1	Froggatt 2(40, 47), Fox(15), Wands(78)	31240
Smith, Westlake, Swift, Cockroft, Gale, Wands, Fox, G.Hunt, Dailey, Froggatt, Slynn					
18 Jan. 1947	Leicester City	Division 2	1–3	Dailey(6)	34858
Smith, Westlake, Swift, Cockroft, Gale, Wands, Ward, G.Hunt, Dailey, Froggatt, Slynn					
25 Jan. 1947	Everton	F.A.Cup 4	2–1	Froggatt(5), Tomlinson(9)	62250
Smith, Westlake, Swift, Cockroft, Gale, Logan, R.Thompson, G.Hunt, Dailey, Froggatt, Tomlinson					
01 Feb. 1947	Millwall	Division 2	3–0	Ward(49), Hunt(51), Dailey(59)	25082
Smith, Westlake, Swift, Ward, Gale, Logan, Slynn, G.Hunt, Dailey, Froggatt, Tomlinson					
20 Feb. 1947	Preston North End	F.A.Cup 5	0–2		50247
Smith, Westlake, Swift, Ward, Gale, Logan, Slynn, G.Hunt, Dailey, Froggatt, Tomlinson					
01 Mar. 1947	Tottenham Hotspur	Division 2	5–1	Dailey 3(2, 30, 61), Tomlinson(60), Hunt(66)	23114
Smith, Westlake, Swift, Witcomb, Gale, Cockroft, Slynn, G.Hunt, Dailey, Froggatt, Tomlinson					
29 Mar. 1947	Birmingham City	Division 2	1–0	Harris(35)og.	27500
Smith, Westlake, Swift, Witcomb, Packard, Cockroft, Marriott, G.Hunt, Dailey, Froggatt, Slynn					
12 Apr. 1947	Nottingham Forest	Division 2	2–0	Ward(16), Slynn(55)	30092
Smith, Westlake, Swift, Witcomb, Packard, Cockroft, Marriott, G.Hunt, Ward, Froggatt, Slynn					
26 Apr. 1947	Newport County	Division 2	2–1	Tomlinson(59), Cockroft(61)pen.	21564
Smith, Westlake, Swift, Witcomb, Packard, Cockroft, Marriott, G.Hunt, Ward, Tomlinson, Slynn					
24 May 1947	Newcastle United	Division 2	1–1	Ward(33)	28405
Smith, Westlake, Swift, Witcomb, Packard, Cockroft, Slynn, G.Hunt, Ward, Tomlinson, Woodhead					
26 May 1947	Manchester City	Division 2	1–0	Ward(17)	33390
Smith, Westlake, Swift, Witcomb, Packard, Cockroft, Slynn, G.Hunt, Ward, Tomlinson, Woodhead					

OTHER GAMES AT HILLSBOROUGH

Date	Match	Home	Away	Att.
26 Aug. 1946	Public Trial Match	Stripes 1	Whites 2	4079
29 Aug. 1946	Inter City	Sheffield 0	Eindhoven 1	6760
31 Oct. 1946	Boys	Sheffield 4	Nottingham 0	5000
08 Apr. 1947	Boys	Sheffield 0	Newcastle 1	5600
17 Apr. 1947	Representative	Sheffield City Police 1	Royal Ulster Constabulary 2	n/k

Date	Opponents	Competition	Score	Scorers	Att.
23 Aug. 1947	Millwall	Division 2	3–2	Ward(35), Froggatt(49), Woodhead(83)	29860
Morton, Westlake, Swift, Witcomb, Turton, Cockroft, Slynn, G.Hunt, Ward, Froggatt, Woodhead					
01 Sep. 1947	Southampton	Division 2	1–2	Dailey(31)	23289
Morton, Westlake, Swift, Witcomb, Turton, Cockroft, Slynn, Lowes, Dailey, Froggatt, Woodhead					
06 Sep. 1947	Barnsley	Division 2	5–2	Dailey 5(4, 42, 60, 68, 87)	33925
Morton, Westlake, Swift, Witcomb, Turton, Cockroft, Slynn, Lowes, Dailey, Froggatt, Woodhead					
13 Sep. 1947	Cardiff City	Division 2	2–1	Woodhead(12), Witcomb(65)	36289
Morton, Westlake, Swift, Witcomb, Turton, Cockroft, Slynn, Lowes, Dailey, Froggatt, Woodhead					
15 Sep. 1947	Bury	Division 2	2–2	Froggatt(3), Dailey(46)	27230
Morton, Westlake, Swift, Witcomb, Turton, Cockroft, Slynn, Lowes, Dailey, Froggatt, Woodhead					
27 Sep. 1947	Nottingham Forest	Division 2	2–1	Lowes(30), Woodhead(75)	33052
Morton, Westlake, Swift, Witcomb, Turton, Cockroft, Slynn, Lowes, Dailey, Froggatt, Woodhead					
18 Oct. 1947	Luton Town	Division 2	1–0	Dailey(80)	40297
Morton, Westlake, Swift, Witcomb, Turton, Cockroft, Slynn, Quigley, Dailey, Froggatt, Woodhead					
01 Nov. 1947	Leicester City	Division 2	1–1	Froggatt(26)	38992
Morton, Westlake, Swift, Witcomb, Turton, Cockroft, Marriott, Quigley, Dailey, Froggatt, Woodhead					
15 Nov. 1947	Fulham	Division 2	2–0	Rogers(17), Quigley(73)	32102
Morton, Westlake, Swift, Witcomb, Packard, Cockroft, Marriott, Rogers, Ward, Quigley, Woodhead					
29 Nov. 1947	Newcastle United	Division 2	1–0	Froggatt(70)	41355
Morton, Westlake, Swift, Witcomb, Turton, Cockroft, Marriott, Quigley, Dailey, Froggatt, Woodhead					
13 Dec. 1947	West Bromwich Albion	Division 2	1–2	Witcomb(62)	36200
Morton, Westlake, Swift, Witcomb, Turton, Cockroft, Marriott, Quigley, Dailey, Froggatt, Woodhead					
26 Dec. 1947	West Ham United	Division 2	5–3	Quigley 4(19, 31, 35, 54), Lowes(50)	37343
Morton, Westlake, Swift, Witcomb, Packard, Cockroft, Slynn, Lowes, Quigley, Froggatt, Woodhead					
03 Jan. 1948	Tottenham Hotspur	Division 2	1–0	Quigley(34)	48007
Smith, Westlake, Swift, Witcomb, Packard, Cockroft, Fox, Lowes, Quigley, Froggatt, Woodhead					
07 Feb. 1948	Bradford Park Avenue	Division 2	3–1	Quigley 2(35, 72), Jordan(68)	36806
Smith, Westlake, Swift, Witcomb, Turton, Cockroft, Ward, Quigley, C.Jordan, Froggatt, Tomlinson					
28 Feb. 1948	Plymouth Argyle	Division 2	1–1	Quigley(70)	27083
Smith, Westlake, Swift, Witcomb, Turton, Cockroft, Fox, Quigley, C.Jordan, Froggatt, Tomlinson					
27 Mar. 1948	Leeds United	Division 2	3–1	Quigley 2(48, 89), Jordan(44)	38557
Smith, Westlake, Swift, Witcomb, Turton, Cockroft, Marriott, Quigley, C.Jordan, Froggatt, Tomlinson					
29 Mar. 1948	Chesterfield	Division 2	1–0	Froggatt(82)	40650
Smith, Westlake, Swift, Witcomb, Turton, Cockroft, Marriott, Quigley, C.Jordan, Froggatt, Tomlinson					
05 Apr. 1948	Doncaster Rovers	Division 2	2–0	Froggatt(41), Quigley(54)	51467
McIntosh, Westlake, Swift, Witcomb, Turton, Cockroft, Marriott, Quigley, C.Jordan, Froggatt, Tomlinson					
10 Apr. 1948	Coventry City	Division 2	1–1	Quigley(10)	38695
McIntosh, Westlake, Swift, Witcomb, Turton, Cockroft, Marriott, Quigley, C.Jordan, Froggatt, Woodhead					
12 Apr. 1948	Brentford	Division 2	1–1	Witcomb(50)pen.	36170
McIntosh, Westlake, Swift, Witcomb, Turton, Cockroft, Marriott, Quigley, C.Jordan, Froggatt, Woodhead					
24 Apr. 1948	Birmingham City	Division 2	0–0		25990
McIntosh, Westlake, Swift, Witcomb, Turton, Cockroft, Marriott, Rogers, C.Jordan, Froggatt, Woodhead					
08 May 1948	Barnsley	County Cup Fl	1–3	Froggatt(53)	22619
McIntosh, Westlake, Swift, Witcomb, Turton, Bannister, Marriott, Quigley, C.Jordan, Froggatt, Woodhead					

OTHER GAMES AT HILLSBOROUGH

30 Oct. 1947	Boys	Sheffield 2	Nottingham 1	3600
10 Jan. 1948	Schools	Sheffield 4	Grimsby 3	n/k
13 Mar. 1948	F.A.Cup Semi Final	Derby County 1	Manchester United 3	60000
30 Mar. 1948	Boys	Sheffield 0	Newcastle 1	20780
01 May 1948	Boys	Sheffield 4	Salford 1	n/k

Date	Opponents	Competition	Score	Scorers	Att.
23 Aug. 1948	West Ham United	Division 2	3–0	Quigley 2(46, 72), Witcomb(51)pen.	35720
McIntosh, Westlake, Swift, Witcomb, Turton, Cockroft, Fox, Quigley, C.Jordan, Froggatt, Woodhead					
28 Aug. 1948	Brentford	Division 2	0–0		36148
McIntosh, Westlake, Swift, Witcomb, Turton, Cockroft, Fox, Quigley, C.Jordan, Froggatt, Woodhead					
11 Sep. 1948	Leeds United	Division 2	3–1	Witcomb(25)pen., Fox(60), Jordan(86)	31479
McIntosh, Westlake, Swfit, Witcomb, Turton, Cockroft, Fox, Quigley, C.Jordan, Froggatt, Woodhead					
13 Sep. 1948	Bury	Division 2	1–2	Quigley(27)	32602
McIntosh, Westlake, Swift, Witcomb, Turton, Cockroft, Fox, Quigley, C.Jordan, Froggatt, Woodhead					
25 Sep. 1948	Southampton	Division 2	2–0	Woodhead 2(65, 68)	38347
McIntosh, Westlake, Swift, Witcomb, Turton, Cockroft, Fox, Quigley, C.Jordan, Froggatt, Woodhead					
02 Oct. 1948	Lincoln City	Division 2	2–2	Froggatt(57), Quigley(85)	42327
McIntosh, Westlake, Swift, Witcomb, Turton, Cockroft, Fox, Quigley, C.Jordan, Froggatt, Woodhead					
16 Oct. 1948	Grimsby Town	Division 2	4–1	Quigley 2(30secs., 66), Froggatt(26), Woodhead(80)	33849
McIntosh, Westlake, Swift, Witcomb, Turton, Cockroft, Fox, Quigley, C.Jordan, Froggatt, Woodhead					
30 Oct. 1948	Fulham	Division 2	1–2	Rogers(65)	33976
McIntosh, Westlake, Swift, Witcomb, Parker, Bannister, Fox, Rogers, C.Jordan, Froggatt, Woodhead					
13 Nov. 1948	Blackburn Rovers	Division 2	3–0	Froggatt(27), Quigley(40), Dailey(63)	29998
McIntosh, Westlake, Swift, Witcomb, Turton, Bannister, Fox, Quigley, Dailey, Froggatt, Woodhead					
27 Nov. 1948	Queen's Park Rangers	Division 2	2–0	Jordan 2(65, 85)	34346
McIntosh, Westlake, Swift, Witcomb, Turton, Bannister, Fox, Quigley, C.Jordan, Froggatt, Woodhead					
11 Dec. 1948	Bradford Park Avenue	Division 2	2–1	Quigley(8), Woodhead(53)	36693
McIntosh, Westlake, Swift, Locherty, Turton, Bannister, Kilshaw, Quigley, C.Jordan, Froggatt, Woodhead					
18 Dec. 1948	Tottenham Hotspur	Division 2	3–1	Jordan 2(37, 51), Woodhead(35)	40251
McIntosh, Westlake, Swift, Locherty, Turton, Bannister, Kilshaw, Quigley, C.Jordan, Froggatt, Woodhead					
27 Dec. 1948	West Bromwich Albion	Division 2	2–1	Tomlinson(52), Quigley(58)	59924
McIntosh, Westlake, Swift, Witcomb, Turton, Bannister, Kilshaw, Quigley, Dailey, Tomlinson, Woodhead					
08 Jan. 1949	Southampton	F.A.Cup 3	2–1	Dailey(25), Quigley(60)	44292
McIntosh, Westlake, Swift, Locherty, Turton, Bannister, Kilshaw, Quigley, Dailey, Froggatt, Woodhead					
15 Jan. 1949	Chelsea	Friendly	2–0	Dailey(8), Woodhead(82)	23114
McIntosh, Westlake, Swift, Locherty, Turton, Bannister(Barnes ht), Kilshaw, Quigley, Dailey, Froggatt, Woodhead					
05 Feb. 1949	Coventry City	Division 2	2–1	Quigley 2(72, 86)	36171
McIntosh, Westlake, Swift, Locherty, Turton, Witcomb, Kilshaw, Rogers, Quigley, Froggatt, Woodhead					
12 Feb. 1949	Sheffield United	County Cup s/f	2–4	Quigley 2(60, 89pen.)	49980
McIntosh, Westlake, Swift, Locherty, Turton, Witcomb, Kilshaw, Rogers, Quigley, Froggatt, Woodhead					
05 Mar. 1949	Barnsley	Division 2	1–1	Froggatt(33)	27725
McIntosh, Westlake, Swift, Witcomb, Turton, Rogers, Kilshaw, Quigley, C.Jordan, Froggatt, Tomlinson					
19 Mar. 1949	Nottingham Forest	Division 2	2–1	Froggatt(31), Woodhead(67)	27870
McIntosh, Westlake, Swift, Gannon, Turton, Witcomb, Kilshaw, Quigley, C.Jordan, Froggatt, Woodhead					
02 Apr. 1949	Plymouth Argyle	Division 2	2–1	Woodhead(6), Jordan(46)	27090
McIntosh, Westlake, Swift, Gannon, Turton, Witcomb, Kilshaw, Fox, C.Jordan, Froggatt, Woodhead					
11 Apr. 1949	Leicester City	Division 2	0–1		25081
McIntosh, Westlake, Swift, Gannon, Turton, Witcomb, Kilshaw, Quigley, Fletcher, Froggatt, Woodhead					
16 Apr. 1949	Cardiff City	Division 2	1–1	Quigley(48)	32374
McIntosh, Swift, Kenny, Gannon, Packard, Bannister, Marriott, Quigley, Fletcher, Froggatt, Woodhead					
19 Apr. 1949	Chesterfield	Division 2	0–0		30293
McIntosh, Swift, Kenny, Gannon, Packard, Witcomb, Marriott, Froggatt, Fletcher, Tomlinson, Woodhead					
30 Apr. 1949	Luton Town	Division 2	0–0		18829
McIntosh, Kenny, Swift, Gannon, Packard, Witcomb, Marriott, Froggatt, C.Jordan, Tomlinson, Woodhead					

OTHER GAMES AT HILLSBOROUGH

14 Aug. 1948	Public Trial Match	Stripes 2		Whites 0	9051
01 Nov. 1948	Boys	Sheffield 4		Nottingham 5	n/k
16 Feb. 1949	Representative	F.A.XI 2		Universities Athletic Union 0	2667
26 Mar. 1949	F.A.Cup Semi Final	Wolverhampton W. 1		Manchester United 1	62250
07 Apr. 1949	Representative	Sheffield Constabulary 0		Royal Ulster Constabulary 0	n/k
25 Apr. 1949	Boys	Sheffield 1		Newcastle 2	2367
04 May 1949	Inter City	Sheffield 3		Eindhoven 1	n/k

1945–46
Robinson, Turton, Pickering, Gale, Lindsay, Wands, Goodfellow, Ward, Froggatt, Swift, Tomlinson.

1946
Cockroft, Swift, Turton, Swift, Kenny, Wands, Powell (trainer); Froggatt, Robinson, Ward, Lowes, Tomlinson.

1947–48
Witcomb, Westlake, Wands, Morton, Swift, Cockroft; Marriott, Quigley, Dailey, Froggatt, Woodhead, Turton.

1948–49
Witcomb, Westlake, McIntosh, Swift, Turton, Cockroft; Fox, Quigley, Jordan, Froggatt, Woodhead.

Date	Opponents	Competition	Score	Scorers	Att.
20 Aug. 1949	Leicester City	Division 2	3–1	Quigley 2(8, 27), Froggatt(11)	35431
McIntosh, Kenny, Swift, Gannon, Packard, Witcomb, Marriott, Quigley, C.Jordan, Froggatt, Woodhead					
29 Aug. 1949	Cardiff City	Division 2	1–1	Froggatt(7)	32873
McIntosh, Kenny, Swift, Gannon, Packard, Witcomb, Fox, Rogers, Fletcher, Froggatt, Marriott					
03 Sep. 1949	Chesterfield	Division 2	4–2	Quigley 4(44, 47, 49, 75)	41159
McIntosh, Kenny, Swift, Gannon, Packard, Witcomb, Fox, Rogers, Quigley, Froggatt, Marriott					
17 Sep. 1949	Sheffield United	Division 2	2–1	Jordan(28), Quigley(39)pen.	55555
McIntosh, Kenny, Swift, Gannon, Packard, Witcomb, Fox, Quigley, C.Jordan, Froggatt, Marriott					
24 Sep. 1949	Hull City	Division 2	6–2	Jordan 4(5, 18, 52, 57), Quigley(20)pen., Froggatt(30)	52869
McIntosh, Kenny, Swift, Gannon, Packard, Witcomb, Marriott, Quigley, C.Jordan, Froggatt, Tomlinson					
15 Oct. 1949	Queen's Park Rangers	Division 2	1–0	Jordan(3)	31748
McIntosh, Kenny, Swift, Gannon, Packard, Witcomb, Marriott, Rogers, C.Jordan, Froggatt, Tomlinson					
29 Oct. 1949	Swansea Town	Division 2	3–0	Rogers(43), Jordan(55), Froggatt(89)	34564
McIntosh, Kenny, Swift, Gannon, Packard, Witcomb, Rickett, Rogers, C.Jordan, Froggatt, Tomlinson					
12 Nov. 1949	Southampton	Division 2	2–2	Froggatt(53), Witcomb(77)	32146
McIntosh, Kenny, Swift, Gannon, Packard, Witcomb, Rickett, Rogers, C.Jordan, Froggatt, Tomlinson					
26 Nov. 1949	Luton Town	Division 2	1–1	Jordan(7)	29533
McIntosh, Kenny, Swift, Rogers, Packard, Witcomb, Rickett, Quigley, C.Jordan, Froggatt, Tomlinson					
10 Dec. 1949	West Ham United	Division 2	2–1	Packard(22), Rogers(32)	26405
McIntosh, Kenny, Swift, Gannon, Packard, Witcomb, Marriott, Rogers, C.Jordan, Froggatt, Rickett					
24 Dec. 1949	Bradford Park Avenue	Division 2	1–1	Woodhead(88)	37851
McIntosh, Kenny, Swift, Gannon, Packard, Witcomb, Rickett, Rogers, C.Jordan, Froggatt, Woodhead					
26 Dec. 1949	Blackburn Rovers	Division 2	2–0	Tomlinson(19), Froggatt(79)	52939
McIntosh, Kenny, Swift, Gannon, Packard, Witcomb, Rickett, Froggatt, C.Jordan, Tomlinson, Woodhead					
14 Jan. 1950	Plymouth Argyle	Division 2	2–4	Gannon(35), Froggatt(46)	39318
McIntosh, Westlake, Swift, Gannon, Packard, Witcomb, Marriott, Froggatt, C.Jordan, Tomlinson, Rickett					
18 Feb. 1950	Brentford	Division 2	3–3	Jordan 2(53, 88), Fox(40)	37923
McIntosh, Kenny, Bannister, Gannon, Packard, Witcomb, Rickett, Henry, C.Jordan, Fox, Woodhead					
11 Mar. 1950	Preston North End	Division 2	0–1		49222
McIntosh, Kenny, Bannister, Gannon, Packard, Witcomb, Marriott, Henry, Dooley, Froggatt, Rickett					
25 Mar. 1950	Leeds United	Division 2	5–2	McJarrow 2(12, 75), Henry 2(28pen., 80), Rickett(70)	50487
McIntosh, Kenny, Bannister, Gannon, Packard, Witcomb, Marriott, Henry, McJarrow, Tomlinson, Rickett					
08 Apr. 1950	Barnsley	Division 2	2–0	Henry(10), Marriott(35)	48119
McIntosh, Kenny, Swift, Gannon, Packard, Witcomb, Marriott, Henry, McJarrow, Tomlinson, Rickett					
10 Apr. 1950	Bury	Division 2	1–0	Henry(17)	30449
McIntosh, Kenny, Swift, Gannon, Packard, Witcomb, Marriott, Henry, McJarrow, Tomlinson, Rickett					
22 Apr. 1950	Coventry City	Division 2	1–1	McJarrow(51)	44035
McIntosh, Kenny, Swift, Gannon, Packard, Witcomb, Marriott, Henry, McJarrow, Tomlinson, Rickett					
26 Apr. 1950	Grimsby Town	Division 2	4–0	Rickett 3(7, 33, 85), McJarrow(12)	40862
McIntosh, Kenny, Swift, Gannon, Packard, Witcomb, Rickett, Henry, McJarrow, Froggatt, Woodhead					
06 May 1950	Tottenham Hotspur	Division 2	0–0		50853
McIntosh, Kenny, Swift, Gannon, Packard, Witcomb, Rickett, Henry, McJarrow, Froggatt, Woodhead					
08 May 1950	Barnsley	County Cup s/f	3–1	Henry pen., Rogers, Tomlinson	11000
McIntosh, Kenny, Swift, Jackson, Barnes, Slynn, Marriott, Rogers, McJarrow, Henry, Tomlinson					
13 May 1950	Sheffield United	County Cup Fl	2–1	Tomlinson(30), McJarrow(89)	31861
McIntosh, Kenny, Swift, Gannon, Packard, Slynn, Rickett, Rogers, McJarrow, Henry, Tomlinson					

OTHER GAMES AT HILLSBOROUGH

Date	Opponents				Att.
13 Aug. 1949	Public Trial Match	Stripes 2	Whites 1		8708
31 Oct. 1949	Boys	Sheffield 5	Nottingham 1		3700
18 Jan. 1950	B International	England 5	Switzerland 0		43053
28 Jan. 1950	Amateur Cup R2	Sheffield 2	Wimbledon 3		10632
11 Apr. 1950	Schools	England 6	Wales 1		40500

Date	Opponents	Competition	Score	Scorers	Att.
21 Aug. 1950	Portsmouth	Division 1	2–1	McJarrow(83), Woodhead(89)	46740
McIntosh, Kenny, Swift, Henry, Packard, Witcomb, Rickett, Froggatt, McJarrow, Tomlinson, Woodhead					
26 Aug. 1950	Burnley	Division 1	0–1		44079
McIntosh, Kenny, Swift, Henry, Packard, Witcomb, Rickett, Froggatt, McJarrow, Tomlinson, Woodhead					
04 Sep. 1950	Stoke City	Division 1	1–1	Tomlinson(80)	37500
McIntosh, Kenny, Swift, Henry, Packard, Slynn, Rickett, Froggatt, McJarrow, Tomlinson, Woodhead					
09 Sep. 1950	Charlton Athletic	Division 1	1–2	McJarrow(57)	40580
McIntosh, Kenny, Swift, Gannon, Packard, Slynn, Rickett, Henry, McJarrow, Froggatt, Woodhead					
16 Sep. 1950	Middlesbrough	Division 1	0–1		46954
Morton, Kenny, Swift, Gannon, Packard, Witcomb, Rickett, Froggatt, McJarrow, Tomlinson, Woodhead					
30 Sep. 1950	Newcastle United	Division 1	0–0		40096
McIntosh, Bannister, Swift, Gannon, Packard, Witcomb, Marriott, J.Jordan, McJarrow, Froggatt, Tomlinson					
14 Oct. 1950	Wolverhampton W.	Division 1	2–2	Froggatt(16), Rickett(65)	47033
McIntosh, Bannister, Swift, Gannon, Packard, Witcomb, Rickett, J.Jordan, McJarrow, Froggatt, Tomlinson					
28 Oct. 1950	Liverpool	Division 1	4–1	Froggatt 3(25, 74, 75), Woodhead(85)pen.	43643
McIntosh, Bannister, Swift, Gannon, Packard, Witcomb, Rickett, Henry, McJarrow, Froggatt, Woodhead					
11 Nov. 1950	Aston Villa	Division 1	3–2	Henry 2(17, 60), Rickett(15)	37160
McIntosh, Bannister, Swift, Gannon, Turton, Witcomb, Rickett, J.Jordan, Henry, Froggatt, Woodhead					
25 Nov. 1950	Bolton Wanderers	Division 1	3–4	Froggatt(12), Howe(24)og., Henry(79)	37033
McIntosh, Bannister, Curtis, Gannon, Swift, Witcomb, Rickett, McJarrow, Henry, Froggatt, Woodhead					
09 Dec. 1950	Tottenham Hotspur	Division 1	1–1	McJarrow(40)	44346
Morton, Bannister, Curtis, Gannon, Packard, Witcomb, Rickett, McJarrow, Henry, Froggatt, Woodhead					
26 Dec. 1950	West Bromwich Albion	Division 1	3–0	McJarrow 2(12, 65), Jordan(42)	44819
Morton, Bannister, Curtis, Gannon, Packard, Witcomb, Marriott, J.Jordan, McJarrow, Froggatt, Woodhead					
30 Dec. 1950	Arsenal	Division 1	0–2		39583
Morton, Bannister, Curtis, Gannon, Packard, Witcomb, Marriott, J.Jordan, McJarrow, Froggatt, Woodhead					
03 Feb. 1951	Huddersfield Town	Division 1	3–2	Froggatt 2(1, 32), Woodhead(30)pen.	40805
Morton, Bannister, Curtis, Kirby, Packard, Witcomb, Marriott, Henry, McJarrow, Froggatt, Woodhead					
10 Feb. 1951	Sheffield United	County Cup s/f	2–0	Marriott(55), McJarrow(85)	40660
Morton, Bannister, Curtis, Kirby, Turton, Witcomb, Marriott, Quixall, McJarrow, Froggatt, Woodhead					
24 Feb. 1951	Chelsea	Division 1	2–2	Hughes(52)og., Quixall(60)	40943
Morton, Swift, Curtis, Gannon, Packard, Witcomb, Finney, Quixall, McJarrow, Froggatt, Woodhead					
26 Feb. 1951	Manchester United	Division 1	0–4		25693
Morton, Swift, Curtis, Gannon, Packard, Witcomb, Finney, Quixall, McJarrow, Froggatt, Woodhead					
24 Mar. 1951	Sunderland	Division 1	3–0	Woodhead(14), Froggatt(62), Rickett(85)	48467
McIntosh, Jackson, Curtis, Gannon, Packard, Witcomb, Marriott, Sewell, Woodhead, Froggatt, Rickett					
07 Apr. 1951	Fulham	Division 1	2–2	Froggatt(27), Sewell(30)	31328
McIntosh, Jackson, Curtis, Gannon, Packard, Witcomb, Marriott, Sewell, Woodhead, Froggatt, Rickett					
18 Apr. 1951	Derby County	Division 1	4–3	Woodhead 2(5, 25pen.), Oliver(13)og., Sewell(80)	40183
McIntosh, Jackson, Curtis, Henry, Packard, Witcomb, Finney, Sewell, Woodhead, Froggatt, Rickett					
21 Apr. 1951	Blackpool	Division 1	3–1	Woodhead(1), Sewell(15), Witcomb(80)	53420
McIntosh, Jackson, Curtis, Henry, Packard, Witcomb, Finney, Sewell, Woodhead, Froggatt, Rickett					
05 May 1951	Everton	Division 1	6–0	Woodhead 2(25, 30), Sewell 2(33, 87), Finney(50), Froggatt(70)	41166
McIntosh, Jackson, Curtis, Henry, Packard, Witcomb, Finney, Sewell, Woodhead, Froggatt, Rickett					
12 May 1951	Doncaster Rovers	County Cup Fl	2–1	Woodhead 2(70, 71pen.)	24081
McIntosh, Jackson, Curtis, Henry, Packard, Witcomb, Finney, Quixall, Woodhead, Froggatt, Rickett					
16 May 1951	Frem	Friendly	0–0		13900
McIntosh, Jackson, Curtis, Henry(Gannon 35), Packard, Witcomb, Finney, Quixall, Woodhead, Froggatt, Rickett					

OTHER GAMES AT HILLSBOROUGH

Date					Att.
12 Aug. 1950	Public Trial Match	Stripes 2	Whites 1		6166
30 Oct. 1950	Boys	Sheffield 5	Derby 3		2581
10 Mar. 1951	F.A.Cup Semi Final	Wolves 0	Newcastle United 0		62250
23 Apr. 1951	Senior Cup Final	Hallam 3	Stocksbridge Works 0		7240
07 May 1951	Yorks. Lge. Cup Final	Farsley Celtic 0	Sheff. Wed. A 3		n/k

Date	Opponents	Competition	Score	Scorers	Att.
18 Aug. 1951	Doncaster Rovers	Division 2	3–1	Woodhead(13), Witcomb(53), Sewell(60)	42005
McIntosh, Jackson, Curtis, Henry, Packard, Witcomb, Finney, Sewell, Woodhead, Thomas, Rickett					
27 Aug. 1951	Leicester City	Division 2	1–0	Sewell(50)	28517
McIntosh, Jackson, Kenny, Gannon, Turton, Witcomb, Finney, Sewell, Woodhead, Thomes, Rickett					
01 Sep. 1951	Southampton	Division 2	3–1	Woodhead 2(23, 87pen.), Witcomb(18)	32016
McIntosh, Jackson, Kenny, Gannon, Turton, Witcomb, Finney, Sewell, Woodhead, Thomas, Rickett					
03 Sep. 1951	Birmingham City	Division 2	1–1	Woodhead(13)	32490
McIntosh, Jackson, Kenny, Gannon, Turton, Witcomb, Finney, Sewell, Woodhead, Thomas, Rickett					
22 Sep. 1951	Rotherham United	Division 2	3–5	Sewell 2(68, 78), McJarrow(87)	54684
McIntosh, Jackson, Curtis, Gannon, Turton, Witcomb, Marriott, Sewell, McJarrow, Henry, Woodhead					
06 Oct. 1951	Barnsley	Division 2	2–1	Dooley 2(50, 77)	34207
McIntosh, Bannister, Kenny, Gannon, Turton, Davies, Finney, Sewell, Dooley, Quixall, Rickett					
20 Oct. 1951	Blackburn Rovers	Division 2	2–0	Sewell(60), Rickett(72)pen.	31454
McIntosh, Bannister, Kenny, Gannon, Turton, Davies, Finney, Sewell, Dooley, Quixall, Rickett					
03 Nov. 1951	Notts County	Division 2	6–0	Dooley 5(53, 65, 68, 70, 85), Sewell(44)	46570
McIntosh, Bannister, Kenny, Gannon, Packard, Davies, Finney, Sewell, Dooley, Quixall, Rickett					
17 Nov. 1951	Bury	Division 2	2–1	Dooley 2(8, 64)	35882
McIntosh, Bannister, Kenny, Gannon, O'Donnell, Davies, Finney, Sewell, Dooley, Quixall, Rickett					
01 Dec. 1951	Coventry City	Division 2	3–1	Dooley 2(38, 58), Froggatt(42)	35739
McIntosh, Bannister, Kenny, Gannon, O'Donnell, Davies, Finney, Froggatt, Dooley, Quixall, Rickett					
22 Dec. 1951	Everton	Division 2	4–0	Dooley 4(51, 70, 84, 88)	38986
McIntosh, Bannister, Kenny, Gannon, O'Donnell, Davies, Finney, Sewell, Dooley, Froggatt, Rickett					
25 Dec. 1951	Nottingham Forest	Division 2	1–1	Rickett(–)pen.	61187
McIntosh, Bannister, Kenny, Gannon, O'Donnell, Davies, Finney, Sewell, Dooley, Froggatt, Rickett					
05 Jan. 1952	Sheffield United	Division 2	1–3	Dooley(22)	65384
McIntosh, Bannister, Kenny, Gannon, O'Donnell, Davies, Finney, Froggatt, Dooley, Quixall, Marriott					
19 Jan. 1952	Leeds United	Division 2	1–2	Dooley(87)	42357
McIntosh, Bannister, Curtis, Gannon, O'Donnell, Davies, Finney, Froggatt, Dooley, Quixall, Rickett					
09 Feb. 1952	Cardiff City	Division 2	4–2	Sewell 4(50, 74, 77, 87)	42881
McIntosh, Bannister, Curtis, Gannon, O'Donnell, Davies, Froggatt, Sewell, C.Jordan, Quixall, Woodhead					
01 Mar. 1952	Hull City	Division 2	6–0	Dooley 4(23, 37, 75, 76), Sewell 2(20, 60)	41811
McIntosh, Bannister, Curtis, Gannon, Turton, Witcomb, Froggatt, Sewell, Dooley, Marriott, Woodhead					
15 Mar. 1952	Queen's Park Rangers	Division 2	2–1	Sewell 2(32, 61)	41706
McIntosh, Bannister, Curtis, Gannon, Turton, Witcomb, Finney, Sewell, Dooley, Quixall, Whitaker					
02 Apr. 1952	Luton Town	Division 2	4–0	Dooley 2(37, 55), Sewell(20), Rickett(52)	25848
McIntosh, Bannister, Curtis, Gannon, Turton, Witcomb, Froggatt, Sewell, Dooley, Quixall, Rickett					
12 Apr. 1952	Swansea Town	Division 2	1–1	Quixall(86)	49002
McIntosh, Bannister, Curtis, Gannon, Turton, Witcomb, Froggatt, Sewell, Dooley, Quixall, Rickett					
14 Apr. 1952	Brentford	Division 2	2–0	Sewell(30), Munro(46)og.	43949
McIntosh, Bannister, Curtis, Gannon, Turton, Witcomb, Froggatt, Sewell, Dooley, Quixall, Rickett					
26 Apr. 1952	West Ham United	Division 2	2–2	Froggatt(57), Dooley(89)	44011
McIntosh, Bannister, Curtis, Gannon, Turton, Witcomb, Froggatt, Sewell, Dooley, Quixall, Marriott					
05 May 1952	Sheffield United	County Cup s/f	1–3	Marriott(78)	20327
McIntosh, Bannister, Curtis, J.McAnearney, O'Donnell, Witcomb, Finney, T.McAnearney, Dooley, Quixall, Marriott					

OTHER GAMES AT HILLSBOROUGH

13 Aug. 1951	Public Trial Match	Stripes 5	Whites 3	3523
31 Oct. 1951	Inter League	Football League 2	Scottish League 1	49075
03 Dec. 1951	F.A.Cup 1–2r	Gateshead 2	Stockport County 1	6834
25 Feb. 1952	Boys	Sheffield 3	Derby 1	n/k
29 Mar. 1952	F.A.Cup Semi Final	Newcastle United 0	Blackburn Rovers 0	65000
15 Apr. 1952	Boys	Sheffield 2	West Ham 0	10156
28 Apr. 1952	Inter League	Lancashire League 0	Northern Intermediate League 1	n/k
01 May 1952	Senior Cup Final	Denaby United 1	Stocksbridge Works 4	n/k

Date	Opponents	Competition	Score	Scorers	Att.
23 Aug. 1952	Newcastle United	Division 1	2–2	Sewell(85), Froggatt(88)	55126
McIntosh, Jackson, Curtis, Gannon, Turton, Witcomb, Froggatt, Sewell, Dooley, Quixall, Rickett					
03 Sep. 1952	Liverpool	Division 1	0–2		41183
McIntosh, Jackson, Curtis, T.McAnearney, Turton, Witcomb, Froggatt, Sewell, Dooley, Quixall, Rickett					
06 Sep. 1952	Charlton Athletic	Division 1	0–3		35203
Capewell, Bannister, Curtis, Gannon, Turton, Witcomb, Froggatt, Sewell, C.Jordan, Quixall, Rickett					
13 Sep. 1952	Tottenham Hotspur	Division 1	2–0	Sewell(65), Finney(87)	42174
Capewell, Kenny, Curtis, Gannon, Turton, Davies, Finney, Sewell, Dooley, Quixall, Woodhead					
17 Sep. 1952	Middlesbrough	Division 1	2–0	Sewell(30), Dooley(70)	41456
Capewell, Kenny, Curtis, Gannon, Turton, Davies, Finney, Sewell, Dooley, Quixall, Woodhead					
27 Sep. 1952	Preston North End	Division 1	1–1	Woodhead(22)	47729
Capewell, Kenny, Curtis, Gannon, Turton, Davies, Finney, Sewell, Dooley, Quixall, Woodhead					
18 Oct. 1952	Derby County	Division 1	2–0	Curtis 2(3pen., 37pen.)	51597
Capewell, Kenny, Curtis, Witcomb, Turton, Davies, Finney, Quixall, Dooley, Froggatt, Woodhead					
01 Nov. 1952	Chelsea	Division 1	1–0	Froggatt(15)	48186
Capewell, Kenny, Curtis, Witcomb, Turton, Davies, Finney, Quixall, Dooley, Froggatt, Woodhead					
15 Nov. 1952	Portsmouth	Division 1	3–4	Curtis 2(46pen., 80pen.), Froggatt(16)	44187
Capewell, Jackson, Curtis, Witcomb, Turton, Davies, Finney, Sewell, Dooley, Froggatt, Woodhead					
29 Nov. 1952	Aston Villa	Division 1	2–2	Dooley 2(29, 38)	30153
Capewell, Kenny, Curtis, Witcomb, Turton, Davies, Finney, Sewell, Dooley, Froggatt, Woodhead					
13 Dec. 1952	Wolverhampton W.	Division 1	2–3	Shorthouse(15)og., Dooley(17)	43108
Capewell, Kenny, Curtis, Gannon, Turton, Witcomb, Finney, Quixall, Dooley, Froggatt, Woodhead					
26 Dec. 1952	West Bromwich Albion	Division 1	4–5	Woodhead 2(3, 27), Froggatt(6), Dooley(47)	59389
Capewell, Kenny, Curtis, Gannon, Turton, Witcomb, Marriott, Sewell, Dooley, Froggatt, Woodhead					
03 Jan. 1953	Cardiff City	Division 1	2–0	Dooley 2(2, 32)	40109
Capewell, Kenny, Curtis, Gannon, Turton, Witcomb, Marriott, Sewell, Dooley, Quixall, Storrar					
10 Jan. 1953	Blackpool	F.A.Cup 3	1–2	Sewell(75)	60199
Capewell, Kenny, Curtis, Gannon, Turton, Witcomb, Marriott, Sewell, Dooley, Froggatt, Quixall					
07 Feb. 1953	Burnley	Division 1	2–4	Sewell(1), Curtis(83)pen.	41864
Capewell, Kenny, Curtis, Witcomb, Turton, Davies, Finney, Sewell, Dooley, Froggatt, Woodhead					
21 Feb. 1953	Stoke City	Division 1	1–0	Sewell(80)	38187
McIntosh, Jackson, Curtis, T.McAnearney, Turton, Davies, Finney, Quixall, C.Jordan, Sewell, Shadbolt					
02 Mar. 1953	Arsenal	Division 1	1–4	Jordan(52)	32814
McIntosh, Jackson, Curtis, T.McAnearney, Turton, Davies, Finney, Sewell, C.Jordan, Froggatt, Shadbolt					
14 Mar. 1953	Blackpool	Division 1	2–0	Sewell(28), Marriott(70)	40904
McIntosh, Kenny, Curtis, Witcomb, O'Donnell, Davies, Marriott, Sewell, Woodhead, Froggatt, Shadbolt					
28 Mar. 1953	Manchester United	Division 1	0–0		31101
McIntosh, Kenny, Curtis, Witcomb, Turton, Davies, Marriott, Sewell, Codd, Froggatt, Woodhead					
06 Apr. 1953	Manchester City	Division 1	1–1	Woodhead(60)	43520
McIntosh, Kenny, Curtis, Gannon, O'Donnell, Davies, Marriott, Quixall, Sewell, Froggatt, Woodhead					
11 Apr. 1953	Bolton Wanderers	Division 1	1–1	Sewell(70)	40158
McIntosh, Kenny, Curtis, Gannon, O'Donnell, Davies, Marriott, Slater, Sewell, Froggatt, Woodhead					
25 Apr. 1953	Sunderland	Division 1	4–0	Sewell 3(12, 48, 50), Aitken(29)og.	45168
McIntosh, Kenny, Curtis, Witcomb, O'Donnell, Davies, Marriott, Quixall, Sewell, Froggatt, Woodhead					
04 May 1953	Doncaster Rovers	County Cup	2–1	Codd(75), Jordan(83)	8100
McIntosh, Conwell, Seemley, Witcomb, O'Donnell, Davies, Codd, Marriott, C.Jordan, Slater, Woodhead					

OTHER GAMES AT HILLSBOROUGH

Date	Competition	Home	Away	Att.
16 Aug. 1952	Public Trial Match	Stripes 2	Whites 0	7987
03 Nov. 1952	Boys	Sheffield 8	Derby 0	n/k
24 Jan. 1953	F.A.Amateur Cup 2	Hallam 1	Dulwich Hamlet 0	13855
09 Feb. 1953	F.A.Cup 4–2R	Notts County 0	Bolton Wanderers 1	23171
07 Apr. 1953	Boys	Sheffield 2	Liverpool 3	n/k
29 Apr. 1953	Boys	Sheffield 3	Doncaster 1	n/k
09 May 1953	Youth	Sheffield & Hallamshire 2	Hampshire 1	3300

1949–50
Gannon, Kenny, Packard, McIntosh, Swift, Witcomb;
Marriott, Henry, McJarrow, Tomlinson, Rickett.

1950–51
Bannister, Turton, McIntosh, Curtis, Froggatt, Witcomb;
Rickett, McJarrow, Gannon, Henry, Woodhead.

1951–52
Gannon, Curtis, Turton, McIntosh, Bannister, Witcomb;
Froggatt, Sewell, Dooley, Quixall, Rickett.

1953–54
Davies, O'Donnell, T. McAnearney, McIntosh, Conwell, Froggatt;
Marriott, Sewell, J. Jordan, Curtis, Woodhead.

Date	Opponents	Competition	Score	Scorers	Att.
19 Aug. 1953	Manchester City	Division 1	2–0	Jordan(10), Sewell(65)	40139
McIntosh, Conwell, Curtis, T.McAnearney, O'Donnell, Davies, Marriott, Sewell, C.Jordan, Froggatt, Woodhead					
22 Aug. 1953	Tottenham Hotspur	Division 1	2–1	Sewell 2(38, 52)	39118
McIntosh, Conwell, Curtis, T.McAnearney, O'Donnell, Davies, Marriott, Sewell, C.Jordan, Froggatt, Woodhead					
02 Sep. 1953	Preston North End	Division 1	4–2	Woodhead(5), Froggatt(15), Shaw(70), Marriott(73)	37528
Capewell, Conwell, Curtis, T.McAnearney, O'Donnell, Davies, Marriott, Quixall, Shaw, Froggatt, Woodhead					
05 Sep. 1953	Charlton Athletic	Division 1	1–2	Woodhead(40)	41723
Capewell, Conwell, Curtis, T.McAnearney, O'Donnell, Davies, Marriott, Quixall, Shaw, Froggatt, Woodhead					
16 Sep. 1953	Bolton Wanderers	Division 1	2–1	Sewell(–), Woodhead(56)	27107
Ryalls, Kenny, Curtis, Gannon, O'Donnell, Davies, Marriott, Sewell, C.Jordan, Froggatt, Woodhead					
23 Sep. 1953	Newcastle United	Division 1	3–0	Jordan 2(3, 24), Marriott(9)	29271
Ryalls, Conwell, Curtis, T.McAnearney, O'Donnell, Gannon, Marriott, Sewell, C.Jordan, Froggatt, Woodhead					
26 Sep. 1953	West Bromwich Albion	Division 1	2–3	Sewell(70), Woodhead(78)	45508
Ryalls, Conwell, Curtis, T.McAnearney, O'Donnell, Gannon, Finney, Quixall, C.Jordan, Sewell, Woodhead					
10 Oct. 1953	Chelsea	Division 1	2–0	Froggatt(20), Shaw(60)	32217
Ryalls, Conwell, Curtis, T.McAnearney, O'Donnell, Gannon, Finney, Sewell, Shaw, Froggatt, Woodhead					
24 Oct. 1953	Portsmouth	Division 1	4–4	Sewell 2(21, 26), Jordan 2(64, 65)	37091
Ryalls, Conwell, Curtis, T.McAnearney, O'Donnell, Gannon, Finney, Quixall, C.Jordan, Sewell, Woodhead					
04 Nov. 1953	South Africa	Friendly	9–3	Shaw 4, Sewell 2, Woodhead 2, Marriott	5298
Ryalls, Conwell, Curtis, Gannon, O'Donnell, Davies, Marriott, Sewell, Shaw, Froggatt, Woodhead					
07 Nov. 1953	Aston Villa	Division 1	3–1	Quixall(9), Shaw(22), Finney(70)	31124
Ryalls, Conwell, Curtis, T.McAnearney, O'Donnell, Gannon, Finney, Quixall, Shaw, Sewell, Woodhead					
21 Nov. 1953	Sunderland	Division 1	2–2	Woodhead(68), Sewell(71)	38120
Ryalls, Conwell, Curtis, T.McAnearney, O'Donnell, Gannon, Finney, Quixall, C.Jordan, Sewell, Woodhead					
05 Dec. 1953	Cardiff City	Division 1	2–1	Froggatt(6), Sewell(48)	28183
Ryalls, Conwell, Curtis, Gannon, Turton, Davies, Marriott, Quixall, Froggatt, Sewell, Woodhead					
26 Dec. 1953	Manchester United	Division 1	0–1		44196
Ryalls, Kenny, Curtis, Gannon, Turton, Seemley, Finney, Quixall, Woodhead, Sewell, Marriott					
02 Jan. 1954	Burnley	Division 1	2–0	Mather(35)og., Woodhead(44)	34040
Ryalls, Kenny, Seemley, Gannon, Butler, Davies, Finney, Quixall, Shaw, Sewell, Woodhead					
09 Jan. 1954	Sheffield United	F.A.Cup 3	1–1	Shaw(46)	61250
Ryalls, Kenny, Seemley, Gannon, Butler, Davies, Finney, Quixall, Shaw, Sewell, Woodhead					
23 Jan. 1954	Sheffield United	Division 1	3–2	Shaw 2(27, 60), Sewell(20)	43231
Ryalls, Kenny, Seemley, Gannon, Butler, Davies, Finney, Quixall, Shaw, Sewell, Marriott					
30 Jan. 1954	Chesterfield	F.A.Cup 4	0–0		46188
Ryalls, Kenny, Seemley, Gannon, Butler, Davies, Finney, Quixall, Shaw, Sewell, Marriott					
06 Feb. 1954	Middlesbrough	Division 1	4–2	Woodhead 2(58, 70), Sewell(55), Shaw(72)	31189
Ryalls, Kenny, Seemley, Gannon, Butler, Davies, Finney, Quixall, Shaw, Sewell, Woodhead					
20 Feb. 1954	Everton	F.A.Cup 5	3–1	Shaw(2), Sewell(85), Woodhead(86)	65000
McIntosh, Curtis, Seemley, Gannon, Butler, Davies, Finney, Quixall, Shaw, Sewell, Woodhead					
24 Feb. 1954	Liverpool	Division 1	1–1	Woodhead(47)	18000
McIntosh, Kenny, Curtis, Gannon, Butler, Davies, Marriott, J.McAnearney, Shaw, Sewell, Woodhead					
06 Mar. 1954	Blackpool	Division 1	1–2	Woodhead(83)	42183
McIntosh, Kenny, Curtis, Gannon, Butler, Davies, Marriott, J.McAnearney, Shaw, Sewell, Woodhead					
13 Mar. 1954	Bolton Wanderers	F.A.Cup 6	1–1	Woodhead(75)	65000
McIntosh, Kenny, Seemley, Gannon, Butler, Davies, Finney, Quixall, Shaw, Sewell, Woodhead					
20 Mar. 1954	Arsenal	Division 1	2–1	Gannon(70), Sewell(72)	42072
McIntosh, Curtis, Seemley, Gannon, Butler, Davies, Marriott, Quixall, Shaw, Sewell, Woodhead					
03 Apr. 1954	Huddersfield Town	Division 1	1–4	Shaw(89)	31106
McIntosh, Kenny, Seemley, Butler, Davies, Finney, J.McAnearney, Shaw, Froggatt, Woodhead					
17 Apr. 1954	Wolverhampton W.	Division 1	0–0		41278
McIntosh, Kenny, Curtis, Gannon, O'Donnell, Davies, Marriott, Quixall, Shaw, Froggatt, Woodhead					
27 Apr. 1954	Rotherham United	County Cup s/f	3–5	McAnearney 2(6, 25), Gannon(20)	9514
McIntosh, Curtis, Seemley, Gannon, O'Donnell, Davies, Marriott, J.McAnearney, Shaw, Froggatt, Woodhead					

OTHER GAMES AT HILLSBOROUGH

15 Aug. 1953	Public Trial Match	Stripes 2	Whites 0		4000
22 Mar. 1954	F.A.Cup 6–2R	Leicester City 1	Preston North End 3		44356
12 Apr. 1954	Boys	Sheffield 2	Doncaster 2		n/k

Date	Opponents	Competition	Score	Scorers	Att.
23 Aug. 1954	Manchester United	Division 1	2–4	Shaw(30), Curtis(60)pen.	38118
Ryalls, Kenny, Curtis, Gannon, O'Donnell, Davies, Finney, Quixall, Shaw, Sewell, Marriott					
28 Aug. 1954	Aston Villa	Division 1	6–3	Sewell 2(13, 33), Shaw 2(29, 44), Quixall(4), Finney(81)	34243
McIntosh, Conwell, Curtis, Gannon, O'Donnell, Davies, Finney, Quixall, Shaw, Sewell, Froggatt					
06 Sep. 1954	Huddersfield Town	Division 1	4–1	Finney(5), Sewell(8), Froggatt(27), Shaw(51)	25825
McIntosh, Conwell, Curtis, Gannon, Butler, Davies, Finney, J.McAnearney, Shaw, Sewell, Froggatt					
11 Sep. 1954	Tottenham Hotspur	Division 1	2–2	Shaw(68), Sewell(87)	34681
McIntosh, Conwell, Curtis, Gannon, Butler, Davies, Finney, J.McAnearney, Shaw, Sewell, Froggatt					
02 Oct. 1954	Blackpool	Division 1	2–1	Sewell(43), Quixall(84)	32107
McIntosh, Conwell, Curtis, Gannon, Butler, Davies, Finney, Quixall, Shaw, Sewell, Froggatt					
09 Oct. 1954	Arsenal	Division 1	1–2	Shaw(52)	39167
McIntosh, Conwell, Curtis, Gannon, Butler, Davies, Finney, Quixall, Shaw, Sewell, Froggatt					
23 Oct. 1954	Burnley	Division 1	1–1	Shaw(20)	30005
McIntosh, Conwell, Curtis, Gannon, Butler, Davies, Finney, Quixall, Shaw, Sewell, Froggatt					
06 Nov. 1954	Manchester City	Division 1	2–4	McAnearney(1), Froggatt(80)	19152
McIntosh, Conwell, Curtis, Quixall, Butler, O'Donnell, Finney, J.McAnearney, Shaw, Froggatt, Howells					
20 Nov. 1954	Chelsea	Division 1	1–1	Sewell(24)	25906
Ryalls, Conwell, Curtis, Gannon, O'Donnell, Shaw, Finney, Quixall, Sewell, Froggatt, Marriott					
04 Dec. 1954	Newcastle United	Division 1	0–3		20221
McIntosh, Conwell, Curtis, Gannon, O'Donnell, Shaw, Marriott, Sewell, Hukin, Quixall, Woodhead					
18 Dec. 1954	Wolverhampton W.	Division 1	2–2	Sewell(15), Marriott(41)	33102
McIntosh, Curtis, Seemley, Shaw, McEvoy, Davies, Marriott, Gannon, Hukin, Sewell, Woodhead					
27 Dec. 1954	Charlton Athletic	Division 1	2–2	Hammond(26)og., Curtis(46)pen.	43114
McIntosh, Conwell, Curtis, Gannon, McEvoy, Shaw, Marriott, Quixall, Hukin, Sewell, Woodhead					
08 Jan. 1955	Hastings United	F.A.Cup 3	2–1	Shaw(57), Greensmith(87)	25965
McIntosh, Conwell, Curtis, Gannon, McEvoy, Turley, Marriott, Quixall, Shaw, J.McAnearney, Greensmith					
15 Jan. 1955	Sunderland	Division 1	1–2	Sewell(61)	16975
McIntosh, Conwell, Curtis, Gannon, McEvoy, Turley, Marriott, J.McAnearney, Sewell, Quixall, Finney					
29 Jan. 1955	Notts County	F.A.Cup 4	1–1	Watson(75)	53138
McIntosh, Conwell, Curtis, Gannon, Butler, Davies, Finney, Sewell, Watson, Quixall, Marriott					
05 Feb. 1955	Sheffield United	Division 1	1–2	Marriott(88)	36176
McIntosh, Conwell, Curtis, Gannon, Butler, Davies, Marriott, Quixall, Watson, Froggatt, Woodhead					
12 Feb. 1955	Portsmouth	Division 1	1–3	Woodhead(37)	21176
McIntosh, Conwell, Kenny, Gannon, Butler, Shaw, Marriott, Quixall, Watson, Sewell, Woodhead					
05 Mar. 1955	Everton	Division 1	2–2	Sewell(48), Marriott(55)	22214
McIntosh, Martin, Curtis, O'Donnell, McEvoy, Davies, Marriott, Quixall, Shaw, Sewell, Woodhead					
19 Mar. 1955	Preston North End	Division 1	2–0	Shaw(83), Marriott(85)	21048
McIntosh, Martin, Curtis, T.McAnearney, McEvoy, Gannon, Finney, Quixall, Ellis, Shaw, Marriott					
02 Apr. 1955	Cardiff City	Division 1	1–1	Curtis(60)pen.	20295
McIntosh, Martin, Curtis, T.McAnearney, McEvoy, Gannon, Finney, Quixall, Ellis, Shaw, Marriott					
11 Apr. 1955	Bolton Wanderers	Division 1	3–2	Froggatt 2(19, 55), Curtis(34)pen.	17267
McIntosh, Martin, Curtis, T.McAnearney, McEvoy, Kay, Finney, Quixall, Froggatt, Sewell, Marriott					
16 Apr. 1955	Leicester City	Division 1	1–0	Froggatt(33)	20539
McIntosh, Martin, Curtis, T.McAnearney, McEvoy, Kay, Finney, Quixall, Froggatt, Sewell, Marriott					
30 Apr. 1955	West Bromwich Albion	Division 1	5–0	Finney 2(62, 75), Curtis(30)pen., Sewell(49), Marriott(50)	16664
McIntosh, Martin, Curtis, T.McAnearney, McEvoy, Kay, Finney, Sewell, Watson, Froggatt, Marriott					
14 May 1955	Rotherham United	County Cup Fl	2–4 aet	Watson(10), McEvoy(87)	11979
McIntosh, Martin, Curtis, T.McAnearney, McEvoy, Kay, Finney, Shaw, Watson, Froggatt, Marriott					

OTHER GAMES AT HILLSBOROUGH :

Date	Type	Home	Away	Att.
03 Nov. 1954	Representative	F.A. XI 1	The Army 1	13794
14 Feb. 1955	F.A.Cup 4–3R*	Doncaster Rovers 0	Aston Villa 0	16117
09 Mar. 1955	Dooley Benefit	Sheffield XI 1	International XI 5	55000
23 Mar. 1955	B International	England 1	Germany 1	32630
26 Mar. 1955	F.A.Cup Semi Final	York City 1	Newcastle United 1	65000
12 Apr. 1955	Boys	Sheffield 6	Newcastle 1	n/k
03 May 1955	Boys	Sheffield 1	Doncaster 1	n/k

*Abandoned after 90 mins due to bad light–result stood

Date	Opponents	Competition	Score	Scorers	Att.
20 Aug. 1955	Plymouth Argyle	Division 2	5–2	Sewell 3(9, 79, 81), Quixall 2(55, 89)	31716
McIntosh, Staniforth, Curtis, Gibson, O'Donnell, T.McAnearney, Finney, Sewell, Shiner, Quixall, Broadbent					
31 Aug.1955	Liverpool	Division 2	1–1	Broadbent(85)	30853
Williams, Staniforth, Curtis, Gibson, O'Donnell, T.McAnearney, Froggatt, Sewell, Shiner, Quixall, Broadbent					
03 Sep. 1955	Bristol Rovers	Division 2	4–2	Shiner 2(56, 66), Froggatt(27), Sewell(46)	30526
Williams, Staniforth, Bingley, Gibson, O'Donnell, T.McAnearney, Froggatt, Sewell, Shiner, Quixall, Broadbent					
12 Sep. 1955	Leicester City	Division 2	1–1	Shiner(61)	25819
McIntosh, Martin, Bingley, Gibson, O'Donnell, T.McAnearney, Froggatt, Sewell, Shiner, J.McAnearney, Broadbent					
17 Sep. 1955	Swansea Town	Division 2	2–2	Sewell 2(60, 88)	29128
McIntosh, Staniforth, Curtis, O'Donnell, T.McAnearney, Froggatt, Sewell, Shiner, Quixall, Broadbent					
24 Sep. 1955	Nottingham Forest	Division 2	1–2	Sewell(85)	29304
McIntosh, Staniforth, Bingley, Gibson, McEvoy, T.McAnearney, Froggatt, Sewell, Shiner, Quixall, Broadbent					
10 Oct. 1955	Vasas Budapest	Friendly	1–7	Quixall(–)	45983
McIntosh, Staniforth, Bingley, Gibson, McEvoy, Kay, Froggatt, Sewell, Shiner, Quixall, Broadbent					
15 Oct. 1955	Leeds United	Division 2	4–0	Shiner 2(15, 88), Sewell 2(32, 61)	28646
McIntosh, Staniforth, Bingley, Gibson, McEvoy, Kay, Froggatt, Sewell, Shiner, Quixall, Broadbent					
29 Oct. 1955	Bury	Division 2	3–3	Quixall(32), Froggatt(33), Sewell(70)	25138
McIntosh, Staniforth, Bingley, Gibson, O'Donnell, Kay, Froggatt, Sewell, Shiner, Quixall, Broadbent					
02 Nov. 1955	Sheffield United	County Cup	2–5	Froggatt(44), Shiner(48)	16158
Williams, Staniforth, Bingley, Gibson, O'Donnell, Kay, Froggatt, Quixall, Shiner, Sewell, Broadbent					
12 Nov. 1955	Middlesbrough	Division 2	3–1	Shiner(14), Wilkinson(20), Gibson(37)	25180
Williams, Staniforth, Bingley, Gibson, Swan, Kay, D.Wilkinson, Quixall, Shiner, Froggatt, Broadbent					
26 Nov. 1955	West Ham United	Division 2	1–1	Shiner(88)pen.	21670
Williams, Martin, Bingley, Gibson, McEvoy, Kay, Finney, Sewell, Shiner, Froggatt, Broadbent					
10 Dec. 1955	Rotherham United	Division 2	0–2		23108
McIntosh, Staniforth, Bingley, T.McAnearney, Swan, O'Donnell, Finney, Quixall, Shiner, Froggatt, Broadbent					
24 Dec. 1955	Stoke City	Division 2	4–0	Shiner(30), Froggatt(46), Broadbent(47), Quixall(55)	23579
McIntosh, Staniforth, Bingley, Gibson, McEvoy, O'Donnell, Finney, Quixall, Shiner, Froggatt, Broadbent					
27 Dec. 1955	Blackburn Rovers	Division 2	5–1	Froggatt 2(25, 43), Broadbent(58), Shiner(72), Finney(86)	31574
Williams, Curtis, Bingley, Gibson, McEvoy, O'Donnell, Finney, Quixall, Shiner, Froggatt, Broadbent					
07 Jan. 1956	Newcastle United	F.A.Cup 3	1–3	Gibson(86)	48198
McIntosh, Staniforth, Bingley, Gibson, McEvoy, O'Donnell, Finney, Quixall, Shiner, Froggatt, Broadbent					
14 Jan. 1956	Doncaster Rovers	Division 2	5–2	Quixall 2(60, 85), Shiner 2(75, 78), Froggatt(53)	18281
McIntosh, Staniforth, Curtis, Gibson, McEvoy, O'Donnell, Finney, Quixall, Shiner, Froggatt, Broadbent					
26 Jan. 1956	San Lorenzo	Friendly	9–0	Finney 3(5, 25, 74), Shiner 3(40, 47, 87), Froggatt(15), Howells(46), Broadbent(49)	8644
McIntosh, Staniforth, Curtis, T.McAnearney, McEvoy, O'Donnell, Finney, Froggatt, Shiner, Broadbent, Howells					
28 Jan. 1956	Luton Town	Friendly	2–2	Finney 2(30pen., 74)	11000
McIntosh, Staniforth, Curtis, T.McAnearney, McEvoy, O'Donnell, Finney, Shaw, Shiner, Broadbent, Howells(Butler 75)					
11 Feb. 1956	Hull City	Division 2	4–1	Shiner 2(16, 75), Froggatt(12), Quixall(87)	19481
McIntosh, Staniforth, Curtis, T.McAnearney, McEvoy, O'Donnell, Finney, Quixall, Shiner, Froggatt, Broadbent					
18 Feb. 1956	Bristol City	Division 2	2–1	Quixall 2(13, 52)	22539
McIntosh, Staniforth, Curtis, T.McAnearney, McEvoy, O'Donnell, Finney, Quixall, Shiner, Froggatt, Broadbent					
03 Mar. 1956	Port Vale	Division 2	4–0	Quixall(6), Shiner(22), O'Donnell(68), Finney(75)	30587
McIntosh, Staniforth, Curtis, T.McAnearney, McEvoy, O'Donnell, Finney, Quixall, Shiner, Froggatt, Broadbent					
21 Mar. 1956	Barnsley	Division 2	3–0	Shiner 2(66, 75), Froggatt(72)	31577
McIntosh, Staniforth, Curtis, T.McAnearney, McEvoy, O'Donnell, Finney, Quixall, Shiner, Froggatt, Broadbent					
31 Mar. 1956	Notts County	Division 2	1–0	Staniforth(73)	32263
McIntosh, Staniforth, Curtis, T.McAnearney, McEvoy, O'Donnell, Finney, Quixall, Shiner, Froggatt, Broadbent					
14 Apr. 1956	Fulham	Division 2	2–3	Shiner(56), Finney(81)pen.	27439
McIntosh, Staniforth, Curtis, T.McAnearney, McEvoy, O'Donnell, Finney, Quixall, Shiner, Froggatt, Broadbent					
28 Apr. 1956	Lincoln City	Division 2	5–3	Shiner 3(8, 12, 71), Finney 2(53, 66pen.)	32129
McIntosh, Staniforth, Curtis, T.McAnearney, McEvoy, O'Donnell, Finney, Quixall, Shiner, Froggatt, Broadbent					

OTHER GAMES AT HILLSBOROUGH

26 Oct. 1955	Inter League	Football League 4	Scottish League 2	37788
31 Oct. 1955	Boys	Sheffield 4	Nottingham 1	n/k
16 Nov. 1955	Inter City	Sheffield 3	Glasgow 2	n/k
08 Feb. 1956	U–23 International	England 3	Scotland 1	n/k
17 Mar. 1956	F.A.Cup Semi Final	Birmingham City 3	Sunderland 0	65107
03 Apr. 1956	Boys	Sheffield 6	Bolton 0	n/k

Date	Opponents	Competition	Score	Scorers	Att.
18 Aug. 1956	West Bromwich Albion	Division 1	4–2	Shiner 2(15, 75), Finney(56), Quixall(69)	22586
McIntosh, Staniforth, Curtis, T.McAnearney, McEvoy, O'Donnell, Finney, Quixall, Shiner, Froggatt, Broadbent					
22 Aug. 1956	Chelsea	Division 1	4–0	Shiner 2(6, 49), Quixall 2(10, 67)	36543
McIntosh, Staniforth, Curtis, T.McAnearney, McEvoy, O'Donnell, Finney, Quixall, Shiner, Froggatt, Broadbent					
01 Sep. 1956	Newcastle United	Division 1	4–0	Finney(39), Broadbent(41), Shiner(44), Quixall(47)	36270
McIntosh, Staniforth, Curtis, T.McAnearney, McEvoy, O'Donnell, Finney, Quixall, Shiner, Froggatt, Broadbent					
12 Sep. 1956	Cardiff City	Division 1	5–3	Froggatt 2(23, 70), Stitfall(20)og., Quixall(60)pen., Finney(72)	38721
McIntosh, Staniforth, Curtis, T.McAnearney, Swan, O'Donnell, Finney, Quixall, Shiner, Froggatt, D.Wilkinson					
22 Sep. 1956	Arsenal	Division 1	2–4	Quixall 2(4, 57)	40629
McIntosh, Staniforth, Curtis, T.McAnearney, Swan, O'Donnell, Finney, Quixall, Shiner, Broadbent, Cargill					
06 Oct. 1956	Sunderland	Division 1	3–2	Shiner(7), Broadbent(48), Froggatt(49)	33423
McIntosh, Staniforth, Bingley, T.McAnearney, McEvoy, O'Donnell, Finney, Quixall, Shiner, Froggatt, Broadbent					
20 Oct. 1956	Blackpool	Division 1	1–2	Broadbent(27)	46539
McIntosh, Staniforth, Curtis, Whitham, McEvoy, O'Donnell, Finney, Quixall, Shiner, Froggatt, Broadbent					
22 Oct. 1956	C.C.A. (Bucharest)	Friendly	3–3	Froggatt 2(19, 40), Broadbent(50)	35811
McIntosh, Staniforth, Curtis, Gibson, McEvoy, O'Donnell, Finney, Quixall, Watson, Froggatt, Broadbent					
29 Oct. 1956	Rotherham United	County Cup	0–1		8912
Hinchcliffe, Curtis, Bingley, Gibson, McEvoy, O'Donnell, Finney, Quixall, Shiner, Watson, Cargill					
03 Nov. 1956	Bolton Wanderers	Division 1	1–2	Watson(65)	24691
Hinchcliffe, Curtis, Bingley, Gibson, McEvoy, O'Donnell, Finney, Quixall, Shiner, Watson, Broadbent					
17 Nov. 1956	Tottenham Hotspur	Division 1	4–1	Finney 3(26, 55, 80), Quixall(11)	32214
McIntosh, Staniforth, Curtis, T.McAnearney, McEvoy, Gibson, Finney, Quixall, Shiner, Froggatt, Cargill					
01 Dec. 1956	Aston Villa	Division 1	2–1	Quixall 2(43, 68)	24353
McIntosh, Staniforth, Curtis, T.McAnearney, McEvoy, Gibson, Finney, Quixall, Shiner, Froggatt, Cargill					
06 Dec. 1956	Zagreb	Friendly	1–1	Shiner(12)	19401
Pllu, Staniforth, Curtis, T.McAnearney, McEvoy, Gibson, Finney, Quixall, Shiner, Froggatt, Broadbent					
09 Jan. 1957	Preston North End	F.A.Cup 3R	2–2 aet	Quixall(25), Shiner(98)	60168
McIntosh, Staniforth, Curtis, T.McAnearney, McEvoy, Finney, Quixall, Shiner, Froggatt, Cargill					
12 Jan, 1957	Charlton Athletic	Division 1	3–1	Froggatt(7), Gibson(17), Finney(33)	24589
McIntosh, Staniforth, Curtis, T.McAnearney, McEvoy, Gibson, Finney, Quixall, Shiner, Froggatt, Broadbent					
19 Jan. 1957	Manchester United	Division 1	2–1	Shiner(15), Quixall(47)	51068
McIntosh, Staniforth, Curtis, T.McAnearney, McEvoy, O'Donnell, Finney, Quixall, Shiner, J.McAnearney, Broadbent					
09 Feb. 1957	Burnley	Division 1	0–0		30385
McIntosh, Staniforth, Curtis, T.McAnearney, McEvoy, O'Donnell, Finney, Quixall, Shiner, J.McAnearney, Broadbent					
23 Feb. 1957	Manchester City	Division 1	2–2	Quixall(5), Ellis(43)	11271
McIntosh, Staniforth, Curtis, T.McAnearney, McEvoy, O'Donnell, Finney, Quixall, K.Ellis, J.McAnearney, Broadbent					
09 Mar. 1957	Wolverhampton W.	Division 1	2–1	J.McAnearney(51), Quixall(60)	30130
McIntosh, Staniforth, Curtis, T.McAnearney, McEvoy, O'Donnell, Finney, Quixall, Shiner, J.McAnearney, Greensmith					
26 Mar. 1957	Leeds United	Division 1	2–3	Quixall(7), Froggatt(19)	33205
McIntosh, Martin, Curtis, T.McAnearney, McEvoy, O'Donnell, Finney, Quixall, Shiner, Froggatt, Broadbent					
06 Apr. 1957	Everton	Division 1	2–2	Quixall(49)pen., Curtis(82)	23258
Pllu, Martin, Curtis, T.McAnearney, McEvoy, O'Donnell, Finney, Quixall, Shiner, Froggatt, Broadbent					
09 Apr. 1957	Portsmouth	Division 1	3–1	Shiner 2(30, 79), Wilkinson(41)	19890
Pllu, Martin, Curtis, T.McAnearney, McEvoy, O'Donnell, D.Wilkinson, Quixall, Shiner, Froggatt, Broadbent					
20 Apr. 1957	Luton Town	Division 1	3–0	Quixall(52)pen., Froggatt(62), Ellis(75)	22497
Pllu, Staniforth, Curtis, T.McAnearney, McEvoy, O'Donnell, D.Wilkinson, Quixall, K.Ellis, Froggatt, Broadbent					
22 Apr. 1957	Preston North End	Division 1	3–1	Quixall 2(15pen., 46pen.), Ellis(77)	21131
Pllu, Martin, Curtis, T.McAnearney, McEvoy, O'Donnell, D.Wilkinson, Quixall, K.Ellis, Froggatt, Broadbent					
29 Apr. 1957	Birmingham City	Division 1	3–0	Ellis 3(30secs., 44, 63)	15307
Pllu, Martin, Curtis, T.McAnearney, McEvoy, O'Donnell, D.Wilkinson, Quixall, K.Ellis, J.McAnearney, Broadbent					

OTHER GAMES AT HILLSBOROUGH

Date	Type	Home	Away		Att.
10 Oct. 1956	Representative	F.A. XI 2	R.A.F. 1		14398
02 Jan. 1957	Boys	Sheffield 3	Hull 3		n/k
23 Mar. 1957	F.A.Cup Semi Final	Birmingham City 0	Manchester United 2		65107
23 Apr. 1957	Schools	England 2	Scotland 0		30177

1954–55
Butler, McIntosh, Davies, Curtis, Conwell, Froggatt;
Finney, Quixall, Gannon, Shaw, Sewell;
Inset: Watson, Marriott.

1955–56
Froggatt, O'Donnell, Broadbent, McIntosh,
McAnearney, Staniforth, Bingley;
Gibson, Shiner, McEvoy, Curtis, Finney, Quixall.

After only one season in the Second Division, Sheffield
Wednesday return to the First. Here is the successful
team : (*Front*) Gibson, Shiner, McEvoy, Curtis, Finney,
Quixall. (*Back*) Froggatt, O'Donnell, Broadbent,
McIntosh, McAnearney, Staniforth, Bingley.

1956–57
Finney, Watson, Baker, D. Wilkinson, Whitham, Ireland, Quixall,
Greensmith;
Walker (ass. trainer), Logan (ass. trainer), Davies, Hukin,
Gregory, McIntosh, Williams, Shaw, Bingley, Powell (ass.
trainer), Marshall (trainer/coach);
O'Donnell, Froggatt, Gibson, Shiner, Staniforth, Taylor (sec.
manager), McEvoy, T. McAnearney, Broadbent, Howells, Curtis.

1957–58
Young, Ellis, Greensmith, Shaw, Quixall, Baker, Ballagher, B. Finney;
Lyttle (staff), Walker (trainer), Curtis, Froggatt, T. Whitham, Bingley,
McIntosh, Pllu, Ryalls, D. Wilkinson, Swan, Broadbent, Powell
(trainer), Marshall (coach);
Logan (trainer), Martin, Finney, Fantham, McEvoy, Taylor (sec.
manager), Shiner, Staniforth, Gibson, T. McAnearney.

Date	Opponents	Competition	Score	Scorers	Att.
31 Aug. 1957	Nottingham Forest	Division 1	1–2	J.McAnearney(24)	31495
Pllu, Staniforth, Bingley, T.McAnearney, McEvoy, O'Donnell, Finney, Quixall, K.Ellis, J.McAnearney, Broadbent
04 Sep. 1957	Newcastle United	Division 1	1–0	Broadbent(51)	23060
Pllu, Baker, Bingley, T.McAnearney, McEvoy, O'Donnell, Finney, Quixall, K.Ellis, J.McAnearney, Broadbent
11 Sep. 1957	Leicester City	Division 1	2–1	J.McAnearney(30), Ellis(60)	18270
Pllu, Baker, Bingley, T.McAnearney, McEvoy, O'Donnell, Finney, Quixall, K.Ellis, J.McAnearney, Broadbent
14 Sep. 1957	West Bromwich Albion	Division 1	1–2	Ellis(43)	23395
Pllu, Baker, Bingley, T.McAnearney, McEvoy, O'Donnell, Finney, Quixall, K.Ellis, J.McAnearney, Broadbent
28 Sep. 1957	Birmingham City	Division 1	5–3	Quixall 2(63, 67), Ellis 2(80, 85), Smith(8)og.	20311
Ryalls, Baker, Bingley, T.McAnearney, McEvoy, Gibson, Finney, Quixall, K.Ellis, Young, Broadbent
12 Oct. 1957	Blackpool	Division 1	0–3		31163
Ryalls, Staniforth, Bingley, T.McAnearney, McEvoy, O'Donnell, Finney, Gibson, Shaw, Clark, Broadbent
26 Oct. 1957	Sunderland	Division 1	3–3	Young(52), Quixall(70), Froggatt(89)	22618
Pllu, Martin, Bingley, T.McAnearney, McEvoy, Hill, Finney, Quixall, Froggatt, Young, Broadbent
04 Nov. 1957	Gwardia (Warsaw)	Friendly	4–4	Shiner 2(–, 83), Froggatt(24), Wilkinson(60)	14735
Pllu, Martin, Curtis, T.McAnearney, O'Donnell, Hill, D.Wilkinson, Quixall, Shiner, Froggatt, Finnney
09 Nov. 1957	Leeds United	Division 1	3–2	Froggatt 2(17, 36), J.McAnearney(16)	22641
Pllu, Martin, Curtis, T.McAnearney, O'Donnell, Hill, D.Wilkinson, J.McAnearney, Shiner, Froggatt, Finney
23 Nov. 1957	Arsenal	Division 1	2–0	Quixall(25)pen., Froggatt(47)	23904
McIntosh, Martin, Curtis, T.McAnearney, O'Donnell, Hill, D.Wilkinson, Quixall, Shiner, Froggatt, Finney
28 Nov. 1957	Juventus	Friendly	3–4	Shiner(–), Quixall(70), Froggatt(88)	44560
McIntosh, Martin, Curtis, T.McAnearney, O'Donnell, Hill, D.Wilkinson, Quixall, Shiner(Cargill), Froggatt, Finney
04 Dec. 1957	Barnsley	County Cup s/f	7–0	Quixall 2(1pen.), Ellis 2, Wilkinson 2, Froggatt	4900
McIntosh, Staniforth, Curtis, T.McAnearney, O'Donnell, Hill, D.Wilkinson, Quixall, K.Ellis, Froggatt, Finney
07 Dec. 1957	Aston Villa	Division 1	2–5	Ellis 2(48, 67)	16144
McIntosh, Staniforth, Curtis, T.McAnearney, O'Donnell, Hill, D.Wilkinson, Quixall, K.Ellis, Froggatt, Finney
21 Dec. 1957	Manchester City	Division 1	4–5	Froggatt(16), Wilkinson(44), Shiner(60), Quixall(80)	22042
Pinner, Martin, Curtis, T.McAnearney, O'Donnell, Hill, D.Wilkinson, Quixall, Shiner, Froggatt, Finney
25 Dec. 1957	Preston North End	Division 1	4–4	Finney 2(–, –), Froggatt(20), Wilkinson(–)	26825
Pinner, Johnson, Curtis, Gibson, McEvoy, O'Donnell, D.Wilkinson, Quixall, Shiner, Froggatt, Finney
11 Jan. 1958	Portsmouth	Division 1	4–2	Quixall(5)pen., Shiner(51), Wilkinson(62), Froggatt(80)	21308
Ryalls, Martin, Curtis, Kay, McEvoy, O'Donnell, D.Wilkinson, Quixall, Shiner, Froggatt, Finney
29 Jan. 1958	Hull City	F.A.Cup 4	4–3	Wilkinson(21), Shiner(60), Durham(63)og., Froggatt(66)	47119
Pllu, Johnson, Curtis, Kay, McEvoy, O'Donnell, D.Wilkinson, Quixall, Shiner, Froggatt, Finney
01 Feb. 1958	Tottenham Hotspur	Division 1	2–0	Wilkinson(36), Shiner(70)	23696
Ryalls, Martin, Johnson, Kay, McEvoy, O'Donnell, D.Wilkinson, Fantham, Shiner, Froggatt, Finney
15 Feb. 1958	Chelsea	Division 1	2–3	Quixall 2(40pen., 72pen.)	17588
Ryalls, Martin, Johnson, Kay, McEvoy, O'Donnell, D.Wilkinson, Quixall, Shiner, Froggatt, Finney
01 Mar. 1958	Luton Town	Division 1	2–1	Shiner 2(55, 70)	17747
Ryalls, Martin, Baker, T.McAnearney, Swan, O'Donnell, D.Wilkinson, Quixall, Shiner, Froggatt, Finney
15 Mar. 1958	Bolton Wanderers	Division 1	1–0	Quixall(18)	25825
R.Springett, Staniforth, Curtis, T.McAnearney, Swan, Gibson, Finney, Quixall, Shiner, Froggatt, Fantham
29 Mar. 1958	Manchester United	Division 1	1–0	Shiner(40)	35608
R.Springett, Staniforth, Curtis, T.McAnearney, Swan, O'Donnell, D.Wilkinson, Quixall, Shiner, Froggatt, Finney
07 Apr. 1958	Burnley	Division 1	1–2	Shiner(14)	23714
R.Springett, Staniforth, Curtis, Gibson, Swan, O'Donnell, D.Wilkinson, Quixall, Shiner, Fantham, Finney
12 Apr. 1958	Everton	Division 1	2–1	Quixall(52), Curtis(62)	18715
R.Springett, Johnson, Curtis, Gibson, Swan, O'Donnell, D.Wilkinson, Quixall, Shiner, Fantham, Finney
26 Apr. 1958	Wolverhampton W.	Division 1	2–1	Wilkinson(16), Shiner(25)	25254
R.Springett, Staniforth, Curtis, T.McAnearney, Swan, O'Donnell, D.Wilkinson, Quixall, Shiner, Fantham, Finney
30 Apr. 1958	Sheffield United	County Cup Fl	0–3		21289
R.Springett, Staniforth, Curtis, T.McAnearney, Swan, O'Donnell, D.Wilkinson, Quixall, Shiner, Fantham, Finney

OTHER GAMES AT HILLSBOROUGH

23 Oct. 1957	Sheffield F.C.Centenary	Sheffield Professional XI 4	England B 5		25000
13 Nov. 1957	Youth	England 2	Belgium 0		7801
31 Mar. 1958	Boys	Sheffield 1	Edinburgh 2		n/k

Date	Opponents	Competition	Score	Scorers	Att.
23 Aug. 1958	Swansea Town	Division 2	2–1	Finney(2), Froggatt(48)	24748
R.Springett, Martin, Curtis, Gibson, Swan, Kay, D.Wilkinson, Froggatt, Shiner, Fantham, Finney					
03 Sep. 1958	Stoke City	Division 2	4–1	Froggatt 2(20, 45), Shiner(7), Wilkinson(9)	23622
R.Springett, Martin, Curtis, T.McAnearney, Swan, Gibson, D.Wilkinson, Froggatt, Shiner, Ballagher, Young					
06 Sep. 1958	Bristol Rovers	Division 2	3–1	Wilkinson 2(20, 30), Quixall(30secs.)	28968
R.Springett, Martin, Curtis, T.McAnearney, Swan, Gibson, D.Wilkinson, Quixall, Shiner, Froggatt, Young					
17 Sep. 1958	Sunderland	Division 2	6–0	Froggatt 3(65, 68, 75), Shiner(14), Quixall(18), Wilkinson(50)	33398
R.Springett, Staniforth, Curtis, T.McAnearney, Swan, Gibson, D.Wilkinson, Quixall, Shiner, Froggatt, Finney					
20 Sep. 1958	Leyton Orient	Division 2	2–0	Froggatt 2(20, 60)	28443
R.Springett, Martin, Curtis, T.McAnearney, Swan, Gibson, D.Wilkinson, J.McAnearney, Shiner, Froggatt, Finney					
04 Oct. 1958	Sheffield United	Division 2	2–0	Froggatt(3), Shiner(86)	46404
R.Springett, Martin, Curtis, Kay, Swan, Gibson, D.Wilkinson, Fantham, Shiner, Froggatt, Finney					
18 Oct. 1958	Grimsby Town	Division 2	6–0	Froggatt 2(39, 49), Player 2(15, 23)og., Wilkinson(35), Fantham(62)	29866
R.Springett, Martin, Curtis, T.McAnearney, Swan, Gibson, D.Wilkinson, Froggatt, Shiner, Fantham, Finney					
01 Nov. 1958	Rotherham United	Division 2	5–0	Fantham 2(48, 58), Curtis(8)pen., Shiner (28), Froggatt(53)	32183
R.Springett, Martin, Curtis, T.McAnearney, Swan, Gibson, D.Wilkinson, Froggatt, Shiner, Fantham, Finney					
05 Nov. 1958	Napoli	Friendly	6–0	Curtis 2(45pen., 83pen.), Finney(1), Fantham(2), J.McAnearney(16), Shiner(41)	29589
R.Springett, Staniforth, Curtis, T.McAnearney, Swan, Gibson, D.Wilkinson, J.McAnearney, Shiner, Fantham, Finney					
15 Nov. 1958	Bristol City	Division 2	2–3	Finney 2(12, 18)	30164
R.Springett, Martin, Curtis, T.McAnearney, Swan, Gibson, D.Wilkinson, Froggatt, Shiner, Fantham, Finney					
29 Nov. 1958	Huddersfield Town	Division 2	4–1	Shiner 2(67, 80), Froggatt(21), Finney(40)	25394
R.Springett, Staniforth, Curtis, T.McAnearney, Swan, Kay, D.Wilkinson, Froggatt, Shiner, Fantham, Finney					
13 Dec. 1958	Middlesbrough	Division 2	2–0	Finney(27), Curtis(51)pen.	28115
R.Springett, Whitham, Curtis, Gibson, Swan, Kay, D.Wilkinson, Froggatt, Shiner, Fantham, Finney					
26 Dec. 1958	Lincoln City	Division 2	7–0	Froggatt 2(21, 86), Fantham 2(25, 31), Shiner 2(35, 51), Finney(43)	36403
R.Springett, Staniforth, Curtis, Gibson, Swan, Kay, D.Wilkinson, Froggatt, Shiner, Fantham, Finney					
03 Jan. 1959	Ipswich Town	Division 2	3–1	Froggatt(34), Finney(50), Shiner(75)	25023
R.Springett, Johnson, Curtis, Gibson, Swan, Kay, D.Wilkinson, Froggatt, Shiner, J.McAearney, Finney					
19 Jan. 1959	West Bromwich Albion	F.A.Cup 3	0–2		50455
R.Springett, Staniforth, Curtis, Kay, O'Donnell, Gibson, D.Wilkinson, Froggatt, Shiner, Hill, Finney					
31 Jan. 1959	Derby County	Division 2	1–1	Moore(80)og.	31199
R.Springett, Staniforth, Curtis, Gibson, O'Donnell, Kay, D.Wilkinson, Froggatt, Shiner, Fantham, Finney					
14 Feb. 1959	Scunthorpe United	Division 2	2–0	J.McAnearney(35), Wilkinson(89)	22877
R.Springett, Staniforth, Curtis, T.McAnearney, O'Donnell, Kay, D.Wilkinson, J.McAnearney, Shiner, Fantham, Finney					
27 Feb. 1959	Charlton Athletic	Division 2	4–1	Finney(7), Fantham(9), Ellis(30), Kay(45)	29470
R.Springett, Staniforth, Curtis, T.McAnearney, Swan, Kay, D.Wilkinson, J.McAnearney, Ellis, Fantham, Finney					
28 Mar. 1959	Brighton & Hove Alb.	Division 2	2–0	Fantham(16), Curtis(60)pen.	20949
Pinner, Johnson, Curtis, T.McAnearney, Swan, Kay, D.Wilkinson, Froggatt, Shiner, Fantham, Finney					
30 Mar. 1959	Fulham	Division 2	2–2	Shiner(31), Fantham(46)	32170
McLaren, Staniforth, Curtis, T.McAnearney, Swan, Kay, D.Wilkinson, Froggatt, Shiner, Fantham, Finney					
11 Apr. 1959	Cardiff City	Division 2	3–1	Shiner 2(58, 64), Fantham(69)	23106
McLaren, Staniforth, Curtis, T.McAnearney, Swan, Kay, D.Wilkinson, Froggatt, Shiner, Fantham, Finney					
14 Apr. 1959	Liverpool	Division 2	1–0	Froggatt(65)	28264
McLaren, Johnson, Curtis, T.McAnearney, Swan, Kay, D.Wilkinson, Froggatt, Shiner, Fantham, Finney					
25 Apr. 1959	Barnsley	Division 2	5–0	Froggatt 2(17, 87), Shiner 2(28, 75), Wilkinson(3)	17917
McLaren, Johnson, Curtis, T.McAnearney, Swan, Kay, D.Wilkinson, Froggatt, Shiner, Fantham, Finney					
28 Apr. 1959	Doncaster Rovers	County Cup s/f	5–2	Griffin 2(15, 25pen.), Curtis(17)pen., Shiner(70), Finney(80)	n/k
R.Springett, Staniforth, Curtis, Gibson, Swan, Kay, Finney, Griffin, Shiner, Kirby, J.McAnearney					
04 May 1959	Sheffield United	County Cup Fl	1–4	Shiner(79)	18221
McLaren, Staniforth, Curtis, T.McAnearney, Swan, Gibson, D.Wilkinson, Froggatt, Shiner, Fantham, Finney					

OTHER GAMES AT HILLSBOROUGH

26 Aug. 1958	Boys	Yorkshire 3	Arnsburg(Germany) 4	n/k
24 Sep. 1958	U–23 International	England 4	Poland 1	38525
21 Oct. 1958	Inter City	Sheffield 6	Belfast 2	9545
29 Dec. 1958	Boys	Sheffield 2	Birmingham 2	n/k
11 Feb. 1959	F.A.Amateur Cup 2–2r	Bishop Auckland 1	Pegasus 0	n/k
14 Mar. 1959	F.A.Cup Semi Final	Aston Villa 0	Nottingham Forest 1	65107
30 Apr. 1959	Junior Cup Final	Ecclesfield Red Rose 1	Manor Social 0	6000

Date	Opponents	Competition	Score	Scorers	Att.
29 Aug. 1959	Manchester City	Division 1	1–0	McAnearney(70)	34093
R.Springett, Johnson, Curtis, T.McAneaerney, Swan, Hill, D.Wilkinson, Froggatt, Shiner, Fantham, Finney					
02 Sep. 1959	Wolverhampton W.	Division 1	2–2	Shiner(15), Froggatt(38)	45145
R.Springett, Johnson, Curtis, T.McAnearney, Swan, Hill, D.Wilkinson, Froggatt, Shiner, Fantham, Finney					
12 Sep. 1959	Blackpool	Division 1	5–0	Fantham(10), Finney(12), Froggatt(70), Wilkinson(75), Shiner(77)	30238
R.Springett, Johnson, Curtis, Gibson, Swan, Hill, D.Wilkinson, Froggatt, Shiner, Fantham, Finney					
16 Sep. 1959	Nottingham Forest	Division 1	0–1		34249
R.Springett, Johnson, Curtis, Gibson, Swan, Hill, D.Wilkinson, Froggatt, Shiner, Fantham, Finney					
26 Sep. 1959	Luton Town	Division 1	2–0	Curtis(8)pen., Fantham(46)	25138
R.Springett, Martin, Curtis, T.McAnearney, Swan, Hill, Quinn, Froggatt, Shiner, Fantham, Finney					
17 Oct. 1959	Tottenham Hotspur	Division 1	2–1	Young(12), Wilkinson(80)	37743
R.Springett, Johnson, Curtis, T.McAnearney, Swan, Kay, D.Wilkinson, Young, Kirby, Fantham, Finney					
31 Oct. 1959	West Bromwich Albion	Division 1	2–0	Ellis(17), Froggatt(70)	26178
R.Springett, Johnson, Curtis, T.McAnearney, Swan, Kay, D.Wilkinson, Froggatt, K.Ellis, Fantham, Finney					
14 Nov. 1959	Burnley	Division 1	1–1	Ellis(3)	19283
R.Springett, Curtis, Megson, T.McAnearney, Swan, Kay, D.Wilkinson, Young, K.Ellis, Fantham, Finney					
23 Nov. 1959	Torpedo Moscow	Friendly	2–1	Finney(26), Ellis(31)	35098
R.Springett, Johnson, Megson, T.McAnearney, Swan, Kay, D.Wilkinson, R.Craig, K.Ellis, Fantham, Finney					
28 Nov. 1959	West Ham United	Division 1	7–0	Fantham 2(3, 9), Finney 2(25, 80), Wilkinson(10), Craig(65), Ellis(72)	38307
R.Springett, Johnson, Megson, T.McAnearney, Swan, Kay, D.Wilkinson, R.Craig, K.Ellis, Fantham, Finney					
12 Dec. 1959	Preston North End	Division 1	2–2	Wilkinson(80), Craig(86)	42614
R.Springett, Johnson, Megson, T.McAnearney, Swan, Kay, D.Wilkinson, R.Craig, K.Ellis, Fantham, Finney					
19 Dec. 1959	Arsenal	Division 1	5–1	Craig 2(65, 68), Finney(15), Kay(80), Ellis(89)	25135
R.Springett, Johnson, Megson, T.McAnearney, Swan, Kay, D.Wilkinson, R.Craig, K.Ellis, Fantham, Finney					
26 Dec. 1959	Fulham	Division 1	1–1	Ellis(65)	50240
R.Springett, Johnson, Megson, T.McAnearney, Swan, Kay, D.Wilkinson, R.Craig, K.Ellis, Fantham, Finney					
09 Jan. 1960	Middlesbrough	F.A.Cup 3	2–1	McAnearney(36)pen., Ellis(46)	49580
R.Springett, Johnson, Megson, T.McAnearney, Swan, Kay, D.Wilkinson, R.Craig, K.Ellis, Fantham, Finney					
16 Jan. 1960	Blackburn Rovers	Division 1	3–0	Fantham 2(55, 62), Craig(12)	27589
R.Springett, Johnson, Megson, T.McAnearney, Swan, Kay, D.Wilkinson, R.Craig, K.Ellis, Fantham, Finney					
30 Jan. 1960	Peterborough United	F.A.Cup 4	2–0	Craig 2(75, 78)	51144
R.Springett, Johnson, Megson, T.McAnearney, Swan, Kay, D.Wilkinson, Fantham, Griffin, R.Craig, Finney					
06 Feb. 1960	Everton	Division 1	2–2	Kay(13), McAnearney(63)pen.	33066
R.Springett, Curtis, Megson, T.McAnearney, Swan, Kay, D.Wilkinson, R.Craig, Griffin, Fantham, Finney					
24 Feb. 1960	Bolton Wanderers	Division 1	1–0	Finney(54)	36392
R.Springett, Johnson, Megson, Swan, Kay, Finney, R.Craig, K.Ellis, Fantham, Young					
27 Feb. 1960	Chelsea	Division 1	1–1	Fantham(16)	41403
R.Springett, Johnson, Megson, T.McAnearney, Swan, Kay, D.Wilkinson, R.Craig, Froggatt, Fantham, Finney					
30 Mar. 1960	Manchester United	Division 1	4–2	Griffin 2(35, 86), Fantham(65), Wilkinson(80)	26821
R.Springett, Johnson, Megson, T.McAnearney, Swan, Kay, D.Wilkinson, R.Craig, K.Ellis, Fantham, Griffin					
06 Apr. 1960	Leicester City	Division 1	2–2	Griffin(28), Ellis(72)	26844
McLaren, Johnson, Megson, T.McAnearney, Swan, Kay, D.Wilkinson, R.Craig, K.Ellis, Fantham, Griffin					
09 Apr. 1960	Leeds United	Division 1	1–0	Finney(15)	28984
McLaren, Johnson, Megson, T.McAnearney, Swan, Kay, D.Wilkinson, R.Craig, K.Ellis, Fantham, Finney					
18 Apr. 1960	Newcastle United	Division 1	2–0	Fantham(37), Froggatt(66)	33332
R.Springett, Johnson, Megson, T.McAnearney, Swan, Hill, Finney, R.Craig, Froggatt, Fantham, Griffin					
23 Apr. 1960	Birmingham City	Division 1	2–4	Wilkinson(16), Froggatt(88)	26218
R.Springett, Johnson, Megson, T.McAnearney, Swan, Hill, D.Wilkinson, R.Craig, Froggatt, Fantham, Finney					

OTHER GAMES AT HILLSBOROUGH

27 Aug. 1959	Boys	Yorkshire Association of Boys Clubs	2	Kreis Soest (W.Germany) 3	n/k
11 Nov. 1959	Inter City	Sheffield 1		Glasgow 1	11728
18 Jan. 1960	F.A.Cup 3–2R	Arsenal 0		Rotherham United 2	56290
23 Jan. 1960	F.A.Amateur Cup 2	Hallam 2		Crook Town 6	5462
16 Mar. 1960	U–23 International	England 5		Holland 2	21163

Date	Opponents	Competition	Score	Scorers	Att.
20 Aug. 1960	West Bromwich Albion	Division 1	1–0	Craig(3)	34177
R.Springett, Johnson, Megson, T.McAnearney, Swan, Kay, D.Wilkinson, R.Craig, Quinn, Fantham, Finney					
31 Aug. 1960	Cardiff City	Division 1	2–0	Quinn 2(30, 31)	28493
R.Springett, Johnson, Martin, T.McAnearney, Swan, Kay, D.Wilkinson, R.Craig, K.Ellis, Quinn, Finney					
03 Sep. 1960	West Ham United	Division 1	1–0	Fantham(50)	28359
R.Springett, Johnson, Megson, T.McAnearney, Swan, Kay, D.Wilkinson, Craig, Quinn, Fantham, Finney					
10 Sep. 1960	Fulham	Division 1	2–0	Finney(40), Craig(85)	27842
R.Springett, Johnson, Megson, T.McAnearney, Swan, Kay, D.Wilkinson, R.Craig, K.Ellis, Fantham, Finney					
14 Sep. 1960	Manchester City	Division 1	3–1	Ellis 2(34, 55), Craig(69)	30221
R.Springett, Johnson, Megson, T.McAnearney, Swan, Kay, D.Wilkinson, R.Craig, K.Ellis, Fantham, Finney					
24 Sep. 1960	Burnley	Division 1	3–1	Ellis(3), Griffin(15), Fantham(32)	37779
R.Springett, Johnson, Megson, T.McAnearney, Swan, Kay, Griffin, R.Craig, K.Ellis, Fantham, Finney					
15 Oct. 1960	Blackpool	Division 1	4–0	Ellis 2(37, 77), Gratrix(28)og., Fantham(82)	34124
R.Springett, Johnson, Megson, T.McAnearney, Swan, Kay, Griffin, R.Craig, K.Ellis, Fantham, Finney					
29 Oct. 1960	Bolton Wanderers	Division 1	2–0	Ellis(38), Griffin(89)	27595
R.Springett, Johnson, Megson, T.McAnearney, Swan, Kay, Griffin, R.Craig, K.Ellis, Fantham, Finney					
07 Nov. 1960	Dynamo Tbilisi	Friendly	5–0	Fantham 4, Ellis	38778
McLaren, Johnson, Megson, T.McAnearney, Swan, Kay, Griffin, R.Craig, K.Ellis, Fantham, Finney					
12 Nov. 1960	Tottenham Hotspur	Division 1	2–1	Griffin(41), Fantham(68)	56363
McLaren, Johnson, Megson, T.McAnearney, Swan, Kay, Griffin, R.Craig, K.Ellis, Fantham, Finney					
26 Nov. 1960	Aston Villa	Division 1	1–2	Griffin(42)	27939
McLaren, Johnson, Megson, T.McAnearney, Swan, Kay, Griffin, R.Craig, K.Ellis, Fantham, Finney					
29 Nov. 1960	Doncaster Rovers	County Cup	3–0	Griffin 2(17, –), Ballagher(25)	4811
Beighton, Johnson, Megson, T.McAnearney, Swan, Kay, Lodge, McMillan, Ballagher, Griffin, Finney					
10 Dec. 1960	Blackburn Rovers	Division 1	5–4	Lodge 2(16, 33), Craig 2(23, 42), Fantham(12)	22455
R.Springett, Johnson, Megson, Young, Swan, Kay, Lodge, R.Craig, K.Ellis, Fantham, Finney					
23 Dec. 1960	Arsenal	Division 1	1–1	Quinn(39)	29311
R.Springett, Johnson, Hill, T.McAnearney, Swan, Kay, Lodge, R.Craig, Quinn, Fantham, Finney					
31 Dec. 1960	Birmingham City	Division 1	2–0	Wilkinson(14), Fantham(55)	24946
R.Springett, Johnson, Megson, T.McAnearney, O'Donnell, Kay, D.Wilkinson, Quinn, K.Ellis, Fantham, Finney					
07 Jan. 1961	Leeds United	F.A.Cup 3	2–0	Quinn(32), Ellis(84)	36225
R.Springett, Johnson, Megson, T.McAnearney, O'Donnell, Kay, D.Wilkinson, Quinn, K.Ellis, Fantham, Finney					
28 Jan. 1961	Manchester United	F.A.Cup 4	1–1	Wilkinson(14)	58000
R.Springett, Johnson, Megson, T.McAnearney, O'Donnell, Kay, D.Wilkinson, Quinn, K.Ellis, Fantham, Finney					
04 Feb. 1961	Preston North End	Division 1	5–1	Griffin 2(29, 59), Fantham 2(31, 77), Ellis(74)	21115
R.Springett, Johnson, Megson, T.McAnearney, O'Donnell, Kay, D.Wilkinson, Griffin, K.Ellis, Fantham, Finney					
21 Feb. 1961	Nottingham Forest	Division 1	1–0	Finney(45)	35199
R.Springett, Johnson, Megson, T.McAnearney, Swan, Kay, D.Wilkinson, R.Craig, K.Ellis, Quinn, Finney					
25 Feb. 1961	Chelsea	Division 1	1–0	Finney(65)	25000
R.Springett, Johnson, Megson, T.McAnearney, Swan, Kay, D.Wilkinson, R.Craig, K.Ellis, Quinn, Finney					
04 Mar. 1961	Burnley	F.A.Cup 6	0–0		55000
R.Springett, Johnson, Megson, T.McAnearney, O'Donnell, Kay, D.Wilkinson, Quinn, K.Ellis, Fantham, Finney					
11 Mar.1961	Wolverhampton W.	Division 1	0–0		35180
R.Springett, Johnson, Megson, T.McAnearney, O'Donnell, Kay, Finney, R.Craig, K.Ellis, Fantham, Meredith					
25 Mar. 1961	Manchester United	Division 1	5–1	Young 3(13, 52, 64), Cantwell(3)og., Craig(77)	35901
R.Springett, Johnson, Megson, T.McAnearney, Swan, Kay, Finney, R.Craig, Young, Fantham, D.Wilkinson					
03 Apr. 1961	Newcastle United	Division 1	1–1	Craig(43)pen	35273
R.Springett, Johnson, Megson, Hill, Swan, Kay, Finney, R.Craig, Young, Fantham, D.Wilkinson					
08 Apr. 1961	Leicester City	Division 1	2–2	Wilkinson(7), Fantham(41)	29904
R.Springett, Johnson, Megson, T.McAnearney, Swan, Kay, Finney, R.Craig, K.Ellis, Fantham, D.Wilkinson					
22 Apr. 1961	Everton	Division 1	1–2	Wilkinson(44)	28521
R.Springett, Johnson, Megson, T.McAnearney, Swan, Kay, Finney, R.Craig, K.Ellis, Fantham, D.Wilkinson					

OTHER GAMES AT HILLSBOROUGH

19 Oct. 1960	Representative	The Army 1	F.A. XI 2		9683
31 Oct. 1960	Boys	Sheffield 2	Nottingham 0		n/k
03 May 1960	Charity	Sheffield Soccer Stars v. Manchester Football Favourites – score n/k			n/k

1958–59
Martin, Fantham, T. McAnearney, R. Springett,
D. Wilkinson, Gibson, Swan;
Finney, Froggatt, Shiner, Curtis.

1959–60
Eggleston (trainer), J. McAnearney, Swan, R. Springett, Kay,
Johnson, Catterick (manager);
D. Wilkinson, Shiner, Froggatt, Finney, Fantham, Curtis.

1960–61
Megson, T. McAnearney, Young, R. Springett,
McLaren, Curtis, Swan;
Froggatt, Craig, Ellis, Finney, Kay, Fantham, D. Wilkinson;
Martin, Johnson.

1961–62
Megson, Kay, Hardy, R. Springett, Swan, Johnson;
Finney, Craig, Fantham, Griffin, Dobson.

Date	Opponents	Competition	Score	Scorers	Att.
23 Aug. 1961	Bolton Wanderers	Division 1	4–2	Ellis 2(75, 76), Craig(3), Wilkinson(35)	36470
R.Springett, Johnson, Megson, T.McAnearney, Swan, Kay, D.Wilkinson, R.Craig, K.Ellis, Fantham, Finney					
26 Aug. 1961	Birmingham City	Division 1	5–1	Fantham 3(47, 70, 78), Ellis(12), Finney(19)	30595
R.Springett, Johnson, Megson, T.McAnearney, Swan, Kay, D.Wilkinson, R.Craig, K.Ellis, Fantham, Finney					
09 Sep. 1961	Fulham	Division 1	1–1	Fantham(89)	35773
R.Springett, Johnson, Megson, T.McAnearney, Swan, Kay, D.Wilkinson, R.Craig, K.Ellis, Fantham, Finney					
20 Sep. 1961	Arsenal	Division 1	1–1	McAnearney(45)pen.	35903
R.Springett, Johnson, Megson, T.McAnearney, Swan, Kay, D.Wilkinson, Dobson, K.Ellis, Fantham, Finney					
30 Sep. 1961	Ipswich Town	Division 1	1–4	Fantham(23)	27565
R.Springett, Johnson, Megson, T.McAnearney, Swan, Kay, D.Wilkinson, R.Craig, K.Elis, Fantham, Dobson					
04 Oct. 1961	Olympique Lyonnais	Fairs Cup 1–L1	5–2	Fantham 2(9, 85), Griffin(14), McAnearney(20)pen., Dobson(78)	30303
R.Springett, Johnson, Megson, T.McAnearney, Swan, Kay, Finney, R.Craig, Fantham, Griffin, Dobson					
07 Oct. 1961	Chelsea	Division 1	5–3	Fantham 2(28, 52), Craig(34), Dobson(49), Griffin(59)	28093
R.Springett, Johnson, Megson, T.McAnearney, Swan, Kay, Finney, R.Craig, Fantham, Griffin, Dobson					
21 Oct. 1961	Blackburn Rovers	Division 1	1–0	Griffin(62)	26491
R.Springett, Johnson, Megson, Hardy, Swan, Kay, Finney, R.Craig, Fantham, Griffin, Dobson					
04 Nov. 1961	Manchester United	Division 1	3–1	Fantham(9), Kay(14), Ellis(83)	36808
R.Springett, Johnson, Megson, T.McAnearney, Swan, Kay, Finney, Griffin, K.Ellis, Fantham, Dobson					
18 Nov. 1961	Tottenham Hotspur	Division 1	0–0		45058
R.Springett, Johnson, Megson, T.McAnearney, Swan, Kay, Finney, R.Craig, Young, Fantham, D.Wilkinson					
29 Nov. 1961	A.S.Roma	Fairs Cup 2–L1	4–0	Young 3(32, 35, 79), Fantham(6)	42589
R.Springett, Johnson, Megson, T.McAnearney, Swan, Kay, Finney, R.Craig, Young, Fantham, D.Wilkinson					
02 Dec. 1961	Nottingham Forest	Division 1	3–0	Young 2(38, 56), Wilkinson(22)	30083
R.Springett, Johnson, Megson, T.McAnearney, Swan, Kay, Finney, R.Craig, Young, Fantham, D.Wilkinson					
16 Dec. 1961	West Bromwich Albion	Division 1	2–1	Dobson(30), Fantham(36)	25168
R.Springett, Johnson, Megson, Hardy, Swan, Kay, Finney, R.Craig, Young, Fantham, Dobson					
09 Jan. 1962	Swansea Town	F.A.Cup 3	1–0	Finney(56)	35184
R.Springett, Johnson, Megson, T.McAnearney, Swan, Kay, Finney, R.Craig, K.Ellis, Fantham, Dobson					
13 Jan. 1962	Everton	Division 1	3–1	Dobson 2(58, 59), Ellis(5)	32130
R.Springett, Johnson, Megson, T.McAnearney, Swan, Kay, Finney, R.Craig, K.Ellis, Fantham, Dobson					
03 Feb. 1962	Sheffield United	Division 1	1–2	Dobson(47)	50937
R.Springett, Johnson, Megson, T.McAnearney, Swan, Kay, Finney, R.Craig, K.Ellis, Fantham, Dobson					
10 Feb. 1962	Leicester City	Division 1	1–2	Finney(75)	28179
R.Springett, Johnson, Megson, T.McAnearney, Swan, Kay, Finney, R.Craig, K.Ellis, Fantham, Dobson					
21 Feb. 1962	Manchester United	F.A.Cup 5R	0–2		65009
R.Springett, Johnson, Megson, T.McAnearney, Swan, Kay, D.Wilkinson, R.Craig, K.Ellis, Fantham, Finney					
28 Feb. 1962	Barcelona	F.Cup QF–L1	3–2	Fantham 2(28, 50), Finney(44)	28956
R.Springett, Johnson, Megson, Hardy, Swan, Kay, D.Wilkinson, Dobson, Young, Fantham, Finney					
03 Mar. 1962	Aston Villa	Division 1	3–0	Dobson 2(44, 55), Wilkinson(3)	23896
R.Springett, Johnson, Megson, Hardy, Swan, Kay, D.Wilkinson, Dobson, Young, Fantham, Finney					
17 Mar. 1962	West Ham United	Division 1	0–0		31403
R.Springett, Johnson, Megson, Hardy, Swan, Kay, Finney, Dobson, Young, Fantham, Holliday					
03 Apr. 1962	Cardiff City	Division 1	2–0	Megson(25), Fantham(47)	18434
McLaren, Johnson, Megson, Hardy, O'Donnell, Kay, Finney, Dobson, K.Ellis, Fantham, Holliday					
14 Apr. 1962	Blackpool	Division 1	3–2	Griffin 2(29, 34), Quinn(4)	20090
McLaren, Johnson, Megson, Hardy, O'Donnell, Kay, Finney, Griffin, Quinn, Fantham, Holliday					
23 Apr. 1962	Manchester City	Division 1	1–0	Finney(53)	22048
R.Springett, Johnson, Megson, Hardy, Swan, Kay, Finney, Dobson, D.Wilkinson, Fantham, Holliday					
28 Apr. 1962	Wolverhampton W.	Division 1	3–2	Wilkinson(16), Holliday(46), Fantham(70)	20079
R.Springett, Johnson, Megson, Hardy, Swan, Kay, Finney, Dobson, D.Wilkinson, Fantham, Holliday					
30 Apr. 1962	Burnley	Division 1	4–0	Dobson 2(12, 54), Fantham(60), Wilkinson(67)	20501
R.Springett, Johnson, Megson, Hardy, Swan, Kay, Finney, Dobson, D.Wilkinson, Fantham, Holliday					

OTHER GAMES AT HILLSBOROUGH

31 Oct. 1961	McMillan Benefit	Sheffield XI 5	Select XI 8		25202
11 Dec. 1961	Boys	Sheffield 1	Hull 1		n/k
15 Jan. 1962	F.A.Cup 3–2R	Bury 0	Sheffield United 2		26941
31 Mar. 1962	F.A.Cup Semi Final	Tottenham Hotspur 3	Manchester United 1		65000

Date	Opponents	Competition	Score	Scorers	Att.
18 Aug. 1962	Bolton Wanderers	Division 1	1–1	Dobson(46)	28036
R.Springett, Johnson, Megson, T.McAnearney, Swan, Hardy, Finney, Dobson, Layne, Fantham, Holliday					
29 Aug. 1962	Leicester City	Division 1	0–3		25307
R.Springett, Johnson, Hill, Eustace, Swan, Hardy, Finney, Kay, Layne, Dobson, Holliday					
01 Sep. 1962	West Bromwich Albion	Division 1	3–1	Dobson 2(5, 31), Fantham(29)	23042
R.Springett, Hill, Birks, Eustace, Swan, Kay, Finney, Dobson, Layne, Fantham, Holliday					
12 Sep. 1962	Fulham	Division 1	1–0	Holliday(41)	21062
R.Springett, Johnson, Birks, Eustace, Swan, Kay, Griffin, Dobson, Layne, Fantham, Holliday					
15 Sep. 1962	Birmingham City	Division 1	5–0	Holliday 2(63, 87), Layne 2(75, 83), Dobson(10)	22255
R.Springett, Johnson, Megson, Eustace, Swan, Kay, D.Wilkinson, Quinn, Layne, Dobson, Holliday					
29 Sep. 1962	Manchester United	Division 1	1–0	Kay(82)	40520
R.Springett, Horrobin, Megson, Eustace, Swan, Kay, D.Wilkinson, Dobson, Layne, Young, Holliday					
13 Oct. 1962	Nottingham Forest	Division 1	2–2	Kay(5), Layne(42)	29784
R.Springett, Johnson, Megson, Eustace, Swan, Kay, Holliday, Griffin, Layne, Fantham, Dobson					
17 Oct. 1962	Ajax	Froggatt Beneft	2–2	Layne(10), Johnson(13)	21810
McLaren, Johnson, Megson, Eustace, Swan, Kay, Holliday, Froggatt(Storf), Layne, Fantham, Dobson					
22 Oct. 1962	Santos	Friendly	2–4	Griffin(30), Layne(33)	49058
R.Springett, Johnson, Megson, T.McAnearney, Swan, Kay, Finney, Dobson, Layne(Young 35), Griffin, Holliday					
27 Oct. 1962	Blackpool	Division 1	0–0		22227
R.Springett, Johnson, Megson, T.McAnearney, Swan, Kay, Finney, Dobson, Young, Fantham, Holliday					
10 Nov. 1962	Aston Villa	Division 1	0–0		20507
R.Springett, Horrobin, Megson, T.McAnearney, Swan, Hardy, D.Wilkinson, Dobson, Layne, Griffin, Hardy					
24 Nov. 1962	West Ham United	Division 1	1–3	Fantham(24)	23764
R.Springett, Johnson, Birks, T.McAnearney, Swan, Kay, Finney, D.Wilkinson, Layne, Fantham, Holliday					
08 Dec. 1962	Liverpool	Division 1	0–2		15939
R.Springett, Johnson, Megson, T.McAnearney, Swan, Kay, Finney, D.Wilkinson, K.Ellis, Fantham, Holliday					
22 Dec. 1962	Everton	Division 1	2–2	Quinn(20), Layne(61)	28279
R.Springett, Johnson, Megson, T.McAnearney, Swan, Kay, Holliday, Quinn, Layne, Fantham, Dobson					
07 Mar. 1963	Shrewsbury Town	F.A.Cup 3R	2–1 aet	Finney(20), Fantham(96)	24207
R.Springett, Johnson, Megson, T.McAnearney, Swan, Eustace, Finney, Quinn, Layne, Fantham, Dobson					
09 Mar. 1963	Manchester City	Division 1	4–1	Layne 3(56, 69, 80), Dobson(39)	19424
R.Springett, Johnson, Megson, T.McAnearney, Swan, Eustace, Finney, Quinn, Layne, Fantham, Dobson					
23 Mar. 1963	Wolverhampton W.	Division 1	3–1	Fantham(39), Layne(60), Dobson(65)	26495
R.Springett, Johnson, Megson, T.McAnearney, Swan, Young, D.Wilkinson, Quinn, Layne, Fantham, Dobson					
08 Apr. 1963	Tottenham Hotspur	Division 1	3–1	Layne 2(30, 47), Fantham(65)	42245
R.Springett, Johnson, Megson, T.McAnearney, Swan, Young, D.Wilkinson, Quinn, Layne, Fantham, Dobson					
15 Apr. 1963	Blackburn Rovers	Division 1	4–0	Layne 2(60, 77), Dobson(25), Young(82)	25707
R.Springett, Johnson, Megson, T.McAnearney, Swan, Young, D.Wilkinson, Quinn, Layne, Fantham, Dobson					
20 Apr. 1963	Ipswich Town	Division 1	0–3		17268
R.Springett, Johnson, Megson, T.McAnearney, Swan, Young, D.Wilkinson, Quinn, Layne, Fantham, Dobson					
23 Apr. 1963	Burnley	Division 1	0–1		25751
R.Springett, Johnson, Megson, T.McAnearney, Swan, Young, Finney, Quinn, Layne, Fantham, Dobson					
04 May 1963	Leyton Orient	Division 1	3–1	Dobson(21), Fantham(60), Finney(70)	19696
R.Springett, Johnson, Megson, T.McAnearney, Swan, Young, Finney, Quinn, Layne, Fantham, Dobson					
15 May 1963	Sheffield United	Division 1	3–1	Layne 2(48, 55), McAnearney(57)	41585
R.Springett, Johnson, Megson, T.McAnearney, Swan, Young, Finney, Quinn, Layne, Fantham, Dobson					
18 May 1963	Arsenal	Division 1	2–3	Fantham(25), Young(88)	20514
R.Springett, Johnson, Megson, T.McAnearney, Swan, Young, Finney, D.Wilkinson, Layne, Fantham, Dobson					

OTHER GAMES AT HILLSBOROUGH

03 Oct. 1962	International	England 1	France 1	35380
14 Nov. 1962	Boys	Sheffield 3	Nottingham 3	n/k
28 Nov. 1962	Representative	F.A.Colts 2	South Yorkshire Amateur League 1	n/k
27 Apr. 1963	F.A.Cup Semi Final	Leicester City 1	Liverpool 0	65000

Date	Opponents	Competition	Score	Scorers	Att.
24 Aug. 1963	Manchester United	Division 1	3–3	Quinn(10), McAnearney(12)pen., Holliday(65)	32177
R.Springett, Johnson, Megson, T.McAnearney, Swan, Young, Finney, Quinn, K.Ellis, Fantham, Holliday					
04 Sep. 1963	Fulham	Division 1	3–0	Fantham 2(47, 68), Layne(88)	20045
R.Springett, Hill, Megson, T.McAnearney, Swan, Young, D.Wilkinson, Quinn, Layne, Fantham, Dobson					
07 Sep. 1963	Ipswich Town	Division 1	3–1	Layne(30secs.), Fantham(40), McAnearney(79)pen.	19127
R.Springett, Hill, Megson, T.McAnearney, Swan, Young, D.Wilkinson, Quinn, Layne, Fantham, Dobson					
28 Sep. 1963	Birmingham City	Division 1	2–1	Fantham(60), Holliday(82)	18903
McLaren, Hill, Megson, T.McAnearney, Swan, Young, D.Wilkinson, Quinn, Layne, Fantham, Holliday					
02 Oct. 1963	Leicester City	Division 1	1–2	Quinn(68)	21420
R.Springett, Hill, Megson, T.McAnearney, Swan, Young, Finney, Quinn, Layne, Fantham, Holliday					
12 Oct. 1963	West Ham United	Division 1	3–0	Dobson(57), Pearson(62), Holliday(82)	23503
R.Springett, Hill, Megson, T.McAnearney, Swan, Young, Finney, Pearson, Layne, Dobson, Holliday					
15 Oct. 1963	D.O.S.Utrecht	Fairs Cup 1–L2	4–1	Layne 3(9, 52, 56pen.), Dobson(16)	20643
R.Springett, Hill, Megson, T.McAnearney, Swan, Young, Finney, Quinn, Layne, Dobson, Holliday					
26 Oct. 1963	Aston Villa	Division 1	1–0	Pearson(39)	20616
R.Springett, Hill, Megson, T.McAnearney, Swan, Young, Finney, Quinn, K.Ellis, Pearson, Dobson					
09 Nov. 1963	Nottingham Forest	Division 1	3–1	Dobson 2(10, 30), Wilkinson(15)	23231
R.Springett, Hill, Megson, T.McAnearney, Swan, Young, Finney, Dobson, D.Wilkinson, Pearson, Holliday					
23 Nov. 1963	Wolverhampton W.	Division 1	5–0	Finney 2(42, 65), Dobson 2(75, 89), Layne(60)	22650
R.Springett, Johnson, Megson, T.McAnearney, Swan, Young, Finney, Dobson, Layne, Pearson, Holliday					
27 Nov. 1963	F.C. Köln	Fairs Cup 2–2L	1–2	Layne(17)	36929
R.Springett, Johnson, Megson, Hardy, Swan, Young, Finney, Dobson, Layne, Pearson, Holliday					
07 Dec. 1963	Blackpool	Division 1	1–0	Holliday(82)	20397
R.Springett, Hill, Megson, T.McAnearney, Swan, Young, Finney, Dobson, Layne, Pearson, Holliday					
21 Dec. 1963	Burnley	Division 1	3–1	McAnearney(31)pen., Layne(77), Dobson(87)	19390
McLaren, Hill, Megson, T.McAnearney, Swan, Young, Finney, Dobson, Layne, Pearson, Holliday					
26 Dec. 1963	Bolton Wanderers	Division 1	3–0	Dobson 2(15, 80), Pearson(27)	31301
McLaren, Hill, Megson, T.McAnearney, Swan, Young, D.Wilkinson, Dobson, Layne, Pearson, Holliday					
18 Jan. 1964	Sheffield United	Division 1	3–0	Wilkinson 2(30, 52), Layne(10)	42898
McLaren, Hill, Megson, Hardy, Swan, Young, Finney, D.Wilkinson, Layne, Pearson, Dobson					
01 Feb. 1964	Everton	Division 1	0–3		30722
R.Springett, HIl, Megson, T.McAnearney, Swan, Young, Finney, D.Wilkinson, Layne, Pearson, Dobson					
15 Feb. 1964	West Bromwich Albion	Division 1	2–2	Layne(7), Fantham(89)	19048
R.Springett, Hill, Megson, T.McAnearney, Swan, Young, D.Wilkinson, Pearson, Layne, Fantham, Dobson					
29 Feb. 1964	Chelsea	Division 1	3–2	McAnearney(12), Layne(25), Finney(72)	20212
R.Springett, Hill, Megson, T.McAnearney, Swan, Young, Finney, Pearson, Layne, Fantham, Dobson					
04 Mar. 1964	Liverpool	Division 1	2–2	Holliday(32), Pearson(47)	23703
McLaren, Hill, Megson, T.McAnearney, Swan, Young, Finney, Dobson, Layne, Pearson, Holliday					
28 Mar. 1964	Blackburn Rovers	Division 1	5–2	Layne 2(40, 59pen.), Hardy(3), Fantham(24), Holliday(35)	20791
McLaren, Hill, Megson, Hardy, Swan, Young, Finney, Dobson, Layne, Fantham, Holliday					
30 Mar. 1964	Arsenal	Division 1	0–4		26433
McLaren, Johnson, Megson, Hardy, Swan, Young, Finney, Fantham, Layne, Dobson, Holliday					
08 Apr. 1964	Stoke City	Division 1	2–0	Dobson(55), Fantham(85)	17487
R.Springett, Johnson, Megson, T.McAnearney, Swan, Young, Finney, Fantham, Layne, Pearson, Dobson					
13 Apr. 1964	Tottenham Hotspur	Division 1	2–0	Wilkinson 2(35, 36)	31377
R.Springett, Johnson, Megson, T.McAnearney, Mobley, Young, Finney, Pearson, D.Wilkinson, Fantham, Dobson					

OTHER GAMES AT HILLSBOROUGH

22 Oct. 1963	League Cup 2–2R	Scunthorpe United 0	Stoke City 1		4900
14 Mar. 1964	F.A.Cup Semi Final	Manchester United 1	West Ham United 3		65000

Date	Opponents	Competition	Score	Scorers	Att.
22 Aug. 1964	Blackburn Rovers	Division 1	1–0	Finney(48)	21620
R.Springett, Hill, Megson, T.McAnearney, Mobley, Young, Finney, Pearson, Quinn, Fantham, Dobson					
02 Sep. 1964	Arsenal	Division 1	2–1	Dobson(30), Pearson(62)	22555
R.Springett, Hill, Megson, T.McAnearney, Mobley, Young, Finney, Pearson, Quinn, Fantham, Dobson					
05 Sep. 1964	Sheffield United	Division 1	0–2		32684
R.Springett, Hill, Megson, T.McAnearney, Mobley, Young, Finney, Pearson, Quinn, Fantham, Dobson					
12 Sep. 1964	Liverpool	Division 1	1–0	Quinn(32)	22701
R.Springett, Hill, Megson, T.McAnearney, Mobley, Young, H.Wilkinson, Pearson, Quinn, Fantham, Dobson					
16 Sep. 1964	Chelsea	Division 1	2–3	Dobson(1), Fantham(60)	18176
R.Springett, Hill, Megson, T.McAnearney, Mobley, Young, H.Wilkinson, Pearson, Quinn, Fantham, Dobson					
23 Sep. 1964	Burnley	Division 1	5–1	Fantham 3(25, 35, 45), Mobley(34), Dobson(36)	17366
R.Springett, Hill, Megson, T.McAnearney, Mobley, Young, D.Wilkinson, Pearson, Quinn, Fantham, Dobson					
26 Sep. 1964	Wolverhampton W.	Division 1	2–0	McAnearney(44)pen., Dobson(89)	19881
R.Springett, Hill, Megson, T.McAnearney, Mobley, Young, Finney, Quinn, D.Wilkinson, Fantham, Dobson					
17 Oct. 1964	Birmingham City	Division 1	5–2	Fantham 2(42, 88), Wilkinson 2(10, 76) Quinn(30)	16161
R.Springett, Hill, Megson, Eustace, Mobley, Young, Finney, Quinn, D.Wilkinson, Fantham, Dobson					
31 Oct. 1964	West Bromwich Albion	Division 1	1–1	Fantham(79)	19004
R.Springett, Hill, Megson, Eustace, Mobley, Young, Finney, Quinn, D.Wilkinson, Fantham, Dobson					
14 Nov. 1964	Fulham	Division 1	1–1	Hickton(87)	18027
R.Springett, Hill, Megson, Eustace, Mobley, Young, Finney, Quinn, Hickton, Fantham, Dobson					
28 Nov. 1964	Stoke City	Division 1	1–1	Fantham(25)	17266
R.Springett, Hill, Megson, Eustace, Mobley, T.McAnearney, Finney, Quinn, Hickton, Fantham, Dobson					
19 Dec. 1964	Blackpool	Division 1	4–1	Dobson 2(27, 88pen.), Hickton(52), Fantham(85)	16172
R.Springett, Hill, Megson, Eustace, Mobley, Smith, Finney, Quinn, Hickton, Fantham, Dobson					
28 Dec. 1964	Leicester City	Division 1	0–0		18046
R.Springett, Johnson, Megson, Eustace, Mobley, Smith, Finney, Quinn, Hickton, Fantham, Dobson					
13 Jan. 1965	Everton	F.A.Cup 3R	0–3		50080
McLaren, Burgin, Megson, Eustace, Mobley, Smith, Finney, Quinn, Hickton, Fantham, Dobson					
13 Feb. 1965	Sunderland	Division 1	2–0	Finney(68), Eustace(85)	17909
R.Springett, Hill, Megson, Eustace, Mobley, Smith, Finney, T.McAnearney, Hickton, Fantham, Dobson					
20 Feb. 1965	Everton	Division 1	0–1		17135
R.Springett, Hill, Megson, T.McAnearney, Mobley, Smith, Finney, Eustace, Hickton, Fantham, Dobson					
06 Mar. 1965	West Ham United	Division 1	2–0	Mobley(48), Hickton(72)	14931
R.Springett, Hill, Megson, Eustace, Mobley, Smith, Finney, Quinn, Hickton, Fantham, Dobson					
08 Mar. 1965	Werder Bremen	Friendly	2–3	Hickton 2(10, 52)	18942
R.Springett, Hill, Megson, Eustace, Mobley, Smith, Finney, Quinn, Hickton, Fantham, Dobson					
15 Mar. 1965	Aston Villa	Division 1	3–1	Hickton 2(5, 60), Quinn(83)	12223
R.Springett, Hill, Megson, Eustace, Mobley, Smith, H.Wilkinson, Quinn, Hickton, Fantham, Dobson					
20 Mar. 1965	Manchester United	Division 1	1–0	Fantham(64)	33549
R.Springett, Hill, Megson, Eustace, Mobley, Smith, H.Wilkinson, Quinn, Hickton, Fantham, Dobson					
03 Apr. 1965	Nottingham Forest	Division 1	0–0		18096
R.Springett, Hill, Megson, Eustace, Mobley, Smith, H.Wilkinson, Quinn, Hickton, Fantham, Dobson					
17 Apr. 1965	Tottenham Hotspur	Division 1	1–0	Eustace(10)	23099
R.Springett, Hill, Megson, Eustace, Mobley, Young, H.Wilkinson, Quinn, Hickton, Fantham, Dobson					
19 Apr. 1965	Leeds United	Division 1	3–0	Fantham 2(3, 25), Hunter(83)og.	39054
R.Springett, Hill, Megson, Eustace, Mobley, Young, H.Wilkinson, Quinn, Hickton, Fantham, Dobson					

OTHER GAMES AT HILLSBOROUGH

27 Mar. 1965	F.A.Cup Semi Final	Leeds United 0	Manchester United 0	65000
22 Apr. 1965	Schools	England 0	Wales 0	10577
28 Apr. 1965	Boys	Sheffield 1	Hull 1	n/k

Date	Opponents	Competition	Score	Scorers	Att.
25 Aug. 1965	Everton	Division 1	3–1	Hickton 2(52, 76), Quinn(83)	26986
R.Springett, Hill, Megson, Eustace, Mobley, Young, Usher, Quinn, Hickton, Fantham, Dobson					
28 Aug. 1965	Newcastle United	Division 1	1–0	Dobson(21)	23391
R.Springett, Hill, Megson, Eustace, Mobley, Young, Usher, Quinn, Hickton, Fantham, Dobson					
11 Sep. 1965	Nottingham Forest	Division 1	3–1	Megson(2), Eustace(39), Hickton(80)	18368
R.Springett, Hill, Megson, Eustace, Mobley, Smith, Usher, Quinn, Hickton, Fantham, Dobson					
09 Oct. 1965	Leeds United	Division 1	0–0		35105
R.Springett, Smith, Megson, Eustace, Mobley, Young, Usher, Quinn, Hickton, Fantham, Dobson					
23 Oct. 1965	Sunderland	Division 1	3–1	Hickton(8), Dobson(53), Irwin(85)og.	21381
R.Springett, Hill, Megson(Ford 8), Smith, Mobley, Young, H.Wilkinson, Quinn, Hickton, Eustace, Dobson					
06 Nov. 1965	Liverpool	Division 1	0–2		24456
R.Springett, Smith, Megson, Eustace, Mobley, Young, H.Wilkinson, Quinn, Hickton, McCalliog, Dobson					
20 Nov. 1965	Fulham	Division 1	1–0	Ford(27)	16030
Wicks, Hill, Megson, Smith, Mobley, Young, Quinn, Ford, McCalliog, Fantham, Dobson					
04 Dec. 1965	Blackburn Rovers	Division 1	2–1	Hickton(55), Finney(75)	15716
R.Springett, Hill, Megson(Quinn 55), Smith, Mobley, Young, Finney, Fantham, McCalliog, Hickton, Usher					
18 Dec. 1965	West Ham United	Division 1	0–0		12996
R.Springett, Hill, Smith, Eustace, Mobley, Young, Usher, Fantham, McCalliog, Hickton, Dobson					
27 Dec. 1965	Arsenal	Division 1	4–0	Hickton 3(9, 11, 61), Usher(20)	33101
R.Springett, Hill, Smith, Eustace, Mobley, Young, Usher, Fantham, McCalliog, Hickton, Dobson					
08 Jan. 1966	Leicester City	Division 1	1–2	Wilkinson(9)	15165
R.Springett, Hill, Megson, Smith, Mobley, Young, H.Wilkinson, Fantham, McCalliog, Hickton, Dobson					
29 Jan. 1966	Manchester United	Division 1	0–0		39281
R.Springett, Smith, Megson, Eustace, Mobley, Young, Usher, Fantham, McCalliog, Hickton(Quinn 75), Dobson					
19 Feb. 1966	West Bromwich Albion	Division 1	1–2	Eustace(15)	18358
R.Springett, Smith, Megson, Eustace, Mobley, Young, Usher, Fantham, McCalliog, Ford, Dobson					
12 Mar. 1966	Sheffield United	Division 1	2–2	Fantham(17), Eustace(74)	34045
R.Springett, Smith, Megson, Eustace, Mobley, Young, Usher(Hickton 78), Fantham, Quinn, Ford, Dobson					
19 Mar. 1966	Northampton Town	Division 1	3–1	Ford 2(40, 86), Fantham(50)	17020
Wicks, Smith, Megson, Eustace, Mobley, Young, H.Wilkinson, Fantham, Quinn, Ford, Dobson					
30 Mar. 1966	Stoke City	Division 1	4–1	McCalliog(30), Ford(46), Dobson(47), Fantham(85)	19898
R.Springett, Smith, Megson, Eustace, Mobley, Young, Quinn, Fantham, McCalliog, Ford, Dobson					
04 Apr. 1966	Blackpool	Division 1	3–0	Ford 2(8, 85), Fantham(75)	20945
R.Springett, Smith, Megson, Eustace, S.Ellis, Young, Quinn, Fantham, McCalliog, Ford, Dobson					
09 Apr. 1966	Tottenham Hotspur	Division 1	1–1	Ford(6)	18009
R.Springett, Smith, Megson, Eustace, S.Ellis, Young, Pugh, Fantham, McCalliog, Ford, Quinn					
27 Apr. 1966	Aston Villa	Division 1	2–0	Fantham 2(67, 71)	28008
R.Springett, Smith, Megson, Eustace, S.Ellis, Young, Pugh, Fantham, McCalliog, Ford, Quinn					
02 May 1966	Chelsea	Division 1	1–1	Davies(40)	27089
Wicks, Hill, Megson, Eustace, S.Ellis, Young, Pugh, Davies, McCalliog, Ford, Quinn					
09 May 1966	Burnley	Division 1	0–2		21049
R.Springett, Smith, Megson, Eustace, S.Ellis, Branfoot, Pugh, Davies, McCalliog, Hickton, Quinn					

1965–66
*Logan (trainer), Eustace, Ellis,
R. Springett, Smith, Young, McCalliog;
Pugh, Fantham, Megson, Ford, Quinn.*

Date	Opponents	Competition	Score	Scorers	Att.
08 Aug. 1966	Bulgarian Select XI	Friendly	2–1	Pugh(5), McCalliog(71)	19441
R.Springett, Smith, Megson, Eustace, S.Ellis, Young, Pugh, Fantham, McCalliog, Ford, Quinn					
20 Aug. 1966	Blackpool	Division 1	3–0	Ford(15), Quinn(17), Eustace(56)	21008
R.Springett, Smith, Megson, Eustace, S.Ellis, Young, Pugh, Fantham, McCalliog, Ford, Quinn					
31 Aug. 1966	Aston Villa	Division 1	2–0	Pugh(7), Fantham(60)	25992
R.Springett, Smith, Megson, Eustace, S.Ellis, Young, Pugh, Fantham, McCalliog, Ford, Quinn					
03 Sep. 1966	Leicester City	Division 1	1–1	Pugh(89)	31252
R.Springett, Smith, Megson, Eustace, S.Ellis, Young, Pugh, Fantham, McCalliog, Ford, Quinn					
14 Sep. 1966	Rotherham United	League Cup 2	0–1		20204
R.Springett, Smith, Megson, Eustace, S.Ellis, Young, Usher, Pugh, McCalliog, Davies, Quinn					
17 Sep. 1966	West Ham United	Division 1	0–2		29171
R.Springett, Smith, Megson, Eustace, S.Ellis, Young, Pugh, Fantham, McCalliog, Ford, Quinn					
24 Sep. 1966	Sheffield United	Division 1	2–2	Munks(40)og., McCalliog(67)	43557
R.Springett, Smith, Megson, Eustace, S.Ellis, Young, Pugh, Fantham, McCalliog, Ford, Quinn					
26 Sep. 1966	All Star XI	Wilkinson TST.	8–7	Springett 4, Ford 2, Quinn, McCalliog	10096
R.Springett(Fantham ht), Smith, Megson, Mobley, S.Ellis, Young, Pugh, Fantham(R.Springett ht), McCalliog, Ford, Quinn					
08 Oct. 1966	Stoke City	Division 1	1–3	Fantham(89)	28047
R.Springett, Smith, Megson, Eustace, S.Ellis, Young, Pugh, Fantham, McCalliog, Ford, Quinn					
22 Oct. 1966	Fulham	Division 1	1–1	McCalliog(8)	20044
R.Springett, Smith, Megson, Eustace, S.Ellis, Young, Pugh, Symm, McCalliog, Ford, Quinn					
05 Nov. 1966	Everton	Division 1	1–2	Fantham(14)	28072
R.Springett, Smith, Megson, Eustace, S.Ellis, Young, Pugh, Fantham, McCalliog, Ford, Quinn					
19 Nov. 1966	Tottenham Hotspur	Division 1	1–0	Ford(85)	32990
R.Springett, Smith, Megson, Eustace, S.Ellis, Young, Fantham, McCalliog, Ritchie, Ford, Branfoot					
03 Dec. 1966	Leeds United	Division 1	0–0		35264
R.Springett, Smith, Megson, Mobley, S.Ellis, Young, Fantham, McCalliog, Ritchie, Ford, Branfoot					
27 Dec. 1966	Manchester City	Division 1	1–0	Young(67)	34005
R.Springett, Smith, Megson, Mobley, S.Ellis, Young, Fantham, McCalliog, Ritchie, Ford, Branfoot					
31 Dec. 1966	Chelsea	Division 1	6–1	Ford 2(42, 88), Ritchie 2(49, 67), McCalliog(18), Fantham(75)	31032
R.Springett, Smith, Megson, Mobley, S.Ellis, Young, Fantham, McCalliog, Ritchie, Ford, Pugh					
14 Jan. 1967	Liverpool	Division 1	0–1		43951
R.Springett, Smith, Megson, Mobley, S.Ellis, Young, Fantham(Symm 16), McCalliog, Ritchie, Ford, Pugh					
28 Jan. 1967	Queen's Park Rangers	F.A.Cup 3	3–0	Ritchie 3(17, 82, 88)	40038
R.Springett, Smith, Megson, Mobley, S.Ellis, Young(Quinn 7), Fantham, McCalliog, Ritchie, Ford, Pugh					
11 Feb. 1967	Southampton	Division 1	4–1	Fantham 3(37, 46, 50pen.), McCalliog(25)	26199
R.Springett, Smith, Megson, Mobley, S.Ellis, Quinn, Fantham, McCalliog, Ritchie, Ford, Pugh					
18 Feb. 1967	Mansfield Town	F.A.Cup 4	4–0	Ritchie 2(6, 50), Fantham(59), McCalliog(80)	49049
Scothorn, Smith, Megson, Mobley, S.Ellis, Quinn, Fantham, McCalliog, Ritchie, Ford, Pugh					
25 Mar. 1967	Nottingham Forest	Division 1	0–2		43118
R.Springett, Smith, Megson, Mobley, S.Ellis, Symm, McCalliog, Ritchie, Ford, Eustace(Usher 28)					
28 Mar. 1967	Sunderland	Division 1	5–0	Ritchie 2(20, 68), Megson(14), Symm(56), Ford(63)	26094
R.Springett, Smith, Megson, Mobley, S.Ellis, Quinn, Symm, McCalliog, Ritchie, Ford, Usher					
10 Apr. 1967	Manchester United	Division 1	2–2	Fantham(53), Ritchie(59)	51018
R.Springett, Smith, Megson, Mobley, S.Ellis, Quinn, Fantham, McCalliog, Ritchie, Usher, Pugh					
19 Apr. 1967	West Bromwich Albion	Division 1	1–0	Ford(54)	23056
R.Springett, Smith, Megson, Mobley, S.Ellis, Quinn, Usher, McCalliog, Ritchie, Ford, Pugh					
22 Apr. 1967	Newcastle United	Division 1	0–0		25007
R.Springett, Smith, Megson, Mobley, S.Ellis, Quinn, Usher, McCalliog, Ritchie, Ford, Pugh(Young 39)					
06 May 1967	Burnley	Division 1	7–0	Ford 3(38, 46, 56), Whitham 2(53, 65), McCalliog(44), Quinn(78)	21103
R.Springett, Smith, Megson, Mobley, S.Ellis, Quinn, Usher(Whitham ht), McCalliog, Ritchie, Ford, Young					
13 May 1967	Arsenal	Division 1	1–1	Ritchie(14)	23222
R.Springett, Smith, Megson, Mobley, S.Ellis, Quinn, Whitham, Symm, Ritchie, Ford, Young					

OTHER GAMES AT HILLSBOROUGH

12 July 1966	World Cup Finals	West Germany 5	Switzerland 0	36000
15 July 1966	World Cup Finals	Switzerland 1	Spain 2	32000
19 July 1966	World Cup Finals	Argentina 2	Switzerland 0	32127
23 July 1966	W.Cup Quarter Final	West Germany 4	Uruguay 0	40007
14 Nov. 1966	Boys	Sheffield 1	Nottingham 2	n/k
28 Nov. 1966	Boys	Sheffield 4	Derby 3	n/k
29 Apr. 1967	F.A.Cup Semi Final	Nottingham Forest 1	Tottenham Hotspur 2	55000

Date	Opponents	Competition	Score	Scorers	Att.
23 Aug. 1967	Leicester City	Division 1	2–1	Ritchie 2(2, 55)	30190
P.Springett, Smith, Megson, Mobley, S.Ellis, Eustace, Usher, McCalliog, Ritchie, Fantham, Quinn					
26 Aug. 1967	Burnley	Division 1	2–1	Fantham(10), Ritchie(15)	29725
P.Springett, Smith(Symm 16), Megson, Mobley, S.Ellis, Eustace, Usher, McCalliog, Ritchie, Fantham, Quinn					
06 Sep. 1967	Fulham	Division 1	4–2	Ritchie 2(56, 71), Mobley(53), Ford(84)	26551
P.Springett, Quinn, Megson, Mobley, S.Ellis, Young, Usher(Fantham 55), Eustace, Ritchie, McCalliog, Ford					
16 Sep. 1967	Manchester United	Division 1	1–1	Usher(32)	47274
P.Springett, Quinn, Smith, Mobley, S.Ellis, Young, Eustace, Fantham(Whitham 65), Ritchie, McCalliog, Usher					
25 Sep. 1967	Sheffield United	R.Springett Tst.	3–2	Whitham(41), Ritchie(80), Eustace(89)	23070
R.Springett(P.Springett ht), Quinn, Smith, Mobley, S.Ellis, Young, Eustace, Usher, Ritchie, McCalliog, Whitham(R.Springett ht)					
30 Sep. 1967	Wolverhampton W.	Division 1	2–2	Mobley(18), Ritchie(65)	35177
P.Springett, Smith, Megson, Mobley, S.Ellis, Young, Usher, Fantham(Quinn 53), Ritchie, McCalliog, Eustace					
07 Oct. 1967	Coventry City	Division 1	4–0	McCalliog(2), Mobley(31), Eustace(44), Fantham(87)	33931
P.Springett, Quinn, Megson, Mobley, S.Ellis, Young, Usher, Fantham, Ritchie, McCalliog(Branfoot 82), Eustace					
11 Oct. 1967	Barrow	League Cup 3	3–1	Fantham 2(27, 85), McCalliog(7)	21829
Wicks, Quinn, Megson, Young, S.Ellis, Symm, Usher, Fantham, Ritchie, McCalliog, Eustace					
23 Oct. 1967	Stoke City	Division 1	1–1	Fantham(90)	33000
P.Springett, Smith, Megson, Mobley, S.Ellis, Young, Usher, Fantham, Ritchie, McCalliog, Eustace					
01 Nov. 1967	Stoke City	League Cup 4	0–0		26001
P.Springett, Smith, Megson, Mobley, S.Ellis, Young, Usher, Fantham, Ritchie, McCalliog, Eustace(Quinn 65)					
04 Nov. 1967	Southampton	Division 1	2–0	Whitham(25), McCalliog(87)	26941
P.Springett, Smith, Megson, Mobley, S.Ellis, Young, Whitham, Fantham, Ritchie, McCalliog, Eustace					
18 Nov. 1967	West Bromwich Albion	Division 1	2–2	Ritchie(34), Williams(54)og.	28256
P.Springett, Smith, Megson, Mobley, S.Ellis, Young, Usher, Fantham, Ritchie, McCalliog, Eustace					
02 Dec. 1967	Manchester City	Division 1	1–1	Fantham(89)	38137
P.Springett, Smith, Megson, Mobley, S.Ellis, Young, Whitham, Fantham, Ritchie, McCalliog, Eustace					
16 Dec. 1967	West Ham United	Division 1	4–1	Ritchie 2(23, 43), Fantham(32), Whitham(59)	24003
P.Springett, Smith, Megson, Mobley, S.Ellis, Young, Whitham, Fantham, Ritchie, McCalliog, Branfoot					
26 Dec. 1967	Leeds United	Division 1	0–1		51055
P.Springett, Smith, Megson, Mobley, S.Ellis, Branfoot, Whitham, Symm, Ritchie, McCalliog, Usher					
06 Jan. 1968	Sheffield United	Division 1	1–1	Fantham(54)	43020
P.Springett, Smith, Megson, Branfoot, Mobley, Young, Whitham, Symm, Ritchie, McCalliog, Fantham					
17 Jan. 1968	Tottenham Hotspur	Division 1	1–2	Fantham(43)	32150
P.Springett, Smith, Megson, Branfoot, Mobley, Young, Whitham, Symm, Ritchie, McCalliog, Fantham					
27 Jan. 1968	Plymouth Argyle	F.A.Cup 3	3–0	Whitham(6), Fantham(38), Ritchie(66)pen.	29283
P.Springett, Smith, Megson, S.Ellis, Mobley, Branfoot, Fantham, Symm(Usher 55), Ritchie, McCalliog, Whitham					
03 Feb. 1968	Sunderland	Division 1	0–1		25004
P.Springett, Smith, Megson, S.Ellis, Mobley, Branfoot, Usher, Fantham, Ritchie, McCalliog(Symm 30), Whitham					
17 Feb. 1968	Swindon Town	F.A.Cup 4	2–1	Smith(65), Ritchie(85)	37457
P.Springett, Smith, Megson, S.Ellis, Mobley, Branfoot, Usher, Symm, Ritchie, McCalliog, Whitham					
02 Mar. 1968	Newcastle United	Division 1	1–1	Whitham(52)	24762
Scothorn, Smith, Megson, Young, Mobley, Eustace, Usher, McCalliog, Ritchie, Whitham, Woodall					
09 Mar. 1968	Chelsea	F.A.Cup 5	2–2	Ritchie(10), Megson(32)	49186
P.Springett, Smith, Megson, Young, Mobley, Eustace, Whitham, McCalliog, Ritchie, Fantham, Usher					
23 Mar. 1968	Liverpool	Division 1	1–2	Ford(79)	32177
P.Springett, Smith, Megson, Eustace, Mobley, Young, Usher, McCalliog, Ritchie, Whitham, Woodall(Ford 57)					
06 Apr. 1968	Chelsea	Division 1	2–2	Ritchie(69), Fantham(90)	26773
P.Springett, Smith, Megson, Young, Mobley, Eustace, Wall, McCalliog, Ritchie, Ford, Fantham					
16 Apr. 1968	Everton	Division 1	0–0		24766
P.Springett, Smith, Megson, Young, Mobley, Eustace, Fantham, McCalliog, Ritchie, Ford, Woodall					
20 Apr. 1968	Nottingham Forest	Division 1	0–0		28496
P.Springett, Smith, Megson, Young, Mobley, Eustace, Fantham, McCalliog, Ritchie, Ford, Woodall					
4 May 1968	Arsenal	Division 1	1–2	McCalliog(51)	25066
P.Springett, Smith, Megson, Young, Mobley, Eustace, Whitham(Fantham 80), McCalliog, Ritchie, Ford, Pugh					

OTHER GAMES AT HILLSBOROUGH

30 Apr. 1968	Senior Cup Final	Hallam 1	Norton Woodseats 0		n/k

Date	Opponents	Competition	Score	Scorers	Att.
14 Aug. 1968	Newcastle United	Division 1	1–1	Ford(16)	27258
P.Springett, Smith, Megson, Young(Whitham 89), Mobley, Eustace, Fantham, McCalliog, Ritchie, Ford, Pugh					
17 Aug. 1968	Coventry City	Division 1	3–0	Fantham 2(20, 70), Ritchie(78)	26235
P.Springett, Smith, Megson, S.Ellis, Mobley, Eustace, Fantham, McCalliog, Ritchie, Ford, Pugh(Whitham 42)					
31 Aug. 1968	Manchester United	Division 1	5–4	Whitham 3(2, 45, 75), Ritchie(17), Stiles(48)og.	51931
P.Springett, Young, Megson, S.Ellis, Mobley, Eustace, Whitham, McCalliog, Ritchie, Ford, Fantham					
07 Sep. 1968	Ipswich Town	Division 1	2–1	Whitham(16), Eustace(64)	27128
P.Springett, Young, Megson, S.Ellis, Mobley, Eustace, Whitham, McCalliog, Warboys, Ford, Woodall					
21 Sep. 1968	Burnley	Division 1	1–0	Whitham(37)	23183
P.Springett, Young, Megson, S.Ellis, Mobley, Eustace, Whitham, McCalliog, Warboys, Ford, Fantham					
05 Oct. 1968	Sunderland	Division 1	1–1	Whitham(59)	27932
P.Springett, Smith, Megson, S.Ellis, Mobley, Young, Whitham, McCalliog, Warboys, Ford, Eustace(Fantham 69)					
09 Oct. 1968	Chelsea	Division 1	1–1	Whitham(82)	30991
P.Springett, Smith, Megson, S.Ellis, Mobley, Young, Whitham, Eustace, McCalliog, Ford, Fantham					
19 Oct. 1968	Wolverhampton W.	Division 1	0–2		23928
P.Springett, Smith, Megson, S.Ellis, Mobley, Young, Whitham(Irvine 56), McCalliog, Warboys, Ford, Eustace					
16 Nov. 1968	Liverpool	Division 1	1–2	McCalliog(63)	31245
P.Springett, Smith, Megson, S.Ellis, Mobley, Young, Fantham, McCalliog, Warboys, Eustace, Ford					
30 Nov. 1968	Stoke City	Division 1	2–1	Ritchie(8), Eustace(34)	23027
P.Springett, Smith, Burton, S.Ellis, Mobley, Young, Fantham, McCalliog, Ritchie, Eustace, Woodall					
14 Dec. 1968	Queen's Park Rangers	Division 1	4–0	Mobley(13), Fantham(49), Ford(60), McCalliog(65)	22004
P.Springett, Smith, Megson, S.Ellis, Mobley, Young, Fantham, McCalliog, Ritchie, Eustace, Ford					
28 Dec. 1968	Southampton	Division 1	0–0		27398
P.Springett, Smith, Megson, S.Ellis, Mobley, Young, Irvine, McCalliog, Ritchie, Eustace, Ford					
04 Jan. 1969	Leeds United	F.A.Cup 3	1–1	Ritchie(44)	52111
P.Springett, Smith, Megson, S.Ellis, Mobley, Young, Irvine, McCalliog, Ritchie, Eustace, Ford					
18 Jan. 1969	Manchester City	Division 1	1–1	Smith(54)	33074
P.Springett, Smith, Megson, S.Ellis, Mobley, Young, Irvine, McCalliog, Ritchie, Eustace, Woodall					
25 Jan. 1969	Birmingham City	F.A.Cup 4	2–2	McCalliog(59), Young(75)	52062
P.Springett, Smith(Branfoot 28), Megson, S.Ellis, Mobley, Young, Irvine, McCalliog, Ritchie, Eustace, Woodall					
01 Mar. 1969	Arsenal	Division 1	0–5		21987
P.Springett, Smith, Megson(Fantham 68), S.Ellis, Mobley, Young, Irvine, McCalliog, Ritchie, Pugh, Ford					
05 Mar. 1969	West Bromwich Albion	Division 1	1–0	Mobley(60)	18960
P.Springett, Smith, Burton, Young, Mobley, Pugh, Irvine, McCalliog, Ritchie, Fantham, Ford					
01 Apr. 1969	Leeds United	Division 1	0–0		34278
P.Springett, Smith, Burton, Eustace, Mobley, S.Ellis, Irvine, McCalliog, Ritchie, Warboys, Fantham					
05 Apr. 1969	West Ham United	Division 1	1–1	Warboys(25)	24268
P.Springett, Smith, Megson, Eustace, Mobley, Young, Irvine, McCalliog, Ritchie, Warboys, Fantham					
07 Apr. 1969	Nottingham Forest	Division 1	0–1		26178
P.Springett, Smith, Megson, Eustace, Mobley, Young, Irvine, McCalliog, Ritchie, Warboys, Fantham					
14 Apr. 1969	Leicester City	Division 1	1–3	Woodall(49)	18155
P.Springett, Smith, Branfoot, S.Ellis, Mobley, Young, Irvine, McCalliog, Warboys, Prendergast, Woodall					
19 Apr. 1969	Everton	Division 1	2–2	Ritchie(42), Woodall(73)	23173
P.Springett, Smith, Burton, Eustace, Mobley, Young, Irvine(Whitham 69), McCalliog, Warboys, Ritchie, Woodall					
12 May 1969	Tottenham Hotspur	Division 1	0–0		28368
P.Springett, Smith, Burton, Young, Mobley, T.Craig, Eustace, McCalliog, Fantham, Warboys(Ritchie ht), Ford					

OTHER GAMES AT HILLSBOROUGH

22 Mar. 1969	F.A.Cup Semi Final	Leicester City 1	West Bromwich Albion 0	53207
23 Apr. 1969	Representative	F.A. Amateur XI 6	Universities Athletic Union 0	n/k

1966–67
Megson, Eustace, Ellis, Wicks, Young, Smith;
Pugh, Fantham, McCalliog, Ford, Quinn.

1967–68
Young, Ellis, Whitham, P. Springett, Mobley, Branfoot, Eustace, Smith;
Fantham, Quinn, Symm, Ritchie, Ford, McCalliog, Usher.

1968–69
Branfoot, P. Springett, Wicks, Whitham, Woodall;
Pugh, Mobley, Fantham, Symm, Warboys, Ellis, Eustace;
Young McCalliog, Mobley, Ritchie, Ford, Smith, Megson.

1969–70
Prendergast, Burton, Pugh, Woodall, Branfoot;
Prophett, Warboys, Wicks, P. Springett, Mobley, Ellis;
Smith, Fantham, Eustace, Megson, Ford, T. Craig, Young.

Date	Opponents	Competition	Score	Scorers	Att.
30 July 1969	Aberdeen	Friendly	2–1	Fantham(8), Ford(28)	10075
02 Aug. 1969	Italian Under–21	Friendly	2–0	Fantham(43), Eustace(85)	8064
04 Aug. 1969	Airdrie	Friendly	1–2	Prendergast(36)	5804
16 Aug. 1969	Wolverhampton W.	Division 1	2–3	Warboys(3), Ford(64)	23167
20 Aug. 1969	Newcastle United	Division 1	1–0	Eustace(35)	19213
30 Aug. 1969	Liverpool	Division 1	1–1	Warboys(25)	33600
03 Sep. 1969	Bournemouth & Boscombe	League Cup 2	1–1	Pugh(40)	14363
13 Sep. 1969	Leeds United	Division 1	1–2	Burton(29)	31998
17 Sep. 1969	Manchester United	Division 1	1–3	Pugh(39)	39938
27 Sep. 1969	Derby County	Division 1	1–0	Warboys(38)	45086
30 Sep. 1969	International XI	Megson Tst.	7–7	Warboys 4(37, 51, 54, 59), Young(35), Whitham(–), Ford(–)	10961
11 Oct. 1969	Southampton	Division 1	1–1	Eustace(69)	20488
25 Oct. 1969	Crystal Palace	Division 1	0–0		19162
08 Nov. 1969	Chelsea	Division 1	1–3	Prendergast(90)	18044
15 Nov. 1969	Stoke City	Division 1	0–2		16444
20 Dec. 1969	Arsenal	Division 1	1–1	Whitham(51)	17165
26 Dec. 1969	Sunderland	Division 1	2–0	Downes(27), Prophett(56)	35126
03 Jan. 1970	West Bromwich Albion	F.A.Cup 3	2–1	Whitham 2(47, 84)	29174
10 Jan. 1970	West Ham United	Division 1	2–3	Craig(51), Prophett(73)	28135
24 Jan. 1970	Scunthorpe United	F.A.Cup 4	1–2	Whitham(4)	38047
28 Jan. 1970	Coventry City	Division 1	0–1		18149
31 Jan. 1970	Ipswich Town	Division 1	2–2	Smith(10), Sinclair(21)	17814
28 Feb. 1970	Burnley	Division 1	2–0	Whitham 2(30, 85)	23188
10 Mar. 1970	West Bromwich Albion	Division 1	2–0	Whitham(8), Warboys(27)	21990
21 Mar. 1970	Nottingham Forest	Division 1	2–1	Craig(70), Warboys(81)	23916
30 Mar. 1970	Tottenham Hotspur	Division 1	0–1		30224
04 Apr. 1970	Everton	Division 1	0–1		30896
22 Apr. 1970	Manchester City	Division 1	1–2	Coleman(65)	45258
25 Apr. 1970	Sheffield United	Young Tst.	3–3	Whitham 2(15, 85), Warboys(88)	12120
02 May 1970	Napoli	Anglo–Italian	4–3	Warboys 2(23, 56), Downes 2(48, 61)	10166
09 May 1970	Juventus	Anglo–Italian	0–0		9495

Lineups (beneath each match row):

- 30 July 1969: P.Springett, Smith, Burton, Young, Mobley, T.Craig, Fantham(Prendergast ht), Eustace, McCalliog(Pugh 70), Ford, Woodall
- 02 Aug. 1969: P.Springett, Smith, Burton, S.Ellis, Branfoot, T.Craig, Irvine, Eustace, Pugh(Woodall ht), Ford, Fantham
- 04 Aug. 1969: P.Springett(Wicks ht), Smith, Burton, Branfoot, S.Ellis, T.Craig, Irvine, Eustace, Prendergast, Ford, Woodall(Fantham 73)
- 16 Aug. 1969: P.Springett, Branfoot, Burton, Young, Mobley, T.Craig, Fantham, Eustace, Warboys, Prendergast, Ford
- 20 Aug. 1969: P.Springett, Branfoot, Burton, Young, S.Ellis, T.Craig, Irvine, Eustace, Warboys, Smith, Ford
- 30 Aug. 1969: P.Springett, Smith, Burton, Young, S.Ellis, T.Craig, Irvine, Eustace, Warboys(Prophett 85), Pugh, Ford
- 03 Sep. 1969: P.Springett, Branfoot, Burton, Young, S.Ellis, Smith, Irvine, Eustace, Warboys, Ford, Pugh
- 13 Sep. 1969: P.Springett, Smith, Burton, Young, S.Ellis, T.Craig, Irvine, Pugh, Warboys, Prendergast, Fantham(Prophett 75)
- 17 Sep. 1969: P.Springett, Smith, Burton, Young, S.Ellis, T.Craig, Irvine, Fantham, Warboys, Ford, Pugh
- 27 Sep. 1969: P.Springett, Smith, Branfoot, Young, S.Ellis, Pugh, Eustace, Warboys, Ford, Woodall(Prendergast 58)
- 30 Sep. 1969: P.Springett, Branfoot, Megson, Young, Prophett, T.Craig, Whitham, Eustace, Warboys, Ford, Fantham
- 11 Oct. 1969: P.Springett, Smith, Branfoot, Young, S.Ellis, T.Craig, Pugh, Eustace, Prendergast, Ford, Coleman(Prophett ht)
- 25 Oct. 1969: P.Springett, Smith, Burton, Young, S.Ellis, T.Craig, Lawson(Pugh 55), Eustace, Warboys, Prendergast, Coleman
- 08 Nov. 1969: P.Springett, Smith, Burton, Young, S.Ellis, T.Craig, Ford, Eustace(Pugh 24), Warboys, Prendergast, Coleman
- 15 Nov. 1969: P.Springett, Smith, Burton, Young, Prophett, T.Craig, Irvine, Pugh, Warboys, Whitham, Coleman
- 20 Dec. 1969: P.Springett, Wilcockson, Megson, Young, Prophett, T.Craig, Sinclair, Pugh(Burton 85), Whitham, Smith, Coleman
- 26 Dec. 1969: P.Springett, Wilcockson, Megson, Young, Prophett, T.Craig, Sinclair, Downes, Whitham(Eustace 67), Smith, Coleman
- 03 Jan. 1970: P.Springett, Pugh, Megson, Young, Prophett, T.Craig, Coleman, Whitham, Warboys, Smith, Lawson
- 10 Jan. 1970: P.Springett, Wilcockson, Megson, Pugh, Prophett, T.Craig, Sinclair, Whitham(Warboys 70), Downes, Smith, Coleman
- 24 Jan. 1970: P.Springett, Pugh, Megson(Burton 72), S.Ellis, Prophett, T.Craig, Sinclair, Whitham, Warboys, Smith, Coleman
- 28 Jan. 1970: Grummitt, Wilcockson, Burton, Smith, Prophett, T.Craig, Sinclair, Whitham, Downes, Pugh(Warboys 57), Coleman
- 31 Jan. 1970: Grummitt, Wilcockson, Burton, Young, Prophett, T.Craig, Sinclair(Whitham 84), Smith, Downes, Coleman, Lawson
- 28 Feb. 1970: Grummitt, Wilcockson, Smith, S.Ellis, Prophett, T.Craig, Sinclair, Young, Warboys, Whitham, Coleman
- 10 Mar. 1970: Grummitt, Wilcockson, Smith, S.Ellis, Prophett, T.Craig, Sinclair, Young, Warboys(Downes 85), Whitham, Lawson
- 21 Mar. 1970: Grummitt, Wilcockson, Smith, S.Ellis, Prophett, T.Craig, Sinclair, Young, Warboys, Whitham, Coleman
- 30 Mar. 1970: Grummitt, Wilcockson, Smith, S.Ellis, Prophett, T.Craig, Sinclair, Young(Coleman 72), Warboys, Whitham, Lawson
- 04 Apr. 1970: Grummitt, Wilcockson, Smith, S.Ellis, Prophett, T.Craig, Sinclair, Young, Warboys, Whitham, Coleman(Prendergast 84)
- 22 Apr. 1970: Grummitt, Wilcockson, Smith(Downes 30), S.Ellis, Prophett, T.Craig, Sinclair, Young, Warboys, Whitham, Coleman
- 25 Apr. 1970: Grummitt, Wilcockson, Megson, Eustace, S.Ellis, T.Craig, Sinclair, Young, Warboys, Whitham, Coleman (Used sub–Mobley)
- 02 May 1970: Grummitt, Wilcockson, Burton, S.Ellis, Prophett, T.Craig, Sinclair, Downes, Warboys(Prendergast 60), Young, Coleman
- 09 May 1970: Grummitt, Wilcockson, Burton, S.Ellis, Prophett, T.Craig, Sinclair, Downes, Warboys, Young, Lawson

OTHER GAMES AT HILLSBOROUGH

| 14 Mar. 1970 | F.A.Cup Semi Final | Manchester United 0　　Leeds United 0 | 55000 |
| 27 Apr. 1970 | Boys | Yorkshire v. Derbyshire – score n/k | n/k |

Date	Opponents	Competition	Score	Scorers	Att.
15 Aug. 1970	Charlton Athletic	Division 2	1–0	Downes(75)	17152
Grummitt, Wilcockson, Smith(Prendergast 65), Young, Prophett, T.Craig, Sinclair, Todd, Downes, Warboys, Lawson					
26 Aug. 1970	Cardiff City	Division 2	1–2	Prendergast(10)	17186
Grummitt, Wilcockson, Burton(S.Ellis 81), Todd, Prophett, T.Craig, Sinclair, Young, Downes, Warboys, Prendergast					
29 Aug. 1970	Blackburn Rovers	Division 2	1–1	Prendergast(14)	15188
Grummitt, Wilcockson, Young, Todd, Prophett, T.Craig, Sinclair, Prendergast, Warboys, Downes, Sissons					
02 Sep. 1970	Bolton Wanderers	Division 2	1–1	Downes(73)	12920
Grummitt, Wilcockson, S.Ellis, Todd, Prophett, T.Craig, Sinclair, Young, Warboys(Downes 68), Prendergast, Sissons					
09 Sep. 1970	Chelsea	League Cup 2	1–1	Sinclair(64)	15869
Grummitt, Wilcockson, Young, Thompson, S.Ellis, Todd, Sinclair, Prendergast(Pugh 56), Downes, T.Craig, Sissons					
12 Sep. 1970	Queen's Park Rangers	Division 2	1–0	Wilcockson(57)	14920
Grummitt, Wilcockson, Young(Prophett 23), Thompson, S.Ellis, Todd, Sinclair, Pugh, Downes, T.Craig, Sissons					
26 Sep. 1970	Carlisle United	Division 2	3–0	Warboys(18), Prendergast(28), Sissons(40)	13181
Grummitt, Prophett(Warboys 16), Wilcockson, Thompson, S.Ellis, Todd, Sinclair, Prendergast, Downes, T.Craig, Sissons					
10 Oct. 1970	Luton Town	Division 2	1–5	Sinclair(69)	15189
Grummitt, Wilcockson, Burton, Thompson, S.Ellis, T.Craig, Sinclair, Prendergast, Downes, Warboys, Sissons					
24 Oct. 1970	Leicester City	Division 2	0–3		23160
Grummitt, Rodrigues, Wilcockson, Thompson, Young, T.Craig, Sinclair, Pugh, Downes(Prendergast 15), Warboys, Sissons					
07 Nov. 1970	Millwall	Division 2	1–0	Todd(6)	12668
Grummitt, Rodrigues, Wilcockson, Thompson, S.Ellis, Pugh, Sinclair(T.Craig 89), Prendergast, Warboys, Todd, Sissons					
21 Nov. 1970	Middlesbrough	Division 2	3–2	Warboys(40), Prendergast(43), Craig(84)pen.	15773
Grummitt, Rodrigues, Wilcockson, Prophett, S.Ellis, Pugh(T.Craig 65), Sinclair, Prendergast, Warboys, Todd, Sissons					
05 Dec. 1970	Watford	Division 2	2–1	Prophett(1), Prendergast(49)	12139
Grummitt, Prophett, Burton, Thompson, S.Ellis, Pugh, Sinclair, Prendergast, Warboys, T.Craig, Todd					
19 Dec. 1970	Oxford United	Division 2	1–1	Warboys(23)	11134
Grummitt, S.Ellis, Young, Thompson, Prophett, Wilcockson, Sinclair, Pugh, Prendergast, Warboys, Sissons					
16 Jan. 1971	Orient	Division 2	2–1	Prendergast(30), Prophett(75)	11149
Grummitt, Rodrigues, Burton, Prophett, S.Ellis, Pugh, Sinclair, Todd, T.Craig(Mullen 75), Prendergast, Sissons					
30 Jan. 1971	Swindon Town	Division 2	2–2	Pugh(22), Sissons(78)	12964
Grummitt, Rodrigues, Burton, Mullen, Thompson(Prophett ht), Pugh, Sinclair, T.Craig, Sunley, Prendergast, Sissons					
13 Feb. 1971	Birmingham City	Division 2	3–3	Prendergast(32), Craig(34)pen., Sinclair(38)	13138
Grummitt, Rodrigues, Burton, Thompson, Pugh, Sinclair, T.Craig, Prendergast, Sunley, Sissons					
27 Feb. 1971	Bristol City	Division 2	2–0	Prendergast 2(10, 39)	12481
Grummitt, Todd, Burton, Thompson, Prophett, Pugh, Sinclair, T.Craig, Sunley, Prendergast, Sissons					
13 Mar. 1971	Norwich City	Division 2	2–1	Prendergast 2(9, 52)	13136
Grummitt, Rodrigues, Burton, Thompson, Prophett, Pugh, Sinclair, T.Craig, Prendergast, Downes, Sissons					
15 Mar. 1971	G.B.Olympic XI	Friendly	3–1	Prendergast(50), Pugh(55), Prudham(65)	3000
Grummitt, Todd, Burton, Mullen, Prophett, Pugh, Potts, T.Craig, Downes, Prendergast, Prudham					
30 Mar. 1971	Portsmouth	Division 2	3–1	Sinclair(77), Prendergast(81), Sunley(90)	14134
Grummitt, Rodrigues, Burton, Thompson, Prophett, Pugh, Sinclair, T.Craig, Sunley, Prendergast, Sissons					
10 Apr. 1971	Hull City	Division 2	1–1	Craig(84)pen.	22150
Grummitt, Rodrigues, Burton, Thompson(Mullen 77), Prophett, Pugh, Sinclair, T.Craig, Sunley, Prendergast, Sissons					
12 Apr. 1971	Sheffield United	Division 2	0–0		47592
Grummitt, Rodrigues, Burton, Thompson, Prophett, Pugh, Sinclair, Sunley, Prendergast, T.Craig, Sissons					
24 Apr. 1971	Sunderland	Division 2	1–2	Prendergast(36)	9720
Grummitt, Rodrigues, Burton, Thompson, Prophett, Pugh, Sinclair(Potts 75), T.Craig, Sunley, Prendergast, Sissons					

OTHER GAMES AT HILLSBOROUGH

13 Oct. 1970	Fantham Testimonial	Sheffield XI 4		John Fantham XI 8	6234
27 Mar. 1971	F.A.Cup Semi Final	Arsenal 2		Stoke City 2	53436

Date	Opponents	Competition	Score	Scorers	Att.
21 Aug. 1971	Bristol City	Division 2	1–5	Prendergast(89)	12738
Grummitt, Rodrigues, Burton, Prophett, Holsgrove(Thompson 30), Pugh, Sinclair, T.Craig, Downes, Prendergast, Sissons					
04 Sep. 1971	Portsmouth	Division 2	1–1	Joicey(4)	13170
Grummitt, Rodrigues, Thompson, Prophett, Holsgrove, Clements, Sinclair, T.Craig, Joicey, Prendergast, Sissons					
18 Sep. 1971	Sunderland	Division 2	3–0	Pugh(47), Joicey(49), Sinclair(70)	13710
Grummit, Rodrigues(Sinclair ht), Thompson, Prophett, Holsgrove, Clements, Pugh, T.Craig, Joicey, Prendergast, Sissons					
02 Oct. 1971	Fulham	Division 2	4–0	Prophett(18), Craig(78), Sissons(83), Joicey(89)	14955
Grummitt, Rodrigues, Clements, Prophett, Holsgrove, Pugh, Sinclair, T.Craig, Joicey, Prendergast, Sissons					
16 Oct. 1971	Queen's Park Rangers	Division 2	0–0		16716
Grummitt, Rodrigues, Clements, Prophett, Holsgrove, Pugh, Sinclair, T.Craig, Joicey, Prendergast, Sissons					
20 Oct. 1971	Carlisle United	Division 2	2–1	Sissons(19), Prendergast(85)	15672
Grummitt, Rodrigues, Clements, Prophett, Holsgrove, Pugh, Sinclair, T.Craig, Joicey, Prendergast, Sissons					
23 Oct. 1971	Swindon Town	Division 2	1–0	Sinclair(88)	19933
Grummitt, Rodrigues, Clements, Prophett, Holsgrove, Pugh, Sinclair, T.Craig, Joicey, Prendergast, Sissons					
06 Nov. 1971	Burnley	Division 2	2–1	Sissons(11), Joicey(32)	23743
Grummitt, Rodrigues, Clements, Prophett, Holsgrove, Pugh, Sinclair, T.Craig, Joicey, Prendergast, Sissons					
16 Nov. 1971	Werder Bremen	Friendly	2–0	Joicey(39), Sinclair(86)	5193
Grummitt, Thompson, Clements, Prophett, Holsgrove, Pugh, Sinclair, T.Craig, Joicey, Prendergast, Sissons					
20 Nov. 1971	Norwich City	Division 2	1–1	Joicey(75)	19902
Grummitt, Thompson, Clements, Prophett, Holsgrove, Pugh, Sinclair, T.Craig, Joicey, Prendergast, Sissons					
04 Dec. 1971	Hull City	Division 2	2–1	Joicey(62), Prendergast(79)	20173
Grummitt, Rodrigues, Clements, Prophett, Holsgrove, Pugh(Thompson), Sinclair, T.Craig, Joicey, Prendergast, Sissons					
27 Dec. 1971	Luton Town	Division 2	2–2	Craig(50)pen., Holsgrove(76)	31391
Grummitt, Rodrigues, Clements, Prophett, Holsgrove, Pugh, Sinclair, T.Craig, Joicey, Prendergast(Thompson 10), Sissons					
08 Jan. 1972	Blackpool	Division 2	1–2	Craig(38)	17113
Grummitt, Rodrigues, Clements, Prophett, Holsgrove, Pugh, Sinclair, T.Craig, Joicey, Sunley, Sissons					
22 Jan. 1972	Millwall	Division 2	1–1	Craig(69)pen.	16829
Grummitt, Rodrigues, Clements, Prophett, Holsgrove, Pugh, Sinclair, T.Craig, Joicey, Sunley, Sissons					
19 Feb. 1972	Watford	Division 2	2–1	Sinclair(47), Joicey(70)	13934
Grummitt, Rodrigues, Clements, Prophett, Holsgrove, Pugh, Sinclair, T.Craig, Joicey, Prendergast(Sunley), Sissons					
23 Feb. 1972	Santos	Friendly	0–2		36996
Grummitt, Rodrigues, Clements, Prophett, Holsgrove(Thompson ht), Pugh, Sinclair, T.Craig, Joicey, Sunley, Sissons (Used Sub–Potts)					
04 Mar. 1972	Preston North End	Division 2	1–0	Craig(75)pen.	12162
Grummitt, Rodrigues, Clements, Prophett, Holsgrove, Pugh, Sinclair, T.Craig, Joicey, Sunley, Sissons					
25 Mar. 1972	Cardiff City	Division 2	2–2	Sissons(41), Craig(50)pen.	12910
Grummitt, Rodrigues, Thompson, Prophett, Holsgrove, Clements, Sinclair, T.Craig, Joicey, Sunley, Sissons					
03 Apr. 1972	Oxford United	Division 2	0–0		13993
Pearson, Rodrigues, Thompson, Prophett, Todd, Clements, Pugh, Taylor(Sinclair), Joicey, Sunley, Sissons					
10 Apr. 1972	Charlton Athletic	Division 2	2–1	Sinclair(24), Sunley(67)	13800
P.Springett, Rodrigues, Thompson, Prophett, Holsgrove, Clements, Sinclair, Pugh, Joicey, Sunley, Sissons					
17 Apr. 1972	Orient	Division 2	3–1	Joicey 3(37, 40, 73)	15188
P.Springett, Rodrigues, Thompson, Prophett, Holsgrove, Clements, Sinclair, Pugh, Joicey, Sunley, Sissons					
26 Apr. 1972	Middlesbrough	Division 2	1–0	Craig(45)pen.	14151
P.Springett, Thompson, Clements, Prophett, Mullen, Pugh, Sinclair, T.Craig, Joicey, Sunley, Sissons					
29 Apr. 1972	Birmingham City	Division 2	1–2	Sunley(58)	28132
P.Springett, Thompson, Clements, Prophett, Mullen, Pugh, Sinclair, T.Craig, Joicey, Sunley, Sissons					

OTHER GAMES AT HILLSBOROUGH

01 Sep. 1971	Division One	Leeds United 5	Newcastle United 1		18623
05 Jan. 1972	League Cup s/f–replay	West Ham United 0	Stoke City 0		46916
15 Apr. 1972	F.A.Cup Semi Final	Birmingham City 0	Leeds United 3		54723
05 May 1972	Boys	Yorkshire 2	Cheshire 0		n/k

Date	Opponents	Competition	Score	Scorers	Att.
12 Aug. 1972	Fulham	Division 2	3–0	Prendergast(14), Holsgrove(31), Joicey(76)	23109
Grummitt, Rodrigues, Mullen, Swan, Holsgrove, Clements, Henderson, T.Craig, Joicey, Prendergast, Sissons					
16 Aug. 1972	Swindon Town	Division 2	2–1	Joicey(78), Craig(83)	20841
Grummitt, Rodrigues, Mullen, Swan, Holsgrove, Clements, Henderson(Sunley 68), T.Craig, Joicey, Prendergast, Sissons					
26 Aug. 1972	Hull City	Division 2	4–2	Joicey 2(40, 80), Sunley(7), Craig(81)pen.	20153
Grummitt, Rodrigues, Clements, Swan, Holsgrove, T.Craig, Sunley, Eustace, Joicey, Prendergast, Sissons					
06 Sep. 1972	Bolton Wanderers	League Cup 2	2–0	Joicey(17), Eustace(39)	15903
Grummitt, Rodrigues, Clements, Swan, Holsgrove, T.Craig, Henderson, Eustace, Joicey, Prendergast, Sissons					
09 Sep. 1972	Portsmouth	Division 2	2–0	Prendergast(36), Sunley(86)	17830
Grummitt, Rodrigues, Clements, Swan, Holsgrove, T.Craig, Henderson(Sunley 17), Eustace, Joicey, Prendergast, Sissons					
23 Sep. 1972	Luton Town	Division 2	4–0	Holsgrove(26), Rodrigues(30), Prendergast(60), Eustace(77)	18913
Grummitt, Rodrigues, Clements, Mullen, Holsgrove, T.Craig(Swan 78), Henderson, Eustace, Sunley, Prendergast, Sissons					
27 Sep. 1972	Huddersfield Town	Division 2	3–2	Prendergast(31), Henderson(70), Craig(75)pen.	22185
Grummitt, Rodrigues, Clements, Mullen, Holsgrove, T.Craig, Henderson, Eustace, Joicey, Prendergast, Sissons					
14 Oct. 1972	Burnley	Division 2	0–1		30197
Grummitt, Rodrigues, Clements, Swan, Holsgrove, Mullen, Henderson, Eustace, Joicey, Sunley, Sissons					
28 Oct. 1972	Nottingham Forest	Division 2	1–2	Sissons(60)	21887
Grummitt, Rodrigues, Clements, Swan, Holsgrove, T.Craig(Sinclair 35), Henderson, Eustace, Joicey, Sunley, Sissons					
01 Nov. 1972	Rotherham United	County Cup s/f	3–0	Sunley(3), Joicey(10), Eustace(58)pen.	6185
Grummitt, Rodrigues, Mullen, Swan, Holsgrove, Clements, Henderson, Eustace, Joicey, Sunley, Sissons					
11 Nov. 1972	Oxford United	Division 2	0–1		13163
Grummitt, Rodrigues, Mullen, Swan, Holsgrove, Clements, Sinclair, T.Craig, Joicey, Sunley, Sissons					
18 Nov. 1972	Middlesbrough	Division 2	2–1	Mullen(45), Craig(60)	16174
Grummitt, Thompson, Clements, Mullen, Holsgrove, T.Craig, Henderson, Eustace, Joicey, Wylde, Sissons					
02 Dec. 1972	Millwall	Division 2	2–2	Joicey(50), Wylde(53)	13906
Grummitt, Rodrigues, Mullen, Thompson, Holsgrove, T.Craig, Henderson, Eustace, Joicey, Wylde(Sunley 70), Clements					
23 Dec. 1972	Aston Villa	Division 2	2–2	Craig(38), Joicey(60)	20961
Grummitt, Rodrigues, Clements, Thompson, Holsgrove, T.Craig, Henderson, Eustace, Joicey, Prendergast, Coyle(Sissons)					
30 Dec. 1972	Queen's Park Rangers	Division 2	3–1	Craig(8), Sunley(68), Joicey(89)	20185
P.Springett, Rodrigues, Clements, Thompson, Holsgrove, T.Craig, Sunley, Coyle, Joicey, Prendergast, Sissons					
13 Jan. 1973	Fulham	F.A.Cup 3	2–0	Prendergast(30), Joicey(55)	21028
P.Springett, Rodrigues, Clements, Thompson, Holsgrove, T.Craig, Sunley, Coyle, Joicey, Prendergast, Sissons					
20 Jan. 1973	Bristol City	Division 2	0–0	*Abandoned after 54mins.–SNOW	11185
P.Springett, Rodrigues, Clements, Thompson, Holsgrove, T.Craig, Henderson, Coyle, Sunley, Prendergast, Sissons					
03 Feb. 1973	Crystal Palace	F.A.Cup 4	1–1	Craig(1)pen.	35156
P.Springett, Rodrigues, Clements, Thompson, Holsgrove, T.Craig, Henderson, Coyle, Sunley, Prendergast(Eustace 18), Sissons					
10 Feb. 1973	Sunderland	Division 2	1–0	Henderson(61)	16949
P.Springett, Rodrigues, Clements, Prophett, Holsgrove, T.Craig, Henderson, Coyle, Joicey(Potts 80), Sunley, Sissons					
24 Feb. 1973	Chelsea	F.A.Cup 5	1–2	Coyle(25)	46910
Grummitt, Rodrigues, Clements, Prophett, Holsgrove, T.Craig, Henderson, Coyle, Joicey, Sunley, Sissons					
28 Feb. 1973	Blackpool	Division 2	2–0	Joicey(77), Craig(83)pen.	13930
Grummitt, Rodrigues, Clements, Prophett, Holsgrove, T.Craig, Potts, Coyle, Joicey, Sunley, Sissons					
03 Mar. 1973	Preston North End	Division 2	2–1	Sunley(75), Prophett(86)	13427
Grummitt, Rodrigues, Clements, Prophett, Holsgrove, T.Craig, Henderson, Coyle(Potts 68), Joicey, Sunley, Sissons					
14 Mar. 1973	Bristol City	Division 2	3–2	Joicey 2(67, 87), Sunley(73)	13819
Grummitt, Rodrigues, Mullen, Prophett, Thompson, T.Craig, Henderson, Coyle, Joicey, Sunley, Sissons(Potts 8)					
17 Mar. 1973	Brighton & Hove Alb.	Division 2	1–1	Joicey(38)	16122
P.Springett(Eustace ht), Rodrigues, Mullen, Prophett, Thompson, T.Craig, Henderson, Coyle, Joicey, Sunley, Potts					
31 Mar. 1973	Orient	Division 2	2–0	Sunley(49), Joicey(76)	10003
Fox, Rodrigues, Clements, Prophett, Thompson, T.Craig, Potts, Coyle, Joicey, Sunley, Sissons					
14 Apr. 1973	Cardiff City	Division 2	1–0	Dwyer(28)og.	10952
P.Springett, Rodrigues, Mullen, Prophett, Thompson, T.Craig, Henderson, Coyle, Joicey, Sunley, Clements					
23 Apr. 1973	Carlisle United	Division 2	0–0		8895
P.Springett, Rodrigues, Clements, Prophett, Mullen, T.Craig, Potts, Coyle, Joicey, Sunley, Eustace					

OTHER GAMES AT HILLSBOROUGH

06 Nov. 1972	Boys	Sheffield 1	Doncaster 1		n/k
07 Apr. 1973	F.A.Cup Semi Final	Sunderland 2	Arsenal 1		55000

SEASON 75　　　　　1973–74　　　　　Division Two (19th)

Date	Opponents	Competition	Score	Scorers	Att.
01 Sep. 1973	Blackpool	Division 2	0–0		15834
P.Springett, Rodrigues, Shaw, Mullen, Holsgrove, T.Craig, Henderson, Eustace, Joicey, Sunley, Sissons					
12 Sep. 1973	West Bromwich Albion	Division 2	3–1	Sunley(51), Potts(55), Joicey(80)	15927
P.Springett, Rodrigues, Shaw, Thompson, J.Craig, T.Craig, Potts, Prendergast, Joicey, Sunley, Knighton					
15 Sep. 1973	Carlisle United	Division 2	1–0	Thompson(77)	15080
P.Springett, Rodrigues, Shaw, Thompson, J.Craig, T.Craig, Potts, Prendergast, Joicey, Sunley, Knighton					
29 Sep. 1973	Crystal Palace	Division 2	4–0	Prendergast 3(9, 22, 68), Sunley(87)	12861
P.Springett, Rodrigues, Shaw, Thompson, Holsgrove, T.Craig, Potts, Sunley, Joicey, Prendergast, Knighton(J.Craig 71)					
03 Oct. 1973	Millwall	Division 2	3–2	Potts(16), Dorney(19)og., Prendergast(79)	13881
P.Springett, Rodrigues, Shaw, Thompson, Holsgrove, T.Craig, Potts, Sunley, Joicey, Prendergast, Knighton(Henderson 29)					
13 Oct. 1973	Portsmouth	Division 2	1–2	Joicey(25)	12690
P.Springett, Rodrigues, Shaw, Thompson, Mullen, T.Craig, Henderson, Kent(Sunley 68), Joicey, Prendergast, Knighton					
15 Oct. 1973	Bournemouth	League Cup 2R	2–2 aet	Craig(42)pen., Prendergast(85)	5883
P.Springett, Rodrigues, Mullen, Kent, Holsgrove, T.Craig(Sunley 70), Potts, Shaw, Joicey, Prendergast, Knighton					
27 Oct. 1973	Notts County	Division 2	0–0		14977
P.Springett, Cameron, Shaw, Thompson, Mullen, Knighton, Henderson, Coyle, Prudham, Sunley, Potts					
29 Oct. 1973	Bournemouth	Lge. Cup 2–2R	2–1 aet	Prudham(62), Prendergast(104)	8894
P.Springett, Cameron, Shaw, Thompson, Mullen, Knighton, Henderson(Joicey 113), Coyle, Prudham, Prendergast, Potts					
10 Nov. 1973	Orient	Division 2	1–2	Joicey(77)	9961
P.Springett, Rodrigues, Shaw, Thompson, Mullen, Eustace, Potts, Sunley, Joicey, Prendergast, Knighton					
24 Nov. 1973	Oxford United	Division 2	0–1		7998
P.Springett, Rodrigues, Shaw, Thompson, Kent, T.Craig, Henderson, Knighton, Joicey, Prendergast, Potts					
08 Dec. 1973	Middlesbrough	Division 2	2–2	Prendergast(18), Joicey(57)	11992
P.Springett, Rodrigues, Shaw, Thompson, Mullen, T.Craig, Henderson, Knighton, Joicey, Prendergast, Potts					
15 Dec. 1973	Fulham	Division 2	0–3		7925
P.Springett, Rodrigues, Shaw, Thompson, Mullen, T.Craig, Henderson, Knighton, Joicey(Sunley 57), Prendergast, Potts					
26 Dec. 1973	Hull City	Division 2	1–1	Prudham(68)	15600
P.Springett, Rodrigues(Prudham 51), Knighton, Thompson, Eustace, Coyle, Potts, T.Craig, Sunley, Prendergast, Sissons					
29 Dec. 1973	Nottingham Forest	Division 2	1–1	Craig(60)	16332
P.Springett, Cameron, Knighton, Thompson, Eustace, Shaw, Potts, Sunley, Prendergast, T.Craig, Prudham					
05 Jan. 1974	Coventry City	F.A.Cup 3	0–0		16799
P.Springett, Cameron, Knighton, Thompson, Eustace, Shaw, Potts, Coyle, Sunley, Prendergast(Joicey 48), T.Craig					
19 Jan. 1974	Swindon Town	Division 2	2–1	Sunley(35), Potts(77)	11944
P.Springett, Cameron, Knighton, Thompson, Eustace, Shaw, Henderson(Potts 74), Coyle, Joicey, T.Craig, Sunley					
26 Jan. 1974	Sheffield United	County Cup Fl	0–0	*Win 4–3 on pens.	18869
P.Springett, Cameron, Knighton, Coyle, Eustace, T.Craig, Potts, Sunley, Joicey(Rodrigues 49), Shaw, Henderson					
10 Feb. 1974	Bristol City	Division 2	3–1	Joicey(12), Henderson(58), Shaw(79)	15888
Ferguson, Cameron, Knighton, Thompson, Eustace(Coyle 60), Shaw, Henderson, Sunley, Joicey, T.Craig, Potts					
23 Feb. 1974	Sunderland	Division 2	0–1		17816
Ferguson, Rodrigues, Shaw, Thompson, Coyle(Prudham 78), Knighton, Potts, Sunley, Prendergast, T.Craig, Henderson					
16 Mar. 1974	Cardiff City	Division 2	5–0	Joicey 2(73, 89), Potts(11), Craig(35), Thompson(80)	13, 841
P.Springett, Rodrigues(Henderson 85), Shaw, Thompson, Holsgrove, Knighton, Potts, Prendergast, Joicey, T.Craig, Cameron					
01 Apr. 1974	Aston Villa	Division 2	2–4	Prendergast(23), Thompson(66)	22094
P.Springett, Rodrigues, Shaw, Thompson, Holsgrove, Knighton, Potts, Prendergast, Joicey, T.Craig, Cameron(Henderson 64)					
13 Apr. 1974	Luton Town	Division 2	2–2	Joicey(7), Potts(46)	16492
P.Springett, Rodrigues, Shaw, Mullen, Holsgrove, Coyle, Potts, Sunley(Prudham 67), Joicey, T.Craig, Henderson					
15 Apr. 1974	Preston North End	Division 2	1–0	Craig(17)	17332
P.Springett, Rodrigues, Shaw, Mullen, Holsgrove, Coyle, Potts, Sunley(Prudham 73), Joicey, T.Craig, Henderson					
27 Apr. 1974	Bolton Wanderers	Division 2	1–0	Knighton(85)	23264
P.Springett, Cameron, Shaw, Mullen, Holsgrove, Knighton, Potts, Sunley(Eustace 78), Joicey, T.Craig, Henderson					

OTHER GAMES AT HILLSBOROUGH

26 Sep. 1973	International	Northern Ireland 0	Bulgaria 0		6292
30 Mar. 1974	FA.Cup Semi Final	Burnley 0	Newcastle United 2		55000

357

Date	Opponents	Competition	Score	Scorers	Att.
24 Aug. 1974	Bristol Rovers	Division 2	1–1	Eustace(86)	14343
P.Springett, Rodrigues, Shaw, Thompson(Brown 77), Holsgrove, T.Craig, Potts, McIver, Joicey, Eustace, Prudham					
07 Sep. 1974	Cardiff City	Division 2	1–2	Lamour(14)og.	9850
P.Springett, Rodrigues, Eustace(Sunley 57), Dowd, Holsgrove, T.Craig, Potts, McIver, Joicey, Knighton, Prudham					
21 Sep. 1974	Nottingham Forest	Division 2	2–3	Craig(45), Joicey(85)	15295
P.Springett, Rodrigues, McIver(Sunley 72), Dowd, Holsgrove, Knighton, Potts, Harvey, Joicey, T.Craig, Brown					
25 Sep. 1974	West Bromwich Albion	Division 2	0–0		12333
P.Springett, Rodrigues, McIver, Dowd, Holsgrove, Knighton, Potts, Harvey, Joicey(Sunley 70), T.Craig, Brown					
02 Oct. 1974	Sunderland	Division 2	0–2		11490
P.Springett, Rodrigues, Shaw, Dowd, Holsgrove, Knighton, Potts, Harvey, Wylde, T.Craig, Sunley					
05 Oct. 1974	Bristol City	Division 2	1–1	Holsgrove(49)	10088
P.Springett, Rodrigues, Shaw, Dowd, Holsgrove, Knighton, Potts, Harvey, Joicey, T.Craig, Sunley(Prudham 71)					
19 Oct. 1974	Hull City	Division 2	2–1	McMordie(37), Harvey(44)	11498
P.Springett, Rodrigues, Knighton, Thompson, Holsgrove, McMordie, Potts, Harvey, Joicey, T.Craig, Brown					
21 Oct. 1974	England All Star XI	Taylor Tst.	0–5		10939
P.Springett, Rodrigues, Knighton, Thompson(Dowd 56), Holsgrove, McMordie, Brown(Shaw 70), McIver, Joicey(Mullen 82), T.Craig, Sunley(Ferguson 56)					
09 Nov. 1974	York City	Division 2	3–0	Ferguson(32), McMordie(62), Potts(89)	12495
P.Springett, Rodrigues, Knighton, Thompson, Dowd, McMordie, Potts, Harvey, Ferguson, T.Craig, Brown(Sunley ht)					
23 Nov. 1974	Fulham	Division 2	1–0	McMordie(49)	12373
P.Springett, Rodrigues, Shaw, Thompson, Dowd, McMordie, Potts, Harvey, Ferguson, T.Craig, Sunley					
07 Dec. 1974	Manchester United	Division 2	4–4	Sunley 2(19, 68), Harvey(23), Shaw(30)	35067
P.Springett, Rodrigues, Shaw, Thompson, Dowd, McMordie, Potts, Harvey, Brown(Wylde 76), T.Craig, Sunley					
14 Dec. 1974	Oldham Athletic	Division 2	1–1	Brown(34)	13339
P.Springett, Shaw, Knighton, Thompson, Dowd, McMordie, Potts, Harvey(Wylde 60), Brown, T.Craig, Sunley					
26 Dec. 1974	Bolton Wanderers	Division 2	0–2		17153
Fox, Rodrigues, Shaw, Thompson, Dowd, Knighton, Potts, Harvey, Brown(McIver 62), Ferguson, Sunley					
18 Jan. 1975	Portsmouth	Division 2	0–2		11032
Fox, Rodrigues, Knighton, Thompson(Ferguson 50), Mullen, Shaw, Potts, Harvey, Sunley, McIver, Brown					
25 Jan. 1975	Burnley	Friendly	1–3	Ferguson(35)	2587
Fox, McIver, Quinn, Thompson, Dowd(Eustace 11), Shaw, Potts, Harvey, Ferguson, Hall, Prendergast					
04 Feb. 1975	Doncaster Rovers	County Cup s/f	1–1	Wylde(27)	2100
Fox, McIver, Shaw, Thompson, Dowd, Quinn, Potts, Eustace, Joicey, Harvey, Wylde					
08 Feb. 1975	Blackpool	Division 2	0–0		14342
Fox, Rodrigues, Quinn, Thompson, Holsgrove, Shaw, Potts, Harvey, Joicey, Henson, Prendergast					
22 Feb. 1975	Notts County	Division 2	0–1		14734
Fox, Rodrigues, Quinn, Thompson, Holsgrove, Shaw, Potts, Harvey(Wylde 13), Joicey, Henson, Prendergast					
15 Mar. 1975	Orient	Division 2	0–1		8492
Fox, McIver, Quinn, Mullen, Dowd, Knighton(Brown 65), Potts, Eustace, Wylde, Henson, Herbert					
29 Mar. 1975	Millwall	Division 2	0–1		8171
Fox, McIver, Quinn(Herbert ht), Mullen, Dowd, Eustace, Potts, Knighton, Wylde, Henson, Sunley					
31 Mar. 1975	Southampton	Division 2	0–1		8505
Fox, Rodrigues(Brown 73), Knighton, Mullen, Thompson, Shaw, Potts, Harvey, Ferguson, Henson, Prendergast					
08 Apr. 1975	Norwich City	Division 2	0–1		7483
Fox, Cameron, Knighton, Mullen, Thompson, Shaw, Potts, Harvey, Ferguson, Henson, Joicey					
14 Apr. 1975	Morton	Friendly	2–0	Sunley 2(5, 53)	1676
P.Springett, Cameron, Knighton(Quinn 56), Mullen, Dowd(Cusack 70), Shaw, Potts, Harvey(Wylde 56), Joicey, Henson, Sunley					
19 Apr. 1975	Oxford United	Division 2	1–1	Joicey(90)	7444
Fox, Cameron, Quinn, Mullen, Dowd(Wylde 9), Shaw, Potts, Harvey, Sunley, Henson, Joicey					
23 Apr. 1975	Aston Villa	Division 2	0–4		23605
Fox, Cameron, Quinn, Mullen, Thompson, Shaw, Potts, Knighton, Sunley, Henson(Wylde ht), Joicey					

OTHER GAMES AT HILLSBOROUGH

05 Nov. 1974	Boys	Sheffield 8	York 0		n/k
05 Apr. 1975	F.A.Cup Semi Final	Birmingham City 1	Fulham 1		55000

Date	Opponents	Competition	Score	Scorers	Att.
11 Aug. 1975	Coventry City	Friendly	0–3		3986
Fox, Cameron, Quinn, Mullen, Thompson, Harvey, Potts, Henson(Knighton 67), Joicey, Prendergast, Brown					
23 Aug. 1975	Brighton & Hove Alb.	Division 3	3–3	Prendergast(6), Joicey(31), Winstanley(87)og.	10326
Ramsbottom, Cameron, Quinn, Mullen, Dowd, McIver, Potts, Harvey(Herbert), Joicey, Prendergast, Henson					
27 Aug. 1975	Darlington	Lge. Cup 1–L1	0–2		7452
Ramsbottom, Cameron, Quinn(Herbert 61), Mullen, Dowd, McIver, Potts, Knighton, Joicey, Prendergast, Henson					
03 Sep. 1975	Darlington	Lge. Cup 1R	0–0 aet	Lost 5–3 on pens.	6276
Ramsbottom, Cameron, Quinn, Mullen, Dowd, McIver, Potts, Harvey(Joicey 85), Herbert, Prendergast, Henson					
06 Sep. 1975	Wrexham	Division 3	1–0	Herbert(79)	7585
Ramsbottom, Cameron, Quinn, Mullen, Dowd, Henson, Potts, Harvey, Herbert, Prendergast, Brown(Knighton 69)					
20 Sep. 1975	Grimsby Town	Division 3	4–0	Prendergast(9), Herbert(13), Gray(61)og., Potts(72)	11345
Ramsbottom, Cameron, Quinn, Mullen, Dowd, Shaw, Potts, Harvey, Prendergast(Proudlove 80), Henson, Herbert					
04 Oct. 1975	Peterborough United	Division 3	2–2	Prendergast(33), Lee(82)og.	11412
Ramsbottom, Shaw, Quinn, Mullen, Dowd, Harvey, Potts, Herbert, Prendergast(Joicey ht), Henson, Proudlove					
11 Oct. 1975	Millwall	Division 3	4–1	Potts 2(40, 50), Henson 2(62, 89)	10144
Ramsbottom, Quinn(Knighton 76), Mullen, Harvey, Dowd, Cusack, Potts, Shaw, Joicey, Henson, Proudlove					
25 Oct. 1975	Shrewsbury Town	Division 3	1–1	Joicey(11)	12045
Ramsbottom, Thompson, Quinn, Dowd, Cusack, Harvey, Shaw, Henson, Joicey, Prendergast, Potts					
05 Nov. 1975	Gillingham	Division 3	1–0	Joicey(70)	8235
Ramsbottom, Shaw, Quinn, Thompson, Cusack, O'Donnell, Harvey, Henson(Herbert ht), Joicey, Proudlove, Potts					
08 Nov. 1975	Port Vale	Division 3	0–3		10880
Ramsbottom, Shaw, Quinn, Thompson, Cusack, O'Donnell, Harvey, Proudlove, Joicey, Sunley(Henson 68), Potts					
22 Nov. 1975	Macclesfield Town	F.A.Cup 1	3–1	Proudlove(26), Knighton(47), Prendergast(53)	12940
Ramsbottom, Shaw, Quinn, Thompson, Cusack, O'Donnell, Knighton, Harvey, Prendergast, Proudlove(Joicey 78), Potts					
29 Nov. 1975	Rotherham United	Division 3	0–0		18691
Ramsbottom, Shaw, Quinn, Thompson, Cusack, O'Donnell, Mullen, Knighton(Proudlove 69), Prendergast, Joicey, Potts					
13 Dec. 1975	Wigan Athletic	F.A.Cup 2	2–0	Sunley(53), Nimmo(88)	12436
Fox, Shaw, Quinn, Thompson, Cusack, O'Donnell, Mullen, Proudlove, Prendergast(Nimmo 72), Sunley, Potts					
20 Dec. 1975	Preston North End	Division 3	2–2	Potts(59), Herbert(85)	8553
Fox, Shaw, Quinn, Thompson, Cusack, O'Donnell, Mullen, Herbert, Proudlove(Wylde 78), Sunley, Potts					
27 Dec. 1975	Mansfield Town	Division 3	0–0		15430
Fox, Shaw, Quinn, Thompson, Cusack, O'Donnell, Mullen, Sunley, Proudlove(McIver 66), Herbert, Potts					
10 Jan. 1976	Hereford United	Division 3	1–2	Shaw(7)	8155
Fox, Walden, Quinn, Thompson, Cusack, O'Donnell, Mullen(Prendergast 62), Shaw, Joicey, Wylde, Potts					
24 Jan. 1976	Swindon Town	Division 3	0–2		8342
Watling, Walden(Nimmo 72), Mullen, Thompson, Cusack, O'Donnell, Shaw, Wylde, Prendergast, Sunley, Potts					
31 Jan. 1976	Chester	Division 3	2–0	Nimmo(7), Prendergast(15)	7558
Fox, Shaw, Mullen, Thompson(Wylde 78), Cusack, O'Donnell, McIver, Henson, Nimmo, Prendergast, Potts					
21 Feb. 1976	Aldershot	Division 3	3–1	Nimmo(27), Prendergast(31), Feely(56)	8286
Fox, Walden, Shaw, Hull, Cusack, O'Donnell, McIver, Wylde, Prendergast, Feely, Nimmo					
06 Mar. 1976	Walsall	Division 3	2–1	Henson(66), Nimmo(87)	9713
Fox, Shaw, Quinn, Mullen, Cusack, O'Donnell, McIver(Nimmo ht), Henson, Prendergast, Feely, Potts					
17 Mar. 1976	Cardiff City	Division 3	1–3	Quinn(89)	8867
Fox, Shaw, Quinn, Mullen, Cusack, O'Donnell, Thompson, Henson, Wylde, Feely, Nimmo(Prendergast 50)					
24 Mar. 1976	Chesterfield	Division 3	1–3	Prendergast(20)	10653
Fox, Walden(Henson 49), Quinn, Mullen, Cusack, O'Donnell, Thompson, Shaw, Prendergast, Nimmo, Bell					
27 Mar. 1976	Colchester United	Division 3	1–0	Henson(71)	6905
Fox, Hull, Quinn, Mullen, Cusack, Wylde, McIver(Nimmo ht), Henson, Potts, Prendergast, Bell					
07 Apr. 1976	Crystal Palace	Division 3	1–0	Prendergast(64)	11909
Fox, Hull, Quinn, Mullen, Cusack, O'Donnell, Wylde, Henson, Prendergast, Bell(Feely 87), Potts					
17 Apr. 1976	Bury	Division 3	1–0	Nimmo(84)	10585
Fox, Shaw, Mullen, Thompson, Cusack, McIver, Wylde, Henson, Prendergast, Feely(Nimmo 66), Potts					
20 Apr. 1976	Halifax Town	Division 3	1–0	Henson(28)	13143
Fox, Walden, Shaw, Mullen, Cusack, O'Donnell, Henson, Wylde, Prendergast, Nimmo, Potts					
29 Apr. 1976	Southend United	Division 3	2–1	Prendergast(29), Potts(35)	25802
Fox, Walden, Shaw, Mullen, Cusack, O'Donnell, Wylde, Henson, Nimmo, Prendergast, Potts					

OTHER GAMES AT HILLSBOROUGH

06 Oct. 1975	Boys	Sheffield 2	Spen Valley 1	n/k
24 Nov. 1975	Boys	Sheffield 2	Durham 1	n/k
26 Jan. 1976	Boys	Sheffield 2	Warley 1	n/k
03 Apr. 1976	F.A.Cup Semi Final	Manchester United 2	Derby County 0	55000

1972–73
Dooley (manager), Rodrigues, Thompson, J. Craig, Grummitt, Prophett, P. Springett, Sunley, Eustace, Mullen, Swan, Staniforth (trainer/coach);
Prudham, Sinclair, Coyle, Joicey, Holsgrove, Clements, T. Craig, Sissons, Potts, Henderson.

1973–74
Staniforth (coach), Knighton, Mullen, J. Craig, Grummitt, Coyle, P. Springett, Shaw, Eustace, Thompson, Egginton (physio), Dooley (manager);
Potts, Sunley, Prudham, Prendergast, T. Craig, Hoslgrove, Henderson, Joicey, Rodrigues, Sissons.

1974–75
Shaw, Coyle, T. Craig, Cameron;
Burtenshaw (manager), Mullen, Dowd, Patterson, P. Springett, Sunley, Potts, Young (coach);
Thompson, Prudham, Knighton, Joicey, Rodrigues, Eustace, Holsgrove.

1978–79
Wylde, Grant, Smith, Turner, Cox, Bolder, Porterfield, Mullen; Toms (trainer), Setters (ass. manager), Tynan, Johnson, Hornsby, Rushbury, Leman, Gregson, Owen, Dowd, Charlton (manager), St John (coach);
Henson, Strutt, Bradshaw, Harrison, McKeown, Nimmo.

Date	Opponents	Competition	Score	Scorers	Att.
31 July 1976	Peterborough United	Shipp Cup	3–2	Feely(4), Prendergast(19), Potts(88)	3275
Fox, Walden, Collins, Mullen, Dowd(Cusack ht), O'Donnell, Henson, Johnson, Prendergast(Wylde 60), Feely, Potts					
04 Aug. 1976	Lincoln City	Shipp Cup	1–0	Potts(24)pen.	3923
Turner, Walden, Collins(Cusack ht), Mullen, Dowd, O'Donnell, Wylde, Johnson, Nimmo, Feely, Potts					
18 Aug. 1976	Grimsby Town	Lge. Cup 1–L2	0–0		10207
Turner, Walden, Collins, Mullen, Dowd, Henson, Wylde, Johnson, Nimmo, Feely, Potts					
21 Aug. 1976	Walsall	Division 3	0–0		12046
Turner, Walden, Collins(Cusack 69), Mullen, Dowd, Henson, Wylde, Johnson, Nimmo, Feely, Potts					
25 Aug. 1976	Northampton Town	Division 3	2–1	Wylde 2(19, 47pen.)	11511
Turner, Walden, Mullen, Cusack, Dowd, O'Donnell, Wylde, Johnson, Nimmo, Feely(Potts 81), Bryant					
04 Sep. 1976	Portsmouth	Division 3	1–1	Prendergast(55)	12131
Turner, Walden, Collins, Mullen, Dowd, O'Donnell, Wylde, Johnson, Prendergast, Feely(Nimmo 64), Potts					
18 Sep. 1976	Chesterfield	Division 3	4–1	Wylde 2(37pen., 86), Tynan(38), Hope(82)	13456
Turner, Walden, Collins, Mullen, Dowd, O'Donnell, Wylde, Johnson, Tynan, Hope, Potts(Henson 83)					
21 Sep. 1976	Watford	League Cup 3	3–1	Potts 2(24, 59), Hope(9)	15787
Turner, Walden, Collins, Mullen, Dowd, O'Donnell, Feely, Johnson, Tynan, Hope, Potts					
05 Oct. 1976	Chester	Division 3	3–0	Wylde(58), Hope(68), Tynan(81)	13209
Turner, Walden, Mullen, Jefferson, Dowd, O'Donnell, Wylde, Johnson, Tynan, Hope, Bradshaw					
09 Oct. 1976	Gillingham	Division 3	2–0	Wylde(4), Feely(68)	15133
Turner, Walden, Mullen, Jefferson, Dowd, O'Donnell, Wylde, Johnson, Tynan, Hope(Henson ht), Feely					
23 Oct. 1976	Shrewsbury Town	Division 3	0–1		17030
Turner, Walden, Mullen, Jefferson, Dowd, O'Donnell, Wylde, Johnson, Tynan, Henson, Bradshaw					
30 Oct. 1976	Mansfield Town	Division 3	0–2		15559
Turner, Walden, Collins, Jefferson, Dowd, Henson, Prendergast(Wylde 55), Johnson, Feely, Hope, Bradshaw					
02 Nov. 1976	Rotherham United	Division 3	1–3	Wylde(32)	18204
Fox, Walden, Collins, Mullen, Dowd, Potts, Wylde, Johnson, Tynan, Hope, Bradshaw					
09 Nov. 1976	Crystal Palace	Division 3	1–0	Bradshaw(7)	14899
Turner, Walden, Rushbury, Cusack, Dowd, Potts, Wylde, Johnson, Tynan, Hope, Bradshaw					
13 Nov. 1976	Burnley	Friendly	2–1	Wylde(43), Tynan(53)	2822
Turner, Walden(Strutt 53), Rushbury, Cusack, Mullen, Potts, Wylde, Johnson, Tynan, Henson, Bradshaw					
20 Nov. 1976	Stockport County	F.A.Cup 1	2–0	Tynan(69), Wylde(85)	13886
Turner, Walden, Rushbury, Cusack, Dowd, Potts, Wylde, Johnson, Tynan, Hope, Bradshaw					
04 Dec. 1976	Tranmere Rovers	Division 3	3–1	Bradshaw(3), Henson(50)pen., Leman(72)	12315
Turner, Walden, Rushbury, Cusack, Dowd, Leman, Henson, Johnson, Tynan, Hope, Bradshaw					
27 Dec. 1976	York City	Division 3	3–2	Leman(2), Tynan(25), Rushbury(42)	22004
Turner, Walden, Rushbury, Cusack, Dowd, Leman, Wylde, Johnson, Tynan, Hope, Bradshaw					
08 Jan. 1977	Brighton & Hove Alb.	Division 3	0–0		17000
Turner, Walden, Rushbury, Cusack, Dowd(Henson ht), Leman, Wylde, Johnson, Tynan, Hope, Bradshaw					
25 Jan. 1977	Bury	Division 3	1–0	Leman(17)	12026
Turner, Walden, Rushbury, Mullen, Cusack, Leman, Wylde, Henson, Tynan(Prendergast 71), Hope, Bradshaw					
05 Feb. 1977	Port Vale	Division 3	1–2	Wylde(55)	12933
Turner, Walden, Rushbury, Mullen, Cusack, Bradshaw, Wylde, Johnson, Tynan, Hope, Prendergast(Henson 65)					
19 Feb. 1977	Swindon Town	Division 3	3–1	Bradshaw(23), Wylde(46), Hope(70)pen.	11265
Turner, Walden, Rushbury, Cusack, Dowd, Leman(Potts 86), Wylde, Johnson, Tynan, Hope, Bradshaw					
21 Feb. 1977	Norwich City	O'Donnell Tst.	2–0	Wylde(52), McKeown(64)	5739
Montgomery(Sunderland), Davis, Rushbury, Dowd(Simmonite ht), Waldron(Man. Utd.), McKeown, Wylde (Prendergast 62), Bremner(Hull City), Potts, Woodward(Sheff.Utd.), T.Craig(Newcastle Utd.)					
05 Mar. 1977	Wrexham	Division 3	3–1	Leman(1), Wylde(6), Hope(61)pen.	13317
Turner, Walden, Rushbury, Mullen, Dowd, Leman, Wylde, Johnson, Tynan, Hope, Bradshaw					
12 Mar. 1977	Lincoln City	Division 3	1–1	Rushbury(13)	14854
Turner, Walden, Rushbury, Mullen, Dowd, Leman, Wylde, Johnson, Tynan, Hope(Potts 74), Bradshaw					
26 Mar. 1977	Reading	Division 3	2–1	Hope(69)pen., Leman(83)	9854
Turner, Walden, Rushbury, Cusack, Dowd, Leman, Wylde, Henson, Tynan(McKeown 67), Hope, Bradshaw					
09 Apr. 1977	Grimsby Town	Division 3	1–0	Wylde(25)	10182
Turner, Walden, Henson, Mullen, Dowd, Leman, Wylde, McKeown, Potts, Hope, Bradshaw					
16 Apr. 1977	Preston North End	Division 3	1–0	Tynan(71)	13217
Turner, Walden, Rushbury, Mullen, Dowd, Leman, Wylde, Henson, Tynan, Hope, Bradshaw(McKeown ht)					
25 Apr. 1977	Leicester City	Prendergast Tst.	2–3	Mullen(71), Nimmo(83)	3179
R.Springett(Turner 70), Walden, Rushbury, Mullen, Swan(Cusack 70), Leman(Potts ht), Wylde(Nimmo 70), Dorman, Prendergast(McKeown ht), Johnson, Tynan					
30 Apr. 1977	Peterborough United	Division 3	4–0	Bradshaw 2(39, 47), Wylde(50), Potts(73)	8727
Turner, Walden, Rushbury, Mullen(Potts 67), Dowd, Leman, Wylde, Johnson, Tynan, Henson, Bradshaw					
14 May 1977	Oxford United	Division 3	2–0	Wylde(50), Tynan(69)	8955
Turner, Walden, Rushbury, N.Owen, Cusack, Henson, Wylde, Davis, Tynan, Johnson, Bradshaw					

OTHER GAMES AT HILLSBOROUGH

25 Oct. 1976	Boys		Sheffield 2	York 0	n/k
16 Mar. 1977	League Cup Final–Rep.		Aston Villa 1	Everton 1	52135
23 Apr. 1977	F.A.Cup Semi Final		Leeds United 1	Man.United 2	55000

Date	Opponents	Competition	Score	Scorers	Att.
06 Aug. 1977	Huddersfield Town	Shipp Cup	0–2		3840
Turner, Walden, Rushbury, Mullen, Dowd(Cusack 60), Leman, Strutt, Johnson, Tynan(McKeown 60), Porterfield, Bradshaw					
13 Aug. 1977	Doncaster Rovers	Lge. Cup 1–L1	5–2	Wylde 3(5, 6, 46), Porterfield(43), Walden(70)	7230
Turner, Walden, Rushbury, Cusack, Dowd, Leman, Wylde, Johnson, Tynan, Porterfield, Bradshaw					
20 Aug. 1977	Swindon Town	Division 3	1–1	Tynan(46)	12095
Turner, Walden, Rushbury, Cusack, Dowd, Leman, Prendergast, Johnson, Tynan, Porterfield, Bradshaw					
27 Aug. 1977	Walsall	Division 3	0–0		10634
Turner, Walden, Rushbury, Cusack, Dowd, Leman, Wylde(McKeown 78), Johnson, Tynan, Porterfield, Bradshaw					
05 Sep. 1977	Blackpool	League Cup 2R	3–1	Bradshaw(6), Tynan(31), Johnson(61)	13260
Turner, Walden, Mullen, Cusack, Dowd, Leman, Darling, Johnson, Tynan, Porterfield, Bradshaw					
10 Sep. 1977	Shrewsbury Town	Division 3	0–1		10324
Turner, Walden, Mullen, Cusack, Dowd, Leman, Darling, Johnson, Tynan, Porterfield(Hope 66), Bradshaw					
24 Sep. 1977	Peterborough United	Division 3	0–1		9620
Turner, Walden, Rushbury, Mullen, Cusack, Leman, Wylde, Johnson, Tynan(Nimmo 56), Hope, Bradshaw					
27 Sep. 1977	Plymouth Argyle	Division 3	1–1	Wylde(43)	8515
Turner, Walden, Rushbury, Mullen, Cusack, Leman, Wylde, Johnson, Prendergast, Porterfield, Bradshaw					
08 Oct. 1977	Chesterfield	Division 3	1–0	Tynan(34)	12920
Turner, Walden, Rushbury, Dowd, Cusack, Mullen, Leman, Johnson, Wylde, Bradshaw, Tynan					
22 Oct. 1977	Lincoln City	Division 3	2–0	Bradshaw(17), Rushbury(31)	13166
Turner, Walden, Rushbury, Dowd, Cusack, Mullen, Wylde, Johnson, Tynan, Porterfield, Bradshaw					
25 Oct. 1977	Walsall	League Cup 3	2–1	Wylde(53), Tynan(75)	18350
Turner, Walden, Rushbury, Dowd, Cusack, Mullen, Wylde, Johnson, Tynan, Porterfield, Bradshaw					
05 Nov. 1977	Carlisle United	Division 3	3–1	Hamilton(4)og., Prendergast(8), Tynan(12)	12285
Turner, Walden, Rushbury, Mullen, Cusack, Porterfield, Wylde, Johnson, Tynan, Prendergast, Bradshaw(Hope 84)					
19 Nov. 1977	Gillingham	Division 3	0–0		9762
Turner, Walden, Rushbury, Dowd, Cusack, Mullen, Wylde, Prendergast, Tynan, Porterfield, Bradshaw					
26 Nov. 1977	Bury	F.A.Cup 1	1–0	Hope(41)	11571
Turner, Walden, Rushbury, Dowd, Cusack, Mullen, Porterfield, Prendergast, Tynan, Hope, Bradshaw					
29 Nov. 1977	Everton	League Cup 4	1–3	Tynan(35)	36079
Turner, Walden, Rushbury, Dowd, Cusack, Mullen, Hope, Prendergast, Tynan, Porterfield, Bradshaw					
03 Dec. 1977	Colchester United	Division 3	1–2	Wylde(63)	9000
Turner, Walden, Rushbury, Dowd, Cusack, Mullen, Wylde, Bradshaw, Tynan, Porterfield(Prendergast 77), Hope					
27 Dec. 1977	Rotherham United	Division 3	1–0	Prendergast(55)	18803
Bolder, Walden, Grant, Rushbury, Mullen, G.Owen(Leman 53), Wylde, Porterfield, Tynan, Prendergast, Bradshaw					
31 Dec. 1977	Hereford United	Division 3	1–0	Wylde(73)	11029
Bolder, Walden, Grant, Rushbury, Mullen, Leman, Wylde, Porterfield, Tynan, Prendergast, Bradshaw					
07 Jan. 1978	Doncaster Rovers	County Cup s/f	1–1	Nimmo(86)	1937
Bolder, Walden, Grant, Rushbury, Cusack(McKeown 61), Johnson, Mullen, Wylde, Leman, Bradshaw, Nimmo					
17 Jan. 1978	Exeter City	Division 3	2–1	Rushbury(27)pen., Wylde(79)	9596
Bolder, Walden, Grant, Rushbury, Cusack, Mullen, Wylde, Porterfield, Tynan, Johnson, Leman					
28 Jan. 1978	Bury	Division 3	3–2	Wylde 2(3, 32), Tynan(40)	9054
Bolder, Walden, Grant, Rushbury, Cusack, Mullen, Wylde, Porterfield, Tynan, Johnson, Leman					
11 Feb. 1978	Port Vale	Division 3	3–1	Leman(11), Mullen(44), Tynan(68)	9516
Bolder, Walden, Grant, Rushbury, Cusack, Mullen, Wylde(Bradshaw 32), Porterfield, Tynan, Johnson, Leman					
25 Feb. 1978	Portsmouth	Division 3	0–0		10241
Bolder, Walden, Grant(Cusack 12), Rushbury, Mullen, Hedley, Bradshaw, Porterfield, Tynan, Johnson, Leman					
07 Mar. 1978	Chester	Division 3	1–1	Grant(4)	10678
Bolder, Walden, Grant, Rushbury, Cusack, Mullen, Prendergast, Hedley, Tynan, Johnson, Bradshaw(Leman 73)					
21 Mar. 1978	Bradford City	Division 3	2–0	Tynan(51), Wylde(85)	12304
Bolder, Walden, Grant, Rushbury, Mullen, Hornsby, Wylde, Porterfield, Tynan, Johnson, Hedley(Leman 35)					
27 Mar. 1978	Tranmere Rovers	Division 3	1–0	Tynan(80)	12976
Bolder, Walden, Grant(Leman 81), Rushbury, Dowd, Mullen, Wylde, Porterfield, Tynan, Johnson, Hornsby					
08 Apr. 1978	Oxford United	Division 3	2–1	Hornsby(45), Mullen(50)	10674
Bolder, Walden, Grant, Rushbury, Dowd, Mullen, Wylde, Porterfield, Tynan, Johnson, Hornsby					
18 Apr. 1978	Preston North End	Division 3	1–0	Tynan(58)	12426
Bolder, Walden, Grant, Rushbury, Dowd, Mullen, Wylde(Leman 80), Porterfield, Tynan, Johnson, Hornsby					
22 Apr. 1978	Cambridge United	Division 3	0–0		11512
Bolder, Walden, Grant, Rushbury, Dowd, Mullen, Wylde(Leman 27), Porterfield, Tynan, Johnson, Hornsby					
03 May 1978	Wrexham	Division 3	2–1	Hornsby(26)pen., Tynan(41)	15700
Turner, Walden, Grant, Rushbury, Smith, Mullen, Wylde, Porterfield(Leman 63), Tynan, Johnson, Hornsby					

Date	Opponents	Competition	Score	Scorers	Att.
04 Aug. 1978	Coventry City	Friendly	1–1	Tynan(20)	3235
Bolder(Turner ht), McKeown(Pet. Shirtliff 73), Grant, Dowd, Cusack, Mullen, Rushbury, Hornsby, Johnson, Porterfield(Harrison 49), Tynan(Strutt 80)					
15 Aug. 1978	Doncaster Rovers	Lge.Cup 1–L2	0–1		8055
Bolder, Pet.Shirtliff(G.Owen 78), Grant, Rushbury, Dowd, Mullen, Wylde, Porterfield, Tynan, Johnson, Hornsby					
26 Aug. 1978	Colchester United	Division 3	0–0		10685
Bolder, Blackhall, Grant, Rushbury, Dowd, Smith, Mullen, Porterfield(Leman 82), Tynan, Johnson, G.Owen					
09 Sep. 1978	Southend United	Division 3	3–2	Hornsby 2(33pen., 54), Grant(40)	11309
Bolder, Blackhall, Grant, Rushbury, Dowd, Mullen, Wylde, Porterfield, Tynan, Johnson, Hornsby					
23 Sep. 1978	Plymouth Argyle	Division 3	2–3	Wylde(42), Nimmo(80)	12088
Bolder, Blackhall, Grant, Rushbury, Smith, Mullen, Wylde, Porterfield, Tynan(Nimmo 71), Johnson, Hornsby					
26 Sep. 1978	Bury	Division 3	0–0		9000
Bolder, Blackhall, Grant, Rushbury, Dowd, Mullen, Wylde, Porterfield, Tynan(Nimmo 66), Johnson, Hornsby					
14 Oct. 1978	Carlisle United	Division 3	0–0		10980
Bolder(G.Owen ht), Blackhall, Grant, Smith, Pickering, Rushbury, Wylde, Porterfield, Leman, Johnson, Hornsby					
17 Oct. 1978	Oxford United	Division 3	1–1	Wylde(28)	9431
Cox, Blackhall, Grant, Smith, Pickering, G.Owen, Wylde, Porterfield, Leman, Lowey(Rushbury 84), Hornsby					
24 Oct. 1978	Exeter City	Division 3	2–1	Hornsby(72), Lowey(86)	11139
Cox, Blackhall, Rushbury, Smith, Pickering, Johnson(Lowey 57), Wylde, Porterfield, Leman, G.Owen, Hornsby					
28 Oct. 1978	Walsall	Division 3	0–2		12019
Cox, Blackhall, Rushbury, Smith, Pickering, Johnson, Wylde, Porterfield(G.Owen 68), Leman, Lowey, Hornsby					
11 Nov. 1978	Lincoln City	Division 3	0–0		12590
Turner, Blackhall, Rushbury, Smith, Pickering, Johnson, Wylde, Porterfield, Leman, Lowey, Hornsby					
28 Nov. 1978	Scunthorpe United	F.A.Cup 1R	1–0	Nimmo(89)	9760
Turner, Blackhall, Rushbury, Smith, Pickering, Johnson, Wylde(G.Owen 63), Porterfield, Leman, Nimmo, Hornsby					
09 Dec. 1978	Chester	Division 3	0–0		8872
Turner, Blackhall, Rushbury, Smith, Pickering, Grant(Wylde), Johnson, Porterfield, G.Owen, Nimmo, Hornsby					
19 Dec. 1978	Tranmere Rovers	F.A.Cup 2R	4–0	Wylde 2(63, 69), Lowey(70), Hornsby(87)pen.	7316
Turner, Blackhall, Rushbury, Smith, Pickering, Johnson, Wylde, Porterfield, Leman, Lowey, Hornsby					
06 Jan. 1979	Arsenal	F.A.Cup 3	1–1	Johnson(47)	33635
Turner, Blackhall, Rushbury, Smith, Mullen, Johnson, Wylde, Porterfield, Leman, Lowey, Hornsby					
03 Mar. 1979	Shrewsbury Town	Division 3	0–0		11284
Turner, Pet.Shirtliff, Rushbury, Mullen, Pickering, Johnson, Wylde, Porterfield(K.Taylor 80), Leman, Lowey, Hornsby					
06 Mar. 1979	Gillingham	Division 3	2–1	Owen(1), Wylde(72)	8205
Turner, Pet.Shirtliff, Rushbury, Mullen, Pickering, Johnson, Wylde, K.Taylor(Porterfield 62), G.Owen, Lowey, Hornsby					
13 Mar. 1979	Brentford	Division 3	1–0	Wylde(14)	10229
Turner, Pet.Shirtliff, Rushbury, Mullen, Pickering, Johnson, Wylde, Porterfield, Leman(G.Owen 63), Lowey, Hornsby					
27 Mar. 1979	Peterborough United	Division 3	3–0	Hornsby(46)pen., Wylde(50), Johnson(81)	9868
Turner, Pet.Shirtliff, Grant, Mullen, Pickering, Johnson, Wylde, Porterfield, G.Owen, Lowey(Nimmo 65), Hornsby					
03 Apr. 1979	Mansfield Town	Division 3	1–2	Nimmo(65)	11065
Turner, Pet.Shirtliff, Grant, Mullen, Pickering, Johnson, Curran, Porterfield, Fleming(Nimmo 63), Lowey, Hornsby					
07 Apr. 1979	Swansea City	Division 3	0–0		12101
Turner, Pet.Shirtliff, Rushbury, Mullen, Pickering, Johnson, Curran, Porterfield, Nimmo, Lowey, Hornsby					
14 Apr. 1979	Chesterfield	Division 3	4–0	Wylde 2(44, 55), Rushbury(41), Johnson(60)	12960
Turner, Pet.Shirtliff, Rushbury, Mullen, Pickering, Johnson, Wylde, Porterfield, Curran(G.Owen 80), Nimmo, Hornsby					
21 Apr. 1979	Tranmere Rovers	Division 3	1–2	Hornsby(4)pen.	9815
Turner, Pet.Shirtliff, Grant, Mullen, Pickering, Johnson, Wylde, Porterfield, Nimmo(Lowey 65), Curran, Hornsby					
05 May 1979	Watford	Division 3	2–3	Hornsby(9), Shirtliff(45)	13746
Bolder, Pet.Shirtliff, Rushbury, Mullen, Pickering, Johnson(G.Owen), Wylde, Porterfield, Curran, Lowey, Hornsby					
07 May 1979	Rotherham United	Division 3	2–1	Mullen(20), Fleming(50)	12094
Bolder, Pet.Shirtliff, Rushbury, Mullen, Pickering, G.Owen, Curran, Porterfield(Johnson ht), Fleming, Lowey, Hornsby					
11 May 1979	Swindon Town	Division 3	2–1	Hornsby(25), Nimmo(73)	9057
Bolder, Pet.Shirtliff, Grant, Mullen, Pickering, Rushbury, G.Owen, Porterfield, Fleming, Nimmo, Hornsby					
17 May 1979	Blackpool	Division 3	2–0	Porterfield(40), Owen(41)	7310
Bolder, Pet.Shirtliff, Grant, Mullen, Pickering, K.Taylor, G.Owen, Porterfield, Fleming, Nimmo, Hornsby(Sterland 78)					
19 May 1979	Hull City	Division 3	2–3	Sterland(20), Hornsby(75)	8950
Bolder, Pet.Shirtliff, Grant, Mullen, Pickering, K.Taylor, Sterland, Porterfield, Fleming, G.Owen(Hornsby 54), Nimmo					

Date	Opponents	Competition	Score	Scorers	Att.
11 Aug. 1979	Hull City	Lge. Cup 1–L1	1–1	Curran(34)	9152
Bolder, Blackhall, Grant, Smith, Pickering, Hornsby, Curran(Porterfield 80), King, Fleming, McCulloch, Mellor					
21 Aug. 1979	Hull City	Division 3	0–0		14376
Bolder, Blackhall, Grant, Smith, Pickering, Hornsby, Curran, King, Fleming, McCulloch, Mellor(Porterfield 79)					
25 Aug. 1979	Blackburn Rovers	Division 3	0–3		14228
Bolder, Blackhall, Grant, Smith, Pickering(Porterfield ht), Hornsby, Curran, King, Fleming, McCulloch, Mellor					
28 Aug. 1979	Manchester City	Lge. Cup 2–L1	1–1	King(67)	24095
Cox, Blackhall, Grant, Smith, Mullen, Hornsby, Curran, Porterfield, Fleming, McCulloch, King					
08 Sep. 1979	Brentford	Division 3	0–2		11612
Cox, Blackhall, Grant, Smith, Mullen, Hornsby, Curran, Porterfield, Fleming(Mellor 60), McCulloch, King					
11 Sep. 1979	Leeds United	Bradshaw Tst.	4–2	Wylde 3(29, 55, 63), Leman(44)	4079
Cox, Williamson, Grant, Smith, Mullen, Johnson, Wylde, Porterfield(Sterland 58), King, McCulloch(Lowey 20 ; Mellor 87), Bradshaw(Leman 15)					
22 Sep. 1979	Swindon Town	Division 3	4–2	Wylde 2(50, 80), McCulloch(3) Smith(37)pen.	11636
Cox, Blackhall, Grant, Smith, Mullen, Hornsby, Wylde, Porterfield, McCulloch, G.Owen, King					
02 Oct. 1979	Millwall	Division 3	2–0	Curran(17), Wylde(52)	12232
Cox, Johnson, Grant, Pet.Shirtliff, Mullen, Leman, Wylde, Porterfield, Lowey, King, Curran					
06 Oct, 1979	Mansfield Town	Division 3	0–0		13072
Cox, Johnson, Grant, Pet.Shirtliff, Mullen, Leman, Wylde, Porterfield, Lowey, King, Curran					
20 Oct. 1979	Oxford United	Division 3	2–2	Wylde 2(6, 64)	13035
Cox, Johnson, Grant, Smith, Mullen, K.Taylor(Mellor 74), Wylde, Porterfield, Lowey, King, Curran					
23 Oct. 1979	Grimsby Town	Division 3	2–0	Mullen(56), Curran(73)	13855
Cox, Johnson, Grant, Smith, Mullen, Leman, Wylde, Porterfield, Lowey, King, Curran					
03 Nov. 1979	Barnsley	Division 3	0–2		23230
Cox, Johnson, Grant, Smith, Mullen, Leman, Fleming(Mellor 61), Porterfield, Lowey, King, Curran					
13 Nov. 1979	Barnsley	County Cup s/f	0–0 *win 5–4 on pens.		1832
Bolder, Strutt(Pl.Shirtliff ht), Williamson, K.Taylor, Pickering, Mullen, G.Owen, Sterland, Mellor, McCulloch, Leman					
17 Nov. 1979	Southend United	Division 3	2–0	Mellor(48), King(54)	10563
Bolder, Pet.Shirtliff, Grant, Smith, Pickering, Hornsby, Wylde, Porterfield, McCulloch, Mellor, King					
24 Nov. 1979	Lincoln City	F.A.Cup 1	3–0	Smith(5)pen., King(56), McCulloch(67)	11226
Bolder, Blackhall, Grant, Smith, Pickering, Hornsby, Porterfield, King, Mellor, McCulloch, Wylde					
08 Dec. 1979	Exeter City	Division 3	0–1		11530
Bolder, Blackhall, Grant, Smith, Pickering, Hornsby, Wylde, Porterfield(Johnson 64), Mellor, King, Curran					
26 Dec. 1979	Sheffield United	Division 3	4–0	Mellor(39), Curran(62), King(64), Smith(86)pen.	49309
Bolder, Blackhall, Williamson, Smith, Pickering, Hornsby, King, Johnson, McCulloch, Mellor, Curran					
12 Jan. 1980	Plymouth Argyle	Division 3	0–1		13287
Bolder, Blackhall, Williamson, Smith, Pickering, Hornsby, King(Leman 65), Johnson, Mellor, McCulloch, Curran					
02 Feb. 1980	Colchester United	Division 3	3–0	Smith 2(9pen., 73pen.), Curran(24)	11958
Bolder, Blackhall, Grant, Smith, Pickering, Hornsby, K.Taylor, Johnson, Mellor, McCulloch, Curran					
05 Feb. 1980	Bury	Division 3	5–1	Curran 2(24, 84), Taylor(25) Grant(45), Smith(55)pen.	12425
Bolder, Blackhall, Grant, Smith, Pickering, Hornsby, K.Taylor, Johnson, Mellor, McCulloch, Curran					
16 Feb. 1980	Chesterfield	Division 3	3–3	Mellor 2(60, 84), Wylde(68)	23433
Bolder, Blackhall, Grant, Smith, Pickering, Hornsby, K.Taylor(King 69), Johnson, Mellor, Wylde, Curran					
23 Feb. 1980	Rotherham United	Division 3	5–0	McCulloch 3(6, 19, 62), Curran(51), King(84)	20557
Bolder, Strutt, Grant, Smith, Pickering, Hornsby, K.Taylor, Johnson, Mellor, McCulloch(King 73), Curran					
08 Mar. 1980	Wimbledon	Division 3	3–1	Curran 2(29, 66), McCulloch(18)	20803
Bolder, Blackhall, Grant, Smith, Pickering, Hornsby, K.Taylor, Johnson, Mellor, McCulloch, Curran					
22 Mar. 1980	Blackpool	Division 3	4–1	Curran 2(54, 71), McCulloch(2), Taylor(59)	19552
Bolder, Blackhall, Grant, Smith, Pickering, King, K.Taylor, Johnson, Mellor, McCulloch(Leman 77), Curran					
01 Apr. 1980	Reading	Division 3	1–1	Curran(25)	20678
Bolder, Blackhall, Grant, Smith, Pickering, Hornsby, K.Taylor, Johnson, Mellor, King, Curran					
07 Apr. 1980	Gillingham	Division 3	1–0	Smith(73)pen.	22717
Bolder, Blackhall, Grant, Smith, Pickering, Hornsby, K.Taylor, Johnson, Mellor, McCulloch, Curran					
19 Apr. 1980	Chester	Division 3	3–0	McCulloch(36), Taylor(74), Curran(89)	19130
Bolder, Blackhall(Leman 82), Grant, Smith, Pickering, King, K.Taylor, Johnson, Mellor, McCulloch, Curran					
03 May 1980	Carlisle United	Division 3	0–0		32734
Bolder, Blackhall, Grant, Smith, Pickering, King, K.Taylor, Johnson, Mellor, McCulloch, Curran					
07 May 1980	Manchester City	Mullen Tst.	3–1	Mullen(15), King(52)pen., Oliver(62)	4531
Bolder, Blackhall, Grant(Sterland ht), Smith, Pickering, Mullen, K.Taylor(Oliver), Johnson, McCulloch, King, Curran					
08 May 1980	Sheffield United	County Cup Fl.	1–2	McCulloch(–)	5430
Bolder, Blackhall, Grant, Smith, Pickering, King, K.Taylor, Johnson, Mellor, McCulloch, Curran					

OTHER GAMES AT HILLSBOROUGH

12 Apr. 1980	F.A.Cup Semi Final	Arsenal 0		Liverpool 0	50174

SEASON 82   1980–81   Division Two (10th)

Date	Opponents	Competition	Score	Scorers	Att.
04 Aug. 1980	Olimpija Ljubljana	Friendly	1–1	Smith(57)pen,	4177
Bolder, Blackhall, Grant(Strutt 24), Smith, Pickering, King, K.Taylor(Oliver ht), Johnson, Mellor, Lowey(Campbell ht), Curran					
09 Aug. 1980	Sheffield United	Lge. Cup 1–L1	2–0	Taylor(10), Johnson(25)	23989
Bolder, Blackhall, Grant, Smith, Pickering, King, K.Taylor, Johnson, G.Owen, McCulloch, Curran					
16 Aug. 1980	Newcastle United	Division 2	2–0	McCulloch(16), Taylor(75)	26164
Bolder, Blackhall, Williamson, Smith, Pickering, King, K.Taylor, Johnson, Mellor, McCulloch, Curran					
30 Aug. 1980	Preston North End	Division 2	3–0	McCulloch 2(25, 43), King(83)	16274
Bolder, Blackhall, Grant, Smith, Pickering, King, K.Taylor, Johnson, G.Owen, McCulloch, Curran					
02 Sep. 1980	Wimbledon	Lge. Cup 2–L2	3–1	Owen(11), Grant(65), Curran(89)	15151
Cox, Blackhall, Grant, Smith, Pickering, K.Taylor, King, Johnson, G.Owen, McCulloch, Curran					
13 Sep. 1980	Bristol City	Division 2	2–1	Pearson(40), King(53)	15054
Bolder, Blackhall, Grant, Smith, Pickering, King, K.Taylor, Johnson, G.Owen(Campbell 78), Pearson, Mellor					
20 Sep. 1980	Queen's Park Rangers	Division 2	1–0	Pearson(29)	15195
Bolder, Blackhall, Grant, Smith, Pickering, King, K.Taylor, Johnson(Oliver 62), G.Owen, Pearson, Mellor					
23 Sep. 1980	Watford	League Cup 3	1–2	Pearson(48)	14085
Cox, Blackhall, Grant, Smith, Pickering, King(Oliver 32), K.Taylor, Mellor, G.Owen, McCulloch, Pearson					
07 Oct. 1980	Blackburn Rovers	Division 2	2–1	Hornsby(22), Curran(40)	16707
Cox, Blackhall, Grant, Smith, Pickering(Mellor 80), Hornsby, K.Taylor, Johnson, King, McCulloch, Curran					
11 Oct. 1980	Cardiff City	Division 2	2–0	Hornsby(34), McCulloch(80)	15396
Bolder, Blackhall, Grant, Smith, Pet.Shirtliff, Hornsby, K.Taylor, Johnson, King, McCulloch, Curran					
25 Oct. 1980	Orient	Division 2	2–2	McCulloch(44), Mirocevic(54)	18018
Bolder, Blackhall, Grant, Smith, Pet.Shirtliff, Hornsby, K.Taylor, Johnson, Sterland, McCulloch(Mellor 64), Mirocevic					
08 Nov. 1980	Wrexham	Division 2	2–1	Curran 2(62pen., 84)	15736
Bolder, Blackhall, Grant, Smith, Pickering(Mellor 34), Hornsby, Curran, Johnson, King, McCulloch, Mirocevic					
11 Nov. 1980	Bolton Wanderers	Division 2	2–0	Jones(14)og., Curran(74)pen.	16262
Bolder, Blackhall, Grant, Smith, Pet.Shirtliff, Hornsby, Curran, Johnson, King, McCulloch, Mirocevic					
29 Nov. 1980	Watford	Division 2	1–0	McCulloch(42)	14761
Bolder, Blackhall, Grant, Smith, Pet.Shirtliff, Sterland, Mirocevic, Johnson, Leman, McCulloch, Curran					
13 Dec. 1980	Bristol Rovers	Division 2	4–1	McCulloch 2(64, 66), Smith(38), Curran(53)	14008
Bolder, Blackhall, Grant, Smith, Pet.Shirtliff, Sterland, Mirocevic, Johnson, Leman(Pearson 68), McCulloch, Curran					
26 Dec. 1980	Shrewsbury Town	Division 2	1–1	Pearson(80)	22863
Bolder, Blackhall, Grant, Smith, Pet.Shirtliff, Sterland, Mirocevic(Pearson 72), Johnson, Leman, McCulloch, Curran					
10 Jan. 1981	Chelsea	Division 2	0–0		25113
Bolder, Blackhall, Grant, Smith, Pet.Shirtliff, Sterland, Pearson, Johnson, Leman, McCulloch, Curran					
31 Jan. 1981	Notts County	Division 2	1–2	Mirocevic(83)	22449
Bolder, Blackhall, Williamson, Smith, Pet.Shirtliff, Sterland, Pearson, Johnson, Leman(Mirocevic 67), McCulloch, Curran					
14 Feb. 1981	Oldham Athletic	Division 2	3–0	Curran 2(6, 75), McCulloch(41)	16679
Bolder, Blackhall, Grant, Smith, Pet.Shirtliff, Sterland, Mirocevic, K.Taylor(Pearson 82), Leman, McCulloch, Curran					
21 Feb. 1981	Swansea City	Division 2	2–0	Sterland(11), McCulloch(69)	17887
Bolder, Blackhall, Grant(Pearson 62), Smith, Pet.Shirtliff, Sterland, Mirocevic, K.Taylor, Leman, McCulloch, King					
07 Mar. 1981	Derby County	Division 2	0–0		28301
Bolder, Blackhall, Grant, Smith, Pet.Shirtliff, Sterland, Mirocevic, K.Taylor, King, McCulloch, Curran					
18 Mar. 1981	Vancover Whitecaps	Friendly	2–1	Mellor(44), Taylor(63)	2385
Cox, Blackhall, Matthewson, Smith(Pickering 55), Pet.Shirtliff(Strutt 55), Johnson(King 55), K.Taylor, Hornsby, Pearson, Mellor, Curran					
04 Apr. 1981	Luton Town	Division 2	3–1	Curran 2(49, 51), Mirocevic(26)	17006
Bolder, Blackhall, Grant, Smith, Pet.Shirtliff, Mellor, Mirocevic, Johnson, K.Taylor(Hornsby 76), McCulloch, Curran					
18 Apr. 1981	Cambridge United	Division 2	4–1	McCulloch 3(53, 81, 83), Taylor(79)	14315
Bolder, Blackhall, Grant, Smith, Pickering, Johnson, Mellor, K.Taylor, Mirocevic, McCulloch, Curran					
28 Apr. 1981	Grimsby Town	Division 2	1–2	Mirocevic(80)	16747
Bolder, Blackhall, Grant, Sterland, Pet.Shirtliff, King, Mirocevic, Johnson, Hornsby(Pl.Sirtliff 72), McCulloch, Curran					
04 May 1981	Barnsley	County Cup s/f	2–1	Curran 2(3, 33)	1276
Bolder, Blackhall, Williamson, Smith, Pickering, Johnson, Mellor, K.Taylor(King ht), Pearson, McCulloch, Curran					
08 May 1981	West Ham United	Division 2	0–1		21087
Bolder, Blackhall, Grant, Smith, Pet.Shirtliff, Johnson, Mellor, K.Taylor, King(Pearson 68), McCulloch, Curran					

OTHER GAMES AT HILLSBOROUGH

20 Jan. 1981	Boys	Sheffield 1	Blackburn 2	n/k
11 Apr. 1981	F.A.Cup Semi Final	Wolves 2	Tottenham Hotspur 2	50174

Date	Opponents	Competition	Score	Scorers	Att.
15 Aug. 1981	Nigeria	Friendly	3–1	Curran(8), Mellor(82), Bannister(89)	4116
Bolder, Blackhall, Grant, Smith, Pet.Shirtliff, Megson, Hornsby, K.Taylor, Bannister, McCulloch(Mellor ht), Curran					
22 Aug. 1981	Middlesbrough	Friendly	0–3		4139
Bolder, Blackhall, Williamson, Smith, Holton, Hornsby, Mirocevic, Megson, Bannister, McCulloch(Pearson 57), Curran					
05 Sep. 1981	Crystal Palace	Division 2	1–0	Bannister(47)	18476
Bolder, Blackhall, Williamson, Smith, Pet.Shirtliff, K.Taylor, Megson, Mirocevic, Bannister, McCulloch, Curran					
08 Sep. 1981	Rotherham United	Division 2	2–0	Williamson(33), McCulloch(52)	26826
Bolder, Blackhall, Williamson, Smith, Pet.Shirtliff, K.Taylor, Megson, Mirocevic, Bannister, McCulloch, Curran					
19 Sep. 1981	Derby County	Division 2	1–1	Megson(88)	23764
Bolder, Sterland, Williamson, Smith, Pet.Shirtliff, K.Taylor, Megson, Mirocevic(Mellor 75), Bannister, McCulloch, Curran					
03 Oct. 1981	Wrexham	Division 2	0–3		18526
Bolder, Blackhall, Grant, Smith, Pet.Shirtliff, K.Taylor(Mellor 75), Megson, Mirocevic, Bannister, McCulloch, Curran					
10 Oct. 1981	Cardiff City	Division 2	2–1	Taylor(66), McCulloch(84)	15621
Bolder, Blackhall, Williamson, Smith, Pet.Shirtliff, K.Taylor, Megson, Mirocevic(Pearson 61), Bannister, McCulloch, Curran					
24 Oct. 1981	Oldham Ahletic	Division 2	2–1	Bannister(53), Shirtliff(81)	17839
Bolder, Blackhall, Williamson, Smith, Pet.Shirtliff, K.Taylor, Megson, Sterland(Pearson 78), Bannister, McCulloch, Curran					
27 Oct. 1981	Blackburn Rovers	Lge. Cup 2–L2	1–2	Bannister(31)	13087
Bolder, Blackhall, Williamson, Smith, Pet.Shirtliff, K.Taylor(Pearson 65), Megson, Sterland, Bannister, McCulloch, Curran					
14 Nov. 1981	Queen's Park Rangers	Division 2	1–3	Bannister(70)	17024
Bolder, Sterland, Williamson, Matthewson, Pickering, K.Taylor, Megson, Mirocevic(Pearson 34), Bannister, McCulloch, Curran					
24 Nov. 1981	Barnsley	Division 2	2–2	McCulloch(51), Taylor(73)	30621
Bolder, Sterland, Williamson, Smith, Pickering, K.Taylor, Megson, King, Bannister, McCulloch(Mellor 75), Curran					
28 Nov. 1981	Watford	Division 2	3–1	Pearson(22), Bannister(35), Taylor(80)	15990
Bolder, Blackhall, Williamson, Smith, Pet.Shirtliff, K.Taylor, Megson, Leman, Bannister, Pearson(Mellor 89), Curran					
16 Jan. 1982	Blackburn Rovers	Division 2	2–2	McCulloch(14), Megson(44)	13120
Bolder, Sterland, Grant, Pickering, Pet.Shirtliff, Smith, Megson, Mirocevic, Bannister, McCulloch, G.Owen					
23 Jan. 1982	Middlesbrough	Friendly	1–2	Megson(11)	2854
Bolder, Sterland(Blackhall ht), Williamson, Smith, Pickering, Mellor(G.Owen ht), K.Taylor, Megson(Pl.Shirtliff 53), Bannister, Curran, Leman					
06 Feb. 1982	Luton Town	Division 2	3–3	Pearson 2(26, 75), Bannister(83)	18012
Bolder, Sterland, Williamson, Pet.Shirtliff, Pickering, Smith, Megson, Pl.Shirtliff, Bannister, Pearson, Mellor(G.Owen 69)					
16 Feb. 1982	Bolton Wanderers	Division 2	0–1		16555
Bolder, Sterland, Williamson, Pet.Shirtliff, Pickering, Smith, Megson(Curran 50), Pl.Shirtliff, Bannister, Pearson, Mellor					
20 Feb. 1982	Grimsby Town	Division 2	1–1	Bannister(39)pen.	14654
Bolder, Pet.Shirtliff, Williamson, Smith, Pickering, K.Taylor, Mellor, Pl.Shirtliff, Bannister, Pearson, Curran					
02 Mar. 1982	Shrewsbury Town	Division 2	0–0		13254
Bolder, Sterland, Williamson, Pet.Shirtliff, Pickering, K.Taylor, Megson, Smith(Pearson 78), Bannister, McCulloch, Curran					
06 Mar. 1982	Charlton Athletic	Division 2	1–1	Taylor(14)	12853
Bolder, Sterland, Williamson, Pet.Shirtliff, Pickering, Smith(Pearson 73), Megson, K.Taylor, Bannister, McCulloch, Curran					
09 Mar. 1982	Rotherham United	County Cup	2–2 aet	Simmons(37), Owen(88) *win 5–3 on pens.	619
Redfern, Blackhall, Williamson, Hornsby, Pet.Shirtliff, Matthewson, G.Owen, Pl.Shirtliff, Mellor, Mirocevic, Simmons					
20 Mar. 1982	Leicester City	Division 2	2–0	Bannister(70), Pearson(88)	18962
Bolder, Blackhall, Williamson, Smith, Pickering, K.Taylor, Megson, Mirocevic, Bannister, McCulloch(Pearson ht), Curran					
27 Mar. 1982	Orient	Division 2	2–0	Taylor(56), Megson(66)	16460
Bolder, Blackhall, Williamson, Smith, Pickering, K.Taylor, Megson, Mirocevic, Bannister, Pearson, Curran(Shelton 70)					
02 Apr. 1982	Stoke City	Friendly	0–0		1984
Bolder, Blackhall, Williamson, Smith, Pickering, K.Taylor, Megson, Mirocevic, Pearson, Shelton, Curran					
12 Apr. 1982	Newcastle United	Division 2	2–1	Shelton(26), Pearson(45)	29917
Bolder, Sterland, Blackhall, Smith, Pickering, K.Taylor, Megson, Shelton, Bannister, Pearson, Curran					
17 Apr. 1982	Cambridge United	Division 2	2–1	Taylor(20), Pearson(48)	18314
Bolder, Sterland, Blackhall, Smith, Pickering, K.Taylor, Megson, Mirocevic, Bannister, Pearson, Curran					
01 May 1982	Chelsea	Division 2	0–0		19259
Bolder, Sterland(Pearson 28), Blackhall, Smith, Pickering, K.Taylor, Megson, Shelton, Bannister, McCulloch, Curran					
15 May 1982	Norwich City	Division 2	2–1	McCulloch(58), Bannister(89)	24687
Bolder, Sterland, Williamson, Smith, Pet.Shirtliff, K.Taylor, Megson, Shelton, Bannister, McCulloch, Curran(Simmons 86)					
17 May 1982	Doncaster Rovers	County Cup s/f	9–1	Simmons 6, Pearson 2, Williamson	n/k
Redfern, Sterland, Williamson, Matthewson, Pet.Shirtliff, S.Mills, Beaumont, D'Arcy, Simmons, Pearson, G.Owen					

1979–80
Lowey, Grant, Pickering, Mellor, Smith, Shirtliff, McCulloch;
Setters (ass. manager), Mullen, Porterfield, Cox, Bolder, King, Strutt, Wylde, Toms (trainer);
Curran, Johnson, Fleming, Leman, Charlton (manager), Blackhall, Taylor, Owen, Hornsby.

1980–81
Toms (trainer), McCulloch, Grant, Smith, Bolder, Mellor, Blackhall, Johnson, Honey (physio);
King, Hornsby, Curran, Charlton (manager), Pickering, Leman, Taylor.

1981–82
McCulloch, Mellor, Redfern, Cox, Pearson, Grant;
Blunstone (coach), Setters (ass. manager), Holton, Smith, Sterland, Matthewson, Blackhall, Peter Shirtliff, Toms (trainer), Honey (physio);
Taylor, Owen, Curran, Hornsby, Mirocevic, Charlton (manager), Leman, Williamson, Paul Shirtliff, King, Bannister.

1982–83
Lyons, Pearson, McCulloch, Peter Shirtliff, Pickering;
Beaumont, Smith, Oliver, Redfern, Bolder, Sterland, Mirocevic, Matthewson;
Shelton, Taylor, Williamson, Megson, Bannister, Owen, Paul Shirtliff.

Date	Opponents	Competition	Score	Scorers	Att.
14 Aug. 1982	Notts County	Friendly	5–0	Bannister 2(32, 51), Pearson 2(55, 68), Shelton(13)	2673

Bolder, Sterland, Bailey, Smith, Lyons(Pickering), Shelton(Oliver), K.Taylor, Megson, Pearson, Bannister(Williamson), Mirocevic

| 23 Aug. 1982 | West Bromwich Albion | Friendly | 2–2 | Bannister(43)pen., Taylor(46) | 4500 |

Bolder, Williamson, Bailey, Smith, Lyons(Pickering 26), Shelton, K.Taylor, Megson(Simmons ht), Pearson, Bannister(Oliver 77), Mirocevic

| 28 Aug. 1982 | Middlesbrough | Division 2 | 3–1 | Pearson 2(69, 72), Bannister(46)pen. | 18611 |

Bolder, Sterland(Simmons 81), Bailey, Smith, Lyons, Shelton, K.Taylor, Megson, Pearson, Bannister, Mirocevic

| 07 Sep. 1982 | Bolton Wanderers | Division 2 | 3–1 | Pearson 2(13secs., 72), Shelton(74) | 17307 |

Bolder, Pet.Shirtliff, Bailey, Smith, Lyons, Shelton, Megson, K.Taylor, Bannister, Mirocevic, Pearson

| 11 Sep. 1982 | Leeds United | Division 2 | 2–3 | Bannister(67), Megson(88) | 29050 |

Bolder, Sterland, Bailey, Smith, Lyons, Shelton, Megson, K.Taylor(McCulloch 56), Bannister, Mirocevic, Pearson

| 25 Sep. 1982 | Chelsea | Division 2 | 3–2 | Shelton(12), Bannister(69)pen., Smith(80) | 18833 |

Bolder, Sterland, Bailey, Smith, Lyons, Shelton, Megson, K.Taylor, Bannister, G.Owen, Pearson

| 09 Oct. 1982 | Wolverhampton W. | Division 2 | 0–0 | | 21519 |

Bolder, Sterland, Bailey, Smith, Lyons, Shelton, Megson, K.Taylor, Bannister, G.Owen, Pearson

| 23 Oct. 1982 | Grimsby Town | Division 2 | 2–0 | Lyons(18), Shelton(73) | 17904 |

Bolder, Sterland, Bailey, Smith, Lyons, Shelton, Megson, K.Taylor, Bannister, McCulloch, Pearson

| 26 Oct. 1982 | Bristol City | Milk Cup 2–L2 | 1–1 aet | Taylor(110) | 7920 |

Bolder, Sterland, Bailey, Smith, Lyons, Pl.Shirtliff(Pickering 67), Megson, K.Taylor, Bannister, McCulloch, G.Owen

| 06 Nov. 1982 | Derby County | Division 2 | 2–0 | Bannister 2(54pen., 80) | 17703 |

Bolder, Sterland, Bailey, Smith, Lyons, Megson, K.Taylor, Bannister, McCulloch, Mirocevic

| 20 Nov. 1982 | Burnley | Division 2 | 1–1 | Taylor(37) | 16117 |

Bolder, Pet.Shirtliff, Bailey, Smith, Lyons, Shelton, Megson, K.Taylor, Bannister, McCulloch, Mirocevic

| 30 Nov. 1982 | Barnsley | Milk Cup 4 | 1–0 | McCulloch(16) | 33354 |

Bolder, Sterland, Bailey, Smith, Lyons, Mirocevic, Megson, K.Taylor, Bannister, McCulloch, Pearson

| 04 Dec. 1982 | Oldham Athletic | Division 2 | 1–1 | Bannister(70) | 15096 |

Bolder, Sterland, Bailey, Smith, Lyons, Mirocevic, Megson, K.Taylor, Bannister, McCulloch, Pearson

| 18 Dec. 1982 | Newcastle United | Division 2 | 1–1 | Haddock(56)og. | 16310 |

Bolder, Sterland, Bailey, Smith, Lyons, Megson, K.Taylor(Pearson 81), Bannister, McCulloch, Mirocevic

| 28 Dec. 1982 | Rotherham United | Division 2 | 0–1 | | 25024 |

Bolder, Sterland, Bailey, Smith, Lyons, Shelton, Megson, K.Taylor, Bannister, Mirocevic(McCulloch 74), Pearson

| 03 Jan. 1983 | Charlton Athletic | Division 2 | 5–4 | McCulloch 2(6, 61), Bannister(54), Gritt(66)og., Lyons(69) | 11799 |

Bolder, Sterland, Bailey(S.Mills 5), Smith, Lyons, Shelton, Megson, K.Taylor, Bannister, McCulloch, Pearson

| 11 Jan. 1983 | Southend United | F.A.Cup 3R | 2–2 aet | Smith(35), Megson(98) | 11093 |

Bolder, Pet.Shirtliff, Matthewson, Smith, Lyons, Shelton, Megson, K.Taylor, Bannister, McCulloch(Mirocevic 32), Pearson

| 22 Jan. 1983 | Carlisle United | Division 2 | 1–1 | Taylor(40) | 12874 |

Bolder, Sterland, Bailey, Smith, Lyons, Shelton, Mirocevic, K.Taylor(G.Owen 70), Bannister, Pearson, Heard

| 24 Jan. 1983 | Southend United | F.A.Cup 3–2R | 2–1 | Taylor 2(14, 56pen.) | 10767 |

Bolder, Sterland, Bailey, Smith, Lyons, Shelton, S.Mills, K.Taylor, Bannister, Pearson, Mirocevic

| 15 Feb. 1983 | Blackburn Rovers | Division 2 | 0–0 | | 11468 |

Bolder, Sterland, Bailey, Smith, Lyons, Shelton, Megson, K.Taylor(Pearson 72), D.Mills, McCulloch, Heard

| 26 Feb. 1983 | Cambridge United | Division 2 | 3–1 | McCulloch 2(17, 36), D.Mills(55) | 12815 |

Bolder, Sterland, Bailey, Smith, Lyons, Shelton, Megson, D.Mills, Bannister, McCulloch, Heard

| 15 Mar. 1983 | Burnley | F.A.Cup 6–R | 5–0 | Shelton 2(17, 28), McCulloch 2(55, 84), Megson(40)pen. | 41731 |

Bolder, Sterland, Bailey, Smith, Pet.Shirtliff, Shelton, Megson, D.Mills, K.Taylor, McCulloch, Heard

| 22 Mar. 1983 | Leicester City | Division 2 | 2–2 | McCulloch(47), Megson(71) | 14036 |

Bolder, Sterland, Bailey, Smith, Lyons, Shelton, Megson, K.Taylor, Pearson, McCulloch, Heard

| 26 Mar. 1983 | Shrewsbury Town | Division 2 | 0–0 | | 14320 |

Bolder, Sterland, Bailey, Pet.Shirtliff, Lyons, Shelton(Pearson 75), Megson, K.Taylor, Bannister, McCulloch, Heard

| 04 Apr. 1983 | Barnsley | Division 2 | 0–1 | | 22427 |

Bolder, Williamson, Bailey, Smith, Lyons, Shelton, Megson, D.Mills, Bannister, McCulloch(Pearson 73), Heard

| 19 Apr. 1983 | Queen's Park Rangers | Division 2 | 0–1 | | 11713 |

Bolder, Pet.Shirtliff, Williamson, Smith, Oliver, Shelton, Megson, D.Mills(Pearson 75), Bannister, McCulloch, Heard

| 30 Apr. 1983 | Fulham | Division 2 | 2–1 | Mills(61), Lyons(90) | 12531 |

Bolder, Sterland, Williamson, Smith, Lyons, Shelton(Pearson 23), Megson, D.Mills, Bannister, McCulloch, Heard

| 14 May 1983 | Crystal Palace | Division 2 | 2–1 | Heard(6), Bannister(64) | 11154 |

Bolder, Sterland, Williamson, Smith, Lyons, Shelton, Megson, D.Mills, Bannister, McCulloch, Heard

OTHER GAMES AT HILLSBOROUGH

| 17 May 1983 | European Yth. Championships | Belgium 0 | Finland 4 | | n/k |

Date	Opponents	Competition	Score	Scorers	Att.
22 Aug. 1983	West Bromwich Albion	Friendly	1–0	Simmons(46)	3409

Hodge, Sterland(Oliver 80), Williamson(Matthewson ht), Pet.Shirtliff(Pickering ht), Lyons, Madden, Megson, K.Taylor(Shelton 61), Bannister(Simmons ht), D.Mills(Dwyer 61), Morris

03 Sep. 1983	Carlisle United	Division 2	2–0	O'Riordan(31)og., Bannister(77)	14544

Hodge, Sterland, Williamson, Pet.Shirtliff, Lyons, Madden, Megson, Bannister, Varadi, Pearson, Shelton

06 Sep. 1983	Cambridge United	Division 2	1–0	Varadi(34)	14947

Hodge, Sterland, Williamson, Pet.Shirtliff, Lyons, Madden, Megson, Bannister(Morris 42), Varadi, Pearson, Shelton

17 Sep. 1983	Chelsea	Division 2	2–1	Lyons(47), Megson(84)	20596

Hodge, Sterland, Williamson, Smith, Lyons, Madden, Megson, Bannister, Varadi, Pearson, Shelton

01 Oct. 1983	Blackburn Rovers	Division 2	4–2	Sterland(28), Bannister(63), Lyons(82), Varadi(87)	16849

Hodge, Sterland, Williamson, Smith, Lyons, Madden, Megson, Bannister, Varadi, Pearson, Shelton(K.Taylor 85)

04 Oct. 1983	Darlington	Milk Cup 2–L1	3–0	Bannister(13), Morris(27), Madden(45)	9060

Hodge, Pet.Shirtliff, Williamson, Smith, Lyons, Madden, Megson, Bannister, Morris(K.Taylor 84), Pearson, Shelton

08 Oct. 1983	Leeds United	Division 2	3–1	Shelton(12), Pearson(47), Morris(69)	26814

Hodge, Sterland, Williamson, Smith, Lyons, Madden, Megson, Bannister, Morris, Pearson, Shelton

29 Oct. 1983	Huddersfield Town	Division 2	0–0		27824

Hodge, Sterland, Pet.Shirtliff, Smith, Lyons, Madden, Megson, Bannister, Varadi, Morris, Shelton

05 Nov. 1983	Barnsley	Division 2	2–0	Smith(10), Sterland(73)pen.	27491

Hodge, Sterland, Pet.Shirtliff, Smith, Lyons, Madden, Megson, Bannister, Varadi, Morris(K.Taylor 83), Shelton

19 Nov. 1983	Newcastle United	Division 2	4–2	Varadi 2(37, 51), Cunningham(71), Bannister(86)	41134

Hodge, Sterland, Pet.Shirtliff, Smith, Lyons, Madden, Megson, Bannister, Varadi, Cunningham, Shelton

03 Dec. 1983	Shrewsbury Town	Division 2	1–1	Varadi(36)	17703

Hodge, Sterland, Pet.Shirtliff, Smith, Lyons, Madden, Megson, Bannister, Varadi, Pearson, Heard

17 Dec. 1983	Cardiff City	Division 2	5–2	Varadi 2(29, 48), Shelton(33), Bannister(39), Lyons(57)	14580

Hodge, Sterland, Pet.Shirtliff, Smith, Lyons, Madden, Megson, Bannister, Varadi(Morris 79), Cunningham, Shelton

27 Dec. 1983	Middlesbrough	Division 2	0–2		24818

Hodge, Sterland, Pet.Shirtliff, Smith(Heard ht), Lyons, Madden, Megson, Morris, Varadi, Cunningham, Shelton

02 Jan. 1984	Oldham Athletic	Division 2	3–0	Varadi(53), Cunningham(76), Bannister(78)	18690

Hodge, Sterland, Pet.Shirtliff, Smith(Heard 89), Lyons, Madden, Megson, Bannister, Varadi, Cunningham, Shelton

07 Jan. 1984	Barnsley	F.A.Cup 3	1–0	Pearson(26)	29638

Hodge, Sterland, Pet.Shirtliff, Smith, Lyons, Madden, Megson, Bannister, Pearson(Morris 86), Cunningham, Heard

14 Jan. 1984	Swansea City	Division 2	6–1	Lyons(16), Pearson(26), Toshack(40)og., Megson(46), Heard(56), Varadi(90)	13787

Hodge, Sterland, Pet.Shirtliff, Smith, Lyons, Madden, Megson, Bannister, Pearson, Cunningham(Varadi 60), Heard

17 Jan. 1984	Liverpool	Milk Cup 5	2–2	Megson(32), Bannister(52)	49357

Hodge, Sterland, Pet.Shirtliff, Smith, Lyons, Madden, Megson, Bannister, Varadi, Pearson, Shelton

30 Jan. 1984	Coventry City	F.A.Cup 4	3–2	Shirtliff(23), Bannister(76), Sterland(82)pen.	26154

Hodge, Sterland, Pet.Shirtliff(Cunningham ht), Smith, Lyons, Madden, Megson, Bannister, Varadi, Pearson, Shelton

11 Feb. 1984	Charlton Athletic	Division 2	4–1	Bannister(6), Shirtliff(47), Cunningham(48), Varadi(73)	18510

Hodge, Sterland, Pet.Shirtliff, Smith, Lyons, Madden, Megson, Bannister, Varadi, Cunningham, Shelton

25 Feb. 1984	Brighton & Hove Alb.	Division 2	2–1	Bannister(22), Varadi(73)	21614

Hodge, Sterland, Pet.Shirtliff, Smith, Lyons, Worthington, Megson, Bannister, Varadi(Pearson 85), Cunningham, Shelton

07 Mar. 1984	Fulham	Division 2	1–1	Pearson(59)	20440

Hodge, Sterland, Pet.Shirtliff, Smith, Lyons, Worthington, Megson(Pearson 20), Bannister, Varadi, Cunningham, Shelton

11 Mar. 1984	Southampton	F.A.Cup 6	0–0		43030

Hodge, Sterland, Pet.Shirtliff, Smith, Lyons, Madden, K.Taylor, Bannister, Varadi(Pearson 73), Cunningham, Shelton

07 Apr. 1984	Portsmouth	Division 2	2–0	Shelton(11), Sterland(71)	20239

Hodge, Sterland, Pet.Shirtliff, Madden, Lyons, Worthington, Megson, Bannister(Pearson 36), Varadi, Cunningham, Shelton

10 Apr. 1984	Derby County	Division 2	3–1	Varadi 2(45, 86), Sterland(78)pen.	21792

Hodge, Sterland, Pet.Shirtliff, Madden, Lyons, Worthington, Megson, Pearson, Varadi, Cunningham, Shelton

21 Apr. 1984	Grimsby Town	Division 2	1–0	Sterland(75)pen.	25828

Hodge, Sterland(Oliver 87), Pet.Shirtliff, Worthington, Lyons, Madden, Megson, Pearson, Varadi, Cunningham, Shelton

28 Apr. 1984	Crystal Palace	Division 2	1–0	Sterland(51)pen.	27287

Hodge, Sterland, Pet.Shirtliff, Madden, Lyons, Worthington, Megson, Pearson, Varadi, Cunningham(Bannister 80), Shelton

07 May 1984	Manchester City	Division 2	0–0		36763

Hodge, S.Mills, Worthington, Pet.Shirtliff, Lyons, Madden, Megson, Bannister, Varadi, Cunningham, Shelton(Williamson 50)

OTHER GAMES AT HILLSBOROUGH

28 Feb. 1984	U–21 International	England 6	France 1		6409

Date	Opponents	Competition	Score	Scorers	Att.
25 Aug. 1984	Nottingham Forest	Division 1	3–1	Sterland(20)pen., Varadi(58), Pearson(82)	31925
Hodge, Sterland, Pet.Shirtliff, Smith, Lyons(Pearson 74), Worthington, Marwood, Blair, Varadi, Chapman, Shelton					
04 Sep. 1984	Southampton	Division 1	2–1	Varadi(39), Shelton(87)	23784
Hodge, Sterland, Pet.Shirtliff, Smith, Madden, Worthington, Marwood(Morris 74), Blair, Varadi, Chapman, Shelton					
08 Sep. 1984	Tottenham Hotspur	Division 1	2–1	Varadi(15), Marwood(32)	33421
Hodge, Sterland, Pet.Shirtliff, Smith, Madden, Worthington, Marwood(Morris 66), Blair, Varadi, Chapman, Shelton					
22 Sep. 1984	Ipswich Town	Division 1	2–2	Marwood(75), Chapman(77)	25558
Hodge, Sterland, Pet.Shirtliff, Smith(Pearson 70), Lyons, Worthington, Marwood, Blair, Varadi, Chapman, Heard					
25 Sep. 1984	Huddersfield	Milk Cup 2–L1	3–0	Sterland(5)pen., Chapman(72), Marwood(73)	16139
Hodge, Sterland, Pet.Shirtliff, Smith, Lyons, Worthington(Morris 30), Marwood, Blair, Varadi, Chapman, Heard					
06 Oct. 1984	Sunderland	Division 1	2–2	Chapman(14), Marwood(43)	27766
Hodge, Sterland, Pet.Shirtliff(Pearson ht), Smith, Lyons, Ryan, Marwood, Blair, Varadi, Chapman, Shelton					
20 Oct. 1984	Leicester City	Division 1	5–0	Varadi 3(6, 24, 59), Blair(77), Ryan(83)	23621
Hodge, Sterland, Pet.Shirtliff, Smith, Lyons, Worthington, Marwood, Blair, Varadi, Chapman, Shelton(Ryan 80)					
30 Oct. 1984	Fulham	Milk Cup 3	3–2	Marwood(25), Lyons(47), Varadi(80)	15665
Hodge, Sterland, Pet.Shirtliff, Smith, Lyons, Worthington, Marwood, Blair, Varadi, Chapman(Pearson 75), Shelton					
03 Nov. 1984	Norwich City	Division 1	1–2	Sterland(86)	21847
Hodge, Sterland, Pet.Shirtliff, Smith, Lyons, Worthington(Pearson 73), Marwood, Blair, Varadi, Chapman, Shelton					
20 Nov. 1984	Luton Town	Milk Cup 4	4–2	Blair 3(15pen., 51pen., 70pen.), Marwood(34)	18313
Hodge, Oliver, Pet.Shirtliff, Smith, Lyons(Morris 75), Worthington, Marwood, Blair, Varadi, Chapman, Shelton					
25 Nov. 1984	Arsenal	Division 1	2–1	Chapman(16), Smith(74)	25575
Hodge, Oliver, Pet.Shirtliff, Smith, Lyons, Worthington, Marwood(Ryan 86), Blair, Varadi, Chapman, Shelton					
08 Dec. 1984	Chelsea	Division 1	1–1	Varadi(86)	29373
Hodge, Oliver, Pet.Shirtliff, Smith, Lyons, Worthington, Marwood, Blair, Varadi, Chapman, Shelton					
22 Dec. 1984	Stoke City	Division 1	2–1	Varadi(33), Chapman(60)	19799
Hodge, Oliver, Pet.Shirtliff, Madden, Lyons, Worthington, Marwood, Blair, Varadi, Chapman(Sterland 62), Shelton					
26 Dec. 1984	Aston Villa	Division 1	1–1	Lyons(88)	30971
Hodge, Oliver(Sterland 65), Pet.Shirtliff, Madden, Lyons, Worthington, Marwood, Blair, Varadi, Chapman, Shelton					
12 Jan. 1985	West Bromwich Albion	Division 1	2–0	Chapman(35), Varadi(55)	24345
Hodge, Sterland, Pet.Shirtliff, Madden, Lyons, Worthington, Marwood, Blair, Varadi, Chapman, Shelton					
26 Jan. 1985	Oldham Athletic	F.A.Cup 4	5–1	Varadi 3(17, 63, 90), Chapman(33), Marwood(59)	24006
Hodge, Sterland, Pet.Shirtliff, Smith, Lyons, Worthington, Marwood, Blair, Varadi, Chapman, Shelton(Oliver 81)					
30 Jan. 1985	Chelsea	Milk Cup 5R	4–4	Lyons(8), Chapman(21), Marwood(45), Sterland(89)pen.	36509
Hodge, Sterland, Pet.Shirtliff, Madden, Lyons, Worthington, Marwood, Blair, Varadi, Chapman(Oliver 109), Shelton					
02 Feb. 1985	Liverpool	Division 1	1–1	Marwood(57)	48246
Hodge, Sterland, Pet.Shirtliff, Madden, Lyons, Worthington, Marwood(Oliver 83), Blair, Varadi, Chapman, Shelton					
24 Feb. 1985	Watford	Division 1	1–1	Lyons(81)	27871
Hodge, Sterland, Madden, Smith, Lyons, Worthington, Marwood, Blair, Varadi, Chapman, Shelton					
02 Mar. 1985	Coventry City	Division 1	1–0	Pearson(36)	20422
Hodge, Sterland, Madden, Smith, Lyons, Worthington, Marwood, Blair, Varadi, Pearson, Shelton					
16 Mar. 1985	Luton Town	Division 1	1–1	Varadi(5)	18856
Hodge, Pet.Shirtliff, Blair, Smith, Lyons(Morris 79), Worthington, Marwood, Jonsson, Varadi, Chapman, Shelton					
30 Mar. 1985	Newcastle United	Division 1	4–2	Chapman 2(26, 58), Marwood(10), Shelton(60)	26525
Hodge, Pet.Shirtliff, Morris, Smith, Lyons, Worthington, Marwood, Blair, Varadi, Chapman, Shelton					
09 Apr. 1985	Manchester United	Division 1	1–0	Chapman(17)	39380
Hodge, Pet.Shirtliff, Morris, Smith, Lyons, Worthington, Marwood(Jonsson 82), Blair, Stainrod, Chapman, Shelton					
23 Apr. 1985	Queen's Park Rangers	Division 1	3–1	Stainrod(44), Marwood(63)pen., Blair(89)	22394
Hodge, Pet.Shirtliff, Morris, Smith, Lyons, Worthington, Marwood, Blair, Stainrod(Varadi 80), Chapman, Shelton					
04 May 1985	Everton	Division 1	0–1		37381
Hodge, Ryan, Morris, Smith, Lyons, Madden, Marwood(Stainrod 79), Blair, Varadi, Chapman, Shelton					
11 May 985	West Ham United	Division 1	2–1	Chapman 2(5, 32)	24314
Hodge, Sterland, Worthington, Smith, Lyons, Madden, Marwood, Blair, Varadi, Chapman, Shelton					

Date	Opponents	Competition	Score	Scorers	Att.
17 Aug. 1985	Chelsea	Division 1	1–1	Lyons(3)	26164
Hodge, Sterland, Worthington, Pet.Shirtliff, Lyons, Hart, Marwood, Blair(Stainrod 68), Chapman, Thompson, Shelton					
26 Aug. 1985	Watford	Division 1	2–1	Sterland(8), Chapman(65)	21962
Hodge, Sterland, Worthington(Chapman 54), Pet.Shirtliff, Lyons, Hart, Marwood, Jonsson, Stainrod, Thompson, Gregory					
03 Sep. 1985	Everton	Division 1	1–5	Marwood(23)pen.	30065
Hodge, Sterland, Worthington, Pet.Shirtliff, Lyons, Hart(Stainrod 71), Marwood, Thompson, Chapman, Jonsson, Shelton					
07 Sep. 1985	West Ham United	Division 1	2–2	Chapman(18), Thompson(57)	19287
Hodge, Morris, Worthington, Smith, Lyons, Madden, Marwood, Thompson(Stainrod 82), Chapman, Jonsson, Shelton					
28 Sep. 1985	Luton Town	Division 1	3–2	Marwood 2(43, 62pen.), Chapman(45)	17887
Hodge, Sterland, Snodin, Smith, Lyons, Pet.Shirtliff, Marwood, Thompson(Chamberlain 77), Chapman, Blair, Shelton					
12 Oct. 1985	Coventry City	Division 1	2–2	Chapman(19), Shutt(44)	19132
Hodge, Sterland, Morris, Smith, Hart, Pet.Shirtliff, Chamberlain, Blair, Chapman, Shutt, Shelton					
15 Oct. 1985	Brentford	Milk Cup 2–L2	2–0	Sterland(10)pen., Chapman(80)	11132
Hodge, Sterland, Morris, Smith, Hart, Pet.Shirtliff, Thompson, Blair, Chapman, Shutt, Shelton(Snodin 30)					
26 Oct. 1985	West Bromwich Albion	Division 1	1–0	Chapman(35)	19873
Hodge, Sterland, Snodin, Shelton, Madden, Hart, Marwood, Blair, Chapman, Shutt, Morris					
09 Nov. 1985	Manchester United	Division 1	1–0	Chapman(84)	48105
Hodge, Sterland, Snodin, Madden, Morris, Hart, Marwood(Chamberlain 82), Blair, Chapman, Thompson, Shelton					
23 Nov. 1985	Southampton	Division 1	2–1	Chapman(18), Marwood(71)	18955
Hodge, Sterland, Snodin, Madden, Morris, Hart, Marwood, Blair, Chapman, Thompson, Shelton					
07 Dec. 1985	Nottingham Forest	Division 1	2–1	Marwood(57), Chamberlain(85)	22495
Hodge, Sterland, Snodin, Madden, Morris, Hart, Marwood, Blair(Chamberlain 79), Chapman, Thompson, Shelton					
21 Dec. 1985	Manchester City	Division 1	3–2	Thompson(13), Megson(24), Sterland(42)	23177
Hodge, Sterland, Snodin, Madden, Morris, Hart, Marwood, Megson, Chapman(Chamberlain 74), Thompson, Shelton					
26 Dec. 1985	Newcastle United	Division 1	2–2	Marwood(41), Thompson(80)	30269
Hodge, Sterland, Snodin(Chamberlain 33), Madden, Morris, Hart, Marwood, Megson, Chapman, Thompson, Shelton					
13 Jan. 1986	West Bromwich Albion	F.A.Cup 3	2–2	Sterland(37), Smith(47)	17042
Hodge, Sterland, Smith, Madden, Hart, Gregory, Marwood, Shutt(Chapman 78), Thompson, Blair, Morris					
18 Jan. 1986	Oxford United	Division 1	2–1	Shotton(18)og., Marwood(85)	18565
Hodge, Sterland, Smith, Pet.Shirtliff, Hart(Chamberlain 15), Megson, Marwood, Shutt, Thompson, Blair, Morris					
25 Jan. 1986	Orient	F.A.Cup 4	5–0	Thompson(1), Chapman(11), Sterland(26), Blair(51), Marwood(79)	19087
Hodge, Sterland, Smith, Pet.Shirtliff(Shelton 42), Madden, Megson, Marwood, Blair, Thompson, Chapman, Snodin					
22 Feb. 1986	Tottenham Hotspur	Division 1	1–2	Thompson(20)	23232
Hodge, Sterland, Morris, Hart, Madden(Shelton 59), Megson, Marwood, Blair, Thompson, Chapman, Snodin					
05 Mar. 1986	Derby County	F.A.Cup 5R	2–0	Shutt 2(43, 83)	29077
Hodge, Sterland, Morris, Smith, Pet.Shirtliff, Shelton, Marwood(Chamberlain 86), Megson, Chapman, Shutt, Snodin					
08 Mar. 1986	Birmingham City	Division 1	5–1	Shutt 3(9, 28, 66), Chapman(42), Chamberlain(65)	17491
Hodge, Sterland, Morris, Smith, Pet.Shirtliff, Shelton(Chamberlain 34), Marwood, Megson, Chapman, Shutt, Snodin					
12 Mar. 1986	West Ham United	F.A.Cup 6	2–1	Worthington(16), Shutt(35)	35522
Hodge, Sterland, Morris, Smith, Pet.Shirtliff, Worthington, Marwood(Chamberlain 81), Megson, Chapman, Shutt, Snodin					
18 Mar. 1986	Leicester City	Division 1	1–0	Sterland(30)	18874
Hodge, Sterland, Morris, Hart, Pet.Shirtliff, Worthington, Marwood, Megson, Chapman(Chamberlain 81), Thompson, Snodin					
29 Mar. 1986	Liverpool	Division 1	0–0		37946
Hodge, Sterland, Morris, Madden, Pet.Shirtliff, Worthington(Chamberlain 41), Marwood, Megson, Thompson, Shutt, Snodin					
08 Apr. 1986	Queen's Park Rangers	Division 1	0–0		13157
Hodge, Sterland, Pet.Shirtliff, Madden, Hart, Shelton(Chamberlain 64), Chapman, Megson, Thompson, Shutt, Snodin					
16 Apr. 1986	Arsenal	Division 1	2–0	Sterland(24)pen., Shutt(66)	16344
Hodge, Sterland, Morris, Madden, Hart, Shelton, Chapman(Chamberlain 65), Megson, Thompson, Shutt, Snodin					
19 Apr. 1986	Aston Villa	Division 1	2–0	Megson(30), Sterland(65)	19782
Hodge, Sterland, Morris, Madden, Hart, Shelton, Marwood, Megson, Thompson, Shutt(Chamberlain 81), Knight					
03 May 1986	Ipswich Town	Division 1	1–0	Marwood(82)	22369
Hodge, Sterland, Snodin, Pet.Shirtliff, Hart, Shelton, Marwood, Megson, Thompson(Chamberlain 78), Shutt, Knight					

1983–84
Cunningham, Smith, Peter Shirtliff, Hesford, Hodge, Pearson, Lyons, Sterland;
Eustace (ass. manager), Madden, Taylor, Bannister, Veradi, Megson, Shelton, Smith (physio);
Paul Shirtliff, Mills, Oliver, Wilkinson (manager), Mossman, Worthington, Morris.

1984–85
Madden, Oliver, Hesford, Hodge, Lyons, Smith;
Eustace (ass. manager), Varadi, Shirtlif, Pearson, Chapman, Worthington, Shelton, Smith (physio);
Marwood, Ryan, Sterland, Wilkinson (manager), Blair, Morris, Mills.

1985–86
Madden, Lyons, Hodge, Hesford, Chapman, Hart;
Eustace (ass. manager), Shelton, Morris, Shirtliff, Thompson, Smith, Blair, Marwood, Smith (physio);
Snodin, Sterland, Worthington, Wilkinson (manager), Jonsson, Chamberlain, Shutt.

1986–87
Chapman, Hart, Hodge, Hesford, Knight, Smith;
Eustace (ass. manager), Shelton, Sterland, Jonsson, Madden, Megson, Worthington, Smith (physio);
Walker, Morris, Chamberlain, Wilkinson (manager), Gregory, Shutt, Snodin.

Date	Opponents	Competition	Score	Scorers	Att.
25 Aug. 1986	Everton	Division 1	2–2	Shutt(12), Hirst(62)	33007
Hodge, Morris, Snodin, Hart, Worthington(Hirst 61), Madden, Marwood, Gregory, Chapman, Shutt, Shelton					
30 Aug. 1986	Chelsea	Division 1	2–0	Chamberlain(23), Gregory(68)	25853
Hodge, Morris, Snodin, Hart, Knight, Madden, Chamberlain, Gregory, Chapman, Shutt, Shelton					
13 Sep. 1986	Leicester City	Division 1	2–2	Chapman 2(14, 67)	21603
Hodge, Sterland, Snodin, Hart, Knight, Chamberlain, Marwood, Megson, Chapman, Shutt, Shelton					
15 Sep. 1986	Sheffield United	Smith Tst.	3–1	Varadi 2(7, 24), Hirst(85)	10800
Hodge(Pressman 76), Sterland, Snodin(Worthington ht), Smith, Lyons(Knight 53), Shelton(Tomlinson 65), Marwood (Chamberlain ht), Megson(Gregory ht), Chapman(Hirst 36), Jonsson, Varadi(C.Walker 75)					
23 Sep. 1986	Stockport County	Littlewoods Cup 2–L1	3–0	Sterland(33), Shutt(57), Marwood(72)pen.	10466
Hodge, Sterland, Worthington, Madden, Knight, Chamberlain(Hirst 72), Marwood, Megson, Chapman, Shutt(Morris 72), Shelton					
27 Sep. 1986	West Ham United	Division 1	2–2	Madden(17), Megson(89)	25715
Hodge, Sterland, Worthington, Madden, Knight, Chamberlain, Marwood, Megson, Chapman, Shutt, Shelton					
04 Oct. 1986	Oxford United	Division 1	6–1	Shutt 2(2, 47), Chapman(35), Chamberlain(41), Shelton(56), Megson(87)	20205
Hodge, Sterland, Worthington, Madden, Knight, Chamberlain, Marwood, Megson, Chapman, Shutt(Snodin 73), Shelton					
25 Oct. 1986	Coventry City	Division 1	2–2	Chapman 2(43, 76)	20035
Hodge, Sterland, Worthington, Hart, Knight, Chamberlain, Marwood, Megson, Chapman, C.Walker(Snodin 65), Gregory					
08 Nov. 1986	Southampton	Division 1	3–1	Chapman 2(71, 75), Marwood(67)pen.	20802
Hodge, Sterland, Worthington, Hart, Madden, Chamberlain(Jonsson 65), Marwood, Megson, Chapman, Hirst, Shelton					
22 Nov. 1986	Luton Town	Division 1	1–0	Megson(73)	21171
Hodge, Sterland, Worthington, Hart, Madden, Jonsson, Marwood, Megson, Chapman, Hirst(Snodin 60), Shelton					
25 Nov. 1986	Portsmouth	Full Members Cup 2	0–1		7846
Hodge, Sterland, Worthington(Chamberlain 34), Hart, Madden, Jonsson, Snodin, Megson, Chapman, Hirst, Shelton					
06 Dec. 1986	Aston Villa	Division 1	2–1	Marwood(38)pen., Chapman(49)	21144
Hodge, Sterland, Worthington, Hart, Madden, Jonsson, Marwood(Snodin 69), Megson, Chapman, Bradshaw, Shelton					
21 Dec. 1986	Newcastle United	Division 1	2–0	Chapman(11), Bradshaw(21)	28897
Hodge, Sterland, Worthington, Hart, Madden, Snodin, Jonsson, Megson, Chapman, Bradshaw(Chamberlain 82), Shelton					
27 Dec. 1986	Liverpool	Division 1	0–1		40959
Hodge, Morris, Worthington, Knight, Madden, Snodin, Jonsson, Gregory, Chapman, Hirst(Shutt 77), Chamberlain					
01 Jan. 1987	Norwich City	Division 1	1–1	Shelton(80)	20956
Hodge, Sterland(Morris 53), Worthington, Knight, Madden, Jonsson, Snodin, Chamberlain, Chapman, Shutt, Shelton					
24 Jan. 1987	Charlton Athletic	Division 1	1–1	Shutt(51)	17365
Hodge, Sterland, Worthington, Smith, Madden, Knight, Marwood, Megson, Chapman, Shutt, Shelton					
26 Jan. 1987	Derby County	F.A.Cup 3	1–0	Bradshaw(31)	25695
Hodge, Sterland(Morris 78), Worthington, Smith, Madden, Knight, Marwood(Chamberlain 78), Megson, Chapman, Bradshaw, Shelton					
04 Feb. 1987	Chester	F.A.Cup 4R	3–1	Chapman(14), Abel(33)og., Bradshaw(60)	20726
Hodge, Morris, Snodin, Smith, Madden, Knight(Jonsson 8), Marwood(Chamberlain 80), Megson, Chapman, Bradshaw, Shelton					
14 Feb. 1987	Arsenal	Division 1	1–1	Chamberlain(52)	24792
Hodge, Sterland, Snodin, Smith, Madden, Worthington, Marwood(Hirst 81), Megson, Chamberlain, Bradshaw, Shelton					
21 Feb. 1987	West Ham United	F.A.Cup 5	1–1	Shelton(40)	31134
Hodge, Sterland(Morris 70), Snodin, Smith, Madden, Worthington, Marwood, Megson, Bradshaw, Hirst(Shutt 70), Shelton					
28 Feb. 1987	Watford	Division 1	0–1		20530
Hodge, Sterland, Snodin(Chamberlain 20), Smith, May, Worthington, Marwood, Megson, Chapman, Bradshaw, Shelton					
14 Mar. 1987	Coventry City	F.A.Cup 6	1–3	Megson(66)	48005
Hodge, Sterland(Morris 63), Snodin, Smith, Madden, Worthington, Marwood, Megson, Chapman, Bradshaw(Hirst 63), Shelton					
21 Mar. 1987	Manchester United	Division 1	1–0	Hirst(90)	29888
Hodge, Sterland, May, Smith, Madden, Worthington, Marwood(Hirst 74), Jonsson, Chapman, Shutt, Snodin					
31 Mar. 1987	H.J.K.Helsinki	Friendly	4–0	Chapman 2(30, 44), Hirst 2(31, 46)	3979
Pressman, Sterland(Morris ht), Snodin, Madden(Smith ht), May, Jonsson, Marwood(Jacobs 58), Megson, Chapman, Hirst(Reeves 80), Hazel					
07 Apr. 1987	Tottenham Hotspur	Division 1	0–1		19488
Hodge, Sterland, Snodin, May, Madden, Worthington, Marwood, Megson, Chapman, Hirst, Shelton					
14 Apr. 1987	Nottingham Forest	Division 1	2–3	Chapman(53), Hirst(61)	18597
Hodge, Gregory(Shutt 83), Snodin, May, Madden, Worthington, Marwood, Megson, Chapman, Hirst, Shelton					
20 Apr. 1987	Manchester City	Division 1	2–1	Marwood(13)pen., Chapman(53)	19769
Hodge, Sterland, Smith, May, Madden, Worthington, Marwood, Megson, Chapman, Hirst(Chamberlain 81), Shelton					
02 May 1987	Queen's Park Rangers	Division 1	7–1	Hirst 2(7, 72), Marwood 2(23, 41), Megson(45), Sterland(64), Chamberlain(83)	16501
Hodge, Sterland, Smith, May, Madden, Worthington, Marwood(Chamberlain 72), Megson, Chapman, Hirst, Shelton					
09 May 1987	Wimbledon	Division 1	0–2		18823
Hodge, Morris, Smith(Chamberlain 68), May, Madden, Worthington, Marwood, Megson, Chapman, Hirst, Shelton					

OTHER GAMES AT HILLSBOROUGH

12 Apr. 1987	F.A.Cup Semi Final	Leeds United 2	Coventry City 3		51372

Date	Opponents	Competition	Score	Scorers	Att.
18 Aug. 1987	Oxford United	Division 1	1–1	Chapman(18)	17868
Hodge, Sterland, McCall, Madden, May, Worthington, Marwood(Bradshaw 15), Megson, Chapman, Hirst, Jacobs(G.Owen 69)					
22 Aug. 1987	Newcastle United	Division 1	0–1		22031
Hodge, Sterland, McCall, Madden, May, Worthington, Hazel, Megson, Chapman, Bradshaw, Hirst					
31 Aug. 1987	Coventry City	Division 1	0–3		17171
Hodge, Sterland, McCall(Bradshaw 44), Madden, May, Worthington, Hazel, Megson, Chapman, Hirst, Galvin					
12 Sep. 1987	Watford	Division 1	2–3	West(39), Chapman(61)	16144
Pressman, Sterland, Worthington, Madden, Fee, Procter, Hazel(Hirst ht), Megson, Chapman, West, Galvin(Jonsson ht)					
26 Sep. 1987	Charlton Athletic	Division 1	2–0	Chapman 2(31, 38)	16350
Hodge, Sterland, Worthington, Madden, May, Procter, Jacobs, Megson, Chapman, West(Bradshaw 77), Galvin					
06 Oct. 1987	Shrewsbury Town	Littlewoods Cup 2–L2	2–1	West 2(34, 59)	8572
Hodge, Sterland, Worthington, Madden, May, Jacobs, Chamberlain(Hirst 77), Megson, Chapman, West, Galvin					
10 Oct. 1987	Manchester United	Division 1	2–4	Robson(10)og., Sterland(84)	32779
Hodge, Sterland, Worthington, Madden, May, Procter, Chamberlain(Hirst 71), Megson, Chapman, West, Galvin					
24 Oct. 1987	Norwich City	Division 1	1–0	Pearson(13)	15861
Hodge, Sterland, Worthington, Madden, Pearson, Procter, Chamberlain(Bradshaw 85), Megson, Chapman, West(Fee 85), Galvin					
10 Nov. 1987	Bournemouth	Simod Cup 1	2–0	Galvin(63), West(90)	3756
Hodge, Fee, Jacobs, Pearson, Madden, Procter, Chamberlain(Hazel 72), Megson, Bradshaw(Chapman 72), West, Galvin					
14 Nov. 1987	Luton Town	Division 1	0–2		16960
Hodge, Jacobs, Worthington, Madden, Pearson, Procter, Chamberlain, Megson, Chapman, West, Galvin(Marwood 73)					
28 Nov. 1987	Queen's Park Rangers	Division 1	3–1	Procter(9), Megson(45), Fenwick(87)og.	16933
Hodge, Sterland, Worthington, Madden, Pearson, Procter, Chamberlain, Megson, Chapman, West, G.Owen					
01 Dec. 1987	Stoke City	Simod Cup 2	0–1		5228
Hodge, Sterland, Worthington, Madden, Pearson, Procter, Chamberlain, Megson(Marwood 60), Chapman, West, G.Owen					
12 Dec. 1987	Wimbledon	Division 1	1–0	Chapman(73)	14289
Hodge, Sterland, Worthington, Madden, Pearson, Procter, Marwood(Bradshaw 88), G.Owen, Chapman, West(Fee 88), Chamberlain					
28 Dec. 1987	Derby County	Division 1	2–1	Chapman(15), West(18)	26191
Hodge, Sterland, Worthington, Madden, Pearson, Procter, Marwood(Chamberlain 75), Megson, Chapman, West, G.Owen					
01 Jan. 1988	Everton	Division 1	1–0	Procter(34)	26433
Hodge, Sterland, Worthington, Madden, Pearson, Procter, Marwood(Chamberlain 70), Megson(Bradshaw 70), Chapman, West, May					
09 Jan. 1988	Everton	F.A.Cup 3	1–1	West(74)	33304
Hodge, Sterland, Worthington, Madden, Pearson, Procter, Marwood, Megson, Chapman, West, May					
16 Jan. 1988	Chelsea	Division 1	3–0	May(41), Marwood(66)pen., Bradshaw(80	19859
Hodge, Sterland(Fee 70), Worthington, Madden, Pearson, Procter, Marwood, G.Owen(Chamberlain 82), Bradshaw, West, May					
20 Jan. 1988	Arsenal	Littlewoods Cup 5	0–1		34535
Hodge, Sterland, Worthington, Madden, Fee(Chamberlain 72), G.Owen, Marwood, Megson, Chapman, West, May					
27 Jan. 1988	Everton	F.A.Cup 3–3R	0–5		38953
Hodge, Sterland, Worthington, May, Pearson, Procter, Marwood, Megson, Chapman(G.Owen ht), West, Chamberlain					
06 Feb. 1988	Southampton	Division 1	2–1	Sterland(78), Chapman(84)	14769
Hodge, Sterland, Worthington, Madden, Pearson(Bradshaw 84), Procter, Marwood, Megson, Chapman, West(Hirst 63), G.Owen					
27 Feb. 1988	Tottenham Hotspur	Division 1	0–3		18046
Hodge, Sterland, Worthington, Madden, Pearson, Procter, Marwood, Megson, Chapman, Hirst(Bradshaw 72), G.Owen(Galvin 82)					
05 Mar. 1988	Nottingham Forest	Division 1	0–1		19509
Hodge, Sterland, Worthington, Madden, Pearson, Procter, Marwood(Chamberlain 73), Megson, Chapman, Hirst, May					
19 Mar. 1988	Portsmouth	Division 1	1–0	Sterland(43)pen.	13731
Pressman, Sterland, Worthington, Madden, Fee, Procter, Chamberlain, Megson, Chapman, Hirst(Marwood 89), Jonsson(Bradshaw 89)					
02 Apr. 1988	West Ham United	Division 1	2–1	Hirst(37), Chamberlain(50)	18435
Pressman, Sterland, Worthington, Madden, Cranson, Procter, Chamberlain(Bradshaw 67), Megson, Chapman, Hirst(Fee 89), Jonsson					
30 Apr. 1988	Arsenal	Division 1	3–3	Sterland(3), Hirst(34), Chapman(36)	16681
Pressman, Sterland. G.Owen(Hazel 73), Madden, May, Procter, West(Fee 73), Megson, Chapman, Hirst, Jonsson					
07 May 1988	Liverpool	Division 1	1–5	Hirst(90)	35893
Pressman, Sterland, Worthington, Madden, May, Procter, West(Galvin ht), Megson, Chapman, Hirst, Jonsson					

OTHER GAMES AT HILLSBOROUGH

22 Feb. 1988	Boys	Sheffield 0	Derby 0		n/k
09 Apr. 1988	F.A.Cup Semi Final	Liverpool 2	Nottingham Forest 1		51627

Date	Opponents	Competition	Score	Scorers	Att.
27 Aug. 1988	Luton Town	Division 1	1–0	Sterland(58)	16433
Pressman, Sterland, Worthington, Pearson, Madden, Harper, Megson, Procter, West, Jonsson, Galvin(Hirst 78)					
10 Sep. 1988	Coventry City	Division 1	1–2	Hirst(86)	15633
Pressman, Sterland, Worthington, Pearson, Madden, Harper(Cranson 14), Megson, Hirst, West, Jonsson, Galvin(Bradshaw 76)					
24 Sep. 1988	Arsenal	Division 1	2–1	Megson(31), Pearson(55)	17830
Pressman, Sterland, Worthington, Pearson, Madden, Cranson, Megson, Hirst(West 86), Reeves, Jonsson, Bradshaw, (Galvin 77)					
01 Oct. 1988	Aston Villa	Division 1	1–0	Hirst(9)	18301
Pressman, Sterland, Worthington, Pearson, Madden, Cranson, Megson, Hirst(West 84), Reeves, Jonsson(Galvin 54), Varadi					
12 Oct. 1988	Blackpool	Littlewoods Cup 2–L2	3–1 aet	Varadi(1), Reeves(57), Hirst(62)	12237
Turner, Sterland, Worthington, Pearson, Madden, Cranson, Megson, Hirst(Galvin 106), Varadi(Reeves ht), West, Procter					
05 Nov. 1988	Everton	Division 1	1–1	Sterland(82)	21761
Turner, Sterland, Worthington, Pearson, Madden, Cranson, Megson(Jonsson 28), West, Varadi(Reeves 69), Hodgson, Procter					
20 Nov. 1988	Tottenham Hotspur	Division 1	0–2		15386
Turner, Sterland, Worthington, Cranson, Pearson, Madden, Jonsson, Procter, West, Reeves, Hodgson(Hirst 66)					
03 Dec. 1988	Derby County	Division 1	1–1	Sterland(32)	20609
Turner, Sterland, Worthington, Cranson, Pearson, Madden, Megson, Jonsson(Harper 70), West, Hirst(Reeves 77), Procter					
26 Dec. 1988	Newcastle United	Division 1	1–2	Hirst(3)	25573
Pressman, Procter, Worthington, Cranson, Pearson, Madden, Megson, Hirst, Varadi(West 65), Sterland, Jonsson					
31 Dec. 1988	Nottingham Forest	Division 1	0–3		20407
Turner, Procter, Worthington(Megson 81), Cranson, Pearson, Madden, Gregory, Hirst(Reeves 22), Varadi, West, Jonsson					
07 Jan. 1989	Torquay United	F.A.Cup 3	5–1	Varadi 2(51, 55), Jonsson(11), Hodgson(39), Procter(74)	11384
Turner, Sterland, Cranson, Knight, Pearson, Madden, Procter, Hodgson, Varadi, West(Reeves ht), Jonsson					
14 Jan. 1989	Liverpool	Division 1	2–2	Procter(5), Varadi(15)	31524
Turner, Sterland, Rostron, Cranson, Pearson, Madden, Procter, Reeves, West, Varadi(Galvin 79), Jonsson					
01 Feb. 1989	Queen's Park Rangers	Simod Cup 3	0–1 aet		3957
Turner, Sterland, Rostron, Cranson, Pearson, Madden, Procter, Hirst(Reeves 84), West, Varadi, Harper(Galvin 105)					
11 Feb. 1989	Manchester United	Division 1	0–2		34820
Turner, Sterland, Rostron, Cranson, Pearson, Madden, Procter, Jonsson, Varadi(Reeves 70), Hirst, Harper					
18 Feb. 1989	Southampton	Division 1	1–1	Procter(89)	16677
Turner, Sterland, Rostron, Cranson, Pearson, Procter, Galvin, Hirst(Reeves 58), Jonsson, Varadi, Harper					
04 Mar. 1989	Charlton Athletic	Division 1	3–1	Hirst(29), Jonsson(76), Galvin(80)	16081
Turner, Harper, Worthington, Wood, Pearson, Cranson, Procter, Jonsson, Whitton(Varadi 87), Hirst, Galvin					
25 Mar. 1989	Queen's Park Rangers	Division 1	0–2		18804
Turner, Harper, Worthington, Palmer, Pearson, Cranson, Bennett, McCall(Galvin 80), Whitton, Hirst, Jonsson					
01 Apr. 1989	Millwall	Division 1	3–0	Whitton 2(70, 83), Palmer(18)	18358
Turner, Harper, Worthington, Palmer, Pearson, Cranson(Jonsson 18), Bennett, Fee, Whitton, Hirst, Barrick					
05 Apr. 1989	Wimbledon	Division 1	1–1	Hirst(54)	15777
Turner, Harper, Worthington, Palmer, Pearson, Jonsson, Bennett, Fee, Whitton, Hirst, Barrick					
09 May 1989	West Ham United	Division 1	0–2		19905
Turner, Harper, Worthington(Galvin 29), Palmer, Pearson, Madden, Bennett(Reeves 79), Fee, Whitton, Hirst, Barrick					
13 May 1989	Middlesbrough	Division 1	1–0	Whitton(66)	20582
Turner, Harper, Wood, Palmer, Pearson, Madden, Bennett(Jonsson 80), Fee, Whitton, Hirst(Galvin 88), Barrick					
17 May 1989	Norwich City	Division 1	2–2	Linighan(75)og., Reeves(83)	16238
Turner, Harper, Wood, Palmer, Pearson, Madden, Bennett, Fee, Whitton, Hirst, Galvin(Reeves 71)					

OTHER GAMES AT HILLSBOROUGH

27 Feb. 1989	Boys	Sheffield 0	London 2		n/k
15 Apr. 1989	F.A.Cup Semi Final	Liverpool 0	Nottingham Forest 0	*Abandoned– 6 mins.	53000

Date	Opponents	Competition	Score	Scorers	Att.
19 Aug. 1989	Norwich City	Division 1	0–2		19142
Turner, Harper, Worthington, Palmer, Pearson, Madden, Bennett, Barrick, Whitton(Hirst 70), Atkinson, Shakespeare					
30 Aug. 1989	Everton	Division 1	1–1	Atkinson(90)	19657
Turner, Wood(Bennett 82), Worthington, Whitton, Pearson, Madden, M.Taylor, Harper, Hirst, Atkinson, Shakespeare					
16 Sep. 1989	Aston Villa	Division 1	1–0	Atkinson(10)	17509
Pressman, Wood, Worthington, Palmer, Pet.Shirtliff, Madden, M.Taylor, Whitton, Atkinson, Hirst, Shakespeare					
20 Sep. 1989	Aldershot	Littlewoods Cup 2–L1	0–0		9237
Pressman, Newsome, Worthington, Palmer, Pet.Shirtliff, Madden, M.Taylor, Whitton(Harper 68), Atkinson, Hirst, Shakespeare					
30 Sep. 1989	Coventry City	Division 1	0–0		15054
Pressman, Newsome(Harper 78), Worthington, Palmer, Pet.Shirtliff, Madden, M.Taylor, Whitton, Atkinson, Hirst, Shakespeare					
28 Oct. 1989	Wimbledon	Division 1	0–1		13728
Turner, Newsome, Harper, Palmer, Pet.Shirtliff, Madden, M.Taylor(Whitton 71), Pearson, Hirst, Atkinson, Barrick(Shakespeare 71)					
11 Nov. 1989	Charlton Athletic	Division 1	3–0	Hirst 2(76, 82), Atkinson(34)	16740
Pressman, Harper, King, Palmer, Pet.Shirtliff, Madden, Bennett, Sheridan, Hirst, Atkinson, Shakespeare					
21 Nov. 1989	Sheffield United	ZDS Cup 2	3–2 aet	Atkinson(19), Palmer(86), Sheridan(94)	30464
Pressman, Pearson, King, Palmer, Pet.Shirtliff, Madden, Bennett(Shakespeare 105), Sheridan, Hirst, Atkinson, Worthington					
25 Nov. 1989	Crystal Palace	Division 1	2–2	Whitton(69), Hirst(89)pen.	17227
Pressman, Pearson(Whitton 57), King, Palmer, Pet.Shirtliff, Madden, Bennett, Sheridan, Hirst, Atkinson, Worthington					
29 Nov. 1989	Liverpool	Division 1	2–0	Hirst(55), Atkinson(90)	32732
Pressman, Worthington, King, Palmer, Pet.Shirtliff, Pearson, Bennett, Sheridan, Hirst, Atkinson, Worthington					
09 Dec. 1989	Luton Town	Division 1	1–1	Dreyer(17)og.	16339
Pressman, Nilsson, King, Palmer, Pet.Shirtliff, Pearson, Bennett(Whitton 87), Sheridan, Hirst, Atkinson, Worthington					
16 Dec. 1989	Queen's Park Rangers	Division 1	2–0	Atkinson(18), Hirst(44)	14569
Pressman, Nilsson, King, Palmer, Pet.Shirtliff, Pearson, Bennett(Whitton 74), Sheridan, Hirst, Atkinson, Worthington					
01 Jan. 1990	Manchester City	Division 1	2–0	Hirst(12), Pearson(78)	28756
Pressman(Bennett 62), Nilsson, King, Palmer, Pet.Shirtliff, Pearson, Carr, Sheridan, Hirst, Atkinson, Worthington					
14 Jan. 1990	Chelsea	Division 1	1–1	Atkinson(52)	18042
Turner, Nilsson(Madden ht), King, Palmer, Pet.Shirtliff, Pearson, Carr, Sheridan, Hirst, Atkinson, Worthington					
28 Jan. 1990	Everton	F.A.Cup 4	1–2	Hirst(12)	31754
Turner, Nilsson, King, Palmer, Pet.Shirtliff, Pearson, Carr(Whitton 81), Sheridan, Hirst, Atkinson, Worthington					
03 Feb. 1990	Millwall	Division 1	1–1	Hirst(6)	17737
Turner, Nilsson, King, Palmer, Pet.Shirtliff, Pearson, Carr(Francis 68), Sheridan, Hirst, Atkinson, Worthington					
17 Feb. 1990	Arsenal	Division 1	1–0	Bould(15secs.)og.	20640
Turner, Nilsson, King, Palmer, Pet.Shirtliff(Madden ht), Pearson, Francis(Carr 72), Sheridan, Hirst, Atkinson, Worthington					
03 Mar. 1990	Derby County	Division 1	1–0	Sheridan(37)	21811
Turner, Nilsson, King, Palmer, Pet.Shirtliff, Pearson, Francis(Madden 90), Sheridan, Hirst(Carr 85), Atkinson, Worthington					
10 Mar. 1990	Brondby	Friendly	3–0	Hirst 2(24, 55), Bennett(12)	3715
Turner(Beresford 62), Nilsson, King(McCall 70), Palmer, Pet.Shirtliff, Pearson, Carr, Sheridan, Hirst, Bennett(Goodacre 55), Worthington					
21 Mar. 1990	Manchester United	Division 1	1–0	Hirst(42)	33260
Turner, Nilsson, King, Palmer, Pet.Shirtliff, Pearson, Carr, Sheridan, Hirst, Atkinson, Worthington					
31 Mar. 1990	Tottenham Hotspur	Division 1	2–4	Hirst(21), Atkinson(53)	26582
Turner, Nilsson, King(Madden 41), Palmer, Pet.Shirtliff, Pearson, Francis(Bennett 60), Sheridan, Hirst, Atkinson, Barrick					
07 Apr. 1990	Southampton	Division 1	0–1		18329
Turner, Nilsson, Madden, Palmer, Pet.Shirtliff, Pearson, Francis, Sheridan, Hirst, Atkinson, Whitton(Bennett 73)					
05 May 1990	Nottingham Forest	Division 1	0–3		29762
Turner, Nilsson, King, Palmer, Pet.Shirtliff, Pearson, Francis(Whitton 81), Sheridan, Hirst, Atkinson, Worthington					

OTHER GAMES AT HILLSBOROUGH

Date	Type	Home	Away		Att.
03 Sep. 1989	Rugby League	Sheffield Eagles 20	St Helens 36		6000
05 Nov. 1989	Rugby League	Sheffield Eagles 10	Wigan 22		7622
22 Jan. 1990	Boys	Sheffield 2	Derby 1		n/k
26 Feb. 1990	Boys	England 2	Northern Ireland 1		2102
11 Apr. 1990	Boys	Sheffield 1	London 3		n/k

1987–88
Sterland, Jonsson, Knight, Pressman, Hodge, Chapman, May, Madden;
Eustace (ass. manager), Marwood, Megson, Worthington, Bradshaw,
Shutt, Gregory, Smith (physio);
Hirst, Chamberlain, Wilkinson (manager), Owen, McCall

1988–89
Pearson, Reeves, West, Pressman, Turner, Knight, Cranson, Madden;
Phelan (coach), Barlow (ass. manager), Galvin, Hirst, Barrick,
Jonsson, Hodgson, Varadi, Smith (physio), Baker (coach);
Megson, Harper, Sterland, Eustace (manager), Worthington, Procter,
McCall.

1989–90
Palmer, Turner, D. Atkinson, Pressman, Shirtliff;
Barker (ass. manager), Madden, Shakespeare, Whitton, Fee,
Worthington, Hirst, Smith (physio);
Harper, Wood, Taylor, R. Atkinson (manager), Pearson, Bennett,
Barrick.

1990–91
Barker (ass. manager), Sheridan, King, Shirtliff, Pressman, Turner,
Palmer, Worthington, Madden, Smith (physio);
Nilsson, Williams, Harkes, Hirst, Atkinson (manager), Pearson,
Wilson, Francis, McCall.

Date	Opponents	Competition	Score	Scorers	Att.
17 Aug. 1990	Sheffield United	Madden Benefit	3–0	Williams 2(9, 55), Shirtliff(54)	15040
Pressman, Nilsson(Wood 36), King, Palmer, Pearson, Madden(Pet.Shirtliff 51), Wilson, Sheridan, Hirst, P.Williams, (Francis 65), Worthington					
01 Sep. 1990	Hull City	Division 2	5–1	Hirst 4(26, 42, 58, 75), Williams(50)	23673
Pressman, Nilsson, King, Palmer, Pet.Shirtliff, Pearson(Francis 80), Wilson, Sheridan, Hirst, P.Williams, Worthington(McCall 87)					
15 Sep. 1990	Watford	Division 2	2–0	Pearson(17), Worthington(47)	22061
Pressman, Nilsson, King, Palmer, Pet.Shirtliff, Pearson, Wilson, Sheridan, Hirst, P.Williams, Worthington					
18 Sep. 1990	Newcastle United	Division 2	2–2	Hirst(42), McCall(90)	30628
Pressman, Nilsson, King, Palmer, Pet.Shirtliff, Pearson, Wilson(Francis 77), Sheridan, Hirst, P.Williams, Worthington(McCall 85)					
26 Sep. 1990	Brentford	Rumbelows Cup 2–L1	2–1	Hirst(51), Pearson(72)	11027
Pressman, Nilsson, King, Palmer, Pet.Shirtliff, Pearson, Wilson(McCall 87), Francis, Hirst, P.Williams, Worthington					
29 Sep. 1990	West Ham United	Division 2	1–1	Hirst(1)	28786
Pressman, Nilsson, King, Palmer, Pet.Shirtliff, Pearson, Wilson(Francis 76), Sheridan, Hirst, P.Williams, Worthington					
13 Oct. 1990	Plymouth Argyle	Division 2	3–0	Sheridan 2(43, 61), Wilson(3)	23489
Pressman, Nilsson, King, Palmer, Pet.Shirtliff, Pearson, Wilson, Sheridan, Francis(Whitton 76), P.Williams, Worthington(McCall 74)					
20 Oct. 1990	Port Vale	Division 2	1–1	Williams(30)	24527
Pressman, Nilsson, King, Palmer, Pet.Shirtliff, Pearson, Wilson, Sheridan, Francis(Hirst 72), P.Williams, Worthington					
31 Oct. 1990	Swindon Town	Rumbelows Cup 3	0–0		13900
Pressman, Harkes, King, Palmer, Pet.Shirtliff, Madden, Wilson, Sheridan, Hirst, P.Williams(Francis 77), Worthington(McCall 90)					
03 Nov. 1990	Oldham Athletic	Division 2	2–2	Sheridan 2(61pen., 82pen.)	34845
Pressman, Harkes, King(Francis 38), Palmer, Pet.Shirtliff, Pearson, Wilson, Sheridan, Hirst, P.Williams, Worthington					
17 Nov. 1990	Swindon Town	Division 2	2–1	Williams(36), Pearson(70)	22715
Pressman, Harkes, King, Palmer, Pet.Shirtliff, Pearson, Wilson, Sheridan, Hirst(Francis 75), P.Williams, Worthington(McCall 85)					
28 Nov. 1990	Derby County	Rumbelows Cup 4	1–1	Hirst(14)	25649
Pressman, Harkes, King(P.Williams 80), Palmer, Pet.Shirtliff, Pearson, Wilson, Sheridan, Hirst, Francis, Worthington					
01 Dec. 1990	Notts County	Division 2	2–2	Sheridan(1)pen, Hirst(45)	23474
Pressman, Harkes, King, Palmer, Pet.Shirtliff, Pearson, Wilson, Sheridan(P.Williams 83), Hirst, Francis, Worthington					
15 Dec. 1990	Ipswich Town	Division 2	2–2	Francis(35), Pearson(66)	20431
Pressman, Harkes, King(Francis 24), Palmer, Pet.Shirtliff, Pearson, Wilson, Sheridan, Hirst, P.Williams, Worthington					
18 Dec. 1990	Barnsley	ZDS Cup 2	3–3 aet	Hirst 3(35, 69, 101) *lost 4–2 on pens.	5942
Pressman, Harkes, Worthington, Palmer, Pet.Shirtliff, Pearson, Wilson, Sheridan, Hirst, Francis(McCall 105), P.Williams					
26 Dec. 1990	Wolverhampton W.	Division 2	2–2	McCall(7), Palmer(22)	29686
Pressman, Harkes, King, Palmer, Pet.Shirtliff, Pearson, Wilson, Sheridan, Hirst, P.Williams, McCall					
29 Dec. 1990	Portsmouth	Division 2	2–1	Hirst 2(5, 79)	22885
Turner, Harkes, King, Palmer, Pet.Shirtliff, Pearson, Wilson(P.Williams 72), Sheridan, Hirst, Francis, McCall(Worthington 61)					
19 Jan. 1991	Charlton Athletic	Division 2	0–0		22318
Turner, Anderson, King, Palmer, Pet.Shirtliff, Pearson, Wilson(Francis 73), Sheridan, Hirst, P.Williams, Worthington					
30 Jan. 1991	Millwall	F.A.Cup 4R	2–0	Anderson(37), Hirst(57)	25140
Turner, Anderson, King, Palmer, Pet.Shirtliff, Pearson, Harkes, Sheridan, Hirst, Francis(P.Williams 83), Worthington					
27 Feb. 1991	Chelsea	Rumbelows Cup S/F–L2	3–1	Pearson(34), Wilson(42), Williams(89)	34669
Turner, Harkes, King, Palmer, Pet.Shirtliff, Pearson, Wilson(McCall 86), Sheridan, Hirst, Francis(P.Williams 69), Worthington					
09 Mar. 1991	West Bromwich Albion	Division 2	1–0	Sheridan(55)pen.	26934
Turner, Anderson, King, Palmer, Pet.Shirtliff, Pearson, Harkes, Sheridan, P.Williams, Francis, Worthington					
13 Mar. 1991	Brighton & Hove Alb.	Division 2	1–1	Anderson(5)	23969
Turner, Anderson, King, Palmer, Pet.Shirtliff, Pearson, Wilson(Hirst 68), Sheridan, P.Williams, Francis, McCall(MacKenzie 85)					
23 Mar. 1991	Bristol Rovers	Division 2	2–1	Clark(48)og., Williams(86)	25074
Turner, Anderson, King, Palmer, Pet.Shirtliff, Pearson, MacKenzie, Sheridan, Hirst, P.Williams, Francis(McCall 87)					
01 Apr. 1991	Oxford United	Division 2	0–2		28682
Turner, Anderson, King, Palmer, Pet.Shirtliff(Mackenzie 56), Pearson, Wilson(Watson 72), Sheridan, Hirst, P.Williams, Francis					
10 Apr. 1991	Blackburn Rovers	Division 2	3–1	Sheridan 2(55, 78pen.), Anderson(54)	23139
Turner, Nilsson, King, Palmer, Pet.Shirtliff, Anderson, Harkes, Sheridan, Hirst, P.Williams, Francis					
13 Apr. 1991	Middlesbrough	Division 2	2–0	Williams 2(85, 87)	30598
Turner, Nilsson, King, Palmer, Anderson, Pearson, Harkes(Mackenzie 85), Sheridan, Hirst, P.Williams, Worthington					
24 Apr. 1991	Leicester City	Division 2	0–0		31308
Turner, Nilsson, King, Harkes(Francis 73), Pet.Shirtliff, Pearson(Anderson ht), Wilson, Sheridan, Hirst, P.Williams, Worthington					
27 Apr. 1991	Barnsley	Division 2	3–1	Hirst(38), Harkes(58), MacKenzie(89)	30693
Turner, Harkes, King, Palmer, Pet.Shirtliff(MacKenzie ht), Anderson, Wilson, Sheridan, Hirst, P.Williams, Francis(Watson 84)					
04 May 1991	Millwall	Division 2	2–1	Hirst 2(31, 51)	30278
Turner, Nilsson, King, Palmer, MacKenzie(Madden 63), Anderson, Harkes, Sheridan, Hirst, P.Williams, Worthington					
08 May 1991	Bristol City	Division 2	3–1	Hirst 2(40, 64), Francis(54)	31706
Turner, Nilsson(Harkes 67), King, Palmer, Madden, Anderson, Wilson, Sheridan, Hirst, Francis(P.Williams 79), Worthington					

OTHER GAMES AT HILLSBOROUGH

07 Oct. 1990	Ladies – League	Sheff.Wed. 3		Chesterfield 1	3000
05 May 1991	Ladies – Lge. Cup Final	Sheff.Wed. 3		Davies Argyle 1	500
12 May 1991	Senior Cup Final	Emley 1		Worksop Town 1 (aet) *Emley win 4–3 on pens.	1300

Date	Opponents	Competition	Score	Scorers	Att.
17 Aug. 1991	Aston Villa	Division 1	2–3	Hirst(3), Wilson(35)	36749
Woods, Nilsson, King, Palmer, Pearson, Warhurst, Wilson, Sheridan(Harkes 87), Hirst, P.Williams(Francis 66), Worthington					
28 Aug. 1991	Everton	Division 1	2–1	Wilson(54), Anderson(87)	28690
Woods, Nilsson, King, Palmer, Warhurst, Anderson, Wilson, Sheridan, Hirst, P.Williams(Francis 72; Mackenzie 88), Worthington					
31 Aug. 1991	Queen's Park Rangers	Division 1	4–1	Palmer 3(5, 42, 45), Sheridan(69)	25022
Woods, Nilsson, King, Palmer, Warhurst, Anderson, Wilson, Sheridan, Hirst(Francis 76), P.Williams, Worthington(MacKenzie 70)					
07 Sep. 1991	Nottingham Forest	Division 1	2–1	Williams(18), Francis(88)	31289
Woods, Nilsson, King, Palmer, Warhurst, Pearson, Wilson, Sheridan, Watson(Francis 72), P.Williams(Anderson 89), Worthington					
21 Sep. 1991	Southampton	Division 1	2–0	Williams(4), Worthington(66)	27291
Woods, Nilsson, King, Palmer, Warhurst, Pearson(Anderson 62), Wilson, Harkes, Jemson(Francis 76), P.Williams, Worthington					
05 Oct. 1991	Crystal Palace	Division 1	4–1	Hirst 2(39, 44), Worthington(8), Palmer(82)	26230
Woods, Nilsson, King, Palmer, Warhurst, Pearson, Wilson, Anderson, Hirst(Francis 88), P.Williams, Worthington					
09 Oct. 1991	Leyton Orient	Rumbelows Cup 2–L2	4–1	Francis 2(74, 87), Anderson(11), Williams(22)	14398
Woods, Anderson, King, Palmer, Warhurst, Pearson, Wilson, Hyde(Wood 69), Hirst(Francis 33), P.Williams, Worthington					
23 Oct. 1991	Manchester City	ZDS Cup 2	3–2	Hirst(12), Hyde(88), Jemson(89)	7951
Woods, Nilsson, King, Palmer, Anderson, Wood, Harkes(Wilson 72), Hyde, Hirst, P.Williams, Worthington(Jemson 81)					
26 Oct. 1991	Manchester United	Division 1	3–2	Jemson 2(70, 81), Hirst(14)	38260
Woods, Nilsoon, King, Palmer, Anderson, Warhurst, Wilson, Sheridan, Hirst(Harkes 88), P.Williams, Worthington(Jemson 63)					
30 Oct. 1991	Southampton	Rumbelows Cup 3	1–1	Hirst(38)	17267
Woods, Nilsson, King, Palmer, Harkes, Anderson, Wilson, Sheridan, Hirst, P.Williams(Jemson 78), Worthington					
02 Nov. 1991	Tottenham Hotspur	Division 1	0–0		31573
Woods, Nilsson, King(Jemson70), Palmer, Warhurst, Anderson, Wilson(Harkes50), Sheridan, Hirst, P.Williams, Worthington					
23 Nov. 1991	Arsenal	Division 1	1–1	Hirst(19)	32174
Woods, Nilsson(Anderson 59), King, Palmer, Pearson, Warhurst, Harkes, Sheridan, Hirst, Jemson(P.Williams 83), Bart–Williams					
07 Dec. 1991	Chelsea	Division 1	3–0	Hirst 2(46, 59), Williams(88)	27383
Pressman, Nilsson, King, Palmer, Warhurst(Harkes 35), Pearson, Bart–Williams, Sheridan, Hirst, Jemson(P.Williams 88), Worthington					
21 Dec. 1991	Wimbledon	Division 1	2–0	Sheridan 2(49pen., 60)	20574
Woods, Nilsson(Anderson 89), King, Palmer, Pearson, Warhurst, Bart–Williams, Sheridan, Hirst(P.Williams 75), Jemson, Harkes					
01 Jan. 1992	Oldham Athletic	Division 1	1–1	Sharp(63)og.	32679
Woods, Harkes, King, Palmer, Pet.Shirtliff, Wilson, Bart–Williams, Sheridan(Hyde 85), Hirst(P.Williams 17), Jemson, Worthington					
12 Jan. 1992	Leeds United	Division 1	1–6	Sheridan(39)	32228
Woods, Nilsson, King, Palmer, Pearson(Harkes ht), Anderson, Watson, Sheridan, Bart–Williams, Jemson, Worthington(P.Williams 64)					
01 Feb. 1992	Luton Town	Division 1	3–2	Hirst(17), Williams(78), Harkes(86)	22291
Woods, Nilsson, King, Palmer, Warhurst, Pearson, Harkes, Hyde, Hirst, P.Williams, Worthington(Francis 64)					
04 Feb. 1992	Middlesbrough	F.A.Cup 4	1–2	Hirst(4)	29772
Woods, Nilsson, King, Palmer, Pearson, Warhurst, Harkes, Hyde, Hirst, P.Williams(Anderson 83), Worthington(Francis 61)					
22 Feb. 1992	West Ham United	Division 1	2–1	Palmer(80), Anderson(88)	26150
Woods, Nilsson, Worthington, Palmer, Anderson, Pet.Shirtliff, Wilson, Hyde(Bart–Williams ht), Hirst, Johnson(P.Williams 72), Harkes					
07 Mar. 1992	Coventry City	Division 1	1–1	Anderson(83)	23959
Woods, Nilsson, King, Palmer, Anderson, Pet.Shirtliff, Wilson, Bart–Williams(Warhurst 74), Hirst, P.Williams, Worthington(Jemson 54)					
11 Mar. 1992	Sheffield United	Division 1	1–3	King(49)	40327
Woods, Nilsson, King, Palmer, Anderson, Pet.Shirtliff, Wilson(Jemson 69), Hyde, Hirst, P.Williams, Pearson(Harkes 72)					
21 Mar. 1992	Notts County	Division 1	1–0	Hirst(74)	23910
Woods, Nilsson, Warhurst, Palmer, Pearson, Pet.Shirtliff, Wilson, Bart–Williams(Hyde 68), Hirst, P.Williams, Harkes(Francis 67)					
11 Apr. 1992	Manchester City	Division 1	2–0	Hirst(55), Worthington(87)	32138
Woods, Nilsson, King, Palmer, Pearson, Warhurst, Wilson, Sheridan(Harkes 89), Hirst, P.Williams(Francis 85), Worthington					
20 Apr. 1992	Norwich City	Division 1	2–0	Nilsson(10), Sheridan(45)	27362
Woods, Nilsson, King, Palmer, Pearson, Warhurst, Wilson, Sheridan(Harkes 89), Johnson(Francis 65), P.Williams, Worthington					
02 May 1992	Liverpool	Division 1	0–0		34861
Woods, Nilsson, King, Palmer, Pearson, Warhurst, Wilson, Sheridan(Francis 77), Hirst, P.Williams(Bart–Williams 12), Worthington					

OTHER GAMES AT HILLSBOROUGH

13 July 1991	World Student Games	Germany 1	Mexico 1		n/k
13 July 1991	World Student Games	Iran 1	Great Britain		n/k
21 July 1991	W.S.Games S/F	Uruguay 1	South Korea 4		n/k
21 July 1991	W.S.Games S/F	Great Britain 0	Netherlands 1		n/k
26 Mar. 1992	Boys	Sheffield 3	Bolton 0		n/k
29 Mar. 1992	Women	Sheff.Wed. 1	Bronte 2		n/k
05 Apr. 1992	F.A.Cup Semi Final	Norwich City 0	Sunderland 1		40102

Date	Opponents	Competition	Score	Scorers	Att.
19 Aug. 1992	Nottingham Forest	Premier League	2–0	Hirst 2(15, 80)	29623
Woods, Nilsson, King(Harkes 78), Palmer, Pearson, Warhurst, Wilson, Bart–Williams, Hirst, P.Williams, Worthington					
22 Aug. 1992	Chelsea	Premier League	3–3	Hirst 2(26, 37pen.), Wilson(82)	26338
Woods, Nilsson, King(Francis 70), Palmer, Pearson, Warhurst, Harkes(Wilson 77), Bart–Williams, Hirst, P.Williams, Worthington					
02 Sep. 1992	Coventry City	Premier League	1–2	Bart–Williams(63)	22874
Woods, Nilsson, Warhurst(Wilson 87), Palmer, Pearson, Pet.Shirtliff, Jemson(Francis 54), Bart–Williams, Waddle, P.Williams, Worthington					
05 Sep. 1992	Manchester City	Premier League	0–3		27169
Woods, Nilsson(Harkes 42), Wilson(Francis 67), Palmer, Pearson, Warhurst, Watson, Bart–Williams, Waddle, P.Williams, Worthington					
16 Sep. 1992	Spora Luxembourg	Uefa Cup 1–L1	8–1	Anderson 2(23, 30), Warhurst 2(32, 74), Bart–Williams 2(61, 81), Waddle(9), Worthington(66)	19792
Woods, Harkes, Anderson, Palmer, Pet.Shirtliff, Warhurst(Jemson 74), Hyde(Wilson 70), Waddle, Francis, Bart–Williams, Worthington					
23 Sep. 1992	Hartlepool United	Coca–Cola Cup 2–L1	3–0	Watson(61), Bright(66), Wilson(89)	10112
Pressman, Harkes, Worthington, Palmer, Pet.Shirtliff, Anderson, Wilson, Waddle, Bright, Bart–Williams, Watson					
27 Sep. 1992	Tottenham Hotspur	Premier League	2–0	Bright(6), Anderson(32)	24895
Woods, Harkes, Worthington, Palmer, Pet.Shirtliff, Anderson, Nilsson(Wilson 77), Waddle, Bright, Bart–Williams, Watson					
17 Oct. 1992	Oldham Athletic	Premier League	2–1	Palmer(10), Bright(18)	24485
Woods, Warhurst, Worthington, Palmer, Pet.Shirtliff, Anderson, Harkes, Waddle(Watson 59), Hirst(Wilson 83), Bart–Williams, Bright					
27 Oct. 1992	Leicester City	Coca–Cola Cup 3	7–1	Bright 2(46, 54), Watson 2(70, 75), Hirst(18), Worthington(33), Bart–Williams(71),	17326
Woods, Harkes, Worthington, Palmer, Pearson, Anderson, Wilson, Waddle, Hirst(Watson 52), Bright, Sheridan(Bart–Williams 66)					
31 Oct. 1992	Blackburn Rovers	Premier League	0–0		31044
Woods, Harkes, Worthington, Palmer, Pearson, Anderson, Wilson, Waddle, Hirst, Bright, Sheridan					
04 Nov. 1992	Kaiserslautern	Uefa Cup 2–L2	2–2	Wilson(27), Sheridan(65)	27597
Woods, Harkes(Nilsson 33), Worthington, Palmer, Pearson(Bart–Williams 77), Anderson, Wilson, Waddle, Watson, Warhurst, Sheridan					
21 Nov. 1992	Ipswich Town	Premier League	1–1	Thompson(16)og.	24270
Woods, Nilsson, Worthington, Palmer, Pearson, Warhurst(Bart–Williams 67), Wilson, Waddle, Hirst, Bright, Sheridan					
02 Dec. 1992	Queen's Park Rangers	Coca–Cola Cup 4	4–0	Bright(31), Hirst(33), Palmer(67), Nilsson(88)	17161
Woods, Nilsson, Worthington, Palmer(Bart–Williams 82), Anderson, Warhurst, Harkes, Waddle, Hirst, Bright(Watson 85), Sheridan					
05 Dec. 1992	Aston Villa	Premier League	1–2	Bright(26)	29964
Woods, Nilsson, Worthington, Palmer, Anderson, Warhurst, Harkes(Bart–Williams 78), Waddle, Hirst, Bright, Sheridan(Watson 81)					
19 Dec. 1992	Queen's Park Rangers	Premier League	1–0	Bright(40)	23164
Woods, Nilsson, Worthington, Palmer, Anderson, Warhurst(Bart–Williams 27), Wilson, Waddle, Hirst, Bright, Sheridan					
26 Dec. 1992	Manchester United	Premier League	3–3	Hirst(3), Bright(7), Sheridan(62)	37708
Woods, Nilsson, Worthington, Palmer, Anderson, Pet.Shirtliff, Wilson(Harkes 74), Waddle, Hirst, Bright, Sheridan					
10 Jan. 1993	Norwich City	Premier League	1–0	Worthington(42)	23360
Woods, Nilsson, Worthington, Harkes, Anderson(Warhurst ht), Pet.Shirtliff, Wilson, Waddle, Hirst(Bart–Williams 85), Bright, Sheridan					
24 Jan. 1993	Sunderland	F.A.Cup 4	1–0	Bright(89)	33422
Woods, Nilsson, Worthington, Harkes, Pearson(Palmer 37), Pet.Shirtliff, Wilson, Waddle, Watson(Bart–Williams 71), Bright, Sheridan					
03 Feb. 1993	Ipswich Town	Coca–Cola Cup 5R	1–0	Warhurst(53)	26328
Woods, Nilsson, Worthington, Palmer, Harkes, Pet.Shirtliff, Wilson, Waddle, Warhurst, Bart–Williams(Pearson 75), Sheridan					
06 Feb. 1993	Everton	Premier League	3–1	Warhurst(16), Harkes(17), Waddle(63)	24979
Woods, Nilsson, Worthington, Palmer, Harkes, Pet.Shirtliff, Wilson(Pearson 67), Waddle, Warhurst, Jemson(Hyde 31), Sheridan					
13 Feb. 1993	Southend United	F.A.Cup 5	2–0	Warhurst 2(43, 55)	26466
Woods, Nilsson, Worthington, Palmer, Harkes, Pet.Shirtliff, Wilson, Waddle, Warhurst(Anderson 90), Bart–Williams(Jemson 83), Sheridan					
20 Feb. 1993	Crystal Palace	Premier League	2–1	Warhurst(28), Wilson(72)	26459
Woods, Nilsson, Worthington, Palmer, Harkes, Pet.Shirtliff, Wilson, Waddle, Warhurst, Bart–Williams(Jemson 58), Sheridan					
27 Feb. 1993	Liverpool	Premier League	1–1	Anderson(81)	33964
Woods, Nilsson, Worthington, Palmer, Harkes, Pet.Shirtliff(Anderson 51), Hyde(Bart–Williams 89), Waddle, Warhurst, Bright, Sheridan					
14 Mar. 1993	Blackburn Rovers	Coca–Cola Cup S/F–L2	2–1	Hirst(68), Bright(74)	30048
Woods, Nilsson, King(Hirst 55), Palmer, Hyde, Anderson, Wilson, Waddle, Warhurst, Bright, Sheridan(Stewart 87)					
17 Mar. 1993	Derby County	F.A.Cup 6R	1–0	Warhurst(23)	32033
Woods, Nilsson, Worthington, Palmer, King(Hirst 76), Anderson, Wilson, Waddle, Warhurst, Bright, Sheridan					
24 Mar. 1993	Wimbledon	Premier League	1–1	Bright(76)	20918
Woods, Nilsson(Watts 50), Worthington, Palmer, Jones, Anderson, Wilson, Waddle, Bart–Williams(Jemson 67), Bright, Sheridan					
12 Apr. 1993	Southampton	Premier League	5–2	Bart–Williams 3(43, 70, 81), Bright(37), King(50)	26184
Pressman, Watts, King, Harkes(M.Williams ht), Stewart, Anderson(Jemson 84), Hyde, Jones, Bright, Bart–Williams, Worthington					
21 Apr. 1993	Sheffield United	Premier League	1–1	Warhurst(78)	38688
Woods, Nilsson, Worthington, Palmer, Harkes, Warhurst, Jones(Hyde 7), Waddle(Bart–Williams 76), Hirst, Bright, Sheridan					
01 May 1993	Middlesbrough	Premier League	2–3	Bart–Williams(52), Morris(78)og.	25949
Woods, Nilsson, Worthington, Palmer, Pet.Shirtliff, Anderson, Harkes, Warhurst, Hirst(Bart–Williams ht), Bright, Sheridan					
04 May 1993	Leeds United	Premier League	1–1	Hirst(90)	26855
Woods, Nilsson, King(Warhurst 74), Palmer, Pet.Shirtliff, Jones, Wilson(Harkes 35), Hyde, Hirst, Bart–Williams, Worthington					
06 May 1993	Arsenal	Premier League	1–0	Bright(19)	23645
Pressman, Harkes, King, Hyde, Anderson, Stewart, M.Williams, Jones, Bright, Bart–Williams(Jemson 71), Sheridan					

OTHER GAMES AT HILLSBOROUGH

12 Nov. 1992	U–13/14 Boys	All Saints R.C.School 3	Boston Spa Comp. 1	n/k
12 Nov. 1992	Boys	Sheffield 1	Derby 0	n/k
25 Apr. 1993	Roulette Cup Final	Bass Regency 1	Park Lane 0	n/k
27 Apr. 1993	Friendly	Sheffield F.C. 1	Queen's Park 3	n/k

Date	Opponents	Competition	Score	Scorers	Att.
07 Aug. 1993	Derby County	Worthington Tst.	1–1	Warhurst(12)	7048

Woods, Nilsson, King(Bart–Williams 62), Palmer(Pet.Shirtliff 84), Pearce, Walker, Worthington, Waddle(Harkes ht), Hirst(Bright 62), Warhurst, Sheridan(Hyde 82)

18 Aug. 1993	Aston Villa	Premiership	0–0		28450

Woods, Nilsson, King, Walker, Pearce, Sheridan, Hyde, Palmer, Worthington, Hirst(Bright 85), Warhurst

21 Aug. 1993	Arsenal	Premiership	0–1		26023

Woods, Worthington, King(Bright 67), Walker, Pearce, Sheridan(Bart–Williams 67), Hyde, Palmer, Sinton, Hirst, Warhurst

01 Sep. 1993	Norwich City	Premiership	3–3	Bart–Williams(51), Bright(59), Sinton(62)	25175

Woods, Nilsson, Worthington, Walker, Pearson, Waddle, Hyde, Sheridan, Sinton, Bart–Williams, Bright

18 Sep. 1993	Southampton	Premiership	2–0	Sheridan(59)pen., Hirst(80)	22503

Woods, Nilsson, Worthington(Bart–Williams ht), Walker, Pearson(Hyde 29), Waddle, Palmer, Sheridan, Sinton, Hirst, Bright

02 Oct. 1993	Manchester United	Premiership	2–3	Bart–Williams(47), Bright(86)	34548

Woods, Nilsson, King, Palmer, Walker, Waddle, Sinton, Hyde, Sheridan, Bright, Bart–Williams

06 Oct. 1993	Bolton Wanderers	Coca–Cola Cup 2–L2	1–0	Bright(81)	16194

Woods, Nilsson, King(Pearce 90), Palmer, Walker, Waddle(Watson 88), Sinton, Sheridan, Hyde, Bart–Williams, Bright

16 Oct. 1993	Wimbledon	Premiership	2–2	Waddle(9), Jones(84)	21752

Pressman, M.Williams, Sinton, Pearce, Walker, Bart–Williams(Poric 79), Jones, Hyde, Palmer, Bright, Waddle

30 Oct. 1993	Leeds United	Premiership	3–3	Waddle(2), Jones(43), Bright(68)	31892

Pressman, Nilsson, Worthington, Pearce, Walker, Palmer, Waddle, Jones, Sinton, Jemson(Sheridan 84), Bright

10 Nov. 1993	Middlesbrough	Coca–Cola Cup 3R	2–1 aet	Watson(16), Palmer(115)	19482

Pressman, M.Williams(Poric 112), Worthington, Pearce, Walker, Palmer, Sinton, Waddle, Jones, Jemson, Watson(Hyde 90)

20 Nov. 1993	Coventry City	Premiership	0–0		23379

Pressman, Nilsson, Worthington, Pearce, Walker, Palmer, Jones, Hyde, Sinton, Waddle, Jemson(Francis 67)

24 Nov. 1993	Oldham Athletic	Premiership	3–0	Watson 2(8, 33), Jemson(64)	18509

Pressman, Nilsson, Worthington, Pearce(Hyde ht), Walker, Palmer, Jones, Sinton(Bart–Williams 43), Waddle, Watson, Jemson

04 Dec. 1993	Liverpool	Premiership	3–1	Ruddock(30)og., Wright(59)og., Bright(81)	32177

Pressman, Nilsson, Worthington, Palmer, Walker, Waddle, Jones, Hyde, Bart–Williams(Poric 72), Bright, Jemson(Coleman 80)

18 Dec. 1993	West Ham United	Premiership	5–0	Marsh(35)og., Bright(47), Waddle(51), Jemson(72), Palmer(87)	26350

Pressman, Nilsson, Worthington, Pearce, Walker, Waddle, Palmer, Hyde, Bart–Williams, Bright, Jemson

29 Dec. 1993	Swindon Town	Premiership	3–3	Watson 2(68, 71), Bright(8)	30570

Pressman, Nilsson, Worthington, Pearce(Jones 63), Walker, Waddle, Palmer, Hyde, Sinton(Bart–Williams 63), Bright, Watson

03 Jan. 1994	Tottenham Hotspur	Premiership	1–0	Bright(4)	32514

Pressman, Nilsson, Worthington, Palmer, Walker, Bart–Williams(Pearce 81), Jones, Hyde, Sinton(Jemson 81), Bright, Watson

08 Jan. 1994	Nottingham Forest	F.A.Cup 3	1–1	Bright(10)	32488

Pressman, Nilsson(Pearce 33), Worthington(Watson 69), Palmer, Walker, Bart–Williams, Jones, Hyde, Sinton, Bright, Jemson

22 Jan. 1994	Sheffield United	Premiership	3–1	Bright(58), Pearce(61), Watson(70)	34959

Pressman, Nilsson, Coleman, Pearce, Walker, Jones, Palmer, Hyde, Sinton(Bart–Williams 84), Bright, Watson

09 Feb. 1994	Chelsea	F.A.Cup 4R	1–3 aet	Bright(38)	26114

Pressman, Nilsson, Coleman, Pearce, Walker, Bart–Williams, Palmer, Hyde, Sinton, Bright, Watson(Waddle 74)

02 Mar. 1994	Manchester United	Coca–Cola Cup s/f–L2	1–4	Hyde(34)	34878

Pressman, Nilsson, Coleman, Pearce, Walker, Bart–Williams, Palmer, Hyde, Sinton(Watson 64), Bright, Hirst

05 Mar. 1994	Newcastle United	Premiership	0–1		33224

Pressman, Nilsson, Coleman, Pearce, Walker, Bart–Williams, Palmer, Hyde(King 24), Sinton, Bright(Jemson 81), Watson

20 Mar. 1994	Blackburn Rovers	Premiership	1–2	Watson(40)	24699

Pressman, Nilsson, Coleman, Palmer, Walker, Bart–Williams, Sheridan(King 69), Hyde, Sinton, Bright, Watson(Jemson 54)

30 Mar. 1994	Chelsea	Premiership	3–1	Bart–Williams(6), Palmer(22), Sheridan(85)pen.	20433

Pressman, Nilsson, Worthington, Pearce, Walker, M.Williams(Watson 64), Palmer, Sheridan, Jones, Bright, Bart–Williams(Hyde 89)

02 Apr. 1994	Everton	Premiership	5–1	Bright 2(81, 87), Jones(11), Bart–Williams(44), Worthington(76)	24096

Pressman, Nilsson, Worthington, Pearce, Walker, M.Williams(Watson 75), Palmer, Sheridan(King 64), Jones, Bright, Bart–Williams

09 Apr. 1994	Queen's Park Rangers	Premiership	3–1	Bright 2(7, 32), Sheridan(21)pen.	22437

Pressman, Nilsson, Worthington, Pearce, Walker(Coleman 74), Bart–Williams, Palmer, Sheridan, Jones, Bright, Watson

23 Apr. 1994	Ipswich Town	Premiership	5–0	Linighan(6)og., Watson(16), Pearce(56), Bart–Williams(69), Bright(90)	23457

Pressman, Nilsson, Worthington, Pearce, Walker, Bart–Williams, Palmer, Sheridan(Hyde 83), Jones, Bright, Watson(Jemson 83)

07 May 1994	Manchester City	Premiership	1–1	Watson(25)	33773

Pressman, Nilsson, Worthington, Pearce, Walker(Hyde ht), Bart–Williams, Palmer, Sheridan, Jones, Bright, Watson

OTHER GAMES AT HILLSBOROUGH

18 July 1993	U-18 European Championship	Hungary 1	Turkey 1		1782
20 Oct. 1993	Boys	Yorkshire 7	North of England 4		n/k
24 Jan. 1994	Boys	Sheffield 4	East Northumberland 3		n/k
03 May 1994	Senior Cup Final	Worksop Town 1	Sheffield F.C. 1		698
		(aet–Sheffield win 6–5 on pens.)			
10 May 1994	B International	England 4	Northern Ireland 2		8281

1991–92

Barker, (ass. manager), King, McCall, Shirtliff, Anderson, Pressman, Palmer, Turner, Warhurst, Worthington, Wood, Watson, Smith (physio);
Nilsson, Williams, Harkes, Hirst, Francis (manager), Pearson, Wilson, MacKenzie, Sheridan

1992–93

Johnson, Shirtliff, Pressman, Anderson, Warhurst, Woods, Watts, Palmer;
Barker (ass. manager), King, Harkes, Watson, Bart-Williams, Nilsson, Worthington, Waddle, Jemson, Smith (physio);
Sheridan, Wilson, Pearson, Francis (manager), Hirst, Hyde, Bright.

1993–94

Warhurst, Pressman, Palmer, Pearce, Woods, Watts;
Barker (ass. manager), Jemson, Watson, Nilsson, Bart-Williams, Worthington, Hyde, Waddle, Smith (physio);
Sheridan, Walker, Pearson, Francis (manager), Hirst, King, Bright.

1994–95

Jones, Linighan, Woods, Coleman, Pearce, Pressman, Watts, Bright;
Barker (ass. manager), Waddle, Watson, Sheridan, Briscoe, Bart-Williams, Poric, M. Williams, Taylor, Galley (physio);
Nolan, Petrescu, Hyde, Walker, Francis (manager), Hirst, Sinton, Atherton, Jemson.

Date	Opponents	Competition	Score	Scorers	Att.
09 Aug. 1994	Sheffield United	Friendly	2–3	Bart–Williams(61), Taylor(69)	13724
Pressman, Coleman, Briscoe, Bart–Williams, Walker(Watts49), Pearce, I.Taylor, Jones(Jemson 61), Watson, Bright, Sheridan					
20 Aug. 1994	Tottenham Hotspur	Premiership	3–4	Petrescu(54), Calderwood(66)og., Hirst(83)	34051
Pressman, Petrescu, Nolan, Walker, Atherton, Bart–Williams, Sheridan, I.Taylor, Sinton, Hirst, Bright(Watson 75)					
31 Aug. 1994	Norwich City	Premiership	0–0		25072
Pressman, Atherton, Nolan, Walker, Pearce, Petrescu, Sheridan, I.Taylor(Bart–Williams 24), Sinton, Hirst, Bright(Watson 61)					
17 Sep. 1994	Manchester City	Premiership	1–1	Watson(77)	26776
Pressman, Petrescu, Nolan, Atherton, Pearce, Bart–Williams, Sheridan, Hyde, Sinton(Ingesson ht), Hirst, Bright(Watson 70)					
21 Sep. 1994	Bradford City	Coca–Cola Cup 2–L1	2–1	Taylor(71), Hyde(81)	15705
Pressman, Petrescu, Nolan, Atherton, Pearce, Bart–Williams, Sheridan, Hyde, Ingesson(I.Taylor ht), Hirst, Bright(Watson 65)					
26 Sep. 1994	Leeds United	Premiership	1–1	Bright(15)	23227
Pressman, Petrescu, Nolan, Atherton, Walker, Bart–Williams, Sheridan, Hyde, Sinton(I.Taylor 79), Watson, Bright(Hirst 85)					
08 Oct. 1994	Manchester United	Premiership	1–0	Hirst(44)	33441
Pressman, Atherton, Nolan, Walker, Pearce, Bart–Williams(I.Taylor 65), Sheridan, Hyde, Briscoe, Bright(Watson 88), Hirst					
26 Oct. 1994	Southampton	Coca–Cola Cup 3	1–0	Bart–Williams(51)	16715
Pressman, Atherton, Nolan, Pearce, Walker, I.Taylor, Sheridan, Hyde, Sinton, Bright, Bart–Williams					
29 Oct. 1994	Chelsea	Premiership	1–1	Bright(67)	25450
Pressman, Atherton, Nolan, Pearce, Walker, I.Taylor, Sheridan(Watson60), Hyde, Sinton, Bright, Bart–Williams(Petrescu 80)					
02 Nov. 1994	Blackburn Rovers	Premiership	0–1		24207
Pressman, Atherton(Petrescu71), Nolan, Pearce, Walker, I.Taylor, Sheridan, Hyde, Sinton, Bright, Bart–Williams(Watson 85)					
19 Nov. 1994	West Ham United	Premiership	1–0	Petrescu(29)	25300
Pressman, Atherton, Nolan, Pearce, Walker, Petrescu(I.Taylor 61), Sheridan, Hyde, Sinton, Bright, Bart–Williams(Watson67)					
03 Dec. 1994	Crystal Palace	Premiership	1–0	Bart–Williams(19)	21930
Pressman, Petrescu, Nolan, Pearce, Atherton, I.Taylor(Waddle 75), Sheridan, Hyde, Sinton, Bart–Williams, Bright					
17 Dec. 1994	Queen's Park Rangers	Premiership	0–2		22766
Pressman, Atherton(Petrescu68), Nolan, Pearce, Walker, Waddle, Sheridan, Hyde, Jones, Bart–Williams, Bright(Ingesson 59)					
28 Dec. 1994	Coventry City	Premiership	5–1	Bright 2(14, 45), Whittingham 2(57, 64), Waddle(38)	26056
Pressman, Atherton, Nolan, Pearce, Walker, Ingesson(Waddle 32), Hyde, Sheridan, Bart–Williams, Whittingham, Bright(Watson 90)					
02 Jan. 1995	Southampton	Premiership	1–1	Hyde(19)	28424
Pressman, Atherton, Nolan, Pearce, Walker, Waddle(Petrescu 73), Hyde, Sheridan, Bart–Williams, Whittingham(Watson 73), Bright					
21 Jan. 1995	Newcastle United	Premiership	0–0		31215
Woods, Petrescu, Nolan, Walker, Atherton, Waddle, Bart–Williams, Sheridan, Ingesson, Whittingham, Watson(Bright 57)					
30 Jan. 1995	Wolverhampton W.	F.A.Cup 4	0–0		21757
Pressman, Atherton, Nolan, Walker, Pearce, Waddle, Hyde, Sheridan(Petrescu 85), Bart–Williams, Whittingham(Watson 68), Bright					
04 Feb. 1995	Arsenal	Premiership	3–1	Petrescu(8), Ingesson(25), Bright(90)	23468
Pressman, Atherton, Nolan, Walker(Sheridan 65), Pearce, Petrescu, Hyde, Bart–Williams(Whittingham 85), Ingesson, Waddle, Bright					
18 Feb. 1995	Aston Villa	Premiership	1–2	Bright(70)	24063
Pressman, Nolan, Briscoe(Whittingham ht), Atherton, Walker, Petrescu, Hyde, Sheridan, Sinton(Bart–Williams 65), Waddle, Bright					
25 Feb. 1995	Liverpool	Premiership	1–2	Bart–Williams(13)	31964
Pressman, Petrescu(Watson 73), Nolan, Atherton, Walker, Waddle(Sheridan ht), Hyde, Bart–Williams, Sinton, Bright, Whittingham					
11 Mar. 1995	Wimbledon	Premiership	0–1		20395
Pressman, Petrescu(Poric ht), Nolan, Walker, Atherton, Pearce, Sinton, Hyde(Whittingham 71), M.Williams, Waddle, Bright					
01 Apr. 1995	Nottingham Forest	Premiership	1–7	Bright(52)pen.	30060
Pressman, Petrescu, Nolan, Walker, Pearce, Bart–Williams, Hyde, Sheridan(Whittingham 77), Sinton, Waddle, Bright					
08 Apr. 1995	Leicester City	Premiership	1–0	Whittingham(38)	22551
Woods, Atherton, Nolan, Walker, Pearce, Waddle, M.Williams, Sheridan, Ingesson(Sinton 60), Hirst(Bright 78), Whittingham					
17 Apr. 1995	Everton	Premiership	0–0		27880
Pressman, Atherton, Nolan, Walker, Pearce, Waddle, Sheridan, Hyde(Ingesson 7), Bart–Williams, Hirst(Bright 87), Whittingham					
14 May 1995	Ipswich Town	Premiership	4–1	Whittingham 2(7, 58), Williams(55) Bright(89)	30213
Woods, Atherton, Nolan, Walker, Pearce, Waddle, M.Williams, Sheridan(Hyde 52), Sinton, Hirst(Bright 69), Whittingham					

OTHER GAMES AT HILLSBOROUGH

09 May 1995	Senior Cup Final	Worksop Town 1	Emley 0		750

Date	Opponents	Competition	Score	Scorers	Att.
23 Aug. 1995	Blackburn Rovers	Premiership	2–1	Waddle(18), Pembridge(83)	25544
Pressman, Petrescu, Nolan, Atherton, Watts, Walker, Pembridge, Sheridan, Waddle(Sinton 69), Hirst, Bright					
27 Aug. 1995	Newcastle United	Premiership	0–2		24815
Pressman, Petrescu(Ingesson 86), Nolan, Atherton, Watts, Walker, Pembridge, Sheridan(Hyde 67), Degryse, Hirst(Sinton 78), Bright					
16 Sep. 1995	Tottenham Hotspur	Premiership	1–3	Hirst(8)	26565
Pressman, Petrescu, Nolan, Walker, Atherton, Watts(Waddle 63), Pembridge, Sheridan(Whittingham 71), Degryse, Hirst, Bright					
23 Sep. 1995	Manchester United	Premiership	0–0		34101
Pressman, Petrescu, Nolan, Pearce, Walker, Atherton, Pembridge(Briscoe 82), Hyde, Waddle, Hirst(Bright 86), Degryse					
04 Oct. 1995	Crewe Alexandra	Coca–Cola Cup 2–L2	5–2	Bright 3(45, 64, 77), Degryse(7), Hirst(17)	12039
Pressman, Atherton, Nolan, Briscoe, Walker, Pembridge, Waddle, Degryse(Whittingham 51), Hyde, Hirst(M.Williams 82), Bright					
15 Oct. 1995	Middlesbrough	Premiership	0–1		21177
Pressman, Nolan, Briscoe, Walker, Atherton, Waddle, Pembridge, Hyde(Sheridan 76), Degryse(Whittingham 70), Sinton, Bright					
28 Oct. 1995	West Ham United	Premiership	0–1		23917
Pressman, M.Williams(Degryse 69), Nolan, Atherton, Walker, Ingesson, Pembridge, Sinton, Waddle, Whittingham(Bright 77), Hirst					
18 Nov. 1995	Manchester City	Premiership	1–1	Hirst(14)pen.	24422
Pressman, Nolan, Briscoe, Atherton, Pearce, Pembridge(Hyde 65), Waddle, M.Williams, Sinton, Degryse, Hirst					
04 Dec. 1995	Coventry City	Premiership	4–3	Whittingham(25), Hirst(39), Degryse(61), Bright(72)	16229
Pressman, Nolan, Briscoe, Nicol, Walker, Atherton, Waddle(Hyde 85), Whittingham, Degyrse, Hirst, Bright					
16 Dec. 1995	Leeds United	Premiership	6–2	Degryse 2(4, 25), Hirst 2(72, 86), Whittingham(18), Bright(67)	24573
Pressman, Nolan, Briscoe, Nicol, Walker, Atherton, Waddle, Whittingham(Hyde ht), Degryse, Hirst, Bright					
23 Dec. 1995	Southampton	Premiership	2–2	Hirst 2(14pen, 50pen.)	25115
Pressman, Nolan, Briscoe, Nicol, Walker, Atherton, Waddle, Whittingham, Degryse(Hyde 83), Hirst, Bright(Kovacevic 83)					
01 Jan. 1996	Bolton Wanderers	Premiership	4–2	Kovacevic 2(22, 45), Hirst 2(54pen., 60)	24872
Pressman, Nolan, Sinton, Stefanovic, Walker, Atherton, Waddle, Whittingham, Degryse, Hirst, Kovacevic(Bright 72)					
13 Jan. 1996	Liverpool	Premiership	1–1	Kovacevic(7)	32747
Woods, Nolan, Briscoe, Nicol, Walker, Atherton, Waddle, Whittingham, Degryse(Hyde 85), Hirst, Kovacevic(Bright 77)					
10 Feb. 1996	Wimbledon	Premiership	2–1	Degryse(50), Watts(85)	19085
Pressman, Nolan, Stefanovic(Watts 80), Atherton, Walker, Nicol, Waddle(Platts 85), Hyde, Whittingham, Kovacevic, Degryse(Bright 80)					
17 Feb. 1996	Queen's Park Rangers	Premiership	1–3	Hyde(22)	22442
Pressman, Nolan, Stefanovic, Atherton, Walker, Nicol, Waddle, Hyde(Bright 76), Whittingham, Kovacevic, Degryse					
02 Mar. 1996	Nottingham Forest	Premiership	1–3	Kovacevic(50)	21930
Woods(Waddle ht), Nolan, Stefanovic(Humphreys 71), Atherton, Walker, Nicol, Hyde(Pembridge ht), Degyrse, Whittingham, Kovacevic, Watts					
16 Mar. 1996	Aston Villa	Premiership	2–0	Whittingham(58), Hirst(87)	22964
Woods, Nicol, Briscoe, Newsome, Walker, Whittingham, Pembridge(Hyde 76), Sheridan, Degryse, Hirst(Kovacevic 87), Blinker					
08 Apr. 1996	Arsenal	Premiership	1–0	Degryse(61)	24349
Pressman, Atherton, Briscoe, Newsome, Walker, Whittingham, Pembridge, Sheridan, Degryse, Blinker(Waddle 83), Hirst(Kovacevic 85)					
17 Apr. 1996	Chelsea	Premiership	0–0		25094
Pressman, Atherton, Briscoe, Newsome, Walker, Whittingham, Pembridge, Sheridan, Degryse, Blinker(Waddle 77), Hirst					
27 Apr. 1996	Everton	Premiership	2–5	Hirst(9), Degryse(64)	32724
Pressman, Nicol, Briscoe, Atherton, Walker, Whittingham, Pembridge(Hyde 74), Sheridan(Waddle 51), Degryse, Blinker, Hirst(Donaldson 81)					

OTHER GAMES AT HILLSBOROUGH

09 June 1996	European Championships	Denmark 1	Portugal 1	34993
16 June 1996	European Championships	Denmark 0	Croatia 3	33671
19 June 1996	European Championships	Denmark 3	Turkey 0	28951

1995–96

Pearce, Bright, Pressman, Watts, Ingesson, Woods, Jones, Waddle;
Begara (coach), Pembridge, Atherton, Sheridan, Williams, Briscoe, Nolan, Worthington, Galley (physio);
Pleat (manager), Hyde, Degryse, Petrescu, Walker, Sinton, Hirst, Barker (ass. manager).

Date	Opponents	Competition	Score	Scorers	Att.
17 Aug. 1996	Aston Villa	Premiership	2–1	Humphreys(54), Whittingham(82)	26861
Pressman, Nolan, Atherton, Stefanovic, Walker, Blinker, Collins, Pembridge(Hyde 72), Whittingham, Humphreys(Oakes 80), Booth					
02 Sep. 1996	Leicester City	Premiership	2–1	Humphreys(25), Booth(51)	17657
Pressman, Nolan, Atherton, Stefanovic, Walker, Blinker, Collins, Whittingham, Humphreys(Sheridan 66), Hirst(Bright 77), Booth					
07 Sep. 1996	Chelsea	Premiership	0–2		30983
Pressman, Nolan, Atherton, Stefanovic, Walker, Blinker, Collins(Trustfull 80), Whittingham(Oakes 69), Humphreys(Sheridan 62), Hirst, Booth					
18 Sep. 1996	Oxford United	Coca–Cola Cup 2–L1 1–1		Whittingham(13)	7499
Pressman, M.Williams, Nolan, Atherton, Newsome(Nicol 86), Pembridge, Blinker, Trustfull(Humphreys 81), Whittingham, Hirst, Booth					
21 Sep. 1996	Derby County	Premiership	0–0		23934
Pressman, Atherton, Nolan, Walker, Stefanovic, Pembridge(Trustfull 34), Blinker(Oakes 68), Hyde, Whittingham, Hirst, Booth(Humphreys 81)					
19 Oct. 1996	Blackburn Rovers	Premiership	1–1	Booth(3)	22191
Pressman, Atherton, Nolan, Newsome, Walker, Carbone(Humphreys 72), Trustfull(Pembridge 77), Hyde, Blinker, Booth, Hirst(Whittingham 88)					
02 Nov. 1996	Southampton	Premiership	1–1	Newsome(14)	20106
Pressman, Atherton, Nolan, Walker, Newsome, Carbone(Humphreys 88), Hyde, Trustfull(Blinker 71), Pembridge, Oakes(Whittingham 80), Booth					
18 Nov. 1996	Nottingham Forest	Premiership	2–0	Trustfull(63), Carbone(86)	16390
Pressman, Atherton, Nolan, Walker, Newsome, Carbone, Hyde(Stefanovic 89), Pembridge, Trustfull(Oakes 80), Blinker, Booth(Humphreys 89)					
30 Nov. 1996	West Ham United	Premiership	0–0		22321
Pressman, Nolan(Oakes ht), Briscoe(Nicol 40), Walker, Atherton, Hyde, Pembridge, Whittingham, Trustfull(Humphreys 70), Carbone, Booth					
18 Dec. 1996	Manchester United	Premiership	1–1	Carbone(57)	37671
Pressman, Nolan, Nicol, Walker, Stefanovic, Atherton, Carbone(Blinker 85), Hyde(Trustfull 44), Pembridge, Whittingham, Booth(Hirst 76)					
26 Dec. 1996	Arsenal	Premiership	0–0		23245
Pressman, Nolan, Nicol, Stefanovic, Walker, Atherton, Whittingham, Oakes(Blinker 57), Pembridge, Carbone, Hirst(Booth 78)					
04 Jan. 1997	Grimsby Town	F.A.Cup 3	7–1	Humphreys 2(14, 48), Booth 2(34, 69), Fickling(45)og., Hyde(55), Pembridge(83)	20590
Pressman, Atherton, Nolan, Stefanovic, Walker, Whittingham, Hyde(Nicol 77), Pembridge, Blinker(Trustfull 62), Humphreys, Booth					
11 Jan. 1997	Everton	Premiership	2–1	Pembridge(22), Hirst(50)	24175
Pressman, Nicol, Nolan, Atherton, Stefanovic, Walker, Whittingham, Pembridge, Hyde, Humphreys, Booth(Hirst ht)					
01 Feb. 1997	Coventry City	Premiership	0–0		21793
Pressman, Nicol, Nolan, Stefanovic, Walker, Atherton, Whittingham(Blinker 71), Hyde, Pembridge, Hirst(Trustfull 80), Booth					
01 Mar. 1997	Middlesbrough	Premiership		Booth(21), Hyde(43), Pembridge(90)pen.	28206
Pressman, Nicol, Nolan, Newsome, Walker, Atherton, Hyde(Stefanovic 90), Pembridge, Carbone(Blinker 78), Booth, Hirst(Humphreys 78)					
09 Mar. 1997	Wimbledon	F.A.Cup 6	0–2		25032
Pressman, Nicol, Nolan, Newsome(Humphreys 13), Walker, Atherton, Whittingham, Hyde(Hirst 36), Pembridge, Carbone, Booth					
12 Mar. 1997	Sunderland	Premiership	2–1	Hirst(42), Stefanovic(63)	20294
Pressman, Nolan, Briscoe, Stefanovic, Walker, Atherton, Whittingham, Pembridge, Carbone(Humphreys 89), Hirst, Booth					
22 Mar. 1997	Leeds United	Premiership	2–2	Hirst(20), Booth(51)	30373
Pressman, Nolan, Briscoe, Stefanovic, Walker, Carbone(Blinker 89), Humphreys(Collins 73), Pembridge, Whittingham, Booth, Hirst					
09 Apr. 1997	Tottenham Hotspur	Premiership	2–1	Atherton(18), Booth(70)	22667
Pressman, Nolan, Briscoe, Nicol, Walker, Atherton, Whittingham(Blinker 68), Pembridge, Carbone, Booth, Hirst(Humphreys 53)					
13 Apr.. 1997	Newcastle United	Premiership	1–1	Pembridge(57)	33798
Pressman, Nicol(Blinker 66), Nolan, Walker(Collins 42), Stefanovic, Atherton, Whittingham, Pembridge, Oakes, Booth(Humphreys 20), Carbone					
19 Apr. 1997	Wimbledon	Premiership	3–1	Trustfull 2(78, 83), Donaldson(42)	26957
Pressman, Nicol, Nolan, Walker, Stefanovic, Atherton, Whittingham, Pembridge, Carbone, Blinker(Trustfull 63), Donaldson					
11 May 1997	Liverpool	Premiership	1–1	Donaldson(75)	38943
Pressman(Clarke 73), Nolan, Humphreys(Oakes 59), Walker, Stefanovic, Whittingham, Atherton, Pembridge, Carbone, Hirst(Donaldson 59), Booth					

OTHER GAMES AT HILLSBOROUGH

16 Apr. 1997	Coca–Cola Cup Final– Rep.	Leicester City 1		Middlesbrough 0 (aet)	39428
22 Apr. 1997	F.A.Cup Semi Final–Rep.	Chesterfield 0		Middlesbrough 3	30339
06 May 1997	Senior Cup Final	Harworth Colliey 0		Worksop Town 7	700

Date	Opponents	Competition	Score	Scorers	Att.
13 Aug. 1997	Leeds United	Premiership	1–3	Hyde(70)	31520
Pressman, Blondeau, Nolan, Walker, Stefanovic, Atherton, Di Canio, Collins(Hyde 58), Humphreys(Oakes 58), Carbone(Donaldson 83), Booth					
30 Aug. 1997	Leicester City	Premiership	1–0	Carbone(56)pen.	24851
Pressman, Nolan(Briscoe 62), Nicol, Walker, Newsome, Atherton, Humphreys(Whittingham 76), Hyde(Collins 16), Di Canio, Carbone, Hirst					
20 Sep. 1997	Coventry City	Premiership	0–0		21087
Pressman(Clarke 22), Nolan, Nicol, Walker, Newsome, Atherton(Collins 17), Di Canio, Pembridge, Magilton(Oakes 73), Whittingham, Hirst					
24 Sep. 1997	Derby County	Premiership	2–5	Di Canio(5), Carbone(12)pen.	22391
Clarke, Blondeau, Nolan, Walker, Newsome(Nicol 28), Di Canio, Pembridge, Magilton, Whittingham(Collins 62), Clough(Hirst ht), Carbone					
01 Oct. 1997	Grimsby Town	Coca–Cola Cup 2–L2	3–2	Di Canio 2(64, 88), Davison(18)og.	11120
Pressman, Nolan, Briscoe, Walker, Stefanovic, Di Canio, Pembridge, Magilton, Whittingham, Collins(Humphreys 57), Carbone(Poric 57)					
04 Oct. 1997	Everton	Premiership	3–1	Carbone 2(79, 82pen.), Di Canio(89)	24486
Pressman, Nolan, Nicol(Briscoe 65), Walker, Stefanovic, Pembridge(Hirst 72), Magilton(Poric 83), Whittingham, Collins, Di Canio, Carbone					
25 Oct. 1997	Crystal Palace	Premiership	1–3	Collins(57)	22072
Pressman, Nolan, Briscoe(Rudi 31), Walker, Newsome, Collins(Poric 73), Magilton, Pembridge, Whittingham(Donaldson 68), Di Canio, Carbone					
08 Nov. 1997	Bolton Wanderers	Premiership	5–0	Booth 3(29, 33, 44), Di Canio(20), Whittingham(26)	25027
Pressman, Nolan, Pembridge, Newsome, Walker, Atherton(Hyde 69), Magilton, Rudi, Whittingham, Di Canio(Blondeau 80), Booth(Donaldson 60)					
22 Nov. 1997	Arsenal	Premiership	2–0	Booth(42), Whittingham(86)	34373
Pressman, Nolan, Pembridge, Newsome, Walker, Atherton, Magilton(Hyde 84), Rudi, Whittingham, Di Canio(Carbone 79), Booth					
08 Dec. 1997	Barnsley	Premiership	2–1	Stefanovic(19), Di Canio(88)	29086
Pressman, Nolan, Pembridge, Stefanovic, Walker, Collins, Rudi, Carbone(Hyde 66), Whittingham, Di Canio, Booth					
20 Dec. 1997	Chelsea	Premiership	1–4	Pembridge(71)	28334
Pressman, Nolan, Stefanovic, Walker, Newsome, Whittingham(Alexandersson 59), Collins(Hyde 59), Rudi, Pembridge, Di Canio(Carbone 68), Booth					
26 Dec. 1997	Blackburn Rovers	Premiership	0–0		33502
Pressman, Nolan, Stefanovic(Collins 68), Walker, Newsome, Atherton, Rudi, Alexandersson, Pembridge, Carbone(Whittingham 83), Booth					
10 Jan. 1998	Newcastle United	Premiership	2–1	Di Canio(50 secs.), Newsome(51)	29446
Pressman, Nolan, Pembridge, Newsome, Walker, Alexandersson, Atherton, Hyde(Humphreys 84), Rudi, Di Canio(Booth 89), Carbone					
14 Jan. 1998	Watford	F.A.Cup 3R	0–0 aet	*win 5–3 on pens.	18707
Pressman, Nolan, Pembridge, Walker(Humphreys 98), Newsome, Atherton, Hyde, Rudi, Alexandersson(Oakes 117), Di Canio, Booth					
26 Jan. 1998	Blackburn Rovers	F.A.Cup 4	0–3		15940
Pressman, Nolan, Pembridge, Walker, Newsome, Atherton, Magilton(Oakes 61), Rudi, Whittingham(Humphreys 61), Di Canio, Carbone					
31 Jan. 1998	Wimbledon	Premiership	1–1	Pembridge(13)	22655
Pressman, Nolan, Hinchcliffe, Walker, Newsome, Atherton, Pembridge, Rudi, Alexandersson(Whittingham 37), Carbone(Mayrleb 74), Booth					
14 Feb. 1998	Liverpool	Premiership	3–3	Carbone(7), Di Canio(63), Hinchcliffe(69)	35405
Pressman, Nolan, Hinchcliffe, Walker, Newsome, Rudi, Atherton, Pembridge(Whittingham 81), Hyde(Magilton ht), Carbone, Di Canio					
21 Feb. 1998	Tottenham Hotspur	Premiership	1–0	Di Canio(33)	29871
Pressman, Nolan(Oakes 38), Hinchcliffe, Walker, Newsome, Pembridge(Stefanovic 89), Rudi, Hyde(Magilton 73), Atherton, Di Canio, Carbone					
07 Mar. 1998	Manchester United	Premiership	2–0	Atherton(26), Di Canio(88)	39427
Pressman, Barrett, Hinchcliffe, Walker, Newsome, Carbone, Stefanovic, Atherton, Pembridge(Whittingham 50), Di Canio(Oakes 89), Booth					
04 Apr. 1998	Southampton	Premiership	1–0	Carbone(79)	29677
Pressman, Barrett, Hinchcliffe, Walker, Sedloski, Carbone, Stefanovic, Atherton, Pembridge(Whittingham 71), Di Canio, Booth					
13 Apr. 1998	West Ham United	Premiership	1–1	Magilton(59)	28036
Pressman, Barrett, Hinchcliffe, Walker, Thome, Carbone, Stefanovic, Magilton, Rudi(Pembridge 84), Booth, Di Canio					
02 May 1998	Aston Villa	Premiership	1–3	Sanetti(89)	34177
Pressman, Barrett(Magilton 72), Hinchcliffe, Thome(Whittingham 34), Walker, Atherton, Pembridge(Sanetti ht), Stefanovic, Hyde, Carbone, Di Canio					

OTHER GAMES AT HILLSBOROUGH

28 Apr. 1998	Senior Cup Final	Emley 3	Parkgate 0		1200

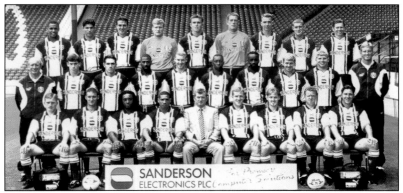

1997–1998
Bright, Stefanovic, Jones, Pressman, Newsome, Clarke, Linighan, Booth, Waddle;
Shreeves (ass. manager), Nolan, Whittingham, Williams, Briscoe, Collins, Donaldson, Sheridan, Humphreys, Galley (physio);
Pembridge, Oakes, Blinker, Walker, Pleat (manager), Atherton, Hyde, Nicol, Hirst.

Date	Opponents	Competition	Score	Scorers	Att.
15 Aug. 1998	West Ham United	Premiership	0–1		30236
Pressman, Cobian, Hinchcliffe, Thome, Walker, Atherton, Jonk, Rudi, Carbone, Di Canio, Booth					
29 Aug. 1998	Aston Villa	Premiership	0–1		25989
Pressman, Cobian(Barrett 63), Hinchcliffe, Thome, Walker, Atherton, Jonk, Rudi, Di Canio, Carbone, Booth					
12 Sep. 1998	Blackburn Rovers	Premiership	3–0	Atherton(18), Hinchcliffe(33), Di Canio(87)	20846
Pressman, Cobian(Barrett 70), Hinchcliffe, Thome, Walker, Atherton, Jonk, Rudi, Di Canio(Sanetti 89), Carbone, Booth					
16 Sep. 1998	Cambridge United	Worthington Cup 2–L1	0–1		8921
Pressman, Cobian, Hinchcliffe, Thome, Walker, Atherton, Jonk, Rudi(Whittingham 67), Di Canio, Carbone, Booth(Sanetti 67)					
26 Sep. 1998	Arsenal	Premiership	1–0	Briscoe(89)	27949
Pressman, Cobian, Hinchcliffe, Thome, Walker, Atherton, Jonk(Magilton 89), Rudi, Alexandersson(Briscoe 59), Di Canio, Booth(Humphreys 19)					
24 Oct. 1998	Everton	Premiership	0–0		26592
Pressman, Atherton, Hinchcliffe, Thome, Walker, Alexandersson, Sonner, Jonk, Briscoe, Humphreys, Booth					
31 Oct. 1998	Southampton	Premiership	0–0		30078
Pressman, Atherton, Hinchcliffe, Thome, Walker, Alexandersson, Sonner(Sanetti 75), Jonk, Briscoe(Rudi 58), Humphreys, Booth					
21 Nov. 1998	Manchester United	Premiership	3–1	Alexandersson 2(14, 73), Jonk(55)	39475
Srnicek, Atherton, Hinchcliffe, Thome, Walker, Alexandersson, Sonner, Jonk, Rudi, Carbone, Booth,					
07 Dec. 1998	Nottingham Forest	Premiership	3–2	Carbone 2(53, 58), Alexandersson(22)	19321
Srnicek, Atherton, Hinchcliffe, Thome, Walker, Alexandersson, Sonner, Jonk, Rudi(Briscoe 79), Carbone(Stefanovic 90), Booth					
12 Dec. 1998	Charlton Athletic	Premiership	3–0	Booth(13), Carbone(64), Rudi(77)	26010
Srnicek, Atherton, Hinchcliffe, Thome, Walker, Alexandersson(Briscoe 59), Sonner, Jonk, Rudi(Stefanovic 79), Carbone, Booth					
26 Dec. 1998	Leicester City	Premiership	0–1		33513
Srnicek, Atherton, Hinchcliffe, Thome, Walker, Alexandersson(Briscoe 67), Stefanovic, Jonk, Rudi, Humphreys(Morrison 67), Booth					
03 Jan. 1999	Norwich City	F.A.Cup 3	4–1	Humphreys 2(18, 33), Rudi(40), Stefanovic(73)	18737
Srnicek, Atherton, Hinchcliffe, Thome(Briscoe 78), Walker, Alexandersson, Jonk(Sonner ht), Stefanovic, Rudi, Carbone, Humphreys					
09 Jan. 1999	Tottenham Hotspur	Premiership	0–0		28204
Srnicek, Atherton, Hinchcliffe, Thome, Walker, Alexandersson, Jonk, Stefanovic, Rudi, Carbone, Humphreys					
23 Jan. 1999	Stockport County	F.A.Cup 4	2–0	Thome(17), Carbone(57)	20984
Srnicek, Atherton, Hinchcliffe, Thome, Walker(Newsome 74), Alexandersson, Jonk, Sonner, Rudi, Carbone, Humphreys(Booth 63)					
30 Jan. 1999	Derby County	Premiership	0–1		24440
Srnicek, Atherton, Hinchcliffe, Thome, Walker, Alexandersson(Pressman 58), Jonk(Newsome 86), Stefanovic, Rudi, Carbone, Booth(Humphreys 55)					
13 Feb. 1999	Chelsea	F.A.Cup 5	0–1		29410
Pressman, Atherton, Stefanovic, Thome, Walker, Alexandersson, Jonk, Rudi(Briscoe 84), Carbone, Sonner(Agogo 90), Booth					
27 Feb. 1999	Middlesbrough	Premiership	3–1	Booth 2(11, 80), Sonner(77)	24534
Pressman, Atherton, Hinchcliffe, Thome, Walker, Alexandersson, Jonk, Sonner, Rudi, Carbone, Booth					
03 Mar. 1999	Wimbledon	Premiership	1–2	Thome(60)	24116
Srnicek, Atherton, Hinchcliffe, Thome, Walker, Alexandersson, Jonk, Sonner(Humphreys 87), Rudi, Carbone, Booth					
13 Mar. 1999	Leeds United	Premiership	0–2		28142
Srnicek, Atherton, Hinchcliffe, Thome, Walker, Alexandersson, Jonk, Sonner(Briscoe 32), Rudi, Humphreys(Agogo 49), Booth					
03 Apr. 1999	Coventry City	Premiership	1–2	Rudi(51)	28136
Srnicek, Atherton, Briscoe, Thome, Walker(Newsome ht), Alexandersson, Jonk(Scott 90), Rudi, Humphreys(Sonner ht), Cresswell, Carbone					
21 Apr. 1999	Newcastle United	Premiership	1–1	Scott(52)	21545
Srnicek, Atherton, Hinchcliffe, Thome, Walker, Alexandersson, Jonk(Scott ht), Sonner, Rudi, Carbone, Booth					
25 Apr. 1999	Chelsea	Premiership	0–0		21652
Srnicek, Atherton, Stefanovic, Thome, Walker, Alexandersson, Jonk, Sonner, McKeever, Carbone, Booth(Cresswell 79)					
08 May 1999	Liverpool	Premiership	1–0	Cresswell(87)	27383
Srnicek, Haslam(Alexandersson 57), Stefanovic, Thome, Walker, Atherton, Jonk, Sonner, Rudi(McKeever 82), Carbone, Booth(Cresswell 80)					

OTHER GAMES AT HILLSBOROUGH

04 May 1999	Senior Cup Final	Emley 0		Stocksbridge Park Steels 1	2000

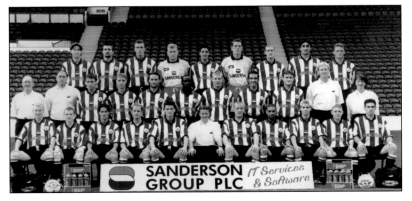

1998–99
Rudi, Thome, Newsome, Pressman, Sanetti, Clarke, Booth, Sedloski, Magilton;
Hodge (coach), Nolan, Haslam, Oakes, Barrett, Humphreys, Di Canio, Hinchcliffe, Galley (physio);
Briscoe, Quinn, Carbone, Hyde, Jonk, Wilson (manager), Atherton, Walker, Alexandersson, Geary, Whittingham.

Supporters
Roll
of Honour

A

Simon Abell
Iain Addis
Philip Adsetts
In Memory of David Allford
Simon Allford
Paul & Lorraine Allum
Dale & Colin Allum
Luke & Suzi Allum
Geoff Allton
M.J. Anderson
Derek Anderson
Martin Andrews
Peter Antcliffe
Mark Appleby
David W. Arbuthnott
Keith Archer
Paul Armitage
Ciaran Armstrong
David John Ashton
Joe Ashton
S. Ashton
M.S. Ashton
Paul Askew
Robert F. Atkinson
David Austin
Robert P. Ayton

B

Walter Bailey
John Baines
Brett Ashley Baker
Steve Ball
Alan Barber
Stuart Barber
Andrew Barlow
Ernest Barron
Steven Bateman
Mrs D.M. Battersby
Ray Battye
Derrick Baugh
George Edward Beadle
A.M. Bedwell
Eric Beech
George M.B. Beevor
Christopher Stephen Bell
Ms Helen Berisford
Enric Bertran
Roger Beynon
Roy Arthur Biggin
Barry Paul Birks
Neil David Blackwell
Mark Blank
Martin Bogue
Rhys Boughen
Alan Bower
R. Brackley

Richard Bradford
R. Bradshaw
Graham M. Bragg
Bryan Bramhill
Ian Brandwood
Jack Breislin
Mark Brewin
Steven Brewster
Wayne Bridgeman
Matt Bridger
G.S. Briggs
Thomas Mark Broadbent
Jonathan Mark Brookes
P. Broomhead
Kenneth T.W. Brown
James Brown
Liam Mark Browne
Ian Brownhill
David Brumby
Ms Sarah Bryan
Martin Bryan
Mark Bryan
Philip Bryan
Joyce Buckley
Mike Buckley
Ian Bull
Vincent Kevin Bullus
Alan J. Burandt
Gary Burditt
A. Burgess
In Memory of Harry Burgess
Robin Burleigh
Martin Burniston
Richard Bursey
Juliet Bursey
Sharon Bursey
Stephen Peter Burton
Peter Butcher
Stuart Butlin
Adrian Button

C

John Caley
June & Robert H. Carr
Ashley Maxwell Carson
Jordan Carson
Chris Carver
John Caselli
Pip Caselli
David Caunt
Marc Chadburn
James Church
Michael Clark
Andrew Richard Clarke
John B. Clarke
G.B. Clarke
Peter Cliffe
Graham Clixby

Neil Clixby
R.W. Coe
Ian Colley
Keith Collins
Jim Cook
Stephen J. Cooper
Peter D. Cooper
Roy Cooper
Ms Jacqueline Cordon
John Corker
Wayne Coulson
F.R.M. Cowper
Tim Cragg
K.E. Creswick
Ms Katherine Cribbes
Richard Crooks
D.J. Cross
Mrs Carolyn Crossland
David Crossland
James Albert Crowder
Mary Elizabeth Crowder
David James Crowder
John Malcolm Cullen
Darren J. Cundey
L. 'Bud' Curtis
Scott Curtis
Chris Curtis

D

Gerald Dailey
Alan Dallman
F. Darley
D.R. Davies
Steven Davies
Barry Shaun Davitt
In Memory of Ernest Deakin
Richard Dean
Philip Dearden
Nills Deleuran
Peter Denton
Paul Derbyshire
T.J. Dix
Simon Donohue
Kate Donohue
Mark Donohue
Dave Dorey
David John Druce

E

Graham Earnshaw
Geoff Eccles
Derrick A. Edwards
W.B. Edwards
B.R. Edwards
Robert Emmett
Douglas H. Emmott
Eric England

Alan John Epton
R.A. Evans
E.W. Evans
Geoffrey E. Evans

F

Robert P. Farmery
Mick Fellows
Andrew Fields
Peter Fieldsend
Paul Finney
Simon Firth
Stephen Fish
J.C. Fisher
Michael J. Flanaghan
Gary J. Fletcher
Alan Fletcher
Barry Ford
Mark & Andrew Ford
Walter Foss
H. Foster
Tom Foster
Ben Foster
Richard W. Foweather
Ian Fraser
K.I. Frith
Eric F. Froggatt

G

M. Gallagher
John C. Gant
Charles Gardner
David R. Giles
David Gingell
Harold Goddard
David Godden
H. Edward Goldthorpe
Ms Yvonne Golland
Nigel Goodison
Yael Gordon
Daniel Gordon
Martin Gordon
R.R. Gould
Charles Richard Grainger
Stephen John Gray
Dennis Gray
Derek Green
Raymond Anthony Green
Ian Gregory
Pam, Bob, Heather & John Grierson

H

Trevor Hall
Chas Handley
Peter Harris
David Harris

A. Harrison
Anthony Kenyon Harrold
Paul S. Harvey
Gary Haselgrove
David Haslehurst
Roy Hatfield
Ian Hawcroft
D.W. Hawksworth
David Hawksworth
Ernest Hawksworth
Sharon & Mark Hawtin
Tony Hayes
Andrew N. Hayes
Jonathan Hayes
Ashley Daulat Haystead
Dean A.S. Hedley
Simon Heeley
Jonathan Hendley
Matthew Herbert
John Andrew Hibberd
Philip Hickinson
Lewis Geoffrey Hides
Geoffrey Hides
Adrian Charles Hides
Adam James Daniel Hills
F.W. Hobson
Brian Hobson
J.N. Hodges
Dave Hodgetts
Angela Rowena Hogg
S. Holland
Jenny Hollingworth
Joe Hollingworth
Ms Catherine A. Hope
J.C. Houltby
Rob Howe
Robert Hukin
The Hulley Family
Paul John Hunsley
Ms Kate Hurley
J.R. Hurt
Sue, Tom & Sally Hutchby
Keith & Steven Hutton

I

Fred Michael Ibbotson
C. Iggo
Jim Illingworth
James William Illingworth
Steven James Ireson
Ian Isaacs

J

George Jacklin
Martin James
Alan Brian Jennings
Barry Jones

Mark R. Jones
Alan Jones
Shaun Jones

K

H.H. Kalman
Roy Kavanagh
H.W. Kay
John Kelly
Mark Kempton
Paul Kenny
C.J. Kershaw
Michael M. Kime
Ronald Keith King
J. King
Cyril Ewart King
David J. Kinns
Gordon Kirk
Steven P. Kirk
In Memory of Harry Kirk
Peter Kitchen
Ms Cheryl Louise Kitchen
Jon Knight

L

Danny Langley
A.W. Large
Darren A. Large
Stuart Laver
Pete & Pam Law
Ms R. Lawson
Anne Leech
Donald Lewin
David J. Lewis
David Thomas Lewis
Peter A.F. Liddle
Luke T.B. Liddle
Jeffrey Lindley
Paul Lindley
Emma Lindley
T.H. Lingard
Darryl Lomas
Thomas Lomas
Graham Lomas
David Loxley
Dennis Lumb
Robert A. Lund

M

David Machan
David Richard Malcolmson
J. Mansfield
In Memory of Rod Marriott
Frank H. Marson
Mrs Jill Matthews
Malcolm G. May

Jacqueline May
Laura Jessica May
Richard James May
Ben McCullogh
Anthony McDermott
Vincent McDermott
Neil McDermott
Sean McDonnell
Kevin McManus
David Mee
Chris Metcalfe
James Mettam
Bill Michie MP
Katie Millar
Robert James Mills
W.A. Milne
David Mitchell
Harry Moore
D. Morley
David Morrall
Frank Morris
Alan Cyril Morton
Peter Motley
Richard Mottram
Martin G. Mullane

N

J.R. Naylor
John Nilen
Graham Norburn
Jonathan Norman

O

Stephen Slink Oldale
Richard Oldfield
Ken O'Neill
Richard Eric Orrin
Michael R. Osbon

P

David Parfitt
Cyril Parker
Ken Parker
Sidney Parker
Glenn Parkin
Robert & Daniel
    James Anthony Parkin
Alan Parkin
David John Parkin
P.S. Pattinson
Ian Peak
Anthony Peal
Ron Pearce
G.T. Pearson
Bryan Pell
Clive John Penfold

Shaun Pennington
Colin Pentland
Philip R. Perry
In Memory of Andrew Peterkin
Kenneth Pitchford
Simon Mark Plant
Tom Pollard
John Poulter
Peter Poulter
Roy Powell
Darryl, Linda & Robert Power
The Prewett Family of
    Hillsborough
I.D. Price
Alan Price
Mrs Eileen Pridmore

R

Paul Radford
Michael Ransford
Steven Rebbeck
Ian Graham Rebbeck
David Ian Rebbeck
Dave Reid
Ben Reilly
Mrs A. Revill
Philip John Rhodes
George Richards
Dave Richards & Family
Ian Richmond
J.B. Riding
Paul Riley
John Rippon
Mrs Jacqueline R. Rippon
Andrew Roach
Miss Susan Roberts
Mark Roberts
Andrew Roberts
Paul Robinson
Andrew C. Robinson
Mr & Mrs P. Robinson & Family
Frank Ronksley
David Roscoe
Aden Rosewarne
In Memory of Laurence
    Stanley Rowan
Simon David Rushton
Trevor Ryals
Nigel Ryals

S

Mark Sadler
Thomas Andrew John Sandham
Leslie Michael Sandham
Mrs J.M. Sanger
David Sayers
Adrian C. Sayliss

Derek Scothern
Roger Scott
J.M. Seago
Martin P. Sedgwick
Max Selby
Mrs C.A. Senior
Christopher Shaw
Joseph Shaw
Stephen Shepherd (Stef)
Matt Sheppard & Family
Norman Shillito
Geoffery Shore
In Memory of Sydney Simmons
Joseph Michael Smith
Barrie E. Smith
Jack E. Smith
Ray H. Smith
Stewart R. Smith
Gary Speight
Brian Steers
Brian Stevenson
David A. Steward
John Stewart
Greg Ashley Stewart
Joseph Stockdale
Ms Jean Anne Stockdale
Joe Stockwell
Ben Stockwell
Mrs Angela P. Straw
Anthony Eric Sturgeon
George B. Swift
George Swindells
Michael B. Sztapka

T

Brian E. Tanner
Janet Tanner

Richard W. Taylor
Allan M. Taylor
R.B. Thomas
Ernie Thompson
Craig Thompson
Neil L. Thompson
Catherine J. Thompson
James E. Thompson
Donald Anthony Thompson
Neil Thompson
Paul Thompson
Alan Thorpe
Graham & Joan Thorpe
In Memory of John Andrew Thorpe
Neil Timmins
Jeffrey C. Toone
John Hayden Townsend
Melvyn David Trigg
Paul Trigg
Ian G. Troops
Albert Truelove
Jack & Oliver Tupling
George Turnbull
David John Turner
Thomas T.T.G. Twigg

U

Stephen J. Ulman
Simon Underwood
Richard Unwin

V

Charles A. Varley
Janet Varley
Lee Vernon

Fred Verso
Karl Verso

W

Peter Wales
Ms Dorothy Walker
Luke A. Walker
Robert Alfred Wallace
Raymond Ward
Michael Ward
John Ward
David Ward
Martyn Ware
Robin Warrender
Graham Wassell
Michael Waterhouse
Ms Barbara Ann Watson
Ian Watson
Tony Watson
A.N. Webster
Harold Webster
Chris Wells
Mick West
Dennis Wheatley
Doug Wheatley
Colin Wheeler
Paul Richard Whitaker
Ian Whitaker
Brian Whitaker
Danny White
Paul Daniel White
Brian Whitehead
Geoffrey Whitehead
Alex Whiteley
Danny Whiteley
Dean Martin Whiteman
In Memory of Michael Whysall

Mrs V. Wilde
Edward Wildsmith
James H. Wilkinson
David C. Williams
Maxine Nicole Williams
Eric F. Williams
Cos Williams
Peter Wilsher
M.A. Wilson
David Winfield
Robert Wiseman
Shaun Wistow
John M. Womersley
Andrew Wood
Shaun Montgomery Woods
Macdara Woods
Michael William Woodward
In Memory of Kenneth Woodward
Andrew Mark Woodward
Paul Woolfson
John Clifford Woolford
Neil B. Woolhouse
Frank Gilbert Worrell
Audrey Wragg
In Memory of Harry Wragg
John Wright
Nicola Jane Wroe
Barry Yeardley

Y

Colin Yeardley
Terry George Yeardley
James Eric Young
Patrick Young

Front cover: An artist's impression of Owlerton in 1913 and a present day aerial shot.

Back cover: The first Sheffield Wednesday team to play at Owlerton and the 1999 team.